W9-BEC-207

Better Teaching
Through
Better Measurement

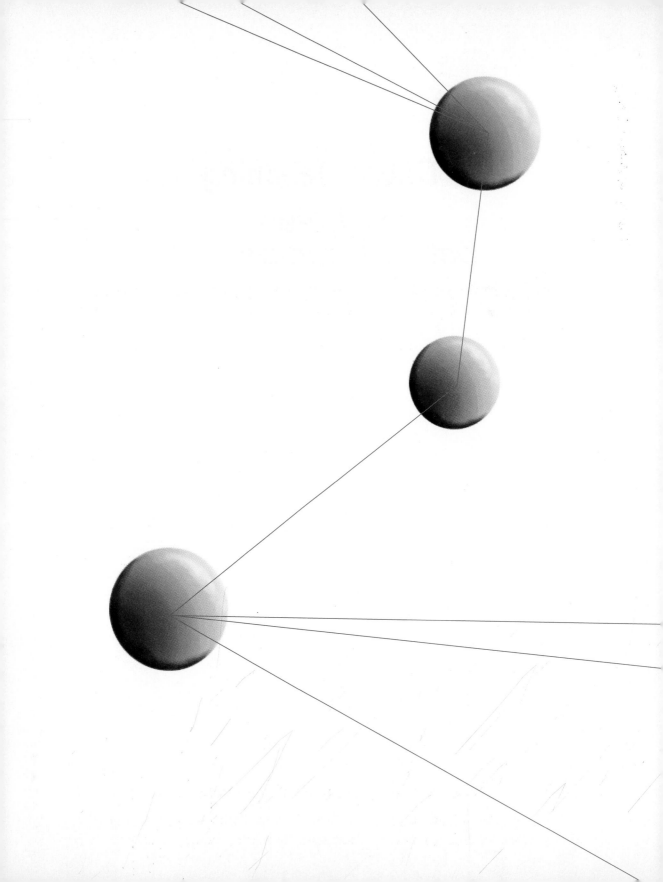

Better Teaching Through Better Measurement

Gerald S. Hanna
Kansas State University

Harcourt Brace Jovanovich College Publishers

Fort Worth   Philadelphia   San Diego   New York   Orlando   Austin
San Antonio   Toronto   Montreal   London   Sydney   Tokyo

To: Atina, Tali, Gladys, and Howie

Editor-In-Chief: Ted Buchholz
Acquisitions Editor: Jo-Anne Weaver
Developmental Editor: Tracy Napper
Project Editor: Barbara Moreland
Production Manager: Cynthia Young
Book Designer: Jeanette Barber
Photo/Permissions Editor: Greg Meadors

Address Editorial Correspondence to: 301 Commerce Street, Suite 3700, Fort Worth, TX 76102.

Address Orders to: 6277 Sea Harbor Drive, Orlando, FL 32887
1-800-782-4479, or 1-800-433-0001 (in Florida)

Printed in the United States of America

ISBN: 0-15-500099-3

3 4 5 6 7 8 9 0 1   039   9 8 7 6 5 4 3 2 1

Preface

*I*ncreasing professional attention has been directed to the acute needs of teachers and other educators for knowledge, skills, and understanding of applied educational measurement. This was recently crystallized in the publication of *Standards for Teacher Competence in Educational Assessment of Students* (Sanders et al., 1990), jointly endorsed by NCME, AFT, and NEA. *Better Teaching Through Better Measurement* is designed to meet those needs and to be the textbook for a first course in educational measurement at either the undergraduate or graduate level. It presumes no background in statistics or mathematics.

Content has been selected, ordered, and structured to help teachers understand that valid student evaluation is an integral part of effective teaching and to provide them with the skills necessary to put this knowledge to use. Thematic emphasis is focused on two ways in which classroom measurement should enhance student learning. First, good assessment data informs professional decisions. Second, student evaluation practices influence student effort; this impact should be harnessed. As the title suggests, this book does not treat tests and other measures as ends in themselves. Neither is it a book about measurement theory per se. Nor is it a book about student assessment as an isolated activity.

I believe an educational measurement textbook should provide bridges to classroom applications. It should be made obvious to students that assessment is central to teaching; the practical utility of topics should not be left to readers to deduce. This book's central thesis is that good measurement enhances effective teaching, while poor measurement interferes with student learning. Therefore, measurement is framed in the broader perspective of classroom instruction. The focus is on measurement, but the perspective is broader.

This book was designed to be singular in providing structure to a set of measurement and instructional topics. The treatment of measurement should be integrated and relationships among topics should be highlighted, not left for readers to divine. For example, students taking their first measurement course typically have previously had a course in educational psychology. They know something about human learning and transfer of learning from the perspectives of both behavioral and cognitive psychology. There are important connections between learning and measurement, and students should be helped to understand the implications of these connections.

In an apparent effort to offend none and please all, many authors treat controversial topics (e.g., criterion referencing or mastery learning) in a nonevaluative, superficial way. They will give the pros and cons of each but offer little help to the unsophisticated reader in choosing among alternative strategies. However, in professional preparation attention should be given to *when* and *why* one should do various things, as well as *how* to do them. My pursuit here of structure and association among topics was undertaken from the perspective of a mainstream, middle-of-the-road orientation. My thinking over the years has benefited greatly by Gronlund's important distinction between two major kinds of instructional objectives, by the writing of Cronbach, Anastasi, R. L. Thorndike, Mehrens and Lehmann, and by the teaching and writing of K. D. Hopkins.

Part I provides a broad, structured view of several important educational issues and shows how they relate to each other and to educational measurement. Chapter 1 illustrates the many ways in which measurement is used in teaching. Chapters 2 and 3 contain the most unusual features of the book. They place measurement topics into an integrated instructional/evaluation model with which readers can organize much of the rest of the book. They also provide meaningful structure to other information from professional education course work so that classroom teachers can harmoniously orchestrate their teaching methods with their student assessment practices.

Part II is devoted mainly to "know how" of classroom test making. Shifting from the more theoretical framework provided in Part I to a very practical, "how to" orientation, Part II is sharply focused on assessment with teacher-made devices. It opens with Chapter 4's unusually comprehensive treatment of planning various kinds of classroom achievement measures. Then Chapters 5 through 8 provide relatively conventional treatments of the various item types, with an entire chapter devoted to performance measures. Chapter 9 takes up test formatting, administration, scoring, item analysis, etc.

Part III concerns classroom use of student achievement measures. Chapter 10 considers teacher uses of formative and summative measures. Chapter 11 provides a simplified core of statistics needed for marking and reporting. Chapter 12 gives rationale and practical techniques of grading.

Part IV moves from the predominant classroom focus that dominates the earlier parts of the book to a broader view that also encompasses published instruments. Here attention to characteristics (e.g., validity and reliability) of effective instruments—both teacher made and published—formalizes, rationalizes, and draws together many of the strands of practical "know how" presented in Part II.

Part V completes the transition from classroom testing to use of published instruments by providing a brief survey of available instruments. Opening with a chapter on derived scores and their appropriate use, the section then provides a chapter each on achievement tests, aptitude tests, and affective measures, along with a few illustrations of each.

Instructors of courses dedicated exclusively to classroom testing may wish to omit some or all of Part V. Those with a purely practical focus may want to skip portions of Part IV as well, particularly the latter sections of Chapter 14. Such truncation may be desirable in some contexts and necessary in others (particularly in shorter courses). The parts of this book have been ordered to accommodate this option without forfeiture of sequence or loss of closure.

On the other hand, instructors of courses (particularly longer ones) that seek a balanced emphasis of teacher-made and published tests and who value emphasis on conventional treatment of core measurement concepts will want to budget time for intensive use of Parts IV and V.

This book contains a wealth of pedagogical features. Quizzes scattered throughout the book are designed to prompt active thinking. Answers and discussion to quizzes provide feedback and, in places, additional instruction. Numerous examples show breadth of application of concepts and connect with readers' prior knowledge. Each chapter ends with a short list of suggestions for further reading. The book is written in a more direct, conversational style than many. I have not tried to hide either my personality or the perspectives I have gained from being a student, a public school teacher, a school counselor, a Peace Corps Volunteer, a parent, an author and editor of published tests, a researcher, and a professor of education.

Those teaching the course will find the Instructors' Manual helpful in at least three ways. First, it offers suggestions concerning structure of a basic course in educational measurement. Second, it provides a description of several kinds of course projects. Finally, it provides sets of objective and essay test questions. In addition, the computerized item bank is available on disk for IBM compatible and for MacIntosh computers.

I am indebted to many people for timely encouragement, assistance, and critical comments. To my students who have taught me so much. To John Steffen for long urging me to undertake this project. To Charles K. Ray and John T. Roscoe for useful ideas. To Les Becklund (San Diego State University), Arlen Gullickson (Western Michigan University), and Bruce Rogers (University of Northern Iowa) for extraordinarily detailed, conscientious, and helpful reviews at early, formative periods in the manuscript's preparation. To C. R. "Bob" DuVall for providing Appendix C. For providing thoughtful and helpful reactions to later drafts of the manuscript, thanks to Donald Barker (Texas A & M University), Ralph Darr (University of Akron), C. R. "Bob" DuVall (Indiana University at South Bend), David Henderson (Sam Houston State University), and Dale Shaw (University of Northern Colorado). And for their editorial assistance, thanks to Julia Berrisford, Jo-Anne Weaver, and Tracy Napper.

Table of Contents

Measurement in Perspective

Measurement and evaluation lie at the heart of effective teaching, permeating all facets of instruction. Yet some teachers may not be aware much of the time that their activities are guided by measures. Similarly, many teachers are not fully cognizant of the extent to which measures shape the activities of their students.

Most educational measurement books are designed to enhance teachers' skills in using educational measures and to make their use a conscious, rational, and professional enterprise. But a hazard lurks on the path to these goals. There is a danger of focusing, for a time, so narrowly on techniques of assessment that one loses perspective on how various technical tidbits fit into the broader scheme of instruction.

The first major section of this book is designed to ensure the reader against this hazard of loss of perspective. It provides a broad, integrated view of several important educational issues and shows how they relate to each other. This preliminary overview also helps demonstrate why it is important for classroom teachers to understand these interrelationships.

In Chapter 1, some of the multitude of ways in which measurement is involved in teaching are noted. In Chapter 2, a model of instruction is outlined. In Chapter 3, this model is expanded into a more comprehensive instructional/evaluation framework within which (a) readers can organize much of the remaining content of this volume; (b) meaningful structure is given to a great deal of information from other professional education coursework; and (c) readers can organize their teaching and evaluation practices into logical and effective patterns.

1

Evaluation and Teaching

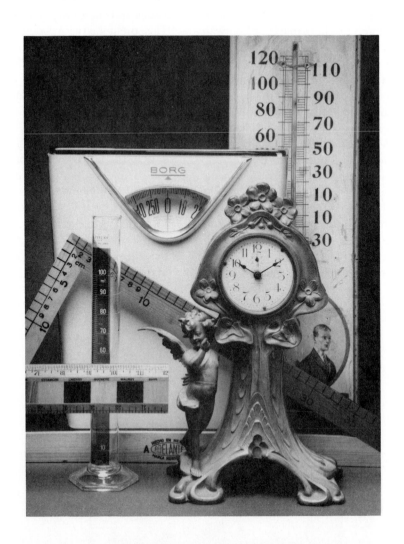

Measurement and evaluation are present in all facets of life. In deciding what clothes to wear in the morning, we observe the weather. In driving to work or school, we measure our speed. In meeting strangers, we assess their physical and social characteristics. In buying a used car, we evaluate its condition. In deciding when to retire in the evening, we measure the time and assess our physical and psychological states. Daily life is saturated with measurement and with evaluation based on it. Measurement is, therefore, an integral part of daily activity, especially in an industrial society where we have the technology to measure so many things. Likewise, measurement is an integral part of teaching, particularly in a technological culture.

This chapter will briefly survey some of the major kinds of measurement activities in which teachers and other educators commonly engage. The function of measurement in decision making will then be considered, with emphasis on the intimate and inseparable partnership between sound measurement and effective instruction. Finally, readers will be invited to take a demonstration test in order to introduce several topics that are previewed in this introductory chapter.

School Uses of Standardized, Published Measures

Some of the assessment conducted in schools is based on commercially prepared instruments. Most such published devices provide for formal, separate, and standardized measurement. That is, measurement is deliberate, planned, separate from other instructional activities, and performed under controlled or standard conditions. A **standardized** device is a measure that is administered and scored under specified, controlled conditions. Much of the measurement that occurs in schools is standardized in this sense. Although some locally developed measures are administered and scored under specified conditions, much of standardized measurement is conducted by use of commercially produced and nationally distributed tests and other instruments. Several examples follow to illustrate the breadth of standardized measurement activities with published instruments.

Prior to kindergarten, pupils are often screened to detect major deficiencies or handicaps. Pre-kindergarten screening commonly includes tests of oral vocabulary, vision, hearing, and motor functions. Such standardized measures are used to identify pupils who may experience early difficulty in school. The purpose, of course, in identifying such children is to enable constructive action on their behalf.

Another example of standardized testing is a first-grade teacher's use of a reading readiness test to help decide which pupils are ready for conventional, formal reading instruction and which would benefit more from additional pre-reading activities. The utility of a reading readiness test, of course, resides in the help it gives teachers in providing each child with the kind of instruction that will be most beneficial.

Standardized, group-administered tests of general academic aptitude (often referred to as "intelligence tests") provide another example of formal school testing with commercially developed instruments. Such tests are routinely used in many schools to provide information about each student's level of present measurable aptitude for regular schoolwork. This kind of information is useful to teachers in arranging for each youngster to be assigned tasks that are both challenging and manageable.

Specialized school personnel such as school psychologists administer standardized individual tests of school aptitude to students needing more intensive evaluation. Such tests are widely used in identifying exceptional children—e.g., the gifted and the mentally retarded—and in evaluating examinees suspected of having learning disabilities and behavioral disorders. By knowing more about an individual's present level of intellectual functioning, school psychologists and other professionals can more wisely suggest instructional programs to suit the student's needs.

Adaptive behavior scales are used in conjunction with intellectual aptitude tests to assess individuals suspected of mental retardation. Adaptive behavior ratings tap such important survival skills as dressing, grooming, shopping, keeping quiet at appropriate times (e.g., instruction, flag salute). Knowledge of a person's mastery of such everyday behaviors helps educators plan appropriate instruction.

Standardized achievement tests are widely used to measure the school achievement of students at all educational levels. Results for such tests help teachers judge the degree to which each examinee has achieved a command of the subject areas tested. This information, of course, can be used to plan instruction of groups and individuals.

Interest inventories will serve as a final example of school use of published standardized measures. Interest scales at the secondary school level help counselors and teachers facilitate better student understanding of their interests. Armed with this dimension of self-knowledge, students can better choose their elective courses, plan their education, and select their future occupations.

One of the principal goals of this book is to help readers understand the issues involved in the selection, evaluation, administration, and interpretation of published, standardized tests. Parts IV and V of this book are particularly relevant to this aim.

Teacher-Made Measures

For a variety of reasons discussed in Part II, most teachers need and wish to construct most of their own measures of student achievement. Examples of teacher-made tests from elementary school to graduate school are sure to be familiar to the reader.

Teacher-made tests play a large role in determining student grades and in showing students what is to be learned. Consequently, teacher-made tests loom large in both teacher and student perception concerning the role of evaluation in education. Teachers use a rich variety of classroom assessment methods, including oral questioning; observation of performance; written exercises, assignments, and projects; and, of course, teacher-made, paper–pencil tests (Gullickson, 1985). Collectively, these activities consume very substantial amounts of class time (Dorr-Bremme & Herman, 1986).

Like published instruments, "homemade" or "customized" teacher-made tests vary greatly in quality. Some teachers use their quizzes and examinations as indispensable features of sound instruction, while others create tests of such deplorable quality that their overall instructional effectiveness is seriously damaged. Fortunately, most teachers realize that their evaluation procedures are important to their teaching. Yet many lack the skills needed to assess students effectively (Gullickson, 1984; Stiggins & Bridgeford, 1985), perhaps because much traditional teacher preparation in measurement has overemphasized large-scale published, paper-pencil testing (Stiggins, 1991).

A major goal of this book is to enable teachers to develop sound tests that will operate in tandem with other features of quality instruction. Parts I, II, III, and IV relate to this goal.

Informal Observations

As vital as relatively formal and standardized teacher-made tests are, it is important to recognize that informal measurement and observation also make a major contribution to effective teaching. This link is especially visible at the primary school level at which formal, standardized measurement by means of commercially prepared and teacher-made tests is at a minimum but prolonged teacher contact with individual pupils is at a maximum. Indeed, teachers' own observations are typically their most important sources of information for assessing their students (Stiggins & Bridgeford, 1985).

An example at the primary level would be the teacher observing that Ralph tends to reverse the numerals "3" and "5" with some frequency; this observation, of course, should lead to corrective efforts. Another example would be the observation that Debbie completes her mathematics assignments with unusual speed and accuracy, which would suggest the possibility of her being accelerated in math. Finally, there is the example of the teacher's observation that Malo is usually the last child in the class to be chosen for any activity in which peer choice plays a part; from this observation the teacher might try to structure situations in which Malo would be perceived by his classmates as a valuable partner or team member.

An example of informal classroom observation at the upper elementary or middle school level would be a music teacher's observation that April seems to be tone-deaf; the teacher could then assign her to percussion instruments rather than to singing during music periods. Then there is the teacher's observation that José's Spanish-language background seems to be interfering with effective oral communication in standard American English. If a teacher did not know how to help José compartmentalize the two languages, a referral could be made to a more specialized professional.

At the secondary level, an English teacher might notice Ann's tendency to use double negatives indiscriminately in oral language but to avoid them successfully in written products; the teacher then could increase efforts to build upon her standard usage in writing and to extend it into her speech behavior on relatively formal occasions. A teacher of beginning woodshop might rate the tie racks made by Jerri and Ian as unusually well built, suggesting that they be assigned to a more demanding and interesting task for their next project. A teacher of German might do much oral questioning. The results would help the teacher ask each student questions that are challenging yet still likely to be answered correctly.

Informal testing and observation at the high school or college level is somewhat less common than at other levels, but it is both prevalent and important. A trigonometry instructor notices that Winnie missed several similar factoring problems in the same manner; correction could take the form of a note in the margin of her homework paper, reference to a section of the text, or a few words with her after the next class period. A drama coach notices Bill's peculiar on-stage walk and undertakes to help him achieve a more natural gait. A counselor observes that Carmen will consider only those occupations that are stereotypically identified as "feminine" jobs; awareness of this tendency could lead the counselor to help broaden her occupational horizons and enlarge the number and variety of her options.

The diversity of the above examples should convey a sense of the pervasiveness of measurement, observation, and evaluation in schools. Measurement and evaluation have something of a symbiotic relationship to the delivery aspects of teaching. On the one hand, measurement, observation, and evaluation arise out of, and are based on, teaching. On the other hand, they provide the feedback to guide teacher efforts. Likewise, measurement and evaluation provide the feedback to guide student efforts. They communicate to students the aims of instruction. In this sense, good evaluation is not merely an adjunct to effective teaching: It is a vital part of good teaching (Sadler, 1983). In addition, of course, measurement and evaluation provide the basis for communicating information about student achievement to parents, students, future teachers, and prospective employers.

Published standardized measures, teacher-made measures, and informal observations have each been shown to make a valuable contribution to teaching. These three sources of information serve different functions. Collectively, they provide the breadth of information teachers need. These sources of knowledge about students are not competitive; rather, each provides information not readily available through the other sources. They complement each other in much the way that each leg of a three-legged stool contributes to supporting and bracing it.

Measurement vs. Evaluation

It will be helpful at this juncture to define formally the word "measurement." Strictly speaking, **measurement** is the systematic assignment of numbers (or names) to attributes. The assignment of numbers (or names) may be made with the benefit of sophisticated apparatus, as in measuring a child's temperature with a thermometer, or it may be conducted with less adequate, but systematic procedures, as in a parent's hand being applied to the child's forehead to estimate the temperature. Measurement can be conducted at various levels of precision; for example, the child's temperature can be reported in tenths of degrees or in crude ranges such as normal, high, or very high.

Each example of measurement provided in the preceding sections of this chapter conforms to this definition of measurement as the systematic assignment of numbers to attributes. Similarly, the classification of newborn babies by gender would clearly conform to the definition of measurement as the naming of attributes. But several of the examples of informal classroom observation lack the assignment of numbers or names. Strictly speaking, the trigonometry teacher's observation that Winnie missed several similar problems is not a measurement; to become one it would need to be quantified—for example, she missed seven such problems. Such use of numbers is an easy next step for the examples offered in the section on informal observations.

As another example, the rough ranges of temperature could be assigned numbers of 1, 2, and 3, respectively. Therefore, such examples are treated in this book. The value of making such assignments arises from the fact that they are subject to the same concerns about reliability and validity[1] as are measurements; thus by including them, the concepts developed in Chapters 14 and 15 can readily be applied to the topics of informal teacher observations as well as to strict instances of measurement.

It is important at this point to draw a distinction between measurement and evaluation. Measurement has been defined as the methodical assignment of numbers or category names to the attributes measured. Measurement, as such, does not involve judgment about acceptability or value of the thing measured. The measurement of the child's temperature—whether done with thermometer or hand—tells nothing about the acceptability of the findings or about the actions that should be based upon the evaluation of acceptability. Neither thermometers nor hands direct the evaluator to consider the temperature acceptable or unacceptable.

Decision making about what to do concerning the temperature follows the evaluation of its acceptability. If the temperature is deemed acceptable, the likely decision would be to do nothing. If it is judged to be unacceptably high, the decision might be to give over-the-counter medication or consult a physician. The decision of what to do follows from the evaluation. **Evaluation** is the application of judgment concerning the results of measurement (or unquantified observation). Thus evaluation is the middle step in the three-step process of measurement, evaluation, and decision making.

The distinction among measurement, evaluation, and decision making is useful because it helps us remember where the data leave off and where our judgment begins. If, for example, the woodshop teacher decides that Jerri and Ian should be moved on to a more advanced woodworking project than the rest of the class, this decision may or may not prove to be a wise one. If it turns out to be unproductive, the problem could lie in the decision concerning the next project to be undertaken or it could lie in measurement error in rating the tie racks in the first place. Sound instructional decisions first require reasonable, valid measurement and then good professional judgment.

The word "assessment" is also used in discussing measurement, observation, and evaluation. **Assessment** is the process of collecting, interpreting, and synthesizing information to aid in decision making. Thus assessment is a broad concept that includes the full range of data that teachers gather—from scores on teacher-made and published tests to findings from formal and informal observations. It also refers to the full range of methods teachers use to gather that information. Finally, it concerns drawing inferences from these data sources (Airasian, 1991). Thus "assessment" is roughly synonymous with "measurement" plus "observation," although it is sometimes used in a broader sense to include connotations of "evaluation."

---

[1]In the early chapters of this book, the flow of ideas will not be interrupted to provide unnecessary technical definitions of terms when "a person on the street" would have a general and sufficient sense of the meaning. Readers who wish to digress to study definitions are directed to the index at the back of the book. As it happens, reliability and validity will be described in the next section of this chapter, but their full consideration will occur in Chapters 14 and 15.

Reliability and Validity

Reliability and validity are concepts central to educational measurement. Although an entire chapter will be devoted to each late in this book, it will be worthwhile at this point to define them a little more clearly than a typical "person on the street" would be able to do.

Validity concerns the extent to which a test or other device measures what it is being used to measure. Moreover, validity concerns the *appropriateness* of inferences and actions that are based on a test's scores (Messick, 1989). Thus, use of a test is valid to the extent that (a) its scores *truthfully* report examinee status on the attribute the test is supposed to measure and (b) the consequences of using the inferences based on these scores are deemed *desirable*.

Suppose a particular bathroom scale is a good measure of weight. If it is used to measure weight, it can be said to be quite valid. That is, its scores tell the truth about people's weight, and this truth leads to socially desirable consequences. On the other hand, if the scale is used to assess height, its use would be much less valid. That is, if used to measure stature, its scores would be much less effective in sorting people on that attribute. And if it were used to ascertain introversion, its use would be even less valid.

Along the same lines, a teacher-made unit test that consists exclusively of knowledge of facts included in the unit might be a valid or truthful measure of factual knowledge. But it would not be as valid a measure of the students' understanding of principles or of their ability to apply the facts and principles to novel situations.

Reliability concerns the consistency with which a test or other device measures whatever it measures. A test is reliable to the extent to which its scores *consistently* report examinees' status on the attribute the test measures. Reliability is *not* related to truthfulness. Reliability is related only to consistency of scores.

Reconsider the bathroom scale. Suppose it is quite reliable as a measure of weight. How reliable is it as a measure of vocabulary? It is just as reliable for one purpose as it is for another. That is, reliability only concerns consistency. Of course, the scale is not a valid measure of vocabulary, but its scores will be just as consistent if they are (falsely) called vocabulary scores as they will be if they are (truthfully) labeled weight scores.

Suppose a teacher-made unit test consists exclusively of knowledge of facts. Assume it is a reliable and valid measure of factual knowledge. How good is it as a measure of student ability to apply principles to novel situations? It depends on what is meant by "good." The test is equally reliable for all purposes. But it would not be valid for measuring application.

Measurement and Decision Making

A basic tenet of educational and psychological measurement is that a test, rating, questionnaire, or inventory should be administered only when its results will tend to help someone make better decisions about something. To be sure, measures can serve worthy purposes other than aiding decision making; for example, tests can stimulate students to study. However, it is almost always true that the proper use of measures is aimed (often among other important things) at improving decision making. Each example of school measurement or observation provided in previous sections of this chapter was accompanied explicitly or implicitly with means by which decision making would be improved. This stress on decision making is an important point. It may be worth the reader's time to re-scan the examples in order to focus on the decision-making payload of each instance of measurement or observation.

The truism that proper use of measurement ordinarily improves decision making extends far beyond the realm of education into other fields that use various kinds of tests. For example, a bridge inspector will examine features of a bridge's construction to determine whether they meet specifications. The decision to be improved, of course, is whether to pass or reject each feature of the structure. Or consider the physician ordering several standard laboratory tests for a patient having a routine physical examination. In this case, the (usually expected) negative results help the physician decide *not* to be concerned about the possibility of certain conditions, while positive results of routine screening measures would suggest further exploration, examination, or laboratory testing. It would be easy to extend examples of how measures and observations almost always should be used, in part at least, to improve decision making. Examples could be drawn from fields as diverse as automobile mechanics, analysis of videotaped athletic performances, horse breeding, or soil analysis; the principle is universal.

Unfortunately, the principle is widely violated. Occasionally a teacher in a measurement class complains that standardized achievement tests are administered in her or his school, but that the results are kept locked in the principal's or counselor's filing cabinet and not used by anyone. The disgruntled teacher sometimes goes on to conclude that altogether too much standardized achievement testing is being done. It is indeed a waste of time and money to test and not use the results; if results are not going to be used to improve decision making, then the test should ordinarily not be used. To ignore test results is as foolish as to order a title search on a house one is about to purchase and then to throw away the results without considering them.

Much of the rhetoric in education regarding "labeling" can be understood in the context of measurement and decision making. Many educators and lay people voice strong objections to labeling students. If one listens carefully to their often vehement attacks on labeling and standardized published tests, it becomes clear that neither testing nor labeling per se is the cause of the distress. What responsible critics cite as indefensible is the use of tests to label students *when no constructive action follows* or when detrimental effects outweigh beneficial ones.

Once the criticism of testing and labeling is delimited in this way, the controversy dissolves. Classifying a person can lead to a stigma; diagnoses or classifications have this very real danger. Although sensitive and thoughtful professional behavior can minimize such stigmas, they may still be present. When labeling students with such terms as "mentally retarded," "hearing impaired," "underweight," "creative," "economically disadvantaged," "gifted," or "learning disabled" is not accompanied by constructive actions, the measurement is indefensible because it invades students' privacy and subjects them to the hazards of stigmas for no constructive purpose. These unnecessary stigmas seem to be a major source of reasoned "antilabeling" sentiment.

Unfortunately, some critics get so caught up in the inappropriate use of tests that they overreact and denounce all labeling. Because labels such as "mentally handicapped" and "learning disabled" have at times been foolishly used, immoderate critics have been known to generalize their criticism to all diagnostic categories and to all standardized testing. This reaction, of course, is as ill-advised as the thing being criticized. To prevent classifications such as "mentally retarded," "overweight," "diabetic," "epileptic," "hearing impaired," and "learning disabled," by use of the best means available for diagnosis—standardized measures—would inevitably deny such persons the benefit of the constructive interventions that are available.

The role of measurement and informal observation in decision making will resurface throughout this book. As teachers, we should strive always to plan and use our measurement activities in such ways as to inform the decisions that we and others make. And we must be able to judge the adequacy of data used in decision making (Stiggins, 1991). The utility of a test to enhance decision making is directly related to the test's validity. For this reason, much attention will be devoted in Part II to building valid teacher-made tests.

Measurement and Evaluation As Components of Teaching

As emphasized above, measurement and evaluation are inseparable components of teaching. It has been observed that education without evaluation is like target practice in the dark. Much research demonstrates that classroom evaluation practices have great impact upon student learning (Crooks, 1988). Teachers should, therefore, pursue *better teaching through better testing*. This task is not always easy; research indicates that assessment is one of the most complex aspects of teaching (Stiggins, Conklin, & Bridgeford, 1986).

Some of the ways in which classroom measurement practices contribute to effective instruction can be previewed at this time. Some of the more obvious contributions that testing makes to student learning involve feedback to teachers and students concerning problems experienced by individuals and groups. Results of tests and informal observations help teachers decide what instruction to pursue for an individual student or for a whole class. Such information is useful in selecting content, in pacing the individual student or the class, in judging when and how much to repeat and review, and in pinpointing specific sources of student difficulties.

Another widely recognized contribution that classroom assessment practices make to effective teaching concerns the fact that tests motivate students to study. If it were not for tests, many students would study much less than they do. That one may deplore this fact does not invalidate it.

Similarly, tests influence when students will study. If tests are administered only infrequently, many learners do not effectively pace their study; some neglect their study until the test approaches and then they "cram." Even at the university level, most students study most diligently when a test is imminent, which may be the reason that a growing body of research findings at the high school and college levels indicate that more frequent classroom testing is associated with enhanced student learning (Bangert-Drowns, Kulik, & Kulik, 1986). The motivational and pacing powers of tests are resources to be aware of and to capitalize on.

Other impacts of classroom testing are less obvious but highly important. One of these is known as the *testing phenomenon* (Glover, 1989). The mere act of taking a test—even if students have had no opportunity to study or review for it—tends, under certain circumstances, to enhance their ability to remember the material. What are these "certain circumstances"? Basically, the testing phenomenon occurs when the testing of studied material takes place after enough time has elapsed for some forgetting to occur but before the material is lost. It appears that the effort of actively retrieving the "fading" material from memory enhances long-term retention.

Another vital way by which classroom assessment contributes to teaching effectiveness is its communication in the kind of material measured of what students' learning aims or goals ought to be. For example, if a teacher habitually tests nothing more than rote recall, students tend to focus their efforts on rote recall. On the other hand, if tests ordinarily emphasize use of the studied material in new applications, then students tend to set their sights on transfer of learning. As Parts II and III of this book will emphasize, this guiding influence that tests have on student actions is something of which teachers need to be keenly aware. It is a tool that should be used expertly. A teacher's tests and other assessment devices do not merely measure student learning after it has taken place; they also help to shape the occurrence of the learning.

Throughout the remainder of this book, measurement and evaluation will be represented as integral parts of teaching. The National Council on Measurement in Education, the American Federation of Teachers, and the National Education Association endorse this view that "student assessment is an essential part of teaching and that good teaching cannot exist without good student assessment" (Sanders et al., 1990, p. 30). These three professional organizations sponsored a Committee on Standards for Teacher Competence in Educational Assessment of Students, which issued a statement of seven standards. Each standard concerned teacher competencies believed to contribute to teachers' ability to obtain information useful in making educational decisions about students and to provide feedback about student achievement. The standards are:

1. Teachers should be skilled in *choosing* assessment methods appropriate for instructional decisions.

2. Teachers should be skilled in *developing* assessment methods appropriate for instructional decisions.

3. The teacher should be skilled in *administering, scoring, and interpreting* the results of both externally-produced and teacher-produced assessment methods.

4. Teachers should be skilled in *using assessment results* when making decisions about individual students, planning teaching, developing curriculum, and school improvement.

5. Teachers should be skilled in *developing valid pupil grading procedures* which use pupil assessments.

6. Teachers should be skilled in *communicating assessment results* to students, parents, other lay audiences, and other educators.

7. Teachers should be skilled in *recognizing unethical, illegal, and otherwise inappropriate assessment methods* and uses of assessment information (Sanders, et al., 1990).

This book is designed to contribute to each of the above skills necessary for effective student assessment—and, therefore necessary for effective teaching.

Similarly, it is designed to help readers achieve the requirements of assessment literacy that have been proposed (Lambert, 1991). The central purpose of the book is to enable teachers to use planned, balanced, and integrated assessment to enhance their teaching effectiveness.

A Demonstration Test

Although tests almost always should be used to help make better decisions, this principle will now be violated with a minor exception. A test will be used purely for instructional purposes.

Since this is a book largely about measuring, you will now take a test to provide a common experience on which to build various topics in subsequent chapters. The test will be on knowledge of state capitals—a topic that is (a) somewhat familiar to most readers and (b) sufficiently low in importance to avoid eliciting anxiety or embarrassment.

QUIZ 1–1

Please number from 1 to 10 on a piece of blank paper. Next to each numeral, write the name of the capital of the state having the same numeral below. Do not consult references or people; do the best you can on your own. Your score will be the number correct.

1. Idaho
2. South Carolina
3. Illinois
4. Connecticut
5. Hawaii
6. Washington
7. New York
8. Colorado
9. Florida
10. New Mexico

After taking the test, score your own answer sheet by use of the key provided at the end of this chapter. Then consider thoughtfully each of the issues set forth below. Finally, read the comments on these issues.

Issues to Contemplate

1.   In scoring a completion test such as this, the issue of spelling invariably arises. Should scoring penalize for spelling errors?

2.   Many readers of this book at one time or another have "mastered" the state capitals. Yet most of these same people score between 3 and 7. What, then, is "mastery"?

3.   If you answered 5 of these 10 questions correctly, is it correct to say that you know 50% of the state capitals?

4.   Is it more meaningful to interpret your score with respect to the fraction of the content you answered correctly or with regard to the fraction of other examinees whose performance you excelled?

5.   When individual test questions are used to infer about a person's competence, how reliable is the inference?

Comments on Issues

1.   Should incorrect spelling be penalized? The answer may depend on the purpose of the test. In a geography unit on state capitals, it would be reasonable to have *partial* loss of credit for errors of spelling, but only partial. It is surely far better to misspell "Tallahassee" than to offer "Miami," "Orlando," or "Disney World" as the answer!

But unlike a geography unit, consider the context in which the test was presented. Had the test been administered by a tutor, it might well have been given orally; the issue of spelling would then be moot. If the intent is to find the fraction of capitals known, then the artifact of test format seems less important than the knowledge. In the context in which this test was presented, I do not penalize for spelling errors when the examinee's intent is clearly correct. But *partial* penalty for spelling errors would not be inappropriate. On the other hand, "Columbus" for Item 2 or "Olympus" for Item 6 would be counted wrong because the misconceptions transcend mere spelling. And, of course, there are always some borderline "calls"; for Item 5, "Honoluuluu" might be tolerated, but what about "Honolu," "Hono," "Honulau," or "Honoluau"?

Along the same lines, I would not penalize a measurement student's misspelling of "symbiotic" on an essay describing the interrelated role of measurement and instruction, although I would mark the error to call it to the student's attention. On the other hand, I would penalize the same spelling error if it were made in a biology class that had just studied the concept, word, and spelling of "symbiosis."

2.   What is *mastery*? Although the word has a ring of definiteness and permanence to it, its meaning is really quite elusive. It is clear to most people from taking this test that "mastered" material may be forgotten unless it is used.

This question raises a very important principle of teaching and testing. Certain kinds of learning, such as generalizations, principles, and applications, tend to be more permanent than rote verbal knowledge. These kinds of meaningful and transferable learning also tend to be more useful in everyday life than nonmeaningful memorized material. It, therefore, makes excellent sense for teachers to stress the higher kinds of learning *both* in their teaching and in their testing. This duality will be a major recurring theme of this book.

3.   If you answered 5 of the 10 questions correctly, is it correct to say that you know 50% of the state capitals? No. Allowance must be made for sampling error. Suppose a person knows 30 of the 50 capitals. Depending on which states happened to appear on the test, the score could be expected to fall somewhere between about 4 and about 8; it could conceivably be anything from 0 to 10. Content sampling error

is thus a major concern to which substantial attention will be given in Chapters 3, 4, and 15. Chapter 3 will take up another dimension of this question—what "know" means.

4.   Is it more meaningful to interpret your score in terms of *content* you answered correctly or the *people* you outperformed? It is a major contention of this book that some measures are suited only to content-referenced (often called criterion-referenced or domain-referenced) interpretations, some are suited only to people-referenced (usually called norm-referenced) interpretations, and some are well suited to both. The State Capitals Test is well suited to both kinds of interpretation. Chapter 3 will treat this issue in depth.

5.   How reliable is a single test item? An answer like, "not very," is a serious understatement. Individual test questions and single informal observations are notoriously inaccurate (Nunnally, 1978). Whether or not an examinee answered a particular question correctly depends in part, of course, upon how much that person knows. It also depends in larger part upon luck. Did the State Capitals Test contain the state in which you now live or a state in which you attended school? If so, you had good luck. If it happened not to sample any state in which you have ever lived, you had bad luck.

A different aspect of luck involves guessing. A guess may or may not be correct. For example, "Boise" is a common guess for Item 1; it happens to be correct. On the other hand, "Chicago" is a frequent guess for Item 3; it is incorrect.

Chapter 15 will show that short tests tend *not* to yield very consistent scores. If a test or subtest is expected to provide reasonably useful scores, then it must be made long enough to provide a relatively broad sample of content so that luck will have less impact on the scores. Similarly, if reliability is wanted for informal observations, then conclusions must be based on multiple observations, not on one or two alone. In this way, the noise of random chance and luck in guessing is reduced so that the signal of the attribute being measured can be clearly detected.

The issues touched on in this section provide a preview of some of the topics with which educational measurement is concerned. As these and other topics are considered in later parts of the book, we shall refer back to the State Capitals Test.

KEY TO STATE CAPITALS TEST

1.   Boise
2.   Columbia
3.   Springfield
4.   Hartford
5.   Honolulu
6.   Olympia
7.   Albany
8.   Denver
9.   Tallahassee
10. Santa Fe

Chapter Summary

Teachers measure and evaluate constantly. Some school measurement is done with published, standardized instruments. More is done with teacher-made tests. Still more is done by means of informal observations. Regardless of the data-gathering methods used, teachers measure in order to gather data about student status and then evaluate by applying judgments to the results of the measurement.

Measurement almost always is designed to *improve decision making*. Educators should not lose sight of the role of school measurement in improving student learning by means of knowledgeable decision making. To forget this goal of measurement causes perversion of its proper and constructive role.

In addition to its role in helping people make wiser decisions, *measurement guides student learning* in several important ways. It prompts many students to study. It influences when they will study. It largely controls whether they will review. It focuses their study on the kinds of learning being tested, and it diverts them from the study of kinds of learning that are not assessed. Measurement is, therefore, a powerful tool with which teachers can enhance their instructional effectiveness.

Suggestions for Further Reading

Airasian, P. W. (1991). *Classroom assessment*. New York: McGraw-Hill. Chapter One, "The Classroom As an Assessment Environment," frames a general perspective to classroom assessment and its integral relationship to instruction.

Ebel, R. L., & Frisbie, D. A. (1991). *Essentials of educational measurement* (5th ed.). Englewood Cliffs, NJ: Prentice-Hall. Chapter One, "The Status of Educational Measurement," gives a general overview of educational measurement in contemporary education. It also introduces several current "hot" measurement topics.

Sanders, J. R., Hills, J. R., Nitko, A. J., Merwin, J. C., Trice, C., Dianda, M., & Schneider, J. (1990). Standards for teacher competence in educational assessment of students. *Educational Measurement: Issues and Practices, 9,* 30–32. Jointly developed by the American Federation of Teachers, the National Council on Measurement in Education, and the National Education Association, this document elaborates each of the seven standards listed in this chapter.

Stiggins, R. J. (1991). Assessment literacy. *Phi Delta Kappan, 72,* 534–539. In this article a persuasive case is made that effective use of classroom assessment should focus on two key questions: What does each assessment tell students about the kinds of achievement teachers value? And what is likely to be the effect on students of each assessment practice used?

Thorndike, R. M., Cunningham, G. K., Thorndike, R. L., & Hagen, E. P. (1991). *Measurement and evaluation in psychology and education* (5th ed.). New York: Macmillan. Chapter One, "Fundamental Issues in Measurement," provides a brief historical perspective of contemporary measurement, an excellent discussion of measurement and decision making, an overview of the measurement process, and an introduction to a few important contemporary measurement issues.

An Instructional Model
That Highlights
Measurement Issues

Classroom measurement does not occur in a vacuum. It takes place in the context of instruction. To understand some of the practical issues and recent developments in classroom assessment, it is necessary to be familiar with the broader instructional context in which it occurs. This chapter addresses several instructional issues that set the stage for classroom measurement.

Among these instructional issues are recent trends, movements, and fads. During the last quarter century, the field of education has experienced several inter-related movements that relate to educational measurement. Use of behavioral objectives crested, criterion or domain referencing came into prominence, the mastery model of instruction attracted considerable attention, performance-based instructional programs proliferated, competency testing for promotion and graduation gained wide political support, measurement-driven instruction came into the limelight, curriculum-based assessment gained support, and several waves of public interest in accountability made headlines.

These mass movements resulted in considerable confusion regarding both the meaning and implications of each one as well as the ways they interrelate, and at times, tangle. Many teachers and administrators have rushed to implement the latest recommended practices in one or more of these areas. At times these efforts have resulted in the mismatching of certain incompatible features, such as some kinds of instructional objectives with some types of subject matter. As noted by the Committee on Standards for Teacher Competence in Educational Assessment of Students, teachers need to be aware that some approaches to classroom assessment are incompatible with certain instructional aims (Sanders et al., 1990). Assessment methods must be appropriately matched with other aspects of instruction.

The purpose of Chapters 2 and 3 is to emphasize practical classroom implications of adopting one or more of several related approaches. Each concerns educational measurement. Yet the topics presented in this chapter are often given little or no emphasis in measurement books. Those discussed in Chapter 3 are almost universally treated, but the relationship among the topics is often neglected. Because of the interrelatedness of the topics, it is helpful to consider all eight. As covered in Chapters 2 and 3, these foci of discussion are:

Manifestations of individual differences

Dimensions of subject matter

Families of Learning Theories

Types of Instruction

Varieties of Instructional Objectives

Kinds of Tests

Types of Test-Score Interpretations

Kinds of Test Scores

As each new topic is addressed, its relationship to previous concepts will be developed. This process will provide a systematic unfolding of a **model (ideational structure) of practical relationships** among these important instructional and measurement considerations. John Muir once said that when one tries to isolate something by itself for scrutiny, it turns out to be hitched to everything else in the universe. Each section of Chapters 2 and 3 focuses on "something," but that thing does not exist in isolation; it is "hitched to everything else" in the assessment-oriented instructional model.

Most of the illustrations used in this book will concern classroom applications of principles. However, a few of the many other potential applications, particularly those germane to counseling, will be pointed out.

While moving from subject to subject, you should experience *déjà vu*. This feeling that "I've been here before" occurs because the eight topics are not only related, but they can also be thought of as providing eight different approaches to, or views of, the same multifaceted reality. This concept is analogous to several photographs of a house taken from different sides. Each contains useful information or perspective that (although often implied) is not explicit from the other angles.

It is important for readers to realize that the following eight topics have *extremely practical implications for effective teaching*. If at times they seem rather theoretical, it should be recalled that nothing is as practical as good theory. The theory is not an end in itself; rather, it is focused on practical classroom applications. Professional practice must always be based on theory—practice without theory lacks rudder and keel. The practical theory provided in Chapters 2 and 3 will provide a coherent framework to "steer a straight course" to effective teaching through effective measurement.

I wish to acknowledge a monumental intellectual debt to Norman E. Gronlund for his book *Stating Objectives for Classroom Instruction*. The kernel of the original ideas that grew into Chapters 2 and 3 is found in his seminal Chapter 6 of the first edition of this superb book.

Individual Differences

From time immemorial, teachers have observed (and often lamented) the fact that students differ. The magnitude of these differences is often great. Some teachers have reacted to the reality of diversity by ignoring the differences and treating all students alike, as though they were alike. Others have reacted to individual differences among their students by trying to wipe them out. (The differences, not the students!) But as Nunnally (1976) humorously observed, the only way to make individual differences vanish is to stick one's head in the sand. For better or for worse, *individual differences cannot be eliminated*. On the contrary, *effective teaching tends to increase individual differences* within a group of students (Feldt & Brennan, 1989, p. 118).

Before this point is amplified, it is worth noting that teachers have a choice as to how individual differences will be manifested. Individual differences can be channeled either into an achievement dimension, into a time-it-takes-to-get-there dimension, or into a combination of the achievement and time dimensions. **This choice of dimensions is of the utmost importance in teaching**, and it will be a recurring issue in this book.

Achievement Dimension

The data shown in Table 2–1 illustrate the results of good teaching. During the year in which these test scores were collected, the teaching of reading was highly effec-

Table 2–1

**Growth of Reading Ability in Three Third-Grade
Classes under Superior Teaching Procedures***

Reading Grade Equivalent	*Number of Pupils*	
	Beginning of Year	*End of Year*
8.1–9.0	0	2
7.1–8.0	0	1
6.1–7.0	1	4
5.1–6.0	2	13
4.1–5.0	7	20
3.1–4.0	37	31
2.1–3.0	38	21
1.1–2.0	8	1

*Adapted from W. W. Cook and T. Clymer, "Accelerating and retardation." In N. B. Henry (Ed.), *Individualizing instruction: The sixty-first yearbook of the National Society for the Study of Education, Part 1*. Chicago: The National Society for the Study of Education, 1962, 190–192.

tive. Teachers provided instruction that both challenged the better readers and was within reach of the poorer ones.

According to the Iowa Tests of Basic Skills, at the beginning of the year some students were reading no better than average first-grade pupils. The top readers, however, did as well as average fifth- and sixth-graders. The range was five grade levels. By the end of the year's instruction in this excellent reading program, the bottom pupil still performed no better than typical first-graders, while the best ones now read as well as average seventh- and eighth-grade students. The achievement now had a range of seven grade levels. *As a result of good teaching, students became more heterogeneous.* That is, they become more variable—their scores spanned a broader range.

Upon reflection, this outcome should not be surprising. When "instruction is equally effective for all groups of students, both the level and the dispersion of outcomes should increase for every group" (Mackenzie, 1983, p. 13). If students vary in capabilities and if teachers assist all to realize their potentials, then the more able will surely gain more than the less able. As Mackenzie indicated, substantial evidence exists that effective schooling expands differences among students rather than contracts them; "rich environments magnify differences in native ability; stultifying environments thwart them" (1983, p. 13). Yet many people are dismayed when they encounter this principle. It seems unfair that the "rich" tend to get "richer," while the "poor" tend to get relatively "poorer."

Arlin (1984) observed that teachers find themselves in an uncomfortable dilemma. They would like to decrease individual differences among students because these differences seem related to inequalities. The lofty tenet exists that all people are created equal, yet teachers are faced daily with individual differences among students, and these differences tend to increase with each year of schooling.

Teachers must recognize, come to grips with, and make constructive use of the reality that individual differences in achievement exist and that they tend to increase during the growing years. To reinforce the importance of this idea, consider two more illustrations of the principle.

Two cars, a vintage Model A Ford and a new Corvette, have a race. Figure 2–1 shows the progress of the race. At the end of the first hour, the Model A has gone 50 miles, while the Corvette has gone 100 miles; although they started together, they are now 50 miles apart. At the end of the second hour, the respective cars have covered totals of 100 and 200 miles; they are now 100 miles apart. At the end of the third hour, they are now 150 miles apart. *The longer they race, the further apart they are.*

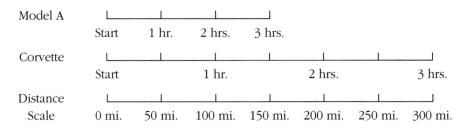

Figure 2–1.   Car Race. The longer they race, the farther apart they are.

It is worth noting that the greater distance traveled by the faster car could be exhibited either in distance from the starting point or in travel on interesting side excursions. Similarly, the greater achievement of some students can be manifested in *level* of achievement and/or in *breadth* of achievement.

Now if you were the mechanic for both of these cars, could you change this outcome? Could you keep the range of distance from increasing with the passage of time? There are two approaches that you could take to attempt this. On the one hand, you could try to make the Model A go faster. But in spite of being in splendid condition, it just does not have the horsepower to go as fast as the new Corvette.

On the other hand, you could try to keep the Corvette from going so fast. You could disconnect a spark plug, substitute kerosene for gasoline, or put sugar in the fuel tank. Clearly, these are not desirable options. A classroom analogy from the reading example would be to prevent the more able readers from reading during the year. These kinds of destructive actions could decrease variability in student achievement over time. In typical teaching situations, however, *it is desirable that all students be helped to achieve their potential.* There are no constructive actions that will decrease individual differences in level or breadth of achievement.

For a final example, consider the increase in individual differences in human height during the growing year. Table 2–2 reports the mean stature of males and females measured at several ages. The amount of individual differences is reported by use of the standard deviation—a widely used measure of variability. For each gender, the general trend is for variability in height to increase during the growing years.

If you were responsible for the diet of these children, could you prevent the individual differences in stature from increasing with the passage of time? Indeed you could. You could see to it that persons taller than average were undernourished. Or, more drastically, once persons attained a height of 5 feet or so you could starve them; this procrustean solution would ensure that most of the children "achieve" very nearly the same height.

Table 2–2

Height in Inches at Selected Ages*

Age	Males		Females	
	Mean	*Standard Deviation*	*Mean*	*Standard Deviation*
1	30.1	1.2	29.6	1.1
3	37.8	1.4	37.5	1.4
6	46.1	1.8	45.8	1.9
18	69.8	2.4	65.1	2.2

*Summarized from three sources: L. M. Bayer and N. Bayley, *Growth diagnosis* (2nd ed.). Chicago: University of Chicago Press, 1976; R. W. McCammon (1970). *Human growth and development.* Springfield, IL.: Thomas; and Pomerance, H.H., & Krall, J.M. (1979). *Growth standards in children.* New York: Harper & Row.

Dismissing such destructive options, all that would be reasonable to do would be to provide the best nutrition available to each short child. But ethically one should do the same for each average child and for each tall child. Thus, differences in height would tend to expand over the growing years.

It is important to note that there is no suggestion that teachers should be content to let low achievers stay low or be fatalistic about the status of individual students. On the contrary, we should strive to maximize the achievement of all students. In addition there is no implication in these examples that one should necessarily treat students of varying abilities in the same manner. As Thomas Jefferson said, there is nothing so unequal as the equal treatment of unequals. A teacher should not give all students the same reading materials, a mechanic should not give the two cars the same kind of gasoline, and a dietitian should not prepare identical diets for people having differing nutritional needs. It is legitimate and appropriate to provide different treatments to different individuals in ways designed to help each attain her or his maximum potential.

These three diverse examples show that when individual differences are channeled into the achievement dimension, they tend to increase during periods of growth. Now consider what happens when individual differences are directed into the time dimension.

Time Dimension

When individual differences are banished from the achievement dimension, they inevitably appear in the time dimension. This occurs when we specify a task that students must be able to perform and work on until it is mastered. For example, one goal could be, "The child correctly spells his or her first name."

Most pupils can be classified quite clearly concerning their mastery or nonmastery of this task. Since most people eventually master it, virtually no individual differences exist in level of achievement. All the readers of this book are equal in spelling their first names correctly.

Although little if any variability is manifested in student *performance*, it nevertheless took individuals varying *amounts of time* to master the task. The individual differences have been channeled into the time dimension. If another task, such as correctly spelling their last names were undertaken, the total amount of instruction required to get all to master both tasks would be more variable than that needed to master only the first task. It is evident that in the time dimension, too, individual differences increase as students proceed through an instructional sequence.

The same three examples will now be re-examined to show how individual differences can be cast in the time dimension rather than in the achievement dimension. If, for the height example, one were to specify that each child is to attain some predetermined height, say 4 feet, 9 inches, one could note when each attained this stature and disregard the extent by which persons missed or surpassed this arbitrary goal or standard. The first of a class-sized group may reach this height by about 8 years of age; the average child might achieve it near age 11; and the last in the group will probably achieve it near age 14. Nearly everybody will reach the fixed height, but the amount of time required to reach it will vary by several years.

In the car example, suppose each car is to be driven a fixed distance of 300 miles. At 50 miles per hour, the Model A will require 6 hours to travel this distance. The Corvette, traveling twice as fast, will need only 3 hours. When distance is held constant, individual differences are manifested entirely in the time dimension. The greater the distance, the more differences will exist between the cars' traveling time.

Finally, in the reading illustration, one could specify that each pupil is to attain a grade equivalent score of at least 3.0. Some children in a typical school may reach this arbitrary goal while they are still in the first grade, while others may be in the sixth grade or beyond before attaining it. It takes people vastly different amounts of time to reach the same level.

Making a Choice

Individual differences, then, are ubiquitous. Moreover, they are here to stay. But teachers and other professionals have to make critical decisions concerning how the differences are channeled—into the achievement dimension, into the time dimension, or into a combination of the two. This choice can be represented by the seesaw shown in Figure 2–2. If the left-hand side of the seesaw goes up as far as possible, then people achieve differing levels and/or breadth of success in a given amount of time. If the right-hand side goes up as far as possible, then people differ in the amount of time it takes them to achieve at a given level and breadth.

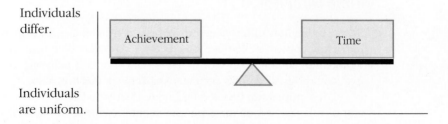

Figure 2–2.   Manifestation of Individual Difference

Of course, it is also possible, and sometimes desirable, to channel some of a group's variability into each dimension. For example, one could decide to have the Model A driven for 8 hours to achieve a distance of 400 miles and have the Corvette driven for 6 hours to cover 600 miles. The cars would then differ in both dimensions, but they would not differ as much in either dimension as they would if the other one were held constant.

Figure 2–2 represents the absolute necessity of individual differences surfacing in some way. It is not possible to have all students reach the same level of achievement in the same amount of time. If equal learning time is desired, as it is in many current forms of schooling, then inequalities in achievement seem inevitable. If equality of achievement is chosen, as it is in mastery learning, then inequality of time seems necessary (Arlin, 1984, p. 83). One side of the seesaw can be depressed *or* the other side can be depressed, but both sides cannot go down at the same time.

Some mastery learning theorists (e.g., Bloom, 1976; Guskey, 1985) have argued that mastery learning strategies offer the potential simultaneously to reduce or eliminate individual differences in both learning rates and achievement levels. But both theory (e.g., Glass & Smith, 1978) and experimental data (e.g., Slavin, 1987b) challenge the realism of such dreams. If teachers pursue mastery learning with the expectation that individual differences in both dimensions will simultaneously be minimized, they are likely to be as disappointed as seekers of the Holy Grail or the Fountain of Youth. It is as futile to declare war on individual differences as it is maladaptive to stick one's head in the sand.

Some Cautions

It was stated earlier that good teaching increases student differences in the achievement and/or the time dimension. Thus the absence of an increase in a group's variability suggests that good teaching has *not* taken place. But the presence of an increase does *not* demonstrate that all is well because individual differences can be increased by undesirable as well as by desirable means. For example, consider the poor readers who could have been deprived of suitable reading material, the Model A that could have been driven on flat tires, or the short children who could have been underfed. Therefore, change in a group's variability during instruction is *not* an appropriate isolated basis by which to evaluate quality of instruction.

A note of caution should also be sounded concerning basic competency testing programs. If it has been (probably ill-advisedly) decided to deny promotion from an elementary school until students have reached a certain level of performance in, say, reading comprehension, then much thought should be given to establishing the level of competence that is to be required. As will be shown, reading comprehension, like much other subject matter, is not well suited to having levels of achievement specified in any way other than statements about students' status in comparison with other people.

Unless care is taken, the standard set may result in far more failures than have been anticipated or are defensible. For example, if it were specified that students' reading comprehension grade equivalent scores on a specified test must be at least at the sixth-grade level (i.e., 6.0 or higher) before graduation from sixth grade, then an appalling 30 to 50% of the sixth-graders in a typical school would be retained! A lower standard would obviously be indicated. Indeed, in view of research findings on the adverse consequences of retention (Shepard & Smith, 1990), it would probably be wiser to refrain from use of standards for this purpose. Great care and sound professional judgment need to be exercised in setting realistic standards for basic competency testing programs. It is very easy to blunder into one or another subtle form of the expectation that everybody will be at least average, to say, for example, "We expect all students to be able to read at grade level." Efforts to bring everyone up to the average tend to be less than successful. They deny the existence of individual differences.

QUIZ 2–1

First answer each of the following questions. Then proceed to the key to score it. For any items you missed, study the explanation.

1. When the author stated that efforts to bring everyone up to the average are prone to be less than successful, he was engaging in

    A. slight exaggeration.
    B. gross understatement.
    C. flagrant falsification.

2. The author takes the position that individual differences in achievement should be

    A. ignored or denied.
    B. minimized.
    C. maximized.
    D. understood and controlled.

3. Into which dimension(s) will good teachers channel individual differences?

    A. The time dimension only.
    B. The achievement dimension only.
    C. Whichever dimension or combination of dimensions is most suitable for the subject matter.
    D. Neither dimension because good teaching will eliminate individual differences.

4. If you were trying to teach a class of monolingual, English-speaking, seventh-grade students to spell 20 Spanish nouns perfectly, about how long would it likely take the slowest student in the class to learn the lesson?

    A. About 10% longer than the fastest student in the class.
    B. About 25% longer than the fastest student in the class.
    C. About 50% longer than the fastest student in the class.
    D. Several times as long as the fastest student in the class.

QUIZ 2–1 (cont.)

5. If a class spent a semester studying high school biology and if all students devoted the same amount of time to the course, then achievement at the end of the semester on a comprehensive test of biology would probably be
   A. more variable than at the beginning of the semester.
   B. about as variable as at the end of the semester.
   C. less variable than at the end of the semester.

KEY TO QUIZ 2–1

Item	Key	Comments
1	B	Such attempts are ludicrous.
2	D	This is a major principle. If you chose Option C, see the first caution on page 23.
3	C	When the subject is vital, individual differences in achievement are best exhibited in the time dimension. Otherwise, individual differences are usually best exhibited in level or breadth of achievement. The following sections will assist in making this important choice.
4	D	This issue was not specifically covered, but the examples cited may enable you to guess the answer. Option D is the only one that is in the right "ball park." Variability is usually great; often it takes slower students 3 to 7 times as long to reach a standard of mastery as it takes faster learners (Gettinger, 1984).
5	A	Variability increases with time during periods of growth. When instructional time is held constant, variability in achievement will increase. See page 21.

Dimensions Of Subject Matter

In view of the enormous diversity of subject matter taught in schools, it is not surprising that methods of instruction that are well suited to some kinds of content may be seriously ill suited to other types. Indeed, it seems naive to expect a particular set of teaching methods (e.g., clinical teaching, discovery learning, mastery learning, cooperative learning) to work well with all kinds of subject matter.

Nor is it surprising that the dimension into which a teacher should elect to channel individual differences for one kind of subject matter may differ from the dimension appropriate for other content. The kind of subject matter being taught and the kind of students being taught should also influence the kind of learning theory upon which instruction is based, the kind of instructional objectives used, the kind of tests given, and the way test results are interpreted. This **subject matter** is not an isolated factor; *it has implications for much of what teachers do.* This section explores some of these implications and lays the foundations for other implications that will be considered later.

Content can be categorized in many ways. Two that are helpful in harmoniously matching kind of subject matter with kinds of individual differences, instruction, tests, and score interpretation are treated in this section. One distinction is between content that can readily be specified in its entirety and content that cannot be laid out in full detail. The other distinction is between subject matter that can, more or less, be mastered and content that clearly cannot be mastered.

Figure 2–3 represents these two dimensions of subject matter. Each dimension ranges from low to high. For convenience, each has been divided into low and high regions. This division yields four cells (one of which will turn out to be empty). Each dimension could have been divided in other ways such as into high, medium, and low regions. Now consider the kinds of content that fit into the respective cells.

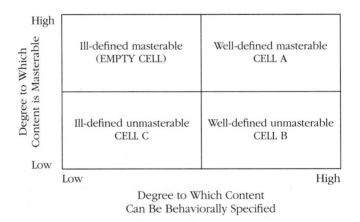

Figure 2–3.   Dimensions for Classifying Content

Easily Specifiable, Masterable Content (Cell A)

Some subject matter can be identified and covered quite adequately by lists of instructional objectives that state (a) what tasks the learner must perform, (b) the circumstances in which the tasks are to be executed, and (c) the levels of proficiency sought. Four examples follow of behavioral objectives for content high in both masterability and specifiability (Cell A in Figure 2–3).

1. When presented with randomly ordered flash cards of the 26 capital letters of the English alphabet, the pupil will orally name at least 25 of the letters correctly.

2. When approaching electric traffic signals on foot, the child will await the green light before crossing each of three different intersections.

3. During free play, the toddler will get to the toilet before urinating with no more than one accident per day.

4. After completing training for the assembly-line job, the worker will correctly install the three bolts on each unit with no more than one faulty installation per 100 units.

For teachers of primary-level pupils or of students who are learning disabled or mentally retarded, the above examples may be rather typical of the kind of content that holds center stage much of the time. It is essential for such material to be learned. It is reasonable and appropriate to demand that students *master* these kinds of tasks. They are *essential* for minimal level functioning and/or for successful study of the material that follows.

When it is essential that students master certain basic material, individual differences should be channeled into the time dimension. The teacher will keep drilling each child on the letters of the alphabet until they are mastered. Society cannot afford variability in how people respond to red and green traffic lights; hence individual differences should be diverted into the time dimension. If it takes one child five times as long as another to learn to stop for a red light, so be it! Each child will eventually master bladder control, but the age at which this is achieved will differ dramatically. Each industrial trainee must master the job before it is profitable to turn her or him loose on the assembly line.

In each of these examples, the content can be mastered. One could, of course, disagree over just how mastery is defined. One could just as well have defined mastery of the alphabet as 24 out of 26 trials instead of 25 out of 26, or allowed the toddler only two or three accidents per week instead of one per day. Nevertheless, the notion of mastery can reasonably be applied to content of this kind. Teachers would have little difficulty in agreeing on which pupils had mastered the names of the capital letters, definition of the six trigonometric functions, bladder control, etc. Likewise therapists would be in substantial agreement concerning clients' success on overcoming bed-wetting or smoking. These kinds of easily specified content can sensibly be said to be masterable.

The concept of **subject matter domain** is helpful in contrasting the kind of content discussed in this section with those of the later sections. For some kinds of instruction, the domain of content is very limited. For example, only 10 Hindu-Arabic numerals exist. In teaching such material, we can drill on every element of the domain. We need not be very concerned with transfer of learning because we can teach everything in the domain.

Before leaving the upper right-hand cell of Figure 2–3, it should be mentioned that not all easily specifiable, masterable content merits being mastered. For example, most readers could master the names and dates of all English monarchs since William the Conqueror or the name of every bone in the human body. Yet few persons need to master such content. When it is vital for learners to master certain foundational subject matter, individual differences should be channeled into the time dimension. But if it is not particularly important for students to achieve mastery of content, even though the content could be masterable, then individual differences should be channeled into the achievement dimension.

Easily Specifiable, Unmasterable Content (Cell B)

Now turn to Cell B of Figure 2–3 and consider content that is easily specified but cannot be mastered. One could reasonably claim to have mastered telephone dialing, the 100 addition facts, or bladder control. It would not be arrogant to claim mastery of these kinds of basic tasks. But could one reasonably proclaim oneself a master at golf, speed keyboarding, or endurance in a unicycling marathon? No.

An important distinction exists between the kinds of content in the two lists in Table 2–3. The left-hand list consists of specifiable content that, for all practical purposes, has a ceiling above which one cannot progress—that is, content that can be mastered. When content of this type is taught, it often is expected that each student will master it.

Table 2–3	

Examples of Masterable and Unmasterable, Easily Specified Content

Masterable	*Unmasterable*
Telephone dialing	Golf
Letter names	Bowling
Multiplication facts	Multiplication speed
Bladder control	Pole vaulting
Trigonometric functions	Keyboarding speed

But when specifiable content like that illustrated in the right-hand side of Table 2–3 is taught, there is no point beyond which we cease to value further achievement of excellence. We are not prepared to set a level so low that virtually everyone will eventually reach it (e.g., keyboard at least 20 words per minute) and be uninterested in advancement beyond that level. We are not content to settle for universal mediocrity. Rather, we wish to enable each student to achieve as much as possible within available time.

A second important distinction between the two kinds of well-defined content illustrated in Table 2–3 is that *masterable content is often, but not always, essential for successful study of subsequent material.* Such subject matter is frequently inherently sequential. Children must know the letter names before learning to spell. Trigonometry students need to know the six trigonometric functions before they can go very far in the subject. Pupils need to know the addition facts before they can efficiently study subtraction or multiplication.

On the other hand, *unmasterable content is usually not essential for successful study of subsequent material.* Such subject matter usually is not inherently sequential. Students need not reach a certain fixed level of skill in golf before learning tennis or before playing golf on a more difficult course. Pupils do not have to be able to multiply at some particular speed before learning to divide. Students do not have to be able to keyboard prose at some predetermined speed before they learn how to keyboard tables.

For subject matter that is not essential for students to master, part or all of the individual differences should be channeled into the achievement dimension. We would not insist that students attain some arbitrary speed in running before allowing them to move on to archery. Rather, we would sensibly hold time constant and let the individual differences be exhibited in level of achievement. Nor would we demand some particular level of achievement in basketball free throws before allowing students to practice dribbling. Here too, individual differences should be channeled into the achievement dimension.

Nonspecifiable, Unmasterable Content (Cell C)

Now turn to the lower-left cell of Figure 2–3 (Cell C). This cell contains the subject matter that properly dominates most teachers' instruction because most subject matter (especially that taught beyond the first two or three years of school) cannot be adequately identified in its entirety by lists of specific behavioral objectives. (It can, however, as will be seen in Chapter 3, be illustrated by specific behavioral examples.) For example:

1. Application of the Bill of Rights to current events
2. Knowledge and attitudes from a third-grade unit on India
3. Resolution of interpersonal conflicts harmoniously and equitably
4. Appreciation from a unit on Beethoven
5. Silent reading comprehension

Such subject matter cannot, with reasonable effort, be specified in detail. The objectives should provide for **transfer of learning**. We should not be content that students merely can perform pre-identified tasks at specified levels. They must be able to *apply* what they have learned to new situations that have not been specifically taught.

Consider, for example, a unit of instruction of the Bill of Rights. We could test an individual's ability to identify or to recall each of the first 10 amendments to the Constitution. But if we were concerned with the meaning, the significance, and the application of these same 10 amendments in contemporary America, how could we meaningfully define and sample from that domain? In this instance the notion of "mastery" slips through our fingers (Thorndike, Cunningham, Thorndike, & Hagen, 1991, p. 166).

Even justices of the Supreme Court have not mastered applications of the Bill of Rights. If they all had, all the relevant decisions would be unanimous.

It is not possible to master such subject matter. Who has achieved the ultimate in conflict resolution, appreciation of Beethoven, or insights concerning India? Nobody! Nor does it seem necessary to achieve at some arbitrary level because such subject matter is not inherently sequential. The major purpose of units like these could have been achieved with entirely different content. Counseling or instruction concerning conflict resolution could be based on content of anything from marital harmony to classroom management to industrial labor relations. A Beethoven unit could, for some purposes, just as well be a unit on Brahms. Most of the important objectives of a unit on India could be attained just as well by a unit on China. Moreover, if both countries were to be studied, it would not matter which was studied first. Thus teachers have great latitude in selecting subject matter to use in pursuit of important learning outcomes.

When subject matter (a) cannot be mastered, (b) need not be handled at a given level of proficiency before students can move on to subsequent content, and (c) cannot conveniently be specified in detail, then individual differences should be channeled largely or wholly into the achievement dimension. Each student should be helped to achieve as much as possible within the available time. There is no point beyond which teachers are uninterested in attainment of greater depth and breadth.

It may be useful to re-emphasize that holding instructional time constant does *not* imply holding instructional method or instructional content constant. A rich variety of content and/or teaching methods could be used in a given unit according to appropriateness for the students. Thus, every attempt is made to help each learner achieve as highly as possible either by using uniform content and teaching methods or, more often, by varying them. But with content that is neither masterable nor highly specifiable, no procrustean attempt should be made to stretch or compress everyone to fit some arbitrary standard of achievement.

In the kinds of teaching that most teachers do most of the time, the domain of content is too large to be covered in its entirety. For example, because many thousands of applications exist for the Bill of Rights, the potential content domain of a unit on it is virtually infinite. Moreover, the boundaries of the domain are not precise. The bright light of consensus around the key elements of a domain (e.g., freedom of speech to criticize government officials) fades into the shadows that define the domain boundaries. Hence the domain is not incisively specifiable. It is debatable whether or not various borderline topics (e.g., obscene speech or student newspapers) are part of the domain. Similarly, the domain of passages that one could read and comprehend is infinite. In teaching this kind of content, we cannot hope to treat each element in the domain. Because we can only teach a small part of the available content, *we must teach for transfer of learning.* In this sense, we seek to develop in students a "latent trait" (in contrast to an overt behavior) such as appreciation.

Subject matter that cannot be specified in detail cannot be mastered. If a domain of content cannot be exhaustively laid out, then the entire domain cannot be mastered. Therefore, the examples of unspecifiable content all fall in the lower left-hand cell of Figure 2–3. The upper left-hand cell is empty.

TO RECAP

The kinds of content will now be related more explicitly to the dimensions of individual differences considered in the last section. Table 2–4 summarizes the relationship between the manifestations of individual differences and the types of subject matter. At the left of Table 2–4 are the letters **A**, **B**, and **C**. These provide labels for the tracks by which we can refer to selected compatible combinations of manifestations of individual differences and types of subject content.

Table 2–4

Model of Relationships between Manifestation of Individual Differences and Types of Subject Matter

Track	Principal Manifestation of Individual Differences	Type of Subject Matter
A	Time dimension	Entire content readily specified, vital, and masterable.
B	Achievement dimension	Tasks readily specified but cannot or need not be mastered.
C	Achievement dimension	Content can neither be tightly specified nor mastered.

You should memorize these lettered tracks at this time. They will be expanded and used as a conceptual framework for numerous classroom measurement issues considered throughout this book.

To review, *Track A is appropriate for situations in which clearly and incisively defined, masterable content is considered essential.* In this case, each student is kept on the content until it is mastered; individual differences are exhibited wholly or largely in the dimension of time it takes to master the task. Examples are adherence to traffic lights, matching the first 10 Roman numerals with the corresponding Hindu-Arabic numerals, certain basic phonic skills, and (for the counselee seeking it) termination of smoking.

Track B is suitable for teaching (a) tightly defined but unmasterable material and (b) specifiable and masterable content that is not deemed essential. In these cases, students are allowed approximately the same amount of time on the content; individual differences therefore appear mainly in achievement. Examples of specifiable but unmasterable material are keyboarding speed and high jumping. Examples of nonessential, well-defined, masterable content are the Gettysburg Address and the square roots to five significant digits of positive integers less than 10.

TO RECAP (cont.)

Track C is appropriate for situations in which the subject matter can be neither tightly specified nor mastered. In this case, students are allowed approximately equal amounts of time for learning; individual differences, therefore, appear mainly in the achievement dimension. Examples are Shakespeare appreciation, knowing human anatomy, parenting, understanding the Bill of Rights, and reading comprehension.

QUIZ 2–2

Below is a modification of Figure 2–3 in which each dimension is divided into three regions. The nine resulting cells are identified by number. Identify the most appropriate cell for each of the following content domains or questions. (It may be wise to check the answers to the first item or two before doing all of them.)

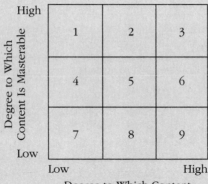

1.   A middle school unit on short stories

2.   Most of the work of an elementary school, remedial reading teacher

3.   A physical education unit on the 100-meter dash

4.   A listening comprehension unit in second-year French

5.   Therapeutic attention to a person's hostility toward authority figures

6.   The topics addressed in this book

7.   A beginning French unit on conjugating regular verbs

8.   A middle school unit on reading directions on medicine bottle labels

9.   Compared with other teachers of the same grade and subject, in which cell should teachers of gifted students spend more time?

10. Which cell has no content?

KEY TO QUIZ 2–2

Item	Key	Comments
1	7	A case might be made for 4 or 8 or possibly for 5. Any other answer is definitely wrong because comprehension and appreciation cannot be fully specified or totally attained. See pages 29–30.
2	3 and/or 2 and/or 6 and/or 5	Remedial instruction tends to focus on essentials basics that are vital for future progress. Remediation is needed only when student deficiencies concern fundamentals.
3	9	The task is very well defined by track regulations, but it certainly cannot be mastered. (The fact that the "score" is kept in seconds of time does not mean that individual differences are exhibited in the time dimension. These are entirely different things.) See pages 28–29.
4	7	Listening comprehension cannot be tightly specified; it is not well defined. One's comprehension depends largely on the content being read. Cells 4, 8, and 5 may possibly be reasonable answers. See pages 29–30.
5	7	Variations in kinds of authority figures and circumstances of interaction render this a huge and fuzzy domain. But, again, Cells 4, 8, and 5 are not unreasonable.
6	7	It is neither tightly specifiable nor masterable. However, some case could be made for 4, 8, or 5. See pages 29–30.
7	3	The content is so important for students of French that it makes sense to keep students on it until they have mastered it. It is clearly and tightly defined and entirely masterable. (*Ir*regular verbs are in or near 7.) See pages 27–28.
8	5 and/or 2 and/or 6 and/or 3	Here the domain has been so drastically curtailed from reading comprehension in general that the content is *relatively* specifiable. It is also *relatively* masterable. There is legitimate room for argument concerning the cell into which it best fits. (General reading comprehension, of course, is Cell 7.)
9	7	Gifted students need less-than-average time to master the basics. They need instruction that takes them far, far beyond the minimal essentials.
10	1	See page 30.

Evaluating Your Score

Obviously the more questions you answered correctly, the greater your comprehension is likely to be. These items were harder than some and easier than others that could just as well have been used. Therefore, there is no implication that you must answer some specified number (for example 9 or 10) correctly before being capable of moving on to other topics. I am willing to let individual differences be exhibited partly in the achievement dimension. Like Cronbach (1977, p. 536), I would not require the tennis player to "master" the forehand drive before engaging in an actual game. But being able to return most of the slow balls that come near is a reasonable expectation. Since the *presentation* of the material is sequenced (even though the material itself is not inherently sequential), it is wise to be at least modestly familiar with the section's content before using it as a foundation for subsequent chapters. If you answered fewer than 8 or so questions in a keyed or identified defensible way, it would be prudent to divert *some* of the individual differences into the time dimension by restudying the chapter.

Families of Learning Theories

Learning theory is another topic that carries implications for classroom assessment practices. As Shepard (1991) has pointed out, some of the most heated contemporary controversies in educational measurement can be traced to the fact that educators' measurement practices relate to their perspective concerning how people learn. Too often the learning theory implications of measurement practices—such as mastery testing—are neither recognized nor understood. This section will fit human learning theories into the model of relationships and make the learning theory-measurement connections explicit.

An abundance of learning theories exists that can leave students overwhelmed by confusion. Fortunately, the field is rendered relatively comprehensible if most of the competing scientific theories of human learning are classified into two major groups—**behavioral** and **cognitive theories**.

Some advocates of particular learning theories (especially early ones) have offered their respective explanations of human learning as the sole or at least the primary explanation of all human learning. This attitude set the stage for expecting teachers to choose between the two major families of theories. Vacillating back and forth between them in organizing one's teaching and testing would have been considered a sign of inconsistency or confusion. In some ways, the expected choice was like a choice of religion; it would not make much sense to be a Hindu each spring, convert to Buddhism in the summer, become a Muslim in the fall, and a Christian come winter.

In contrast to this stance, the position taken in this book is that each of the two families of learning theories is highly appropriate to *some* teaching and testing situations and less suited to others. I believe teachers should be situationally consistent, using each orientation where it makes sense and avoiding it where it is unsuitable. Thus, an analogy of wardrobe would be better than one of religion. It is perfectly appropriate to wear different kinds of clothes in each season. There can and should be consistency between what is worn and when it is worn; that is, the clothes should match the season. It would be foolish to wear the same kind of apparel, irrespective of weather. The nature of the subject matter one is trying to teach is a useful basis for determining which orientation toward learning is best suited for one's needs.

This section sketches the two major groups of learning theories. Each will be related to the kind of subject content to which it seems most congenial. Although sufficient diversity exists within each family of theories to render precise comparisons hazardous, it is nonetheless helpful to characterize each general orientation by means of several topics. The following contrasts are drawn mainly from Bigge and Shermis (1992) and Hergenhahn (1988).

Behavioral Learning Theories

What Is Learned?

In describing what is learned, behaviorists focus on observable **behaviors**. They use terms such as "stimulus-response association," "habits," and "reinforcement contingencies." Teachers of this persuasion usually specify educational goals in behavioral terms and then organize instruction to prompt the desired behaviors.

What Does Reinforcement Do?

Reinforcement is a central notion in contemporary behaviorism. Reinforcement causes **organisms** to form stimulus-response associations. It causes organisms to learn contingencies (i.e., what happens if . . .). Behaviorists emphasize various conditions of reinforcement that influence rate of responding and likelihood that responses will occur in the future.

How Are Problems Solved?

Behaviorists tend to view a problem's degree of difficulty as a function of its similarity to other problems the learner has experienced in the past. If an attempted solution fails or if the learner has never encountered such a problem, she or he resorts to **trial-and-error** until a solution is chanced on and reinforced.

What Is the Actional Nature of Learners?

Behaviorists tend to accept Locke's position that the mind begins like a blank slate. They, therefore, emphasize the paramount role of environmental input via sensory experience in forming the content of the mind. Teachers accepting this position view the learner as a *passive receiver* of what is taught.

Perspective

Behaviorists view learning as the **acquisition of behaviors**, not as some unobservable happening in a vague construct called "mind." Their perspective is mechanical in that the organism's learning is thought to be similar to a machine's "programming." They tend to be reductionistic in that they are prone to analyze a complex task into its simplest components and then to consider the whole to be no more than the sum of its component parts.

Behaviorist teachers tend to see learning hierarchies as linear sequences of component parts, each step of which must be completed in turn in order to develop higher-order learning. From this perspective it is appropriate to analyze the task to be learned, to reduce it to its simplest elements, and then to organize these elements into the best sequence. This procedure is similar to building a block tower; each block must be in place before the next one is added. An important practical consequence of this model of instruction is that higher-order learning is delayed until the prerequisite skills have been mastered (Shepard, 1991, p. 5).

Cognitive Learning Theories

What Is Learned?

Cognitive theorists describe what is learned in terms of **mental constructs** such as information, expectancies, understandings, appreciations, principles, and insights. Teachers of this persuasion tend to identify mental as well as behavioral educational goals and then to organize their teaching to help students enlarge, clarify, and reorganize their cognitive framework.

What Does Reinforcement Do?

Most cognitive theorists think learning takes place independently of reinforcement. They view reinforcement as important mainly because it provides the **person** with information; this information acts as a means by which the individual thinks or reasons about a problem.

Notice the contrast between the two orientations in their references to the "organism" and the "person." The different connotations of these words catches much of the difference in orientation between behaviorists and cognitive learning supporters.

How Are Problems Solved?

Cognitive theorists tend to believe that students "think" about a problem until they gain insight into its solution. In contrast to behaviorist emphasis of behavioral trial and error, cognitivists emphasize the person's **cognitive activity** or **thought**.

What is the Actional Nature of Learners?

Cognitive theorists think the mind is an **active processor** of information while reacting to and interacting with environmental events. Teachers holding this position view the learner as an **interacter** with what is learned.

Perspective

Cognitive perspective is mental. Cognitive theorists see learning as more than the acquisition of responses; it is perceived as the **integration** of new content and insights into what was previously known. To them, learning involves the reorganizing of cognitive structures. Meaningfulness receives much attention. Some are attracted to the notion of intellectual scaffolding, or connecting new material with old material. Cognitive-oriented teachers see learning hierarchies as complex structures like scaffolds with which one can build. But there is no one necessary way for the scaffold to be erected. This perspective reduces (but does not eliminate) the importance of instructional sequences. Some cognitive psychologists view excessive attention to task analysis as a fetish. This attitude was humorously stated long ago by Samuel Johnson:

There is no matter what children should learn first, any more than what leg you should put into your breeches first. Sir, you may stand disputing which is best to put in first, but in the meantime your backside is bare. Sir, while you stand considering which of two things you should teach your child first, another boy has learn't 'em both.

Matching Subject Matter with Learning Theories

The position taken in this book is that the nature of the subject matter one teaches has great bearing on the utility of various orientations toward human learning. It seems reasonable to use different conceptions of learning for different kinds of subject matter. The three kinds of subject matter identified in the previous section will now be revisited.

Easily Specifiable, Masterable, Vital Content (Track A)

Some content can be clearly described in its entirety, is masterable, and is important enough to merit mastery by each student. Examples are:

The 10 Hindu-Arabic numerals

The letters of the Hebrew alphabet

Each of these is a crystal-clear content domain with easily identified boundaries. Each is vital for subsequent learning. The numerals are essential for all students; the Hebrew alphabet is vital, of course, only for those studying Hebrew.

This kind of material typically does not have much inherent meaning. The need is to form sets of paired associations between stimuli and responses. There is little in such content to involve one's personal interpretation or style, or with which to meaningfully interact. Students can very reasonably be viewed as passive receivers of this kind of information. Behavioral learning theories are therefore congenial to such content.

Most of the examples provided by behaviorist educators of the utility of task analysis and linear learning hierarchies use content for which such approaches make good sense. Content such as the alphabet or numerals is *inherently sequential.* When intrinsic sequence exists for subject matter, learning theories that provide for careful task analysis are attractive.

Specifiable Content That Cannot or Need Not Be Mastered (Track B)

Some content can be specified in its entirety, but either (a) it cannot be mastered or (b) it is not generally deemed to be important enough to merit mastery. Examples, respectively, of the two types of specifiable content are:

Pole vaulting

Your state's counties and county seats

With regard to the mostly psychomotor content of the first type of specifiable subject matter (the first example), one may consider two approaches. First, a behavioral learning theory orientation seems most suitable for the early phases while attention is on conditioning standard techniques; but a more cognitive approach seems more appropriate in the later stages when attention shifts to such outcomes as self-analysis of performance and development of personal style. Second, a learning theory that emphasizes the importance of demonstration and imitation of modeled behaviors would be attractive; such a theory (Bandura, 1977) does not fit neatly into the behavioral-cognitive dichotomy.

With regard to content of the second type of specifiable subject matter (the second example above), a straight behavioral approach is indicated. Such material lacks inherent meaning. The task is to condition rote associations between county names and the names of their seats. Students cannot meaningfully interact with meaningless material. Better to treat learners as passive receptacles of this kind of information. The only thing that separates content such as the second example from Track A (see Table 2–4) is someone's judgment that it is not important enough to warrant channeling individual differences into the time dimension until all learners master it. Therefore, the learning theory choice is the same as it would be for most Track A content.

Content That Can Neither Be Specified Nor Mastered (Track C)

Much subject matter is low in both specifiability and masterability. For example:

> Application of the Bill of Rights
>
> Critical thinking

Such content contains much inherent meaning with which learners can and should interact. Working with such content causes learners to weave it into their cognitive structures. Not much inherent sequence or structural hierarchy exists here; particular elements need not ordinarily precede others and be mastered before one can succeed with the others. Instructional emphasis should be on principles, insights, meaning, connections, and understanding.

TO RECAP

The correspondence between subject matter and learning theories discussed in this section and the match between subject matter and teaching methods outlined in the following section are not as neat as the correspondence between subject matter and manifestation of individual differences developed previously. Yet there is sufficient consistency to make the following generalizations useful, even though they are not universally applicable.

When content is taught that lacks inherent meaning and/or when a person's goals are truly behavioral, then a mechanistic orientation to learning seems to make good sense. Conditioning of desired stimuli and behavioral responses is indicated. In addition, when the subject matter is inherently sequential, task analysis is attractive.

When one is teaching content that is richly meaningful and/or when one's aims are not mere behaviors, then cognitive orientations to learning are usually more functional. Instruction focuses on meaningful, insightful integration of new content into the learner's prior cognitive structure to enhance understanding, appreciation, etc.

Kinds of Instruction

A central thesis of this chapter is that various kinds of subject matter are best taught in different ways. Teaching effectiveness can be seriously jeopardized by mismatching content and instructional methods. The three kinds of subject matter will now be re-examined and matched with suitable methods of instruction. These methods arise from the learning theories on which they are based. It is, of course, beyond the scope of this book to focus on details of instructional methods or theory. Readers wishing to delve into these topics should consult general educational psychology texts and books concerning methods of teaching the subject matter and grade level in which they are interested.

Specifiable Masterable Content (Track A)

When subject matter can be adequately specified in its entirety in behavioral terms, it is both *limited* in size and *closed*, as Figure 2–4 demonstrates. The dots represent the small number of domain elements. The figure is closed, or complete, to signify that the well-defined subject matter is stable and fixed.

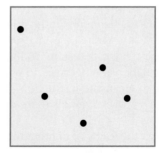

Figure 2–4.   Limited, Closed Content Domain Suitable for Mastery Teaching

Examples of small, closed domains include:

1. Matching names of the three primary colors with appropriate color chips
2. Making change from a dollar for items costing less than a dollar
3. Focusing a given microscope
4. Measuring objects less than a foot long to the nearest eighth of an inch
5. Naming the members of a certain school class
6. Avoiding bed-wetting

Drill is a primary technique by which many such domains are taught. The specific drill is limited to the exact content that has been specified in the detailed objectives. Each of the five elements shown in Figure 2–4 would be (a) explicitly identified, (b) directly taught, and (c) explicitly tested. Thus *teaching and testing in Track A are sharply focused.*

Many such domains lack inherent meaning. Examples 1 and 5 above are not meaningful. In teaching such limited, closed domains, attention can be directed to such issues as massing and distributing practice, desirable degree of overlearning, and provision of periodic review. The less inherent the meaning in the subject matter, the more dominant will such considerations become.

Other specifiable, masterable domains are amenable to task analysis in which subelements are identified and carefully sequenced. Examples 2, 3, 4, and 6 might well be pursued via task analysis.

Behavioral learning theories tend to be congenial to instruction in small, closed content domains. Even in Example 6 above, in which drill would not be applicable, such behavioral techniques as task analysis, conditioning, counterconditioning, and punishment are likely to be considered.

The amount of time a student should spend on an essential, well-defined, masterable unit of content is whatever amount of time it takes to master it. With material of this kind, the goal of teaching and testing is mastery. Individual differences are relegated wholly or largely into the time dimension.

Specifiable Content that Cannot Be Mastered or Is Not Important Enough to Master (Track B)

When it comes to channeling individual differences, both delimitable material that is not masterable and delimitable masterable content that is not important enough to master can be treated the same. Individual differences are best channeled into the achievement dimension because no particular level of achievement exists at which it makes sense to terminate instruction. "Subtleties in human performance will always exist to make some individuals more masterful than others" (Cox & Dunn, 1979, pp. 28–29).

Although the kinds of content that lie in Track B of Table 2–4 are conveniently lumped together for most purposes, it will be worthwhile to divide them for the present purpose of considering teaching methods.

Teaching Specifiable But Unmasterable Content

Some content lies in Track B because it is not masterable. Most such content is psychomotor as was already mentioned. Examples of content that can be tightly or clearly specified by behavioral terms but that cannot be mastered include:

1.   Weight lifting
2.   Spelling all words in a particular dictionary
3.   Bowling

Content of this kind can be taught *in the early phases* in a manner quite similar to the way specifiable, masterable material is taught. Teachers guide student effort, reinforce desired behaviors, and provide for suitable distributed practice. Desired behaviors are conditioned; undesirable ones eliminated. Where appropriate, as in Example 2 above, the teacher will also teach for the attainment of positive transfer of learning and/or the avoidance of negative transfer.

After instruction is well under way, the role of the teacher may become less active. The advanced speller and the good bowler can continue to improve their performance without a teacher's continual guidance. Advanced students become able to criticize their own performance, thereby becoming relatively self-sufficient. Behavioral approaches seem more suitable for the early phases, while cognitive approaches seem to many teachers to be more appropriate to the later stages.

Teaching Specifiable and Masterable But Nonessential Content

Some content is put in Track B because of the value judgment that it is not important enough to merit mastery. Examples of content that is specifiable and masterable but of insufficient import to merit mastery are:

1. All the county seats in California
2. The value of pi to 100 digits
3. Names and terms of all Vice Presidents of the United States

Such content can be taught by the same methods as vital, masterable Track A content. When material lacks inherent meaning, drill is a key teaching method. The only difference in the methods of teaching this kind of content and teaching Track A content is that here mastery need not be sought.

Content That Can Neither Be Fully Specified Nor Mastered (Track C)

When subject matter cannot be adequately laid out in its entirety in behavioral terms, it is *broad or unlimited* in scope *and/or open*. Figure 2–5 represents a very large and open content domain. The dots represent the multitude of elements of the domain. The figure is open, or incomplete, to represent the everchanging subject matter of this dynamic domain. The boundaries of the domain have some gaps because it is not entirely clear whether certain content is in the domain. For example, are pornography and flag burning protected by the Bill of Rights? Since the domain contains a great number of present and/or future elements, it is not feasible to specify each. Even if it were possible, teachers can put their time to much better use than by generating cumbersome, exhaustive (and exhausting) lists of specific behavioral objectives.

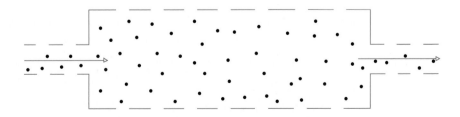

Figure 2–5.   Broad, Open Content Domain Requiring Teaching for Transfer

This kind of subject matter occupies most of the instructional time of most effective teachers. Examples of large, open domains include:

Current events

Crosscultural knowledge and tolerance

Reading comprehension

Understanding the concept of "mammal"

Establishing and maintaining counseling rapport

Art appreciation

Automobile engine diagnosis

Cognitive theories are congenial to such content. Teaching methods include emphasis on understanding, provision of different content for different students, group processes, use of problem solving, and discovery learning. Techniques such as group discussion help learners assimilate new information and accommodate their pre-existing cognitive structures to the new material. Much exists in such subject matter with which a person can interact.

Transfer of learning receives primary attention in teaching and testing nonspecific, unmasterable content. The central role of transfer will be now illustrated with a fifth-grade unit on mammals.

In selecting the specific content for such a unit, perhaps only one point is vital—all mammal species provide milk for their young. The teacher could write one or more specific masterable behavioral objectives about this point because that characteristic of mammals is closed. Other important characteristics of mammals, such as having backbones and being endothermic, could also (although need not) be declared essential. We could develop a short set of Track A type objectives for these content elements.

It is wise to devote most concern and instructional time to concept formation and the enhancement of transfer of learning about mammals, and, more broadly, transfer in general. For example, one approach might be analysis of root words to divine the meaning of "endothermic." *Teaching and testing in Track C are not narrowly targeted.*

The contrasting domains of *illustrative* mammals and of *sample* nonmammals are virtually infinite. Hence, we must teach only a *sample* of the domain. We would want to pick a few instances of the concept of mammal to show its breadth. Cows might be studied, for example, because they are well known as producers of milk; dogs as a familiar example of carnivorous mammals; mice as an example of rodents and small mammals; bats as flying mammals; kangaroos as marsupials; seals as aquatic mammals; elephants as herbivorous and large mammals; humans as a species that has special significance to us, and monkeys because they are especially interesting to children. Having picked these examples to demonstrate the variety of the concept, teachers would go on to select with equal care several noninstances of the concept in order to show its limits.

The particular teaching examples are chosen not because they are more important than others that could just as well have been selected (e.g., dolphins instead of seals or hamsters instead of mice), but because of their convenience and utility in maximizing positive transfer of learning and in minimizing negative or inappropriate transfer. After pupils study instances and noninstances of the concept by use of the original sample, new examples would then be selected to *provide instructional practice in transferring* what students have learned. Pictures of animals not previously studied might be presented, and pupils then asked to classify the animals as mammals or nonmammals. Or, if the class has previously studied fish, amphibians, and reptiles, we could present pictures of animals not previously studied and have students classify them into these four classes, thereby integrating review and new learning. In short (as will be seen in Chapter 3), transfer would be the focus of our goals, teaching, and (as will be seen in Chapter 4) testing.

It is not mastery of what is specifically sampled to be taught that is sought; rather *it is insight, understanding, and transfer or generalization throughout the domain that is desired.* One therefore could not sensibly specify some level of achievement in the specific sample of material that happened to be taught and demand that all students come up to that standard. No particular level of competence exists (either with the examples used in instruction or with the general content domain) that a student needs to attain before proceeding to the study of birds. Therefore, teachers can best let individual differences be exhibited in the achievement dimension.

Chapter Summary

Boyer (1987) stressed that a college education should be connected—that instruction should reveal the connections among areas of study. Why? To make the learning meaningful and to render it transferable. An educated person does not keep each area of knowledge in an isolated compartment. On the contrary, he or she is aware of the rich network of relationships among fields and understands the connectedness of topics.

This chapter has laid a broad, instruction-oriented foundation for the study of educational measurement. Why? Because *classroom measurement is connected to the subject matter taught, to the way in which individual differences are best treated, and to the way the material is most effectively taught.* Educational measurement is connected to human learning and to teaching methods. This chapter has "broadened the picture" enough to show these connections with educational psychology and methods courses. This understanding should enable educated professionals to better comprehend the relationships among several of their professional educational courses and to better transfer their learning among the related areas of professional preparation.

Table 2–5 summarizes the connections among topics that have been treated in this chapter. As in Table 2–4, at the left are the A, B, and C labels to designate various compatible combinations of these four variables. For example "Track C" will be used throughout this book to refer to situations in which individual differences are exhibited in level and breadth of achievement in subject matter that cannot be specified in its entirety and is taught for transfer of learning by means suggested primarily by cognitive learning theories.

Table 2–5

Relationships among Individual Differences, Subject Matter, Learning Theories, and Kinds of Instruction

Track	Main Manifestation of Individual Differences	Type of Subject Matter	Family of Learning Theory	Kind of Instruction
A	Time dimension	Entire content of small, closed domain readily specified in behavioral terms; content vital and masterable.	Behavioral	Much specific training
B	Achievement dimension	Tasks specified in behavioral terms, but cannot be mastered or do not merit mastery	Mixed	Specific training in early phases
C	Achievement dimension	Content of large and/or open domain cannot be specified in its entirety or mastered	Cognitive	Primarily teaching for understanding and transfer

QUIZ 2–3

In this list appear content units. Designate each as Track A, B, or C (See Table 2–5). Each track may be used once, more than once, or not at all.

1. A high school unit on Shakespeare
2. Conjugation of regular Spanish verbs (for students of Spanish)
3. Mark Antony's funeral address in a literature unit
4. An elementary school unit on making change
5. A fourth-grade unit on Tibet
6. A first-grade unit on careers

KEY TO QUIZ 2–3

Item	Key	Comments
1	C	Neither the comprehension nor the appreciation objectives have a limit beyond which the teacher would not value more achievement. The domain is large and lacks clear boundaries. Transfer of both appreciation and understanding to additional works of Shakespeare and to other authors would be most teachers' main intent of the unit.
2	A	This goal is minimally essential knowledge for students of Spanish. It can be mastered and it merits mastery. Teaching is sharply focused.
3	B	The content domain is clear; hence it could be treated as Track A. However, most teachers would not view its importance to be sufficient to warrant mastery because it is neither prerequisite to successful study of subsequent topics nor necessary for daily life. It, therefore, fits best in Track B for literature students. (For the actor playing Mark Antony, the content would be Track A.)
4	A	The content is relatively specifiable, relatively masterable, and important enough to merit mastery.
5	C	The specific content matters little; the principal aim should transcend the specifics of Tibet. Teaching is not narrowly focused. Transfer of learning is the major goal.
6	C	The specific content is too expansive and too dynamic to be explicitly defined. Although a class may study only five "community helpers," the occupations chosen constitute a mere sample of an enormous domain. Transfer is sought.

Suggestions for Further Reading

Gronlund, N. E. (1985). *Stating objectives for classroom instruction* (3rd ed.). New York: Macmillan. Chapter 6, "Relating Objectives to Classroom Instruction," presents the relationship among two kinds of instructional objectives and several elements of teaching and testing. This relationship was the seminal concept that grew into this book's Chapters 2 and 3.

Salomon, G., & Perkins, D. M. (1989). Rocky roads to transfer: Rethinking mechanisms of a neglected phenomenon. *Educational Psychologist, 24,* 113–142. This insightful article contrasts two competing research traditions that focus on transfer of learning. The authors contend that distinct kinds of transfer exist and that these are best sought by different teaching methods. Their "Low Road" Transfer fits nicely into our notion of Track A learning and transfer, while their "High Road" Transfer is very congenial to this book's description of Track C.

Shepard, L. A. (1991). Psychometricians' beliefs about learning. *Educational Researcher, 20,* 2–16. Shepard astutely brings to light some of the long-ignored (if not hidden) assumptions about learning that underlie sharp differences of opinion about measurement issues.

Thorndike, R. M., Cunningham, G. K., Thorndike, R. L., & Hagen, E. P. (1991). *Measurement and evaluation in psychology and education* (5th ed.). New York: Macmillan. Pages 165–167, "Day-to-Day Instructional Decisions," briefly relate the issues of domain clarity to educational decision making.

3

An Integrated
Instructional/Evaluation Model

Chapter 2 developed a conceptual structure that identifies the harmonious combinations of four factors: (a) the expressions of individual differences, (b) kinds of subject matter, (c) groups of learning theories, and (d) methods of instruction. In Chapter 3, this instructional model is given a measurement focus and interfaced with four more factors: (e) kinds of instructional objectives, (f) kinds of tests, (g) kinds of interpretations, and (h) kinds of scores. These latter topics are of universal concern to educational measurement. Together, the eight topics provide an integration of several issues that are intricately related to effective teaching and effective student evaluation.

The perspective of this chapter, and book, is that evaluation does not occur in isolation. Enlightened student evaluation is an integral part of good teaching. This book's contribution to effective teaching is to assist teachers in providing *better teaching through better measurement.*

Instructional Objectives

Instructional objectives are now emphasized to explore how they relate to the other seven topics. Much of this section has been adapted from Gronlund's (1985) insightful and informative *Stating Objectives for Classroom Instruction.*

Instructional objectives can be stated in nonbehavioral terms (e.g., "knows" calculus) or in behavioral terms (e.g., "dials" telephone). Pioneer educators have urged the use of behavioral objectives since the 1930s (Tyler, 1931). Since the publication in 1962 of the first edition of Mager's (1975) delightful and popular book, *Preparing Instructional Objectives,* most educators have become acquainted with behavioral objectives. Some writers (e.g., Mager, 1975; Popham & Baker, 1970) have taken an orthodox behaviorist view that all instructional objectives ought to *be* behavioral, while others (e.g., Gronlund, 1970, 1985; Mehrens & Lehmann, 1991) have taken the broader view that all instructional objectives should be phrased *in terms of* observable behaviors.

Before these two views are contrasted, it will be worthwhile to focus on their "common ground." Most scholars agree that instructional goals should be framed in terms of **terminal student behaviors**. These three crucial words will be examined one by one.

Unless instructional objectives are stated in terms of what *students* do, they miss the target. To cause student learning, a teacher may provide drill, assign reading, show films, lecture, or prompt group discussion. But these activities are the means, not the ends, of instruction. The aim of teaching is student learning. Learning is evidenced by student behaviors. In planning a lesson, a teacher surely should plan the content and methods; these are vital. But subject matter and teaching techniques are only the means of achieving objectives. They are not the actual goals. Thus instructional objectives should be stated in terms of terminal *student* performance.

Consider the word "terminal." Instructional goals should focus on student behaviors at the conclusion of instruction, not on what they do at the beginning or on the learning activities in which they are to engage. For example, contract systems of grading create problems if they allow students to earn points merely for engaging in learning activities (e.g., writing papers, participating in discussions, or reading books) rather than for demonstrating competence. It is a serious error to assess only whether students engage in activities that are intended to cause learning rather than to assess terminal student performance (McKeachie, 1986). The objective would become the process rather than the outcome. Although initial student behaviors are important considerations in establishing realistic goals and in developing appropriate content and learning activities, neither initial learner behavior nor instructional activities is the output of the teaching endeavor. The objectives should be phrased in terms of *terminal* learner behavior.

Finally, consider the word "behaviors." Throughout history, most goals have been so vague as to be virtually useless. Teachers have pursued such goals as student *appreciation* of Homer, *knowledge* of the Civil War, and *understanding of* and *commitment to* the Bill of Rights. Similarly, counselors have sought to develop client *positive self-concept* and *peace of mind.* Objectives that stop with verbs such as "understand," "know," and "appreciate" are hopelessly ambiguous. What does it mean to "appreciate" Poe? To be able to *state* his nationality and age at death? To be able to *name* and *date* his works? Customarily to *sit* quietly when his works are read? To *go* voluntarily to see productions of his works? To *say* "I like Poe"? In short, the word "appreciate" obscures more than it reveals because it can mean any and all of these and other student behaviors. "Appreciates" does not indicate what is sought. In order to communicate, **active behavioral verbs** such as "state," "sit," "go," "list," and "compute" are needed. Behavioral verbs avoid the ambiguity that haunts unqualified nonbehavioral verbs. Thus instructional objectives ought to be stated in terms of **observable behaviors** by use of active verbs.

Minimum Essential Behavioral Objectives

One way to state instructional objectives is to list all the specific behaviors that students should exhibit at the end of a unit of instruction. The key words in the preceding sentences are "all" and "specific." In teaching young children to spell their first names, one can specify the goal quite precisely by use of a behavioral objective. For example,

1. When told to spell his or her first name, the pupil will do so orally without error.

    Note how clear and unambiguous this goal is. Almost anyone could determine whether a pupil had reached it. While one could debate all week as to what such free-floating aims as "understands the Bill of Rights" or "appreciates Shakespeare" mean, sensible people would agree at once concerning the meaning of this behavioral objective. A major advantage of behavioral objectives of this kind is the ease and clarity with which one can determine *whether* the student has reached the goal. This clarity is a major contribution of behavioral learning theories to education.

    Other examples of specific behavioral objectives that all, or nearly all, pupils can be expected to master are:

2. Given a standard wall telephone, the pupil can dial at least 4 out of 5 seven-digit telephone numbers correctly on the first trial.

3. When orally presented with pairs of one-digit numbers, the student can correctly state the sum within two seconds of at least 95 of the 100 addition facts.

4. When approaching standard electric traffic signals, the child will stop when the light is red at least 49 times in 50.

5. Given two trials on a pogo stick, the student will, in the better attempt, jump at least 100 times on level cement without falling off.

Notice that, where it is needed, the examples indicate the circumstances in which the behavior must occur; for example, it would not be clear what kinds of surfaces the student of the pogo stick is expected to be able to manage, so "level cement" is specified. At other times, indicating the details of the circumstances would be needlessly laborious. For example, it hardly seems necessary to specify that the child is expected to respond to the traffic signal only when weather conditions render signals visible; no sensible person would test the child during a blizzard. Similarly, it is understood that pupils are not expected to pass their days in dialing telephones; clearly, this behavior is to be performed only on command. Therefore, conditions are specified only in reasonable detail.

Finally, notice that each of the above objectives indicates the level of performance that is expected—for example, "4 out of 5," "49 times in 50," and "100 times without falling off." This standard enables one to determine whether each student has *reached* the goal, that is, mastered the objective.

Suitable Use of Minimum Essential Objectives

Minimum essential behavioral objectives are admirably suited to certain teaching situations, marginally suited to other kinds of content (including that specified in the pogo stick objective above), and extremely ill-suited to many other situations. *Minimum essential behavioral objectives are best used in situations where mastery of fundamental material is crucial,* no matter how much time such mastery may require. The first four objectives above concern content of this kind. Bloom noted several characteristics of content that is most suitable for mastery teaching and the accompanying use of minimum essential objectives; such content tends to be (a) essential, (b) sequential, and (c) closed (Bloom, 1971).

To summarize, minimum essential instructional objectives are behavioral, mastery objectives. They state (a) what terminal behavioral learners are expected to exhibit, (b) the circumstances in which the behavior is to occur, and (c) the standard that must be met. Minimum essential behavioral goals channel individual differences entirely into the time dimension. They are suitable for small domains of subject matter that are specifiable, masterable, and vital. Such domains can normally be mastered in relatively short periods of specific, focused training on each element of the domain. Behavioral approaches may be best suited to such content.

In teaching for mastery, teachers may provide lists of such micro-objectives when they want students to *master the specific points* covered by the objectives *and nothing else* (Cronbach, 1977). Teaching based on minimal essential objectives trades breadth of coverage for mastery (Slavin, 1987b).

Limitations of Minimum Essential Objectives

In many circumstances content domains are not totally specifiable, and/or are not masterable, and/or not important enough to warrant mastery. As Cronbach (1971) noted, the concept of mastery is severely limiting—it seems to imply that one can get to the end of what it is desirable to learn. On the contrary, educational development should be open-ended.

For content that cannot be explicitly specified, it is impossible to set a meaningful standard and label it "mastery." In limited, closed-content domains, sharply focused training can produce mastery of the entire specified domain. But in a large and/or open domain, no amount of instruction can cover it all. Focusing on minimum essential objectives can chop off incidental learning of material that is not included in the list (Cronbach, 1977).

For large open subject matter domains, reliance must be placed largely on transfer of learning to develop competence throughout the domain. Interest is not restricted to the particular content that happens to be used in teaching. For example, "there is no way of describing the limits of the range of transfer of the application of a principle like Boyle's law nor of specifying the number of situations to which the student should be able to apply it" (Krathwohl & Payne, 1971, p. 23). Therefore, valid tests for such content must involve tasks that require students to apply their learning to new, unstudied situations. Of the myriad of possible test questions that could be asked for most such domains, the difficulties vary widely. In this context, it does not make good sense to use objectives that attempt to specify level of achievement that must be met, for example, "answer 80 percent of Boyle's law application items correctly." If the items are easy, this "standard" is modest; if the items are very hard, this pseudostandard may be unreasonably demanding.

For subject matter that cannot be mastered, mastery does not exist. Moreover, we would not wish to specify a level beyond which we are indifferent to further achievement. We are interested in helping each student *develop as much as possible. Our goal is maximum individual development.*

Most large or open subject matter domains are not sequential to the extent that students must reach some particular level of achievement before being "ready" to proceed to the next domain. Therefore, instruction that is not inherently sequential is normally best organized to channel individual differences primarily into the achievement dimension.

What is needed then are instructional objectives suitable for situations in which we do not narrowly focus instruction on content domains that are small, closed, masterable, and essential. What kinds of objectives are suitable for use in Tracks B and C?

In answering the question, it will be useful to recall that minimum essential behavioral objectives (i.e., the type suited for Track A), must:

1. State the learning outcome in terms of terminal student behavior,
2. Indicate the conditions under which the behavior is to occur, and
3. Specify the standard or level of achievement that must be attained.

These three requirements of minimum essential behavioral objectives serve as a convenient point of departure in evolving objectives to suit the types of learning appropriate for Tracks B and C.

Behavioral Developmental Objectives

The only thing that renders minimum essential behavioral objectives ill suited for Track B is the third requirement—the setting of a standard. In Track B, it makes little sense to set a rigid standard. Because the subject matter is not ordinarily inherently sequential, there is no need to insist that all students reach some predetermined level. Moreover, because we wish to help students develop their skills to the fullest extent possible, it would be counterproductive to ignore excellence beyond the point established by an arbitrary standard. The critical points are that we should neither (a) channel individual differences into the time dimension nor (b) be satisfied with universal mediocrity.

If the third requirement is dropped, behavioral objectives are rendered suitable for Track B wherein we aspire to help each student achieve *maximum development* within the time available. This kind of behavioral objective is *developmental.* Table 3–1 displays the relationship between minimum essential behavioral objectives and behavioral developmental objectivess. The goals are identical except for the need to set a minimum standard in the former.

Table 3–1

Comparison of Minimum Essential Behavioral Objectives and Behavioral Developmental Objectives

Minimum Essential Behavioral Objectives (Track A)	*Behavioral Developmental Objectives (Track B)*
Are terminal student behaviors.	Are terminal student behaviors.
State the conditions under which the behaviors are to occur.	State the conditions under which the behaviors are to occur.
Contain minimum standards that must be reached by each student.	Avoid arbitrary standards; the more the achievement, the better.

Examples of behavioral developmental objectives are:

1. Types rapidly
2. Plays golf well on a given course
3. When given the names of all Vice Presidents of the United States, arranges them into the order of their terms of office
4. Recites Mark Antony's funeral address

TO RECAP

Behavioral developmental objectives (a) state what terminal behaviors learners are expected to exhibit at as high a level as available study time enables and (b) indicate the circumstances under which the behavior is to be elicited. Behavioral developmental objectives channel individual differences largely or wholly into the achievement dimension. They are suitable for two rather different kinds of subject matter: (a) motor skills that are neatly specifiable, but not masterable (e.g., Examples 1 and 2 above) and (b) masterable material that a teacher judges not to be important enough to demand mastery from all (e.g., Examples 3 and 4 above).

Nonbehavioral Developmental Objectives

The first distinction between minimum essential objectives and either behavioral or nonbehavioral developmental objectives concerns masterability. It does not seem sensible to set a standard for the behavioral developmental objectives that are needed for Track B. This is even more true of the kind of objectives needed for Track C. Because the content of large and/or open domains is normally not highly sequential, students do not need to reach some arbitrary minimum standard on prerequisite units before attempting advanced ones. In writing goals for Track C, then, teachers should aim to channel individual differences largely or wholly into the achievement dimension and focus their attention on maximizing, within available time, the achievement of each student rather than on merely assuring minimum achievement.

The second difference between the minimum essential behavioral objectives appropriate for (Track A) small, closed, vital content domains and the kind of objectives needed to do justice to (Track C) large and/or open subject matter domains concerns the issue of specifiability. *Large, open content domains cannot be specified in their entirety.*

This limitation of behavioral objectives has generated much conflict. Although those who advocated the moderate use of behavioral objectives have long recognized this limitation, some of the radical champions of the behavioral objective movement of the 1970s and the accountability movements of the 1980s have zealously urged that *all* instructional goals be behavioral and have set standards. This popular but extremist stance was often perceived as the only position favorable to the use of behavioral objectives. As such, it elicited a substantial negative reaction.

Some of the conflict can be understood and resolved when it is recognized that people who advocate the exclusive use of narrow, behavioral minimum essential objectives are often thinking of subject-matter fields (e.g., arithmetic) for which Track A is appropriate; for well-defined content, all objectives can indeed be behavioral. Such persons usually have a preference for behavioral learning theories. On the other hand, people who denounce all use of behavioral objectives usually are thinking of content areas (e.g., humanities) for which Track C is suitable; for unspecifiable subject matter, objectives indeed cannot be behavioral. (But, as will soon be shown, they can be illustrated behaviorally.) Such people often find cognitive theories of human learning to be more congenial.

Two examples of large content domains will be used to show how the major advantages of behavioral objectives can be obtained without compromising the size, openness, or richness of the domains. We seek the clarity of behavioral objectives, but shun the limitations that often accompany them.

For the first example, recall the elementary school unit on mammals. Chapter 2 emphasized the fundamental need to teach this Track C unit for transfer of learning because its potential content is enormous. Undesirable consequences would occur, however, if teachers were to follow the advice of those who would use only minimum essential behavioral objectives and if we were to attempt to write the objectives, teach, and test as though the domain were small and closed. Several minimal essential behavioral objectives could be written, such as:

1.   Writes the definition of a mammal
2.   Lists the four major characteristics of mammals

3. When orally given the names of animals studied in the unit, students state whether each is a mammal with at least 90% accuracy.

4. Lists at least 7 of the 8 mammals studied

Notice how narrow, rote, and sterile the unit becomes. The goals of having pupils achieve understanding of the concept of mammal by means of meaningful verbal learning has been lost in the shuffle of minimal essential behavioral objectives. Moreover, if this list were given to students in advance, it would notify them that they need not understand or be able to transfer their knowledge to new applications. The "rules" for Track A mastery teaching are that teachers inform learners exactly what they must be able to do, teach them to do it (and nothing else), and test to see if they have mastered it (and nothing else). Neither the teaching nor the testing in Track A goes below the surface. Hence, it would not be legitimate to ask students in a test to classify pictures of animals studied or verbal descriptions of animals not studied. This prohibition is clearly undesirable; narrow, shallow mastery has been attained at too great a cost in breadth.

True, we could expand our list of behavioral objectives to include:

5. When shown pictures of animals studied in the unit, students will classify them as mammals or nonmammals with at least 95% accuracy.

6. Given written descriptions of animals not studied in class, students will label them mammal or nonmammal with at least 75% accuracy.

Now more problems surface. It still would be taboo to test with pictures of animals that were not studied or with descriptions of ones that were. This is ridiculous! If we persist, we can again "patch up" the list by adding:

7. When shown pictures of animals not studied in the unit, students will classify them as mammal or nonmammal with at least 80% accuracy.

8. Given written descriptions of animals studied in the unit, students will label them mammal or nonmammal with at least 90% accuracy.

Persistence will only dig a deeper pit of problems. Teachers could now lament they still cannot test with orally described animals, pictures of imaginary animals, or even with real animals brought to class!

We could lengthen the list indefinitely, but our efforts would never eliminate all the problems. For instance, Objective 1 refers to *the* definition of a mammal. Yet several ways exist to define a mammal, and these ways vary in adequacy. Such an objective is not simply passed or failed—mastered or not mastered; it is attained to some extent. Similarly, Objective 2 refers to *the* four features of mammals. Why exactly four? Are three no better than none? And are not five or six better than four? Objectives 1 and 2 are of the type that often really mean, "By rote give back on the test the exact material I gave you; you will not be tested to see if you understand what you are parroting." Such an objective may be useful for *training*, but it has limited place in *educating* students.

Aside from this problem, if we persevered in lengthening the list, we would end up with such a long one that it would be ignored by teachers and students alike. Even after such a great investment of effort, the list would still be more limited than the size and wealth of the domain merited, and it would still contain meaningless standards for the significant objectives that reflected transfer of learning (e.g., Objectives 6 and 7 above). To pursue the exclusive use of minimum essential behavioral objectives and the mastery model of teaching (i.e., Track A), teachers would have to pay the unthinkable price of forsaking concern with student ability to apply learning to new situations.

What is needed, then, for unspecifiable content is a kind of nonbehavioral objective. The real goal is for students to *understand* the concept of mammal. The behavioral "objectives" that could be written for the unit are not really the aims; *the true goals are mental, not behavioral.* Student behaviors such as the eight listed above are potentially useful as *evidence* or *indicators* of understanding, but they are not the actual objectives.

A good solution is to accept nonbehavioral verbs for *general* instructional objectives for Track C. But leaving it at that would forsake the clarity that behaviorism offers. That is, general, nonbehavioral verbs tend to be vague. How can we have our cake and eat it too?

Gronlund (1970, 1985) provided a great gift to education in the insight that most of the clarity of behaviorism can be secured without using restrictive behavioral objectives. Instead, active or behavioral verbs can be used as **examples** or **indicants** of the kinds of behaviors that one would accept as evidence of student attainment of mental objectives. The "rules of the game" thus do not limit test content to the exact material used as examples; rather, they limit the content to the general types of material used as indicants. Each general objective is accompanied by enough behavioral indicants to convey a good idea of the extent and limits of the large domain. For example, two general objectives with accompanying indicants for the mammal unit might be:

1.   Knows basic terms.

    1.1.   Matches terms that have the same meaning.

    1.2.   Selects the term that best fits a particular definition.

    1.3.   Distinguishes among terms orally or in writing.

    1.4.   Uses terms correctly orally and in writing.

    1.5.   Gives original examples of the meaning of terms.

2.   Understands the concept of mammal.

    2.1.   Writes a correct definition.

    2.2.   Lists several characteristics of mammals.

    2.3.   When given the names of familiar animals, classifies them as mammals or nonmammals.

    2.4.   Classifies pictures of familiar or unfamiliar animals as mammals or nonmammals.

    2.5.   Classifies real or imaginary animals as mammals or nonmammals from oral or written descriptions.

The absence of minimum standards in the indicants and objectives reflects the unmasterable nature of the subject matter. Open-endedness of the lists of behavioral indicants (i.e., examples) reflects the openness and/or large size of the content domains and the need to teach and test them for depth of understanding and transfer. *Neither teaching nor testing should be narrowly targeted at the indicants.*

For another example of a large, open content domain, consider a high school music unit. Some of the unit's general objectives would probably concern knowledge and understanding of composers and performers, their more famous works, the cultural and historical context in which their works developed, etc. These cognitive objectives are similar to the kinds illustrated in the last example. But what of appreciation? How can one write behavioral indicants for the affective objective of music appreciation?

The key lies in continuing to make a very sharp distinction between objectives and indicants. Indicants are not conclusive; they only provide circumstantial evidence that objectives have, to some measurable extent, been attained. The circumstantial evidence provided by indicants tends to be stronger in cognitive domains than in affective ones. This is mainly because feelings, attitudes, interests, and so forth can usually be faked.

If we were at a loss concerning affective indicants, we could ask, "How do people who clearly appreciate music differ from those who clearly do not?" The answer to this useful question can be phrased as indicants. For example:

1.   Appreciates music.
   1.1.   Orients ears toward source of music.
   1.2.   Does not chat during concert.
   1.3.   Spends own money and time attending concerts voluntarily.
   1.4.   When a tape is played, student does not throw spit balls.
   1.5.   Checks tapes out of library.
   1.6.   Discusses content of major works and own reactions to them.

At this juncture, the devoted teacher of music, art, literature, or other humanities is likely to explode, "But that's not what appreciation is! Appreciation is *felt*, not *behaved*!"

Precisely! That is why an affective objective is used rather than a behavioral one. That is also why behavioral indicants are written rather than behavioral objectives. Although these and similar indicants are not individually very much of the "stuff" of which appreciation is made, the point is that they provide a needed means of evaluating learning.

In well-funded research on the effects of a music appreciation unit, the list of behavioral indicants could be expanded to include indicants that are observable only with special apparatus and that are not easily faked. For example, samples of persons believed to be high and low respectively in appreciation could be measured during a concert with polygraphs, blood samples, electroencephalographs, and so on. Marked group differences would likely emerge at different parts of the concert in such things as the galvanic skin response, pulse rates, blood pressure, respiratory rates, brain waves, and hormone levels. These observable (with apparatus) behaviors could then be considered indicants of music appreciation. (They would not, of course, be practical for classroom teachers to use in evaluating individual students.)

It should be reiterated that these indicants are not, individually or collectively, "appreciation." The purpose served by indicants is to provide evidence (albeit not proof) concerning appreciation. Without behavioral statements, there can be no empirical evidence.

Table 3–2 shows the relationship between minimum essential behavioral objectives and nonbehavioral developmental objectives. Like behavioral developmental objectives, cognitive and affective developmental objectives contain no minimum standards. In addition, such developmental objectives, to be suitable for the large and/or open content domains found in Track C, are not behavioral. Instead, these objectives contain behavioral examples to illustrate the meaning of the general nonbehavioral objective.

TABLE 3–2

Comparison of Minimum Essential Behavioral Objectives and Nonbehavioral Developmental Objectives

Minimum Essential Behavioral Objectives (Track A)	*Nonbehavioral Developmental Objectives (Track C)*
The behavioral objective states a terminal student behavior.	The nonbehavioral objective is illustrated by use of terminal student behaviors.
The behavioral objectives state the conditions under which the behavior is to occur.	The behavioral indicants give the conditions under which the behaviors are to occur.
The objective states a minimum standard that must be reached by each student.	The objective avoids arbitrary standards; the greater a student's achievement, the better.

TO RECAP

In nonbehavioral developmental objectives for either cognitive or affective content: (a) nonbehavioral verbs express goals, (b) indicants exemplify the kinds of behaviors that evidence achievement of the objective, and (c) achievement of the goals is sought at as high a level as possible. Cognitive and affective developmental objectives enable openness and flexibility in teaching that are not found in the narrow and shallow shaping that characterizes teaching of minimum essential objectives (Gronlund, 1985). They channel individual differences into the achievement dimension. Nonbehavioral developmental objectives are suitable for large and/or open content domains that are neither specifiable nor masterable. They set the stage for use of teaching methods that are based mainly on cognitive learning theories.

Three Other Contrasts

It is now appropriate to consider three additional topics that concern objectives. Although these topics are not central to the model of relationships developed in Chapters 2 and 3, each topic is important.

Levels of Objectives

Krathwohl and Payne (1971) and Payne (1992) identified useful levels of educational objectives. The first level is the most abstract, and includes the long-term, global goals toward which a school might strive. An example would be, "Students shall attain fundamental skills in reading." Such goals are inclusive, tending to transcend single classes or units. Objectives at this level are useful for district and school curriculum planning, for policy-making bodies, and for public statements of goals.

The second level is more concrete, consisting of statements that translate the global objectives into more focused learning outcomes cast in terms of terminal student behavior. For pupils completing elementary school, the above general objective might be broken down into a dozen or more narrower, more concrete goals such as, "Knows the letters of the alphabet," "Understands simple news stories," and "Adapts reading techniques to purpose (e.g., enjoyment, locating an item of information, or following a logical argument)." This level of objective is often used in Track C.

The most specific of the three levels pinpoints precise student behaviors. Second-level objectives can ordinarily be broken down into third-level ones. For example, the above second-level objective, "Knows the letters of the alphabet," can give rise to such specific objectives as "When shown a printed lower-case letter, names it within three seconds," "Recites the alphabet correctly," and "When shown the upper-case alphabet, can point to any letter on command." When a standard is used in a third-level objective, the result may be a Track A minimal essential objective. When an objective of this level is used without a standard, the result may be either a Track B developmental behavioral objective or a Track C indicant.

Cognitive, Affective, and Psychomotor Objectives

Educational objectives can be sorted into three main groups on the basis of the kind of learning they address. The following three names for groups of objectives are widely used (Krathwohl, Bloom, & Masia, 1964).

Cognitive objectives concern intellectual skills. They involve memory and thinking processes. Most of the objectives that teachers use are cognitive. Because they are relatively easy to measure with tests, cognitive objectives may tend to be overemphasized.

Affective objectives concern emotional or feeling states. They involve such attributes as personal-social adjustment, preferences, esthetic appreciations, interests, and commitments. Affective objectives are vital to much of education. For example, teachers want students to "like" to read as well as be able to do so, to "respect" as well as to know traffic laws, to "enjoy" as well as to understand music, and to "appreciate" as well as to understand the Bill of Rights. Affective goals are the hardest to measure because, among other reasons, their achievement can be faked. They concern how students typically respond rather than how they can respond under conditions of testing. Affective assessment is seriously neglected in most school settings.

Psychomotor objectives concern muscular or motor skills, manipulation of material and objects, and acts requiring coordination. Examples are pushups, handwriting, skateboarding, keyboarding, and driving. Psychomotor goals can be tested quite directly, but doing so is often inconvenient because it may require individual testing rather than group paper-pencil assessment.

Cognitive and affective components are, of course, usually involved in psychomotor skills. For example, one must "know" the letters in order to perform the motor task of producing them, and their neatness is often more a function of affect toward the task than of enabling motor skill. Pitching a baseball clearly involves knowledge not only of game rules and pitching techniques, but psychomotor skills in executing the techniques, and affect toward the game.

Classifications Systems for Objectives

The Cognitive Domain.   The most widely used classification system for cognitive objectives was developed by a committee chaired by Bloom (Bloom et al., 1956). Their *Taxonomy of Educational Objectives Handbook I: Cognitive Domain* provides a classification scheme. The lower levels of behavior are the simplest and least complex. The six categories and condensed descriptions are:

Knowledge is the ability to recall or recognize facts, principles, methods, etc. Little is demanded besides bringing to mind the material. This level tends to be seriously overemphasized in classroom testing (e.g., Fleming & Chambers, 1983).

Comprehension is the ability to grasp the meaning of messages, to paraphrase, to explain or summarize in one's own words, to "translate" among mathematical symbols, English, pictures, etc.

Application is use of ideas, rules, or principles in a new situations.

Analysis is the ability to break apart the component parts of a concept or message and show the relationship among the parts.

Synthesis is the ability to put elements together into coherent wholes in ways not experienced before.

Evaluation is the ability to assess the value of goals, methods, works, materials, etc., and to judge how well they meet established criteria.

Most classroom teachers find the *Taxonomy* to be too complex for their tastes. Chapter 4 will provide several examples of alternative ways by which cognitive learning can be classified. Nonetheless, the *Taxonomy* has done much to make educators aware that their tests tend to overemphasize seriously the lowest level or two and to largely neglect the higher levels.

The Affective Domain.   The *Taxonomy of Educational Objectives Handbook II: Affective Domain* (Krathwohl, Bloom, & Masia, 1964), provides a classification scheme for affective goals. The categories, ordered from lower level to higher level, are: Receiving, Responding, Valuing, Organization, and Characterization by a Value or Value Complex.

The Psychomotor Domain.   Although classification schemes have been devised in the psychomtor domain (e.g., Harrow, 1972), none has achieved the primacy enjoyed by the cognitive and affective *Taxonomies*.

QUIZ 3–1

1. What kind of objective establishes a standard?

    A. Minimum essential behavioral.

    B. Behavioral developmental.

    C. Nonbehavioral developmental.

2. Which kind of objective is most consistent with a need to teach and evaluate for transfer of learning?

    A. Minimum essential behavioral.

    B. Behavioral developmental.

    C. Nonbehavioral developmental.

3. Which kind of objective uses behavioral indicants?

    A. Minimum essential behavioral.

    B. Behavioral developmental.

    C. Nonbehavioral developmental.

4. Which kind of objective causes individual differences to be exhibited in the time dimension?

    A. Minimum essential behavioral.

    B. Behavioral developmental.

    C. Nonbehavioral developmental.

5. Which kind of objective is best suited to subject matter that is well defined, but not masterable?

    A. Minimum essential behavioral.

    B. Behavioral developmental.

    C. Nonbehavioral developmental.

6. Which kind of objective is most appropriate for content that is both well defined and masterable?

    A. Minimum essential behavioral.

    B. Behavioral developmental.

    C. Nonbehavioral developmental.

7. Which kind of objective is best suited to content that is neither specifiable nor masterable?

    A. Minimum essential behavioral.

    B. Behavioral developmental.

    C. Nonbehavioral developmental.

QUIZ 3–1 (cont.)

8. Which kind of objective would be most suited to a teacher who is using behavior modification to eliminate undesirable student behaviors?

    A. Minimum essential behavioral.

    B. Behavioral developmental.

    C. Nonbehavioral developmental.

9. Which kind of objective would be most suitable for a conventional psychotherapist?

    A. Minimum essential behavioral.

    B. Behavioral developmental.

    C. Nonbehavioral developmental.

10. Behavioral indicants should be used instead of behavioral objectives when

    A. subject matter is closed.

    B. goals are not observable student behaviors.

    C. teachers do not believe in behavioral objectives.

11. When nonbehavioral developmental objectives are used, should special instructional attention be devoted to the behaviors that are listed?

    A. Yes, because they are the only aims.

    B. Yes, because they are the goals on which students are likely to work the hardest.

    C. No, because they are unimportant.

    D. No, because they are only a sample of the kinds of evidence that could be listed.

12. Why should no standard be set for certain objectives?

    A. Standards never make sense.

    B. The content cannot or need not be mastered.

    C. The objectives are minimal.

    D. The objectives are behavioral.

13. Which of the following verbs is behavioral?

    A. Knows.

    B. Says.

    C. Values.

    D. Visualizes.

QUIZ 3–1 (cont.)

14. Which of the following verbs is nonbehavioral and cognitive?
    A. Comprehends.
    B. Lists.
    C. Runs.
    D. Values.
15. Which of the following verbs is nonbehavioral and affective?
    A. Counts.
    B. Knows.
    C. Likes.
    D. Matches.

KEY TO QUIZ 3–1

Item	Key	Comments
1	A	See pages 49–50.
2	C	See pages 53–57.
3	C	See pages 53–57.
4	A	See pages 49–50.
5	B	See pages 51–52.
6	A	See pages 49–50.
7	C	See pages 53–57.
8	A	See pages 49–50.
9	C	See pages 53–57.
10	B	See page 55–57.
11	D	See page 56. If we do, then the indicants become the students' goals. This issue will be examined more closely in the next section.
12	B	See pages 50–52.
13	B	See page 49.

KEY TO QUIZ 3–1 (cont.)		
14	A	"Lists" and "runs" are behavioral verbs; "comprehends" is nonbehavioral and cognitive; "values" is nonbehavioral and affective.
15	C	"Counts" and "matches" are behavioral verbs; "knows" is nonbehavorial and cognitive; "likes" is nonbehavioral and affective.

Kinds of Tests

We return now to the integrated instructional/evaluation model that is being unfolded. Several kinds of subject matter have been identified. For each we have examined the appropriate manifestation of individual differences, relevant learning theory, suitable teaching methods, and functional kinds of instructional objectives. The next step is to consider the kind of measure best adapted to each teaching-learning situation.

Measuring instruments can be classified in many ways—essay versus objective, performance versus paper-pencil, group versus individual, speed versus power, cognitive versus psychomotor versus affective, formative versus summative, and so on. For purposes of the model of instruction, the most useful distinction is between mastery tests and discriminatory tests.

Mastery Tests

In Track A, where a small, closed body of content is well defined, masterable, and vital, teaching is aimed directly at "stamping in" the specific content. Goals for surface learning of this kind of material are best communicated by means of minimum essential behavioral objectives. These objectives set specific levels of mastery that all normal learners can expect to meet. Such goals, therefore, dictate that individual differences shall be exhibited solely as the time it takes to master the content.

In this context, a test is used to determine *whether examinees have mastered the material.* A **mastery test** yields an all-or-nothing score, indicating that the examinee has or has not reached the pre-established standard (Anastasi, 1988). Since content domains are small, tests can often include each domain element. Where the entire domain can be tested, we do not have to be concerned with representativeness of test content. Such tests are easy to construct, and their scores are easy to interpret. Figure 3–1 represents a domain that is taught and tested in its entirety.

Questions in a mastery test are easy for adequately prepared examinees. The minimum essential behavioral objective lays out exactly what students must do. The training is then focused exclusively on the specified content until the standard is met. Students are therefore able to answer nearly all the questions correctly. Since

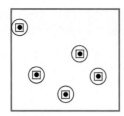

Figure 3–1. Typical Track A, Small, Closed Domain. Each element taught is circled, and each element tested is enclosed in a square.

individual differences are not expressed in the achievement dimension, mastery tests do not need to reveal differences in student attainment. Indeed, once the domain is mastered by all students, there are no achievement differences to be revealed.

The purpose of a mastery test is to determine for each student whether more instructional time is needed. If a person's performance on a mastery test does not meet the established standard, then he or she should be provided with more instruction. This is the famous teach-test-reteach cycle.

In this context, nothing may be wrong with the same test items being reused to reassess achievement after further study. In Track A, test security is not much of a concern because all the specified test content is typically known in advance from the minimum essential objectives.

Discriminatory Tests

As Anastasi observed, *mastery testing is not appropriate beyond the basic skills.* For advanced levels of knowledge in less highly structured subjects, it is neither practicable nor desirable to formulate highly specific objectives. "At these levels, both the content and the sequence of learning are likely to be much more flexible" (Anastasi, 1988, p. 103). Assessing all-or-none attainment of rigidly sequenced objectives is unnecessary when (a) the content is not inherently sequential and (b) achievement is not dichotomous.

In Tracks B and C, individual differences are exhibited mainly or wholly as level and/or breadth of achievement. "Thus, it is appropriate and realistic to recognize and document that some people are somehow better than others at certain skills" (Cox & Dunn, 1979, p. 28). Tests of such skills should reveal the differences that exist among students' achievement. In other words, Tracks B and C tests should *discriminate* among students to reveal the individual achievement differences that exist.

The word "discriminate" elicits negative reactions from some people because one of its meanings connotes prejudice or treatment of persons on bases other than merit. However, the word's primary meanings concern making clear distinctions, perceiving differences, and differentiating among them. The word is used here in this way with regard to achievement. Note that it is not the "evil test maker" who makes people unequal. Rather, the tester's job is to measure the differences that exist with **discriminatory tests**.

Discriminatory Tests for Track B

When specifiable but unmasterable skills are taught, effort is devoted to helping, within available time, each student perform as well as possible. No arbitrary level of achievement exists above which further excellence is either impossible or unsought, or if there is (e.g., bowling score of 300 or golf score of 18), virtually nobody consistently attains it. Tests suitable for Track B (e.g., typing speed and long-jumping) therefore need enough "ceiling" to reveal how well the best students perform and enough "floor" to reveal how poorly the worst ones perform. That is, Track B tests need to reveal the individual differences in achievement that exist.

The purpose of Track B discriminatory tests is to *reveal individual differences in the extent to which objectives have been achieved.* Since the subject matter is well defined, students should ordinarily know ahead of time exactly what can be tested or sampled. In Track B, as in Track A, there frequently need not be a very sharp distinction made between practice material and testing material; they are often identical. The specifiability of the content makes test construction easy.

It should be noted that an occasional Track B (or even Track A) domain is too large to be conveniently tested in its entirety; in this case, the test must sample the domain. Consider a fifth-grade unit on state capitals. If this well-defined domain is deemed by the teacher to be vital, then it is put in Track A. If it is considered to be nonessential, then it is put in Track B. In either case, the 50 states could be stratified in some sensible way(s) (e.g., by difficulty and/or by region of the country), and a sample could be randomly drawn from each stratum or cell.

When an entire domain is to be tested, test security is not an issue. But when a domain is to be sampled, then students should not, of course, know ahead of time precisely which elements of the domain are to be tested.

Discriminatory/Survey Tests for Track C

In Track C, where large and/or open content domains are neither well defined nor masterable, instruction is directed at broadly educating students with some of the content so that they will be able to go beyond what is explicitly studied and transfer their learning to parts of the domain that were not covered. Goals for such cognitive and affective content are developmental. When developmental objectives are used, individual differences are exhibited largely or wholly in level and/or breadth of achievement.

The purpose of a test in this setting is to measure individual differences in the extent to which objectives have been achieved throughout a large and/or open domain. To do this, the test must not only discriminate, but it must also *survey.* A **survey test** *samples* only part of the domain's content. Because of the size and/or openness of Track C domains, it is not possible for the test to cover all the possible content.

Along these lines it is important to understand that when the objectives involve students' ability to generalize, then repeated retesting on exactly the same material is ill advised. Similarly, suppose a student recycles a written theme after receiving feedback from the teacher. A point of view is clarified, punctuation errors are corrected, etc. The assumption might be made that the student now has the ability independently to punctuate and use written communication strategies to present various viewpoints adequately. However, this student may have only been following blindly what the teacher indicated should be done. Without a demonstration of these abilities on a new theme, unaccompanied by teacher assistance, no guarantee exists that the presumed capability truly exists (Cox & Dunn, 1979, p. 26).

It was seen in Chapter 2 that it is not possible to cover everything in a large and/or open domain. Only a sample can be taught. Effective teachers, therefore, adopt the strategy of teaching for transfer. *When teaching has been aimed primarily at transfer* of learning rather than at mere surface knowledge of the exact material taught, *testing should be for transfer.* As Thorndike stated:

> The crucial indicator of a student's understanding of a concept, a principle, or a procedure is that he is able to apply it in circumstances that are different from those under which it was taught. Transferability is the key feature of meaningful learning. So if we are to test for understanding, we must test in circumstances which are at least part new (Thorndike, 1969, p. 2).

Track C testing should involve transfer for two compelling reasons. First, since content sampling is central to Track C testing, the tests must provide broad and balanced samples of the domains described by the objectives. Since the units are taught for broad transfer of learning, the tests will not be valid unless they assess transfer. Put differently, Track C nonbehavioral objectives and the accompanying behavioral indicants are designed to avoid extreme focus on specifics of content (Gronlund, 1985). They should be saturated with novel applications. Since the goals emphasize transfer, the tests cannot assess achievement of these objectives unless they also stress transfer.

The second compelling reason why Track C tests should assess transfer concerns the fact that *tests influence what students learn.* Like it or not, most students from primary school through graduate school try to learn what they think will be tested. This is a powerful force for good or for bad. If this force works against us, much of our teaching is doomed to failure. For example, if a history teacher consistently tests only factual knowledge (e.g., names and dates), then students work mainly to memorize this kind of low-level material. On the other hand, if the teacher also consistently assesses such learning outcomes as analyses, syntheses, applications, and evaluations, then students will also pursue these higher-level objectives.

Evaluation exerts an enormous influence on student effort. Research indicates "that the use of higher level questions in evaluation enhances learning, retention, transfer, interest, and development of learning skills" (Crooks, 1988, p. 442). Wise teachers harness this force to make it work for them rather than against them. The motto might well be, "Harness Test Power." To do this, teachers must go to pains to assure that they assess what they want students to learn.

That this is a topic meriting attention is demonstrated by research which reveals that teacher-made tests often fail to reflect the teacher's own instructional objectives and often require little more than repetition of material that was presented in the textbook or class (Fleming & Chambers, 1983). In Tracks A and B, this is the specific material taught. In Track C, however, teachers want learners to be able to apply what they have learned; they must, therefore, test for *transfer.* Since most teaching concerns Track C subject matter, testing for transfer is critically important to most teachers. Part II of this book provides assistance in testing students' ability to use what they have learned in new situations.

Figure 3–2 shows a domain such as a mammal or Bill of Rights unit. The domain is large, open, and has fuzzy boundaries. Only part can be taught and only part can be tested. Care is needed to avoid excessive overlap between the portions taught and the portions tested.

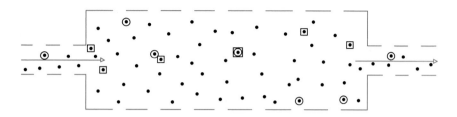

Figure 3–2.   Typical Track C, Large, Open Domain. The elements taught are circled, and the elements tested are enclosed in squares.

Like most educational achievement tests, most psychological tests address large, ill-defined, open content domains. For example, psychological tests designed to measure **constructs** or latent **traits** such as academic aptitude, mechanical aptitude, outdoor interest, impulsivity, and extroversion need to sample broadly from fuzzy content domains. In its focus on achievement testing, this model emphasizes the instructional nature of Track C. It should be recognized, however, that the kinds of content, interventions, goals, tests, interpretations, and scores involved in Track C teaching are also involved in Track C counseling.

Should Teachers Teach to the Test?

Another aspect of sampling merits special attention—the old debate regarding the legitimacy of "coaching," or "teaching to the test."

It is clear to many teachers that a survey test (i.e., a Track C test) is a *sample* of student performance. Its purpose is to enable *generalization* from the sample to the domain. The generalization concerns student achievement in the *entire* domain. It is prudent to generalize from a sample only when the sample is representative of the domain. To enable this kind of inference, tests are carefully built to sample widely and evenly from the entire domain. Now if a teacher were to "peek" at the test before instruction in order to give *dis*proportional emphasis to the specific content that happens to be tested, three undesirable consequences would follow.

First, the test questions would no longer constitute a balanced sample of the studied and unstudied parts of the domain; inference from the test would be biased. Teaching to a survey test has the purpose of rendering inferences from its scores misleading. Second, the test would no longer adequately measure transfer of learning from these students; hence, its validity would be compromised. Third, because the test would not give sufficient emphasis to transfer, students would, in the future, strive less for transfer. *In the context of Track C education, teaching specific content of a test merely because it is on a test is counterproductive.* This statement applies equally to teacher-made and to published devices. Likewise, it applies to instruments used to assess individual students and to those used to evaluate programs.

To other teachers, this line of reasoning has long seemed devious and nefarious. In the context of Track A and Track B training, teaching the content of a test is entirely appropriate and professional. For content in which the test taps the entire domain—not just a sample of it—it is legitimate to teach the test, the whole test, and nothing but the test. For example, if pupils were to memorize "do, re, me, fa, so, la, te, do," one would teach and test it in its entirety. Test security would not be an issue because sampling and transfer are not central concerns. Strictly speaking, the curriculum should not be derived from the test; rather, both the content taught and the content tested should be based on the instructional objectives. Nevertheless, *in the context of Tracks A and B, content taught and content tested may be identical.*

Some of the disputes regarding "teaching to the test" arise from failure to recognize the instructional implications of different kinds of subject matter and goals. What is effective for one may be ineffective for another (Sanders, et al., 1990). *Effective teachers are able to function skillfully with each kind of subject matter.*

Other aspects of the "teaching to the test" dispute reflect the different meanings the phrase has. In the context of Track C, use of the term is usually pejorative, referring to instructional overemphasis of that which is sampled in the test. Yet some educators take the phrase to mean teaching to the general domain of knowledge sampled by the test (Shepard, 1990). Therefore, those who wish to discuss the topic should either first define the term or avoid using it.

Two Other Contrasts

Before concluding the discussion of kinds of tests, it will be worthwhile to consider briefly pretesting vs. posttesting and the contrast between formative and summative evaluation. Appropriate uses of pretesting, posttesting, formative testing, and summative testing will be related to the three tracks. However, these topics do not have the same key relationship to other elements of the model that exists for mastery and discriminatory tests.

Pretests and Posttests

A **pretest,** of course, *is a test given before instruction, while a* **posttest** *is one administered at the end of an instructional segment.* Unless otherwise indicated, both terms typically refer to achievement tests.

Track A.   In teaching for mastery, learners must have the entry behaviors needed for successful new learning. Requisite entry behaviors are often preidentified. If they are essential, then their presence should definitely be verified. This verification commonly takes one of two forms. If recent prior instruction has been organized on a mastery model, then posttests for prior requisite units would certify each examinee's readiness. Otherwise, the teacher would need to use one or more mastery pretests to determine whether each student was ready for the new material.

In mastery learning of suitable subject matter, an essential sequence of content exists; for example, one must be able to count before learning to add, and add before learning to subtract, multiply, or divide. If, in this context, a teacher discovers that a student lacks vital requisite learning, then the new material is *not* presented; rather, remediation is undertaken. In Track A, pretests provide vitally important information, and their results should be used to make instructional decisions about individual learners.

In mastery learning, posttests are used to ascertain *whether* critical achievement standards have been met. If they have, then instruction proceeds to the next unit. If a standard has not been met, then recycling occurs in order to remediate the difficulty. Posttesting in Track A is *diagnostic* and *prescriptive*. That is, it is designed to pinpoint problems and to provide information useful in correcting these problems.

Tracks B and C. In Tracks B and C, pretests are much less important. Since subject matter is not highly sequential, learners need *not* meet specific, rigorous entry standards. Hence many teachers appropriately dispense with pretests altogether when teaching Track B and C content.

On the other hand, many other teachers of Track B and C content use pretests to good advantage to gain some idea of learners' level of functioning. Pretesting enables them to assign appropriate instructional material.

An example is an elementary teacher's decision to assign pupils to groups for mathematics instruction. In the absence of other data, a pretest for this purpose would make good sense. The pretest would be designed to discriminate among different *degrees* of competence. Or a baseball coach might want to ascertain that team members have some grasp of rules. If no other data were available, a pretest of rules would be appropriate. This pretest would be designed to discriminate among different *degrees* of knowledge of rules. The pretest's results could be used (a) to decide what instruction is necessary for the team as a whole and/or (b) to identify any individual players who may be so deficient that they need remedial instruction.

In Track B and C instruction, posttests are used to determine students' degree of competence. Results provide a record of achievement and may be useful in making future instructional decisions. But because no particular level of achievement is vital to future progress (provided that level of instruction is matched with student capabilities), no specific diagnostic or remedial use is made of posttests.

Formative and Summative Tests

A **formative test** *is used to provide information that will aid ongoing instruction.* It is diagnostic in nature, designed to identify specific areas that need further study. Because pinpointing weaknesses is especially important with basic, essential content, formative tests are ordinarily mastery tests. Results can be used by teacher and/or student to prescribe remediation of deficiencies. Scores of formative tests are *not* ordinarily used for grading.

A **summative test** *is designed to provide information at the end of a unit's instruction.* It provides information about students' terminal achievement. A mastery summative test is designed to indicate *whether* a standard has been met, while a discriminatory summative test is intended to reveal *degree* or *level* of performance. Scores of summative tests are usually used for grading.

In Track A, much use is made of ongoing formative testing. In Tracks B and C, less use is made of formative testing. Summative tests are important, of course, in all tracks. Chapter 10 will explore the instructional uses of formative and summative testing in greater depth.

Table 3–3

Model of Relationships among Content, Individual Differences, Instructional Objectives, Learning Theories, Teaching Methods, and Kind of Test

Track	Type of Subject Matter	Principal Manifestation of Individual Differences	Type of Instructional Objective	Group of Learning Theories	Type of Instruction	Kind of Test
A	Entire content of small domain readily specified in behavioral terms; content vital and masterable	Time dimension	Minimum essential behavioral	Behavioral	Much specific training	Mastery—student has prior knowledge of the exact domain to be tested (usually in its entirety)
B	Tasks readily specified in behavioral terms, but cannot or need not be mastered	Achievement dimension	Behavioral developmental	Mixed	Specific training in early phases and/or varied	Discriminatory—student has prior knowledge of exact tasks that will be tested (usually in their entirety)
C	Content of large and/ or open domain cannot be specified in detail, but can be illustrated in behavioral terms; content not masterable	Achievement dimension	Nonbehavioral developmental	Cognitive	Mainly teaching for under-standing and transfer	Discriminatory/survey—student has prior knowledge of the general domain to be sampled, but not of the exact test questions

TO RECAP

In this section, appropriate kinds of tests were matched with curricular content, individual differences, instructional objectives, learning theories, and teaching methods. These relationships are summarized in Table 3–3, which revises the material contained in Table 2–5 to include the topics that have been addressed in Chapter 3. In addition, the columns have been rearranged from the pedagogically convenient order in which they were introduced to the logistically convenient order in which a classroom teacher might best consider them in planning a unit.

QUIZ 3–2

1. Which track of Table 3–3 does *not* require a test that reveals individual differences in achievement?
   A. Track A.
   B. Track B.
   C. Track C.

2. Content sampling is most frequent in tests designed to assess achievement of
   A. minimum essential behavioral objectives.
   B. behavioral developmental objectives.
   C. nonbehavioral developmental objectives.

3. "Harness Test Power" was used on page 66 to mean
   A. Let's harness the power of students' prior knowledge of exact test content as a means of controlling what they will study.
   B. Let's harness the power of tests to control what students study.
   C. Let's come to terms with the fact that most students are not influenced by teacher-made tests.

4. To reveal individual differences in achievement, test questions need to be
   A. so easy that nearly everybody passes each item.
   B. of medium difficulty.
   C. so hard that nearly everybody misses each item.

5. In which track is transfer of learning the most important?
   A. Track A.
   B. Track B.
   C. Track C.

QUIZ 3–2 (cont.)

6. What kind of test should be derived from minimum essential behavioral objectives?

    A. A mastery test.

    B. A discriminatory test that covers the entire domain.

    C. A discriminatory/survey test.

7. For which track is it normally *not* legitimate to teach all of the specific content that will be tested?

    A. Track A.

    B. Track B.

    C. Track C.

8. Which track's tests are most related to tests of psychological traits or constructs?

    A. Track A.

    B. Track B.

    C. Track C.

KEY TO QUIZ 3–2

Item	Key	Comments
1	A	See pages 63–64.
2	C	See page 65.
3	B	See page 66. Option C is the antithesis of the intended meaning. Option A would be good for Tracks A and B, but would be wholly inappropriate and educationally disastrous with large and/or open content domains. Option B is appropriate in Track C because students' knowledge that the test will demand transfer of learning will prompt them to try to enhance their ability to apply their learning; Option B is also appropriate for Tracks A and B in the special-case sense verbalized by Option A.
4	B	See page 65. If everybody received nearly the same score, be it high (from very easy items in tests lacking adequate ceiling) or low (from very hard questions in tests having insufficient floor),

		KEY TO QUIZ 3–2 (cont.)

		the test could not reveal individual differences in achievement; it could not discriminate among people whose achievement differs. This will be more fully treated in Chapters 4, 9, and 15.
5	C	See pages 65–67.
6	A	See pages 63–64.
7	C	See pages 66–68.
8	C	See page 67.

Kinds of Score Interpretations

The last section concerned the type of test appropriate for each track of the model of relationships. Attention is now turned to the type(s) of interpretation that can meaningfully be given the scores of each kind of test.

If a measure is to serve any useful purpose whatsoever, it is necessary for its scores to have at least one basis for interpretation. Two major bases of score interpretation will first be introduced. They will then be matched with the three tracks of the model.

Bases for Score Interpretation

Domain Referencing

A **domain-referenced (or criterion-referenced or content-referenced or objectives-referenced)** *statement tells how a person handled certain well identified content.* For example:

Performed CPR on a dummy in the standard, prescribed way.

Keyboarded at the rate of 37 words per minute.

Correctly read the time to the nearest minute from five different standard clocks that vary in face design.

Made 14 out of 20 basketball free throws.

To be useful, a domain-referenced interpretation must relate to a well-defined content or skill domain. "The domain definition should be sufficiently detailed and delimiting to show clearly what facets of behavior are included and what facets are excluded" (American Psychological Association, 1985, p. 26).

Unfortunately, some test authors lose sight of this essential requisite for meaningful domain or criterion referencing. In pursuit of being able to describe examinee status with regard to content, they attempt referencing to ill-defined domains. Everyone agrees that it *would* (note the conditional tense) be desirable to have educational measures that accurately describe what examinees can and cannot do. The problem is that this simply is not possible *unless* the content domains are well described (Forsyth, 1991).

Due to this oversight, "Some tests referred to as criterion referenced simply do not define a domain of behavior, and thus they cannot form the basis for referencing test performance in the manner considered here" (Nitko, 1980, p. 464). For instance, it is not useful to know that Al correctly answered 7 out of 10 items on the test for the War of 1812, or that Jill correctly spelled 95% of the words on a test. Such statements are referenced to ill-defined domains; the test items could range from very easy to unreasonably difficult.

But when a content domain or skill is highly specifiable, then the interpretation can be *content referenced* (i.e., domain referenced). The interpretation can reveal *what the examinee can do.* The clear delimitation of test content provides a "measuring stick" against which an examinee's performance can be compared.

This tightly specified content "measuring stick" is called a "criterion" by some writers (e.g., Popham, 1990). In this usage, **criterion** is defined to mean "basis of comparison" or "continuum of knowledge acquisition, ranging from no proficiency at all to perfect performance (Glaser, 1963, p. 529). Unfortunately, the word "criterion" suggests a point on the continuum and is used by many people to mean "required level of achievement." The term "criterion" thus lends itself to misunderstanding and is widely misinterpreted (Jeager, 1987; Mehrens & Lehmann, 1991). "It carries surplus associations to mastery learning that are best avoided by using the more general term 'domain' instead" (Hively, 1974, p. 5). This ambiguous usage of "criterion" is avoided in this book in order to maintain clarity. **Domain** is used to refer to a body of content or skills, and **standard** is used to denote the level of achievement specified in a minimum essential behavioral objective.

The point was made above that some tests alleged to be criterion or domain referenced or to be referenced to behavioral objectives fail to define domains of behavior in a clear-cut manner. Such tests are therefore not usefully referenced to the domains. A corollary follows.

Some so-called mastery tests are not referenced to objectives that are incisive enough to make the standard meaningful. An example is the objective that "students will correctly match the time shown on standard clocks with the time written in colon notation at least 3 times out of 4." If this goal were given to three test makers, tests of markedly different difficulty might result. Tester X might base all the items on large clocks having 12 Hindu-Arabic numerals and 60 clearly demarcated minutes and provide absurd incorrect choices. Meeting the 3-out-of-4 "standard" of mastery would be relatively easy on this test. Tester Y might base items on small clocks having 4 or fewer Roman numerals and set off only in five-minute intervals and provide very attractive incorrect options. Meeting the mastery standard on this test would be relatively difficult. Tester Z might prepare items that span the possible range of difficulty. The phrasing of the clock example above represents an attempt to direct teaching and testing along these lines. But even this does not "tie down" the difficulty of the test; it could still vary substantially.

Unfortunately, many so-called mastery or diagnostic tests are not referenced to objectives that are precise enough to enable meaningful domain referencing. "The fruitfulness of the orientation in terms of domain mastery depends on the possibility of defining a domain clearly and incisively, so that the range of performances that lie within the domain can be fully specified and agreed on" (Thorndike, 1982, p. 2).

Norm Referencing

A **norm-referenced (or people-referenced)** *statement tells how a person's performance compares with that of a group of other people.* For example:

Obtained a grade equivalent of 4.7 from the national reference group on a reading comprehension test.

Won the keyboarding speed contest.

Answered more questions correctly on the World War I test than 40% of the class.

Obtained a WISC–III IQ of 114.

To be useful, a norm-referenced interpretation must compare the examinee's performance with the performance of a *well-identified and relevant* group of people. It would not ordinarily be useful to be told that tenth-grade Maria answered more questions correctly on an oral reading test than 74% of a national sample of third-grade students; this reference group is not likely to be relevant for a tenth-grade student. Nor would it be useful to know that Nickoli did better on an algebra test than 10% of some undescribed sample of other people; unless a reference (or norm) group is clearly described, it does not enable meaningful comparisons to be made.

But when a reference group is both adequately described and relevant to the purpose of the interpretation, then the interpretation can be *people referenced* (i.e., norm referenced). It can describe examinee status in comparison with a significant group of other people.

Some published tests alleged to be norm referenced are not accompanied by data for reference groups of people that are well described and/or relevant to the purpose of interpretation. The mere presence of normative tables in a test manual does not ensure the usefulness of the data. The adequacy of normative samples must be thoughtfully judged by prospective test users. This topic will be addressed more fully in Chapters 13 and 17.

Choosing Appropriate Bases for Interpretation

It may be helpful to refer back to Table 3–3 to consider the kind(s) of test-score interpretation that go(es) with each combination of type of subject matter, exhibition of individual differences, kind of instructional goal, family of learning theories, type of instruction, and kind of test.

Track A

Where subject matter domains are small and closed, the content is clear and masterable. If it is important for all students to master a domain, then individual differences should be directed into the time dimension by means of a minimum essential behavioral objective in which a standard of mastery is established. Instruction often consists of specific drill on each element in the domain, and teaching methods tend to be based on behavioral learning theories. Achievement is best tested with a mastery test designed to show whether examinees have reached this minimum standard. In these circumstances, the interpretation should be referenced to (a) the incisively defined content domain and (b) the standard. The interpretation is domain referenced to reveal what the examinee does, and it is referenced to the minimum essential standard to indicate whether mastery has been attained.

Examples of such domain-referenced, mastery interpretive statements are:

Herbie successfully counted each group of objects ranging in number from 2 to 10.

When given a standard combination lock and its combination, Anita opened the lock within the one-minute time limit.

These statements are domain referenced because each refers to an exact domain or task (e.g., counting up to 10 objects). Each statement is also referenced to a minimum standard because it indicates whether a given level (e.g., opened in one minute) was attained.

Track B

Where learning tasks can be adequately specified in behavioral terms but cannot be mastered or are not judged to be important enough for everyone to have to master them, individual differences are best relegated to the achievement dimension by means of behavioral developmental objectives that describe the domains but do not set minimum standards. Achievement is best assessed with tests that discriminate among persons having various amounts of competence in the tasks. The resulting scores may be given either norm-referenced and/or domain-referenced interpretations. Norm-referenced statements reveal how examinees compare with other people, while domain-referenced statements indicate what examinees can do. These interpretations are not referenced to standards.

Examples of such domain-referenced statements are:

John Adams lived to be 90 years old.

Max lifted a weight of 74 kilograms.

These statements are domain referenced because they refer to clear domains or tasks (i.e., staying alive and standard weight-lifting rules). They are not referenced to minimum standards. Rather, they report *degree* of achievement.

The results of these same tests can also be given norm-referenced interpretations. For example:

John Adams holds a record for longevity among United States presidents.

Max (aged 14) lifted a weight equal to the amount the average 14-year-old Iowa male can lift.

These statements are norm referenced because they compare the performance of the examinees to that of well-described reference groups of other people (i.e., all United States presidents and 14-year-old Iowa boys).

Note that it is the *interpretations* given test scores, not the tests themselves, that are domain or norm referenced (American Psychological Association, 1985; Feldt & Brennan, 1989). A given test can, if its content is clearly defined, be given both a domain-referenced *and* a norm-referenced interpretation. In Track B, both are often useful.

Track C

Finally, where content domains are large and/or open, the subject matter cannot be specified in detail. Individual differences are best directed to the achievement dimension by means of nonbehavioral developmental objectives. Instruction should be aimed at understanding and transfer of learning. Achievement is best assessed with broad-spectrum survey tests that reveal individual differences in breadth and depth of achievement. Under these conditions, test scores must be given norm-referenced interpretations to show how examinee performance compares with that of some well-described and relevant group of people.

Examples of such norm-referenced, interpretive statements are:

Khalaf answered more items on the mammal unit test than did 8% of the pupils in his class.

Angela did as well on the test in geography, culture, and religions of India as the average eighth-grade student in the country.

These statements are norm referenced because they compare examinee performance to that of specified groups of other people.

Results of such tests could not meaningfully be domain referenced because the content domains are open-ended and fuzzy. Referencing tests to ill-defined, open domains is like anchoring a ship to a floating platform.

TO RECAP

In Track A teaching, small, closed, vital content domains require minimum essential objectives and mastery tests. Mastery tests reveal *whether* examinees have reached a predetermined standard of competence in tightly specified, masterable domains; interpretations are thus *dichotomous.* Interpretations suitable for scores of such tests are referenced both to domain content and to established standards of mastery.

Track B content is clearly defined, but either (a) is unmasterable or (b) is not judged to be important enough to warrant mastery. Such content is best specified by behavioral developmental goals and assessed by discriminatory tests that reveal *level* of achievement. Interpretations given the scores may be domain referenced to the specifiable content domain. Interpretations may also be norm referenced to performance of some well-described group of other examinees. Thus the interpretations of tests used to assess individual differences in the extent of achievement of behavioral developmental objectives may appropriately be domain referenced and/or norm referenced.

In Track C teaching, unspecifiable, unmasterable content calls for cognitive or affective developmental objectives. Achievement of such objectives is assessed by tests that survey or sample content domains to reveal the *breadth and level* of achievement. Interpretation given to such scores cannot be meaningfully referenced to the domains because they are not clearly identified. They, therefore, should be people referenced. These norm-referenced interpretations indicate how examinee performance compares to that of relevant groups of other people.

QUIZ 3-3

For Items 1–8, indicate whether each statement is true or false.

1. All interpretations that are referenced to a minimum standard are also referenced to content domains.

2. Scores of some tests can meaningfully be given both norm-referenced and domain-referenced interpretations.

3. When norm-referenced interpretations are used, individual differences are exhibited in the achievement dimension.

4. Percentage grading systems can be meaningful in courses such as Introductory Psychology, Survey of American Literature, and Introductory Biology.

5. Domain referencing came into American education in the 1960s.

6. Technically, a *test* can be norm referenced.

7. Large, open content domains are compatible with referencing to minimum standards.

8. When tests tap higher mental processes, interpretations can ordinarily meaningfully indicate whether or not examinees have met a standard.

For Questions 9–15, indicate whether each of the following statements is norm referenced or domain referenced.

9. Mike's oral temperature is 37.2° C.

10. Mike's oral temperature is within the normal range.

11. Enrico is the best-liked boy in his class.

12. April knows only 18 of the multiplication facts.

13. May has more mechanical interest than 98% of eleventh-grade girls.

14. June won the chess game.

15. Tim answered 72% of the questions correctly on the final examination in Principles of Educational Measurement.

KEY TO QUIZ 3-3

Item	Key	Comment
1	True	See pages 75–76.
2	True	Track B tests are often given both domain- and norm-referenced interpretations. See page 76.

KEY TO QUIZ 3–3 (cont.)

Item	Key	Comment
3	True	Norm-referenced interpretations are meaningful only in combination with developmental objectives that channel individual differences into the achievement dimension. See page 75.
4	False	Such courses concern enormous, ill-defined domains. Thus, test item difficulty is not well anchored to the content domains. Hence, domain referencing or "absolute" percentage grading systems are free-floating and lack inherent meaning. This topic will be examined in depth in Chapter 12. See pages 76–79.
5	False	Tests of arithmetic facts, typing speed tests, track events, etc., have long been given domain-referenced interpretations.
6	False	Strictly speaking, it is the interpretation, not the test, that is norm and/or domain referenced. See page 76.
7	False	This is a very serious (albeit common) mismatch. Referencing to a standard makes sense only where the standard is (a) meaningful because the content domain is clearly and tightly described and (b) necessary because the subject matter is highly sequential. Neither of these conditions is descriptive of large, open content domains. See page 74.
8	False	Higher mental processes are found in large, open content domains. Therefore, no meaningful domain standard can be established. Achievement of the objectives is a *matter of degree*, not a "whether or not." See the several italicized "whether" statements in this section. Only in Track A, where a standard can meaningfully be set, does such a dichotomous "whether or not" interpretation make any sense. In Tracks B and C, where objectives are developmental, interpretations should reflect *level* or *degree* of achievement. In Track C, *breadth* also should be assessed.
9	Domain referenced	
10	Norm referenced	

KEY TO QUIZ 3–3 (cont.)

Item	Key	Comment
11	Norm referenced	
12	Domain referenced	
13	Norm referenced	
14	Norm referenced	
15	?	This is an unfair question. The attempt clearly was to domain reference the interpretation, but this is an example of the very common source of confusion. Because the content domain is large, open, and ill-defined, test interpretations cannot meaningfully be anchored to it. It would be foolish to anchor a ship to a floating iceberg in an attempt to remain stationary. Yet how many teachers attempt to anchor inter-pretations of tests of large, fuzzy domains to some "absolute standard" represented in a percentage grading system? Alas, many. This issue will be treated more fully in Chapter 12.

Kinds of Scores

All that remains to bring closure to the model of relationships is a brief consideration of the types of test scores used in the various kinds of teaching-testing-interpreting situations.

Raw Scores

A **raw score** *is the number of points earned.* Examples are:

Twenty-three letters of the alphabet correctly named.

Forty-nine points on a current-events test.

(Occasionally, raw scores are obtained by adjusting the original number of points by a so-called correction-for-guessing formula. For example on a true–false test, the raw score could be considered either to be the number of questions answered correctly or the number right minus the number wrong.)

Closely related to raw scores are percentage scores. Examples are:

Eighty percent of the 100 addition facts answered correctly.

Seventy-three percent of the questions on the literature test answered correctly.

For interpretive purposes, raw scores and percentage scores are highly similar.

In Track A where content domains are very clearly defined, raw and percentage scores carry inherent meaning; they convey domain-referenced information. For example, "Rich correctly named 23 letters of the alphabet," and "Yar answered 80% of the addition facts correctly," provide meaningful information about what the examinee can do.

Similarly in Track B, where tasks are well defined, raw scores (but less often percentage scores) are inherently meaningful because they convey domain-referenced information. For example, "Ellen made 6 out of 10 basketball free throws" and "Jack ran 100 meters in 11.8 seconds," provide meaningful information about what the examinee can do.

The first examples in the above pairs for raw and percent scores on page 80 are well suited to domain-referenced interpretation; the domains are clear-cut. Both second statements are not appropriate for domain-referenced interpretation; the domains are only vaguely identifiable. These scores need to be converted into derived scores in order to enable norm-referenced interpretation.

Derived Scores

Useful as they are in making domain-referenced interpretations, neither raw nor percentage scores communicate norm-referenced information. To show how examinees' performances compare with that of relevant and clearly described reference groups, raw scores are converted into derived scores. Many kinds of derived (i.e., converted or norm-referenced) scores exist. (An explanation of the meaning, derivation, and use of the respective derived scores is provided in Chapter 16.)

The major kinds of derived or converted scores are:

Grade equivalents and age equivalents.

Simple ranks and percentile ranks.

Standard scores (e.g., *z*-scores, stanines, and deviation IQs)

The feature that all **derived scores** share is their *capacity to render people's performance comparable to that of other people.*

In Track C where content domains are not tightly described, derived scores are needed for meaningful interpretation. These interpretations must, of course, be norm referenced. For example,

Roy's reading comprehension score equaled that of the average beginning sixth-grade pupil in the state.

Nellie's adaptive behavior rating equaled that of an average three-year-old in the country.

Avis' United States History test score was better than those of 64 out of every 100 students in a national sample of other ninth-grade students.

Compared with others in his English class, Guy obtained a *z*-score of +1.7 on the vocabulary test.

Psychological constructs also lack clearly identified boundaries. Therefore, derived or converted scores are necessary to provide meaningful norm-referenced interpretations. For example, "Warrick's self-report anxiety inventory score exceeds

Table 3–4

Model of Relationships among Subject Matter, Individual Differences, Instructional Objectives, Learning Theories, Teaching Methods, Tests, Scores, and Interpretations

Track	Type of Subject Matter	Principal Manifestation of Individual Differences	Type of Instructional Objective	Family of Learning Theories	Type of Instruction	Kind of Test	Type of Score	Type of Interpretation
A	Entire content of small, closed domain readily identified in behavioral terms; content vital and masterable	Time dimension	Minimum essential behavioral	Behavioral	Much specific training	Mastery—students have knowledge of the exact domain that will be tested	Raw or percent	Domain-referenced and referenced to a standard of mastery
B	Tasks readily specified in behavioral terms, but cannot be mastered or are not important enough to merit mastery	Achievement dimension	Behavioral developmental	Mixed	Varied and/or specific training in early phases	Discriminatory—students have prior knowledge of exact task or domain to be tested or sampled	Raw and derived	Domain-referenced and norm-referenced
C	Content of large and/or open domain cannot be specified in detail, but can be illustrated in behavioral terms; content not masterable	Achievement dimension	Nonbehavioral developmental	Cognitive	Mainly teaching for understanding and transfer	Discriminatory/survey—students have prior knowledge of general domain to be sampled, but not of exact items	Derived	Norm-referenced

that of 98 out of every 100 men in the country" and "Cara's IQ score on the nationally normed test was 107."

Similarly in Track B, where the objectives are developmental and mastery either does not exist or is not sought, derived scores *can* be given norm-referenced interpretations. For example,

> Bertha's strength of grip was greater than that of 71% of a national sample of girls in her grade.
>
> Tim won the bowling tournament.
>
> Ian's high jump placed him in the seventh stanine in his physical education class.

(As seen in the previous section, it is also possible to give Track B raw scores domain-referenced interpretations.)

TO RECAP

Table 3–4 summarizes the eight interrelated topics that have now been treated. Chapters 2 and 3 have considered ways in which the topics are interwoven and the evolution of the three tracks into which the eight aspects of teaching and testing are harmoniously interfaced. The columns of Table 3–4 are arranged in the order in which a teacher engaged in planning instruction would most likely consider the topics.

Table 3–4 provides a succinct summary of Chapters 2 and 3 and will serve as a handy reference to the model of relationships for the remainder of the book. You may want to mark the page to enable its quick location.

QUIZ 3–4

By now, the contents of Table 3–4 should be internalized. Try to answer the following questions without reference to the table, but feel free to use it if you get stuck. For Questions 1–10, choose among the following three options: Track A, Track B, or Track C.

1. For which kind of teaching should one set a level of excellence up to which each student is expected to come?
2. For which kind of content is it vital to distinguish between indicants and objectives?
3. For which kind of material does logic lead to use of norm-referenced interpretations?
4. For which track are percent scores most suitable?
5. In which track is attainment of behavioral developmental objectives interpreted by means of either raw scores or derived scores?

QUIZ 3–4 (cont.)

6. For which kind of content does logic suggest use of domain-referenced interpretations?

7. In which track is achievement of clearly defined but unmasterable content compared with reference groups of other people or with content or skill domains?

8. In which track is it *not* appropriate to "teach to the test"?

9. In which track is it *un*necessary for tests to reveal individual differences in achievement?

10. In which track does it require the most effort to assure that tests contain suitably balanced samples of content?

11. Which applied measure would have to be norm referenced?

    A. Age.

    B. Blood pressure.

    C. Height.

    D. Self-concept.

12. Which applied measure could sensibly be domain and/or norm referenced?

    A. Academic aptitude.

    B. Dependability.

    C. Liberalism.

    D. Weight.

KEY TO QUIZ 3–4

Item	Key	Comments
1	A	See pages 49–50.
2	C	See pages 53–57.
3	C	See pages 76–77.
4	A	See pages 80–81.
5	B	See pages 80–81.
6	A	See pages 76–77.
7	B	See page 76.
8	C	See pages 67–68.

	KEY TO QUIZ 3–4 (cont.)	
Item	**Key**	**Comments**
9	A	See pages 63–64.
10	C	See pages 65–67. Chapter 4 focuses largely on meeting this challenge.
11	D	Self-concept is a vague, ill-defined psychological construct. The other three domains are clear and could be either norm and/or domain referenced.
12	D	Weight is clear. The other three domains are ill defined. Hence only weight can properly be domain referenced. Measures of the other three domains can be meaningfully interpreted only through norm referencing.

Amphibians, Hybrids, and Other Exceptions

This and the previous chapter have presented a usable model of relationships among eight topics that are integral to effective instruction. These chapters have provided the core content of the model and have brought it to reasonable, albeit somewhat simplistic, closure. This section amplifies and enriches the core contents.

The purpose of the presentation has been to bring the patterns or tracks of *compatible combinations* of eight elements into focus. In pursuit of this end, differences among the tracks were emphasized by use of carefully selected illustrations. But by examining only neat, clear-cut illustrations of the respective tracks, reality was oversimplified. It is now time to confront some not-so-neat cases. This section examines four types of legitimate departures from clear-cut, single-track teaching: teaching characterized as amphibious, hybridized, double-exposure, and multilevel.

Amphibious Teaching

Some subject matter is best handled in one track early in training and then shifted to another track for more advanced instruction. The analogy would be the tadpole's developmental shift from water to land. In some instances this amphibianlike change of form reflects the inherent nature of the content, while in other cases a teacher elects to start in Track A for reasons of safety.

Inherently Amphibious Material

In teaching people to play chess, the first tasks concern teaching (a) the names of the six chess pieces, (b) the starting position of each piece, (c) the moves allowed each piece, (d) certain vocabulary, and (e) the basic rules of the game. Each of these content domains is well defined, masterable, and essential for subsequent progress. Individual differences should therefore be channeled into the time dimension. Minimum essential behavioral objectives are indicated. Instruction should consist of specific training. Raw scores should be used with mastery tests to give domain-referenced interpretations of whether mastery of each objective has been attained.

So far, this is Track A teaching. But once these essentials are mastered, things change. Reference to Table 3–4 may be useful. The domain of intermediate chess is not small, closed, specifiable, rigidly sequential, or masterable; hence, the content clearly no longer fits into Track A.

Moving on to the next topic of Table 3–4, individual differences in excellence in chess must be exhibited in the achievement dimension. Developmental objectives are obviously appropriate. Cognitive-oriented learning theory would foster instruction for understanding and transfer of learning—this clearly is Track C. Tests consist of games in which players do not have advanced knowledge of the moves that opponents will make; this too sounds like Track C.

The next column of Table 3–4, type of score, provides little help; a game lost or won is a score, but to classify it as either a raw or derived score may not be easy. Since winning is relative to the other person, the interpretation given the score is clearly norm referenced; this indicates either Track B or C.

Analysis has shown Track A to be wholly inappropriate for intermediate or advanced chess instruction. Although several of the topics were of little help in deciding between Tracks B and C, only Track C seems compatible with each topic. It is, therefore, the only suitable approach.

This analysis has shown that in teaching chess one might best start in Track A with several minimum essential objectives. As soon as the student has mastered each of these vital goals, the teacher should ascend directly to Track C. This shift is reminiscent of the "graduation" of the tadpole from the water onto the land; in this sense, chess is an "amphibious" subject.

For another example of subject matter that can be viewed to be inherently amphibious, consider a common approach to teaching reading. In the early primary years, much of the instructional effort devoted to reading is often considered to be Track A. For instance, learning such things as letter names, standard sound–symbol correspondences, and common prefixes and suffixes can well be taught by use of the mastery model. However, once the average reader advances beyond second grade or so, the emphasis shifts from these mechanical features to reading comprehension. This more advanced level of reading instruction clearly belongs in Track C.

Learning to play many musical instruments follows a similar sequence. These examples illustrate the fact that some subject matter should, by virtue of its inherent nature, be recognized as being Track A —> Track C amphibious.

Safety-Induced Amphibious Treatment

Other subject matter, although not inherently amphibious, may be *treated* as amphibious for reasons of safety. For example, Judy Wright is a swimming instructor who believes floating on the back to be an unnecessary skill before learning to swim. Indeed, she believes that it may be possible to become an expert swimmer without ever learning passive floating. However, she teaches swimming in a large, deep pool, and she thinks it prudent to insist that each student be able to float before entering the big pool. She, therefore, establishes a minimum essential objective of floating for two minutes. No student is allowed to enter the big pool before "mastering" this task. After this minimum standard is met, her attitude becomes "the-longer-the-better." Her amphibious instruction is therefore Track A —> Track B.

Driver education provides an example of a safety-motivated Track A —> Track C, amphibious sequence. Before allowing beginning students to embark on the psychomotor tasks of operating a car, Mike Klabunde first demands mastery of cognitive knowledge of traffic and basic safety rules. Although knowledge of these rules is not sequentially related to controlling a vehicle, he believes their prior mastery reduces the hazard of accidents.

Hybridized Teaching

As the sophisticated reader may have suspected all along, some content cannot be assigned to a uniquely correct track. While most subject matter falls quite clearly into one track or another, some is about equally suited to each of two tracks, falling in borderline regions. Still other content is within one track yet near one of its neighboring regions.

The proximity of each track to each other track is represented in Figure 3–3. Each track is adjacent to each other track. Note that Track B is *not* "between" Tracks A and C on a linear continuum; Tracks A and C are adjacent.

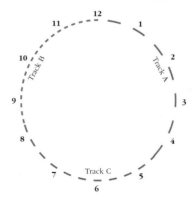

Figure 3–3. Continua of Track Characteristics

The separation of one track from another is not sharp; rather, a gradual shading occurs of one region into the next. To facilitate discussion, 12 regions of Figure 3–3 have been numbered to correspond to the numerals on a clock face. A borderline situation for each pair of tracks will now be illustrated.

Track A/B Border

Recall Judy Wright's unit on floating, and use Table 3–4 to analyze this unit. The content is adequately defined, but its masterability is questionable. For some purposes (such as admission into a big pool), she would prefer to classify people as floaters or nonfloaters. But her standard of mastery must be very arbitrary. How long must a "master floater" be able to float? Two minutes? Half an hour? All day? Although she could convincingly argue that floating is unmasterable, she could also persuasively maintain that for most purposes no one is very interested in achievement beyond a few minutes. Corresponding ambivalence enters into her consideration of individual differences. Similarly, all that she can insist on concerning appropriate objectives is that they should be behavioral. She decides that learning theory and her instructional methods should rely more on training than on transfer of learning. Test content is known in advance, and she can use either raw or derived scores to make domain- or norm-referenced interpretations, respectively.

These considerations leave her a choice of Track A or B. She could appropriately choose the option that best suits her preferred teaching style. A unit on back floating would be located in Figure 3–3 at or near Region 12.

Track A/C Border

For an example of an A/C borderline content domain, consider the part of Max Abernathy's unit on the United Nations that concerns its membership. The list of member nations is substantial in size. It is masterable at any point in time, but the domain is open because membership keeps changing. Although he would like students to know a few major members such as the United States, United Kingdom, and People's Republic of China, he does not believe that every student must know the name of every obscure member. Therefore, his consideration of subject matter does not place him in a particular track.

Regarding instructional goals, he reasons that he wants cognitive *knowledge* of membership. Students could be expected to do such things as list, choose, or recognize members and nonmembers. However, if he wants to be able to establish a standard (e.g., permanent members of Security Council plus 20 other members), he would have to settle for specific behavioral objectives rather than behavioral indicants; this might not seem in this particular unit to be an unreasonable price to pay for the means of establishing a standard. On the other hand, there is no reason for him to accept a behavioral rather than a cognitive objective unless he is pursuing a standard.

Choice of behavioral versus cognitive learning theory parallels the choice of behavioral versus nonbehavioral objective. Likewise, instruction can either be aimed at Track A mastery of some modest standard or at Track C memory of as much of the list as time permitted. Memory could be evidenced in any of several ways that would be suggested by indicants.

His test can be used either to judge the attainment of the standard (for Track A) or to discriminate among students whose achievement differs (for Track C). He can give the raw scores domain-referenced interpretations (for Track A or B) or convert them into derived scores for norm-referenced interpretation (for Track B or C).

This leaves him a reasonable choice between Tracks A and C. Competent teachers could elect differing tracks within these limits because the particular topic falls in Regions 3 to 5 in Figure 3–3.

Track B/C Border

For an example of a B/C borderline topic, consider spelling accuracy. If the content of interest for an advanced spelling unit were all words in a particular dictionary, the domain would be well defined, but so large as to be unmasterable. Its unmasterability would preclude putting it in Track A. Its specifiability in combination with its virtual unmasterability suggest Track B. Yet there was an artificiality in specifying only entries in a particular dictionary. Had the domain been less provincially defined to be all words in the English language, then its openness and the fuzziness of its boundaries would have demanded Track C classification.

Individual differences in spelling should clearly be directed largely into the achievement dimension. Concerning kinds of objectives, we would probably consider such things as being able to spell orally or in writing and being able to recognize correct and incorrect spelling to be indicants of nonbehavioral knowledge; this suggests Track C. Yet a good case can be made that the real goal is the behavior of correct written spelling; this suggests Track B. Teaching would quite clearly be of Track C type with emphasis on pursuit of positive transfer and avoidance of negative transfer. Concern would not be limited exclusively to the material studied. This orientation draws heavily on cognitive learning theories.

Tests would sample the domain rather than assess all of it. Results could be given domain-referenced interpretations by use of percentage scores (e.g., can spell approximately 60% of the domain). But to justify this type of inference, great care would be necessary to assure that the words tested were representative in difficulty of the domain. It might be better to give results norm-referenced interpretations by use of derived scores.

The analysis yields the conclusion that the subject matter is perhaps best categorized as Track B, while the instruction, testing, and probably objectives clearly belong in Track C. The topic is a hybrid at or near Region 8 in Figure 3–3; it just does not fit neatly into the model.

Double-Exposure Teaching

The addition (or multiplication) facts present an interesting variant. This content is neither amphibious nor hybrid, yet its instruction transcends a single track. The subject matter consists of *two separate domains.* The first to be taught is the straightforward, Track C domain concerned with understanding addition; it has a heavy emphasis on meaningfulness and transfer of learning.

Later, pupils need to be liberated from the need to compute common addition facts. They should be able to *figure out answers,* but should not be obliged to spend time doing so. Pupils should *memorize* the addition facts. Rapid, rote recall of the addition facts is clearly Track A content.

Addition and multiplication facts thus need double exposure, once as material to be studied meaningfully and understood and later as training content to be memorized. Although either the Track A or the Track C domain could come first, good reason exists to present the meaningful Track C treatment first. It helps to establish the mental set that mathematics is inherently meaningful.

Multilevel Teaching

Before completing the discussion of legitimate departures from single-track teaching (i.e., teaching from the perspective of just one place on the circle depicted in Figure 3–3), the legitimacy and desirability of **multilevel teaching** should be noted. Attention has been focused on the unique objectives or primary concern of various instructional units. Yet good teaching also is directed toward the simultaneous achievement of secondary and tertiary objectives as well as the primary ones. A set of objectives for a given unit should often include goals from more than one track.

For example, consider a Track A unit on telling time. The primary objectives are minimum essential. But progress should also be sought on such Track C developmental objectives as oral communications and peer relations. It is highly desirable to pursue the Track A objectives on one level along with the Track C objectives on another level.

Similarly in a Track C unit on the New Deal, it would be good to pursue attainment of such hybrid Track A/C objectives as use of library catalogs and of such Track C objectives as reading comprehension. Educators should avoid tunnel vision; they should exploit instructional units for all they are worth.

Finally, consider a unit on AIDS. Some key objectives would most emphatically be behavioral and minimum essential. For example, a critical behavioral goal would be to teach avoidance of exchanges of body fluids (except with low-risk, monogamous partners). A few "don'ts" would greatly reduce risk. In addition, one would seek higher-level (Track C) understanding and application so that students could transfer their learning to untaught, unanticipated situations (e.g., avoid "blood brother" rituals or needle sharing for home ear-piercing). One would also want to develop connections between current instruction and students' prior knowledge of viruses and to foster ever-higher levels of understanding of such biological material; this, of course, concerns Track C.

Chapter Summary

Chapters 2 and 3 present an integrated instructional/measurement framework that equips educators with *a foundation of theory upon which to base important professional decisions.* This framework enables teachers to orchestrate assessment with instruction. Table 3–4 summarizes this model.

The cornerstone of the model is the subject matter. *Characteristics of subject matter determine the kind of instructional objectives one should use, the way the material is best taught, and the kinds of tests, scores, and interpretations that are most meaningful.*

When subject matter domains are highly specifiable, masterable, and essential, objectives should demand mastery. Individual differences should, therefore, be exhibited as time needed to master. Behavioral approaches to learning and instruction are usually best suited to such content. Student assessment should be designed to certify mastery. Such tests are interpreted with reference to the content domains and the mastery standards by means of raw or percent scores.

When skill or content domains are highly specifiable but either unmasterable or nonessential, objectives should reflect a "the-more-the-better" attitude. Individual differences should therefore be exhibited as level of achievement. Students should be assessed with tests designed to discriminate among differing levels of achievement. These tests can be interpreted with reference to the well-defined content domains by use of raw scores and with respect to the performance of other examinees by means of derived scores.

When, as is most often the case, subject matter is not very specifiable, master-able, or essential, objectives should foster as much achievement as available time permits. Individual differences should therefore be manifested in level and breadth of achievement. Cognitive approaches to learning and instruction are typically well suited to such content. Assessment should be designed to reveal the achievement differences that are present. Such tests are interpreted with reference to the performance of other examinees by means of derived scores.

Suggestions for Further Reading

Gronlund, N. E. (1985). *Stating objectives for classroom instruction* (3rd ed.). New York: Macmillan. At a time when many educators were leaping on the band-wagon of indiscriminate use of Mager's type of behavioral objectives and when others were resisting attempts to clarify educational goals, the first edition of this book in 1970 provided an extraordinarily balanced and reasoned perspective. Gronlund's classic position argues for use of minimum essential objectives in (and only in) contexts where they are appropriate and for the use of non-behavioral developmental objectives accompanied by behavioral examples in other teaching situations.

Kirst, M. W. (1991). Interview on assessment issues with Lorrie Shepard. *Educational Researcher, 20,* 21–23, 27. This interview with a noted educational researcher touches on a number of current topics such as measurement-driven instruction. Shepard takes a scholarly, middle-of-the-road perspective in pointing out consequences of various innovative assessment practices and in noting some of the problems associated with the use of mandated assessment to force educational reform.

Mehrens, W. A., & Kaminski, J. (1989). Methods for improving standardized test scores: Fruitful, fruitless, or fradulent? *Educational Measurement: Issues and Practice, 8,* 14–22. This discussion of teaching-to-the-test applies the thinking summarized in this chapter to published tests.

Mehrens, W. A., & Lehmann, I. (1991). *Measurement and evaluation in education and psychology* (4th ed.). Fort Worth: Holt, Rinehart and Winston. Chapter 3, "The Role of Objectives in Educational Evaluation," and Chapter 2, "Norm- and Criterion-Referenced Measurement," provide sound introductions to several of the topics treated in this chapter.

Payne, D. A. (1992). *Measuring and evaluating educational outcomes.* New York: Macmillan. Chapter 4, "Specifying Educational Outcomes," provides an informative discussion of educational objectives from several significant perspectives.

Developing and Using Teacher-Made Achievement Measures

Creating effective classroom measures requires at least five attributes. First, teachers need a grounding in theory and knowledge to guide sound professional judgment concerning when and how to use various kinds of tests. The integrative theoretical framework provided in Chapters 2 and 3 serves as a foundation on which teachers can plan and implement sound assessment practices. Chapter 4 will relate the instructional/evaluation model to the topic of planning classroom measures. Other topics related to effective use of various kinds of assessment devices will be considered in Part III.

A second attribute of teachers who develop effective achievement measures is possession of basic techniques of test construction. This "how to" information is provided in Part II.

Third, test makers need to know the subject matter well enough to avoid stumbling on content issues while assessing examinee command of it. Next, teachers must be familiar with student characteristics such as reading level and ability to cope with separate answer sheets. Finally, those who create outstanding tests need a measure of creativity. Although some attention will be directed to the refinement of these last three attributes, relatively little time is devoted to them because these aspects of professional qualification are already present in the vast majority of teachers. Vital as they are, deficiencies in these attributes are not often the cause of inadequate classroom testing practices.

Part II focuses on those attributes most often lacking. The rationale that guides test planning is discussed in Chapter 4, while Chapters 5 to 9 are devoted largely to "know how." Teachers who are armed with both theory and technical skills are equipped to use classroom assessment as an integral part of effective teaching.

Planning Teacher-Made Achievement Measures

The aim of this chapter is to enable readers to plan useful and valid classroom achievement measures that are compatible with other features of good teaching. Attainment of this general goal requires attention to two themes that were introduced in Chapter 1. First is the principle that tests should be used to improve decision making. The kind of test best suited to a given situation depends on the kind of decisions it is intended to inform. This principle and the theory presented in Chapters 2 and 3 enable teachers to choose appropriately between formative tests and summative tests, and between mastery and discriminatory tests. The theory also enables wise professional decision making between domain- and norm-referenced interpretations.

The second theme that is central to the use of measurement as an integral part of effective teaching is this: Classroom assessment devices and practices influence what, when, and how students will try to learn. "Classroom evaluation has powerful direct and indirect impacts, which may be positive or negative, and thus deserve very thoughtful planning and implementation" (Crooks, 1988, p. 438). The kind of tests a teacher gives communicates to students what their learning goals ought to be. Tests are, therefore, a powerful force in teaching.

Teacher-Made Tests vs. Published Tests

As mentioned in Chapter 1, published tests assess achievement over a wide span of subject matter and grade levels. The first issue in planning for classroom achievement testing is when to use ready-made, published instruments and when to use customized, teacher-made ones. Properly used, of course, either teacher-made or published tests "are potent educational tools that enhance the instructional process" (Nitko, 1989, p. 446).

Published Achievement Tests

By-and-large, published achievement tests are summative. Moreover, they tend to encompass large bodies of content, not short units. For example, a published test on fifth-grade map reading would probably span all the basic map skills; separate tests would not likely be available for units such as identifying land forms or estimating distance. Similarly, a published test in first-year algebra would be expected to give balanced coverage to the entire year-long course; one would probably not find separate tests for specific units, such as rationalizing denominators or graphing linear equations.

Some of the advantages of published achievement tests to be addressed in Chapter 17 can be anticipated. Commercially prepared instruments can be developed and reviewed by specialists; thus they provide high-quality item writing and reliability. Moreover, normative data external to the individual classroom are available for published achievement tests having norm-referenced interpretations.

Teacher-Made Achievement Tests

Teacher-made tests are customized to meet the needs of their makers. Therefore, they are highly adaptable. This flexibility is the key virtue of "home-made" tests.

In global competence assessment, such as reading comprehension, biology, or algebra, teachers often have a choice between published and teacher-made tests.

While published instruments tend to excel in technical adequacy and to have external normative data, teacher-made tests have the advantage of being sensitive to local curricular emphases. Flexibility to reflect local peculiarities in content is, in some cases, important in subjects such as biology or United States history; it seems less likely in algebra or reading.

At the unit level (in contrast to whole-course summative testing), the advantage of the teacher-made test is great. Teachers can tailor unit tests to reflect local content and to allocate desired weight among content topics. For example, biology teachers in Alaska, Florida, and Oregon who have respectively used the walrus, manatee, and seal as prime examples of sea mammals can fashion their tests to reflect these desirable local flavors in curriculum.

Teacher-made achievement tests are most widely used to assess unit achievement. Some units are small, highly sequential instructional segments characteristic of Track A mastery teaching. In such cases, formative and summative mastery teacher-made tests are needed. Other units are in Track B and cover delimitable content that is not taught for mastery. In these cases, summative discriminatory teacher-made tests are called for. Tests of these kinds are relatively easy to plan and construct owing to the high degree to which their content domains are specified.

More often, units concern larger Track C content domains that are taught with transfer of learning as the primary goal. In these cases, summative discriminatory teacher-made tests are fashioned to provide the desired balance of emphasis among various objectives. Discriminatory survey tests that assess a variety of mental processes are the most demanding to develop; their planning will, therefore, receive the most attention in this chapter.

Two Orienting Principles for Planning Teacher-Made Tests

As mentioned before, learning is enhanced by student assessment when teachers are cognizant of two guiding principles. Namely, (a) testing should improve decision making and (b) assessment practices should be used to influence student effort in desired ways. This section expands these ideas.

Testing and Decision Making

With only rare exception, *a test should be used only when there is reason to expect a better decision to result from its use than would occur without it.* This simple principle is of fundamental importance. As noted in Chapter 1, adherence to this principle precludes much misuse of tests.

Tests can facilitate various kinds of decisions, but a test well suited for one kind of decision may be ill suited for another. Therefore, before getting very far into planning a test—before considering difficulty level, length, item type, etc.—teachers should address such questions as "Why am I giving this test? What kind(s) of decision(s) should it improve?"

Attention at this time will be restricted to kinds of decisions teachers commonly make with teacher-made tests. Decision types will be identified that correspond to the three tracks in the instructional/evaluative model.

Decisions That Call for Track A Testing

In Track A teaching, most material is highly sequential. In this context it is important to ensure that each learner has sufficient mastery of the present unit to be able to progress to the next. An example would be "Is each pupil in this primary class ready to move beyond addition of two one-digit numbers?" A simple yes–no answer is needed. This kind of decision is best made by use of a mastery test.

As noted in Chapter 3, teachers place some material in Track A for reasons of safety even though it is not inherently sequential. It may be important to deny students access to certain activities until they have acquired certain requisite safe behaviors. For example, "Does each shop student put on the safety goggles before turning on the power drill?" Here too, a dichotomous yes–no answer is desired for each student. Mastery tests are well suited to provide this kind of answer.

Decisions That Call for Track B Testing

"Which four students should the coach enter in the 100-meter sprint?" Assume the only criterion is speed. To answer the question, the coach needs a discriminatory test to separate students on the basis of how rapidly they run 100 meters. A norm-referenced interpretation is, of course, needed since only the top four sprinters can be entered in the meet.

"How rapidly can each student type?" In this Track B context, a discriminatory test is needed. A domain-referenced interpretation is necessary to answer the question.

Decisions That Call for Track C Testing

In each of the above examples, the content domain was clear; hence the choice of test content would be relatively simple. This is the case for Tracks A and B content, but less clearly identified Track C domains present much greater difficulty in constructing adequate tests. The following questions relate to such less delimitable content.

"Which pupils will benefit most from initial placement in each of the three reading groups that a teacher is planning?" Here the content domain is neither specifiable nor masterable, so mastery testing is out of the question. Needed is a test designed to reveal the individual differences in level of achievement. This Track C context requires a test that broadly samples reading skills.

"Which students should receive each letter grade in an American history class?" Here too, the content is neither masterable nor specifiable, so discriminatory survey tests make sense. Such tests should sample the course content broadly and representatively.

Testing Influences Student Learning

A test is somewhat like the ring in the nose of a bull; the ring permits the bull to be led. Although the beast is relatively unresponsive to such things as shoves from behind and shouts, it is sensitive to the slightest tug on the ring. In similar fashion, many students at all levels of school are relatively unresponsive to many kinds of teacher efforts to guide their learning, but they are highly sensitive to student evaluation practices. As one writer concluded, *"An examination is a revealing statement by a teacher about what is important"* (Ericksen, 1983, p. 135).

I draw an example from my own first semester as a community-college student many years ago. A required literature course was taught by an interesting, dedicated, talented teacher who did much to spark our interest in the subject. Her goals clearly focused on understanding and appreciation. During the first third of the semester, she got us interested in the literature. To prepare for the stimulating class discussions that involved higher-level cognitive and affective objectives, we studied the literature and we thought about it. It was a good course.

Then came the first test. It consisted largely of matching exercises—matching authors with their works, matching works with their publication dates, matching authors with their nationalities. Rather than assessing the understanding and appreciation to which the teacher's objectives and methods had been directed, the test measured only rote recall of facts.

What impact do you suppose this test had on our future study? It seriously undermined the instructor's otherwise excellent teaching. After we "psyched her out," we began to study for such simple memory outcomes as who wrote what when. The higher mental processes such as understanding and appreciating the literature "were not important" because they were not tested. If a student wanted a good grade, the expedient thing to do was to memorize and "waste" no time on deep learning.

Readers could supply examples from their own experience of instances where poor testing seriously eroded what was otherwise good teaching. They could also cite cases in which inappropriate student evaluation practices made poor teaching ever poorer. It is not unusual for testing practices to divert student effort from the pursuit of instructional objectives.

Some people lament that students are such rudderless and expedient creatures who are so easily diverted from study emphasis of what both they and their teachers may deem important. They gnash their teeth and call it deplorable. But it remains a fact of life that *most students are influenced by what they think will be assessed. Because evaluation is such a powerful force in driving student effort, it should be harnessed.*

Testing is one of a teacher's most powerful means of influencing what content students study, how they pace their study, and what kind of learning outcomes they pursue. *Assessment is a teaching tool* having enormous power (Crooks, 1988). "If teachers test recall, students learn the facts; if teachers test more, students prepare themselves to deliver more" (Stiggins, Rubel, & Quellmalz, 1986, p. 5). This is part of the reason why testing is an integral part of teaching.

It should also be mentioned that my literature instructor's test was an educational disaster for another quite separate reason. The test did not assess student attainment of the course objectives—it did not measure what she had been trying to teach. Its validity was therefore gravely compromised.

Why Are Teacher-Made Tests Not Better?

Many teachers from primary level through graduate school use tests of very modest quality due to both their extreme emphasis on lower-level learning (Fleming & Chambers, 1983) and to their failure to measure achievement of their own instructional objectives (Haertel, 1986; Nitko, 1989). Why is this the case? The tests are often not valid measures of student achievement of the more important instructional objectives. They often fail to provide useful and timely information with which to improve student and/or teacher decision making. They also often fail to focus student effort on attainment of the more important instructional objectives. Alas, such tests often actively divert students from pursuing significant learning. Why are teacher-made tests so often counterproductive?

A major reason is that the kinds of test questions that are easiest to write—be they objective or essay—measure rote knowledge, not higher-level processing. It is natural for busy teachers to take the easy road and to "crank out" items that "flow" easily. If one does not engage in thoughtful preliminary planning concerning balance between memory questions and items that tap higher mental processes, the test will likely turn out to give more emphasis than the teacher would have wanted on memory and less on such things as understanding, thinking, transfer of learning, and appreciation.

A related reason that many teacher-made tests are poor can be found in the quality of test questions provided by publishing companies to accompany textbooks. Often contained in "teachers' manuals," these collections of questions keyed to the texts are convenient for busy teachers to use. Unfortunately, many such sets of questions are of very modest quality. They are often written by persons who have no special competence in educational measurement—often by graduate assistants of the textbook's author. If, for example, it is a history text, the graduate assistant is pursuing an advanced degree in history and may have never had an education course, let alone one in educational measurement. Items created in this context are likely to overemphasize simple learning outcomes and neglect higher mental processes.

Publishers often give little attention to the quality of such free accessory products. Test questions are rarely if ever given the same level of careful editorial scrutiny as the text itself. Yet some teachers, not realizing this, view the test questions as meriting the same confidence that they accord the text.

Does this caution about free accessory "teachers' manuals" of test items mean that one should not use them? Not at all. The caution means that one should not use the items indiscriminately. If one picks and chooses, it is usually possible to get several good items. Too, some of the less adequate items suggest ideas that can lead to creation of good questions. Others can be revised. Teachers with test plans can use the supply of questions to develop the parts of the tests that the items satisfy and then develop their own items to complement those supplied free.

Knowledge is power. The natural "drift" is for casually produced tests to overemphasize rote learning and underemphasize deep learning. Teachers who know this can avoid the hazard by thoughtful test planning.

But planning is not enough. Student evaluation practices should be planned at the appropriate point in time—when other aspects of instruction are being designed. Thus another factor that limits the effectiveness of much classroom testing is the lateness of its planning. Too often, conscientious teachers who plan their tests do so after much of the instruction has taken place. By then it is too late to effectively integrate evaluation into the total instructional package. As teachers initially design instruction, some of the planning should concern methods of assessing achievement; test content; mental processes to be measured; timing and frequency of testing; timeliness for decision making of information secured from evaluation; and the impact that evaluation practices will have on amount, pacing, and direction of student effort (Nitko, 1989).

TO RECAP

One of the two guiding principles for ensuring that teacher-made testing contributes to effective instruction highlights the wisdom of always planning tests in light of the decisions the tests are used to improve. The instructional/evaluation model provides a framework. Track A testing is aimed at improving decisions concerning whether students are ready for the next instructional segment. Mastery tests interpreted with respect to a standard are well designed for this purpose. Track B testing is used to improve decisions regarding either (a) how well students perform on content that is specifiable but either unmasterable or not important enough to master or (b) how they compare with others in handling such content. Discriminatory tests interpreted respectively (a) in domain-referenced or (b) in norm-referenced fashions are suitable for these purposes. Finally, Track C testing is designed to improve decisions concerning how examinees compare with others on content that is neither specifiable nor masterable. Tests well suited for this kind of use are discriminatory tests that sample content thoughtfully from the loosely defined domains and that are given norm-referenced interpretations.

The other guiding principle of classroom assessment highlights the "fact of life" that student evaluation practices influence what students try to learn. "Evaluation is a dominating aspect of educational practice. It strongly influences what students attend to, how hard they work, how they allocate their study time, and what they can afford to get interested in" (Sadler, 1983). This power should be harnessed to contribute maximally to effective teaching. Teachers should seek excellence in using "test power."

QUIZ 4–1

1. Mr. Ambrosius teaches a unit on first aid as part of an eighth-grade health class. He is eager for all students to learn and be able to get a good grade. He does not want a "bias" in favor of the brighter students. In an effort to enable any conscientious student to earn an "A," Mr. Ambrosius decides to base the unit's grades entirely on notebooks. The unit will have no test.

   What impact will this evaluation practice likely have on (a) validity of grades as measures of student knowledge, understanding, and ability to apply the material and (b) student learning?

2. The point has been made that tests exert a powerful influence on student performance. This point could be generalized to state that any means of evaluating any group of people will tend to influence the performance of those evaluated. Is this generalization of "test power" also true? If not, why not? If so, provide two examples.

KEY TO QUIZ 4–1

1. Such a grading practice will prompt motivated students to prepare good notebooks. While it will cause them to try to get much good material in their notebooks, it will *not* give them reason to try to get much into their heads! They may, but it will be only incidental to their effort to earn good grades.

   The notebook should be recognized as Mr. Ambrosius' *means* of getting students to learn material. It should not be an *end* in itself. By making it the basis of grading, it becomes the end. The proper objectives should focus on terminal student status with regard to knowledge, understanding, and ability to apply first aid. This status is testable.

   This mismatch between the objectives and the method of evaluating student achievement has two undesirable consequences. First, it renders the grades less valid than they would be if they were based on terminal student status. Second, it fails to use the driving power of evaluation to achieve what the teacher wants students to achieve—to *know, understand, and be able to apply* first aid in an emergency, not merely to have a notebook reference to appropriate first-aid procedures.

2. Yes! People in a wide variety of contexts are influenced by the means by which they are evaluated. Of course, exceptions exist, but the generalization states a powerful truth. The emphasis in this book concerning the influence on students of classroom evaluation practices is only a special case of a profoundly important general principle.

   Several examples will illustrate the generalizability of the principle that evaluation affects performance. First, consider new factory workers who have not yet completed a probationary period of employment. If their supervisor is known to place heavy emphasis on amount of work completed, then most of the workers will aim to do a lot of work. On the other hand, if the supervisor places primary emphasis on quality of work completed, then most workers will try to trade off some quantity for greater quality.

   Next, consider a softball game at a local park. The umpire is calling strikes on pitches nearly as low as the batters' ankles. The pitcher notices this eccentricity of the umpire and starts to pitch low, knowing that the low ones will be (incorrectly) called strikes rather than balls. Soon the batters realize what is happening and start swinging at the low ones. The umpire's evaluation of the pitches has great impact on how the adaptive pitcher pitches and how adaptive batters respond to the pitches.

   Third, consider teacher evaluation. If a school district ignores assessment skills in evaluating its teachers, then its teachers are likely to display lower levels of assessment skills than they otherwise would. Indeed, Hills (1991) contended that this is part of the reason that assessment literacy among teachers is not higher. If a principal emphasizes classroom management in evaluating teachers, then the teachers are likely to attend more closely to their classroom management than they

KEY TO QUIZ 4–1 (cont.)

otherwise would. If the district emphasizes lesson plans, then adaptive teachers will produce better lesson plans than they otherwise would. If the evaluation includes ratings of teacher-produced handouts, work sheets, assignments, and tests, then the teachers will tend to produce better materials of these kinds than they otherwise would. This is not to say that teachers lack self-direction; it is only to point out that most of us are sensitive to the means by which we are evaluated and will ordinarily accommodate ourselves to those means of evaluation to a greater or lesser degree.

Finally, consider a point made in *Scientific American* (Berger, et al., 1989). It was observed that American industry has failed to invest enough in long-range research to keep up with other industrial countries. One reason for this neglect concerns our general principle. Business executives are often compensated with benefits that reflect *current year's* profits. An executive whose compensation is directly linked to the company's financial performance in the current year will naturally stress *short-term* results over long-term research and development investment.

The principle that evaluation tends to influence those evaluated has application wherever people are evaluated. The potential of this power to pressure people to engage in undesirable activities is as great in other fields as it is in the classroom. The benefits that accrue from harnessing this power are also as great in other fields as they are in classroom evaluation.

Measures of Maximum Performance vs. Measures of Typical Performance

The third-graders are taking a teacher-made summative test on the posture unit they have just completed. Mike "sits" slumped down in his seat so that his weight is on his back rather than his rump. One leg is slung atop his desk. He thoughtfully completes the test and turns it in. It is perfect! If you were the teacher, would it distress you to have to give him an "A"?

It depends, doesn't it, on your instructional objectives for the unit. A very useful distinction can be made between objectives and tests concerned with maximum performance and those that address typical performance. *Tests of maximum performance assess what the examinee can do. Measures of typical performance assess what the examinee ordinarily does do* (Cronbach, 1990). To paraphrase, in tests of maximum performance, we ask examinees to do their best work; achievement or aptitude is being assessed. In measures of typical performance, "we hope to obtain some ideas as to what the examinees really like or what they actually do, rather than what they are capable of doing" (Lyman, 1991, p. 9).

If, on the one hand, some or all the posture unit's objectives focused on maximum performance, then student attainment should be assessed with **tests of maximum performance**. This might include paper-pencil tests of knowledge about proper posture and/or performance tests wherein pupils are asked to show the proper way to sit, stand, or walk while they are rated. Focus would be on what pupils *can do* when they know they are being evaluated and are motivated to do their best. In this context, the "rules of the game" are to represent oneself at one's best.

If, on the other hand, some or all of the unit's goals concerned typical behavior, then student attainment should be assessed with **measures of typical performance**. These measures would require rating pupils when they are unaware they are being observed in order to assess their characteristic or typical posture. Focus would be on what pupils *ordinarily will do* when they are not especially mindful of posture or motivated to be at their best. In this context, we need a representative sample of what each child ordinarily does do—a measure that is not influenced by the fact that the behavior is being observed.

Which kind of learning outcome is proper for a third-grade posture unit? Most of us would answer "both." If this is the case, then our objectives should address both maximum performance and typical performance. For example:

1. Knows proper sitting posture at desk.

    1.1.   When shown pictures of several children seated at desks, can identify the child exhibiting the best or worst posture.

    1.2.   Demonstrates good sitting posture on request.

    1.3.   Describes orally or in writing the proper way to sit at a desk.

This objective focuses on what children *can do* when they know they are being assessed, are expected to do their best, and want to do their best. In this context of maximum performance, faking is not an issue.

2. Typically exhibits good posture at desk.

    2.1.   Sits appropriately when reading.

    2.2.   Exhibits good desk posture during class discussions.

    2.3.   Shows good posture when doing paper-pencil seat work.

This objective focuses on what children *typically do* when they do not know they are being observed and are not motivated to be at their best.

Assessment of the second objective is much more demanding than the first. To evaluate pupil achievement of this goal, the teacher will have to make *several observations* of each child *without his or her knowledge*. To provide a good sample of behavior, observations should be distributed over several activities, over several times of day, and over several days.

Some authors limit the word "test" to measures of maximum performance because the word connotes to many people a situation in which people are to do their best. Thus we test knowledge of posture, typing accuracy, running speed, knowledge of spelling, understanding of history, or ability to use correct grammar. We use other devices to measure characteristic posture, typical typing accuracy, typical spelling, or ordinary grammar.

The most vivid distinction between tests of maximum behavior and measures of typical behavior came to my attention during the late afternoon of the last day of my first year of teaching. As we faculty sat in the lounge, Jim ran outside the window shouting to a friend, "No, I ain't got none neither." My colleague Mr. Halliday threw up his hands and cried, "Good Heavens, I've just given him a 'B' in English!" One can infer that Mr. Halliday's objectives included typical oral language usage; apparently his assessment devices did not. Assessment was likely limited to tests of *maximum performance* of written language usage.

QUIZ 4–2

Consider a social-studies citizenship unit. Would the more important unit objectives involve maximum behaviors or typical behaviors? Do the more important objectives concern student status at the immediate conclusion of instruction or at some more distant future point?

KEY TO QUIZ 4–2

Clearly, interest resides in typical behaviors at some future time. For example, we are more concerned in students' ultimate citizenship practices than in their present ability to answer factual test questions correctly.

Although the questions are easy enough to answer, the ramifications are complex. It obviously would not be practical to postpone awarding grades in such units until years or decades after the courses were completed. Even if it were feasible, we would have no practical way by which to gather undistorted information concerning students' typical practices.

The feeble substitutes for which teachers have to settle concern such things as *requisite* knowledge, understanding, ability to analyze, and ability to apply. These kinds of (mainly higher mental process) *maximal* behaviors are testable. Educators reason that if students lack such maximal behaviors, they will necessarily lack the corresponding typical behaviors. This seems like a logically sound enough case.

But the inverse does not logically hold. It does not follow that having the maximal behaviors will assure the desired corresponding typical behaviors. (Witness Mr. Halliday's student Jim.) Yet there is not much that classroom teachers can do about this worrisome problem in evaluating individual students' achievement of some very important objectives.

Fortunately, program evaluation (in contrast to evaluation of individual students) can address this question of degree of student attainment of ultimate objectives concerning typical behaviors. Follow-up surveys under conditions where former students have no motive to distort or falsify their self-reported behaviors can cast light on the effectiveness of instruction.

Planning Track A Measurement

Some instructional content is clearly identified, masterable, and important enough to merit mastery by all. In this case, minimum essential behavioral objectives are used to set minimal standards. Individual differences are directed into the time dimension so that each student will be able to reach the standard. Raw or percent scores of mastery tests are referenced to both the content domains and to the standards.

Planning to Answer Useful Instructional Questions

In the Track A context, pretests can help teachers answer such important questions as: "Does each student need this unit or module?" "If so, is the entire unit needed or will an abbreviated version suffice?

Formative tests should help students answer such questions as: "Am I ready to take the summative test for this objective? If not, what specific content have I not mastered?"

The question that summative tests are designed to help teachers answer is: "For this minimum essential objective, does the student meet the standard that indicates readiness to move on to the next instructional segment?"

This kind of "yes-no" information from a summative posttest score is needed separately for each minimum essential objective. This point is widely overlooked by teachers and measurement textbooks alike. Here is the logic. Each objective is minimally essential. It is therefore necessary to determine whether each objective has been mastered. Combining data for several objectives obscures this needed information.

For example, suppose there are five minimal essential objectives and a standard of 85% has been set for each. Marge's status on the respective objectives is 100%, 60%, 95%, 100%, and 95%. Her mean percentage is 90; this is safely above the 85% standard. But she has not mastered the second objective. If it is truly a minimal essential, then it is not appropriate for her to be advanced to the next unit before mastering it.

Therefore, in Track A testing, *it is necessary for a separate test (or subtest) to provide a separate score (or subscore) for each minimum essential objective.* Failure to assess achievement of each minimum essential objective separately contradicts the contention that the goals were truly essential.

Figure 2–4 on page 39 represents a typical Track A content domain. Few elements exist in such small domains. The instructional decisions are usually best based upon complete testing of the entire domains as shown in Figure 3–1 on page 64. When there are so few items in a domain, it is practical and useful (a) to teach each and every one of them and then (b) to test all of them.

Planning Guidance of Student Effort

Recall the second guiding principle in test planning—tests should guide student study in desirable directions. In Track A, this guidance is most constructive if knowledge of exact test content directs study to each one of the important elements in the domain.

Two qualifications should, however, be added. First, students ordinarily should not have advance knowledge of item order because it would enable them to memorize a test key without necessarily achieving the objective. For example, if an individually administered oral test is to ask the child to name each lower-case letter of the English alphabet when shown it, the child obviously should not know ahead of time the order in which the items will be presented. Similarly, the order should be varied between formative and summative forms of the test.

Second, in unusual Track A domains where there are more items than one may choose to test at one time, the test may sample the domain. For example, an objective concerning the 100 addition facts presented both horizontally and vertically might reasonably be assessed with a 50-item sample of the 200 possible items. In this case it would, of course, *not* be appropriate for pupils to have advance knowledge of which 50 addition facts were to be sampled on a particular form of the test. Likewise, the particular items sampled should be varied from form to form.

Aside from these qualifications, it is generally productive for students to have advance knowledge of exact test content when they are expected to exhibit mastery of small, closed, well-defined, essential domains. *The advance knowledge prompts them to do what we want them to do*—study and master the entire domain.

Mastery for How Long?

The State Capitals Test at the end of Chapter 1 demonstrated that material mastered at one point in time may not remain mastered. What then is mastery? The word has a connotation of permanence that is often unjustified.

When we declare certain content to be essential, we would do well to consider whether or not mastery is likely to be sustained over time. Mastery of some material holds up well, while other content tends to erode. The main thing that makes the difference is whether or not the learning is used.

Much Track A material is used constantly. The 10 Hindu-Arabic numerals are encountered daily; the addition facts are used frequently; stopping at red lights and going at green ones occurs far too often for people to forget the arbitrary association. When the content of minimum essential objectives is likely to come into frequent use in everyday living or in future schoolwork, then it seems adequate for teachers to demand mastery before moving on to the next unit and not to worry about re-assessment of mastery over and over again for years or decades to come.

Other Track A material is not used constantly. Examples are emergency telephone numbers and how to administer CPR. *When the content specified by minimum essential objectives is not likely to come into frequent use in everyday living or in future schoolwork, then it is important to ensure that mastery is permanent.* Mere passing of a mastery test on one occasion does not guarantee permanent mastery.

Two well-known ways exist to enhance the permanence of mastery. One is **overlearning**; this is achieved by continuing drill after the established standard of mastery has been met. This prolonged drill tends to improve long-term retention.

The other technique for enhancing long-term mastery is **review**; this is achieved by re-learning after some forgetting has had time to occur. Figure 4–1 shows how review can bolster long-term retention far in excess of the amount of time the review requires. The value of review in enhancing long-term memory is by no means limited to the kind of content found in Track A.

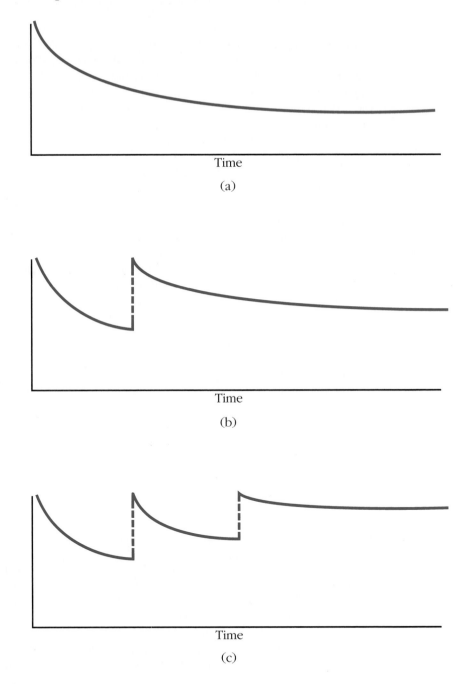

Figure 4–1. Hypothetical Retention Curve with (a) No Review; (b) One Review; and (c) Two Reviews

If content is essential, but not likely to be practiced in ordinary living, then steps should be taken to provide for permanence of mastery. Overlearning and review provide means of ensuring more than fleeting mastery. This issue is often neglected by advocates of mastery learning strategies. The next paragraph provides a hint as to the reason for some of the neglect.

Before we rush to provide overlearning and/or excessive review of mastered content not likely to be practiced in daily living, we would be well advised to reconsider whether the content was truly essential in the first place. If the content concerns low-frequency emergency procedures (e.g., being prepared to stop one's car when a ball rolls out from behind a parked car), then it probably merits overlearning and/or review. Otherwise, it may prove to be some oft-memorized content that really was not essential. Examples are the state capitals, the names of U. S. Presidents, the algorithm for extracting square roots, and the Gettysburg Address. It is often a mistake to classify such content as essential. It would be a double mistake to ensure permanence of its retention. The mastery approach to teaching and testing is best reserved for what is truly essential.

Planning the Test Content

Tests that validly measure student achievement match the instructional content and objectives. In the case of a mastery test (or subtest) suitable for a Track A minimum essential objective, validity concerns the extent to which the test measures mastery of the appropriate content domain and answers the question concerning *whether* students have mastered the objective.

Minimal essential behavioral objectives used for Track A subject matter combine both content and statement of objectives. The objective contains all that is needed to know what the test (or subtest) should contain. This renders test construction for Track A mastery tests relatively easy. Four examples follow.

Sentence Capitalization

Miss Shoop is teaching her primary class that the first word of a sentence is always capitalized. This content is vital, simple, and masterable. The first draft of her behavioral objective is:

> When writing from dictation or composing, pupils capitalize the first word of each sentence at least 90% of the time.

Before continuing, please pause and consider this objective. What is wrong with it from the perspective of the last section?

It is not clear whether the objective concerns (a) maximum performance when pupils are aware they are being tested for mastery of this objective or (b) typical performance when pupils are attending to something else, such as a coherent written account of a recent field trip to the zoo. Most teachers would feel that the issue of typical versus maximal performance is adequately addressed by simply inserting the word "can" or the phrase "typically will" before the word "capitalize." Or Miss Shoop could be more explicit.

The above draft objective contains another flaw. What if a pupil were to capitalize every word? In this case, Miss Shoop would not want to give credit for capitalizing the first words of sentences. To accommodate these two points, she revises the objective to read:

When writing from dictation or composing in situations where no special emphasis is directed to the issue of capitalization, pupils typically will selectively capitalize the first words of sentences at least 90% of the time.

All Miss Shoop needs to do is to obtain samples of work done for other reasons and determine whether the initial words of each child's sentences are capitalized at least 90% of the time (and that most other words are not). The children should not, of course, know ahead of time which samples of their work will be used to measure mastery of this objective.

What about the issue of permanence? Need Miss Shoop use overlearning or focused review? Probably not. Everyday schoolwork provides more review than necessary to make mastery of this objective permanent. She might best monitor written work for the rest of the school year for capitalization of first words; thus when a pupil slips, it is caught and corrected. Subsequent teachers can also be depended on to monitor maintenance of this objective.

This has been a rather straightforward example of a Track A unit and test. The next two examples are less clear-cut.

Name Capitalization

Mr. Albrecht's class is learning to capitalize first and last names. Two things about this content make it atypical of Track A. First, the domain of names is neither small nor closed. Second, not all surnames are capitalized for example, deCosta, de la Vega, and van der Steevenhoven are not. This content really isn't masterable. But Mr. Albrecht wisely decides to stick to names that conform to the rule and treat the unit as a mastery unit in spite of its borderline status. (He would do well to mention in passing that exceptions to the rule do exist. If such occur in his class, they would probably be learned, but their exceptionality would be noted.)

Having decided to treat the content (at least mainly) as a mastery unit, Mr. Albrecht writes the following minimum essential objective:

When composing or writing from dictation, students will, at least 90% of the time, selectively capitalize the name(s) of any persons mentioned.

Clearly, what he needs to do is dictate some suitable material to his students and include in it some names. He comes up with this:

Mrs. Jones drove to school to pick up Jane and her friends Mary Smith and Jim Armstrong. Their teacher, Miss Ann Green, had been sick that day. Mary said that the principal, Mr. Short, had taught their class.

Mr. Albrecht can score each test to see if the child capitalizes at least 9 of the 10 names (without indiscriminately capitalizing all words). Those who do are judged ready to move on to another objective. The others should spend more time on this mastery objective. Those who need to study more will take *another form* of the test when they are ready. The other form should not contain the same names or sentences. Because of the open-ended content of this domain, students should not know ahead of time the exact test content.

This unit exemplifies a borderline Track A/C content domain, somewhere in the 3 to 4 range in Figure 3–3 on page 87. Yet it is best taught mainly as a Track A unit because the rule is masterable and very widely applicable.

Roman Numerals

Next consider a much less clear-cut, borderline Track A/C unit. Ms. McAlpine is teaching the first dozen Roman numerals to her fourth-grade class. Her tentative minimum essential behavioral objective for this small, closed, incisively defined, important, and masterable content domain is:

> When shown one of the first 12 Roman numerals, the pupil will write the corresponding Hindu-Arabic numeral with at least 95% accuracy.

Here too, it would be simple to create a mastery test based on this clearly stated minimum essential behavioral objective. Although Ms. McAlpine could elect to sample the 12 elements of this small domain, she decides to test all of the elements. One form of her test is shown in Figure 4–2.

Below are some Roman numerals. Next to each write the Hindu-Arabic numeral that has the same meaning.

VIII _____	III _____	XI _____	X _____
I _____	XII _____	VI _____	V _____
_____ IX _____	VII _____	II _____	IV _____

Figure 4–2. Adequate Test of A (Too) Limited Objective

Ms. McAlpine might well create several forms of this test so that one could be used as a pretest to enable some students to "test out" of the unit and others could be used formatively to let students know when they were ready for a summative test. Students will, of course, have prior knowledge of the exact 12 items that will appear on the test, but not the order in which the items will appear; this should be varied from form to form.

In this way, Ms. McAlpine will develop a test that validly assesses her objective. Prior knowledge of the nature of the test will also serve to guide students to do what the teacher wants—know the first dozen numerals.

This unit exemplifies borderline Track A/C content (somewhere in the 4 to 5 range in Figure 3–3) that has been *restricted artificially* to fit the format of mastery learning. Many practicing teachers would handle the unit in this way. (The quiz at the end of this section provides an opportunity to consider how the unit might better be taught.)

Now that two not-so-obvious units have been considered, consider again a clear-cut, Track A situation for our final example.

Driver Education

Mr. Sudds teaches driver education and wants each student to remember that the switch for the emergency blinkers on most cars is on the right-hand underside of the steering column several inches below the steering wheel. Although this knowledge is not sequentially requisite to driving, he decides to demand mastery of it because of its importance in emergencies. Accordingly, he writes the following minimum essential objective:

On command to do so, the student will turn on the emergency blinkers within five seconds while driving the car without taking eyes off the road.

As in almost all clear-cut Track A units, it is easy to create the test once the objective is well written. When a student is driving, Mr. Sudds need only unexpectedly say, "Turn on the emergency blinkers," and see if the task is executed within five seconds. (True, we could quibble about the difficulty of this task varying somewhat with traffic conditions when the command is given. Yet most of us would elect to treat this as Track A content in spite of this slight limitation of specifiability of task difficulty.)

QUIZ 4–3

1. In the Roman numerals unit, Ms. McAlpine confined the unit to a small, closed domain. She taught the material mainly by rote and demanded mastery of the first 12 written Roman-to-Arabic conversions.

    Some teachers do just this; they focus on securing rote mastery of *artificially delimited* content domains. This makes for sterile units that do little to encourage thinking. (Indeed, such units subtly communicate that school is a place to memorize, not a place to think!) I weep for their students! Were you uncomfortable with Ms. McAlpine's approach? If one were more inclined to favor a Track C approach, how might the entire approach to the unit differ? In considering your answer, you may find it useful to consider the concept of amphibious material and the notion of multilevel teaching.

2. Is Question 1 above a Track A, Track B, or Track C question? Why?

KEY TO QUIZ 4–3

1. Is it appropriate to require translation from Roman to Hindu-Arabic numerals, but not the reverse? (That is what Ms. McAlpine did.) Should one arbitrarily pick exactly 12 Roman numerals? Are the first 12 really vital? Are others unimportant? Is this content as void of meaning and transfer as is common in Track A material? The answers are all "no" or "probably not." Roman numerals do not best belong in Track A.

    The domain of Roman numerals is highly specifiable, closed, and masterable, but uncommonly large. Clearly mastery is not necessary for the entire domain, yet mastery (via rote learning) of the first few *symbols* (e.g., I, V, and X) seems vital. For these basics, individual differences would best be channeled into the time dimension. But beyond that, it is not reasonable to demand mastery. This is like the amphibious unit on chess discussed in the last chapter. The instructional strategy

KEY TO QUIZ 4–3 (cont.)

implied is to demand mastery of the first three symbols—to treat them as Track A, then to move on to higher-level aspects of the topic.

But the plot thickens. It is also important for pupils to master the *basic system* (e.g., the difference between IV and VI and the meaning of XVII). They need to understand and be able to transfer or extend the system to larger Roman numerals if and when additional symbols (e.g., L and C) are introduced. The Roman *system* is large, but quite simple. It is moderately important and relatively masterable. The system might best be treated as Track A/C border material or as Track A material to be mastered before moving on. Thereafter, instruction in Roman numerals would be in Track C.

Transfer is also important from another angle. A little work with arithmetic using Roman numerals does much to instill a profound appreciation of two major features of our Hindu-Arabic number system—place value and zero. Without going outside the familiar system with which one has grown up, it is difficult to grasp the "breakthrough" significance of these features. It would be a pity to study Roman numerals without exploiting this opportunity to build appreciation and understanding of the Hindu-Arabic system through contrast. This consideration suggests multilevel teaching.

Another multilevel benefit to be sought from a study of Roman numerals is the knowledge of the monumental contribution of Islamic and Hindu cultures to European civilization. Understanding and appreciating this Hindu-Arabic heritage would be an important outcome of the unit. Yet it would be lost in a sterile mastery approach to the topic.

Since the first 12 numerals are important for using some clocks, should they be mastered? Some could well answer "yes," but I would not. Rather I would rely on mastery of the first three symbols and mastery of the system to produce *meaningful command* of the first 12—indeed the first 39—Roman numerals. By emphasizing the meaningfulness and downplaying the ability to memorize the first dozen numerals, I would hope to establish the attitude that this unit consisted of material to be understood, not merely memorized.

2. The above analysis was hard and required much transfer of learning. The question definitely tapped high-level Track C content and processes.

Planning Track B Measurement

Some teaching material is incisively identifiable, but unmasterable. Other material is clearly definable and masterable, but insufficiently important to warrant mastery. In either case, behavioral developmental objectives direct individual differences into the achievement dimension. Raw or derived scores of discriminatory tests are referenced, respectively, to the content domains or to reference groups of other people.

Planning to Answer Useful Instructional Questions

In Track B teaching, the instructional questions that pretests should help answer involve such issues as: "Into which distance-running instructional group would Sylvia best be placed?" "Which bowling league should I join in order to be challenged, but still competitive?" The kinds of questions that formative tests help students answer are: "How would I do if I were to take the summative basketball free-throw test now?" "Has my keyboarding speed improved since last week?" The kinds of questions that summative posttests are designed to help teachers answer are: "How well does Alex handle the content specified in this objective? How does his performance compare with that of others in this content?"

Planning Guidance of Student Effort

As emphasized before, teachers' use of tests should be designed to direct student study in desired ways. In Track B, the two kinds of content lead to somewhat different recommendations. Some Track B content is very delimitable yet unmasterable (as in basketball free throws or archery). In this case, the guiding function of tests is ordinarily most effective if students have prior knowledge of the exact content. Planning and developing such tests follow very simply from well-stated behavioral developmental objectives.

Other Track B content is specifiable and masterable but not important enough to require students to master (e.g., knowledge of names and terms of all United States presidents). In this case, the way to maximize the study-driving force of the test depends upon whether the test will cover the entire domain or merely sample it. If the test is to assess the whole domain, then test security is no concern. The behavioral developmental objective identifies the exact domain, it is taught in its entirety (but not to the point of mastery), and it is tested in its entirety (without expecting mastery).

If the test is to assess only a sample of the domain, then test security is important. Again the behavioral developmental objective specifies the exact domain, it is taught in its entirety (albeit not to mastery), and it is tested *by sampling*. In this case, the sample tested should be *representative* of the entire domain. If students had prior knowledge of the material to be sampled (e.g., particular presidents), they would tend to learn these better than the rest. Indeed, some students would not bother to study the rest at all! The test would thereby be rendered *un*representative of the domain, and interpretations of its scores would *mis*represent student status. This is a double bind. Prior knowledge of what a test samples can both (a) compromise the test's validity in answering the instructional questions it was designed to address and (b) divert students from the kind of study the teacher wants.

Planning the Test Content

Behavioral developmental objectives for Track B subject matter combine both content and the statement of goals. This makes test construction for Track B discriminatory tests relatively easy. Two examples follow.

Swimming

Mr. Mathews coaches swimming and wants each member of the team to be able to swim a 100-meter freestyle as rapidly as possible. This developmental behavioral objective concerns skills that are highly specifiable (by means of swim-meet regulations) but clearly unmasterable. Developing the test is simple; the test and the practice activity are indistinguishable.

Eurasian Countries and Capitals

Mrs. Sprong's seventh-grade geography class is studying Eurasia, and she would like students to have some familiarity with the countries and their capitals. This material is well specified and masterable so it could be taught for mastery. But, realizing that memorized material such as this tends to be quickly forgotten, Mrs. Sprong judges the material not to merit mastery. She therefore puts it in Track B.

Mrs. Sprong has to decide whether to test all of the countries or only to sample them. If she chooses to test them all, then exact test content is not confidential.

If she elects to sample the countries, then test content must be kept secure. If students knew which countries are to be tested, then both guiding principles of classroom achievement testing would be violated. Some students would now study the tested countries to the exclusion of the rest. Hence, the test would be rendered an *un*representative sample of the content domain and would thereby provide *misleading* information for decision making. Moreover, the test would not prompt students to do what the teacher desires—learn as many of the countries and their capitals as feasible.

In selecting which countries to include on her test, Mrs. Sprong divides the list into three equally long portions on the basis of country importance. She wants major countries to have greater probability of being tested than minor ones. She decides to select from the respective strata of the list 60%, 30%, and 10% of the countries to be tested.

Information about the existence and degree of this "toploading" should be given to students. Doing so helps to harness test power. Such information will help them know the extent to which she wants them to give priority to certain countries and will cause most of them to comply.

She considers the following developmental behavioral objectives:

1. Given an outline map of Eurasia, students will pronounce the names of the countries.
2. Given an outline map of Eurasia, students will write the names of the countries.
3. Given an outline map of Eurasia, students will match the numerals of countries with their names.

Since these goals are not deemed to be essential, their assessment can be combined into a single test. Thus she must address how achievement involving each objective would be measured and the weight it should carry.

To assess achievement of Objective 1, she would likely use an outline map with numbered countries and have students individually pronounce the names of countries. To measure their achievement of Objective 2, she would have them write the names of countries on an answer sheet. These procedures both measure student ability to *retrieve* names from memory and to *produce* them.

To assess achievement of Objective 3, she would again use the outline map with countries numbered, but names of countries would be supplied for students to match with numbers. This taps student ability to *recognize* and *match* names. Mrs. Sprong values this less than their ability to produce the names.

If she has only a few students in the class, she might plan for a 25-item test with, say, 8 items administered individually to sample student command of Objective 1; 9 group-administered questions to measure their attainment of Objective 2; and 8 group-administered items to estimate their achievement of Objective 3. In this case, her test plan might resemble Table 4–1. Along the right-hand side, she has controlled the 60–30–10 percent ratio among strata. The bottom of the table shows her maintenance of near-equal balance among her three objectives. Having no reason to depart from proportional representation among cells of the table, she departed only enough to round to whole items.

Table 4–1

Planned Questions on a Geography Test for a Small Class

Strata	Oral Items	Completion Items	Matching Items	Total
Top	5	5	5	15
Middle	2	3	2	7
Bottom	1	1	1	3
Total	8	9	8	25

But if Mrs. Sprong has many students, she might conclude that individual testing would divert too much time from instruction. In this case, her test plan might resemble Table 4–2. Here, she has decided to abandon Objective 1 because of its inconvenience, coupled with her belief that the other two objectives get at similar learning.

Table 4–2

Planned Questions on a Geography Test for a Large Class

Strata	Completion Items	Matching Items	Total
Top	8	7	15
Middle	3	4	7
Bottom	2	1	3
Total	13	12	25

In de-emphasizing or eliminating Objective 1, Mrs. Sprong considers the impact of so doing on student study efforts. If the weight of both Objectives 1 and 2 were to be drastically reduced, students might try to learn more for recognition than for retrieval. Moreover, they would neglect spelling; this could be a serious concern. However, she judges that the maintenance of Objective 2 at 50 percent of the total would not impact gravely on student effort.

This example illustrates why test makers sometimes consider using a less-than-ideal item type to assess learning. The example has shown that, within limits, it is reasonable to alter testing practices in order to be cost- and time-effective. But it has also pointed out the need to be aware that bowing too much to expediency may cause "test power" to pull in the wrong direction.

QUIZ 4–4

Suppose you were a fifth-grade teacher charged with teaching the state capitals as a small part of the year's social studies work. Suppose also that you agree with the rationale developed at the end of Chapter 1 which suggests that students need not master the 50 state capitals in order to lead full lives and be good citizens. This would lead you to treat the content as Track B material. How might you best plan to test it?

You have decided to give the unit limited emphasis over a five-week interval and to give a 12-item quiz on five different occasions during the unit. How might you best develop a plan that would be helpful in creating each of these five quizzes?

KEY TO QUIZ 4–4

Several things should be considered in planning for these quizzes. First is proportionality among regions of the country. This could be achieved by dividing the country into a few regions and selecting for each form of the quiz a suitable number of states from each region.

Second is difficulty. If the results are going to be given only norm-referenced interpretations, then the relative difficulty of the several forms does not matter. But if the results are to be given domain-referenced interpretation, then it is important to select for each form of the quiz states of representative difficulty. Otherwise if Quiz 2 happened to sample mostly easy states and Quiz 3 chanced to include several difficult states, then pupils would appear to know less in Quiz 3 than in Quiz 2; this could be quite demoralizing. Ideally, one would have prior data on the relative difficulty of the states and would stratify the states in each region to include some states at each of several difficulty levels. Lacking this, one might simply use one's

KEY TO QUIZ 4–4 (cont.)

judgment concerning relative difficulty and thereby attempt to maintain a very crude equivalence of difficulty among the five forms of the quiz.

Third is importance. Some states may be judged to be more important than others. One might well demand mastery of the students' own state. And one might want to give more emphasis to very populous states than to others.

Table 4–3 provides one reasonable way of taking account of all three of these factors. The teacher has (arbitrarily) specified the five states having the largest population and the students' own state as ones that will have relatively high probability of being included on any given form of the test.

Table 4–3

State Capitals Quiz Specifications

Five Big States plus Local State	4	
Region of Other 44 States	*Easier*	*Harder*
11 Northern	1	1
11 Eastern	1	1
11 Southern	1	1
11 Western	1	1

In developing the five forms of this quiz, the teacher ought to *avoid behaviors that enable students to guess which items will appear in a given form.* For example, one ought not to systematically rotate through the states in each region. If New Mexico and Oregon happen to be the western states sampled in Quiz 1, then these two states should have no more and no less likelihood of appearing on another form of the quiz than do states such as Arizona and Washington that happened not to be sampled in Quiz 1. Students are quick to pick up on such teacher behaviors as avoidance of retesting states. Therefore, one should be careful *not to be predictable* beyond the level specified in the test plan.

Planning Track C Measurement

Some instructional content is broad in scope, not very delimitable, unmasterable, and not sequentially necessary for study of subsequent topics. In this case, nonbehavioral developmental objectives are used to channel individual differences into level and breadth of achievement. Derived scores of discriminatory survey tests are referenced to the performance of other people.

Planning to Answer Useful Instructional Questions

In this Track C context, pretests could be used to help answer such instructional questions as "Which approach to the subject will capitalize on relevant background information that students have?" "What important prerequisite learning is present? Absent?" "Into which instructional group might each student best be placed?" Formative tests have less use in Track C than in Track A, but they can help students and teachers cope with such questions as "What grade would I receive on a summative test if I (the student) studied no more?" "Is there a subdomain in which my (norm-referenced) status is especially weak?" Is there an especially important part of the unit (such as conjugation of a particularly important irregular Spanish verb) on which I am still weak? On which I (the teacher) needs to devote more class time?"

Most Track C testing, of course, involves summative tests designed to help teachers answer such questions as "What grade should I assign to each student?" "How has the class as a whole achieved relative to other groups?" "Are there especially important subdomains on which student achievement seems weak?" "How has the new teaching approach on a certain topic worked?"

Since developmental objectives are suitable for Track C content, student mastery of each objective is not an issue. It therefore is not necessary to obtain a separate measure of student achievement of each objective. Several objectives are ordinarily combined into a single score.

Planning to Guide Student Effort

For open-ended, unmasterable Track C content of the type that most of us teach most of the time, students definitely should *not* have prior knowledge of the exact test content. Figure 3–2 on page 67 shows how a discriminatory survey test can only sample a Track C domain. Such content is taught for transfer; it therefore should be tested for transfer. A test assesses student ability to generalize only if some of its content is novel—that is, if the content has *not* been studied in the exact way in which it is tested. "One cannot claim to have engaged a student in any higher level cognitive process without presenting in the question a situation that is different in important respects from situations the student has previously encountered during learning" (Terwilliger, 1989, p. 18).

A teacher can guide student effort to emphasize some content more than others simply by announcing that it is more likely to be tested. For example, the teacher of the state capitals unit discussed in the previous section might wisely tell the pupils that their own state and the five largest states are much more likely to be tested and re-tested than are other states. This is "test power" at its best; it causes students to do what the teacher wants—give priority to certain states. Likewise, the "top loading" of the Eurasia test would be publicized with the intent of guiding student effort.

Teachers also should direct student study effort to emphasize some *mental processes* more than others. Track C units typically contain some material that can be memorized by rote and other content that requires higher mental processing. We want students to do far more than be able to recite the facts taught them; we want them to be able to use the information. "We want them to think" (Stiggins, Rubel, & Quellmalz, 1986, p. 5). If we want students to be able to engage in such processes as application, analysis, and synthesis, they should know this. A powerful way to get students to pursue such outcomes is to *tell them they will be tested.*

It will now be profitable to review the characteristics of nonbehavioral developmental objectives and to emphasize some additional features of this very important kind of instructional goal statement.

Nonbehavioral Developmental Objectives for Track C

A Little Review

It is helpful if cognitive and affective developmental objectives, like other instructional aims, are stated in terms of terminal student behaviors. Even though they are not ordinarily behavioral, they can be given relative clarity by use of behavioral examples. These behavioral indicants illustrate the kinds of evidence that the teacher would accept concerning degree of student attainment of the nonbehavioral objective. In other words, indicants illustrate some of the ways in which the objectives may be assessed.

The format consists of a general nonbehavioral statement for each terminal student goal. Under it are listed several behavioral indicants that would evidence achievement of the goal (Gronlund, 1985). For example:

1. Knows basic terms.
    1.1. Matches terms with definitions.
    1.2. Writes acceptable definitions of terms.
    1.3. Uses terms correctly in extemporaneous speech.
    1.4. Uses terms correctly in written work.
    1.5. Selects the term that fits a given studied definition.

2. Understands basic terms.
    2.1. Given flawed definitions of terms, identifies the problems.
    2.2. Selects the term that best fits a given paraphrased definition.
    2.3. Arranges terms in order from most to least inclusive.
    2.4. Uses terms correctly in extemporaneous speech.
    2.5. Uses terms correctly in written work.
    2.6. Given a passage in which terms are used, identifies correct and incorrect usages.
    2.7. Explains relationships among terms.
    2.8. Shows relationships among terms with representations such as outlines and Venn diagrams.

3. Understands the concept of mammal.
    3.1. Orally provides a correct definition.
    3.2. Lists several major characteristics of mammals.
    3.3. Given names of familiar but unstudied animals, classifies them as mammals or nonmammals.

3.4. Given verbal descriptions of exotic animals, classifies each as a mammal or nonmammal.

3.5. Classifies pictures of zoo animals as mammals or nonmammals.

4. Applies Bill of Rights to contemporary events.

4.1. When given a relevant current event not previously studied, identifies violations, if any, of Bill of Rights.

4.2. Given a fictitious scenario, identifies which, if any, of the first 10 amendments are relevant and provides a reasoned opinion concerning whether they have been violated.

4.3. Lists governmental actions in any recently studied country that would, in the United States, be violations of the Bill of Rights.

4.4. Given a fictitious political campaign speech, points out advocated legislation that would violate and/or would safeguard the Bill of Rights.

A New Emphasis

An important feature of instructional objectives deserves emphasis. Recall that they are phrased in terms of *terminal* student behavior. This means that they focus on what the student can do or typically does do at the end of instruction. Therefore, they do *not* involve methods of achieving the objectives. They focus on ends, not means.

This is an extremely important point for two distinct groups of reasons. The first major reason why nonbehavioral developmental objectives should be stated in terms of terminal student status concerns the separation of means and ends. It is helpful to make a sharp distinction between instructional objectives on the one hand and teaching methods and materials on the other. By focusing on the goal or destination, all options are left open concerning means of pursuing it.

An analogy may be helpful. If you plan to fly to Mexico City, it is helpful to indicate the goal or destination as Mexico City and to avoid confounding the objective with the means by which you plan to reach it. Thus if the air-traffic controllers should go on strike, you can change your means and not be thwarted in the attainment of the objective.

Similarly in teaching, it is wise to keep one's goals separate from the means of pursuing them, that is, to distinguish between terminal student status on the one hand and teaching methods and instructional materials on the other. To illustrate, suppose you were a first-year primary teacher who had developed a modest unit on Eskimos to pursue such important objectives as understanding and appreciating that some cultures provide ways different from our own of solving major life problems, of reducing ethnocentrism, of understanding our linguistic heritage from Eskimo (e.g., the word "kayak"), and of knowing some specific geographic information about Eskimo habitat and culture.

Now suppose the retiring teacher across the hall has truly outstanding materials on a similar unit on India and offers to give you the materials. Would you change units? Most of you would.

Would your important objectives change? Mostly not. You would still strive to show that various cultures have differing ways of solving life's problems. You would still try to use the unit to reduce ethnocentrism. You would still show that English is heir to other languages for some of its words, although you would now want to show our indebtedness to Hindi (e.g., "guru"). You would change the geographic and cultural information from arctic to India. All in all, many of your objectives would remain unchanged. And it tends to be the more important objectives that would survive.

The point is this: Compared with behavioral objectives, *nonbehavioral objectives usually should be less content-specific.* To explore this important point further, please re-examine the four objectives on pages 118–119. The first two are completely *content free.* The third is focused on the content of mammals, but it does not specify which mammals or nonmammals will be tested. Moreover, it could readily be converted into an objective on fish or spiders. Thus it is *content-reduced.* Of the four, only the last objective is relatively content-specific, and even it avoids locking in specific examples.

Some advocates of curriculum-based assessment (e.g., Choate et al., 1992) overlook this distinction between objectives and the methods and curriculum that teachers use to pursue them. In Track A, where objectives are quite properly content-saturated, the distinction is of relatively minor importance. But in Track C, where many means exist for pursuing each objective, the distinction is important.

The second set of reasons why goals should focus on terminal student behaviors is relevant to objectives for any track. Each kind of objective should be stated in terms of *terminal* student status rather than in terms of *change* in student status. A common fault in the phrasing of instructional objectives for any track is the use of verbs that denote change. For example:

Pupils will *learn* the first 10 Roman numerals.

Members of 4-H will *grow* in self-concept.

Students will *develop* greater appreciation of Bach.

Learners will *improve* their listening comprehension.

Patients will *lose* weight.

Runners will *increase* endurance.

Students will *gain* in vocabulary.

Compelling reasons exist for avoiding verbs that denote change in student status. First, to measure change, teachers would be obliged to pretest, to posttest, and to compute the difference; this would be inconvenient. It also would introduce sources of measurement error that will be considered in Chapter 15 as well as some technical problems that are beyond the scope of this book (e.g., see Cronbach & Furby, 1971).

Another consideration is that gain can easily be faked. Suppose grades for the 100-meter dash were to be based on gain rather than on terminal status. Some students would "fake bad" on the pretest in order to enhance their potential gain. This would reduce such a grading system to a farce!

Yet another difficulty with using change of status for goals can be illustrated by the first objective above. What if Omar already knows the first 10 Roman numerals before the unit is taught? He does not "learn" them in the unit. Should he then fail the unit because the objective was not met? Of course not. Most teachers who "paint themselves into this corner" by use of change verbs would ignore the logical problem, "walk on the wet paint," and give the student an "A." This suggests that terminal status was really the teacher's objective and that the verb "learn" did not reflect the intent. It would be better to state the objective in a way that captures the intent (e.g., "Pupils will *know* the first 10 Roman numerals.").

Implications for Test Planning

Track C objectives are often not content-saturated as are objectives in Tracks A and B. *The objectives provide information that is somewhat independent of that contained in the content*. Plans for Track C tests therefore need to take into account both (a) the *mental processes* specified by the objectives and (b) the *content* with which the mental processes interact.

This is commonly accomplished by means of a **two-way grid**. The subject matter topics are listed along the left-hand side. The mental processes are listed at the top. If several objectives all use the same key verb (e.g., "understands" or "applies"), they can often be combined into a single column headed by that verb. Table 4–4 illustrates such a grid.

This grid or **table of specifications** is used to ensure that Track C tests *maintain desired proportionality* among the several (a) content topics and (b) mental processes.[1] It enables a test maker to specify how much weight to give each topic and how much weight to allocate to each mental process. Such a plan enables a teacher's intent to guide his or her action. The teacher thoughtfully decides on the desired proportionality of content among topics and mental processes and then sets out to make the test conform to this intent.

The value of developing such a table of specifications or test blueprint is that it makes the teacher's wishes concerning weight allocations explicit and enables her or him to keep track of tendencies to depart from the intended weights. As discussed before, teacher-made tests are prone to overemphasize lower mental processes and to neglect higher levels of thinking. Test specifications can prevent this. Thoughtfully developed test plans enhance test validity by improving the adequacy with which content domains are sampled. In addition, they help harness test power.

Planning the Test Content and Mental Processes

This section illustrates how tables of specifications "lock in" weight allocation of (a) content topics and (b) mental processes. Two points should be understood in examining the examples that follow.

First, recognize that it is the classroom teacher—not some "higher" authority—who is dictating test content. In this sense, a test blueprint is a "contract" that a teacher makes with herself or himself. It functions much like a blueprint for a house that has been developed by the owner. It is a means of ensuring that the final product turns out as intended. It guides the building process to obtain the results that the planner wants.

Second, in the examples that follow, notice how the number of mental processes and content topics were kept small in order to avoid making the tables of specification too complicated and cumbersome to use. In planning for objective tests, it is common to have from three to twelve content topics and about three mental

---

[1]As is common and "quite adequate in most practical situations" (Tinkelman, 1971, p. 68), it will be assumed in this chapter that the relative weight contributed by groups of items that assess various topics and mental processes is proportional to the number of items. Actually, as will be seen in Chapter 12, variability rather than number of points is the key determiner of weight. However, practical use of this information is beyond the reach of most classroom teachers, owing to data limitation and time constraints. Therefore, the approximation based on the above assumption will be used.

processes. Test makers most often use mental process categories of (a) knowledge, (b) comprehension or understanding, and (c) something involving problem solving, "the key feature of which is transfer of existing knowledge and skills to situations that the student has not met before" (Crooks, 1988, p. 441). In planning for essay tests (in which there are fewer test questions), fewer rows and columns are desired.

Fifth-Grade Science

Mrs. Pambookian's fifth-graders have been studying vertebrate animals, the major characteristics of each class of vertebrates, and classification of vertebrates into the major five groups. She has provided students with much practice in transferring their learning by giving students new animals to classify, considering their tentative classifications, and discussing criteria for classification. Some of her examples have been presented with names and others with pictures. Still others have been presented by means of verbal descriptions. A few have even been real animals at hand, for example, the class hamster, the class goldfish, and the pupils themselves. In addition to studying the five classes of vertebrates, the class has studied the distinction between vertebrates and invertebrates.

Because of her teaching emphasis on transfer of learning, Mrs. Pambookian wants to give substantial test emphasis to student ability to classify novel examples, not just ones they have studied. By making pupils aware that they will be required to transfer their learning on the test, she has guided their study efforts in this direction.

Concerning content, more class time has been devoted to mammals and birds than to amphibians. Accordingly, Mrs. Pambookian wants the test to reflect these weights. After considering all of these issues, she develops the table of specification shown in Table 4–4.

Table 4–4

Item Specifications for a Fifth-Grade Science Test

Topic \ Process	Knowledge of Characteristics	Classification of Studied Examples	Classification of Unstudied Examples	Totals
Mammals	3	2	5	10
Birds	2	2	4	8
Reptiles	2	2	2	6
Amphibians	1	1	0	2
Fish	2	1	3	6
Invertibrates	0	2	6	8
Totals	10	10	20	40

Notice that 20 of the test's 40 items are devoted to assessing transfer of learning (i.e., classification of animals, presented via picture or verbal descriptions, that were not studied in class). Mrs. Pambookian believes this reflects the emphasis she has given to transfer in class.

She will test student knowledge of the characteristics specified in the first column either by use of short-answer questions or with matching exercises. For the second and third columns, she will use five-option multiple-choice items for the top five rows to require pupils to classify vertebrates into classes. She plans to use alternate-choice items for the bottom row to have pupils classify animals as vertebrates or invertebrates.

This example is typical of Track C summative posttests. It illustrates the principle that a test should ordinarily provide about the same relative weight to the various topics as they received in the unit. Similarly, the relative weight allocated to teaching and working with various mental processes should usually dictate corresponding weights in the test. Although there are times when a teacher might thoughtfully depart from this parallelism of relative weights between a unit and its test, a good rule of thumb is to devote as much emphasis in the test to each topic and process and as you did in the unit.

Third-Grade Mathematics Pretest

On the first day of the year, Mr. Clark wants to assess his third graders' arithmetic skills after a summer without practice. Accordingly in the week before school opens, he has developed the test plan shown in Table 4–5.

This table contains more detail than most teachers would have time to develop. To illustrate how topics could be collapsed, Mr. Clark could have used as few as two rows, one for adding one-, two-, and three-digit numbers without regrouping and one for subtracting without regrouping. But since he had the time to plan his test more fully, he chose to specify the content in more detail.

Mr. Clark plans two uses of the pretest results. First, he will use them to decide how much review to plan. Second, the scores of this test will provide part of the information he will use after a week or so to tentatively divide his class into two or three instructional groups for mathematics.

He does *not* plan to use this test to diagnose specific weaknesses for individual pupils. It is not long enough to provide dependable information such as, "Mary can subtract when problems are presented in vertical format, but not when they are given horizontally" or "Max can set up thought problems, but makes many careless errors in routine computations." At best, his test might provide weak clues along such lines. Additional testing and/or informal observation would be needed to substantiate or refute such hints.

This example illustrates the use of a Track C test plan for a pretest. It also reinforces the principle that tests are used to improve decision making.

Eleventh-Grade United States History

Each year Mrs. Orr teaches three or four sections of eleventh-grade United States history. She has collected a rich assortment of multiple-choice and essay questions for use in her tests. She stores her items in a personal computer and finds it relatively

Table 4–5

Specifications for a Third-Grade Arithmetic Pretest

Content \ Process	Routine Computation		Thought Problems	Totals
	Vertical	Horizontal		
Addition of two one-digit numbers	2	5	1	8
Addition of a one-digit number and a two-digit number without regrouping	2	2	1	5
Addition of two two-digit numbers without regrouping	2	1		3
Addition of a one-digit number and a three-digit number without regrouping	2	1	1	4
Addition of a two-digit number and a three-digit number without regrouping	3		1	4
Addition of two three-digit numbers without regrouping	3			3
Subtracting a one-digit number from a one-digit number	2	2	1	5
Subtracting a one-digit number from a two-digit number without regrouping	3	1	1	5
Subtracting a two-digit number from a two-digit number without regrouping	2		1	3
Subtracting a one-digit number from a three-digit number without regrouping	2		1	3
Subtracting a two-digit number from a three-digit number without regrouping	2		1	3
Subtracting a three-digit number from a three-digit number without regrouping	3		1	4
Totals	28	12	10	50

easy to produce two or more forms of each test to prevent students from transmitting test information between periods. (See Appendix C for a discussion of item banking with personal computers.)

Mrs. Orr keeps her items in order to reuse them. Good test items are hard to find and hard to create. They can be reused many times. Of course, she does not reuse whole tests in consecutive years. If she did, much information about her test content would "get out." (Indeed she does not ever reuse whole tests because she always wants a few items to relate history to current events.) But she is able to re-cycle individual questions with little danger of compromising test security.

She uses multiple-choice questions to test lower-level knowledge of history as well as to assess some understanding, analysis, and application. She reserves essay items for those things that are not well assessed by objective item (e.g., she uses questions such as, "What lessons might the history of . . . teach us about the current situation of . . . ?" "How was the President's recent decision to . . . inconsistent with President Truman's decision to . . . ? What justification could a defender of both of these presidents offer to justify the inconsistency?").

Use of such integrative questions is likely to prompt students to look for con-nections as they study. Test power can motivate students to seek meaning, relation-ships, or relevance.

For several years Mrs. Orr has used a plan shown in Table 4–6 for a two-hour comprehensive final exam, which she counts one-fifth of the second-semester grade.

Table 4–6

Eleventh-Grade U.S. History Examination Specifications

Topic \ Objective	Knowledge	Understanding	Application	Total
Pre-contact to Revolution				10%
Revolution and early national				13%
Antebellum, Civil War, and reconstruction				15%
Gilded Age and Progressive Era				8%
World War I				5%
Depression and New Deal				14%
World War II				10%
Cold War to Bicentennial				10%
Recent and present				15%
Totals	40%	35%	25%	100%

All forms of this test have 60 multiple-choice items. While most forms have two 20-point essay questions, she occasionally uses two 15-point and one 10-point essays or one 20-point and two 10-point essays. A typical essay question involves understanding and/or application of two historical periods.

In building each form of the test, Mrs. Orr first selects or creates the essay questions and distributes the points for each among the rows and columns to which it relates. She then retrieves from computer storage enough one-point multiple-choice items to complete each form of the test in a way that conforms to her plan. To maintain the flexibility needed to accommodate the two or three big essays, she does not specify the exact percentage of weight for each cell of the table. Instead she settles for keeping the sums of rows and the sums of columns in conformity with the plan.

Last summer, Mrs. Orr took a graduate course in social-science curriculum development that raised her awareness of the need to give adequate teaching coverage to historical topics (e.g., military, economic, and social) as well as to historical periods. In Table 4–6, she specified her test in terms of a chronological approach to history rather than topical approach. This has served her well in insuring balance among periods (e.g., in avoiding overemphasis of World War I, which she has always found fascinating). But has she maintained an appropriate balance among various topics?

To find out, she developed the alternative test plan shown in Table 4–7 to reflect her best judgment concerning weights the various topics should receive *in both the course and the examination.* She then scanned her lesson plans and found that some topics had not in the past received as much emphasis as she now believed them to merit. Moreover, some topics had been even more seriously underemphasized in her tests. The worst example was economic history—her own weakest suit. She believes that it should comprise about 15% of the course and final exam. She esti-

Table 4–7

Alternative Test Plan for Eleventh-Grade U.S. History Examination

Objective / *Topic*	*Knowledge*	*Understanding*	*Application*	*Total*
Intellectual and cultural				15%
Social				15%
Political				25%
Economic				15%
Military				20%
Diplomatic				10%
Totals	40%	35%	25%	100%

mated that in the past she had only given it 9% of the course emphasis and only 3% of the weight in her tests.

To correct this, she committed herself to give economics a little more attention in the course and much more attention in the final exam. She wrote several economic test items to add to her file of questions.

She wonders which table she should use in building next year's final examination. Ideally, she would like the features of both. This could be achieved with a three-dimensional grid, but such a complex table of specifications would be more trouble than it would be worth. Instead she decides to use Table 4–7 next year to establish appropriate balance among topics. Then she will revert for a year to Table 4–6 to make sure that the content does not drift away from the desired balance among periods.

This example illustrates several things. It shows the need for looser constraints in planning essay tests than in planning objective exams. It provides an example of one way in which a test can be planned to mix essay and objective items. It illustrates how tests can be specified in terms of percentages of total weight (as in Tables 4–6 and 4–7) as well as in terms of numbers of raw score points (as in previous tables). It shows that test plans are useful for final examinations as well as for unit tests. It reveals that there is sometimes more than one sensible way to structure specifications. Finally, it illustrates how test planning is not separate and distinct from planning instruction; the two processes go arm in arm.

This is a good place to define the terms "alternate forms," "parallel forms," or "equivalent forms" of a test. Although some writers make minor distinctions among these terms, they are used interchangeably in this book. **Alternate forms** *of a test are forms that conform to common specifications*, but that are not systematically more similar than their specifications dictate. **Parallel**, **equivalent** or **alternate forms** *therefore have identical weight allocations among topics and mental processes, but the particular test questions differ.*[2]

An analogy with house plans is again helpful. If two or more houses are built from the same set of blueprints, the houses will be alike in those attributes that are specified in the plans. They will, for example, have the same floor plans, but they will not likely be the same color, have the same bathroom colors, or the same carpeting.

Alternate forms are interchangeable in the sense that Mrs. Orr can use any of several forms for testing a given class. All forms are parallel in the balance or mix of content and mental processes. Yet their raw scores should *not* be considered to be interchangeable because the forms will likely have chance differences in difficulty and variability.[3]

---

[2]Ideally, parallel forms should also have equivalent raw score means, variability, distribution shapes, reliabilities, and correlations with other variables. Although these features can be approximated in professionally prepared published tests, even these instruments' derived scores require statistical fine-tuning to achieve interchangeability (Petersen, Kolen, & Hoover, 1989, p. 242).

[3]Thus one could not use an alternate form of a Track C test for make-up purposes if the raw score of the makeup form were to be interpreted by use of the reference group used for the regular form. Yet in Track A formative and summative testing, it is customary to treat the raw scores of alternate forms as interchangeable. This is reasonable to the extent that the small, well-described Track A domains inherently determine test difficulty. In Track A, the tightly specified domain usually does this fairly well. In Track C, the loosely specified domain does not determine test difficulty, and it is inappropriate to treat raw scores of alternate forms of Track C tests as equivalent.

Upper-Division Educational Psychology

Dr. Gomez uses a combination of essay and objective items in most of his tests. Because he has very little time to get his grades computed after his final examination, he relies solely on multiple-choice items for the two-hour final.

Dr. Gomez uses the *Taxonomy of Educational Objectives: The Cognitive Domain* (Bloom et al., 1956) to organize his table of specifications. As mentioned in Chapter 2, many scholars find its categories useful in classifying test questions, but most classroom teachers find its six categories to be cumbersome. Liking the categories, but preferring fewer, Dr. Gomez combines Knowledge with Comprehension

Table 4–8

Educational Psychology Final Examination Specifications

Content \ Process	Knowledge and Comprehension	Application	Analysis and Synthesis	Evaluation	Total
Research methods	3	2	3	1	9
Learning theories	5	4	3	1	13
Retention and information processing	5	4	3	1	13
Problem solving	3	2	3	3	11
Motivation	3	2	3	3	11
Classroom dynamics	2	1	1	1	5
Class management and discipline	2	2	1	0	5
Instructional objectives	2	0	1	2	5
Instructional theories	3	2	2	2	9
Individual differences	3	2	2	0	7
Measurement and evaluation	4	4	3	1	12
Totals	35	25	25	15	100

and Analysis with Synthesis; this yields four columns for a test plan. Since he is planning a relatively long final exam, he uses more rows for content topics than he would for a shorter unit test. Table 4–8 displays his specifications.

Since his educational psychology students have studied the *Taxonomy,* instructional objectives, and classroom testing practices as part of the course content, Dr. Gomez distributes his table of specifications as a class handout. In this way he exerts maximum influence on what students emphasize in preparing for his final exam. As is common at the college level, Dr. Gomez counts the final examination more than would be appropriate at the elementary or secondary level; it will constitute 35% of the course grade. Therefore, students are prone to take it very seriously and to prepare for it.

This example illustrates the use of the *Taxonomy* in planning a test so that the content it samples will correspond with the teacher's objectives and instructional emphases. It again shows that test specifications can be used for cumulative review examinations as well as for unit tests. It reminds us that tests are used to improve decision making—about grading in this case. It shows how tables of specification are as useful at the college level as at other levels. It illustrates how information about a test can be used effectively to guide students' study. Finally, it emphasizes the role of tests in prompting review as well as stimulating original study.

Junior High School Music

Mr. Martin teaches a ninth-grade survey course in music appreciation. One of the units in this required course is "Music around the World," in which students listen to, study features of, and seek to appreciate the distinctive and common features of music from four diverse cultures. Mr. Martin places much teaching emphasis on such objectives as understanding, application, analyzing, transferring, and appreciating. He is eager to develop a test that will go far beyond measuring mere rote learning.

Of course he also wants to test knowledge and comprehension of features of the four music styles. He does this with conventional multiple-choice items. The first column of Table 4–9 shows the weight he assigns to each kind of music for learning outcomes that involve knowledge and comprehension.

Now to assess higher-order learning. One method would be to provide pictures of instruments accompanied by objective questions on aspects of the sounds the instruments are likely to produce. Another would be to play recordings of music from the various cultures and ask students to analyze in essays various features of the music. Yet another method of testing would be to play short excerpts from two different kinds of music and ask students to compare and contrast them. The second column of Table 4–9 involves these kinds of learning outcomes. To allow flexibility for longer essay questions, Mr. Martin does not fill in the separate cells in the separate column.

He also expects students to be able to recognize typical music from each of the four cultures when they hear it. By using selections for testing that were not used in class, he taps more than mere recall. The third column in his specifications concern this means of testing for transfer.

Finally, he requires two projects—one done in class and one out of class. For each project each student must create and perform (on any instrument or voice) an original composition in one of the music styles studied. The two projects must focus

Table 4–9

Music Around the World Assessment Plan

Processes — Content	Paper–Pencil Responses			Original Productions
	Knowledge and Comprehension	Application and Analysis	Auditory Category Recognition	
Oriental	9%		5%	Use rating forms to assess two original productions played by each student
African	8%		5%	
Slavic	7%		5%	
Polynesian	6%		5%	
Totals	30%	20%	20%	30%

on different styles. A rating form is used to assess various facets of these original compositions. These projects are local legend—the thing for which his class is famous. The final column of his test plan indicates how much weight he allocates to this means of assessing higher-level learning.

Mr. Martin estimates that about 40% of students' total time on the unit is spent in developing their projects. The rule of thumb for weight allocation would specify that 40% of the evaluation should be allotted to the projects. But Mr. Martin has three reservations concerning the projects. First, he suspects that some students receive more help in developing their out-of-class project than is desirable; he is therefore hesitant to count it very much. Second, occasionally he suspects plagiarism. Third, he believes that the reliability with which he evaluates the projects is not as high as that of his unit test; he is therefore reluctant to give too much weight to items that contain considerable error of measurement. In view of these misgivings, he would prefer to give the projects only about 20% of the total weight to the projects.

But test power must also be considered. Evaluation guides effort. If the projects do not carry much weight, students will neglect them. And he values them; they get students actively engaged in the ethnic music. In addition, he believes that their more intensive study of the two music styles enables students to perform better on the novel classification items specified in the third column of the table. Balancing his inclination to count the projects only 20% with the practical need to make them important in students' eyes, he compromises with a 30% weight.

This example illustrates the use of a table of specification for a summative unit posttest of a domain that will be assessed by joint use of paper-pencil test and performance ratings. It provides another example of planning for a variety of test item types—in this case a rich diversity. It also illustrates a situation in which a teacher considers departing from the rule of thumb that suggests parallel weights in a unit and on its test. Finally, it reviews the fundamental principle that tests and other means by which students are evaluated influence what they will study.

QUIZ 4–5

1. On page 119, the statement was made that "this is an important point that instructors are likely to test." What purpose does this statement serve?

2. If Mrs. Orr gave different forms of her final to different sections, could she combine the distributions of raw scores into one large distribution?

3. Why do Dr. Gomez and Mrs. Orr give final examinations? He already has three unit tests, a paper, and a project for each student. She has four unit tests, a term paper, several homework assignments, and class participation for each student. Each could compute defensible grades without even having a final. The finals are inconvenient for the teachers. They are gravely inconvenient (not to mention sources of anxiety) to their students. Why not do the "popular" thing and eliminate the finals?

KEY TO QUIZ 4–5

1. The statement is intended to attract reader attention. It is a deliberate use of naked test power to guide student effort. In this case, I am handicapped by not having control over the tests that instructors use, but the statement still serves to focus reader attention on the issue.

2. No. In Track C, domain description is not tight enough to "lock in" test difficulty. If she wishes to be able to combine the distributions of her several sections, she should give the same form to all sections. If she wishes to administer different forms to different sections, she should interpret scores in the respective distributions separately.

   Chapter 12 will address appropriate ways of securing larger reference groups than individual classes.

3. The dominant reason Dr. Gomez, Mrs. Orr, and many other teachers give finals and count them substantially is *to prompt review*. As emphasized before, review enhances permanence of learning. (See Figure 4–1.) Relatively little time devoted to review can greatly improve long-term retention. Of course, unit tests also stimulate review.

   In addition to causing students to review—and integrate—course content, final examinations also provide teachers with another basis on which to make decisions concerning the award of valid grades.

Deciding Which Item Types to Use

The next four chapters focus on various kinds of assessment devices that are useful in classroom testing. Different kinds of test items serve varied purposes. An item type well suited to assessing some kinds of student status may be wholly inappropriate for assessing other student attributes. Teachers therefore need to have a command of the several major kinds of items so that each can be used when it is most useful and avoided when it is not a good match with one's needs.

Testing techniques can be grouped into three broad categories:

Objective items (e.g., true–false, matching, completion, and multiple-choice)

Essay and other product measures (e.g., essay tests, math proofs, shop products, computer programs, and works of art)

Performance measures (e.g., behind-the-wheel driving, oral tests, dramatic try-outs, musical contests, debates, high diving, machine operation)

Although most of the criteria by which a teacher can best decide when to use each method of assessing student status will be left to the remainder of Part II and to Parts III and IV, a rule of thumb can be given at this time. It is not the only consideration and should not be used in isolation, but it takes into account many of the major issues that should enter into decisions concerning what kind of test to plan.

By the time this guiding rule is reviewed, its full rationale will have been developed. For now, the decision rule will be previewed without benefit of its rationale. It consists of three statements:

1. Those instructional objectives that can be assessed with objective items ordinarily should be.

2. Of the remaining instructional goals, those that can be assessed with essay and other product measures ordinarily should be.

3. Only the remaining objectives need to be assessed by means of performance measures.

Chapter Summary

To achieve better teaching by means of better student measurement, teachers need to use testing carefully. *Testing is part of teaching.* Poorly constructed tests or inappropriate kinds of measures can undermine other facets of teaching. Well-planned, carefully crafted achievement measures enhance student learning.

The first step in developing effective classroom tests is to make theoretically sound *professional decisions* concerning kind(s) of tests that are appropriate to the situation. This professional decision making is aided by use of the model of relationships developed in Chapters 2 and 3.

The second step in devising good measures of student achievement involves careful *planning.* By thoughtful planning, teachers can obtain desirable balance among content topics and among mental processes. Without deliberate planning, imbalance is likely. *Planning also takes into consideration the effect that assessment practices will have on student effort.*

The final step in developing effective teacher-made tests is to apply specific item-writing skills. The next four chapters are devoted to this topic.

Suggestions for Further Reading

Ebel, R. L., & Frisbie, D. A. (1991). *Essentials of educational measurement* (5th ed.). Englewood Cliffs, NJ: Prentice-Hall. Chapter 7, "Achievement Test Planning," provides sound, brief coverage of much of the material considered in this chapter.

Gronlund, N. E. (1988). *How to construct achievement tests* (4th ed.). Englewood Cliffs, NJ: Prentice-Hall. Parts of Chapter 1, "Achievement Testing and Instruction," highlight the integral relationship of testing to instruction. Chapter 2, "Planning the Test," provides a brief and sound treatment of the topic of test planning.

Mehrens, W. A., & Lehmann, I. (1991). *Measurement and evaluation in education and psychology* (4th ed.). Fort Worth: Holt, Rinehart and Winston. Chapter 4, "Classroom Testing: The Planning Stage," covers much of the material treated in this chapter in addition to some topics that preview contents of the next four chapters.

Stiggins, R. J., Rubel, E., & Quellmalz, E. (1986). *Measuring thinking skills in the classroom*. Washington, DC: National Education Association. This booklet is a practical and readable guide for planning assessment of a variety of mental processes. It provides helpful illustrations of the use of oral questions to tap thinking skills.

Tinkelman, S. N. (1971). Planning the objective test. In Thorndike, R. L. (Ed.), *Educational measurement* (2nd ed.). Washington, DC: American Council on Education. This thorough treatment of test planning relates more to published tests than to classroom ones, but much of the content is applicable to the latter. It considers planning somewhat more broadly than this chapter does, including treatment of issues that will surface in Chapters 9 and 15.

5

Developing Completion, Alternate-Choice, and Matching Items

The preceding chapters have provided information to help teachers decide what evaluation practices best contribute to student learning. Since no single outlook on student assessment serves all situations, three different perspectives were developed to meet the needs of various kinds of teaching-learning situations. The emphasis was on theoretical analysis of situations and professional decision making. Just as surgeons must first use professional judgment to decide what, if any, operation is called for, *educators need professional judgment* to choose appropriate student evaluation practices.

Once a surgeon decides that a given operation should be performed, a specialized set of surgical skills must be invoked for the operation to be successful. Likewise, once a teacher decides on a given means of assessing students, specialized instrument-construction skills are needed to develop measures that will do the job satisfactorily.

Chapters 5 to 8 concern instrument-development skills. These chapters complement the earlier, more theoretically oriented material with a body of rather specific "how to" information.

This chapter concerns completion and short-answer items, alternate-choice items, and matching exercises. In general, these item types are suitable for assessing examinee status on relatively simple behavioral objectives and behavioral indicants. That is, these item types tend to be more useful for measuring examinee command of lower-level learning than for assessing their use of higher mental processes.

Each of these item types is helpful in developing effective tests. At times, one of them will suffice for a valid test of Track A or Track B content. In Track C testing, each of these kinds of items is sometimes well suited to assess some of the objectives or indicants. Yet it is unusual for any single type or combination to be sufficient for the variety of mental processes sought in a well-designed, Track C test.

In general, these three item types are somewhat easier to construct and to use than are multiple-choice items, essay and other product-assessment instruments, and performance tests. They are combined in this one chapter, while a chapter each is devoted to the latter item types.

What Are Objective Items?

This and the next chapter consider various kinds of objective items. Before proceeding, one might ask, "What is an objective item?"

Objective questions are so named because they are *objectively scored*. But objective items are somewhat misnamed because they are objective in only that one sense—scoring. In other respects, "objective items" are just as subjective as other item types.

In planning a unit test, a teacher contemplates test content and mental processes. The teacher decides to allocate content weight in a given way and to assign relative weights to various processes specified in a test plan. The teacher decides to use a particular item type or blend thereof and, finally, which particular questions to ask. All of these decisions are equally subjective whether the test decided on is "objective" or essay.

The one element that differs between essay and objective tests is the objectivity with which the answer sheets are scored. Judgment is required in marking essays as well as other product measures and performance assessments. Much inaccuracy can creep into the scoring process of such devices. Chapters 7 and 8 devote considerable attention to minimizing subjectivity of scoring in order to enhance reliability.

In contrast, marking objective test answer sheets is relatively easy, fast, and reliable. Once the test maker has decided which option of a question is to be keyed, then the determination of whether each examinee has selected that keyed option is entirely objective. Comparing examinee answer sheets with the key does not require professional knowledge, just clerical accuracy. The scoring of objective tests can be relegated to conscientious teacher aides, competent clerks, or even machines.

In seeking to delimit the meaning of the adjective "objective," emphasis was placed on what was not objective about so-called objective tests. This is an important point that helps to deprive objective tests of any inappropriate aura of scientific infallibility.

On the other hand, the feature that *is* objective is extremely important. This marking feature enables objective tests to be scored more reliably than is usually possible with other kinds of tests. Moreover this reliable scoring is rapid and does not demand professional qualifications. These are major virtues. Indeed, these were most of the factors that led, at the end of Chapter 4, to recommendation that objective items ordinarily be used to measure all instructional outcomes for which they are adequate. The ease and accuracy of scoring is so important that it should be sought whenever feasible.

Completion and Short-Answer Items

The first of the simple item types considered in this chapter are **short-answer** items and **completion** questions. They share so many features that they will be considered together.

Paper-pencil test items are often classified into two groups—objective and essay. Short-answer and completion items are categorized as objective because of the objectivity with which they are scored, yet they differ from other objective item types in an important respect.

Examinees responding to completion or short-answer questions must *produce* their own answers (like examinees responding to essay questions); they must *recall* and *supply* their responses. In contrast, examinees responding to alternate-choice, matching, or multiple-choice items must *select* the correct or best options. Thus completion and short-answer questions are objective items that share with essay items the demand that examinees *produce* their own answers rather than *recognize* and *select* correct answers when they see them.

What Do Completion and Short-Answer Items Measure?

Figure 5–1 provides several sample short-answer items and completion questions. While some exercises are best cast as completion items, others are more easily phrased as questions to be answered with a short answer. Still others can be written either way about equally well. For example, Item 3 could have been "What is the

1. What was the name of the author of *Hamlet?* _____ _____
2. The set of events that brought the U.S. and the U.S.S.R. to the brink of war during the Kennedy Administration is best known as the _____ .
3. The chemical symbol for gold is _____ .
4. The name of the most important prophet in Islam was _____ .
5. The planet having the greatest mass is _____ .
6. Which political party controlled most of the South during the period of the New Deal and the Fair Deal? _____
7. $\dfrac{56}{8} =$ _____
8. A 15-kg child sits 4 m from the center of a seesaw. A 20-kg child sits on the other side so that they are in perfect balance. The second child must therefore be _____ m from the center.
9. If $x^2 - 3x - 10 = 0$, then the roots are _____ and _____ .

Figure 5–1. Sample Short-Answer and Completion Items. (See text for discussion of which items would better be cast in other formats.)

chemical symbol for gold? _____ or Item 6 could have been, "During the periods of the New Deal and the Fair Deal, most of the South was controlled by the _____ party."

Completion and short-answer items all require examinees to produce answers. But beyond that, important differences are present. Some questions require students only to retrieve answers from long-term memory without much processing. Others require examinees to figure out the answers.

Each item in Figure 5–1 assesses learning that can be measured with a completion or short-answer item. Some are *best* assessed with such items, while others would better be measured by use of other item types.

The first six questions require examinees to retrieve answers from long-term memory. Questions 2, 3, and 4 are particularly well suited for the completion or short-answer format because students who do not know the answer are not likely to have available much material from which to guess. Very few students will guess these questions without some relevant knowledge.

For Item 4 in Figure 5–1, only a few viable alternatives exist, for example, Abraham, Moses, Jesus, and Mohammed. A multiple-choice format could be used. However, an argument for the completion format among students raised in a predominantly Judeo–Christian culture is that they will be less likely to know the name of the right answer—Mohammed; it may therefore be better not to provide them with this name, which would enable correct guessing. This situation is reminiscent of the completion item "South Carolina" on the State Capitals Test on page 12. People not knowing the capital miss the completion item more often than they would miss the corresponding multiple-choice or matching items in which they have a chance to guess the correct answer.

Although Items 1, 5, and 6 are also suitable for completion format, they could well be cast in easier-to-score formats. Almost anyone would realize that Shakespeare was a possibility; indeed, the poor student may know his name and his alone among reasonable authors. In this case, framing the item in a format that provides other options may actually make it harder for students who do not know the answer. This is reminiscent of Idaho on the State Capitals Test; some people get it right because Boise (which happens to be the correct answer) is the only Idaho city they know. Formats that provide other options might cause more persons who do not know the capital to miss the item.

For Item 5, only nine possibilities exist. For the student knowing the names of the planets (which is requisite to knowing relative facts about them), the short-answer or completion item requires a multiple-choice mental selection. It might be better if the item were cast in multiple-choice or matching format.

For Item 6, only two reasonable alternatives exist; therefore, for the student, the task is really to choose between two, alternate choices. Better that the item be cast as such (possibly along with several similar items).

Items 7, 8, and 9 require that students figure out answers, that is, actually produce them. This is a demand that completion and short-answer items are particularly well suited to making. Some teachers, especially math teachers, make a sharp distinction between student ability to *produce* an answer and student ability to *select* or *recognize* a correct answer. They contend that students not knowing how to solve a problem might know how to check alternative answers for it. For example, a pupil unable to divide 8 into 56 might know that multiplication is the inverse operation of division. Thus each option provided in a multiple-choice format can be checked by multiplication to see if it is correct. Such a pupil could use elimination to select correct answers to such questions if they were in multiple-choice format, but could not produce the correct answers if the problems were cast in completion format.

The logic of this worry seems unassailable. Yet other teachers dismiss the argument with the observation that virtually any student astute enough to systematically check options in this way is also proficient enough to solve the problem in the first place.

Nonetheless, many math and physical science teachers prefer completion and short-answer items to other item types mainly for this reason. It is not unusual to see an entire Track C math test framed in completion and/or short-answer format. Some such tests contain questions that demand higher mental processes. Item 8 in Figure 5–1, for example, requires application of a principle. Such tests are important exceptions to the generalization offered in the introduction of this chapter that completion items rarely were adequate for entire Track C tests.

Another reason that some math and science teachers prefer completion and short-answer items is the ease with which they can require students to show their work. Having students show their formulas and calculations has several possible uses. That is, it improves several kinds of decision making. It can provide a basis for awarding partial credit to some questions. It gives teachers an opportunity to mark papers to show students where and how they went astray. It provides teachers with feedback about what may need review. Finally, it provides insight to teachers concerning common misconceptions; this can improve future instruction.

For testing spelling, most teachers prefer short-answer items over other objective item types. Being able to *produce* a correctly spelled word orally or in writing is not the same thing as being able to *recognize* which of several options is correct, being able to *discriminate* between correct and incorrect spellings, or being able to *identify* which words in a passage are misspelled. Most elementary teachers would consider their instructional objectives for spelling to be much better assessed by items that require pupils to produce correct spellings than by items that assess how well they can recognize correct spelling, identify incorrect spellings, etc.

Some Rules for Constructing Completion and Short-Answer Items

A set of rules will be provided for each of the several item types considered in this and subsequent chapters. Before considering these rules, it is appropriate to acknowledge that they do not rest on a solid foundation of empirical research. Rather, they "are based primarily on common sense and the conventional wisdom of test experts" (Millman & Greene, 1989, p. 353).

Before enumerating specific rules for constructing various item types, it is important to recognize a cardinal rule that applies to all item types: *Start with an important item idea*. Every test question begins as an idea in the mind of the item writer (Wesman, 1971, p. 86). After one has in mind some *significant* element to be assessed, then one is ready to choose an item type and to draft the item. We all need to be sure we put our brains in gear before engaging our hands.

Following are a number of item-writing rules that apply to short-answer and completion items.

1. **Phrase items so that blanks fall at or near the end of statements**. A completion task is more easily understood when the missing part occurs at the end of a sentence than when it falls early in the statement. Therefore, blanks should come as near the end as possible without contorting sentences.

Example of rule violation: _____ are animal species that provide milk for their young.

Improved version: Animal species that provide milk for their young are called _____ .

2. **Blanks should be of a uniform length**. Variable lengths of blanks provide clues to examinees.

Example of rule violation: What was the most famous thing that Thomas Jefferson ever wrote?

____ _____ ____ _____

A student about to write in "The United States Constitution" would be clued by the lengths of the blanks.

Improved versions: What was the most famous thing that Thomas Jefferson ever wrote?

_____ _____ _____

_____

What was the most famous thing that Thomas Jefferson ever wrote?

_____

The most famous thing that Thomas Jefferson ever wrote was the _____ _____

_____ .

Notice in the second improved version that the item writer did not provide the clue of number of words in the correct response.

3. **There should be only one correct way to answer an item**. Some items can be correctly completed in so many correct ways that they are worthless.

Example of rule violation: The drafter of the Declaration of Independence was _____ _____.

The intended answer may have been Thomas Jefferson, but correct answers include "a man," "an American," "a Virginian," "a patriot," "a radical," and so on.

Improved version: What is the name of the person who drafted the Declaration of Independence?_____

_____

4. **Completion questions should not ordinarily be lifted from textual material without editing**. One of the worst ways to create a completion item is to indiscriminately lift a sentence from a text, deleting a word or two. Such items usually violate the cardinal principle of item writing by failing to measure important learning. Moreover, such items often have many correct ways by which they can be completed. The examples of poor items for Rules 1 and 3 above could well have been lifted verbatim from a text.

5. **Avoid excessive numbers of blanks in completion items**. When several blanks occur in the same item, there usually is no one correct way to fill them in. The following example illustrates the kind of multilation sometimes found in completion items. Such items usually are the result of mindless lifting of material from a textbook in violation of Rule 4.

Example of rule violation: The most decisive battle in the _____ War was between General _____ and General _____ at _____.

6. **Use completion and short-answer items to measure ability to recall significant factual information** (in contrast to recognizing it). If recognition and recall seem to be about equally appropriate indicants for a given objective, then it is usually easier to assess students by use of multiple-choice or matching exercises than with short-answer or completion items. On the other hand, if recall is the greater concern, then completion or short-answer items are indicated. In this case, of course, one *should expect recall only of significant material.*

7. **Decide ahead of time how to handle spelling errors, and be consistent with this decision**. As discussed in the quiz at the end of Chapter 1 on page 13, the context should determine whether spelling should count. It often should, but only for partial credit. For example, a student who answers the question, "The name of the most important prophet in Islam was _____," with "Mohamed" rather than "Mohammed" surely deserves more credit than one who answers "Confucius."

8. **If units of measure (e.g., dollars, miles per hour) are required, decide how to handle omissions and errors for each item, and be consistent with this decision**. Omission and errors of units in math and science often should be penalized, but (like spelling errors) usually only for partial credit. If this issue is not important to the test maker, then it is best avoided by including the unit in the item as was done with Item 8 in Figure 5–1.

9. **Avoid grammatical clues**. Common grammatical clues indicate whether a missing word is singular or plural or whether the initial letter is a vowel or a consonant.

Example of rule violation:	Each self-governing nation in the Commonwealth of Nations is called a _____.
Improved versions:	Each self-governing nation in the Commonwealth of Nations is called a(n) _____.
	What is each self-governing nation in the Commonwealth of Nations called?_____

The second improved version illustrates an advantage of the direct question over the completion format: It is less likely to provide clues.

    10. **Format to make scoring easy and accurate**. If examinees fill in the blanks where they naturally occur, scoring is tedious and error-prone. Yet this may be the best approach in lower primary grades because it is less complicated for pupils. Above the primary grades, two better solutions exist. First, a column of blanks can be provided along the right-hand side of the test booklet. The blank for each item is positioned to the immediate right of the blank embedded in the item. This enables a strip answer key to be used for rapid and accurate scoring. Second, a separate answer sheet can be used to provide a similar arrangement of easy-to-score answers. In either case the blanks may be retained in the items (as shown in Figure 5–1), and examinees are instructed where to record their answers.

    11. **Avoid overuse of completion and short-answer items**. In general (aside from mathematics and certain physical-science tests), completion items tend to be limited to measuring recall of factual information. Some factual recall is important in most Track C units, and completion and short-answer items provide a good way by which to measure some of it. But Track C tests typically should measure much more than mere recall. To tap higher mental processes, consider the techniques discussed in the next three chapters.

Directions to Accompany Completion and Short-Answer Items

The directions that precede a set of items should inform examinees of several things. They should be told where they are to write their answers. They should often be reminded to write or print clearly. They should be informed whether such things as spelling and capitalization will count. In quantitative tests, examinees should be cautioned if units of measure will count. In most cases, directions should indicate that each item (in contrast to each blank) is worth one test point.

QUIZ 5–1

1. At several places in this section, emphasis was placed on techniques to cause students who do not know an answer to miss the item. Is it appropriate for teachers to try to cause some students to miss test questions? Aren't teachers supposed to be helping students?

2. What two major problems arise when completion items are overused?

KEY TO QUIZ 5–1

1. Persons irritated by efforts to cause items in Track C tests to discriminate between students who know more and those who know less can be said to suffer from a "Track A hangover." That is, they are applying a rationale that is suitable for Track A teaching to a Track C testing context in which it is inappropriate.

   Tests in Tracks B and C are designed to reveal the individual differences that are present among examinees in level and breadth of achievement. That is, the tests are supposed to discriminate among persons on the basis of the attribute measured by the test. For example, a 100-meter race is supposed to discriminate against slow sprinters.

   In this context, a sharp distinction between one's teaching function (where one tries to enable all students to do as well as possible) and one's testing function (where one tries to reveal how well each examinee can perform) is necessary. The function of the test is to reveal examinee status. Where examinees differ in status, the test should show it. The information revealed by such tests can then be used to enhance student learning.

2. Serious overuse of completion and short-answer items is common. Tests consisting mainly of such items (aside from math and some science tests) usually measure little beyond factual recall. As was seen in Chapter 4, tests that overemphasize lower mental processes have two major failings. First, they are not valid measures of student ability to handle a wider spectrum of mental processes. Second, they communicate to students that only rote learning is important to success and that ability to understand, apply, analyze, etc. are not important.

Alternate-Choice Items

The key distinctions among selection-type items are the number of options per item and how they are formatted. As the name implies, **alternate-choice** items offer two options. Multiple-choice items offer three or more options, usually three to five, and the options usually differ from one self-contained item to another. Matching exercises are formatted into sets and usually provide more than five options, but occasionally fewer.

What Do Alternate-Choice Items Measure?

Alternate-choice items are appropriate whenever there are exactly two possible answers to be considered. What they assess, of course, is examinee ability to correctly choose between the two alternatives. Wide variation exists as to what the two choices are. The most common alternatives are "true" and "false." Before taking up the true-false item type, we will first consider some of the other kinds of alternate-choice items.

Miscellaneous Alternate-Choice Items

Alternate-choice items sometimes provide the best single way to assess student achievement of certain rather limited objectives and indicants. They can often be used to assess examinee ability to engage in higher levels of thinking. Miscellaneous alternate-choice items are by no means limited to assessment of rote recall. They could be used more widely to good advantage.

However, Track C units usually encompass a broader spectrum of objectives and indicants than can be measured adequately with alternate-choice items. Therefore, Track C tests should not ordinarily be limited to such questions.

Following are some examples of how miscellaneous alternate-choice items can be appropriately used in a wide variety of contexts.

A kindergarten class that has been building the concepts of "plant" and "animal" could well be given alternate-choice items in which the two options were "plant" and "animal." Items could be presented orally or visually. If the test is to be individually administered, pupils could respond orally. If group administration is desired, pupils could respond on answer sheets by circling the word "plant" or "animal" if they have learned to recognize these two words. If not, the answer space for each item could contain small pictures of two sets of organisms, one of which is to be circled. One set might contain three dissimilar animals (e.g., a cow, a grasshopper, and a worm), and the other might contain three plants (e.g., a blade of grass, a tree, and a carrot). The items could be statements of characteristics (e.g., "are usually able to move themselves from place to place") or names or pictures of plants and animals. Items using the exact organisms studied in class may measure no more than recall; items involving examples not used in class measure ability to apply principles of classification.

An elementary school class that has studied the distinction between fact and opinion might well be tested with alternate-choice items. Each item would consist of a statement. The directions would instruct pupils to circle "Fact" if the statement is a fact and "Opinion" if the statement is an opinion.[1] Fact-opinion items can measure transfer of learning if the stimulus statements are novel to the students.

If important behavioral objectives or behavioral indicants concern student ability to discriminate between correct and incorrect things (e.g., health practices, sewing procedures, math answers, statements of class rules, or punctuations), then correct-incorrect alternate-choice items may be useful.

Alternate-choice items have several other uses in language arts. In considering capitalization of words, there are only two natural alternatives—upper case or lower case. A set of items can be based, for example, on a passage in which selected words are underlined and numbered. For each, students indicate whether the word should be capitalized.

Alternate-choice items are also suitable for certain word-choice situations. They provide an excellent way to test student ability to choose correctly between "who"

---

[1]Test makers should avoid the confusion that is present in this item type in several state minimum competency tests. An incorrect factual statement is ambiguous. For example, "Mars is the planet nearest the sun." Does one consider this to be an incorrect statement of fact or to be an opinion? At an advanced level this could be addressed in the test directions, but in elementary treatments of the topic it often is not.

and "whom," "me" and "I," etc. For example, examinees can be instructed to circle their choice in items such as:

(Us, We) students took a test today.

It is (I, me).

Please turn your application in to Mrs. Dunzeczky or to (me, myself).

Give it to (whoever, whomever) most deserves it.

Of course alternate-choice items should only be used where one choice is clearly the better. In this regard, what is wrong with the following item?

The faculty presented (their, its) recommendations.

A teacher preparing this item might have intended "its" to be the correct answer. But British teachers would key "their" (and so possibly might American ones if various faculty members offered different recommendations).

True-False Items

By far the most common variety of alternate-choice question is the **true-false** item. True-false questions provide a suitable way to assess student achievement of certain rather restricted objectives and indicants. They can be used to measure ability to use higher levels of thinking, but they rarely are used to do so. Testing more than rote recall with true-false items requires skillful item construction and can usually be achieved more easily and more adequately with other item types.[2]

Track C units almost always encompass a wider variety of objectives than can be assessed adequately with true-false items. Consequently, Track C tests should rarely if ever consist exclusively of true-false questions.

Figure 5-2 provides several true-false items that are formatted in an easy-to-score manner. Students would be directed to circle the **"T"** if the statement is true and the **"F"** if the statement is partly or wholly false. Note that these items are not ideal ones; some contain faults that will serve as examples in the following discussion.

T	F	1.	Most insects have six legs.
T	F	2.	All presidents of the United States must be at least 35 years of age.
T	F	3.	There are more hours of daylight in June than in November.
T	F	4.	Mohammed is to Islam as Jesus is to Christianity.
T	F	5.	If it is 7:00 A.M., in five hours it will be 12:00 o'clock.
T	F	6.	It is generally warmer in the summer than in the winter mainly because the sun is nearer during the summer.
T	F	7.	Water boils at 100 degrees C.
T	F	8.	Meals should not ordinarily consist entirely of fruits.

Figure 5–2. True-False Items of Variable Quality

---

[2]This rather unfavorable assessment of true-false items is the view held by most measurement authorities. Yet Robert Ebel long championed this item type and capably argued that it could be used efficiently to assess student command of significant verbal learning (e.g., Ebel, 1975).

Some Rules for Constructing True-False Items

1. **Use only statements that are categorically true or false**. This require-ment eliminates from consideration most important content in most fields of study because most statements have exceptions. This is an important reason why true-false items are so limited with regard to the kinds of Track C objectives and indicants they can effectively assess. The sample true-false items in Figure 5–2 contain several vio-lations of this basic rule.

In Item 3, it is unclear whether the question is intended to address the whole world or just the Northern Hemisphere.

In Item 4, Mohammed and Jesus have *somewhat* parallel places in Islam and Christianity, but not identical. Mohammed is considered to be the greatest prophet by far. Jesus is considered to be much more than a prophet. This item keyed "false" might be quite acceptable after a thorough study of Islam that stressed this difference, but for a superficial middle school study of Islam, the issue would probably be too technical. In this case, it would be wrong to key it **"T"** because it is not true; to so key it would deny credit to students who "know too much." And it would be wrong to key it **"F"** because so answering requires knowledge beyond that provided in text or class.

In Item 5, the correct time would be 12:00 *noon*. Again the examinee does not know whether the teacher writing this item would key it true or false. If one were intent on assessing the technical (and widely violated) point "noon," then a multiple-choice item offering options of 12:00, 12:00 A.M., 12:00 P.M., 12:00 noon, and 12:00 midnight would be preferable.

In Item 7, the hapless student is left to wonder whether the teacher intends it to be false because it is not true at all altitudes (or more technically, at all pressures) or whether the teacher simply overlooked this important issue. If the latter, then the stu-dent who "knows too much" may miss the item. Indeed, this is the problem with all true-false items that fail to be absolutely true or false. If they are keyed in the sim-plistic way (which happens to be "true" in each of the four examples here discussed), the student who responds from a more sophisticated perspective than that of the item writer will miss the item. On the other hand, if the item is keyed in the more techni-cal way, then it may be "picky" or "tricky."

2. **True-false items should not ordinarily be lifted verbatim from textual material**. One of the worst possible ways to develop true-false items is to unthink-ingly lift sentences from a text and call them true-false test questions. For example, "Grapefruits are similar to oranges."

It is equally inappropriate to insert (or delete) a negating word to make such a sentence false. Statements that may be acceptably true in the context in which they appear in a text are often ambiguous when presented in isolation. Moreover, such items usually fail to assess important learning. Good true-false items are usually cre-ated from scratch.

This item-writing rule is merely a special case of the cardinal principle of item writing. One should always start with an item idea in mind.

3. **Avoid consistent clueing with specific determiners**. A **specific deter-miner** is a word that tends to be found much more often in true items than in false ones or vice versa.

Absolute words such as "always," "never," "every," "none," and "all" provide clues that a true-false item is apt to be false. This is because item writers often use such words to make an otherwise ambiguous item false. For example, a high school physics teacher might alter Item 7 in Figure 5–2 to read, "Water always boils at 100 degrees C." Now the item is categorically false, but it contains the clue "always." A better solution might be, "Regardless of altitude, water boils at 100 degrees C."

The other class of specific determiners are qualifying words such as "usually," "most," "tend," and "generally." They are most often found in true items because item writers often have to qualify statements to some extent in order to make them categorically true. For example, the writer of Item 1 in Figure 5–2 had to say "most" in order not to get hung up on injured individual insects or mutants. The word "ordinarily" is needed in Item 8 to make the statement true in spite of possible exceptions.

Many students are aware of the clues provided by specific determiners and thereby consistently improve their test scores. Thus their scores reflect test wiseness as well as the attributes the test is designed to measure. This erodes the validity of the test as a measure of instructional objectives. Consider Item 1 as an example. A student who is test wise will get the question right even if she or he knows nothing whatsoever about insects.

This caution about specific determiners does *not* dictate that they be avoided, only that they not be used in a manner that provides consistently helpful clues. Items 2 and 6 in Figure 5–2 exemplify skillful use of specific determiners in ways that will misclue test-wise students who know nothing of the subject matter. Item 2 concerns an absolute constitutional requirement for eligibility. It is no less true with the "always" than without it, but the "always" causes some test-wise students who are ignorant of the constitutional provision to miss the item. Similarly, Item 6's use of "generally" and "mainly" tends to make the test-wise, content-ignorant student respond "true"; since the item is false, this misclue is useful.

Skillful use of specific determiners to provide misclues achieves two things. Obviously, it improves the quality of the items themselves. In addition, it enables one to resort to use of an occasional specific determiner in the conventional clue-providing way with impunity. For example, the "ordinarily" was needed in Item 8 to make it categorically true. The important thing is that the test maker avoid careless use of specific determiners in ways that provide test-wise students with predominantly helpful clueing.

4. **Avoid clueing with item length**. Unless effort is made to avoid it, true items will, on average, be longer than false items. This is because more qualification is often necessary to make an item indisputably true. The remedy is to edit true statements carefully to render them as succinct as clarity allows. If this does not suffice to make the average lengths of true and false statements equal (and it often does not), then "pad" a few of the false statements to make them longer.

5. **Avoid double-barreled items**. Each true-false item should focus on the truth or falsity of one statement, not several. For example, "California is a western state having more people than any other state," is a double-barreled question. Better that each important fact be measured by a separate true-false item. Or consider Item 6 in Figure 5–2, which involves three issues: the truth of the first clause, the truth of the second clause, and the causal link between the clauses. A multiple-choice item offering several reasons why it is generally warmer in the summer would be preferable.

6. **Avoid negative items**. Negative statements, such as Item 8, require double negative thinking. For example, examinees must ask, "Is it *false* that salt water will *not* freeze at 32 degrees F?" This becomes logically taxing.

If one were going to use a negative item, one should underline, bold face, capitalize, or italicize the negating word to ensure that it will not be overlooked. However, the most desirable means of editing such an item is usually to rephrase it, for example, "It is ordinarily appropriate for meals to consist solely of fruit." (Notice the use of "ordinarily" in this version will tend to misclue the content-ignorant but test-wise examinee.)

7. **Maintain balance between true and false statements**. Many teachers tend to develop more true items than false ones. This is doubly undesirable. First, it enables ignorant examinees to guess with better-than-average luck. Second, false items consequently tend to be a bit more valid than true ones (Cronbach, 1942).

A few teachers have the opposite quirk. Either way, some students catch on to a teacher's item-writing peculiarities, and this provides a clue to the test-wise. It is therefore necessary to check sets of true-false items to assure that approximate balance is maintained.

8. **Format sets of true-false questions to make scoring easy and accurate**. If examinees cursively write "true" or "false," much grief will be experienced in reading their writing. Likewise, capital cursive **"T"** and **"F"** look much alike. Even manuscript **"T"** and **"F"** can be troublesome. To avoid wasted time and disputes, have examinees circle the letters **"T"** or **"F"** or the words "true" or "false." If answers are to be recorded in the test booklet, then these letters or words should be arranged in a single column to the left of the items (as in Figure 5–2) or at the extreme right-hand side of the page. This enables use of a scoring strip for accurate and rapid scoring. Better still (for older students), a separate answer sheet can provide a column of item numbers with **"T"** and **"F"** letters to be circled. This makes for even faster scoring with no need to turn pages.

9. **Avoid overuse of true-false items**. True-false items have their rightful place and should occasionally be used by most teachers. In general, they are most effective for measuring recognition-type recall of factual information. Some such recall is important in most Track C units, and true-false items provide one reasonable way to measure some of it. But Track C tests should measure much more than mere recall of facts. Therefore, the rightful place of the true-false item is a limited place.

Directions to Accompany True-False Items

The directions that precede a set of true-false questions should achieve several things. They should inform students that an item is to be marked true only if the statement is always true. It is to be considered false if it is always false, sometimes false, or partially false.

In most cases, the directions should inform examinees of how much each item will count. This is usually one point each. It is seldom if ever worth the trouble to provide differential weights to objective test items. If the topic on which an item is based is deemed important enough to merit more credit than is assigned to other items, then the topic merits more questions.

Directions should also inform examinees of how and where they are expected to record their answers.

Finally, if the issue of guessing is not addressed in the general directions at the beginning of the test, examinees should, at the beginning of the first selection-type section, be given clear directions concerning the circumstances under which they should or should not guess if they do not know the answers to questions. Since this issue is intimately related to methods of scoring, its consideration will be postponed until Chapter 9.

QUIZ 5–2

1. What major problems would occur if an eighth-grade American history teacher were to use tests made up exclusively of true-false items developed mainly by "lifting" sentences from the textbook and negating about half of them?

2. Can alternate-choice items measure higher levels of reasoning and transfer of learning?

KEY TO QUIZ 5–2

1. The tests will tend seriously to overemphasize recognition of factual material. Factual material "lifted" from the text is likely to consist mainly of trivia (for example, the exact number of brothers that Mrs. Lincoln had fighting in the Confederacy rather than the important fact that the Civil War divided families, even the First Family).

   This causes two problems that relate directly to the two guiding principles discussed in Chapter 4. First, the test will not be a valid measure of the broader domain of learning that was likely intended by the teacher. Second, tests of this kind communicate to students that the way to "succeed" is to memorize trivia and that time spent in understanding principles, trends, contemporary applications, etc., is time "wasted."

2. Definitely! Each alternate-choice item type *can* measure higher mental processes. This is more true of the miscellaneous alternate-choice items than of the true-false questions, but true-false items assuredly *can* measure understanding of meaningful verbal knowledge. But in practice, they usually do not. Tests and quizzes consisting largely of true-false items often assess little beyond recognition of factual information. Teachers who know how to use true-false items effectively tend also to know how to use other item types where they are better suited.

Matching Exercises

Another objective item type is the **matching exercise**. Matching items are actually a special case of multiple-choice items in which the items are similar in content and the same options are used for all items in a set.

What Do Matching Exercises Measure?

Matching exercises provide a good way to test recognition-type recall when it is appropriate to test several homogeneous elements. Figures 5–3, 5–4, and 5–5 contain matching exercises. Notice that each requires examinees to *recognize* associations, not to produce them. Notice too that each exercise consists of several items having very similar content.

Figure 5–3 exemplifies the use to which matching exercises are most often put—the measurement of factual knowledge of several highly similar items. This can be either desirable or undesirable. If a whole unit of an advanced-placement literature course had been devoted to utopian literature, then the set shown in Figure 5–3 might be a suitable way to sample knowledge of who wrote what. Of course other item types should be used to assess student achievement of the more important objectives of the unit. But if only 10% of a five-week unit had focused on utopian literature, then the exercise grievously overemphasizes author-work associations.

Below is a list of books and a list of authors. For each book in the left-hand column, identify its author. Record each answer by printing the capital letter that goes with the author's name in the space provided to the left of the book. Each author may match one, more than one, or none of the books.

Works	Authors
_____ 1. *News from Nowhere*	A. Francis Bacon
_____ 2. *We*	B. Edward Bellamy
_____ 3. *Walden II*	C. Theodor Herzka
_____ 4. *A Modern Utopia*	D. Aldous Huxley
_____ 5. *Brave New World*	E. Jack London
_____ 6. *New Atlantis*	F. Thomas More
_____ 7. *A Visit to Freeland*	G. William Morris
_____ 8. *Looking Backward, 2000–1887*	H. George Orwell
_____ 9. *The Iron Heel*	I. Plato
_____ 10. *Nineteen Eighty-four*	J. B. F. Skinner
_____ 11. *Utopia*	K. Henry David Thoreau
_____ 12. *The Republic*	L. H. G. Wells
	M. Yevgeny Zamyatin

Figure 5–3.   Matching Exercise on Utopian Literature. It probably overemphasizes (a) the topic and (b) author-works associations.

Such distortion often occurs when a teacher has in mind one or two particularly important associations (e.g., Thomas More's *Utopia* and Plato's *Republic*), and then realizes that similar (although less important) associations could be included in a matching exercise. As a result, the test ends up having excessive emphasis in this area, while other important facets of achievement may be seriously neglected (Wesman, 1971, p. 99).

The best protection against overuse of matching exercises is obtained by developing and using carefully considered test plans as discussed in the last chapter. Thoughtful test specifications for a survey literature course might call for a few author-works associations, but certainly not a dozen. If the plan called for two items, then one would want to *sample*, probably from the better known of the Utopian authors. Multiple-choice or completion items might be considered.

Figure 5–4 provides an example from Mr. Martin's "Music around the World" unit (described on pages 129–130) of the use of matching exercises to assess Track C learning that goes well beyond rote recall of facts. These items constitute Mr. Martin's assessment of the third column of his table of specifications shown on page 130. Recall that he wanted to measure transfer of learning; therefore all eight selections will be ones that were *not* used in class and ones with which he has no reason to believe many students have had prior contact. Of course, if familiar selections were used, then the exercise would measure only the recognition recall of factual information.

Several short selections of music will now be played. Each will be identified by a number. In the blank for each selection, print the capital letter that precedes the kind of music the selection exemplifies.

_____ Selection 1   A.   African
_____ Selection 2   B.   Oriental
_____ Selection 3   C.   Polynesian
_____ Selection 4   D.   Slavic
_____ Selection 5
_____ Selection 6
_____ Selection 7
_____ Selection 8

Figure 5–4.   Matching Exercise on "Music around the World"

Figure 5–5 provides another example of how matching exercises can measure more than rote recall. Assume in this case that the teacher had not stressed memorization of dates of these or other events, only that students are expected to have a "ball park" notion of when events occurred and a sense of how much of the content of a history course focuses on the recent past. Under these conditions, this matching exercise provides a good assessment of students' time perspective. It should be noted, however, that most matching exercises that are based on dates involve only rote recall.

Some Rules for Constructing Matching Exercises

1. **Include in a given matching exercise only homogeneous material**. Matching exercises are poorly suited to topics meriting only one or two items. If they are used for such topics, one of two things is likely to result. First, dissimilar materials (e.g., some meanings of terms, some dates, and some people's names) may be organized into a matching set. In this case, the dissimilarities among the options make guessing relatively easy. Second, the topic may be expanded to provide a full matching exercise containing homogeneous content. In this case, the topic is overemphasized.

2. **Prevent examinees from guessing the answer to one of the options by means of elimination**. That is, do not create matching exercises having the same number of elements in each column in which each option is used exactly once. One way to reduce guessing is to provide more options than items. Another is to provide

Below is a timeline that is divided into several lettered periods. The beginning and end of each period are identified by dates. Below the timeline are significant events in world history. To the left of each event, print the capital letter of the period during which it occurred. Each letter may match one, more than one, or none of the events.

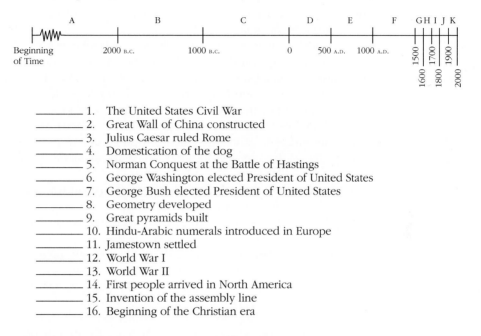

_____ 1. The United States Civil War
_____ 2. Great Wall of China constructed
_____ 3. Julius Caesar ruled Rome
_____ 4. Domestication of the dog
_____ 5. Norman Conquest at the Battle of Hastings
_____ 6. George Washington elected President of United States
_____ 7. George Bush elected President of United States
_____ 8. Geometry developed
_____ 9. Great pyramids built
_____ 10. Hindu-Arabic numerals introduced in Europe
_____ 11. Jamestown settled
_____ 12. World War I
_____ 13. World War II
_____ 14. First people arrived in North America
_____ 15. Invention of the assembly line
_____ 16. Beginning of the Christian era

Figure 5–5. Matching Exercise on Historical Time Perspective

fewer options than items; in this case, options obviously may be used more than once. Finally, directions can state that each option may be used once, more than once, or not at all. Of course, such directions can be used in combination with either of the other methods. Figure 5–3 shows use of the first and third methods. Figure 5–4 illustrates the second technique. Figure 5–5 demonstrates the second and third methods.

3. **Place the shorter or simpler elements in the right-hand column**. Which set of elements is considered to be the items and which is deemed to be the alternatives is often an arbitrary assignment. For example in Figure 5–3, the columns could be reversed except for the issue addressed by this rule—ease and speed of test taking. The easier-to-read elements are best defined as the options because they have to be scanned repeatedly as each item is attempted.

An occasional matching set is formatted by some means other than the conventional two columns. For example, Figure 5–5 presents the options in a time line. Similarly, options can be located in a diagram, map, etc.

4. **Sequence options in a manner that makes them easy to find**. If the options are dates, put them in chronological order. If they are numbers, put them in numeric order. If they are such things as people, cities, or products, alphabetize them. If they are events, put them in chronological order unless this would provide clues. In any way possible, sequence the options in ways that will make them easy to scan and locate.

5. **Keep matching exercises to reasonable lengths**. Ordinarily, there should be no more than 10 or 12 items in a matching exercise, and there usually should be fewer. There are two reasons for this rule. First, it is only rarely appropriate to devote more emphasis to a single set of homogeneous items. Second, for most kinds of content, it becomes tedious to work through a lengthy set of options over and over again for each item.

The matching exercise shown in Figure 5–3 is long, but this might be tolerable in view of the capabilities of the students in an advanced-placement class. Nonetheless 12 items probably overemphasizes the topic. The exercise shown in Figure 5–4 could be made longer *if* it were desirable to devote more items to the objective measured by this set. Exceptional length would be acceptable because the number of options would remain very small. The exercise shown in 5–5 is longer than this rule suggests. Since the time-line options are very easy to scan, this might be acceptable *if* the test specification called for so many items on this kind of content.

6. **Be sure that there is one clearly best option for each matching item**. Unless care is taken, it is easy to create matching exercises in which one or more items can be defensively answered by two or more options. This, of course, is to be avoided.

7. **Keep each set of matching items on a single page**. Much annoyance is caused and time wasted by requiring examinees to flip back and forth between pages. Items can often be rearranged to enable each matching exercise to fit on a single page. If necessary, part of a page can be left empty in order to start a matching exercise on a new page so that it will fit thereon.

8. **The directions should specify the basis for matching**. In some matching exercises the basis for matching is self-evident, but if there can be any doubt, the issue should be addressed in the directions.

9. **Number the item stimuli and letter the options**. Figures 5–3 and 5–4 illustrate typical layout, numbering, and lettering of items and options.

10. **Avoid overusing matching exercises**. As Figures 5–4 and 5–5 reveal, matching exercises can be used to assess higher mental processes, but they only rarely are. The typical matching exercise distorts test emphasis with respect both to mental processes (overemphasizing recognition recall) and to content (overemphasizing the kinds of material conducive to being included in matching exercises). This item type should, therefore, be used sparingly and thoughtfully.

QUIZ 5–3

Identify the major faults with the following matching exercise.

Draw a line to connect each person in the left-hand column with the corresponding entry in the right-hand column.

1.	Theodore Roosevelt	A.	Republican
2.	Lyndon Johnson	B.	Democrat
3.	George Washington	C.	Assembly line
4.	John Philip Sousa	D.	Election of 1904
5.	Leonard Bernstein	E.	Steamboat
6.	Francis Scott Key	F.	Mark Twain
7.	*Uncle Tom's Cabin*	G.	Harriet Beecher Stowe
8.	*Tom Sawyer*	H.	"Stars and Stripes Forever"
9.	Henry Ford	I.	Election of 1788
10.	Robert Fulton	J.	"The Star-Spangled Banner"
11.	Dwight D. Eisenhower	K.	Election of 1964
12.	Richard M. Nixon	L.	*West Side Story*
13.	James E. Carter		
14.	George Bush		

KEY TO QUIZ 5–3

This matching exercise is a disaster. First, the content is not at all homogeneous; inventors, composers, presidents, and authors are all mixed into one exercise. Since there are not enough items of any one of these subsets to make up a good matching exercise, other item types should be considered.

If one were (undesirably) going to mix such diverse persons, one would want to move the two authors into the same column as the other persons. One would also want to place the three elections together and put them in chronological order. At least two items lack a clearly preferable option. Item 1 can be answered defensively either with Options A or with Option D. Options B and K are each correct for Item 2.

The basis for matching is not specified. This makes the mental processing of all the items more difficult than necessary, and it creates the problem noted in the previous paragraph for Items 1 and 2.

The method of drawing lines to show responses is sometimes useful with young children with very short exercises, but it would result in a tangled visual nightmare for a set of this length.

Finally, this matching exercise, like most poorly constructed ones, taps one thing only—rote knowledge. While nothing is wrong with measuring knowledge of any of the facts covered in this exercise, one certainly hopes that there would be more to a unit and its test than rote memorization.

Chapter Summary

This chapter has provided the techniques with which teachers can produce effective completion and short-answer items, alternate-choice items, and matching exercises. Each of these item types has its list of "dos" and "don'ts" that aid in item development.

In general, these simple item types are most effective for assessing student achievement of simple learning outcomes, that is, of lower mental processes. They are especially suited for assessing student recognition or recall of factual knowledge. In addition, each of these kinds of test questions can at times be effectively used to assess student facility in the use of higher mental processes.

In assessing student recall of factual information, *test makers should remember the importance of measuring significant information*. These item types (among others) are too often used to measure trivia. At their best, they are used to assess important information that students should know.

Because of the inherent limitations of each of these item types, they are not individually or collectively sufficient for most well-designed paper-pencil tests. Although such simple item types make a valuable contribution to many excellent tests, they usually are best used in combination with multiple-choice items and/or essay items.

Suggestions for Further Reading

Ebel, R. L., & Frisbie, D. A. (1991). *Essentials of educational measurement* (5th ed.). Englewood Cliffs, NJ: Prentice-Hall. Chapter 8, "True-False Test Items," presents a case that true-false items have more potential than is generally accorded them by measurement experts. The chapter provides a good avenue to pursue that potential.

Gronlund, N. E., & Linn, R. L. (1990). *Measurement and evaluation in teaching* (6th ed.). New York: Macmillan. Chapter 6, "Constructing Objective Test Items: Simple Forms," parallels this chapter's discussion and provides additional examples of item faults and their avoidance.

Mehrens, W. A., & Lehmann, I. (1991). *Measurement and evaluation in education and psychology* (4th ed.). Fort Worth: Holt, Rinehart and Winston. Chapter 6, "Writing the Objective Test Item: Short-Answer, Matching, and True-False," provides another set of examples illustrating rules similar to those presented in this chapter. A helpful checklist is presented for each item type.

Wesman, A. G. (1971). Writing the test item. In Thorndike, R. L. (Ed.), *Educational measurement* (2nd ed.). Washington, DC: American Council on Education. This classic, scholarly, and practical treatment of objective items provides a wealth of information and perspective.

Developing Multiple-Choice Items and Interpretive Exercises

With three relatively simple item types previously discussed, more complex kinds of test questions remain. Attention is directed in this chapter to the multiple-choice item and to sets of questions that are presented along with material to be interpreted (e.g., a reading passage or map).

It has been noted that the simpler item types tend to be most effective in assessing surface learning, such as knowledge of terms and recall of facts. To be sure, important exceptions exist in which simple item types tap deeper learning. Examples would be classifying unstudied organisms into animals and plants or matching unfamiliar statements with the public figure who would be most likely to make them. By and large, however, completion and short-answer items, alternate-choice questions, and matching exercises are best suited to measuring lower mental processes.

More complex kinds of questions are generally better suited for measuring higher mental processes such as making applications, formulating logical arguments, or recognizing the ethnic origins of unfamiliar works of art. Of course, the potential of an item type for measuring more significant learning does not ensure that all items will necessarily realize this potential. Poorly written multiple-choice and essay tests may never penetrate beneath surface learning, but thoughtfully planned multiple-choice and essay tests can assess a wide variety of significant kinds of learning.

Developing Multiple-Choice Questions

The **multiple-choice** question is by far the most widely used objective item type. This popularity is a result of its versatility. Multiple-choice items are appropriate for measuring an exceptionally wide array of mental processes. They are also effectively used with an amazing variety of subject matter. Finally, they are suitable for educational levels ranging from lower elementary school through graduate school.

Some Key Terms

The Parts of the Multiple-Choice Item. Each multiple-choice item has two major parts. The **stem** is the part in which the question is asked or the task is set. By the time examinees finish reading the stem, they should ordinarily know what is expected and what the question is designed to measure. Following the stem are the **options**, which are also commonly referred to as choices or alternatives. The three or more options are the possible answers among which examinees must choose.

One of these options, if chosen, yields credit; it is called the **keyed response**. The keyed response is the right answer or the best answer. The other options are called **distractors**, **decoys**, or **foils**.

These names are richly descriptive of the function the wrong options serve. For students who do not know the material on which the item is based, the purpose of the wrong options is to *distract* examinees away from the keyed response. That is, the wrong choices are designed to *decoy* or to *foil* examinees who are ignorant of the content. Note that educators do not try to foil examinees who have a command of what the item measures, only those who do not.

Even so, some teachers may find these terms offensive. If so, they may be confusing their teaching role with their testing role. In teaching, of course, educators do not aim to distract, decoy, or foil any students; they try to enable all learners to find best or right answers. However, in testing teachers *aim to discriminate.* All tests are designed to discriminate. In Track A, the need is to distinguish students who have mastered a minimal essential objective from those who have not. (If the instruction in Track A has been successful in bringing all students up to mastery, then the mastery test's scores will not discriminate among those taking the test. Track A tests, nonetheless, should be able to discriminate between *masters* and *nonmasters* (e.g., between instructed and uninstructed examinees). In Tracks B and C the need is to differentiate among students who have achieved various amounts of competence on developmental objectives. Educators always want students who know what an item measures to get it right, and teachers always want those who do not know what the item measures to get it wrong. In this way the items yield information about examinee achievement.

Two Major Formats of Multiple-Choice Exercises. Some multiple-choice items are phrased as questions. In Figure 6–1, Items 1 and 2 both have stems that are complete questions. The stems end with question marks. The options can either be punctuated as complete sentences as shown in the left-hand column or left unpunctuated as styled in the right-hand column.

Sample Items	**Alternative Styles**
1. Who was the third President of the United States?	1. Who was the third President of the United States?
A. John Adams.	(1). John Adams
B. John Quincy Adams.	(2). John Quincy Adams
C. Andrew Jackson.	(3). Andrew Jackson
D. Thomas Jefferson.	(4). Thomas Jefferson
E. James Madison.	(5). James Madison
2. Which of the following foods provides the best combination of nutrients?	2. Which of the following foods provides the best combination of nutrients?
A. Applesauce cake.	1. applesauce cake
B. Banana split.	2. banana split
C. Pineapple milkshake.	3. pineapple milkshake
D. Pumpkin pie.	4. pumpkin pie
3. The third President of the United States was	3. The third President of the United States was:
A. John Adams.	a. John Adams.
B. John Quincy Adams.	b. John Quincy Adams.
C. Andrew Jackson.	c. Andrew Jackson.
D. Thomas Jefferson.	d. Thomas Jefferson.
E. James Madison.	e. James Madison.
4. Of the following foods, the one that provides the best combination of nutrients is a(n)	4. Of the following foods, the one that provides the best combination of nutrients is
A. applesauce cake.	(a) an applesauce cake.
B. banana split.	(b) a banana split.
C. pineapple milkshake.	(c) a pineapple milkshake.
D. pumpkin pie.	(d) a pumpkin pie.

Figure 6–1. Complete-Question and Incomplete-Sentence Multiple-Choice Items

Other multiple-choice items are phrased as incomplete sentences. Items 3 and 4 have incomplete sentence stems. Each option provides a way to complete the sentence. Therefore, the options *per se* are not capitalized, and each must end with a period. Some item writers end the incomplete sentence stem with a colon as shown in the right-hand column version of Item 3.

The right-hand side of Figure 6–1 also illustrates various ways by which the options can be designated—by numerals, capital letters, and lower-case letters. The test maker is free to go with her or his preference on such matters. Of course, however, the items within a given test should be styled consistently.

Some item ideas are more easily developed into complete question stems, while other ideas are better given expression as incomplete sentence stems. There is no reason to try to force items into one format or the other. Nor is there need for sets of multiple-choice items to be consistent; the two kinds of items can be mixed.

However, many item ideas are equally suited to either phrasing. This is certainly true of the two item ideas illustrated in Figure 6–1. In this case, it is better to opt for the complete-question format because it has fewer potential pitfalls. The problems avoided in complete questions include those of grammatical consistency (a) between the stem and the options and (b) among the options. An example is Item 4 in which the articles "a" and "an" could easily have been botched to provide a grammatical clue. This hazard did not exist in the complete-sentence format illustrated with Item 2.

Two Major Kinds of Multiple-Choice Content.   In some items, the keyed response is clearly the only right answer. For example, in Items 1 and 3 of Figure 6–1, Option D is categorically right and the other options are decisively wrong. In such cases, the keyed response may also be called the *right answer.* In other items, the keyed response is not categorically right and the other options are not absolutely wrong; rather the keyed response is only the *best answer* available. Items 2 and 4 illustrate best-answer items.

Right-answer multiple-choice questions are suitable for purely factual information and for computation problems in which one option is clearly right and the rest are absolutely wrong. The directions that accompany such items instruct examinees to select the *one right answer* for each item. In this context, it is permissible to offer options such as "All of the above," "More than one of the above," and "None of the above."

Most test content is not appropriate for right-answer directions. Most subject matter domains consist mainly of material for which some options are better than others, but for which none is categorically right. Items 2 and 4 in Figure 6–1 are a case in point. Option D is clearly the best option because pumpkin pie contains all four food groups, but it is certainly not the ideal or best possible way to balance the four food groups. The directions that accompany sets of best-answer multiple-choice items instruct examinees to select the one *best answer* to each question.

Fortunately, it is *not* necessary to segregate these two kinds of items into separate test sections or to provide a set of directions for each kind. The two kinds of items can be mixed. A mixed set should be preceded with best-answer directions.

What Do Multiple-Choice Items Measure?

Figure 6–2 illustrates the breadth of content and mental processes that multiple-choice items can assess. In every case, examinees must *recognize* and *select* (in contrast to produce) the best option from those presented. Yet the level of mental processing varies greatly. In the first item, the task is mainly that of retrieving information from long-term memory. If it had been mentally encoded in exactly the same words used in the question, then Item 1 would tap only rote surface learning. If the wording of instruction and the item differ, then the learning outcome measured would not be quite as shallow.

1. The Marshall Plan was announced shortly after the end of the
   A. Revolutionary War.
   B. Civil War.
   C. First World War.
   D. Second World War.
   E. Korean Conflict.

2. You are going to eat two eggs. Which method of preparation will produce the *fewest* calories?
   A. Fried.
   B. Omelet.
   C. Poached.
   D. Scrambled.

3. Draw a circle around the *smallest* box.

4. An explorer found an animal species that has not been classified before. It has warm blood. It takes good care of its young and provides milk for them. It can fly very well, can swim a little, but cannot get around well on land. What kind of animal is it?
   A. An amphibian.
   B. A bird.
   C. A fish.
   D. A mammal.
   E. A reptile.

5. A patent is to a new kind of mousetrap as a copyright is to a new
   A. kind of copy machine.
   B. medical drug.
   C. musical composition.
   D. surgical procedure.
   E. variety of rose.

6. A mammal's hair is most like a fish's
   A. bones.
   B. fins.
   C. gills.
   D. scales.

7. People who believe in capital punishment offer several reasons to support it. Some of these reasons reflect values. Others are based on testable facts. Which of the following reasons could best be tested?

    A. Capital punishment reduces crime.

    B. Society should be protected from criminals.

    C. Victims of crimes should be compensated.

    D. Wrongdoers deserve to be punished for their crimes.

8. What was the public reaction to the choice of George Bush as president?

    A. Disagreement by a large minority with the system by which the choice was made.

    B. Disagreement by the majority with the choice.

    C. Overwhelming agreement with the choice.

    D. Overwhelming support of the system by which the choice was made.

9. Some people support the use of lie detectors in hiring government workers. They admit that the use of lie detectors invades the privacy of job applicants, but they believe that national security justifies this invasion of privacy. What is the *unstated assumption* in their rationale?

    A. National security is *not* improved by use of the devices.

    B. The devices are *not* valid.

    C. The devices do *not* invade privacy.

    D. The devices are valid.

    E. The devices invade privacy.

10. Which of these body parts is a *joint*?

    A. Your head.

    B. Your knee.

    C. Your nose.

    D. Your thumb nail.

    E. Your tongue.

Figure 6–2.   Illustrative Breadth of Content and Mental Processes That Multiple-Choice Items Can Tap

Items 2 through 10 involve more complex thought processes, *provided that instruction did not use the same words or examples.* In examining these items, assume that wording, examples, or cases, are new to examinees. Item 2 requires examinees to relate egg-cooking methods to calories.

Item 3 requires the identification of an example of "smallest." Although it should be relatively easy for young children who have learned the concepts of "smallest" and "largest," the question clearly requires some mental processing that evidences understanding of the concept.

Item 4 involves the classification of a novel example. It taps a slightly deeper variety of meaningful verbal learning. No amount of mindless memorization would enable pupils to answer this item correctly unless they understand the meaning of the options. Such understanding, of course, comes in degrees. Some of the novel examples that could be used for test items would be very easy to classify, while others would be much more demanding.

Item 5 also requires more than rote recall. In addition to recognizing an example of a category (of copyright), the examinee must address the relationship between copyrights and patents. Similarly, Item 6 requires consideration of a relationship (between hair and scales). This goes beyond mere knowledge that fish have scales, gills, or fins.

Notice that when items require more than rote knowledge, requisite knowledge may be needed. In Item 5, students must know the categories of things that are patentable and those that can be copyrighted. Similarly for Items 2 and 4, examinees need to know the meaning of the terms used in the options. To deal with the relationship in Item 6, the child must know what scales are. Therefore, such items still measure knowledge. Their virtue is that meaningless knowledge alone does not suffice; examinees must be able to *use* or *process* what they "know."

Item 7 taps one dimension of the distinction between value statements and statements of fact. It might be a good item in a context where instruction had focused on helping students recognize which kinds of statements are philosophical and which are empirical.

Item 8 requires examinees to make sharp distinctions between the process of decision making in a democracy and satisfaction with the decision. Assuming this particular application was not used in class, it measures student ability to transfer learning. This item also requires basic factual background before the higher levels of reasoning can come into play.

Item 9 involves examinee ability to recognize an unstated assumption. If the example is not one previously encountered, such an item measures relatively high levels of reasoning. Of course, domain-specific knowledge is usually needed as well. Item 9 presupposes familiarity with lie detectors and with the concepts of invasion of privacy and national security.

Item 10 returns to material that might be measured at the elementary school level. It requires pupils to recognize an unstudied example of a concept. Answering this item correctly requires more than merely being able to parrot a definition of a joint or to recognize a definition drilled in class. If the example is not one previously studied, the item measures understanding of the concept.

These examples illustrate some of the many kinds of thinking that multiple-choice items can measure. As mentioned above, multiple-choice items are highly versatile. At times it would be appropriate for an entire test to consist of multiple-choice items.

But some cognitive attributes are not tapped with their use. Multiple-choice items do not measure how well examinees can produce, generate, or create. They do not assess how well students can express their ideas in their own words. They do not show how well learners can operate a car or how well teachers can control a class. For that matter, they are not even well suited to measuring how well teachers can write multiple-choice items! As good as the potential of multiple-choice items is, they do not provide an adequate means of measuring everything. Later chapters will address other methods of assessment that get at some of these kinds of learning outcomes.

Some Rules For Constructing Multiple-Choice Items

Following are several rules for developing multiple-choice items.

1. **Measure significant student learning**. The rule stating multiple-choice items should test only significant learning derives directly from the two themes of

Chapter 4. The first of these concerns the issue of validity. To make tests valid, measure what you have been trying to teach. The second theme concerns the power that tests have in influencing student effort. Students tend to study what they think will be tested. To harness test power (truthfully) give students reason to believe that evaluation will focus on significant content rather than on trivial rote learning.

In spite of the obvious merit of this cardinal item-writing rule, it is sadly true that many teacher-made tests measure little beyond rote learning (Fleming & Chambers, 1983) and fail to match the teachers' own aims (Nitko, 1989). It is necessary, therefore, for all of us to be ever vigilant against the temptation to "crank out" items that easily "flow" rather than to craft items that assess significant learning outcomes.

As an example, suppose a history textbook explained that President John Tyler, the first vice president to succeed to the office, established that the successor shall exercise all the duties of the office, rather than merely head a caretaker government. Suppose the text also happened to mention that, Tyler had 14 children—a presidential record. Both of these testable features are only facts, but one concerns an important historical precedent, while the other is trivial. The items in Figure 6–3 illustrate how either fact can be developed into a technically sound multiple-choice item. The second item, however, is far more valid and is much superior in signaling students to focus on important facts rather than on inconsequential ones.

Item Measuring Trivial Fact	**Item Measuring Significant Fact**

1. Which U. S. president had the most children?
 	
  A. Cleveland.
  B. Hayes.
  C. Madison.
  D. Tyler.
  E. Washington.
	1. Which U. S. president established that a vice president who succeeds to the office shall exercise the full powers of the office?
	
	  A. Chester Arthur.
	  B. Andrew Jackson.
	  C. Andrew Johnson.
	  D. Lyndon Johnson.
	  E. John Tyler.

Figure 6–3.   Technically Sound Items That Measure Both Trivial and Significant Facts

2. **Formulate the issue in the stem**. By the time examinees finish reading a multiple-choice item stem, the nature of the required task should be clear. It should not be necessary to wade through several options before being able to divine what one is expected to do. The flawed version of Item 1 in Figure 6–4 illustrates a stem that fails miserably to formulate an issue.

Stems that fail to formulate tasks are often written before their authors have good item ideas. One should not start composing an item until achieving a clear focus on what is to be measured. The author of Item 1 probably lacked an item concept other than the wish to "have a question on" cows. Once such a vague stem as "cows" is created, the item writer often merely completes the so-called multiple-choice item with several unrelated true or false statements. If the test maker could not develop a coherent idea for a multiple-choice item, it would be better to develop one or more true-false items than to package several of them in the guise of a multiple-choice item.

Flawed Items	**Improved Versions**
1. Cows	1a. How many young do cows most often give birth to at a time?
A. are marsupial mammals.	A. 1
B. are rodents.	B. 2
C. are used for their milk.	C. 3
D. have single, undivided hooves.	D. 4 or 5
E. usually give birth to two or three calves at a time.	E. 6 to 10
	1b. To which major group of mammals do cows belong?
	A. Monotreme.
	B. Marsupial.
	C. Placental.
2. Which of the following is true of pine wood?	2. How is pine classified in terms of hardness?
A. It is quite hard.	A. Hardwood.
B. It is quite soft.	B. Medium wood.
C. It comes from trees that grow mainly in the tropics.	C. Softwood.
D. It is quite dark.	

Figure 6–4. Stems That Fail to Formulate the Issue and Improved Versions of the Stems

Since no coherent item idea exists in Item 1, no one right way exists to fix the item. Improved version 1a focuses on number of births, while 1b concerns varieties of mammals. Other ideas could focus on cows being mammals rather than other kinds of vertebrates or on the structure of cattle feet.

Item 2 in Figure 6–4 provides a less extreme case in which the issue is not fully formulated in the stem. In this case, the item writer had an idea of wanting to test something about pine wood, but did not have a clear notion of what. The improved version focuses on one particular attribute of pine.

3. **Express ideas clearly, unambiguously, and briefly at as low a readability level as feasible**. The reading difficulty of an item should not cause some students to miss it. (This statement is least true in reading tests, but even there, the reading difficulty is usually incorporated into the passage, rather than the item.) Of course, items may rightly contain hard words and expressions that are part of the content to be tested, but in other respects, items should not be harder than necessary to read. If some pupils taking an arithmetic test cannot solve the verbal application problems because they cannot read them, then the test is (invalidly) measuring reading as well as mathematics. If several history students cannot understand what test questions are asking, then the test is contaminated to that extent.

Isolated objective test items stand on their own without clarifying context. This situation creates a hazard of ambiguity and misunderstanding. Great care is necessary to avoid use of words or phrases that can reasonably be interpreted in more than one way. Item 1 in Figure 6–5 illustrates ambiguity. What does "about the same" mean? Within a few months? Within a decade? The improved version of the item eliminates this ambiguity. It also achieves greater brevity in the stem. As long as the clarity is not compromised, shorter stems are clearly preferable to longer ones.

Flawed Items	**Improved Versions**
1. Compared with the average life span of American females, the average life span of American males is A. shorter. B. about the same. C. longer.	1. Compared with American females, the average life span of American males is A. shorter. B. within a year of being the same. C. longer.
2. The sun sets in the A. East. B. North. C. South. D. West. E. None of these.	2. The sun sets in the A. East. B. North. C. South. D. West.

Figure 6–5.   Ambiguous Items and Their Improved Versions

Item 2 in Figure 6–5 illustrates other sources of ambiguity. Strictly speaking, the sun does not set; the earth rotates. Students who understand this have to guess the sophistication of the item writer. If the item is naively conceived in everyday language, Option D is keyed, but if the item hinges on the earth's rotation, then Option E is keyed.

Assuming the teacher intends the first meaning, then the ambiguity is removed by eliminating the "none of the above" option. The sophisticated examinee still may grumble at the naivete of the item, but she or he will not miss it because of ambiguity.

Another compelling reason exists to eliminate the "none of the above" option. In most places at most times of the year, the sun does not "set" exactly in the West. In the northern hemisphere it tends to "set" in the Southwest. Therefore, "none of the above" may be the best option. The "none of the above" is a serious source of ambiguity that should be eliminated.

Even after purging the item of the "none of these" option, a problem still remains. In some places, such as Fairbanks, Alaska, in the winter, the direction is more South than West; therefore, South would be the best answer in some places. What to do? The stem could be modified to read, "In most places, the sun sets in the" or the issue might be ignored in most places.

4. **Be sure that each item has one option that is clearly best**. The basic criterion is that experts in the subject should be able to agree on the best option. As the last few paragraphs have demonstrated, ambiguity is one source of problems. Another major source of difficulty is differences of expert opinion. If the keying of an item hinges on an issue on which experts lack consensus, the item violates this rule.

It should be noted that this rule does not prohibit use of opinion items. One common way is to transform them into knowledge items with wording along the lines, "In the opinion of the author,. . . . " In addition, it is legitimate to focus items on opinion *when expert consensus is present*. Thus it might be permissible to ask which of four presidents was the best (or, to be safer, to ask which is generally considered to be best) if the options are Grant, Harding, Lincoln, and Pierce; but it would be unreasonable to use the same stem if the options were Cleveland, Monroe, Polk, and Van Buren.

5. **Avoid clueing with position or length of keyed response**. Most test makers have item-writing quirks. Many of these quirks are fairly common. Test-wise students who know these common tendencies are able systematically to use this knowledge to obtain scores higher than their achievement merits (Cronbach, 1984). Test makers should do everything within their power to prevent this invalid, unfair advantage. The remedy is for the item writers to be test-wise as well, and to use this knowledge to ensure that test wiseness does not provide a systematic advantage.

One such feature is location of the keyed response. Many teachers seek to "hide" it among other options, hating to "give" it as the first option or to call attention to it by locating it as the last option. They thus "bury" it among the middle options. Such a teacher making a 40-item, four-option, multiple-choice test might end up with only about 5 questions keyed "A," about 15 keyed "B," about 15 keyed "C," and about 5 keyed "D." In this teacher's class, a student can benefit much by adhering to the following rule: "If I think I know an answer, choose it; otherwise select a middle option."

Another feature is option length. Naive, careless, or rushed item writers tend to produce keyed responses that are, on average, longer than the decoys. This arises from the need to qualify the keyed response more in order to make it distinctly the best option. Test-wise students can gain a consistent unearned advantage by following this rule: "If I think I know an answer, choose it; otherwise select the longest option." Of course, more sophisticated examinees will have operational rules that incorporate both of these features. For example, "If I think I know an answer, choose it. Otherwise, pick the longer or longest of the middle options."

Teachers can use several ways to avoid such clueing. When options are numerals, they should be put into numerical order unless doing so would provide a clue (as in the items "Choose the smallest of the following numbers," or "Which historical event happened first"). A method applicable to a wide variety of content is to use a random process, such as rolling a die, to assign response positions (e.g., A, B, C, D) to options. Another is to put the options into alphabetical order. Such methods do much to assure that the item writer avoids getting into unconscious patterns that provide clues. It will be instructive to re-examine Figures 6–1 through 6–5 to consider how this issue of option ordering was handled in each.

Even after using one of the above processes, it often happens that one or more option in a given test is seriously underused or overused. As a last step, it is wise to tally the frequency with which options are keyed. If the options are used with approximately equal frequencies, leave them alone. If the frequency is very uneven, however, then a few options can be changed to bring about approximate balance. This last check is also useful in avoiding having a "long run" of consecutive items that have the same keyed responses.

6. **Avoid clueing with familiarity of keyed option**. Many teachers write keyed responses that contain the exact phrases drilled in class (Wesman, 1971). When this occurs, students who have learned the pat phrases by rote can get items correct without necessarily understanding them.

Here is an example. Suppose science students have studied the law of buoyancy and have learned Archimedes' Principle: "Any object floating or submerged in a fluid is buoyed up by a force equal to the weight of the displaced fluid." The teacher intends, of course, that students understand its meaning. Item 1 in Figure 6–6 fails to assess understanding; rote memorization of the statement would suffice.

1. Which of the following is a correct statement of the law of buoyancy?
    A. Any object that has sunk in liquid will weigh the same amount as the displaced liquid.
    B. Any object that is floating in a gas will weigh the same amount as the displaced gas.
    C. Any object floating or submerged in a fluid is buoyed up by a force equal to the weight of the displaced fluid.
    D. The weight of an object is not affected by whether it is in a fluid.

2. Which of the following is a correct statement of the law of buoyancy?
    A. When an object is put into a gas or liquid, it replaces some of the gas or liquid. This is true whether the object sinks or floats. This replaced gas or liquid has some weight. The object is pushed up by the same amount of force as the weight of the replaced gas or liquid.
    B. When an object is put into a gas or liquid, it replaces some of the gas or liquid. This is true whether the object sinks or floats. This replaced gas or liquid has some weight. The weight of the object will be increased by an amount equal to the weight of the replaced gas or liquid.
    C. When an object is put into a gas or liquid, it replaces some of the gas or liquid if it sinks but not if it floats. This replaced gas or liquid has some weight. The weight of the object will be increased by an amount equal to the weight of the replaced gas or liquid.
    D. When an object is put into a fluid, it displaces some of the fluid if it sinks, but not if it floats. This displaced fluid has some weight. The object will be buoyed up by a force equal to the weight of the displaced fluid.

3. A balloon is filled with salt water. It is then submerged in several fluids. In which fluid would it weigh the *least?*
    A. Carbon dioxide
    B. Helium
    C. Pure water
    D. Vegetable oil

4. A car went off a bridge into a deep river. At first it floated, then it sank. Why did it float at first?
    A. It floated until the engine was cooled by the cold river water.
    B. It floated until the people in the car had used up the oxygen trapped in the car.
    C. The gasoline in the tank was lighter than the river water.
    D. The water that the car replaced weighed more than the car.

5. A car had a full tank of gas, three people in it, and its windows closed. It went off a bridge into a deep, cold river. At first it floated, then it sank. Why did it finally sink?
    A. Because the air in the car leaked out and was replaced by water.
    B. Because the engine was cooled by the river water.
    C. Because the gasoline in the tank was lighter than the river water.
    D. Because the people in the car had used up most of the oxygen trapped in the car.

6. A wood block has a volume of 5 cubic centimeters and weighs 4 grams. Five cubic centimeters of a certain liquid weighs 3 grams. If the block is placed in this liquid, how much will it weigh?

    A.   1 gram

    B.   2 grams

    C.   3 grams

    D.   4 grams

    E.   5 grams

7. A wood block has a volume of 6 cubic centimeters and weighs 4 grams. Six cubic centimeters of a certain liquid weighs 3 grams. If the block is placed in this liquid, how much will it weigh?

    A.   1 gram

    B.   2 grams

    C.   3 grams

    D.   4 grams

    E.   5 grams

Figure 6–6.   Avoiding Rote Associations. See text for discussion of flaws in Items 1 and 6.

This item has multiple flaws. It violates Rule 5 as well as Rule 6. Even if a content-ignorant student is not test-wise enough to choose the longest option when it is in a middle position, he or she is likely to answer the item correctly simply because Option C "sounds familiar."

"Sounding familiar" can be turned into an advantage by clever item construction. Effective foils can be created by use of familiar phrases where they do not belong. Option D of Item 2 is a case in point; it uses the familiar-sounding words "buoyed" and "displaced fluid." The keyed Option A conveys the correct idea without using the familiar wording.

A teacher who has carefully planned the test and considered the relative weight to be given to various mental processes is less likely to create an item like Item 1. Planning the test and considering mental processes would probably sensitize one enough to be able to recognize that Item 1 does not delve beneath the surface.

The test plan may call for an item dealing with a correct statement of the law of buoyancy. If so, Item 2 in Figure 6–6 might be used to require students to distinguish between correct and incorrect paraphrases. Item 2 goes past rote learning to the comprehension level of the *Taxonomy*. In spite of its appalling length, Item 2 is better than Item 1. In addition to demanding comprehension rather than rote recall, in Item 2: (a) the longest option is not the best one, (b) a middle option is not the best one, and (c) the most familiar wording is not in the keyed response.

The teacher who has given careful thought to planning the test may or may not decide to use a question like Item 2. In either case, the plan would likely call for some questions that assess still higher mental processing. Item 3 in Figure 6–6 measures ability to *use* the principle to predict an outcome. Item 3 would be a good item (a) if this particular application is novel and (b) if examinees have the requisite knowledge that salt water is heavier than carbon dioxide, helium, pure water, and vegetable oil and that pure water is heavier than all the options.

Item 4 requires less requisite knowledge. However, in addition to ability to apply the principle, it requires students to sort out relevant from irrelevant information. Item 5 takes this process a little further. Of course, Items 4 and 5 are too similar for both to be included in the same test.

Items 6 and 7 in Figure 6–6 get at applications that require simple computation. These two items are also too similar to be used together.

Items 2 to 7 are consistent with each of the above rules. Persons who mindlessly commit material to memory without processing it will not know how to attack the problems and will rightfully get most of them wrong. Yet most of these items should be relatively easy for students who understand the principle.

7. **Use only plausible distractors**. Item 6 in Figure 6–2 illustrates this rule. Each distractor (like the keyed response) is a fish part. Any distractor that was not a part of fish anatomy (e.g., wings or antlers) would not be plausible.

For another illustration of adherence to this rule, examine Item 5 in Figure 6–6. Each decoy is designed to be attractive to students who do not understand the generalization. Option B states an obvious but irrelevant fact. Option C states a less obvious fact, but one whose impact would contribute (negligible) to buoyancy, not to sinking. Option D is most likely the poorest of the foils; the respiration of the passengers does not seem very plausible to those who keep the issue of flotation in mind. To examinees who lose sight of the issue, however, the option may be attractive because people in a closed car would indeed consume oxygen.

Now consider Item 6. Each of its foils could also well be chosen by a student who does not understand the principle. Option A, of course, is the keyed response (4 g minus 3 g). Option B can be obtained by subtracting 3 g from 5 cc, Option C by simply using the 3 g, Option 4 by using the 4 g, and option E by using the 5 cc.

Notice that Items 5 and 6 do not have the same number of options. Some item writers feel compelled to develop the same number of options for each multiple-choice item in a test. This seems unwise. Some items exist for which only three or four plausible options can be generated. In the case of Item 5, I was out of ideas after four options. Creating additional ones that will fail to attract any examinees seems pointless. If you can generate only three good options, stop there. Indeed there are times when no more options are logically possible, as in math items involving the three possibilities: greater than, equal to, or less than. At other times it is possible to generate five or even more options that are attractive and functional. If so, it may be desirable to do so because a larger number of options reduces the chances of examinees selecting the keyed response by guessing.

How should you devise plausible decoys? Some experts recommend that multiple-choice stems first be administered as completion items in order to learn what wrong answers students actually produce. These wrong answers are subsequently used as the distractors in multiple-choice items. Research does *not* support this advice (e.g., Johnson, 1976; Loree, 1948); teachers can do about as well with much less work by thinking up the distractors themselves.

Recall three attributes of good item writers that help in developing plausible distractors. First, effective item writers know the subject matter in considerably more depth than the test will assess. This knowledge helps one to know what is important and how to avoid content pitfalls. It also helps one to know content that can (and cannot) be used as foils. Recall Item 2 in Figure 6–5 concerning the direction of the sunset. To avoid these pitfalls, the teacher would need to know quite a bit more about geography and astronomy than the item seems superficially to measure.

Second, good item writers know the technology of crafting items. Such knowledge helps one avoid the kinds of pitfalls covered in these rules.

Finally, excellent item writers know students and the kinds of errors they make. This knowledge enables test makers to know which distractors will be attractive to students who lack the knowledge assessed by an item. Consider first-year algebra as an example. Suppose students have just learned to multiply literal numbers that are raised to powers, such as $(x^5)(x^2)$. Every algebra teacher knows how common it is for students to multiply the exponents and answer x^{10}. (Recall that the correct way is to add the exponents; therefore, the correct answer is x^7.) Multiplying the exponents is a high-frequency conceptual error in first-year algebra. Thereafter, it is more likely to be a careless error, but it remains a common one. Knowledge of frequent student error will enable the algebra teacher to include x^{10} as a distractor.

8. **Avoid items in which incorrect reasoning yields the keyed response**. A frequent cause of good item ideas "going sour" lies in a keyed response that can be obtained by an incorrect process. This applies to all item types, not just multiple-choice questions. Four examples follow. Notice in each how the problem is best avoided by the item writer knowing the kinds of errors that students commonly make.

In algebra, the test maker would want to avoid the item stem, $(y^2)(y^2)$. This item will malfunction in either completion or multiple-choice format because students who do the wrong thing and multiply the exponents will get the right answer. Thus the item will not effectively discriminate between those who know how to perform the multiplication and those who do not.

Item 6 of Figure 6–6 on page 167 provides a second example. Students can get the right answer by the wrong process. Recall that the proper way to obtain the answer was to subtract 3 from 4. Unfortunately, the student who subtracts 4 from 5 (doing violence to nonequivalent units in the process) will also get the right numeric answer. Item 7 has been modified to correct this flaw.

Map work at the elementary level provides another example of this flaw. A common misconception is that all rivers flow south. In some parts of the country, it results from overgeneralizing from local rivers. The other basis for the misconception lies in the reasoning that "north is up on a map; south is down. Water flows downhill. Therefore, water flows south."

Suppose a teacher is making an imaginary map to test students' map skills. A test item is to ask the direction of a certain river, and the four options are to be the four primary compass directions. The teacher would be well advised to avoid a river that flows south because some pupils would get the item right via their *miscon*-ception.

For the final example, consider the flawed Item 1 and its improved version in Figure 6–7. Why is the second item better? The issue here is that some pupils have the misconception that the antecedent to a pronoun is the noun that *immediately* precedes the pronoun. Therefore, the item writer should be careful not to create items in which this misconception will result in correct answers. In the flawed version, the misconception happens to yield the right answer for the wrong reason; this will limit the extent to which the item can discriminate between those who can correctly identify the antecedent of a pronoun and those who cannot. The improved version of the item is free from this fault.

Flawed Items	**Improved Versions**
1. "After rushing through the gate into the yard, the dog dug up the bone and settled down to enjoy **it**." The "**it**" in the last sentence stands for	1. "The dog rushed through the gate and hid the bone in the yard where no other dog would find **it**." The "**it**" in the last sentence stands for the
A. the gate.	A. dog.
B. the yard.	B. gate.
C. the dog.	C. bone.
D. the bone.	D. yard.
	E. other dog.
2. A polygon with six sides is called a	2. A polygon with six sides is called a/an
A. hexagon.	A. hexagon.
B. pentagon.	B. pentagon.
C. octagon.	C. octagon.
D. quadrilateral.	D. quadrilateral.
E. triangle.	E. triangle.
	3. The title of the presiding officer of the United States House of Representatives is
3. The presiding officer of the United States House of Representatives is the	A. chair.
A. chairman.	B. president.
B. chairperson.	C. president pro tem.
C. chairwoman.	D. speaker.
D. president.	
E. speaker.	4. A moa was a giant
4. A moa was a giant	A. amphibian.
A. bird.	B. bird.
B. dog.	C. fish.
C. mammal.	D. mammal.
D. reptile.	E. reptile.
E. turtle.	5. At the end of the story, Ray Short was
5. At the end of the story, Ray Short was	A. dead.
A. dead.	B. insane.
B. married.	C. married.
C. poor.	D. poor.
D. rich.	E. sad.
E. sad.	

Figure 6–7. Item Flaws and Their Corrections

The improved version of 1 also moves the word "the" to the stem. In general, whenever a word or phrase appears at the beginning of each option, it should be moved to the end of the stem.

Both versions of Item 1 illustrate a sensible ordering of options. By putting them in the order in which they occurred in the stem, students would have less trouble finding them than they would with any other order.

9. **Avoid grammatical clues**. Clues of number or gender can enable examinees to eliminate some options as implausible. Likewise, the articles "a" and "an" enable students to reject options that start with vowels or consonants, respectively. The flawed version of Item 2 in Figure 6–7 shows how failure to attend to this detail enables examinees to eliminate Option C. The improved version of Item 2 shows one way by which this clue can be avoided. The two versions of Item 4 in Figure 6–1 on page 157 illustrate other ways.

10. **Create options that are noninclusive of each other**. Item 3 of Figure 6–7 illustrates the problem of an option that includes other options. In the flawed question, the student could reason that neither "chairman" nor "chairwoman" could be correct because if it were, then "chairperson" would be too. Hence, the person not knowing the answer would have only three options among which to choose.

Item 4 also illustrates the problem with options that include other options. Even if the student has no idea what a moa is, he or she would have better-than-chance odds of guessing the right answer. Being test wise, the student could reason that it could not be a turtle because if it were, the item would have to be double keyed for reptile. Likewise, it could not be a dog because that would also make mammal correct. Therefore, it must be either a bird, mammal, or a reptile. (It was an enormous, now-extinct bird that lived in New Zealand.)

11. **Avoid unskilled use of options that are opposites**. Novice item writers are apt to have one of a pair of opposite options as the keyed response more than its share of the time. Item 5 in Figure 6–7 illustrates this. Opposite Options C and D are the best guesses, especially since they are among the middle options. Similarly, the flawed version of Item 2 in Figure 6–4 on page 163 provided this clue.

Of course, opposites can be used skillfully to misclue those who do not know what an item is designed to measure. It is sometimes useful to use a pair of opposite options provided that both are wrong.

Another way of using opposite options without providing helpful clues is shown in Item 8 of Figure 6–2 on page 160. Options A and D are opposite; so are Options B and C. Thus there is no clue. Similarly, Item 9 in Figure 6–2 used two sets of opposites, thereby providing only minimal clueing.

12. **Avoid negative stems where possible. Where they are used, call attention to the feature that makes them negative**. In general, test questions should focus on what is right, not on what is wrong. Item 1 in Figure 6–8 illustrates the typical use of negative stems. If a history class has studied the accomplishments of Franklin Roosevelt's first two terms, it is easier for the item writer to place several accomplishments and one nonaccomplishment in a list and ask examinees to identify the latter. Yet this is usually a poor practice. The improved version represents a more desirable approach—that of focusing on what is true rather than on what is false. The improved version also illustrates how a key word or phrase can be made conspicuous.

Yet at times it *is* appropriate to use negative stems. When teaching has emphasized what *not* to do, then negative stems are desirable. For example, "Which of the following would be an UNsafe way to use the lathe?" Or "If you find an unconscious person who has fallen from a ladder, you should *not*. . . . " Or "Which behavior tends to make others **dis**like a person?"

If, for any reason, a negative stem is used, then a safeguard is needed to prevent examinees from failing to notice the one minor word or prefix that reverses the

Flawed Items	**Improved Versions**
1. Which of the following events did not occur during Franklin Roosevelt's first two terms?	1. Which of the following events occured during Franklin Roosevelt's *first two* terms?

A. Attack of Pearl Harbor.
   B. Bank Moritorium.
   C. Creation of the SEC.
   D. Creation of the WPA.
	A. Attack of Pearl Harbor.
	   B. Bank Moritorium.
	   C. Election of Harry Truman as Vice President.
	   D. Roosevelt stricken by polio.

2. Liability insurance for a given car in a certain city will likely cost least if the only driver of the car is a	2. Liability insurance for a given car in a certain city will likely cost LEAST if the only driver of the car is a

A. 17-year-old female with good grades.
   B. 17-year-old female with poor grades.
   C. 17-year-old male with good grades.
   D. 17-year-old male with poor grades.
	A. 17-year-old female with good grades.
	   B. 17-year-old female with poor grades.
	   C. 17-year-old male with good grades.
	   D. 17-year-old male with poor grades.

Figure 6–8.   More Item Flaws and Their Corrections

stem's meaning. In one way or another, attention should be called to the negative word or prefix. It can be printed in bold face, italicized, printed in capital letters, or underlined. Some of these options were used in the previous paragraph's examples.

It is also good practice to highlight other words that may reverse examinees' mental set. For example, "Which of the following is *smallest?*" Item 2 in Figure 6–8 shows another way of making such unexpected words conspicuous. So does Item 3 in Figure 6–6 on page 166.

Double negatives should always be avoided. If a negative stem is used, no negative options should follow.

13. **Avoid inappropriate use of options such as "none of the above," "all of the above," and "A and C above".** Recall that such options are perfectly acceptable in *right-answer*, multiple-choice questions, but have no place in the *best-answer* items that populate most tests. Such options violate logic and grammar by asking examinees to select the *best* option and then offering them such choices as "none of the above," and "all of the above" as the "best."

Unskilled item writers who use such options tend to employ them as the keyed response too much or too little. This provides yet another basis for test-wise examinees to guess answers without knowing content. For example, many teachers who use "all of the above" in multiple-choice items have it as the keyed response in at least half of the items in which it appears. This gives rise to the guessing rule, "If I think I know the answer to an item, choose it; otherwise choose 'all of the above' if it is an option."

Such options are so frequently misused that they have a bad reputation even where they are legitimate. Note that the recommendation is to avoid *inappropriate* use of the options, not to avoid all use of the options.

When testing content that is categorically right or wrong under "right-answer" directions, such options may be used. Suppose, for example, that a multiple-choice algebra test has directions to choose the right answer to each question. An item having the stem, "$3 + 5 \times 4 - 2 \times 6 = $," might be followed by four numeric options such as 11, 63, 96, and 180 and a final option, "none of the above." The value of the "none of the above" option is its capacity to encompass all other errors that examinees can possibly make. Without the "none of the above" option, an examinee making an error that does not appear among the options (e.g., 20, 126, or 78) is clued that he or she has erred.

Even when used correctly with "right-answer" content, the "none of the above" option is hazardous. If used in five-option items, it should, of course, be the keyed response about one-fifth of the time. Yet difficult items keyed for "none of the above" usually violate Rule 8 above. That is, a student who obtains an unusual incorrect response will choose the "none of the above" option for the wrong reason and thereby get unearned credit. Such items tend to provide poor discrimination between high- and low-achieving examinees. As a result, the item writer is caught in a difficult situation. On the one hand, if the option is not keyed correct its share of the time, then the test-wise will benefit from avoiding it. On the other hand, when the option is keyed correct for a difficult item, it usually fails to discriminate well. A remedy is to establish the credibility of the "none of the above" option by using it as the keyed response a few times early in the test with easy items and thereafter to use it very little.

14. **Write options that are grammatically parallel to each other**. A "nicety" of item writing is parallel construction among the options, particularly in the incomplete-sentence variety of multiple-choice items. Item 1 in Figure 6–9 illustrates an awkward item that is improved by developing parallel construction of the options. In addition to having options that are not grammatically consistent, both versions of Item 1 also violate Rule 2; the issue is not provided in the stem. When all the options are similar (e.g., names of cities), then this issue is of little consequence, but since the options of the flawed version all "go off in different directions," this violation of Rule 2 is worrisome.

This is a good place to mention that several of these rules should, at times, be violated. When a good reason exists for doing so, it may be wise to violate an item-writing rule. The rule concerning parallel construction is a case in point. While it is usually good to adhere to this rule, some items exist for which forcing parallel construction is awkward. If the results would be contorted, it is better to tolerate minor nonparallelism among the options. In the case of Item 1, there is no need to tolerate it; the stem can be improved as shown in Item 2.

15. **Beware of humor**. Item 2 in Figure 6–9 illustrates an attempt at humor. It often leads to trouble. In this case, "Short Beach" (whether or not it is humorous) will not be very plausible to children in Long Beach, California (which was founded by a Mr. Fillmore) because its beach is not short. The more blatant attempt at humor, "Holdless," will also be chosen by few if any pupils who do not know the right answer.

Another problem with humor in test items is that it often backfires. Students who, under the stress of the test situation, fail to recognize the teacher's attempt to be cute, are often seriously irritated after the test when they realize that credit has been lost as a result of the teacher's playfulness. To them, it is *not* funny.

Flawed Items	**Improved Versions**
1. Our city was first named	1. Our city was first named
A. before anyone lived in it.	A. Baytown.
B. by its first resident.	B. Fillmore City.
C. Fillmore City.	C. Long Beach.
D. in honor of its first minister.	D. Oceanville.
E. to attract settlers.	E. Winter Resort.
2. What was the first name given our city?	2. What was the first name given our city?
A. Fillmore City	A. Baytown
B. Holdless City	B. Fillmore City
C. Long Beach	C. Long Beach
D. Short Beach	D. Oceanville
	E. Winterburg
3. The Cuban Missile Crisis took place when the USSR shipped missiles to	3. A major international crisis took place when the USSR shipped missiles to
A. Cuba.	A. Cuba.
B. India.	B. India.
C. Mexico.	C. Mexico.
D. Yugoslovia.	D. Yugoslovia.
4. To *inaugurate* is to	4. To *inaugurate* is to
A. elect.	A. elect.
B. install.	B. incarcerate.
C. lock up.	C. put in place.
D. remove.	D. vindicate.

Figure 6–9. Additional Examples of Item Flaws and Their Corrections

16. **Avoid clueing with similar phrasing in stem and keyed response**. If important words or phrases in the keyed response also appear in the stem, students who lack knowledge and are grasping for clues will be attracted to the option that looks most similar to the stem. The flawed version of Item 3 in Figure 6–9 provides an obvious illustration of this problem.

Like several other hazards, this one can be turned to advantage. Item 5 of Figure 6–2 on page 159 illustrates how a key word can be used to misclue. The use of *copy* machine in Option A provides an irrelevant association with *copy*right in the stem and may render this option more attractive to those lacking knowledge of what the item is intended to assess.

Prefixes present a particular hazard of clueing. The flawed version of Item 4 in Figure 6–9 would be guessed by many people lacking the knowledge because of the prefix "in-." Note in the improved version that this clue has been eliminated. In addition, two misclues have been used. The prefix "in-" is now associated with an incorrect option, and the ending "-ate" is associated with two incorrect options.

17. **Do not let one item clue other items**. As a test maker focuses on developing one item at a time, it is natural to fail to have in mind all the other items in the test. This creates the hazard that the content of one question will give away the

answers to other questions. Interitem clueing, of course, is a problem not only with multiple-choice items, but for other item types as well. Most teachers are sensitive to the need to have items in close proximity avoid clueing each other. They tend to violate this rule more frequently, however, as item types change and/or as items are further apart in a test.

For example, a test might contain a multiple-choice question asking the identify of the most influential person in preventing the United States from joining the League of Nations. In an earlier section, a true-false item might concern whether or not the United States joined. A student who did not know the answer to the true-false item might, upon reading the subsequent multiple-choice question, realize that it provides the answer to the earlier item.

QUIZ 6–1

Think of your own experience in taking multiple-choice examinations. You have probably often been able to deduce an answer when you did not know it. Most of the ways you did so are discussed in the above set of rules. Can you think of any additional methods you have used that are not treated in the rules? In order words, what additional item-writing rules might the lists well have included?

KEY TO QUIZ 6–1

Although the above 17 rules were designed to cover most of the important issues, they are not exhaustive. Nor can this discussion cover every possible means of foiling test-wise examinees.

Your thought on this issue may enhance your item-writing skills. You may also have an opportunity to propose any additional rules to other students or to your instructor for reaction.

Developing and Polishing Items

In the discussion that accompanied Figures 6–1 through 6–9, mention was made of various features of items that serve to make them effective. A few illustrative items will now be examined for some "tricks of the trade" that enable them to be polished. It is obvious, of course, that good item writing is a Track C, career-long endeavor.

Example 1.   The second version of the item in Figure 6–3 on page 162 will be used to illustrate the process by which foils are thoughtfully selected. Of all the potential foils, which would work best to discriminate between examinees who know and those who do not know this fact? Other vice presidents who succeeded to the presidency would be the obvious set. We would probably restrict ourselves to this set unless there were good reason to enlarge it. This gives us John Tyler, Millard Fillmore, Andrew Johnson, Chester Arthur, Theodore Roosevelt, Calvin Coolidge, Harry Truman, Lyndon Johnson, and Gerald Ford. Tyler is the right answer, so which others should we select?

Andrew Johnson comes to mind because of the difficulties he had with a hostile Congress over his attempt to follow precedent. By good fortune the list of possible distractors contains another Johnson (Lyndon Johnson). The double occurrence of the Johnson name will make it more attractive and distract away from Tyler students who lack the key knowledge. First names are now needed to distinguish between the two Johnsons. The list now contains Andrew Johnson, Lyndon Johnson, and John Tyler.

At this point, Andrew Jackson comes to mind even though he did not attain office by succession. His name serves to provide two Andrews as well as two Johnsons. Some students who do not know the content of an item look for recurring features among the options. One might reason, "There are two Andrews. The test maker is trying to tempt us with a wrong Andrew; therefore, the right answer is probably one of them. Likewise for two Johnsons. One option has both Andrew and Johnson; it is the best one to guess."

If a fifth option is desired—and since options are both plentiful and brief, a fifth one can be added to make lucky guessing less likely. Gerald Ford might be used since he was not even elected to the vice presidency; Theodore Roosevelt because his name would be among the most familiar on the list and might therefore "draw" some of the students lacking the knowledge. Chester Arthur might be chosen because his name is relatively obscure, and might be chosen by some students who are acutely aware they will not recognize the right name. There is no apparent superiority of one of these over the others.

Example 2. For another example consider the math item from the last section having the stem: $3 + 5 \times 4 - 2 \times 6 = $ _____ .

To get desirable options, we would work the problem in the most likely incorrect ways. The most likely error may be 180, which is obtained by working from left to right with no regard for order-of-operation rules. Another error would be 20, obtained by (wrongly) first adding 3 and 5 and then proceeding correctly. Another is 126, obtained by correctly adding the product of 5×4 to 3 and then wrongly subtracting 2 and multiplying the difference by 6. Another would be 96, obtained by reversing the order-of-operation rule.

Figuring out these options was a bother. And even after going to the trouble, we are left to worry that some students will make still different errors. "None of the above" could be considered as a catch-all option, but it has the problems discussed above. These considerations help us to understand why many algebra teachers very properly would prefer to use this stem in a completion item rather than as a multiple-choice question.

Example 3. Now consider the evolution of an item idea. Sometimes the idea for an item that assesses higher mental processes springs directly to mind. At other times, it gradually evolves as an item is revised through several drafts. In Figure 6–6 on page 166, Item 2 could have evolved out of a reconsideration of Item 1. Likewise, Items 3, 4, and 5 might have evolved out of dissatisfaction with the low level of thinking required in Item 1 and the length of Item 2.

Example 4. For a final example, consider an elementary level reading passage that described how the Mennonites migrated to Kansas from Russia. They brought a variety of wheat called Turkey Red. Turkey Red started Kansans in growing hard winter wheat—the variety that today makes Kansas the "Breadbasket of the Nation."

One of the items drafted for this reading passage concerned the country from which the Mennonites came to Kansas. What options would you use?

Russia, of course, would be the keyed response. At first, foils like England, Poland, and Spain were drafted. On review, however, Turkey came to the item writer's mind because of the name of the wheat variety. Still later, the author had the creative idea of Mennon; although there is no such country, it certainly sounds plausible that Mennonites would come from Mennon. Thus the final item, after much evolution contained the distractors "Turkey" and "Mennon." These two distractors proved to be extraordinarily effective in discriminating better readers from less capable ones.

Directions to Accompany Multiple-Choice Items

As is true for other item types, the directions that introduce a set of multiple-choice items should inform examinees of several important things. They should indicate the relative credit of the items. Objective items should ordinarily be equally weighted. If a topic merits more weight, it typically should be assessed with more items.

Multiple-choice directions should forcefully indicate that only one answer may be selected for each item. (The variety of multiple-choice item that instructs students to mark each option that is true is generally not recommended because it suffers from several problems. First, it can only be used with right-answer items, never with best-answer items. Second, such items are usually more effective if recast into true-false items. Third, no uniquely defensible way exists to score the many possible combinations of incorrectly marked decoys and unmarked keyed responses.)

Examinees should be told how to mark their answers. Common ways are by circling or underlining option letters or numerals either in the test booklet or on a separate answer sheet, by printing option letters (or numerals) either on the test itself or on a separate answer sheet, and by filling in circles (or marking an **X** in them) on a separate answer sheet. When tests are administered by computer—as is becoming more common—examinees respond by pressing a keyboard key or using a "mouse."

Finally, the topic of guessing should be fully addressed either at the beginning of the test or in the respective sections of objective items. Chapter 9 will address this issue. For now, suffice it to say that the directions concerning guessing should honestly inform examinees when it is or is not in their best interest to guess.

Developing Interpretive Exercises

An **interpretive exercise** is a set of test items based on some stimulus material that is presented with them. The purpose is to determine how well examinees can *extract meaning from* or *interpret the unfamiliar* Track C content. Since examinees have not previously studied the stimuli upon which items are based, interpretive exercises measure examinee ability to process new material.

Most reading comprehension tests exemplify school use of interpretive exercises. Students are presented with a reading passage followed by several objective questions *based on the passage*. The purpose is to determine how well students can obtain meaning from the passage.

Map skills are also traditionally measured with interpretive exercises. The stimulus is a map that is unfamiliar to the examinees. It is followed by a set of objective items—usually multiple-choice. Each question should be based on the map so that it cannot be answered without reference to it. Hence, the items assess student ability to secure information from the map.

This section shows how interpretive exercises provide a powerful way to measure higher mental processes in a wide variety of subject matter and grades. In addition, their use in classroom tests sends the important message to students that school learning should enable them to obtain meaning from realistic, novel material. That is, by measuring transfer of learning, *interpretive exercises communicate that transfer is an important objective.*

What Do Interpretive Exercises Measure?

Interpretive exercises are as varied as the imagination and ingenuity of their creators. The stimuli on which they are based can vary widely, and a variety of item types can be referenced to the stimuli.[1] Following are descriptions of a wide variety of interpretive exercises. To demonstrate the breadth of this means of testing, the examples will range from the commonplace to the exotic.

Reading Comprehension.   The ability to extract meaning from written material (either in native tongue or in a second language) is usually measured by material to be read accompanied by multiple-choice questions about that material. Length may range from a sentence to long passages. Passages can be excerpted from existing sources or specially created for a test. Most authors of reading tests prefer to create their own stimulus passages because they can be developed and revised to serve the testing purposes.

A critical attribute of a reading comprehension test is that the information necessary to answer questions be unfamiliar to examinees. If they already knew the answers, there would be no way to know whether correct answers were based on the prior knowledge or on ability to derive meaning from the passage. For example, a passage about Cleopatra and her brother in a middle-school reading test might be accompanied by a question asking the name of her country. The problem is that many students know this without reading the passage; hence, the ability to answer the item is probably not **passage dependent**. On the other hand, an item asking the name of her brother would be more acceptable because few students would have that prior knowledge. The need to ensure passage dependence has received considerable attention in the field of reading comprehension (e.g., Pyrczak, 1972; Tuinman, 1974). The way to build passage dependence into a test is to base reading tests on passages that do not contain material already known to examinees.

---

[1]Most discussions of interpretive exercises make an explicit or implicit assumption that only multiple-choice items are used in exercises. Test makers need not be constrained by any such assumption. While most interpretive exercises best employ multiple-choice items, the full gamut of items can, on occasion, be used to advantage.

Interpreting Tables.   The ability to "read" tables and charts is also well measured with interpretive exercises. Figure 6–10 provides an example of an interpretive exercise based on a table.

Items 1–3 are based on the table below.

Tudor Monarchs

Henry VII	1485–1509
Henry VIII	1509–1547
Edward VI	1547–1553
Mary I	1553–1558
Elizabeth I	1558–1603

1.   How long did the Tudors reign?
    A.   24 years
    B.   45 years
    C.   118 years
    D.   128 years
    E.   218 years

2.   Which Tudor had the longest reign?
    A.   Henry VII
    B.   Henry VIII
    C.   Edward VI
    D.   Mary I
    E.   Elizabeth I

3.   Elizabeth I was 25 years old when she became queen. About how old was she when she died?
    A.   30
    B.   31
    C.   49
    D.   63
    E.   70

Figure 6–10.   Interpretive Exercise Based on Table

Novelty of the stimulus material is just as important in other kinds of interpretive exercises as it is in reading. Student ability to answer items correctly should be a function of their ability to decode the stimulus, not a function of their prior knowledge. The general term is **context dependence**.

Context dependence is a function of the familiarity of the material. It can be judged by considering the likelihood of familiarity to the kinds of examinees for whom an exercise is intended. The information contained in Figure 6–10 would probably not be very well known to students, hence it might be acceptable. Greater assurance of context dependence would be easy to obtain, however, by making up the data. For example, the table could report the lengths of reigns of monarchs of Hertoslovia (a fictitious country).

Listening Comprehension.   Ability to obtain meaning from the spoken word is a vital skill. Its measurement is best accomplished with interpretive exercises in which passage stimuli are read or played. Paper-pencil multiple-choice items are often the best way to assess student grasp of what they hear.

Study Skills.   Interpretive exercises are particularly well suited to measuring student ability to use resources such as dictionaries, card catalogs, and book indices. Figure 6–11 contains a set of matching items for elementary children concerning use of the encyclopedia.

Directions: Below is a picture of the volumes of an encyclopedia. Each volume has information about subjects that begin with the letters shown. Questions 1 – 4 below are based on this picture. To the left of each question, write the number of the volume that answers the question. Each volume may be used once, more than once, or not at all.

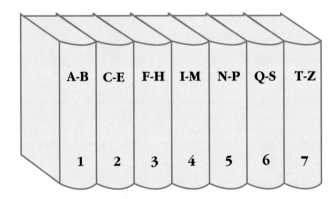

_____ 1.   Which volume would be the best to find whether Catherine the Great ruled Austria, France, or Russia?

_____ 2.   Which volume would contain information about grasshoppers, crickets, and butterflies?

_____ 3.   Which volume would give you the most information about Bertrand Russell, a famous English mathematician?

_____ 4.   Which volume would be most likely to have pictures of a poodle, a Saint Bernard, and a German shepherd?

Figure 6–11.   Interpretive Exercise on Encyclopedia Use

Printed Music.   Another example of interpretive exercises would be printed music followed by objective questions. Again, the test maker should ensure that the passage was not previously known to examinees.

Objective questions can efficiently measure such basic skills as ability to decode time, key, and how long notes are held. Advanced topics such as analysis of mood, techniques, period, influences, and style can be addressed with either multiple-choice or essay questions.

From another angle, printed music can be used as the stimulus for a performance test. If the test is designed to determine how well each student can read music while performing it, an unfamiliar selection can be given to each student to perform.

Auditory Music.   If a music appreciation class were studying musical analysis or evaluation, a useful way to test these higher cognitive processes might be to play a tape of an *unfamiliar* passage of music. The accompanying questions would most often be printed multiple-choice items, but essay questions would also have potential. For that matter, even oral questions could be used.

Interpreting Maps.   Map skills are commonly assessed with interpretive exercises because they provide a realistic simulation of real-life map usage. If, for example, the test maker wants to know if pupils can use the key to determine distance, a multiple-choice question can ask how far it is from one city to another. Here again, it is important to ensure that students do not have the prior knowledge. For example, one would not want to ask how far New York City is from Chicago; too many students already know this without the map. It would be better to use a map of an obscure place (e.g., Zanzibar) so that few if any would have the prior knowledge of the distance between two cities. Better still to create a map of an imaginary place; then we can be sure that none has prior knowledge. This technique has the added advantage of enabling the map to be altered to fit the testing needs.

Although interpretive exercises based on maps usually rely exclusively on multiple-choice items, a broader variety of item types could be used. For example alternate-choice items could focus on which of two countries was better suited to grow various crops or develop specified industries. Or an essay item could ask students to compare and contrast the pros and cons of two potential sites for a steel mill.

Such questions raise the issue of whether stimulus materials must be sufficient to enable examinees to answer questions without other knowledge. No, they need not, provided that the requisite knowledge is either (a) universally known to examinees or (b) course relevant. An example of needed knowledge that might *not* be fair would be found in a map skills question asking which city would provide the best location for a ski resort. If all the students in the class know that skiing is done in high, cold places, all is well. But if some students have not had the opportunity to learn this and if it has not been part of the course, then it would be unfair to presume it.

An example of necessary knowledge that could well be course relevant is found in a map-interpretation item asking which city would be the best location for a steel mill. This question cannot be answered solely on the basis of information contained in the map. Examinees also have to know that steel production requires coal and iron, that transportation of raw resources and finished products is needed, and that a labor force is necessary. If this information has been part of the social studies course, then it is fair and valid to create interpretive exercise items that require both the ability (a) to decode raw resource, population, and transportation indicators on a map and (b) to integrate this information with the requisite knowledge.

A similar issue attends Items 2 and 4 in Figure 6–11. Is it fair to assume that pupils know that grasshoppers, crickets, and butterflies are insects? Assuming the science curriculum has covered this, then it seems very appropriate to tap pupils' ability to use superordinate categories on a test; this simulates use of the encyclopedia in real life.

Interpreting Cartoons.   Unfamiliar political cartoons provide a splendid way of measuring student knowledge and understanding of social studies or other content. For example, an *un*captioned cartoon can be accompanied by a multiple-choice item asking "Which of the following would be the best caption of this cartoon?" or "The point of this cartoon is." Or a cartoon can be accompanied by an item asking the name of the person or group to which it is sympathetic or hostile. A single cartoon may give rise to one or more items.

Analyzing Art Objects.   An art appreciation course or unit might well use interpretive exercises to assess important learning outcomes. Each stimulus could be either an art object such as a watercolor painting or mobile or a picture of it. Multiple-choice or essay items could be chosen to assess such things as student ability to identify, analyze, and/or evaluate such features as theme, style, technique, balance, movement, and period.

Critiquing Cooking.   Suppose a cooking class had studied how to analyze the features of a cake to judge what is right and what is wrong with it. A good way by which the teacher could test this skill would be to prepare batches of miniature cupcakes in which some things were deliberately done incorrectly. At the beginning of the test they would be distributed, one of each batch per examinee. Students could be directed first to eat the white cupcake and then to answer the multiple-choice items or essay question based on it. Then they would be instructed to eat the cherry-chip one and to answer the questions about it. Finally they would eat the chocolate cupcake and answer the items based on it.

Interpreting Blueprints.   Suppose a high school industrial arts class has studied "reading" blueprints. The most suitable way to test student skill in obtaining meaning from blueprints would be to provide a blueprint stimulus and to ask several questions about it.

A given print should not, of course, be used both for instruction and for testing. The instructor should keep secure those that are to be retained for testing.

Interpreting Experiments.   Student ability to interpret results from scientific experiments is very effectively measured by interpretive exercises. Experiments can either be pictured or described in words.

Interpreting Charts and Graphs.   One of the most common uses of context-dependent exercises involves the interpretation of charts and graphs. Figure 6–12 provides an example.

POPULATION CHANGES IN FIVE CITIES

Instructions: To the right is a chart that shows the population of five cities during a 100 year period. Use the information in the chart to answer the multiple choice questions that follow it.

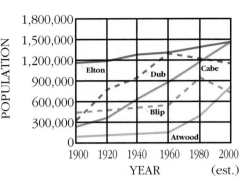

1. Which city grew the most during the century shown?
   A. Atwood
   B. Blip
   C. Cabe
   D. Dub
   E. Elton

2. Which city is expected to grow the most between 1980 and 2000?
   A. Atwood
   B. Blip
   C. Cabe
   D. Dub
   E. Elton

3. Which two cities had the same population in 1960?
   A. Atwood and Blip
   B. Blip and Dub
   C. Blip and Cabe
   D. Cabe and Dub
   E. Dub and Elton

4. Which city grew the least during the century?
   A. Atwood
   B. Blip
   C. Cabe
   D. Dub
   E. Elton

5. Which city had a decline in population before 1980?
   A. Atwood
   B. Blip
   C. Cabe
   D. Dub
   E. Elton

6. Which city has had the most steady growth?
   A. Atwood
   B. Blip
   C. Cabe
   D. Dub
   E. Elton

7. Which city is expected to be *smallest* in 2000?
   A. Atwood
   B. Blip
   C. Cabe
   D. Dub
   E. Elton

8. In 1950, the population of Dub was about
   A. 100,000
   B. 400,000
   C. 1,100,000
   D. 1,300,000
   E. 1,500,000

9. By about how many people did the population of Blip increase between 1960 and 1975?
   A. 100,000
   B. 350,000
   C. 450,000
   D. 750,000
   E. 900,000

10. In about what year did Cabe overtake Blip in size?
    A. 1900
    B. 1928
    C. 1960
    D. 1981
    E. 2000

Figure 6–12. Long Interpretive Exercise Based on Chart

Evaluating Performances.   Some school learning is designed to enable students to evaluate or judge performances. For example, a debate coach might want students to learn to analyze strong and weak points in debates. Interpretive exercises provide a good way to evaluate how proficient examinees are in judging. The stimulus might be a videotaped debate. The test items might be multiple-choice (e.g., "Which of the four debaters was strongest in so and so?"). Or alternate-choice items might be used (e.g., "Following are eight elements of a debate. Rate which team was superior in each."). Or students could be asked to list the two or three strongest points and the two or three weakest points for each team.

Suggestions for Developing Interpretive Exercises

1. **Find or create relevant stimulus materials**. When teaching is based on cognitive or affective developmental instructional objectives, Track C teaching and testing should concern transfer of learning. We want students to be able to apply their learning to new situations that are similar, but not identical, to those studied. If pupils have been studying how to use pie graphs, then the way to test their skills is to have them interpret *different or new* pie graphs. If the teacher has 12 pie graphs with which to teach and test the unit, then a couple might best be set aside for use in testing. The novelty of those to be used for testing should not be compromised by "teaching to the test." That is, no special teaching emphasis should be devoted to features found in the test graphs. If the teacher happened to end up using all 12 for teaching, then new stimuli should be created for testing purposes.

The same might be said for interpreting works of art, comprehending blueprints, or understanding cartoons. The need always exists to obtain some new interpretive exercise stimuli for testing. Where to get them?

Good stimulus materials should be collected, saved for use, and saved for re-use. They can be found in all sorts of places such as supplementary textbooks and newspapers. The best ones are often *created* specifically for testing.

When it comes to creating interpretive exercises, few teachers can sustain prolonged creative marathons. Rather, good item ideas more often occur one or two at a time. It is useful to jot down ideas when they occur. If an idea for a good interpretive exercise occurs while reading the evening paper, taking a shower, or driving to work, it should be cut out or jotted down. It is wise to keep a file of ideas for test items on each unit.

2. **Ensure context dependence**. When a teacher is creating interpretive exercises, she or he may easily slip and produce some that are answerable without reference to their stimuli. Prior knowledge should *not* be sufficient to answer items correctly. The purpose of context-dependent exercises is to assess examinee ability to obtain information from stimuli. To achieve this kind of assessment, the ability to answer each item must depend on correctly interpreting its stimulus.

3. **Modify the stimulus materials to suit testing purposes**. As one drafts test items, ideas often occur concerning how the stimulus could be altered to advantage. A stimulus might be edited to eliminate an ambiguity in a test item. Or a stimulus could be changed to provide an opportunity to add an item or two. The entire interpretive exercise is best viewed as fluid until all parts of it are completed. Successive refinements of items lead to revision of the stimulus, and conversely. The

test maker should move back and forth in "fine tuning" until the entire exercise is perfected.

For example, the exercises shown in Figure 6–12 started as a published chart of seven Australian cities' growth between 1931 and 1981. It was modified beyond recognition as the items were written and the total "package" evolved. This freedom to alter an original stimulus to suit one's testing purposes enables test makers to obtain more good test items from a given stimulus than might otherwise be possible.

4. **Seek sufficient numbers of items per stimulus**. It would not do to have students study a two-page reading passage that is followed by only one or two multiple-choice items. Nor would it be efficient to have examinees engage in detailed study of a complex map if only two or three questions are based on it. In selecting and developing stimulus materials, test makers should use only those that can support enough test questions to compensate for the time it takes to examine the material. A very short stimulus, such as a cartoon, may be justified if it only yields an item or two. A long stimulus, however, would have to produce several items in order to be cost effective with regard to examinee time.

5. **Avoid letting blocks of items depart from the weights specified in the test plan**. Interpretive exercise items, like matching exercise items, come in sets. It is possible to get so carried away in producing a block that sight is lost of the desired number of questions specified in a given cell of the test plan. With matching exercises, the items of which are generally easy to generate, this danger is great. With interpretive exercises, the items of which are generally difficult to produce, the problem is less likely to occur. Test makers nonetheless should always keep their test specifications in mind and resist temptation to depart from them (unless, of course, they have new insights that lead them to thoughtful revision).

Figure 6–12 contains 10 questions based on a single chart. Is this too many? Quite possibly; the test plan may not have indicated that many items for interpreting charts. Even if the specifications called for that many questions on charts, it would probably be better to have two shorter sets, based on somewhat different kinds of charts. The shorter sets would provide for more adequate content sampling, and would also make it easier to avoid items that clue other items.

Yet there is certainly no fault in generating as many items as shown in Figure 6–12; doing so provides more from among which to select the ones desired for final use. In this illustration, the last four questions developed (Items 7–10) contained somewhat different ideas than the more redundant first seven. If a teacher only needed five items for a test, being able to select a balanced five from the ten generated would be highly desirable.

6. **Adhere to standard item-writing rules**. One should observe the ordinary rules, such as avoiding careless use of specific determiners, preventing items from answering each other, and maintaining grammatical consistency between stem and options.

The standard rule that prohibits splitting an item between two pages has a corollary for interpretive exercises. Where possible, the entire exercise should be printed on one page, or at least on facing pages. Examinees should not have to turn pages back and forth between a stimulus and its items.

A rule often violated in interpretive exercises involves reading difficulty. For tests designed to measure any kind of achievement *other than* reading, it is important to keep the reading demands low. If students miss items on a social studies or science test because they have difficulty reading the stimulus materials, then the test is measuring their reading achievement in addition to their social studies or science achievement. In this context, the measurement of reading is *in*valid; it contaminates the exercise as a measure of social studies or science.

7. **Provide appropriate directions at the beginning of each exercise**. Ordinarily, each interpretive exercise should open with a statement that indicates the numbers of the items that are based on the stimulus. For example, "Items 7–12 are based on the map shown below. Use it to answer the questions." Or, "Carefully read the following newspaper ad, and then answer the three questions that follow it." Or, "Below is part of the Table of Contents from a book. Questions 1–6 are based on it. After you read each question, refer to the Table of Contents to decide which page would contain the beginning of the section you are to find."

QUIZ 6–2

Following is an interpretive exercise. A reading passage is accompanied by a set of questions. You are asked to critique the items. In addition to multiple-choice questions, the exercise contains item types discussed in the last chapter, thereby providing an opportunity to apply the material in Chapter 5 as well as Chapter 6.

The set as a whole has problems of directions to examinees and item type order. You need not address these topics; they will be taken up in Chapter 9.

Your task is limited to identifying what is wrong with each separate test item. Many of the questions suffer from multiple faults. Simply note what is wrong with each item; you need not try to revise it. Indeed, many of the items in this exercise are so fundamentally problematic that they should be discarded rather than revised.

Passage

As Lewis ate his "ham on rye" sandwich, he wondered what "rye" was. Later that afternoon at the library he looked it up in an encyclopedia and learned the following.

Rye cereal grass grows to be about five feet tall and produces an edible grain. This grain is used to make flour for bread, as animal feed, as a pasture plant, and for making alcoholic beverages. The plant's strong straw is used for animal bedding and roof thatching and for making cardboard, hats, and other products.

QUIZ 6–2 (cont.)

Rye is a relative of wheat that was long considered to be a weed because it invaded prehistoric wheat patches. But, as people migrated northward, the cold-resistant rye could survive where the wheat could not. It thus became a valued grain crop rather than an unwelcome invader. It probably originated in Asia Minor and gradually spread throughout Asia and Europe where it is now cultivated extensively.

Rye is sometimes called the "grain of poverty" because it grows in poor soils that will not support wheat. Although not quite as rich in protein as wheat, rye flour usually is made from the whole grain and therefore is richer in protein that white wheat flour.

Test Questions

1. What would be the best title for this passage?

    A. A Useful Weed   B. The Grain of Poverty

    C. Wheat's Poor Cousin   D. Ham on Rye

2. The author of the passage is

    A. feeling sorry for rye because of its bad reputation.

    B. concerned with rye's nutritional features.

    C. interested in the history of rye.

    D. trying to proselytize the use of rye.

3. "It" in line 2 refers to

    A. ham sandwich

    B. afternoons

    C. libraries.

    D. rye.

4. Rye is not as rich in protein as wheat because

    A. it will not grow where wheat grows.   C. it has more uses.

    B. it provides variety to diet.   D. it is easy to grow.

5. Rye

    A. originated in Africa.

    B. stalk is used for thatching roofs.

    C. used for making pumpernickel bread.

    D. has a bad reputation.

6. The word "cultivated" means

    A. refined.

    B. nurtured as a desired domestic crop.

QUIZ 6–2 (cont.)

    C. hoed.

    D. grown.

7. T F Wheat is always more nutritious than rye.

8. T F Because it is more susceptible to cold, wheat is not as desirable as rye.

9. Rye is sometimes called _____ .

10. Lewis looked "rye" up in the _____ in the _____ in the _____ .

KEY TO QUIZ 6–2

Preliminary Considerations

Two general problems can be noted. Both will be addressed in Chapter 9. One concerns the lack of directions for the exercise, including directions concerning guessing. The other concerns order of items types. In general, the multiple-choice items should be placed after the completion and true-false items.

Item Flaws

These items have many, many flaws. You are not expected to catch all of them. They are roughly ordered from most serious to least worrisome.

1. No clear best answer exists. Too, the basis by which "best" is to be judged is not specified. Finally, some measurement specialists recommend a vertical arrangement of options, like that found in Item 3. Other authorities are open to horizontal arrangement of options provided that they are arranged consistently among items.

2. First, there is no best answer. (That the item calls for an inference is not a fault, but there needs to be a good basis for making the inference.) Next, the vocabulary level of "proselytize" is quite high. (This is less worrisome in a reading test than it would be elsewhere, but even in a reading test, the difficulty is intended to reside primarily in the passage.) Fourth, the issue is not formulated in the stem. (Are we seeking the author's nationality, gender, age, motive, or what?) Finally, the options are not grammatically parallel.

KEY TO QUIZ 6–2 (cont.)

3. First, "it" is singular, but some of the options are plural; this provides a powerful clue. Second, finding the "it" in the passage should be made easy by numbering lines, bold facing the word, etc. Third, each option should end with a period.

4. There is no best answer; indeed the options do not address the reason for rye having less protein than wheat. Too, the negative "not" in the stem should be highlighted in some way. Next, the negative in Option A creates a double negative with the stem—a taboo. Also, the options are not only arranged in a nonvertical format, but one differing from that of Item 1. Finally, the word "it" should be moved to the stem to avoid repetition in each option.

5. No best answer exists among Options B, C, and D; the correctness of Option C is problematic because this correct fact is not presented in the passage; it requires specialized external knowledge. The issue is not formulated in the stem. Option C lacks a verb. The options are not parallel.

6. There is no one best answer; if this item were intended to refer to the meaning of "cultivated" in the passage's context, it should so state. Assuming that Option B is the keyed response, it is conspicuous by virtue of its length. The options are not parallel. "Cultivated" should be highlighted in the passage to make it easy to locate. In addition, an item should never be split between two pages (or even between two columns); it is too easy for examinees to overlook the options on the next page.

7. The "always" clues false, which the item is.

8. Triple-barreled item! (1. Is wheat more susceptible to cold? 2. Is wheat less desirable than rye? 3. If "yes" to both of the above, then is susceptibility to cold the reason for the lesser desirability?) Ambiguous (by virtue of point 3). Also ambiguous with respect to geographic location where it would be desirable.

9. No one best response ("A Cereal Grass," "A Weed," "The Grain of Poverty"?)

10. No one best response. Unreasonable number of blanks! Inconsistent length of blanks.

Chapter Summary

For good reason, the multiple-choice item is the most widely used objective item type. Some of its simpler forms are comprehensible to very young elementary school aged children. Some of its more complex forms are suitable for complex advanced subject matter.

Multiple-choice items are also appropriate for measuring a wide variety of mental processes. They can tap lower-level learning. They can also assess many kinds of higher mental processes. And they are well suited for use with novel stimuli such as reading passages, maps, charts, tables, and graphs.

Multiple-choice items—indeed objectives in general—are efficient. They provide much information per unit of testing time. Properly used, they enable broad-range content sampling.

As will be stressed in Chapters 7 and 8, many important outcomes of school learning exist that are not adequately assessed by multiple-choice items. While they are by no *means* a panacea to all measurement needs, they are so versatile that they merit their great popularity.

The construction of multiple-choice items requires much skill in item writing as well as knowledge of examinees and good grasp of subject matter. Good items are not produced in a hurry or under pressure. Like other professional products, meritorious multiple-choice items grow out of careful preliminary planning of the total product (i.e., table of specifications for the total test), insightful and/or creative forethought about the individual elements (i.e., generating good item ideas), and thoughtful, skillful, and creative revision to fashion each element (i.e., item).

None of us will ever fully master this challenging literary form. Developing good multiple-choice questions that *contribute to our teaching effectiveness* is a career-long *developmental* objective.

Interpretive exercises enable teachers to measure some (but not all) higher mental processes in more effective ways than individual multiple-choice items or essay questions allow. The great virtue of interpretive exercises is the *realism* with which they represent or simulate *applications* of school learning. By basing several items on a single stimulus, reasonable efficiency can be achieved even if the stimulus is complex and consumes quite a bit of examinee time.

Interpretive exercises require more time, effort, and skill to prepare than do other item types. But their superb capacity to assess transfer of learning—and to signal its importance—renders them well worth the effort.

Suggestions for Further Reading

Educational Testing Service. (1973). *Multiple-choice questions: A close look.* Princeton, NJ: Educational Testing Service. Presents an excellent, brief general discussion of multiple-choice items and provides some of the most widely reproduced samples in the literature of fine interpretive exercises.

Gronlund, N. E., & Linn, R. L. (1990). *Measurement and evaluation in teaching* (6th ed.). New York: Macmillan. Chapter 7, "Constructing Objective Test Items: Multiple-Choice Forms" provides a fine elementary discussion and set of rules for constructing multiple-choice items. Chapter 8, "Measuring Complex Achievement: The Interpretive Exercise," is unusual in being devoted wholly to this important kind of test question and in providing a superb discussion of it.

Hopkins, K. D., Stanley, J. C., & Hopkins, B. R. (1990). *Educational and psychological measurement and evaluation* (7th ed.). Englewood Cliffs, NJ: Prentice-Hall. Chapter 9, "Constructing Objective Tests," presents sound advice for constructing various kinds of objective items, including multiple-choice questions and interpretive exercises.

Wesman, A. G. (1971). Writing the test item. In Thorndike, E. L. (Ed.), *Educational Measurement* (2nd ed.). Washington, DC: American Council on Education. Provides a richly illustrated discussion of three distinct kinds of context-dependent items.

Developing and Scoring Essays and Other Product Measures

The essay is the oldest form of paper-pencil test question. Its use dates back to ancient times. Until the first part of the twentieth century, essay and short-answer items were virtually the only written item forms used.

The popularity of the newer objective items attests to several serious limitations of the essay item type. Essays take more time to administer, require more time to mark, can sample fewer items of content per unit of testing time, and tend to provide less reliable results than objective items. Yet the rise of objective item types has not rendered essays obsolete. They remain popular and useful. Essays retain their place in educational testing because they are superior to objective items in measuring certain educational outcomes.

Actually, essays belong to a larger category of item types called **product measures**. In product measurement the examinee is directed to create a specified product, which is then assessed. Thus a product measure is simply an assessment of a product *after* it has been completed. Some products are created under tightly managed, standard conditions. Others are produced under the uncontrolled conditions of everyday life. The assessment can be analytic, objective, and detailed, or it can be impressionistic and global. This chapter concerns product measurement, with special attention to its most widely used special case, the essay.

The Nature of Product Measures

Variety

Measurement of educational achievement is enriched by a wide variety of product measures. Some examples will illustrate the breadth of practices that come under this heading.

A primary class has been studying manuscript writing. Each child copies a sentence from the chalkboard and creates a written product that can be evaluated for quality of writing. In this case, the products are developed under uniform conditions.

A keyboarding teacher is interested in how accurately and how rapidly each student can keyboard. Each student is provided with a copy of a given passage and directed to keyboard as much of it as the time limit allows under highly standardized, timed conditions. The resulting copy is a product that the teacher can examine to determine how accurately and how rapidly each student performed.

Students in a woodworking class have spent several weeks making sturdy, four-legged, wooden, stepping stools to conform to specified plans and drawings. The instructor assigns grades for this project by examining each student's finished stool and rating it on each feature of concern (e.g., strength of joints, smoothness, squareness of corners, and uniformity of wood stain application).

An art teacher who has been instructing pupils in certain techniques gives them an assignment that involves use of these methods. The products of this assignment are then examined to judge how well pupils use the techniques. If the assignment is completed in class, then the conditions under which each pupil completes it are relatively standard; in this case, a relatively strong basis exists for assessment. On the other hand, if the assignment is given for homework, then the circumstances under which pupils undertake the assignment may vary widely; in this case the less uniform conditions render the assessment less than ideal for judging pupils' skills.

High school students may be given a demanding assignment to produce a research paper. When completed, these products are graded by the teacher. Like homework, out-of-class assignments, major compositions, and so on, this is a case in which conditions are not well controlled. Thoughtful teachers are acutely aware that the amount of assistance (legitimate and questionable) differs greatly from student to student. Yet it is not practical to have students complete long, complex projects under tightly controlled conditions. Thus a judgment is often made that the loss of standard conditions is an acceptable trade-off for the realism of the work conditions under which a project is completed outside of class.

A cooking teacher is interested in how well students can follow a new recipe. This ability to transfer prior learning is tested by giving each student a copy of the recipe and sufficient ingredients, equipment, and time to use it. Assessment is then made of the finished products. In addition to visually inspecting the cooked products, the teacher also tastes each student's dish in order to judge its other qualities.

Students are given a social studies essay exam. The teacher examines the essays produced under highly standardized conditions to assess each person's command of the topic.

These examples illustrate the variety of product measures. Chapter 10 will address how these and other kinds of measures can be used both (a) formatively to enhance learning and (b) summatively to improve learning.

Product Measures vs. Objective Measures vs. Performance Measures

The above examples illustrate the rich diversity that exists among product measures. The defining feature they share is their focus of measurement and evaluation on the final *product* of examinee labor, *not* on the production *process* or on *questions about* the work.

To sharpen this distinction, reconsider the keyboarding test. On the one hand, the teacher could have given an objective test about how to keyboard. This would provide a useful method of assessing *knowledge* of such things as proper margin size. **Objective items** could also measure *understanding* of why certain things are or are not recommended, *analysis* of the likely impact of doing various things, *evaluation* of pages, etc. An objective test, however, would *not* provide a valid means of assessing students' actual *skill* in typing.

On the other hand, the teacher could have observed each student as he or she keyboarded. Such a **performance measure** would be a useful and authentic means of assessing certain aspects of performance, such as posture, hand positioning, and eye activity. However, it would not provide a direct measure of what each student's finished page looks like. Moreover, it would be much more time consuming to observe each student separately while he or she reproduces the entire page than to test all at the same time and then only inspect the finished product.

When to Use Product Measures

Recall the three-step decision rule provided in Chapter 4:

1. Those instructional objectives that can be assessed with objective items should be.

2. Of the remaining objectives, those that can be assessed with essay and other product measures should be.

3. Only the remaining objectives should be assessed by means of performance measures.

Recall also that these rules should not be used in isolation and that other criteria should be considered. The rationale of these rules can be developed a little more at this time.

Three examples will be used to illustrate simple use of this three-step evaluation rule. Then two more examples will introduce other considerations that should contribute to a teacher's thoughtful professional judgment concerning which method(s) of student evaluation to use.

Interpreting and Constructing Graphs.   Suppose a class has been studying the *interpretation* and *construction* of charts, tables, and graphs. What method(s) should the teacher use to assess student achievement?

As noted in the last chapter, context-dependent items based on such things as charts, tables, and graphs provide an excellent means of measuring higher-order learning outcomes involving student ability to *interpret* the stimuli (Terwilliger, 1989). To assess this objective, we need not move beyond the first step of the decision rule. Because of the novelty of the material presented for interpretation, it is possible to test higher mental processes with objective items. True, one could use essay questions about charts, tables, or graphs, but they would be much less efficient in terms of (a) testing time, (b) marking time, and (c) breadth of coverage than would well-constructed objective items.

The best way to measure people's ability to *construct* charts, tables, and graphs is to have them do it. A teacher could, for example, provide data in prose or tabular form and direct students to construct pie or bar graphs to represent the data. (Depending on the teacher's objectives and the class's experience with computers, the test directions might or might not permit use of computers and graphics software.) Their resulting products would then be assessed. This evaluation of each examinee's graph will take more time than marking several objective items, but it is worth it. Teachers simply cannot measure student ability to *construct* graphs with multiple-choice or other objective items. Thus this goal demands a move to the second step of the three-step decision rule.

Composing Coherent Paragraphs.   A second example of the three-step decision rule is the ability to *compose* well-developed, purposeful paragraphs. If a teacher, an educational institution, or a prospective employer wants to know how well a given person can write, then there is one clearly superior way to find out—have the person write and then assess the results.

True, we could ask objective questions about mechanics of construction. Alternate-choice items are better than essays to determine whether a student can correctly choose between "whom" and "who" or can correctly capitalize. Similarly, multiple-choice items are excellent for assessing skill in editing composition such as deciding which elements in a sentence are acceptable or choosing which of several ways would be the best to express an idea.

If our aim had been to measure mechanics of construction, we could have "jumped off" at the first step of the decision rule. However, since the goal is to assess how well people actually compose paragraphs, students must compose. This results in a product—the second step in the decision rule.

Driving a Car. A driver education teacher might consider the three-step decision-making rule for assessing students' driving. Before doing so, it may be useful to discriminate between *knowledge* of driving laws and safety rules and *skill* in driving. Both are important. Indeed, a student must be able to exhibit both in order to be licensed.

Concerning the knowledge aims of driver education, the first step in the decision rule provides the means of assessment. Knowledge can be adequately assessed with paper-pencil objective testing. Therefore it should be. Yes, essays could be used, but they would be an inefficient means of measuring the kinds of knowledge required for driving. Using essays would cost more time and effort and would produce less valid assessment of knowledge.

Concerning driving skills, the first step of the rule does not end the quest for an appropriate measurement method. Objective paper-pencil items will *not* adequately assess how well a person can operate a car. So we go on to the second step. Product measures are not much better. Paper-pencil products such as essays would be no more satisfactory than objective items. Accident and citation records could be considered as products. Indeed insurance companies use such data in establishing people's insurance rates. However, the driver education teacher does not have this option. Driving records take much time to accumulate, and the teacher must make evaluation decisions before students have amassed records.

Thus the teacher must move on to the final step of the decision-making rule. This move leads to performance measurement—observing the student as the car is driven and rating various facets of the performance. Unfortunately, this method is even more time consuming (and unnerving) than reading essays, but it is the only authentic way to measure driving skills. Thus the teacher would elect it. Chapter 8 is devoted to performance measures.

History. Recall from Chapter 4, Mrs. Orr's detailed plans for her history final. Admirably, she used multiple-choice items to assess lower-level knowledge of history as well as to assess some understanding, analysis, and application. She reserved essay questions for those things that are not well assessed by objective items.

She may well have had an additional reason for using some essay items. Some students typically do better on objective tests, others on essay tests. It seems fairer for tests to contain both item types in order not to give a systematic advantage to either group of students. This issue of balance is one reason why the above decision-making rule should not be used in isolation.

When should the principle of **balance** be invoked? When should it not be? Balance should *not* be considered when there is only one sensible way to measure instructional objectives. The driver education instructor should *not* seek balance between essay and objective items in assessing knowledge of driving laws. Nor should the person seeking to learn how well a job candidate can compose paragraphs. The criterion of balance should be invoked only when there is more than one valid way by which to measure the objectives.

Balance can be considered whenever one's general, Track C objectives can be assessed reasonably well by either essay or objective items. Consider the following developmental objective and its indicants.

Understands historical terminology.

1. Matches terms with correct, but novel, definitions.
2. Given a novel situation, selects from several options the term that best describes the situation.
3. Provides original examples of a given term's applications.
4. Uses terms correctly in writing.

The first two indicants point to objective items. The last two examples point to essay items. Which to use?

The first step in the decision-making rule leads to objective items. The criterion of balance leads to mixed objective and essay tests. Still other considerations such as teacher preference and class size may pull one way or the other. The point is that the above decision-making rule alone does not suffice. Other things, such as assessment balance, logistics, and teacher preference, should also be considered.

Cooking an Omelet.   Suppose a home economics teacher needs to assess student ability to cook a simple omelet. Objective questions could be used to measure knowledge about how it is cooked. Or the final omelet could be inspected, tasted, and rated. Or the performance of cooking the omelet could be witnessed, scrutinized, and rated. Which is best?

Of course, from a formative, *instructional* perspective, watching the process and giving diagnostic feedback have much merit. However, this is often impractical. Neither the woodshop instructor, the keyboarding teacher, nor the cooking teacher can be everywhere at once, observing all the students simultaneously. Fortunately, it is often possible to tell in retrospect what processes were faulty; thus formative, diagnostic feedback can often be provided from retrospective assessment of products. For example, if the wax on the wood stool is gummy, the instructor can quite soundly deduce that adequate drying time was not allowed between coats.

From a summative evaluation perspective, the decision-making rule's first step leads to the question of how well the essence of omelet cooking can be captured by objective items. Actually, the skill of omelet cooking (unlike that of driving) consists of relatively simple components on which students already have good motor control. The main difficulty of the task involves *knowing* how much margarine to put in the skillet, how much water to mix with the beaten eggs, how to judge when the skillet reaches the right temperature for pouring in the eggs/water mix, etc. It is more a matter of simple cognitive knowledge than of complex, integrated cognitive/motor control. These relatively simple knowledge elements can be tested quite satisfactorily with objective items.

Another angle in this example is the speed with which omelets deteriorate. Unlike a stack of essays, omelets cannot be stored until they can conveniently be examined and tasted. This issue renders product assessment less attractive than it otherwise would be.

In view of these issues, the teacher might well decide to test omelet cooking with an objective, paper-pencil test rather than with a performance or product measure.

One important issue remains to be considered, however. It is the recurring theme of this book that *classroom evaluation practices impact on student effort.*

Before deciding on objective testing of omelet making, the teacher should ask, "Will knowledge that they will be tested on paper rather than at the range cause students to study differently? If so, is the difference desirable?" The likely answer to the first question is "yes," so the second question must be addressed.

If the teacher believes that changes in student study caused by a shift to paper-pencil testing are either desirable or neutral, then he or she could proceed without misgivings. However, if the answer to the second question is "no," then use of objective items would *not* be a good idea. Although economical of testing time and teacher time, and likely to yield more reliable results than would alternatives, objective items would have negative consequences.

Developing Product Measures

Developing effective product measures is, at times, quite simple. More often, however, their formulation requires skill and time. Suggestions will be offered in this section to assist teachers in devising measures that (a) validly assess their teaching objectives and (b) influence student efforts in desirable ways.

Rules for Writing Effective Essay Questions

1. **Use essays mainly to measure higher mental processes**. Essays do not provide a reliable or cost-effective means of assessing factual recall. They can be used to measure it, but it is not efficient to do so.

Suppose a science teacher wants to assess student knowledge of the names of the three main kinds of blood vessels and understanding of their respective functions. The knowledge objective would best be assessed by means of select- or supply-type objective questions. The understanding objective could well be assumed either with multiple-choice or essay items.

Items 1 and 2 in Figure 7–1 exemplify essays that tap higher mental processes. In focusing on the complementariness of arteries and veins (presumably in terms somewhat different from those used in instruction), Item 1 penetrates beneath mere surface knowledge. Novelty plays a larger role in Item 2 insofar as it presents an impossible situation. Students who understand circulation should find it relatively easy to analyze the case presented in Item 2 and detect why it is not possible.

For another example, suppose an upper elementary class has been studying a particular work of fiction with a focus on the concept that everybody has problems. Class discussion has focused on each character's problems with consideration that some of the problems were obvious to other people. Other problems, however, were apparent only to the character. Items 3 and 4 in Figure 7–1 illustrate the use of essay questions that measure mental processes higher than the mere statement of the principle that "everybody has problems." It must be assumed, of course, that class discussion has not focused on the exact applications referenced in Items 3 and 4; to measure higher mental processes, some item novelty is necessary.

2. **Phrase items so that examinees know what is expected**. Regardless of whether students are able to respond well to an essay question, they should know what the charge is. Said differently, the basis on which responses will be evaluated

1. Briefly explain how arteries and veins complement each other. That is, tell how they work together to make up an effective system of circulation. Focus your discussion on arteries and veins, but mention briefly how the capillaries fit into the system.

2. Suppose a certain animal's circulation system consisted of arteries and capillaries, but no veins. What key problem would this create? In other words, why would this circulation system **not** work?

3. Remember when we read "Jim and the Oak Tree." Jim's sister Synthia was usually unpleasant to Jim and his friends Mick and Joe. The boys thought Synthia was "just plain mean." Think of two problems that could have caused Synthia to act the way she did to the boys. List these two possible problems in at least a complete sentence each.

4. Think of someone you have known whom you never thought of as having any problems, or at least not big ones. Now use what we have learned about everybody having problems to identify two problems that this person probably had. Explain why you think each problem was likely.

Figure 7–1. Sample Essay Items That Measure Higher Mental Processes

should be clear. Figure 7–2 provides examples of vague items that have been revised to provide clearer instruction. When ambiguity is removed, some of the alternative ways of interpreting an item are eliminated. The purpose is to eliminate those that the test maker does not desire, causing students to focus on those issues that the test maker wants. Other improved versions would, of course, be possible.

In Item 1, ambiguity is caused by the fact that three Kennedy brothers (not to mention the possibility of others having that surname) each served in the United States Senate. Another dimension of ambiguity is the issue of which senate, national, state, or foreign. Even if students realize the item is intended to refer to John F. Kennedy, a third difficulty lies in the fact that he was twice elected to the United States Senate.

Item 2 refers to a long period of history (before Pope John XXIII in the 1960s) when Roman Catholics gave up meat on Fridays for religious reasons. Here is the ambiguity: Because many markets carried fish on Thursdays and Fridays to accommodate Catholic customers, the best selection of fish was for Fridays. However, many non-Catholics who liked fish chose to eat it on Friday. The revised version of Item 2

Ambiguous Items	**Improved Versions**
1. Describe the election of Mr. Kennedy to the Senate.	1. Describe the election of John F. Kennedy to his first term in the United States Senate.
2. Why did many people used to eat fish on Fridays?	2. What was the religious reason why many people used to eat fish on Fridays?
3. What causes the price of an item to go up?	3. In general, if more people want to buy an item, what happens to its price? In a well-written paragraph, explain why.

Figure 7–2. Ambiguous Essay Items and Their Improved (But Still Poor) Revisions

eliminates this excess reason for why in many communities more non-Catholics than Catholics ate fish on Fridays.

For an elementary class that has studied the effect of demand on price, Item 3 is ambiguous for students who know more than this one relationship. Other factors (e.g., supply) affect prices. The revised version focuses on the relationship between supply and price.

These three items have been improved by clear thinking and careful wording. Other ways of eliminating ambiguity are delimitation of topics and structuring of questions. Provision of appropriate delimitation and structure will be the next two suggestions. These topics obviously overlap.

Even though ambiguity has been eliminated from the three items in Figure 7–2, their quality is still only very modest. They measure nothing more than the recall of material. To be sure, the content is meaningful, but the three improved items require nothing more than retrieval of material from memory. Therefore, they tend to violate Rule 1.

3.   **Delimit topics appropriately**. First drafts of questions are often absurdly open-ended, giving little or no hint to hapless examinees concerning what they are to address in their limited time. Figure 7–3 provides examples of both inadequately delimited questions and some improved versions. To emphasize the obvious point that there are often many possible ways to focus an item, the first two examples have each been delimited in alternative ways.

Inadequately Delimited Items	**Improved Versions**
1. Discuss modern communication in the United States.	1a. Describe how modern communication in the United States helps business.
	1b. How has family life in the United States been influenced by the invention of the airplane and the telephone?
2. Describe the growth of the American Labor Movement from the Industrial Revolution to the present.	2a. Public and government attitudes toward organized labor have changed in the United States from the Industrial Revolution until the present. Contrast the early public attitudes with current ones.
	2b. Describe two major problems faced by early American labor organizers that are no longer big problems. How was each of the problems overcome?
3. How has Spanish culture influenced life in the United States?	3. Imagine that Columbus had been financed by Henry VII of England and that Spain never became a major New World power. Describe some likely ways in which our Standard American English language in the United States would be different than it now is.

Figure 7–3.   Inadequately Delimited Items and Their Improved Versions

How well do the improved items in Figure 7–3 conform to Rule 1 and measure higher mental processes? If the class's study has not focused on family or business in its study of modern communications, then improved Items 1a and 1b call for some original thinking beyond mere recall. Similarly, for the improved Items 2a and 2b, the adequacy of the questions depends on how closely they parallel instruction. If some novelty characterizes the items, they may tap higher mental processes. Finally, improved Item 3 seems the most likely to require original (yet fairly easy) thinking; however, even here one cannot be certain that the item measures higher mental processes without knowing that the instruction did not specifically treat this idea.

4. **Provide appropriate structure**. The amount of organizational guidance that is desirable depends on the maturity of the examinees and the skill to be measured. If the teacher wants students to respond along relatively uniform lines, then it is generally desirable to provide the components of the answer. On the other hand, if one wants to assess ability to select the elements, then, of course, the elements should not be provided in the question.

Item 1 in Figure 7–4 provides two levels of structure for an elementary school science item. The structure of the improved version achieves several things. Student discussion is focused on what the teacher has in mind; thus the item is a more valid measure of what it is intended to assess. Second, the accuracy of marking the answers is enhanced because all pupils will attempt to respond to the same elements; otherwise some comparability is lost when some examinees respond to different elements than others. Third, pupil ability to bluff is impeded. That is, those who lack the desired knowledge are not as able to "talk around the topic" in highly structured questions as they are in relatively open-ended items. (Or if they try to, their bluff is more transparent.)

Items 2 to 4 in Figure 7–4 provide other examples of use of structure. By providing the guidance, the teacher assures that the desired points will be addressed by those students who are able to do so, that they will be given the intended relative emphasis, and that individual students will not digress onto unintended topics.

How well do the items in Figure 7–4 require thinking beyond mere recall? Improved Item 1 seems to, provided that pupils have not been instructed to memorize the comparison and contrast. Improved Items 2 and 3 seem mainly to require recall. Such learning could probably better be assessed with objective items. Improved Item 4 clearly requires transfer of learning.

5. **Phrase questions to elicit the desired responses**. The wording of essays is important. It can make the difference between questions that elicit verbatim retrieval of meaningless information and ones that require mindful processing of meaningful information. Between these extremes are many items that require recall of meaningful material such as Improved Items 2 and 3 in Figure 7–4. Such items are not really bad items, yet they fail to rise above mediocrity.

Wording or phrasing, then, is the means of following the first suggestion to use essay questions for the measurement of higher mental processes. Figure 7–5 provides two lists of essay item phrases. In most contexts, the items in the first list would prompt nothing more than recall. The phrases in the second list are apt, in many situations, to demand higher levels of thinking.

Another perspective of this rule concerns obtaining the *desired study activities.* Because students tend to study in ways that reflect the kind of learning their teachers assess, it is important to phrase a suitable fraction of test items—be they objective or essay questions—in ways that elicit higher mental activities. This guides students

Inadequately Structured Items	**Improved Versions**
1. Compare caterpillars to true worms.	1. Compare and contrast caterpillars and true worms. Explain how they are alike and different in: (a) the major group of animals to which each belongs, (b) their methods of locomotion ("walking"), and (c) their life stages.
2. Describe life insurance.	2. Describe life insurance with about a paragraph each explaining (a) its purpose, (b) how it works, and (c) what kinds of people most need it.*
3. Tell about the peanut and its uses.	3. Describe the peanut and its uses, using about one paragraph each for (a) its nutritional value, (b) its effect on soil, and (c) its uses and their origin.*
4. How has Spanish culture influenced life in the United States?	4. Spanish culture has influenced life in the United States, even for those who have no Spanish or Mexican ancestry. Give one example each of its influence on our (1) food, (2) language, (3) place names, and (4) recreation. **Your examples must be ones that were NOT used in class.**

*Although improved from the perspective of structure, this item still seems to fail to assess more than mere knowledge.

Figure 7–4. Inadequately Structured Essay Items and Their Improved Versions

to more deeply process what they try to learn rather than merely to commit it to memory.

6. **Indicate the relative weight of essay questions**. The value or weight of each question in a test should be indicated. This can be accomplished in several ways. If all the questions carry the same weight, the directions can so indicate. If items have unequal number of possible points, then this information should accompany individual items. Notice is often given with an indication of number of points possible in parenthesis at the end of each question. Or relative importance can be communicated by suggesting number of minutes to be allocated for each item. This is especially helpful for students who are not very accomplished in budgeting their test time.

7. **Sample learning as fully as feasible**. Essay questions take longer to answer than do objective questions; therefore, essay tests must contain fewer items. These larger sampling "chunks" often lead to serious imbalance of test content; tested topics tend to be overemphasized, while unsampled ones are neglected. Although this limitation of the essay item type is inherent, and to some degree has to be tolerated, it should be kept to a minimum.

One way to maintain content balance in essay tests is to devise questions that span more content. For example, if a class has studied the presidential elections of the twentieth century, a question could span three elections by asking: "Evaluate the

Phrasing Likely to Require Only Recall

What were the three major causes of the Civil War?
Define an "out" in softball.
Describe the battle of New Orleans.
Explain how to convert inches into centimeters.
How does photosynthesis work?
Outline the fall of Rome.
Explain "balance of nature."
Identify the major exploits of Alexander the Great.
List the key events in the Watergate scandal.
Quote FDR's two most famous lines.
Describe the nutritional value of sugar.
Reproduce Mark Antony's funeral address.
Who was Hamlet?
What is relativity?

Phrasing Likely to Call for Higher Levels of Thinking

In what important ways does a . . . differ from a . . . ?
Compare and contrast . . . .
Analyze the reasoning behind the recommendations to . . . .
If . . . , what would be the likely effect on . . . ?
What would happen if . . . ?
Judge the importance of . . . . In explaining, focus on . . . .
A new kind of . . . has these features: . . . . Evaluate its likely value.
Why is it difficult to achieve both . . . and . . . at the same time?
Identify the major assumptions underlying the case for . . . .
What values are likely to motivate people to . . . ?
How would . . . likely have responded to the proposal to . . . ?

Figure 7–5. Essay Phrases Likely to Prompt Recall vs. Higher Levels of Thinking

relative importance of the 'Catholic Issue' in the elections of 1920, 1960, and 1988. Make a case either that the differences do or do not represent a trend in voter religious tolerance or intolerance."

Another way to enhance content balance in essay tests is to provide brief-response rather than the long-answer questions. A larger number of more delimited items enables broader content sampling. This solution tends to be quite attractive in content areas in which emphasis is in assessing student command of some area *other than* ability to write. By providing more structure and focus, teachers of social studies, literature, science, health, etc., can specify relatively sharply targeted responses that require less time. However, if a language arts teacher is interested in testing student ability to *organize* and *structure* content for themselves, the use of more restrictive essay questions would not be attractive.

Devising Other Kinds of Effective Product Measures

General rules for devising effective product measures closely parallel those for developing essay examinations. Because essays are a special case of product measures, this similarity is hardly surprising.

1. **Use product measures to assess achievement that is not more easily assessed by other means**. Consider the ability to produce geometric proofs. It is not possible to test this ability with objective item types. Although objective items *about*

proofs can be used for some purposes, teachers who are keenly interested in student ability to *develop their own proofs* have no alternative to proof items. Or consider the metal shop teacher interested in student ability to *drill* a hole. Objective items will not do. Or the art teacher who wants to know if primary students can *mix* primary colors to obtain the desired shades. The most straightforward way to measure this objective might be to provide sample shades and the three primary pigments and ask each pupil to match the shades.

Before embarking on the extra difficulties inherent in product measures, it is prudent to ask if some of the learning outcomes could be approached with objective items. If so, then product measures might be reserved to supplement objective items rather than used exclusively. For example, the geometry teacher might use multiple-choice items to determine if students can identify from verbal statements what is given and what is to be proved. The metal shop teacher could show pictures of persons drilling and ask objective questions to see if examinees can recognize what is right or wrong about the procedures pictured. The art teacher could show a picture of a particular color (e.g., a yellow-green) and a picture of a target color (e.g., a mid green). Students might be asked which primary color needs to be added to the first picture to approach the second.

It is efficient to use product measures only when objective items, for one reason or another, will not do the job. Moreover, it is sensible to resort to product measures for only those parts of the job for which objective items are not well suited. However, where objective items do not suffice, it is necessary to use product measures in spite of the logistical difficulties they introduce.

2. **Delimit and structure tasks clearly so that examinees know what is expected**. Suppose a home economics class has been studying a particular sewing stitch. To obtain a summative measure of student skill in producing this stitch, a product assessment would be in order. Students would each be given cloth, needles, and thread. Instructions should clearly specify what aspects of the product are going to be evaluated.

Or consider an elementary science assignment to summarize a current science event. Does clarity of expression count? Does spelling? Neatness? Length? Well-phrased questions address most such issues.

3. **Indicate relative weight of performance tasks**. Suppose a woodshop class is given the stool assignment described earlier. This task has several facets, and the relative weight of features such as joint strength, adequacy of sanding, smoothness of varnish, and dryness of wax should be clearly indicated in advance. This guides student effort.

Or consider the art test in which the students are asked to create five simple products. Their relative weight should be known to the students so that they can budget their time appropriately. This not only enhances fairness, it also harnesses test power.

4. **Sample learning as fully as possible**. A more complete sample of the breadth of student skill can usually be obtained from several, varied, short tasks than from one long one. For example in the art test described in the preceding paragraph, several simple or partial tasks provide a more complete picture of each student's skills than would one complex or full product.

On the other hand, there are times when it seems more valid to have students fully complete an integrated product. Where this is the case, be it a work of art, a mathematical proof, the preparation of a complex meal, or the development of a research paper, it is important for the teacher to choose the product with care. The one selected should encompass as many of the component skills as possible. Thus the woodshop stool project that involved measuring, drilling, gluing, decorating, planing, sanding, varnishing, and waxing would be superior to a project that involved fewer skills.

Some Instructional Issues

As has been mentioned repeatedly, the means by which students (or other people) are to be assessed tends to influence the direction their efforts will take. This section examines the probable instructional impact of two sets of practices that are commonly used with essay tests and other product measures.

Giving Students a Choice of Tasks

Most teachers who use essay examinations or other product measures often provide students with more questions or other tasks than they are required to address; this allows examinees a choice. For example, a geometry test might consist of four formal proofs from which each student is instructed to prove three. Or an essay exam in English might consist of five questions, with instructions to respond to any four.

The popularity of this practice resides mainly in two issues. First, without question, the practice is popular with students. Students (and sometimes teachers) think that students are being given something. This is illusory. Here is why. Product measures are usually used to assess Track C content. Recall that such content must be provided norm-referenced interpretations. The raw score is thus an immaterial artifact; the important issue about people's performance is their status relative to performance of other people. Therefore, providing a choice of tasks does not give examinees anything in a norm-referenced sense because each has the same "advantage."

Second as noted above, essay tests, having relatively few items, tend to provide less balanced and less comprehensive sampling. These limitations tend to make teachers uncomfortably aware that their essay tests lack comprehensive content coverage. Here is a common scenario. The unit consists of six main topics. The test plan calls for a question on each. The teacher, therefore, develops the six essay questions. Then to her or his dismay, the realization sinks in that answering all six would take much more time than the test period. What to do? Ah! Do the popular thing and give students a choice of four of the six questions. The students are happy in the illusion that they have been given something for nothing, and the teacher is happy in the illusion that content balance has been preserved. Actually, of course, it has not. The four questions that each examinee selects provide just as imbalanced a coverage of the total unit as would have resulted from the teacher's choice of four items.

The common reasons that most often lead to offering a choice of tasks are therefore not sound. What else is to be said for and against the practice?

The conventional wisdom expressed in measurement books is that choice of tasks should *not* be offered. Here is the thinking behind the admonition. When different people perform different tasks, the basis of comparability is reduced. To illustrate, consider an extreme example. At a track meet, Hank competes only in the pole vault and Joe only in the 100-meter dash. The two events have no common contestants. Each comes in second in his event. Who performed better?

Who knows! There is no basis provided by which to compare them. If we wish to make comparative (i.e., norm-referenced) statements about people (as we often do for Track B content and as we always do for Track C content) then we need a basis by which to compare each examinee's performance with that of a relevant group of other examinees. To the extent that different students perform different tasks, the basis of comparison—that is, the basis of norm referencing—is compromised.

The reasoning that leads to the taboo on choice of tasks is clearly correct. No doubt about it; offering a choice of essay questions or other tasks always reduces reliability.

However, reliability is not the only issue. Another extremely important issue concerns impact of evaluation practice on student effort. To consider that (frequently neglected) dimension of the problem, return to the scenario in which the teacher ended up offering students a choice of four out of six questions. Suppose some astute members of the class have her or him "psyched out" and correctly anticipate a question on each of the six topics and then a choice of questions. They therefore reason that they can safely neglect one or two of the topics from their study and reallocate the time saved to the other topics. Would this appall you? *That* is the main question.

In many settings, it would indeed be undesirable. If each of the six topics is important, if the topics are quite sequential (as might be the case in geometry or Spanish), or if a level achievement profile for the six topics is the main concern, then you would be dismayed that an evaluation practice was leading students away from a study practice deemed desirable. In that case you should, of course, not offer a choice of questions.

In other situations, however, it would not distress you that some students were opting out of one or two of the topics with immunity. For example, in a unit on contemporary short stories, a teacher might not mind if a student studied four of the stories more intensively. There is nothing vital about any one of the stories. The content is not particularly sequential. Uniform knowledge of them is no particular virtue. In this context, if you are not appalled, then decide whether you feel indifference or a favorable attitude to the more concentrated study of only four of the topics. If neutral, you should probably discontinue the practice of providing choice of questions because of its cost in reliability. If favorable, you should go ahead and provide a choice of questions, but let all students know ahead of time how they will be tested. There should be no special academic benefit to those who "psych you out."

Providing Questions or Tasks in Advance

Two additional practices are common enough to warrant attention. One involves giving out the exact questions or other tasks ahead of time so that students can prepare for them. Is this advisable?

The answer depends on the nature of the subject matter. If the subject matter is a small, closed, vital content domain (i.e., Track A content), then each student must master it in its entirety. In that context, test content is no secret. (It is unlikely, however, that one should be using essay questions to assess this kind of content. Objective items are more efficient in assessing simple knowledge.)

On the other hand, if the subject matter is an expansive, unmasterable domain (i.e., Track C content), then the essence of good testing is unbiased content sampling. This is ordinarily the case when essays are suitable. In this context, test content must be kept secure if the test is to provide a basis for valid inference about examinee status on the total domain. It is thus inappropriate to "teach to the test" by providing questions ahead of time (or by other ways). Doing so only renders the test results *mis*leading.

The other practice meriting mention concerns giving students a longer list of questions from which a few will be selected for inclusion on an essay test. This too tends to be tantamount to "teaching to the test," albeit in a diluted manner. To the extent that the practice focuses student study on a subsample of the domain that will be tested more than on other possible subsamples of equal importance, the test content is rendered *un*representative of the domain and its results will lead to *mis*representation of examinee status with respect to the whole domain.

QUIZ 7–1

Following are test information dissemination practices of five teachers. Judge the appropriateness of each practice from the perspective of its impact on student study. Assume that each teacher is teaching a Track C biology unit on food chains and that the test will consist of six short essay or other tasks.

1. Teacher A gives the six questions to students ahead of time so that they can do well on the test.

2. Teacher B provides students with the parallel forms of the test that were used for the past two school years. This year's form will be parallel to the previous two forms.

3. Teacher C provides students with a list of 15 questions from which the six to be tested will be randomly selected.

4. Teacher D gives students a list of 50 questions from which the six to be tested will be randomly selected.

5. Teacher E hands out a list of five particularly important questions with the information that two of them will appear on the test.

KEY TO QUIZ 7–1

1. Teacher A's practice in effect reduces the originally rich and diverse content domain into a mere six elements. That will tend to be all that is important to the students. Learning to transfer their learning is not valued by Teacher A—at least that is the clear message conveyed by the

KEY TO QUIZ 7–1 (cont.)

testing practice. When teachers do not value and reward student ability to apply their learning, students tend not to seek it.

2. Teacher B's practice provides students with useful guidance concerning item types, test coverage, and mental processes tested, but it does not provide them with a means of focusing on the particular items of information that will be sampled in the test more than on other equally important items that happen not to be sampled. By giving students the parallel forms for two previous years (rather than only one), the teacher may better enable them to realize that exact items are not repeated (or at least not with greater-than-chance frequency).

3. Teacher C's practice is similar to that of Teacher A, but it is less outrageous because it has reduced the content domain to 15 items rather than to only six. However, the practice is still deplorable because it prompts memorization rather than learning with an aim to be able to transfer.

4. Teacher D's practice further dilutes the evils of the practice to one of frantically and mindlessly trying to memorize all 50 answers rather than trying to be able to apply their learning.

5. Apparently Teacher E believes the five items handed out are especially important. The practice will certainly achieve its aim of focusing student study on these five questions. It also has the virtue of informing students of just how much of the test (two of six essays) will be drawn from this important subsample of content.

    On the negative side, students are apt to memorize the answers to these five distributed items rather than to try to understand them and be able to apply the underlying concepts; this is clearly undesirable. The teacher's intent would likely be better served if students were told that *the topics addressed* by two of these five distributed items will appear in the test, but that the exact wording and other detail of the items will be altered to ensure that they *understand the underlying concepts*. One could even provide students with examples of how content can be altered; that is, one might provide them with two or three forms of some of the distributed questions.

Scoring Product Measures

Stories about the scandalous unreliability with which some essay tests are scored are legend. Some essay tests deserve this bad reputation. The problem of unreliability of scoring essays was publicized 80 years ago when Starch and Elliot (1912) showed that a student's English essay test might receive an assessment anywhere from failing to outstanding depending on which English teacher marked the paper. One year later, they published studies in which over 100 math teachers independently marked a geometry exam and over 100 history teachers graded a history test. The unreliability of marks was found to be as great in one subject as in another.

Recognizing the chaotic status then common in marking product measures, Starch and Elliot asked what could be done to secure greater objectivity of marking. This section presents the rules that have evolved over the ensuing decades to enable teachers to mark essays much more reliably.

Rules for Marking Product Measures

Fortunately, the rules for marking essay examinations are also generally applicable for assessing other kinds of products, and their discussion here is combined. To illustrate these rules, it will be useful to refer to four varied examples of product measures:

1. A conventional essay test in a content area (e.g., science, social studies, or literature) consisting of several questions

2. The woodshop stool project

3. A home economics homework assignment consisting of planning a balanced meal to meet certain criteria

4. A drafting test consisting of several separate tasks

1. **Maintain examinee anonymity during scoring**. Ideally, a teacher marking essays or other products would not know whose work was being marked until after the assessment was completed. This protects the process from the contaminating influence of the teacher's prior expectations.

To illustrate why this protection is needed, suppose a teacher encounters an ambiguous paragraph in an essay or a slightly faulty process in a drafting task. If, on the one hand, the teacher knows the student to be very capable, then she or he is very prone to project meaning and sense into the ambiguous material. If, on the other hand, the teacher believes the student to be inept, then she or he is apt to interpret the ambiguous material as nonsense.

To protect the integrity of evaluation processes from this source of contamination, it is important to mark papers without knowing whose paper is being marked. (Of course, if a teacher knows that only Carolyn uses green ink, her anonymity is compromised, but one should take reasonable measures to achieve anonymous marking.) This state is usually best achieved by having students place their names on a part of their tests (e.g., back of last page) that is not examined in reading the essays.

2. **Developing marking criteria**. At the time each essay question or other product measure is created, the teacher should develop scoring criteria that can be applied systematically to all products. Marking bases can be more fully detailed when items are highly structured than when they are less structured. The items in Figure 7–6 illustrate highly structured items that are amenable to analytic scoring.

One reason for this rule is that demanding marking criteria focuses the teacher's attention on the need to establish the *relative importance of an item's elements*. Without this thought, a teacher may be inconsistent from student to student in the relative weight given to the component parts. For example, the elementary teacher scoring Item 1 in Figure 7–6 might be so impressed with a pupil's enumeration of over a

Item 1: Describe the peanut and its uses, using about one paragraph each for (a) its nutritional value, (b) its effect on soil, and (c) its uses and their origins. (20 points)

Scoring Key: (*a*) Good source of protein (3 points, or if peanut protein is distinguished from animal or complete protein, 4 points), carbohydrate (2 points), and fat or oil (3 points). Maximum: 7 points.

   (*b*) Roots produce nitrogen products (2 points) that fertilize or revitalize soil (3 points), making it very useful in crop rotation (2 points). (A good discussion of either revitalization or rotation could adequately imply the other.) Maximum: 6 points.

   (*c*) The peanut is used to make peanut butter (2 points), edible peanuts (1 point), animal food (1 point), peanut oil (2 points), and other (specified) use(s) (1 point), and the plants make hay for animals (2 points). Many of the uses were invented to create a need for the plant because of its benefit to soil (2 points). Maximum: 7 points.

Item 2. Woodshop, four-legged, square, stepping stool project from directions that include drawings and model. (50 points)

Scoring Key: Correct dimensions—5 points
         Fit of joints including invisible pins—7 points
         Glueing of joints—5 points
         Smoothing of top and legs from
             Planing—4 points
             Sanding—9 points
         Decorative grooving—3 points
         Staining—5 points
         Varnishing—5 points
         Waxing—7 points

Figure 7–6.   Sample Scoring Keys for Product Measures

dozen uses of peanut products that he or she overlooks the fact that the answer did not address the effect on soil. Or the woodshop teacher marking a stool might be so annoyed with a student who had applied three coats of wax without allowing adequate drying time between coats that he or she penalizes too severely the student who made an otherwise excellent stool.

   Another benefit of marking criteria is the help they provide in focusing marking on the *content* of the answers, rather than on excellence of expression. Answer outlines provide the teacher with substantial immunity from being "snowed" by an eloquently written essay that says little.

   Yet another reason for this scoring rule concerns **drifting standards**. Teacher expectations often differ from what students actually deliver. We often expect more than students produce. Unrealistic expectations may be especially common early in our careers. As a teacher works through a set of products, her or his standards tend to become more referenced to the group's performance—i.e., standards may descend. It is obviously undesirable to have "standards" that are not uniformly applied. Pre-established scoring criteria help to prevent drift.

   Two reasons for clarifying the bases for marking at the time questions are devised are (a) the relative ease of doing it then rather than having to re-establish the mind set at a later time and (b) the impact the process can have on the item. Thinking about how an item will be scored often leads one to clarify phrasing or to specify in the item itself how much weight will be given to the various parts of the answer. In Item 1 in Figure 7–6, for instance, it was in thinking about scoring that the idea occurred to me that students might well show their knowledge that many peanut uses were developed to create a market in order to prompt crop rotation. This thought led to the addition of the last three words of the item.

This item illustrates a practice that some teachers find useful. Maximum credit in each part of the answer can be secured in somewhat different ways. In part (c), for instance, the sum of the possible points is 11, yet it would be unrealistic and probably unreasonable to expect pupils to cover all of these subtopics in a brief paragraph. Therefore, earning any 7 of these 11 points secures maximum credit. Doing more in part (c) would not compensate for deficits in either other part.

Item 2 illustrates other features of a scoring key. The teacher purposely placed relatively much credit on an important, skill-demanding part of the product—fit of joints. This emphasis was designed to enable the project to differentiate among students having different skills. Yet relatively little credit was given to the less skill-demanding decorative grooving because (a) the teacher deemed this a less important wood-working skill and (b) single slips of the hand can cause marring of the product. Substantial weight was assigned to sanding and waxing in order to assess conscientious effort; these are tasks that can be done well by virtually any diligent student regardless of higher level skills.

One final point remains to be made concerning scoring criteria for relatively structured items. Their publication is an effective way of harnessing test power. For instance, it would be foolish for the woodshop teacher to keep secret the way the stool project would be graded. Far, far better that the bases for scoring be given to students at the time the project is assigned, enabling student effort to be directed into those activities that the teacher deems important.

How about Item 1 in Figure 7–6? Should the item specify the relative weight of the three elements of the answer? Perhaps. Without it, pupils will likely assume the three parts to be equal. Because that is, in fact, the case in this item, there may be no absolute need to indicate the relative weight. However, if the parts were given substantially unequal weight, then this should clearly be made known to the examinees.

3. **Examine several students' work on each task before marking any**. This cross-checking serves two purposes. First, it lessens the tendency of standards to drift—or more precisely, it enables much of the drift to occur before the real assessment begins. Second, examining several (ideally all) products can enable the teacher to pick up inadequacies in the scoring criteria before the marking commences. It is common for a teacher to notice that some student has made a good point in an essay that was overlooked in the criteria. Or in the drafting test, a student may have made an error that the teacher did not anticipate and provide for. It is nice to be able to refine the criteria before scoring is started.

4. **Mark one task at a time**. In marking a set of essay exams, the teacher should mark each student's Item 1 before proceeding to anyone's Item 2. Then all the next item should be evaluated before going to the third, etc.

Marking one item at a time is clearly appropriate for essay exams, for mathematics problems such as formal proofs that might involve any subjectivity of assessing, for drafting tests consisting of several separate tasks, etc. But what of integrated products, such as the home economics assignment to plan a balanced meal, an art project, or the woodshop stool? In the cases of the balanced meal assignment or some art projects, the adequacy of each element is not wholly independent of the other elements; each should be considered in the context of the others. These would be exceptions to the rule. In this case, each student's product should be considered in its entirety. It would be especially important to use a scoring key with criteria in order to maintain as much objectivity of marking as possible. It would also be especially important to examine several products before marking any in order to minimize standard drift.

As for the wood stool project, the rule of marking one element at a time might well be applied. If there were a whole set of stools to be marked, then the teacher could set them out in a row on workbenches. A marking card or rating form could be placed next to each. The teacher could then move down the row marking the first element—correct dimensions—for each stool. Then he or she would work back up the row marking the second element—fit of joints. Then down the row to judge the glueing, and so on.

On the other hand, if the stools are handed in one at a time as each is completed, then delaying feedback to students until a whole set of stools have accumulated would probably be too high a price to pay for the enhanced objectivity that would result from anonymity and avoidance of interelement effect. In this case the use of a rating form would be especially helpful in "anchoring" the teacher's marking criteria.

Although the topic of rating forms will be considered more fully in Chapter 8, a few comments will be helpful at this point. Rating forms can be used for either domain-referenced or norm-referenced interpretations. When the content to be rated lies in Track A, interpretations need to be domain referenced. When Track C content is being assessed, interpretation needs to be norm referenced. Track B content can be meaningfully interpreted via either type of referencing.

Woodworking involves mainly Track B content, so the teacher would have a choice of how to devise rating forms. Figure 7–7 illustrates domain-referenced ratings for the first element in evaluating the wooden stools. The ratings are domain referenced because they are made with respect to well-specified content—the dimensions of the stool. While this approach can be used, it tends to introduce problems, because it is extremely difficult to fully specify all of one's criteria. For example, suppose a student had two measurements that were off by just over ¼" but all others were virtually perfect—within ¹⁄₃₂". Would one really want to assign a zero? Probably not. Yet if we persisted in trying to specify fully all possible scoring situations, more time and effort would be devoted to developing the form than is fruitful; moreover, the resulting form would be so detailed that it would be cumbersome to use.

Correct dimensions. Circle the numeral that best describes the stool's measurement.

5   All within ¹⁄₁₆"
4   Most within ¹⁄₁₆" and none off by more than ⅛"
3   All within ⅛"
2   Most within ⅛" and none off by more than ¼"
1   One off by more than ¼"
0   More than one deviation over ¼"

Figure 7–7. Sample Domain-Referenced Rating Form

Student Name: _____   Total Score: _____

For each aspect of the stool, circle the numeral that best represents the student's work in comparison with other students who have taken this course. To obtain the total score, add the nine circled numbers.

	Poor		Fair		Good		Outstanding		
Dimensions	0	1	2		3	4	5		
Joints	0	1	2	3	4	5	6	7	
Glueing	0	1	2		3	4	5		
Planing		0	1	2	3		4		
Sanding	0	1	2	3	4	5	6	7	8	9
Grooving		0	1		2		3		
Staining	0	1	2		3	4	5		
Varnishing	0	1	2		3	4	5		
Waxing	0	1	2	3	4	5	6	7	

Figure 7–8. Sample Rating Form for a Wood Stool

Figure 7–8 illustrates one way in which the wooden stool rating form could be structured in a norm-referenced manner. Although the form itself need not indicate what the reference group is, it would probably be understood to be the students in all of the teacher's classes in this and recent years.

One reason to mark only one item at a time is to prevent the **halo effect**, the tendency to be influenced on one item by a person's performance on other items. Each essay or other task should ordinarily provide an *independent* source of data. To maintain this independence, the way one task is evaluated must not influence judgment concerning other tasks. Each drafting task or each essay should be judged on its own merits, not on the merits of the examinee's performance on other tasks.

Halo effect can be a serious source of contamination. Imagine that the fourth essay or drafting task has some unusual flaw that renders it incorrect, yet worthy of partial credit. A teacher who knows that a student's first three items were superior is likely to deem the error in the fourth item to be minor. However, a teacher who remembers the first three items as inferior is more prone to judge the error in the fourth item more harshly.

A second reason for evaluating one item at a time is economy of teacher time and effort. It is easier to retain in mind the scoring criteria for one item than for a whole test.

A third reason for judging each item separately concerns the possibility that standards may drift. If a teacher were to evaluate the whole test rather than one item at a time, a disadvantage could exist for students being marked at particular parts of the process. By judging one item at a time, the order of marking papers can be varied. This prompts the next suggestion.

5. **Systematically vary the order in which papers or projects are evaluated**. In following the rule of marking one task at a time, the set of papers or projects should *not* be examined in the same order in each cycle. By varying the order, we prevent the influence of drifting standards from accruing to the consistent advantage of some students at the expense of others.

Moreover, if the same order were maintained, then the evaluation would likely be influenced by an **order effect**. If one has just read a brilliant essay, worked through an elegant proof, or examined a magnificently crafted stool, then the next paper, proof, or stool will suffer from comparison. On the other hand, if one has just examined several successive disastrous efforts, the next one, even if only fair, is likely to seem superior (e.g., Hales & Tokar, 1975).

Fortunately it is possible to prevent contamination from halo effect, order effect, and drifting standards by simple procedures. After marking the first item or task, work through the set of second tasks in reverse order; this equalizes the influence of drifting standards. Then shuffle the set to minimize order effect and to help in maintaining anonymity. After working through a third time, reverse for the fourth pass. Then shuffle again, and so on. Note that the shuffle should be added to the procedures described above for the woodshop teacher.

6. **Do not ordinarily penalize for poor handwriting or mechanics of expression**. Several studies have shown such variables as handwriting and grammar to influence scoring of essays (e.g., Chase, 1968; Marshall & Powers, 1969). This influence can occur even when readers are directed to score on content alone (Marshall, 1967).

This rule is perhaps the most controversial one offered in this section. Three points are to be made. First, important exceptions exist. Second, the rule has a sound rationale. Third, if you decide not to follow it, these factors must be included in the scoring criteria.

First, the exceptions. Language arts teachers would, by and large, be better advised to count spelling, punctuation, and grammar than would other teachers. When it is part of the content of English courses, such material obviously merits testing. While one would not be inclined to dispute this line of reasoning, it might also be pointed out that essay questions do *not* provide a good way to assess mechanics of expression. Examinees can avoid hard-to-spell words by paraphrasing or using synonyms; if some students avoid while others do not, the spelling component of the test may be as much a measure of test-wiseness as of spelling. If a teacher wants to test spelling, dictated items with written responses provide a superior way to do so.

The other major class of exceptions to this rule involves content-specific words. For example the biology class that has been studying human circulation would probably be responsible for spelling "veins," "arteries," and "capillaries"; thus some penalty of misspelling these words would clearly be appropriate. The teacher's using the peanut question (Item 1 in Figure 7–6) could well have taught the spelling of "peanut," "protein," "nitrogen," and "legume." If so, there should be a penalty for misspelling these terms.

Aside from such exceptions, the rationale for the rule is this: A history test should measure command of history; a driver education test should measure knowledge, understandings, and skills relevant to driving, etc. To count mechanics of expression in such tests is to introduce a contaminant. Yes, it is an educationally significant contaminant, but it is not what the test is designed to measure. Therefore, by and large, mechanics of expression should not count in the content scores of essay tests. (It is, of course, useful and appropriate to point out the errors.)

Much the same can be said for excellence of handwriting. However, if a student's mechanics or handwriting is so deficient that the reader literally cannot decode the essay, then, of course, these factors must take their toll.

If spelling errors of content-specific words are to be counted, then a decision must be made concerning how much. Likewise, teachers who decide they cannot agree with this rule should also make a conscious decision concerning amount of penalty for poor handwriting and mechanics of expression. Rule 2 applies here: If spelling and handwriting are counted, then the scoring criteria should specify their weight.

7. **If the results are especially important, use multiple evaluators**. This practice is not ordinarily practical for classroom teachers. However, reliable scoring is vital if the results of a product evaluation are to contribute significantly to a major decision, such as college admissions, licensing to practice law, high school graduation, etc. In this case, having several markers *independently* assess each essay or other product would enable the final decision to be based on their pooled judgment.

Special Issues for Essays Measuring Self-Expression and Individualized Assignments or Projects

English and advanced foreign language teachers occasionally need to test how well students can *express themselves*. Examples of such test items are "explain how you spent last summer" and "write a persuasive essay taking a forceful position on any of twenty topics supplied in the attached list." In order to assess how well students can express themselves, it is essential that the question concern some topic with which each student is very familiar. Often the best way to achieve this is to allow a choice of topics. Each student did different things last summer, hence each is writing on different things. Each will select a familiar topic for the persuasive essay. Under these conditions, scoring criteria cannot be very detailed.

(It should be understood, of course, that teachers of language also often want to test command of content [e.g., literature] much like teachers would in science or history. In this case, all of the above rules apply. In the present section, however, cases are addressed in which the language teacher wants to assess students' ability to express themselves.)

Similar individuality is found in certain assignments (a) designed to relate to the interests and needs of individual students or (b) designed to be realistic. For example, a high school term paper might be written on any (approved) topic of the student's choice. Or a journalism assignment may be for each student to cover a different story. Or a vocational automotives course may have a project of repairing a real car. Or each art student may be instructed to create an original collage. Or a college measurement class may have a project of developing a teacher-made test suitable for the grade level and subject matter that the student is preparing to teach.

Clearly, a loss of comparability will occur among students in such essays, papers, or projects. However, the gain in relevance to the interests and needs of individual students will far outweigh the loss of reliability. So the teacher must bite the bullet and assess the diverse products as reliably as she or he can in spite of the diversity of products.

In general, this assessment involves **holistic** (meaning wholistic) or **global marking**, in which one forms an overall impression of each product and marks it accordingly. Holistic assessment is at one end of a continuum, while highly analytic assessment with detailed objective scoring criteria is at the other end. Most essays and other products fall somewhere on the analytic side of the continuum, although the degree to which they lend themselves to explicit, objective marking criteria differs. Other products, however, such as those considered in this section, lie nearer the holistic end. Some of these are amenable to limited analytic procedures. For example, the journalism assignment of covering a story can be analyzed in terms of "who," "what," "why," "when," "where," and "how" coverage. On the other hand, the art collage will be less amenable to analytical marking, although some would still be possible (e.g., use of color or balance).

However, even when measures must be scored almost entirely globally in terms of the total, indivisible unity, or gestalt, steps can and should be taken to enhance accuracy of marking so that grades are not awarded capriciously. Objectivity of marking is maximized by the use, to varying degrees, of the marking suggestions provided above. The rules are reconsidered below.

The rule for protecting examinee anonymity is often just as feasible in holistic marking as it is for more analytic marking, and the need for the rule is greater. In evaluating collages, one may be more vulnerable to being influenced by one's overall impression of the creator than would be the case in, say, scoring either item from Figure 7–6 on page 208. The reduced objectivity of criteria renders anonymity more important.

The rule for establishing clear and detailed bases for marking is relevant, albeit less feasible. It is not possible to develop detailed marking criteria along the lines illustrated in Figure 7–6. Nonetheless, it is almost always possible to formulate *some* marking criteria. For example, even in the most creative writing exercises requiring the greatest degree of evaluative reaction to the gestalt, one can still address such issues as the extent, if any, to which poor handwriting or spelling errors will be penalized.

The suggestion to examine several products before marking any of them is especially important in holistic marking. To the extent that one's marking criteria in global assessment are less firmly anchored, one is especially vulnerable to drift of standards.

In holistic marking it is not possible to mark one task at a time or to vary the order in which tasks are examined, so these rules are not applicable.

The case against penalizing for poor handwriting (provided it can be read!) is the same in creative writing essays as in content-specific essays.

The benefits of using multiple evaluators to enhance marking reliability are even greater in holistic marking than in analytic. Unfortunately, in most classroom settings, it is impractical. However, in borderline cases, multiple markers should be given more consideration for global marking than for analytic marking because of the greater subjectivity in the former.

QUIZ 7–2

Below are listed the seven suggested rules for evaluating products.

1.　Protect examinee anonymity.

2.　Develop marking criteria.

3.　Examine several products before marking any.

4.　Mark one task at a time.

5.　Systematically vary the order in which students' products are marked.

6.　Do not ordinarily penalize for poor handwriting or mechanics of expression.

7.　If results are especially important, use multiple markers.

Some of the marking rules are almost always relevant, while others are more appropriate for some products than for others. For each of the eight product evaluation tasks described below, consider the applicability of each of the seven rules. For each marking task, do three things: (1) Note the rules, if any, that may not be relevant. (2) Note the rules, if any, that may be unusually important because other rules are not fully relevant. (3) Note the rules, if any, that do not seem practical to use in the context described.

I.　Secondary history students are given an essay test consisting of four questions.

II.　High school biology students are each to prepare a slide of the same thing as per specific directions.

III.　Third-graders are to write a thank you letter to a guest speaker after studying the parts of such a letter.

IV.　Sixth-grade students are each to choose a work of fiction and prepare a report according to specific instructions.

V.　Middle school students are each to write a news story for the school paper.

VI.　Seventh-grade cooking students have an assignment to mix and bake a batch of cookies by use of a certain recipe.

VII.　A 4-H club has a contest to see which member can create the most interesting display or arrangement using various parts of the wheat plant.

VIII.　High school geometry students are given a homework assignment consisting of five formal proofs.

KEY TO QUIZ 7–2

The following key offers the way I would rate each rule for each task. Since the ratings have a number of "close calls," you should not worry if some of your ratings differ slightly from the key. Your answers should, of course, be close to—never opposite from—the key.

I. Rule 7 is irrelevant and impractical. All the rest apply.

II. Rules 4 and 5 may not be as relevant here as in essays. Rules 6 and 7 seem irrelevant. Rule 7 is impractical.

III. Rules 4 and 5 may not be relevant. Rule 6 is irrelevant—perhaps spelling and handwriting should count. Rule 7 is irrelevant. Rules 1, 4, 5, and 7 seem impractical.

IV. Because marking may not be as analytic as for some products, Rule 3 is extremely important. Rules 4, 5, and 7 seem largely irrelevant and impractical. Depending on the teacher's integration of spelling and other language arts activities, Rule 6 may or may not be relevant.

V. Rule 2 can be used less analytically than sometimes, so Rule 3 is extremely important. Rules 4, 5, and 7 are irrelevant and impractical. Rule 6—spelling—is probably irrelevant, i.e., spelling probably should count.

VI. Rules 4 and 5 seem only moderately relevant and practical. Rules 6 and 7 are irrelevant.

VII. Rule 2 will be hard to use; consequently Rule 3 is unusually important. Rules 4, 5, and 6 are irrelevant. If a lot of volunteer help is available, Rule 7 might, for once, be practical.

VIII. This task is very similar to a typical essay test. All rules are relevant and practical except Rule 7.

Maximum vs. Typical Products

A distinction was made in Chapter 4 between measures of maximum performance and measures of typical performance. **Maximum behavior** is measured when examinees know they are being assessed, are motivated to do well, and the "rules of the game" enable them to do their best. Examples are paper-pencil tests, art contests, and swim meets. **Typical behavior** is measured when examinees do *not* know they are being assessed or are motivated to represent themselves as they most typically are. Examples are observations of student deportment, an interest inventory, and ratings of sporting behavior when students do not know they are being observed and have no special reason for behaving unusually well.

Some products are developed in situations that will prompt the student to "put the best foot forward." Others originate in circumstances that elicit more typical results. Which kind of product is best used for product assessment?

If we always had our choice, we would answer "it depends." To use drafting or cooking as examples, sometimes we want to know how good a sketch or meal students *can produce* under conditions of maximum effort. At other times, we want to know what kind of sketches or meals students *ordinarily do produce.* To tap the limits of a person's skill, maximum product assessment is called for. To get a picture of representative products such as would interest the drafting student's future employer or the cooking student's future spouse, typical product assessment is in order. There are legitimate needs and uses for each kind of measure.

However, teachers often lack unrestricted choice. It is often inconvenient or impossible to obtain good representative measures of typical performance. Most teachers of posture units would be more interested in children's typical posture than in their posture when they knew they were being graded. However, because of the impracticalities and limitations in reliability of a few "spot checks" of posture, most such teachers feel pressured to make serious compromise with practicality. As a result, their assessment techniques for the posture unit would be weighted toward maximum performance.

So it is too with product assessment. We usually measure products produced under conditions that yield maximum effort.

Nonetheless, advice can be offered for those situations in which products are created under conditions that prompt only typical effort. Examples are an elementary teacher's spot check of math homework for grading, a sewing teacher's occasional inspection and rating of each student's ongoing work, or a drafting teacher's aperiodic collection of class assignments for grading. In addition to the usual considerations involved in marking products, an additional topic merits attention—the representativeness of the products assessed. The teacher needs to go to pains to be *un*predictable. The elementary teacher must *not* avoid collecting homework on Tuesdays because it is the faculty bowling night. The students will soon catch on to this and their performance the other nights will be a little better than average, while their effort on Tuesdays will be much less than average; thus the sample assessed would not be representative. The sewing teacher should *not* work down the rows or through the class in alphabetical order of names. Otherwise, students will be at their best when their "turns" approach. The drafting teacher should not give any hints in the ways the assignments are made that would clue which will be collected for grading.

What are the purposes of these three teachers' actions? They are not using a sampling technique because they believe it to be superior to assessing every product. On the contrary, they resort to it because they do not have time to check every product that is produced every day. They engage in sampling for one or both of two quite separate reasons. First, they may want to use typical product measurement as part of their grades because they believe it reflects an important dimension of student achievement. That is, they use typical product assessment to enhance the validity of grades.

Second, they probably do their various kinds of spot checking in an effort to keep students on task. They understand that *evaluation procedures drive much student effort.* They know if they do not count the products, students will not produce them with the same diligence. They use aperiodic product assessment to prompt high, stable effort. Along these lines, what is known about schedules of reinforcement is helpful. Initial learning (in this case, to do homework) is fastest under conditions of continuous reinforcement. This suggests that spot checking might best be very frequent near the beginning of the course. Once established, high, stable response rates that are resistant to extinction are best maintained with variable schedules of reinforcement. This phenomenon suggests totally unpredictable spot checking.

Fortunately, the teachers' two possible motives of securing valid data for grading and of prompting continuous effort are both best pursued by the same means, unpredictable product collections with higher frequency near the beginning of the course and somewhat reduced frequency later.

Directions for Product Measures

Directions for product measures serve to inform examinees how they will be evaluated and thereby to put all of them on equal footing. Instructions are especially helpful in enabling examinees to budget their time.

If all items in an essay test are given equal weight, then it may be easier to indicate this in the directions rather than to show the number of points possible in each item. On the other hand, if the questions in an exam or the elements in some other product are to be given markedly unequal weight, then the directions might well alert examinees to the need to note item weights as they read individual items.

Directions for product measures should make the rules explicit concerning allowable resources. In essay tests, no doubt should exist about whether dictionaries may be used. In the drafting test, students should know exactly what instruments are permitted. In the meal planning assignment, students should know whether consulting resources about nutritional attributes of various foods is legitimate.

(Should it be? If the assignment is to be done out of class, the teacher cannot control use of resources. In this case, it seems fairest to explicitly allow them so all students operate on the same rules. If the work is to be done in class, the teacher should consider its purpose in deciding for or against the use of resources.)

Directions should provide necessary logistic information. Essay test directions should tell students where to write their name (e.g., on the back of the last page). Instructions for the wood stool project should specify when and how the finished products are to be turned in and how ownership should be identified. If a teacher insists that essays be written in ink or that term papers be typewritten or computer printed, then directions should so specify. (Of course, if class rules concerning these issues have been published and have become habitual, then they need not be repeated on each assignment or test. However, if any possible doubt exists, information is best repeated.)

Directions for each assignment or product should make due dates absolutely clear. Will late projects be accepted? If so, what penalty will be assessed for unexcused delinquency? (Here too, if class rules already make this clear, then directions for each assignment need not necessarily repeat them.) Veteran teachers can attest that much conflict is avoided by having these kinds of rules *in writing*. "Paving a paper trail" (i.e., protecting oneself with documentary evidence of some course of action—in this case providing timely notice of deadlines and penalties) serves two very useful purposes. First, as indicated above, written rules are fair; they prevent most potential misunderstandings, problems, and conflicts from occurring. Second, it usually gives the teacher the winning hand on the rare occasions when conflicts or appeals do occur.

Chapter Summary

Product measures provide for the assessment of many extremely important educational outcomes that cannot be adequately measured by objective item types. In general, the kinds of instructional objectives best assessed by product measures have two attributes. First, the focus is on student ability to *produce* something. Being able to *develop* a plan for a successful party differs from being able to evaluate an existing plan. The latter could be measured with objective or essay items. The former can be assessed only with essay or other product assessment. Being able to plan and produce a formal geometric proof differs from being able to match steps of an existing proof with the justification for each. The latter can be measured with matching or other objective test items. The former can be assessed only by having students produce proofs. Being able to write a coherent paragraph differs from being able to specify the best order for existing sentences. The latter can be assessed with multiple-choice items. The former can be assessed only by having examinees write.

Second, the kind of objectives best assessed by essay or other product measures are such that adequate data can be secured by examining the finished product. Thus it is *not* necessary to witness the performance of the task. The keyboarding teacher can adequately judge what the student's processes were by examining the finished product. Likewise, the geometry or history teacher can follow the mental reasoning of the student by examining the finished proof or essay without having watched its development.

Product measures have an inherent tendency to be less reliable than objective tests. For that reason, it was suggested that when instructional objectives can adequately be assessed with objective items, they ordinarily should be. However, when learning is more validly measured with product measures, then they should be used, and used as reliably as possible. Reliability is maximized by carefully developing the production task to *measure* as *broadly* as feasible within the content domain and by *marking* as *objectively* as possible.

Skillful use of product assessment thus involves two related components. Directions and items first have to be developed to elicit relatively broad samples of skills. This requires skillful phrasing of questions or assignments. Then the finished products have to be assessed in a manner that yields reliable, valid results. A number of techniques enhance the marking process without significantly increasing time demands on the teacher. Use of these methods of accurate marking can do much to enhance effective use of product measures.

The kind of essay tests a teacher uses communicates to students what it is important for them to learn. If questions demand nothing more than the recall of unprocessed information, then the test power channels student effort in that direction. On the other hand, if questions require higher levels of mental processing, then the evaluation practices channel student effort toward the pursuit of learning that tends to be more permanent, more meaningful, and more practical. The same can be said of objective questions. Item type and format (e.g., essay vs. objective) seem to have less impact on students' effort and achievement than do their expectations of the mental processes and content to be measured (Crooks, 1988).

Suggestions for Further Reading

Gronlund, N. E., & Linn, R. L. (1990). *Measurement and evaluation in teaching* (6th ed.). New York: Macmillan. Chapter 9, "Measuring Complex Achievement: The Essay Test," presents a very helpful discussion and set of rules for writing and scoring essay tests.

Hopkins, K. D., Stanley, J. C., & Hopkins, B. R. (1990). *Educational and psychological measurement and evaluation* (7th ed.). Englewood Cliffs, NJ: Prentice-Hall. Chapter 8, "Constructing and Using Essay Tests," provides a thorough, research-based treatment of essay test use.

Linn, R. L. (1971). Essay examinations. In Thorndike, R. L. (Ed.). *Educational measurement* (2nd ed.). Washington, DC: American Council on Education. This chapter offers detailed consideration of advantages and disadvantages of essay tests and offers sound bases for improving them.

Stiggins, R. J. (1987). Design and development of performance assessments. *Educational Measurement: Issues and Practices, 6,* 33–42. This self-contained instructional module provides an excellent introduction to what this book calls product and performance assessment.

Developing and Scoring Performance Measures, Including Oral Tests

Even more ancient than the essay exam, the oral test dates to antiquity, yet its utility is limited for a number of reasons. Compared with written essay or objective examinations, oral tests take much more examiner time to administer, limit the practicality of asking all examinees to respond to the same questions, suffer from serious problems of test security, and provide less reliable results. Yet oral tests continue to be used because they are superior to other item types in measuring certain kinds of outcomes.

Actually, oral exams belong to a larger category of tests known as **performance measures**, which involve observing and rating student behavior and require that students actually demonstrate proficiency. Some relatively structured observations are "designed to include prespecified purposes, exercises, observations, and scoring procedures." Other observations arise spontaneously and lead teachers to judgments about student proficiency (Stiggins & Bridgeford, 1986, p. 471). Thus performance measurement is simply assessment of performance *while* it is in progress. This assessment can be highly detailed, analytic, and objective, or it can be global and impressionistic.

Performance assessment plays a major role in day-to-day classroom achievement measurement. "Teachers rely at least as much on observation and judgment in evaluating student achievement as they do on paper-and-pencil assessment strategies" (Stiggins, 1987, p. 33). This chapter will address the nature of this important means of assessment, offer suggestions for developing effective performance measures, provide methods of enhancing the reliability and validity with which they are scored, and discuss implications for better teaching via better use of classroom performance assessment.

The Nature of Performance Measures

Performance measurement is indispensable to the assessment of a rich variety of achievement, ranging from preschool to graduate school. Yet, performance assessment is not typically our method of choice—*if* we have a choice. It has been emphasized that when objective tests can adequately assess learning, they should ordinarily be given priority. If objective tests will not suffice, then product measures should be considered. A teacher should ordinarily resort to performance measures only when product measures also will not do the job.

This decision rule leads teachers to assess performance for purposes of both formative and summative decision making. In **formative evaluation**, teachers want to see what is right or wrong with specific elements of a student's performance in order to *provide helpful diagnostic feedback* for improvement. Performance measures are used when it is necessary to witness the performance, not just inspect the final product, in order to pinpoint problems. Here are several examples of formative uses of performance assessment:

1. The band director listens to each trombone player's performance *in order to offer suggestion for improvement.*
2. The cooking teacher observes the mixing of the cookie recipe, noting and *making suggestions* regarding such things as whether the baking soda is first mixed with the flour before being added to the wet mix.

3. The elementary physical education instructor watches each kickball player kick the ball and *makes suggestions for improvement.*

4. The metal shop teacher observes students using the metal drill *to ensure that each uses goggles.*

5. The keyboarding teacher moves around the room as students keyboard, observing their posture and *making suggestions* that will reduce fatigue of hands, wrists, arms, and back.

6. The driver education instructor provides continuous feedback about students' early, behind-the-wheel driving *in order to increase safety and identify and alter bad driving habits while they are still in the formative stage.*

7. The swimming coach videotapes each student's high dive *in order to go over it with the student to identify strengths and weaknesses.*

8. The primary teacher watches children as they copy a written exercise from the chalkboard. *Specific suggestions are provided* to individual pupils concerning posture, positioning of paper on the desk, and grasp of the pencil.

All the above examples are alike in that the purpose of the observation is improvement; in pursuit of this improvement in performance, the feedback is ongoing. There is, however, another dimension in which the examples differ. In some cases, performance measurement is virtually the only way by which one could assess student performance; this is the case with Examples 1, 3, 4, 6, and 7. In other cases, such as Examples 2, 5, and 8, performance assessment is used only to supplement other means of assessment.

The other context in which teachers use performance measures to enhance decision making involves **summative evaluation** in which judgments are made concerning the status of student achievement. In most cases, at least some of a unit's summative evaluation can be made by use of the more economical and reliable methods—objective tests or product assessment, yet some aspects cannot adequately be evaluated by these methods. In this case, it is appropriate to use performance assessment to "fill in the gaps" left by the other methods. At times, however, most or all of a unit's achievement can be measured only by means of performance measure. Of course, in this case it is necessary to rely heavily on performance measurement to evaluate achievement.

Several examples follow that parallel those provided above for formative evaluation. The difference in the examples that follow is that the decisions concern terminal level of student performance—not improvement. (Recognize, however, that in practice the distinction between formative and summative evaluation is not always sharp. Even while grading, teachers often provide feedback aimed at improving student performance.)

1. The band director listens to each trombone player's performance *in order to assign chairs* for the next nine weeks.

2. The cooking teacher observes the mixing of the cookie recipe, *grading* such things as whether the baking soda is first mixed with the flour before being added to the wet mix.

3. The elementary physical education teacher watches each kickball player kick the ball *to rate/grade the adequacy* of kicks.

4. The metal shop instructor observes students using the metal drill *to pass or fail* each on use/nonuse of goggles.

5. The keyboarding teacher moves around the room as students keyboard, *rating their posture.*

6. The driver education teacher fills out a rating form about various aspects of each student's behind-the-wheel driving in order to have a sound *basis for grading and/or awarding licenses.*

7. The swimming coach videotapes team members' high dives in order to compare them and *choose the three students to attend the meet.*

8. The primary teacher watches children as they copy a written exercise from the chalkboard. *Ratings are made* for use in report cards of specific performance features, such as posture, positioning of paper on desks, and grasp of the pencils.

QUIZ 8–1

Following are four applied problems in classroom measurement. For each, apply the decision rule to decide which to use: objective tests, product measures, and/or performance measures. Also consider whether each teacher would be concerned mainly with formative evaluation, mainly with summative evaluation, or about equally with both.

1. The director of the school play must, for each major part, select the student to be cast in it.

2. Once casting is completed, the director of the school play holds several rehearsals.

3. Consider Mr. Martin's unit on "Music around the World" described on pages 129–130 in Chapter 4.

4. A teacher of Spanish is developing a final examination to assess student achievement in (a) reading comprehension, (b) writing, (c) listening comprehension, and (d) speaking.

KEY TO QUIZ 8–1

1. Paper-pencil objective tests are ill-suited to the job of casting. So are essay tests and other kinds of product measures. Therefore the director will have to endure the problems associated with performance measurement. (Later in this chapter these problems will be considered in greater detail, as well as how to cut losses from each.)

   This would likely be considered to be a straightforward case of summative evaluation—of selecting the one or two highest achievers for each role. Germane to casting is an issue that few teachers have to

KEY TO QUIZ 8–1 (cont.)

face—the matter of *match* of person to role. Thus students' summative evaluation is not just their achievement in the abstract, but their achievement *in relation* to the role being cast.

Another dimension might possibly enter into the director's casting—student "coachability." That is, the teacher might want to estimate how quickly students can modify their acting to conform to instruction. If the tryout were to pursue this dimension, performance measurement would also be used with several critiques and re-performances per student. Would this be formative or summative evaluation? *During* the process it is formative, but *after* the last round of critique and performance, the director must make the summative decision concerning who gets the part.

2. The way to provide ongoing diagnostic feedback concerning student's performance of their parts is to have them perform and to critique their efforts. Neither objective items nor product measures have anything to offer to this formative evaluation endeavor.

3. Mr. Martin used objective paper-pencil tests to assess all that was assessable with such devices. Thus knowledge/comprehension and auditory category recognition were tested with objective items. His application and analysis objectives were not as amenable to objective items, so he used essays for them. Finally, he used performance measurement only to "fill in the gaps." Since the original productions had to be produced in order to be judged, he had to rely on performance evaluation for this dimension of his unit. (For the accomplished composer, the creation of the score of the music would yield a product that could be evaluated as such. Mr. Martin's beginning students would probably have to perform the work in order to communicate what they had created.)

    The focus of Mr. Martin's end-of-unit assessment is, of course, *summative,* yet the application/analysis section and the original production section would probably have some formative flavor (e.g., mention of strengths and weaknesses).

4. By virtue of its being a final examination, all four modes of communication would be assessed summatively. However, most teachers would use the occasion of an oral test also to provide some formative instruction.

    Reading comprehension can adequately be assessed with objective items; it is well suited to interpretive exercises. Therefore, the decision rule dictates that it be assessed with objective items.

    Writing cannot be well measured with any procedure other than having students write. Thus the decision rule demands the use of essay product measurement for assessing student ability to write.

    Listening comprehension is nicely measurable with objective items (most often multiple-choice) based on an auditory stimulus.

Therefore, the decision rule suggests objective items in interpretive exercises.

Finally, speaking must be performed. Answering objective questions cannot measure ability to speak, nor can work in the written language assess facility in producing oral language. The only way to measure students' ability to speak Spanish is to have them talk! This leads to all kinds of logistic and measurement problems, but there can be no compromise. Much of the remainder of this chapter is devoted to coping with the difficulties of performance measures.

Developing Performance Measures

The task of developing some performance measures is so obvious as to require little comment. For example, the keyboarding teacher's need to assess posture is accommodated without special arrangements. Students' posture is there to be observed almost any time, and one time may be about as good as another. Or the kindergarten teacher's need to screen children for speech disorders might be achieved without much special arrangement beyond the need for the teacher to be sensitive to potential speech problems.

Other instances of performance measurement occur in contrived situations. For example, the teacher casts students for parts in the play in auditions. Similarly, the swim coach must bring the camcorder to the pool and set it up to record dives, and the Spanish teacher must organize sufficient class time to enable individual oral testing. In these cases, the teacher not only has to go to the trouble of organizing for the measurement, but there is a degree of artificiality about the context during the performance. That is, students trying out for the play may be more self-conscious and anxious than they would be during most performances. The divers' performance may well be altered by the mere knowledge that they are being recorded. And the Spanish students' "conversations" with the teacher during the test are likely to have rather different content and style than their typical conversations.

Two issues inherent in performance measurement merit attention. One is the *realism* of the context in which performance is exhibited and the various costs associated with the pursuit of realism. The other issue is the presence or absence of *interaction* with others during the performance. Teachers can develop better performance measures by carefully considering these issues.

Realism and Reliability

The artificiality of the context of some performance assessment is an undesirable, invalidating feature. Put positively, we seek *realism* in the circumstances in which performance is exhibited (Fitzpatrick & Morrison, 1971).

However, when the context for performance measurement is realistic, it also frequently is unstandardized. Different students have to perform in different contexts, and comparability is sacrificed. When this happens, reliability of measurement is eroded. Both realism and reliability are desirable. Teachers should therefore carefully consider the tradeoff between them, and seek to enhance each only to the extent that it does not cost too much of the other.

To illustrate, the Spanish teacher's oral test of conversational Spanish probably entails a moderate loss of realism. The teenager's performance in conversing with the formidable teacher may differ a great deal from an unthreatening conversation with a peer, parent, or shopkeeper. Yet practical considerations preclude the teacher's observation of each student in casual Spanish conversation (partly because most students of Spanish as a foreign language do not have casual Spanish conversations with anyone!). Moreover, even if this were feasible, the different demands of the various conversations that students would have would render the teacher's job much more difficult. Informal adjustments would have to be made for the unequal difficulties of various conversations. The lack of standardization of tasks would reduce the reliability with which the discriminatory test revealed individual differences in achievement. Therefore, although this contrived conversation with the teacher would suffer from some loss of realism, it would probably be the best compromise available between realism and reliability.

For another illustration of the realism-reliability tradeoff, consider an element of driving a car. When a green traffic light turns yellow, the driver must judge whether there is time to move completely through the intersection before it turns red. This judgment needs to take account of (a) the speed of movement and (b) the speed limit (which will have determined the yellow light's duration). The teacher or examiner needs to assess how good the student is in judging when to drive through and when to stop. Would this skill best be measured in a natural context or in a contrived one?

In the natural context, the examiner simply has the examinee drive and hopes that a light turns yellow as the student is in the "decision zone." This provides realism, but one might have to drive for quite some time before an opportunity presents itself to assess this skill even once.

In the contrived context, the examiner might use simulation. Of the many ways in which this could be organized, suppose that there is a three-block-long stretch of private road on which a special remote-control, radio-operated traffic light is located. As the student approaches the signal, the examiner could control exactly when (and if) the light turns yellow, thereby enabling the assessment of the student's judgment and skill. Now in a small fraction of the time that would be required to get a trial or two under real driving conditions, the examiner could obtain several relatively standardized trials with the light turning yellow when the car is at various distances from the intersection and when it is moving at various speeds.

Alternative means of simulation can be found in stationary simulators or trainers that have speedometers, realistic hand and foot controls, and a screen display of traffic and signal conditions. With electronic apparatus no more sophisticated than that of many a video computer game, good, standardized simulation can be achieved along with electronic scoring of performance and formative feedback to examinees.

Both simulations provide superior means of either teaching or testing the skill. It can be done far more reliably with simulations than in real traffic. Nonetheless, contrived simulations are accompanied by some costs in realism; the simulations do not contain all the elements—such as traffic conditions—that are present in the real world. In this case, the loss of realism is not very great in comparison with the gains in standardization and reliability. Not to be overlooked, however, is another kind of cost—money. Some simulations are expensive. That might be the greatest cost in this example.

Finally, consider an elementary school test on the first aid topic of stopping severe bleeding. Here simulation is clearly indicated even though the realism will be feeble indeed. Directions to show the tester how the examinee would stop bleeding from a deep gash in Mike's forearm may elicit affective, cognitive, and psychomotor reactions very different from those of a real accident. In some respects, it might be preferable to see how pupils perform in real accidents rather than how they act in a play-acting context.

Not only is such an attempt at realism impractical, unsafe to the victim, and potentially distressing to the examinee, but in one important regard—task standardization—real accidents would not be as good for testing first aid performance as would a simulation. Real accidents yield different first aid needs. Even if students could be presented with real accident victims, each examinee would be confronted with a different set of needs. Some would get easier tasks than others. Comparability would be severely limited, and resulting reliability would suffer. In light of this consideration, the feeble simulation does not seem quite as bad by comparison as it otherwise would. Hence, we are willing to endure a huge cost in realism to secure reliability and practicality.

These examples illustrate the kinds of tradeoffs teachers should make. They show that in addition to realism and reliability, features such as cost, practicality, danger, and ethics also enter into consideration.

Interactive vs. Noninteractive Performance Measures

It will be helpful to consider performance assessment from the perspective of the model of relationships developed in Part I. Performance measurement takes place in all three tracks. Some examples will be considered as well as the extent to which the performance measures in each track require examinees to interact with other people.

Tracks A and B

Track A subject matter is sharply delimited, masterable, and vital. Its masterability implies that it is *not* interactive. For example, unlocking a combination gym locker is a task that students can and should master. Pronouncing the name of each letter of the alphabet is also vital and masterable. Rating forms and check lists designed to assess such specifiable and masterable performance tasks should, of course, be domain referenced.

Track B subject matter is clearly delimited, but is not vital. Examples are free throws in basketball and knowledge of state capitals (for teachers who do not deem it vital), track events, or keyboarding speed tests.

Tasks in Tracks A and B tend to be noninteractive. Thus the examiner's job is relatively easy. The performance tests are easy to create, easy to score, and uncomplicated by any demands of realism that they be interactive with the behavior of other people. Relatively high realism can be achieved along with relatively high reliability. There is little need to trade off one against the other. True, some situational factors exist (e.g., the noise and distractions in the dressing room when the locker is being unlocked, or the audience behavior in a track event). Hence removing the performance from the natural context would somewhat enhance standardization and reliability at the expense of realism. However, the issue is not usually a very big one in Tracks A and B because (a) the natural context does not cost much in standardization of influences and, (b) if simulation is elected, it can be quite realistic.

Track C

Track C subject matter is not very specifiable and cannot be mastered. Track C performance assessment is very often interactive. Indeed, it is the inherently interactive nature of many Track C tasks that makes it impossible to specify fully either their difficulty or the context in which they must be performed. For example, playing a role in a musical, playing a game of tennis, participating in a class discussion, or conversing in Spanish all involve interaction with other people. The actions of these other people influence the difficulty of the performance task. In Track C performance measurement, the uncontrolled features of the performance—often resulting from the role of other persons in the activities—require that interpretation be norm referenced in order to be meaningful.

The tradeoff between realism and reliability is often painful. The more realistic a task is, the less reliable it tends to be (Fitzpatrick & Morrison, 1971); conversely, the more reliable a task is, the less realistic it tends to be. Consider the Spanish teacher's oral test in conversation. It has already been noted that the realism was somewhat limited by the artificiality of the context. Thus a price in realism has been paid.

Now consider that the way the teacher responds to the conversational efforts of various students will have to reflect and follow from what they say. This necessary interaction clearly limits the extent of standardization of task requirements and the equality of task difficulty.

Moreover, many teachers would also be concerned about potential compromise of test security resulting from the passage of test information from previously tested to yet-to-be-tested students. To prevent this, they might vary the conversation from student to student more than would otherwise be necessary. This lack of uniform content further compromises comparability and reliability. Thus a price in reliability has also been paid.

This example highlights the fact that in Track C performance assessment the teacher often faces multiple problems. The need to examine one student at a time can consume a great deal of time. The need to interact reduces task standardization, comparability, and reliability. The need to protect test security further limits comparability and reliability. The logistics of what to do with students while they are not being tested can be troublesome. And the realism of the performance tasks often is only modest. In devising Track C performance measures, one should thoughtfully consider all the problems and use good judgment concerning the best balance among the considerations.

With all these disadvantages, why do teachers use Track C performance measures? Because that is the only valid way by which to assess student attainment of some important instructional objectives. Yet awareness of these multiple problems highlights the rationale of the decision rule: Performance measures should ordinarily be used only when objective measures and product measures will not do the job.

QUIZ 8–2

Following are five applied measurement problems. For each, decide on the best way to assess the instructional objective.

1. In teaching primary children the Pledge of Allegiance, the teacher wants each child to be able to recite it.

2. An elementary school has been studying principles and practices to be used in case of a school fire.

3. A scout leader wants scouts to know the proper way to fold the flag.

4. A university wants to be assured that foreign students be able to speak understandable English before being employed as graduate teaching assistants.

5. A driver education teacher wants students to recognize and properly respond to various traffic signs by their shapes.

KEY TO QUIZ 8–2

1. The way to find out if Mary can recite the Pledge of Allegiance is to have her recite it. Clearly a performance measure is in order. (With older, literate students, having them write the Pledge of Allegiance might be an attractive alternative.)

2. Consider first the simple, normal route of exit a child is supposed to use. One could test this with paper and pencil (e.g., draw the route of exit), but most teachers would want to enhance realism by having a performance measure. In this simple (but unrealistic) Track A case, the task is masterable and has little interaction with circumstances.

   Now consider a better simulation in which some people are highly excited and in which the normal route of exit is blocked. The task now becomes interactive with circumstances and people and clearly falls in Track C. Here too, one could test this with paper and pencil, but most teachers would again want to enhance realism by having performance acted out. To become very realistic however would be difficult because it would require a whole school full of accomplices who would act excited, yell that the exit was blocked, etc. Even then it would be a poor simulation. And, of course, it would not be practical.

3. Although paper-pencil testing has the attraction of enabling one to test several people at once, the nature of the task would be quite different. In other words, the simulation is poor. Hence, the leader would likely opt to have each scout tested separately by a performance test. Fortunately, test security is not an issue with such Track A content. One person's test can provide vicarious practice to others.

KEY TO QUIZ 8–2 (cont.)

4.   The *only* way to measure how well people speak is to have them speak. Paper-pencil tests are *not* an adequate substitute. Yet a university might face a grave logistical problem of needing to award graduate teaching assistantships to foreign applicants before they leave their jobs and travel to the United States. It would be unconsciencable to wait until they arrived before deciding whether to award assistantships. What to do?

I would consider telephone testing. A five- or ten-minute phone call abroad may seem expensive, but its cost is trivial compared to the educational costs of employing persons to teach whose English is not comprehensible to their students. What logistic problem does telephone interviewing/testing present?

An applicant might have a more fluent substitute take the phone interview/test. To protect against this possibility, one could record the phone conversation so that if the person who shows up for the job is clearly less fluent that the person interviewed on the phone, voice print analysis could prove that misrepresentation had occurred. All of this should be made known to candidates before the phone conversation (and would provide the proverbial ounce of prevention).

5.   There is no need to endure the various costs of a performance measurement. The learning can adequately be assessed by paper-pencil testing. Application of the decision rule would lead one to use objective items to measure achievement of this goal. A matching exercise might do the job best. In one column would be the shapes of the various traffic signs; in the other column would be the words telling what they say, e.g., "stop" and "yield."

One might be concerned by the issue that the objective items would test maximum performance, while the goal of teaching involved typical responses as well as ability to respond. This is a good thing to be concerned about. A later section of this chapter takes up this subject. But this concern does not lead one to use a performance test over a paper-pencil test because a behind-the-wheel performance measure would be just as much a test of maximum performance as would the matching exercise.

Scoring Performance Measures

The last chapter discussed problems associated with the reliability of scoring products where the products "stand still" to be evaluated. Greater problems are associated with the reliability of scoring performance where the performance "flies by" at one point in time. Fortunately, however, "the relatively low reliability of performance tests is not an entirely universal or necessary characteristic" (Fitzpatrick & Morrison, 1971, p. 268).

The greater difficulty of achieving reliable and valid assessment of performance measures renders it necessary for teachers to be better prepared to make the crucial observation while the performance is under way. That is, teachers must know exactly what they are looking for *before* they start evaluating student performance measures.

Developing Clear Criteria

The primary suggestion for providing reliable and valid assessment of performances is to *develop clear evaluation criteria*. The elements of the task should be thoughtfully analyzed. Then a decision should be made regarding whether assessment will be global or analytical.

Some performance tasks are well suited to analytical marking in which various elements of the task are identified and each is rated and given the desired weight. Examples are tying a shoe or stick-shifting a car. Other performance tasks seem to defy fully analytical assessment. An example is skill in making informal conversation. Most raters would want to reserve some credit for their global or holistic assessment of a person's conversational skills. Yet even the most difficult of tasks can be broken down into components for some degree of analytical assessment. Various aspects of making casual conversation can be identified, and these can be assigned desired weights. Scoring adequacy is enhanced by analytical assessment to as great an extent as the tasks being evaluated lend themselves to analysis. Four examples will illustrate use of the above principle of using clear evaluation criteria as analytically as the task allows. "Our goal is to be sure that performance ratings reflect the examinee's true capabilities and are *not* a function of the perceptions and biases of the person evaluating the performance" (Stiggins, 1987, p. 33).

Cooking an Omelet.   In Chapter 7, the task of cooking a simple omelet was considered from the framework of the decision model. It was concluded that the relatively simple motor tasks could adequately be assessed with objective paper-pencil testing. However, it was noted that the teacher should consider the impact of paper-pencil assessment on student study. Suppose a cooking teacher has decided to use a performance test in order to prompt students to practice making omelets rather than to sit and memorize verbiage. The test will be the task of making a simple, two-egg omelet.

This task is well suited to analytical assessment. It is possible to list the criteria quite fully. Figure 8–1 represents the teacher's analysis of the task. Each step is listed. As the student performs the task, the teacher would have ample time to observe and record each element.

Learning is enhanced if students have advanced knowledge of the criteria. Regardless of whether the actual rating form is distributed to students, the teacher would certainly want to be sure that they know each criterion on which evaluation would be based. Thus test power is constructively harnessed.

The rating form displayed in Figure 8–1 provides no means of arriving at a total score. It was designed solely for formative evaluation. Its items are diagnostic in nature; it is suitable for providing instructional feedback. If it were to be used summatively, point values could be assigned to each place where a check mark could be made. But does this make sense?

Is the finished omelet no more than the sum of its parts? It was asserted above that omelet making was well suited to analytic assessment. That is true in the sense

Student's Name: _____

For each item, place a check mark in the one place that best describes the student's performance.

1. Select Skillet
    _____ Too small
    _____ OK
    _____ Too large

2. Margarine or Butter in Skillet
    _____ Much too much
    _____ Too much
    _____ OK
    _____ Too little
    _____ Much too little

3. Breaking Eggs
    _____ Egg(s) miss(es) bowl
    _____ Shell in egg
    _____ OK

4. Water Added to Egg
    _____ Much too much
    _____ Too much
    _____ OK
    _____ Too little
    _____ Much too little or none

5. Salt
    _____ Much too much
    _____ Too much
    _____ OK
    _____ Too little
    _____ Much too little or none

6. Pepper
    _____ Much too much
    _____ Too much
    _____ OK
    _____ Too little
    _____ Much too little or none

7. Heat Skillet
    _____ Much too cool
    _____ Too cool
    _____ OK
    _____ Too hot
    _____ Much too hot

8. Pouring
    _____ Too fast splatter/slop
    _____ OK
    _____ Too slow

9. Shaking
    _____ Too violent/slops
    _____ OK
    _____ Too gentle

10. Puncture/run through
    _____ Too rough
    _____ OK
    _____ Insufficient
    _____ Not done

11. Fold
    _____ Broken
    _____ OK
    _____ Partial
    _____ Not done

12. Doneness of Exterior
    _____ Raw
    _____ Underdone
    _____ OK
    _____ Overdone
    _____ Burnt

13. Doneness of Interior
    _____ Raw
    _____ Underdone
    _____ OK
    _____ Overdone
    _____ Burnt

Figure 8–1.   Formative Evaluation of Making a Simple Omelet

that its elements can be broken apart and separately identified along the lines shown in Figure 8–1. However, when it comes to judging the final product, the gestalt, the whole is more than the sum of its parts. A serious defect in any one element (e.g., much too much salt or serious burning) can overshadow all other elements, no matter how excellent they might be. Any one element could well prevent one from winning a cooking contest.

However, grades are not quite the same thing as a contest. A student might burn the exterior and ruin the product completely, yet that error is unlikely to be repeated.

Partial credit for those elements competently performed would provide a better summary of the student's total skill and a better prediction of future omelet-making performance. Thus a case can be made after all for analytic assessment. However, a case can also be made for one additional item on the rating form—an item calling for global appraisal of the overall performance. If such a holistic item were added to the form, one might well want to weight it more than most other items.

This was a relatively simple illustration of performance assessment. Simple omelet making might best be thought of as a noninteractive skill classified in Track B, perhaps near the Track A/B border. The realism of the performance test is rather good.

Making an Oral Book Report.   For the next example, consider an upper elementary level oral book report, a relatively noninteractive performance. At a more advanced level, sensitivity to audience might receive much emphasis, but here it might be treated more like a static performance. Even so, it is a Track C task because there are as many book reports as there are books and because there is no one best way to report on any one book. Figure 8–2 displays a form that might be used for this performance.

An important feature of the book report performance is that it consists of two quite separate features that ordinarily should *not* be mingled or summed. The content of the report is something quite apart from the style of the report's delivery. Actually, the content could better be assessed with a product assessment—a written report. However, the teacher wanted to give pupils experience in speaking before the class, and the book report was chosen as the content to be presented. The items within each major part of the rating form can be summed.

This rating form serves several purposes. First, by being analytical in assessing the performance, greater reliability and validity will likely be achieved. Second, the form provides each pupil with useful information that can be used for improvement; hence this summative performance rating also has good formative utility. Third, by telling students how they will be rated, the teacher can communicate priorities. For example, anticipating that talking too rapidly will be the major problem for children, the teacher explains that speed will count more than any other element of presentation. It is also explained that it is much more serious (and more common) to talk too fast than it is to speak too slowly and that the resulting point ratings reflect this. The same point can be made about the problem of speaking inaudibly. Thus, prior knowledge of how they will be rated enables the assessment to influence pupil learning.

Seeking Information on the Phone.   Suppose a middle school language arts teacher has a unit on seeking information on the phone. One means by which students are evaluated is to give each student a real phone call to make to obtain specific information (e.g., "Does your store stock monophonic earphones with a quarter-inch jack for use with electric guitar amplifiers?").

The teacher could provide a relatively realistic task (individualized to fit individual student's interests) of making real phone calls. Unfortunately this might create public relations difficulties in the business community or logistic difficulties in getting access to real phones during class time. It would also yield results that were not very comparable from student to student because of variable difficulty of tasks. Alternatively, the teacher could provide the same task for each student and play the role

Pupil: _____

For each step, record the numeral that best represents the pupil's performance.

CONTENT	**PRESENTATION**
Title Provided	Speed
_____ (0) No	_____ (4) Slow
_____ (1–3) Partial	_____ (5) Good
_____ (4) Yes	_____ (2–4) Rather Fast
	_____ (0–1) Very Fast
Author Provided	
_____ (0) No	Articulation
_____ (2) Yes	_____ (0) Poor
	_____ (1) Fair
Description of Book	_____ (2–3) Good
_____ (0) None	_____ (4) Excellent
_____ (1–2) Scant	
_____ (3–5) Good	Volume
_____ (2–3) Excessive	_____ (0-1) Inaudible
	_____ (3) Hard to Hear
Illustrative Anecdotes	_____ (4) Good
_____ (0) None	_____ (3) Too Loud
_____ (1–2) Scant	
_____ (3–5) Good	Language Usage (Word Choice, Sentence
_____ (1–3) Excessive	Structure, and Grammar)
	_____ (1) Poor
Summary Evaluation	_____ (2) Fair
_____ (0) None	_____ (3) Good
_____ (1–2) Scant	_____ (4) Excellent
_____ (3–4) Good	
_____ (2–3) Excessive	Posture and Gestures
	_____ (0) Poor
	_____ (1) Fair
	_____ (2) Good
	_____ (3) Excellent
CONTENT TOTAL: _____	PRESENTATION TOTAL: _____

Figure 8–2.　Summative Rating Form for Oral Book Report

of the person(s) on the other end of the line. This approach is much more practical in that it does not bother business people, does not require access to phones, etc. It will also provide better reliability owing to the better comparability among students. The price, of course, for these benefits would be loss of realism.

Suppose the teacher elects the second option, but tries to protect test security by altering the conversations. For example, in some calls the teacher plays the part first of a switchboard operator who must route the call and then of the sales clerk in the appropriate department. In other calls, the teacher acts the part of the clerk who answers the phone in a smaller store having no operator. Similarly, the clerk is played as more competent in some conversations than others to see how well students can cope with unforseeable contingencies. All these attempts to add realism to the task—features that make the performance distinctly Track C and realistically interactive—have a cost. They reduce comparability.

Figure 8–3 provides a form with which student performance on this task might be rated. Use of the form requires considerable judgment. For example, if the person answering is also the relevant clerk, the first and second items blend into one another. Or if the clerk is competent and polite, it is easier to be polite than it is in the face of a rude, incompetent person on the line. The teacher making the ratings would need to make allowance for issues of this kind. Nonetheless, the form does lend itself to summing for a total score.

Student: _____

For each item, circle the numeral that best represents the student's performance.

Provides appropriate information to person answering for routing (e.g., "the department that sells headphones").	Much Too Little	Too Little	About Right	Too Much
	0	1	3	2

Provides appropriate detailed information to department (e.g., "monophonic earphones with quarter-inch jack for use on electric guitar amplifier").	Much Too Little		About Right	Much Too Much
	0 1 2 3 4		3	2

Secures and records desired information (e.g., availability, variety, price(s)).	No	Some	Most	All
	0 1 2	3 4	5	6

Enunciation	Poor	Fair	Good
	0	1	2

Politeness	Poor	Fair	Good
	0	1	2

TOTAL SCORE: _____

Figure 8–3.   Summative Rating Form for Making an Information-Seeking Telephone Call

Making Small Talk with Strangers.   The final example of the use of well-considered criteria for assessing performances involves making casual conversation. Suppose a secondary teacher has a unit on this art. Making small talk is clearly a highly interactive, Track C task. It cannot be tightly specified; therefore, it is not very amenable to analytic marking. It will be seen, however, that its evaluation is enhanced by being as analytic as feasible.

Figure 8–4 was designed by the teacher to focus rater attention on various aspects of the "performance." But few real conversations give rise to opportunity to exhibit all the possible component subskills. It is therefore necessary to have a "no opportunity to observe" or an "irrelevant" category with which the rater can avoid rating something that was not observed.

It is important to note that Figure 8–4 calls for a holistic rating. But before making this global assessment, the rater's attention is sequentially focused on various elements of informal conversation with strangers. In this way, much of the subjectivity is avoided. Also, use of the several items in the form helps the rater avoid overreacting to one particularly good or bad feature of the student's performance.

Yet in the end, the task of making casual conversation with a stranger is highly

Student: _____

Elements: Fill in a circle for each.

	Poor	Fair	Good	Irrelevant
Self-introduction	O	O	O	O
Casual openers (e.g., weather)	O	O	O	O
Asks good questions	O	O	O	O
Answers questions appropriately	O	O	O	O
Reflects questions	O	O	O	O
Graceful termination	O	O	O	O
Other (specify) _____	O	O	O	O

Comment:

Global Score: Circle one. (This rating is to be your overall impression. It should take all the above elements into account, but it is not to be a mere sum of them. This rating is to reflect your holistic judgment about the gestalt.)

    1   2   3   4   5   6   7
   Low   Average   High

Figure 8–4. Summative Rating Form for Making Informal Conversation

dependent on the stranger's conversational characteristics. For example, some totally monopolize the conversation to the extent that the student would never have a chance either to ask or even to answer a question; in this case being a polite, attentive listener and making a speedy, graceful escape may be called for. Others would never ask a question or answer one with more than a phrase; this would call for more of a monologue on the part of the examinee than would otherwise be appropriate. The final global judgment should take such features into account. That is, the holistic rating is not a rating of the student's performance in the abstract; rather it is a rating of her or his performance in the interactive context.

    This example provides another opportunity to consider the tradeoff between realism and reliability. The teacher could seek real-life conversations, but this would probably prove impractical; thus simulations would likely be elected. The easiest simulation would be for the teacher to play the role of the other party—not himself or herself, but a *role*. This could maximize teacher control over directions the simulation takes and minimize time costs in that the teacher could simultaneously role-play and rate.

    The next question is whether to play the same role with all students or to achieve several benefits by varying the role from student to student. These benefits are (a) protection of test security, (b) protection of the teacher from excessive boredom, and (c) ability to individualize the task's difficulty to reflect the ability of individual students. If the task is varied from student to student, one might consider having students observe each other's performance. This might be attractive for its instructional value and/or because it would solve the problem of what to do with the class as each is given an individual, oral test.

In this case there would be instructional value in having students critique or rate each other. Teaching students to be effective raters often is an excellent *instructional* strategy. As they internalize performance criteria, they see how the criteria apply to their own and each other's performance. This helps them become better performers (Stiggins, 1987). In addition, training students to be raters is often an excellent *evaluation* strategy in that it provides more sources of formative feedback to students than the teacher alone could provide.

Of course, if students observe each other's performance, the last to be tested will also be the most instructed students—a great advantage. Some adjustment could be made for this in judging adequacy of performance. Alternatively, the role the teacher plays could become progressively more conversationally challenging as the end of the list is approached. This has the potential of making for good instruction, but poor, unstandardized evaluation. If the evaluation stakes are low and if multiple trials are possible for each student (such as by working back through the class in reverse order), then it might be adequate for the teacher to use the rating form presented in Figure 8–4 to rate each student at least twice while the teacher progresses through a series of roles from skillful conversationalists to painfully shy ones or monopolizing bores.

An issue that was implicit in the above examples should be made explicit. *Good records should be kept of observations.* Mental recordkeeping, although common, is ill-advised because (a) useful information is forgotten, (b) recalled incidents are attributed to the wrong students, (c) subsequent observations will influence recall of earlier observations of the student, and (d) interpretations of subsequent observations of a student are biased by the student's earlier events (Stiggins, 1987). Thus it is wise to maintain careful, systematic records of performance data.

Two Potentially Useful Suggestions

Much attention has been given to the one major rule for evaluating performance measures—identify the criteria and be ready to observe them while the performance is under way. Two other suggestions can be offered for occasional use. One is to electronically record the performance when it will serve instructional or summative evaluative purposes. If the assessment is serving a formative purpose, the recording can often help the student to improve. Or if a summative assessment is particularly important, then being able to view the performance more than once may enable the teacher to make better judgments than would otherwise be possible.

The other suggestion is to use multiple raters of performances when the decision is especially important. Actually, this is commonplace in many kinds of contests. Multiple judges in the final rounds of debate tournaments or swim meets are more the rule than the exception. However, in classroom settings, the use of multiple raters is not usually practical. It might be noted, however, that if performances are electronically recorded, the logistical problems of securing multiple raters is often lessened because each can work when it is convenient.

An additional situation exists in which multiple raters are practical, even when the decision to be made concerning the measurement is not unusually important. That is the situation noted above when there is instructional value for students to rate each other. It is common in speech, debate, and driver education classes, for example, for students to critique each other's performances. The purpose is not only to provide constructive feedback to the performer, it is also to sensitize student raters to the importance of the features of the tasks. This is yet another way in which student familiarity with the bases of grading can favorably impact learning.

Maximum vs. Typical Performance

It is time once again to consider the distinction between what a student *can do* under conditions that produce maximum effort and what he or she ordinarily *does do* under typical conditions. In some performance measures, the distinction is very important because most people do not consistently perform at their best. Teachers using performance measures should carefully consider whether they should assess students' maximum performance and/or their typical performance. Several issues enter into this decision. Three examples will show how the issues operate.

Consider first the omelet-making performance test (or, if the teacher had elected, the paper-pencil substitute for it). The teacher might reason that students who decide to make omelets in everyday situations will be motivated to do a good job. Hence there is no pressing need to distinguish between students' maximum efforts and their typical efforts; the two will not differ sharply. In this case the teacher would not need to worry about assessing omelet making under typical conditions.

Consider next the safety goggles in the shop class. The teacher would reason that students who use the power equipment in everyday situations will often be tempted to take shortcuts. Moreover, the possible adverse consequences of doing so are dire. Hence an important distinction exists between students' maximum efforts and their typical efforts, and the two may differ. In this case the teacher would want to assess students' typical use of the safety goggles when they are under work conditions as commonplace as can be arranged. Fortunately, as long as students are in the class, the instructor is in a position to observe their typical behavior; therefore assessment of this typical performance is relatively practical.

Finally, consider the teacher of music appreciation whose developmental objective was:

1. Appreciates music.
    1.1 When a tape is played, does not throw spit balls.
    1.2 Orients ears toward source of music.
    1.3 Does not chat during concert.
    1.4 Spends own money and time attending concerts voluntarily.
    1.5 Checks tapes out of library.
    1.6 Discusses content of major works and own reactions to them.

Achievement of this objective, like most affective ones, is easily faked. The teacher might reason that some students will not develop much appreciation, but will "go through the motions" to satisfy the course requirements. Fortunately, no dire adverse consequences will result from failing to appreciate music. Hence the teacher might well decide not to measure typical performance for grading purposes because it would be excruciatingly impractical to do so.

Another reason a teacher might decide to neglect assessment of this important objective for grading purposes reflects the potential that the assessment process has to become perverted. For example, if students discover that they are being graded on the number of tapes they check out of the library, many will start checking out large numbers without listening to them. Librarians will be burdened, patrons who really want the tapes will be unable to secure them, and the grading practice will be invalid. This anecdote illustrates the issue behind the admonition: "Do not let indicants become the students' objectives." Checking out tapes is a useful indicant of appreciation *only* if it is measured under typical conditions. The moment it is measured under maximum conditions—as it would be if it were known to be used for grading—it ceases to be a legitimate indicant.

However, for the purpose of *program evaluation,* one might be interested in obtaining performance measures based on several such indicants. That is, if the school is investigating the extent to which a music appreciation course influences typical student behavior, then some of the above indicants could be used in a research study. Indeed if the study is done to evaluate the music education program rather than to evaluate individual students, then students probably would *not* be motivated to fake. In this context, regular self-reporting procedures, asking such questions of former students as "Did this course give you a greater appreciation of music?" would probably be even more useful than the performance indicants.

It is useful to consider performance measurement of typical behaviors from the perspective provided by the distinction among the three kinds of content and instructional objectives presented in Chapters 2 and 3. Track A content is vitally important. This is the kind of content that teachers should feel compelled to assess when it is possible to do so, even if doing so is awkward.

Concerning Track B content, teachers can best take a "the more the better" stance. Where one can assess student achievement of such typical performance objectives, one would; where it is impractical to do so well, one need not be compulsive. This flexibility results from the fact that Track B behavioral developmental objectives are not essential.

Track C content likewise is not vital; hence one need not feel compelled to assess every aspect of its typical performance dimensions. Moreover, as shown in the music appreciation example, the very act of assessing certain indicants of an affective developmental objective can lead to undesirable consequences. Under some such circumstances it seems a lesser evil to neglect (for grading purposes) the assessment of such an objective than to assess it.

QUIZ 8–3

Following are several instructional objectives, some from each track (although a standard would have to be added to make proper mastery objectives). The objectives all suffer from a fault—they do not make clear whether they reference maximum performance, typical performance, or both. For each objective, first decide whether the teacher's primary *goal(s)* should concern maximum performance, typical performance, or both.

QUIZ 8–3 (cont.)

Then consider the importance of the objective and the practical difficulties of assessing it to decide whether the teacher should focus formative and summative *evaluation* of individual students on maximum performance, typical performance, or both. In making the second judgment, consider practical issues. Maximum behavior is so much easier to measure than is typical behavior that it often makes sense for teachers to exhibit a consistent bias favoring maximal performance. On the one hand, a "tilt" toward the expedient is sensible. On the other hand, we should not completely "sell out" to expediency where doing so (a) is not necessary or (b) is too costly in terms of test validity and/or misdirected test power.

For both tasks, use the following key:

M = Mainly or exclusively *maximum* performance
T = Mainly or exclusively *typical* performance
B = *Both* maximum performance and typical performance

1. When walking, the pupil stops for red traffic lights.
2. Thinks critically.
3. Turns off room lights when they are not in use.
4. The driver does not "jump" lights.
5. Places a direct dial, long distance telephone call.
6. Starts a car.
7. Makes basketball free throws.
8. Is fiscally mature.
9. Writes neatly.
10. Turns away from other people while sneezing.

KEY TO QUIZ 8–3

1. Goal: T (or B); evaluation: B

   The teacher's real interest is in out-of-school, safe pedestrian behavior. This is a minimum essential, Track A objective. How well the child can perform on a test of maximum performance is really unimportant except for one thing. A performance test of maximum behavior reveals which children *can do* the desired thing. Those who cannot do it clearly will not ordinarily do it; for them, more instruction is obviously needed. Once they can do it, then the issue becomes whether they ordinarily actually do it.

KEY TO QUIZ 8–3 (cont.)

It would be quite inconvenient for the kindergarten teacher to assess typical behavior when the children do not know they are being observed. Yet the importance of this objective makes it desirable for the teacher to go to reasonable lengths to assess it (e.g., note how they perform on a field trip when attention is not focused on the issue, observe how they perform in simulations when they are somewhat distracted by other events, and systematically observe how they act on the way to and from school).

2. Goal: B; evaluation: M

Teachers obviously want students to be able to think rationally on command as well as in their ordinary activities. Assessment of student achievement of this Track C objective is much easier under maximum performance conditions than under typical performance conditions. Thus the teacher might reasonably (yet not ideally) "cut corners" and assess only under conditions that tap maximum performance.

3. Goal: T; evaluation: M (or B)

The economy is achieved from the routine habit of turning off the lights. Yet it will probably not be practical for the teacher to assess each child's degree of achievement of this Track B objective. Nor is it essential to do so. Therefore, the "tilt" operates toward the assessment of maximum performance.

4. Goal: T; evaluation: B

The driver educator would probably consider this an essential attribute of safe drivers. Yet, as in Item 1, maximum behavior is prerequisite to typical behavior. Therefore some maximum performance testing is useful to determine if students have the necessary knowledge.

Over and above this rationale for some maximum performance assessment, the teacher would probably have to bend somewhat to the impracticality of getting good observational data on each student's typical driving behavior. Together these two considerations would create a "tilt" toward maximum performance assessment. At a minimum, however, the teacher could assess this objective when the student's attention was more focused on other aspects of driving, thereby getting closer to typical behavior.

5. Goal: M, T, or B; evaluation: M

Since people who can make the call correctly ordinarily will do so, the distinction between maximum and typical performance is not very important. Hence the teacher of this Track A objective need not complicate life; simple mastery performance tests of maximum performance are very adequate.

KEY TO QUIZ 8–3 (cont.)

6. Goal: M, T, or B; evaluation: M

    Same as Item 5.

7. Goal: M; evaluation: M

    Here the teacher can be confident that students will ordinarily do their best, so maximum performance testing suffices.

8. Goal: T; evaluation: M (or B)

    What is fiscal maturity? Clearly it involves cognitive and affective developmental Track C material. And it is one's typical behavior that counts. So the objective mainly concerns typical behavior. But for the familiar two reasons, student evaluation shifts somewhat toward maximum behaviors. First, certain knowledge is a necessary but not sufficient condition to enable desired typical behaviors. Second, maximum behavior is much more easily and reliably assessed.

9. Goal: T; evaluation: B

    The reasons for shifting evaluation of this Track B objective somewhat toward maximum behavior are the same as those just reviewed. For some typical performance objectives, such as Items 3 and 8, there are few if any practical ways by which the teacher could reliably assess typical behavior. For other typical performance goals, there is, fortunately, the possibility of practical and consistent assessment. The metal-shop teacher is in a good position to monitor student use of safety goggles. Likewise, the elementary teacher is in a good position to consistently monitor neatness of handwriting.

10. Goal: T; evaluation: M

    Here again we encounter practical difficulties in assessing pupil typical behavior. Although a teacher does (and should) occasionally make an opportunistic observation of this behavior and use the results therefrom, opportunities are very limited. For assessing individual pupils, one would likely have to settle on paper-pencil testing of knowledge and/or on play acting performance testing under conditions of maximum behavior.

Directions and Procedures for Performance Measures

Directions ordinarily are designed to serve several purposes. They should inform examinees of the conditions under which they are to work, clarifying such issues as time limits and allowable aids such as tools, instruments, and references. Instructions should ordinarily indicate what criteria will be used in assessing the performance. The relative weight of various aspects of a performance or the relative weight of various performance tasks should be specified. In general, instructions should inform examinees of all the things that would enable an expert in the task who is not familiar with the testing conditions to achieve an excellent rating.

To some extent, however, the directions that should accompany performance measures depend on the nature of the task. Measures of maximum performance should ordinarily have directions and procedures quite different from measures of typical performance. Too, the instructions and procedures suitable for interactive performance assessments are not necessarily the same as those appropriate for non-interactive assessments.

Instructions and Procedures for Measures of Typical Performance

Measures of maximum performance ordinarily present no special problems. Their directions generally conform to each of the above points.

On the other hand, measures of typical performance present special problems. If examinees are to be assessed when they are operating as they most typically function, then *they should not know when their performance is being observed.* Therefore, instructions should *not* tell students when they will be observed. If, for example, instructions were to inform the driving student (intentionally by word or unintentionally by action) when she or he is being observed for "jumping" lights, then the performance measure would not be one of typical behavior; it would become one of maximal behavior.

It often makes the best sense in typical performance measurement to provide information about how performance will be assessed but to separate this information from the time at which the assessment will take place. An example of relatively formal measurement of typical performance would be an elementary teacher's statement to a class that each pupil will be rated on six different occasions for seat posture and that these observations will be made when students are not necessarily expecting them. The teacher might then make a point to systematically rate every child's posture at his or her desk on three different days at different times of the day while the class is engaged in different kinds of desk work. An additional systematic observation might be planned during the showing of a film, one during a paper-pencil test, and a final one during a class discussion. This should provide an assessment of typical sitting posture that is acceptable in both reliability and realism.

Another example is observation of students' interpersonal skills in class discussion of issues. A teacher might systematically rate each student a specified number of times. In both examples, students would be kept ignorant of when they were going to be observed.

These examples provide an opportunity to emphasize an important point. In both cases, the teachers *systematically* rated each student. In the second (and harder) case, the teacher might resolve to rate each participant's first contribution on a certain day. This protects against the tendency for raters to choose to rate those occasions in which a student's behavior conforms to the rater's preconceptions. For example, if the teacher had the preconception (founded or unfounded) that John's posture was very poor and that Sam's was good, then the teacher might tend to "catch" John in poor posture and to "catch" Sam in good posture. Conscientious teachers are systematic in order to guard against such biased, unnecessarily opportunistic observations.

A third example of formal and systematic observation of typical behavior introduces a slightly different twist. A shop teacher might wisely make a point of glancing up whenever a power tool is switched on to see if the user is using appropriate safety equipment (e.g., goggles). The instructor's motives are three-fold. First and foremost is the desire to prevent accidents; whenever a violation of this safety rule is observed, it must be promptly halted. Under these conditions of formative evaluation, students will assuredly know they have been observed to err. Second, the teacher would probably also use the results summatively for grading purposes. Third, the instructor would hope and expect the immediate corrections or reprimands of errant students would foster observational learning in others.

These examples of posture, discussion skills, and use of safety equipment illustrated systematic and formal observation of typical performance. In each of these cases, the students could know ahead of time how they were going to be assessed. Other examples could illustrate somewhat less systematic observation such as the driving instructor's careful observation of student tendency to "cut" corners even though the number of opportunities to observe this behavior might be small during any given driving session.

In still other circumstances, however, observation cannot be fully anticipated or planned; rather it has to be opportunistic. Pupil sneezing behavior, for example, can only be observed when the child sneezes. For some, it will likely never be observable by the teacher; for others, alas, numerous opportunities may exist to observe it.

Another example of opportunistic observations concerns the cautionary driving behaviors appropriate when a Frisbee lands in the street ahead of the car the student is driving. What directions should be given concerning such observations? Students can know that they will be observed, rated, and graded if and when opportunity to observe cautionary actions occurs. But transfer of learning is expected. Instruction might have touched on balls rolling out from behind parked cars or animals often being followed by children, but it likely would not have addressed Frisbees, badminton shuttlecocks, etc. Needless to say, the lack of student-to-student comparability will seriously limit the reliability of such measures.

Since such behaviors can only be observed opportunistically, we do not condemn opportunistic observation. Protection against systematic bias in selection of episodes can be provided by a teacher resolving to observe and record *every* episode of relevant behavior that opportunity presents.

Instructions and Procedures for Interactive Performance Measures

Interactive performance measures present valuable opportunities to probe and delve into selected aspects of performance in a manner tailored to the particular examinee. For example, a major advantage of oral tests over essay tests is the examiner's ability to pose follow-up questions. That is, oral tests typically are interactive. Along these lines, the Spanish teacher conducting an oral test in conversational Spanish might, upon hearing a student's use of the wrong word for a verb, act surprised and ask in Spanish something to the effect "Really? He did what? Remarkable!"

Such follow-up questions or clues reveal whether the student can adeptly correct the error with a minimum of damage or, with more directed probing and hints, manage to correct the error with somewhat more damage to his or her rating. Follow-up questions or tasks also enable the examiner to verify whether a student really has a serious misconception or merely misspoke. They thus help to assess the gravity of a particular examinee's problem.

Interaction is not limited to oral performance measures. A life-saving test might well have the student "save" the instructor from "drowning." How the "victim" acts would depend upon how the examinee approached the "victim." The individualization of the task is contingent on the examinee's behavior; this has the potential to enhance considerably the realism of the performance test.

Yet another variety of follow-up task is illustrated by a first aid test I recently witnessed. The task was to stop severe bleeding of a deep wound on the upper arm. The desired behaviors were (a) direct pressure on the wound, (b) elevation of the wounded arm, and (c) pressure on a pressure point. The examinee carefully, slowly, and neatly bandaged the wound loosely without doing any of the desired things. At this point, the examiner wondered if the student had misunderstood the rather verbose directions. So the follow-up situation was posed in which the victim had a severed foot; this situation was described rather graphically in very simple language. Again the examinee slowly provided a neat, loose covering to the "truncated" lower leg. The individualized follow-up task greatly enhanced the confidence with which the examiner decided to fail the student.

What directions or understandings should accompany these kinds of interactive performance measures? We would want to reassure examinees that follow-up questions or tasks are sometimes used only to check their confidence in a correct answer. They should also realize that follow-up questions provide an opportunity to recover partial credit for mistakes.

Chapter Summary

Performance measures enable teachers to assess many important outcomes that cannot be adequately measured by either objective items or product measures. Instructional objectives that are best matched with performance measures focus on student ability to do something. Being able to execute a performance differs from being able to plan it or being able to evaluate how well somebody else performs it. If we want to know if a student can play a given selection of music, sprint 100 meters, or speak French, the only way to find out is to have the student do it. It may be inconvenient or expensive, but it is the only valid way to assess achievement of the objective.

Performance tests are best for assessing attainment of goals that require witnessing the performance rather than by inferring it by examining its results. For example, if we want to know how well a student of fishing can fly-cast, we learn more by watching several casts than by counting the day's catch (which is influenced by a number of other factors).

Performance measures tend to be much less reliable than objective tests. For this reason, they ordinarily should be used only when they clearly provide the best way of assessing objectives. *Since reliability of performance measures is limited, its enhancement is important.* The establishment of clear marking criteria helps much. Multiple measures of a repeatable performance (such as a gymnastics feat) and the use of multiple raters (such as judges at a gymnastics contest) also enhance reliability.

Skillful use of performance measures involves two related components. The directions and the performance tasks have to be devised so as to elicit a realistic sample of the behavior of interest. This is achieved with thoughtful and careful crafting of the task to be tested and the situations in which it will be observed. Then the performance has to be assessed in a way that can produce reliable, valid ratings.

The kinds of performance measures a teacher uses communicate what students must be able to do. The appropriate use of performance measures to supplement objective testing and product assessment not only provides for well-balanced student assessment, but also provides for communicating to students the relative importance of various educational objectives.

Suggestions for Further Reading

Berk, R. A. (Ed.). (1986). *Performance assessment: Methods and applications.* Baltimore: Johns Hopkins University Press. A relatively advanced and comprehensive consideration of performance assessment methodology.

Fitzpatrick, R., & Morrison, E. J. (1971). Performance and product evaluation. In Thorndike, R. L. (Ed.), *Educational measurement* (2nd ed.). Washington, DC: American Council on Education. This chapter provides a thoughtful, research-based analysis of performance and product assessment with particular emphasis on simulation. The discussion helps identify some important tradeoffs (e.g., realism and reliability).

Payne, D. A. (1992). *Measuring and evaluating educational outcomes.* New York: Merrill. Chapter 9, "Using Observation and Simulation with Rating Scales to Assess Process, Performance, and Product Outcomes," provides a solid introduction to these topics along with good examples of rating forms.

Priestly, M. (1982). *Performance assessment in education and training: Alternative techniques.* Englewood Cliffs, NJ: Educational Technology Publications. An introductory textbook on performance assessment.

Stiggins, R. J. (1987). Design and development of performance assessments. *Educational Measurement: Issues and Practice, 6,* 33–42. A step-by-step description of how to develop performance measures appropriate for classroom use.

Editing, Producing, Administering, Scoring, and Analyzing Teacher-Made Tests

Previous chapters have focused on planning evaluation methods and developing valid items and tasks to assess student achievement of instructional goals. This final chapter of the section addresses disparate issues involving assembling, editing, producing, administering, and scoring tests. Also considered are ways in which scores can be analyzed to improve the test, and ways in which test items can be filed and appropriately reused.

Assembling the Teacher-Made Test

After a teacher creates or compiles the items necessary to satisfy the table of specifications, these questions have to be sequenced and formatted into a well-designed test and provided with appropriate directions. These "final touches" contribute significantly to the overall quality of the measure and are well worth the time and effort they require for careful execution.

Organizing the Mixed Test

Tests that foster student learning across a broad spectrum of mental processes often consist of more than one item type. The simple kinds of questions are seldom sufficient to give appropriate emphasis to higher-order learning. Multiple-choice items, in contrast, can be more adequate by themselves, yet even they often need to be complemented by other kinds of items. Essay questions are less commonly found as the sole kind of item in well-designed tests because some of the outcomes to be measured can often be tapped with easier-to-use and more reliable item types.

Therefore, Track C paper-pencil tests should often include more than one kind of test question. There is no virtue, however, in systematically using each major item type in a test; this leads to short, choppy sections. Just as a surgeon or carpenter should not feel compelled to use every available tool for any one operation or job, the teacher should use only those item types that are appropriate for a given test.

This section concerns the organization of tests that contain a mixture of item types. There are three obvious ways in which such tests could be structured: by item type, by content or instructional objective, and by difficulty.

Organizing by Item Type. Ordinarily the superordinate organization is by item type. Thus, all the questions of a given kind are grouped together and *accompanied by directions* (Millman & Greene, 1989). The simpler item types are located early in the test in order to get examinees off to a secure start and to make sure they reach all the items they would likely have the least need to ponder. This criterion gives rise to the following rules.

1. If completion, short answer, and/or alternate-choice items are used, their separate section(s) should precede the rest of the test. If more than one of these item types are used, their sections may appear in any order.

2. If multiple-choice and/or matching items are used, their separate section(s) should come next, in either order.

3. If interpretive exercises are used, they usually should be next.

4. If essay questions are used, they should appear in the last section.

Organizing by Content or Objective.   It is rarely useful to organize tests by content. Tables 4–6, 4–7, 4–8, and 4–9 exemplify test plans in which segregation by content would be neither necessary nor helpful. However, in other situations (such as those illustrated in Tables 4–1, 4–2, and 4–9), desirable organization by objectives is some-times automatically achieved by the use of different item types and directions for dif-ferent kinds of learning outcomes.

In those unusual situations in which a test maker wishes to keep topics or instructional objectives separate, the task is usually best accomplished by segregating the topics or learning outcomes within item type. That is, one would not have sev-eral sections for any item type, but would instead locate the items on a given topic or objective together within each section. This arrangement requires no special head-ings or directions.

Organizing by Difficulty.   Of the three ways of structuring typical tests, item difficulty is the subordinate concern. It is given attention only after questions have been orga-nized by item type.

The rule is to arrange the questions of each type in order from easiest to hard-est (Millman & Greene, 1989). However, a teacher usually does not know the exact order of item difficulty. In this case, the rule is applied as best one can by estimating or guessing how difficult each question is. Although it is not vital that item order closely parallel item difficulty, it is good for the first few items within each section to be relatively easy ones on which examinees can get off to a secure start. It is also desirable for any items that are clearly the most difficult to come at the ends of their respective sections in order to minimize the possible impact of discouragement on student effort.

Most educators want most tests to measure power *much* more than speed. Yet, as will be seen in Part IV, some degree of speed is common for logistic reasons. Therefore, test makers often seek to minimize its impact. If a test is at all speeded (i.e., if any examinees lack sufficient time to attempt all items), then there is an addi-tional reason why the hardest items in the last section should be located at the end. It minimizes the impact of speed. Examinees who do not have time to attempt the last few questions are penalized least if the unattempted items are the ones they would have had the poorest chances of answering correctly.

Providing Appropriate General Directions

Every test should open with general instructions. These directions should tell how much total working time is available. They should also indicate how and where stu-dents are to mark their answers. If separate answer sheets are used, examinees should be reminded to put their names on the answer sheets. Finally, general instruc-tions should often instruct examinees who have questions to remain at their desks and let the teacher come to them.

The general directions should bring to examinees' attention any peculiar fea-tures of the test. Any unusual provisions (e.g., allowing students to use their notes) should be explained in the directions and made known to students at least one day before the test to enable them to prepare appropriately.

Directions should indicate which, if any, resource materials (e.g., dictionaries) and tools (e.g., hand calculators) may be used. This too should be known by students before the test. This kind of prior knowledge not only reduces anxiety, but also serves to guide student effort. As an example, suppose a science teacher does not value formula memorization and accordingly decides to write all the needed ones (and perhaps some additional ones to ensure that students can identify the relevant one) on the chalkboard. If the teacher kept this intent secret, then some students would devote study time to memorizing formulas rather than to practicing their use—the thing the teacher values more. Hence, test power is better harnessed by telling students ahead of time what they do and do not need to memorize.

Finally, the directions should address the issue of guessing. Students should be informed whether it is in their best interest to guess on items about which they know nothing. This topic will be addressed later in this chapter.

Additional directions are necessary whenever there is a change of item type. Those instructions that are peculiar to each item type are presented at the beginning of the appropriate sections. The general directions address only those issues that apply to the entire test.

Editing the Final Test

After questions have been ordered, the entire test should be subjected to a final round of editing. This careful scrutiny of individual items will probably reveal some content flaws and item construction faults that have previously escaped notice. However, the additional purpose of this final editing is to identify items that provide answers or clues to other items. This need reflects the fact that previous editing probably focused at the item level. Yet when several individually excellent items are assembled into a test, some will usually clue others.

This final round of editing to eliminate interitem clueing is equally important for teacher-originated items, handed-down items from colleagues, or items obtained from teachers' manuals that accompany textbooks. Regardless of the source of questions, the probability is great that some will clue others.

The final round of editing should also attend to issues of balance. While item writing and item selection focus on adequacy of individual items, when a group of items of high individual quality are assembled, various kinds of imbalance are still likely to result.

Content imbalance is one such problem. Some topics are likely to be overrepresented, while others go untested. Of course, adherence to a test plan will have prevented much of this problem, yet few plans are detailed enough to prevent all forms of content imbalance. For example, a mechanics of expression quiz may specify four items on comma usage, but not specify *which* comma uses. This might result in a quiz having two items each on commas in introductory dependent clauses and commas in series, but none on other uses. The teacher who notices this in the final editing would probably replace two items with others (e.g., one measuring commas in compound sentences and one on commas and parenthetical content).

Another kind of balance concerns stereotyping people by such traits as gender, ethnic group or age. For example, an arithmetic application test might have a number of story problems. It would be wise to tally the number of stereotypic portrayals versus nonstereotypic ones. Are the boys usually cast with jobs of newspaper delivery and grocery store sacking, while the girls do dishes, iron, and baby-sit? Or has the teacher "leaned over backward" to avoid this to the point of creating reverse stereotyping? A tally of traditional versus nontraditional portrayals will help achieve balance. At the same time, this final check provides a last chance to ensure that one has not slipped into use of outdated, gender-limiting occupational titles such as "box boy," "mailman," and "stewardess."

Yet another kind of balance concerns use of response options. To assess this, the key to objective sections should be made. Although it is not needed for scoring until after the test has been administered, the key should be developed at this time in order to tally the frequency with which various responses are used. For example, in a true-false section, there should be approximate equity between true and false items; if serious imbalance is found, a few items can be altered or replaced.

Similarly, each multiple-choice option should be keyed roughly the same number of times. Suppose a tally of 30 four-option, multiple-choice items were 5 As, 9 Bs, 11 Cs, and 5 Ds. This imbalance is great enough to be a concern. The teacher should seek ways to alter some of the items keyed B and C into items keyed A and D. After modifying several items, suppose the resulting tally is 7 As, 9 Bs, 7 Cs, and 7 Ds. Is this close enough to equal use of options? Probably so, provided the teacher is not guilty of a pattern of consistently overusing response position B. Exact balance is neither practical nor desirable; it would provide a basis for guessing. Approximate balance is all that is sought.

Many textbooks suggest asking a colleague to critique one's test and to make a key at this point. The process of having to think through each question enough to answer it forces a more careful scrutiny than is otherwise likely to occur. Most teachers, however, do not find it practical to impose on a colleague in this manner; nor do they wish to incur the obligation of rendering the same service for the other teacher. However, those who do form such reciprocal arrangements often report that other professionals catch many problems and save them from many a poor question.

Creating the Master Copy and Reproducing Teacher-Made Tests

Tests should almost always be reproduced. Writing a test on the chalkboard (even a short essay quiz) is rarely adequate. Likewise, dictating objective tests is not acceptable, even for brief true-false, completion, or short answer quizzes. (Spelling tests are, of course, an obvious exception; dictation is often the best possible way to present spelling items.)

Once questions have been arranged into the desired order, they need to be laid out page by page. In doing this, items should not be split between two pages, nor should the set of items in an interpretive exercise. Nor would one locate the directions to a section at the bottom of a page.

In developing a style, one should be consistent. Figure 6–1 on page 157, for example, illustrated some of the many acceptable ways of formatting multiple-choice items. One style may be about as good as another, but students should not be subjected to shifts of style within a given test.

When the master copy of a test is to be produced, a decision must be made whether it is to be handwritten, typed, or computer printed. When might each be best?

The master copy of short quizzes or tests—such as those that will fit easily on one side of one piece of paper—can be handwritten (although they need not be). This is especially attractive at the elementary school level, where quizzes tend to be quite short and where teachers often have extremely legible handwriting.

Longer objective tests should almost always be typed or computer printed. The only exceptions to this rule would be for certain science, math, and foreign language courses for which the typewriter or printer lacks necessary symbols. Even here, it would ordinarily be preferable to have a printed test with those symbols inserted by hand.

The decision between typewriting or computer printing will, of course, depend mainly on the teacher's skills, the available equipment, and the availability of secretarial assistance in test production. Most often, of course, teachers have to rely on their own skills. Where teachers have word processing skills and access to a personal computer with a good printer, their use is far preferable to a typewriter.

Indeed, if the teacher maintains an item file on a computer disk, the creation of a test is greatly simplified and it does not have to be re-keyboarded. Page layout and formatting is also much easier with word processing than with typing. Moreover, with word processing, the final round(s) of editing can also serve as proofreading. As more teachers gain skills in use of personal computers for word processing and item banking, these methods will probably become the dominant ways by which teacher-made tests are prepared and the master copy printed. (Appendix C provides further discussion of use of personal computers for item banking.)

Whatever method is used, the master copy should be neat, highly legible, and uncrowded. Examinees have enough to contend with in taking a test without experiencing difficulty in deciphering illegible material. They should be able to focus their attention on the test content.

Even if the master copy is neat, attractive, and legible, there can still be many a slip in its reproduction. Copy machines are commonly used to reproduce classroom tests. In using a copy machine, the operator needs to ensure that the glass cover is clean and that the adjustments are appropriate. The same is true of offset printing—an inexpert or careless operator can turn a neat, clean original into an unattractive, illegible copy. A few schools still use ditto masters to reproduce tests. This method makes it a little harder to produce neat, legible tests; however, it is still possible.

Administering Teacher-Made Tests

There is more to proper test administration than a casual observer might notice. The teacher or other examiner should attend to several important considerations even before the examinees arrive. Perhaps the most obvious is adequate working space. Examinees need room to lay out their tests and answer sheets. Desks or tables are preferable, but armchairs can suffice when necessary. Seating should be sufficiently spaced so that it is difficult—not easy and tempting—to look at another's answer sheet.

Other needs to which the teacher should attend before the test include provision for reasonable climate control, freedom from glaring light, and insulation from interruption. Hence, one should set the thermostat (if the room is equipped with one) well ahead of time. The shades should be checked to ensure that direct sunlight does not shine in students' eyes or on their desks. If a clock is not visible to students, it is a good practice to put time information on the chalkboard during the test. If regulations permit, the teacher might turn off intercommunication with the office or send a note asking that interruptions during the testing time be kept to a minimum. Finally, a notice on the classroom door announcing the test helps to minimize interruptions. Such a notice might read, "PLEASE DO NOT DISTURB: Test in Session."

Once students are assembled, necessary supplies (e.g., scratch paper, pencils, and resources and tools such as dictionaries and rulers) may need to be distributed. If adequate preparation and announcements have been given beforehand regarding what to bring and what may be used, much less confusion is likely to result at the time of the test.

As students are about to start the test, they should be helped to feel relaxed, yet serious. Care should be taken to avoid making the experience any more threatening than necessary. At the same time, a serious tone should be sounded, encouraging students to work hard and to do their best.

Standard classroom testing practice should be established concerning what students are to do if they have questions during a test. It would be nice if tests were so perfect that no questions would ever be legitimate, but that is not the case. Hence, some provision for asking questions needs to be made.

Students with questions should be instructed to remain in their seats and to raise their hands until the teacher comes to them. They should *not* be allowed to speak up with their questions; such behavior not only creates interruptions, but will often clue other students. It is usually ill-advised to allow students to come to the teacher's desk; they create traffic noise, can obstruct the teacher's view of the class, can waste time standing in line, and can look at other students' answers.

Once the teacher comes to an examinee who has a question, the student should *whisper* the question to the teacher. The teacher must decide "on the spot" whether the item is seriously flawed. If the student's question arises from "knowing too much" and/or spotting a flaw in the item, it should be answered. If the question reveals a typographic error of consequence, it should be corrected. If the question points out an ambiguity, it should be clarified. When the teacher decides to answer or clarify a question, the answer should be given to all students; a general announcement is in order.[1] (In such cases, the teacher should make a note to correct the flaw before reusing the item.)

If examinees see each other getting reinforced with answers to questions, they ask more questions; the testing environment deteriorates. This is the well-known *ripple effect.* (Hence every effort should be made ahead of time to prepare high quality tests for which few, if any, legitimate questions can arise.) If the teacher decides that an answer to a student question is not needed, she or he might best whisper something to the effect, "I cannot answer that," or "The question is correct," *and nothing*

---

[1]Some educators would take exception to this advice on the grounds that it ill prepares students to take standardized tests, where items can never be clarified. They would prefer to make it clear that questions on test content are never allowable. Although this may seem rigid, it need not be *if* provision is made at the time the test is discussed later for students to challenge faulty items. At that point, items could be double keyed, voided, etc.

else. By whispering this rather loudly, other students will see that the student did not benefit from questioning. As a consequence, they will be less likely to ask inappropriate questions.

A major job of the teacher giving a test is to ensure that each student does his or her own work—that no cheating occurs. Teachers can do several things to *prevent* problems of unauthorized help. Adequately spacing students is one. Another is requiring desks to be cleared of items not used in the test. Too, students should be directed to keep their eyes on their own desks. Another, of course, is to have standard classroom rules that prohibit communication (i.e., talking, passing notes, signing, etc.) during tests. Such rules not only help to prevent cheating, but they prevent distractions and interruptions as well.

The most important single thing a teacher can do to prevent cheating is to *be attentive and alert*. The teacher should sit or stand in a place where each student's head is visible; if this is not possible, the teacher should move very frequently to monitor the class. It is tempting to use testing time to do other things such as mark assignments, read, visit with a colleague in the hall, or clean the closet. All such activities distract the teacher from the job at hand—supervision. In addition, some activities distract examinees. Teachers who decide to read, mark papers, or perform other tasks during a test should be very mindful that *their primary duty is supervision*. They should glance up frequently to scan the class.

In supervising a test, one should *not* wander unnecessarily around the room or stand by an examinee's desk looking at her or his paper. At best, this is distracting; at worst, it creates anxiety, causing the youngsters to think the teacher suspects them of cheating. The idea is to be an attentive, but unobtrusive monitor.

When an examinee is considering looking at another's paper, he or she usually first assesses the risk. Is the teacher watching? When such a person glances up and sees an alert, attentive teacher in the front of the room, the student usually decides not to risk cheating.

When a teacher suspects a student of looking at another's paper, the best approach is usually to increase surveillance of that individual. Most such examinees will glance up from time to time to see if the examiner is watching. When this happens, the teacher should *be looking directly at him or her*. This may recur several times during the test. If their eyes meet each time, the problem will usually be "nipped in the bud," and there will be no disciplinary problem that requires overt action. When it comes to cheating, *prevention is better than cure*.

In spite of reasonable precautions, a rare student will still cheat. In such cases, it is best *not* to disrupt the class with an emotionally charged scene in which the offender is humiliated. Rather, the situation should ordinarily be handled later in private.

Many of the topics considered in this section concern various aspects of standardization. In order to be able to interpret people's performance on a test (in either a domain- or norm-referenced manner), the test has to be *administered* and *scored* under standard conditions. Each person must undertake the same tasks under the same conditions of difficulty. At the middle school or high school level, additional aspects of standardization are relevant if the same test is used in more than one section of a course. Attention should be given to assuring equal amounts of working time, equal *lack* of advance access to test content, and so forth.

Scoring Teacher-Made Tests

Chapters 7 and 8 addressed issues and made recommendations for scoring essay tests, other kinds of product measures, and performance measures. This section addresses issues relevant to scoring objective tests.

Separate Answer Sheets

Separate answer sheets usually significantly reduce the labor of scoring objective tests. Of course, no practical advantage to their use exists unless a test or quiz exceeds one page in length, printed front and back.

Unfortunately, separate answer sheets increase the complexity of the examinee's task. A very young child should not be expected to cope with them. A rule of thumb might be: Answer sheets should not be used below Grade 3; they should be used in Grade 3 only with average or higher classes that have been well instructed and supervised in their use; and they can ordinarily be used in Grade 4 and above with appropriate instruction and supervision.

When older examinees are given longer tests, much scoring time can be saved if the scorer does not have to flip through each student's test booklets to find the answers. The great economy achieved by use of separate answer sheets is that all the items for a test can fit on a single page. Figure 9–1 illustrates an answer sheet that was "customized" for a particular teacher-made test. Figure 9–2 provides an example of a more "generic" answer sheet that might be used for various multiple-choice tests consisting of 50 or fewer items having five or fewer options.

Accuracy of Scoring, Converting, and Recording

Recall that the defining characteristic of objective items concerns the reliability with which they can be scored. Once a key has been made, a set of answer sheets can be scored with little or no need for any subjective judgment. This is a major advantage of so-called objective items. Yet the fact that objective items *can* be scored accurately does not ensure that they *will be*. The possibility of error always exists in the scoring process.

The job of the person scoring a set of objective tests (teacher, clerk, aide, etc.) is to ensure complete accuracy of scoring. This job is made easier if the layout of the test or answer sheet is done with the needs of the scorer in mind. For example, completion items are much easier to mark if the answers are written in a single column of blanks provided along the right-hand side of the test booklet or on a separate answer sheet (such as those shown in Figure 9–1) than if they are embedded in the questions. Another thing the test maker can do to make scoring easier and more accurate is to avoid having students write or print **T** or **F** in true-false items or A, B, C, etc., in multiple-choice or matching items. Figures 9–1 and 9–2 illustrate ways to render students' responses less ambiguous.

Even if a test or answer sheet has been designed to make scoring easy and accurate, effort is still necessary to ensure accuracy. Some people make many clerical errors in counting number of items marked correctly. All of us occasionally err

Name: _____

Directions: Circle the **T** or the **F** for each true-false item.

1. T F	5. T F	9. T F	
2. T F	6. T F	10. T F	
3. T F	7. T F	11. T F	
4. T F	8. T F	12. T F	

Directions: Neatly write or print the word that best goes in each blank.

13. _____

14. _____

15. _____

16. _____

17. _____

18. _____

Directions: Circle the letter of the one best answer for each multiple-choice item.

19.	A	B	C	D	E		28.	A	B	C	D	
20.	A	B	C				29.	A	B	C		
21.	A	B	C	D			30.	A	B	C		
22.	A	B	C	D	E		31.	A	B	C	D	E
23.	A	B	C	D			32.	A	B	C	D	E
24.	A	B	C	D			33.	A	B	C	D	
25.	A	B	C	D	E		34.	A	B	C		
26.	A	B	C	D	E		35.	A	B	C	D	E
27.	A	B	C	D	E							

Figure 9–1.   Sample Customized Answer Sheet

when scoring a test. Another place where errors can creep in is in the conversion of raw scores into derived scores or percentage scores. Arithmetic mistakes can lead to serious errors. A final place where errors can occur is in recording scores in a grade book. Entry of data in the wrong row and numeral transposition are especially common errors.

Teachers in some schools have access to optical scanners that can rapidly and (if properly used) accurately score special answer sheets (that usually are as "generic" as the one shown in Figure 9–2). Where such answer media are used, students should be well instructed and supervised in properly and neatly using them. If coupled to computers, such technology can also make needed conversions and record scores in grade rosters.

Name: _____

Instructions: Indicate your answer for each multiple-choice question by filling in the circle under the letter of the one best answer.

	A	B	C	D	E			A	B	C	D	E			A	B	C	D	E
1.	O	O	O	O	O		18.	O	O	O	O	O		34.	O	O	O	O	O
2.	O	O	O	O	O		19.	O	O	O	O	O		35.	O	O	O	O	O
3.	O	O	O	O	O		20.	O	O	O	O	O		36.	O	O	O	O	O
4.	O	O	O	O	O		21.	O	O	O	O	O		37.	O	O	O	O	O
5.	O	O	O	O	O		22.	O	O	O	O	O		38.	O	O	O	O	O
6.	O	O	O	O	O		23.	O	O	O	O	O		39.	O	O	O	O	O
7.	O	O	O	O	O		24.	O	O	O	O	O		40.	O	O	O	O	O
8.	O	O	O	O	O		25.	O	O	O	O	O		41.	O	O	O	O	O
9.	O	O	O	O	O		26.	O	O	O	O	O		42.	O	O	O	O	O
10.	O	O	O	O	O		27.	O	O	O	O	O		43.	O	O	O	O	O
11.	O	O	O	O	O		28.	O	O	O	O	O		44.	O	O	O	O	O
12.	O	O	O	O	O		29.	O	O	O	O	O		45.	O	O	O	O	O
13.	O	O	O	O	O		30.	O	O	O	O	O		46.	O	O	O	O	O
14.	O	O	O	O	O		31.	O	O	O	O	O		47.	O	O	O	O	O
15.	O	O	O	O	O		32.	O	O	O	O	O		48.	O	O	O	O	O
16.	O	O	O	O	O		33.	O	O	O	O	O		49.	O	O	O	O	O
17.	O	O	O	O	O									50.	O	O	O	O	O

Figure 9–2.   Sample Generic, Multiple-Choice Answer Sheet

Scoring Formulas and Directions Regarding Guessing

In deciding whether to use a so-called correction for guessing scoring formula, one should first understand the problem the formula is designed to redress. Then one should consider the alternative acceptable ways of solving this problem. Finally, one should understand the need to have compatibility between a test's directions and the way in which it will be scored. This section addresses these three matters.

The Problem

Suppose that Mary and Joan are taking an 80-item, four-optioned, multiple-choice test. Each knows the answers to 44 of the items and is ignorant of the answers to the remaining 36. Further suppose (a bit simplistically) that when they guess that average luck yields right answers exactly one-fourth of the time (since each item has four options). Clearly Joan and Mary have the same knowledge and deserve the same final score.

Mary is a timid creature who always leaves blank those questions for which she does not know the answers. In contrast, Joan is a bold soul who never leaves an item unanswered; if she does not know the answer, she always guesses. In analyzing their performance it will be useful to count (a) the number of items each answers correctly (Number Right, or **R**), (b) the number each answers incorrectly (Number Wrong, or **W**), and (c) the number each does not attempt to answer (Number Omitted, or **O**). Recall that each knows 44 of the answers and is totally ignorant of the remaining 36.

Mary will get 44 right and omit the remaining 36. Hence her status is:

	R	W	O
Mary	44	0	36

Joan, on the other hand, will get correct the 44 items she knows and will guess on the remaining 36. With average luck she will get one-quarter of these 36 right (i.e., another 9 items for a total of $44 + 9 = 53$ right) and three-quarters wrong (i.e., 27 items). Thus, her status is:

	R	W	O
Joan	53	27	0

Now they deserve the same score because they know the same amount. They differ only in propensity to guess. However, if the teacher does nothing to render their test-taking behavior more similar and scores for number right, they will obtain different scores. Moreover, Joan's advantage will not be limited to this test; it will be consistent over time and across different subject areas.

The problem, then, is that student differences in personality and/or in test-taking sophistication give some a systematic advantage over others of equal knowledge. This is a major affront to fairness and to validity.

Two Ways to Deal with the Guessing Problem

Educators have pursued several scoring methods intended to give people like Mary and Joan the equal scores they deserve. The two general approaches are (a) to provide a test with directions that cause all students to adopt the same behaviors with respect to guessing and (b) to adjust the final scores in an attempt to remove the benefits that some examinees gain from guessing. Before considering workable versions of these two general approaches, we might best mention a method that does *not* work.

Some test makers try to get all students to act like Mary and to avoid guessing. To accomplish this, they instruct students not to guess. The directions can be strong (e.g., "Do not guess") or moderate (e.g., "Guess intelligently, but not wildly"). The fundamental problem with such directions is that some students violate them. Joan will probably still guess, wildly when necessary. The directive is not enforceable because students missing an item claim (often truthfully) that they really thought they knew the answer. Thus such directions, by themselves, cannot solve the problem. Fortunately, two general approaches are serviceable in obtaining justice.

Solution via Directions.　We have just seen that directing all students to avoid guessing is ineffectual because it is to their advantage to violate such directions. However, directing all students to mark every item, guessing wildly if necessary, is effective because it is to their advantage to conform. At the high school level, such directions can read something like, "Your score will be the number correct. It is therefore to your advantage to mark every item." For younger examinees, the idea requires more explication. For example, "Answer every question. If you know the answer to a question, mark it. If you do not know the answer, make the best guess you can. Your score will be the number of questions you answer right, so be sure not to leave any answers blank. Mark every item."

Such instructions are "enforceable" in the sense that students who omit answers thereby clearly identify themselves as violators of the "answer every item" directions. The teacher can point out to them that they penalized themselves in not following directions; thus, teacher and student have common motives of getting the student to follow the directions in the future. Pupils quickly learn to comply. People like Mary are thereby caused to adopt the more test-wise practice of people like Joan, and the injustice is righted.

This solution works very well. Educators who like it perceive guessing as a behavior that is appropriate in some situations and inappropriate in others. Such teachers define a test as a place where guessing is permissible and see no significant risk of transfer of guessing behaviors to places where it is maladaptive. They like the simplicity of the solution of directing examinees to answer every item and then scoring for number right.

Although this method works admirably and is the preferred solution of most measurement authorities, some teachers have reservations about directing students to guess wildly. They fear that it will teach poor practices. Such teachers therefore seek another solution to the problem.

Solution via Scoring Formula.　Teachers who are unwilling to direct students to mark every item (thereby effectively demanding that they guess wildly when necessary) need another way to solve the injustice. Fortunately, other ways exist, but they are less adequate and require more work. These methods involve use of scoring formulas designed to remove the impact of guessing. They seek to take away the extra points that students like Joan obtained from guessing.

The most widely used formula is: $FS = R - \dfrac{W}{C-1}$

where *FS* is the final score, *R* is the number right, *W* is the number wrong, and *C* is the number of options per item. To see how the formula works in (simplified) theory, reconsider Joan who answered 53 items right and 27 wrong. Inserting these values into the formula yields,

$$FS = R - \frac{W}{C-1} = 53 - \frac{27}{4-1} = 53 - \frac{27}{3} = 53 - 9 = 44.$$

The result of 44 is the same score Mary obtained without guessing. Thus, in (over-simplified) theory, the scoring formula removed the impact of guessing.

Alas, the theory is not very tenable, in part because most guessing is not random (Thorndike, 1971, p. 59). Much guessing is based on partial knowledge, and examinees usually perform better than chance. Yet the formula only corrects for *wild* or *random* guessing. Hence, it systematically *under*corrects for guessing; it is only a partial solution.

Since informed or "intelligent" guessing typically yields better-than-chance results, students should not be directed to refrain from all guessing. Those doing so are penalized. Rather, when the scoring formula is used, students should be instructed only to avoid completely *wild* guessing.

At the secondary level, it is often sufficient for directions to announce use of the above formula with a statement that "your score will be the number correct minus a fraction of the number wrong. Therefore, it is to your advantage to guess intelligently, but not wildly." At the elementary level or with examinees who are not sophisticated in test taking, directions ought to go into more detail. For example, "Your score will be the number right minus a fraction of the number wrong. If you have any idea at all of what the best answer is, then mark it. This kind of intelligent guessing is to your advantage. But if you have absolutely no idea of what the best answer might be, then it is best to omit it. In other words, guess intelligently, but not wildly."

For a number of reasons, including those considered above, "formula scoring is generally inappropriate for classroom testing" (Frary, 1988, p. 37). The main exception to this generalization involves highly speeded tests.

Recall that a speeded test consists of very easy items that most people can answer correctly if given sufficient time. Such tests measure *how fast* examinees can work. If directions were issued to answer every item in a speeded test, then much guessing would occur as the time ran out and much more error of measurement would be introduced. Therefore, directions in speeded tests should be to guess intelligently, but not wildly. In order that scoring be compatible with these directions, scoring formulas are recommended for such instruments (American Psychological Association, 1974, p. 19).

Honesty of Test Directions

It is to this issue of consistency between directions and scoring procedures that attention is now directed. *Test directions should honestly tell examinees what to do to maximize their scores* (Thorndike, 1971, p. 61). The best strategy for maximizing scores depends, of course, upon how the test is to be scored. Authors of both classroom tests and of published tests realize they have a choice of directions regarding guessing. They also realize they have the option of scoring for number right or by formula. Unfortunately, many test makers exercise these two choices independently without realizing that the two choices must be compatible.

If scoring is to be done the easiest way—for number correct—then the directions must tell examinees to mark every item. In this context, it is unethical to urge them to avoid wild guessing because those who follow such directions will tend to answer fewer item correctly than they would if they violated the directions. Educators should not reinforce violations of rules.

The top section of Figure 9–3 summarizes this set of compatible directions and scoring procedures. Teachers can have the convenience of scoring power tests for number right *if* they can live with directions that instruct students to mark every item, even if this requires wild guessing.

Directions	Scoring Method
Mark every item.	Number right
Guess intelligently, but not wildly.	Formula

Figure 9–3.   Compatible Combinations of Test Directions and Scoring Methods

Some teachers cannot live with such directions. They believe it is wrong to instruct students to guess wildly. Teachers can avoid directing examinees to answer every item *if* they use the scoring formula to remove the advantage that some students would otherwise obtain from violating directions that discourage wild guessing. The bottom section of Figure 9–3 summarizes this set of honest and compatible directions and scoring procedures.

The goal of directions should be to convey information on the relative effectiveness of various strategies and thus to provide all examinees with an equal opportunity to perform optimally (American Psychological Association, 1985, p. 28). The point to be emphasized is that a mismatch of directions and scoring procedures can give a systematic advantage to people like Joan and a consistent disadvantage to those like Mary. Many tests instruct examinees to guess intelligently but not wildly and then score for number right. This is unethical in teacher-made tests and in published ones alike.

QUIZ 9–1

1. The conventional scoring formula is, $FS = R - \dfrac{W}{C-1}$. We have seen that for four-option, multiple-choice items this works out to be,

   $$FS = R - \frac{W}{3}.$$

   What is the formula for five-option, multiple-choice items?

2. What is the formula for alternate-choice items?

3. What is the formula for items in an eight-option matching exercise?

4. For which objective item type would use of the formula have the greatest impact? Why?

QUIZ 9–1 (cont.)

5. Some writers refer to the formula, $FS = R - \dfrac{W}{C-1}$, as a *correction for guessing formula*. This is a poor name because it seriously overstates what the scoring formula does. How so?

6. Some test authors do not address the issue of guessing in the directions because they do not wish to tell students to guess wildly. Then they score for number correct because this is the most convenient way to score. Is this an honorable "way out" of the guessing "problem"?

KEY TO QUIZ 9–1

1. $FS = R - \dfrac{W}{4}$

2. $FS = R - W$

3. $FS = R - \dfrac{W}{7}$

4. The formula has the greatest impact in alternate-choice items because $C =$ only 2; hence, $C - 1 = 1$, and the formula simplifies to $FS = R - W$. It is because guessing has the greatest impact in alternate-choice items that teachers most often use the formula with them.

5. The formula, on average, corrects or adjusts only for wild guessing. When guessing is intelligent—as it often is—the formula undercorrects. Here is an example.

    On a 70-item, three-option, multiple-choice test Sam knows 30 items and is able to eliminate an average of one of the three options on each of the remaining 40 items before guessing. Hence, he will likely answer about half of these 40 questions correctly for an additional 20 points. So his scores are:

    $R = 30 + 20 = 50$

    $W = 20$

    $O = 0$

    Therefore, $FS = 50 - \dfrac{20}{3-1} = 50 - 10 = 40$.

    He only knew 30 of the items, but his "corrected" score is 40; hence, in a sense, the formula has *under*corrected. It is not undesirable that his partial knowledge should yield the extra 10 points. The point is that the formula does not correct for all guessing, only for wild guessing.

6. No! If test directions make no mention of what to do about guessing, then the Marys will not guess and the Joans will; the problem is not solved. Sticking one's head in the sand does not solve problems.

Keeping an Item File

Creating effective classroom tests is an important aspect of effective teaching (Sadler, 1983). Tests not only measure student achievement, they also shape it (Crooks, 1988). Most students try to learn what they have reason to believe will be assessed. To capitalize on this powerful force, teachers should give primary emphasis to those learning outcomes that they most value. This typically concerns higher mental processes.

Unfortunately, creating test items that effectively measure deep learning is not easy. It requires effort, creativity, test-making skills, competence in the subject matter, and knowledge of learner characteristics. Even then, many of the questions we create turn out to be ineffective in one way or another. Since good items are so hard to come by, it behooves us to retain those that function well. It is wise to establish a file of test items for each unit. Then when it is time to build a new test, one need not start from scratch. One can select from the file most of the needed items from those that have been used in the past. New questions need only be created either to fill in the cells of the table of specification that are inadequately represented or to create alternative items for purposes of test security.

To attain such efficiency, teachers need systematically to file used test items. The file can be as simple as a folder containing old tests. This, method, however, renders keeping track of individual items very awkward. A better, but very old-fashioned, method is to have a file box of note cards on which individual questions appear. This method is much better for sorting items and assembling new forms.

The best approach for increasing numbers of teachers in this era of the personal computer is a computer file of items for each unit, classified by content topics and mental process. Even the simplest computer file (using nothing beyond word processing software) liberates the teacher from the need to keyboard and proofread each time an item is used. Computerized item storage, test assembling, and item editing should be seriously considered by any teacher who has convenient access to a personal computer and who has basic skills in word processing. Additional skills and computer software enable more sophisticated activities such as access of items by their classification categories and maintenance of records of items' past effectiveness directly in the file. Appendix C treats this topic in greater depth.

Retention and reuse of test *items* is helpful. Habitual reuse of *whole tests* is often ill-advised, especially at the secondary level. For one reason, unit content often does and should change from year to year. For another, students can pass old tests along to younger students, enabling them to "study to the test." This risk would be greatest if teachers allowed students to keep their old tests. For Track A tests, as well as certain Track B tests, this is little problem because the entire domain is often tested, and test security is not a major concern. In Track C tests, however, as well as Track B tests that sample a larger domain, test security is important.

Allowing students to keep their old tests is usually ill-advised even when tests are substantially revised from one year to the next (Terwilliger, 1989, p. 19). Little reason exists to let students keep their old tests. One would ordinarily want to return students' tests while going over the results and discussing various issues, but the tests usually should be re-collected at the end of this session.

Aside from seeking to violate test security, why are some students eager to keep their tests? Mainly for three reasons. First, they expect individual questions to be reused later in a course, such as on a final examination. In Track C content, items should *not* be reused the same term. Each test is a mere sample of the content domain; teachers should do nothing (such as retesting with the same items) to encourage students to focus their study emphasis on what happened to have been sampled in the past (Gronlund & Linn, 1990, p. 260).

Second, some students wish to restudy and "remediate" their errors item-by-item. In Track C, individual items are not essential and need not be remediated. Other material that happened not to have been sampled in the test could be studied just as advantageously. Moreover, test items are not a good focus for study; they tend to be atomistic and isolated, and they do not provide structure for learning. Test items are not designed to be study aids, and they are not as effective in this respect as materials that are designed with this aim in mind.

Third, some pupils may wish (or be expected) to bring tests home to report to their parents. This is not necessary; parental monitoring of Track C work can be done with scores and grades without full tests. Parents might better be encouraged to keep informed about their children's studies by looking at curricular materials. And, of course, parents are always welcome to inspect their children's tests during parent-teacher conferences.

As test items are used, a record of their effectiveness should be kept. Good items can be retained, while poor ones should be discarded or revised. This is the next topic.

Item Analysis

It is possible to collect various kinds of numeric data regarding the performance of individual test items. Some item information concerns reliability (treated in Chapter 15); other information concerns validity (considered in Chapter 14). A few of these kinds of data are reasonably collected for teacher-made tests, while most are not. This section addresses only information that is easily secured for classroom tests. This delimitation focuses attention on traditional item analysis applied to Track C tests (and to those Track B tests that sample a large masterable domain that is not important enough to master). The kinds of data for which collection is practical only for published tests will be discussed in Chapters 14 and 15.

The Nature and Limitations of Traditional Item Analyses

Traditional **item analysis** concerns the extent to which information secured from each item agrees with information obtained from the total test to which it belongs. In other words, the kinds of item analyses considered in this chapter address the contribution of each question to the total score's ability to measure differences in examinee status.

Recall that in Tracks C and B teaching, individual differences are channeled into the achievement dimension. Thus students ordinarily differ markedly in achievement. Tests are designed to measure those differences. Tests are supposed to discriminate among those who know more and those who know less. The main point of traditional item analysis is to determine *how much each item contributes to the discriminatory power of the test*. Hence, the topic is pertinent only to tests that are intended to discriminate.

The concern, then, is with how well the score of each item of a test agrees with the score of the whole test. How consistent is each item's score with the total test score? It is important to note that this question concerns reliability, not validity. Item analysis data do not directly address the issue of whether or not items measure what they are intended to measure. For this reason, item analysis data should always take a back seat to judgment about item validity. What item analysis data can do is focus attention on questions that function peculiarly; the resulting scrutiny often draws attention to validity issues that would otherwise go unnoticed.

A **discrimination index** is a measure of an item's agreement with the total score. If a computer is doing the work, the best kind of discrimination index is a correlation coefficient between the item score and the total score. Most teachers, however, do not have the combination of three things needed for the computer to do the work, namely, computer access, test data in computer readable form, and item analysis software. (Appendix C provides relevant material for teachers who do have the three things.) Therefore, this section will introduce a kind of discrimination index that is a crude, yet serviceable, approximation to correlation coefficients that can be calculated quite easily by hand.

Conducting An Item Analysis by Hand

Increasing numbers of teachers have access to computers, computer programs, and computer readable answer media. And while they need not conduct item analyses by hand, recent surveys suggest that existing item analysis programs may be too difficult for typical practitioners (Baker, 1990; Hsu & Yu, 1989). So for the present, most teachers who want to use the information provided by item analysis will have to obtain it by hand themselves.

Following is a relatively simple way to *estimate* the correlation between each item's score and the total score. The steps will be more meaningful when the reader follows them through the examples that follow. Indeed, "walking through" the procedures may well prove instructive even to those fortunate individuals who have computer capability to conduct item analyses for their classroom tests. The insights gained help make for better item writing.

1. After you score all the tests or answer sheets (using either Number Right or Formula scoring), arrange them in order of scores from high to low.

2. Take out the highest 27% of the answer sheets (because this fraction yields the most stable results). Round a bit, if desired, to make the number more convenient for computing decimal fractions. Take out exactly the same number of the lowest answer sheets.

3. For each item, tally the number of persons in the high group who responded to each option. Do the same for the low group.

4. Convert these tally marks for the respective groups into numerals and then into decimal fractions.

5. Estimate the item *discrimination index* by subtracting the fraction of the low group that responded correctly from the fraction of the high group that answered correctly. Do the same for each distractor.

6. Estimate the *fraction passing* the item by computing the mean of the fraction of the two groups that answered correctly (i.e., add the two fractions and divide by 2).

Although item analyses are most commonly performed on multiple-choice questions, they can also be used for completion, alternate-choice, and matching exercises. Item analysis will first be illustrated with some data from the State Capitals Test from the end of Chapter 1.

A class of 36 took the test. First, 27% of 36 is computed. The product, 9.72, is rounded to 10. The top 10 and the bottom 10 answer sheets are therefore used. (In the event of tying at the bottom score for the high group or the top score of the low group, randomly select the number of answer sheets needed.) The number in each group answering each item correctly is tallied, then converted into a decimal fraction. This is shown in Figure 9–4.

	Tally High	Tally Low	Fraction High	Fraction Low	Disc. Index	Proportion Passing
ID	8	5	.8	.5	.3	.65
SC	3	1	.3	.1	.2	.20
IL	8	4	.8	.4	.4	.60
CT	7	5	.7	.5	.2	.60
HI	10	10	1.0	1.0	.0	1.00
WA	6	4	.6	.4	.2	.50
NY	9	4	.9	.4	.5	.65
CO	10	9	1.0	.9	.1	.95
FL	7	4	.7	.4	.3	.55
NM	9	1	.9	.1	.8	.50

Figure 9–4. Item Analysis for State Capitals Test

For Idaho, 8 of the 10 high scorers got the item right, while 5 of the bottom 10 answered it correctly. Thus 8 of 10 converted into the decimal fraction .8; similarly, 5 out of 10 = .5. The difference between these fractions (.3) is the discrimination index of the item produced by this particular class. The mean of the .8 and the .5 provides an estimate of the fraction of the total group that answered the item correctly ($\frac{.8+.5}{2} = .65$).

Notice that very easy items do not discriminate well. If everyone answers an item correctly, it cannot differentiate at all between those who know more and those who know less. Likewise, if an item were missed by everyone in high and low groups alike, it would not discriminate. The least satisfactory items from the perspective of revealing differences among examinees' achievement were Hawaii and Colorado.

What difficulty level enables good discrimination? A perfect positively discriminating item would be answered correctly by everyone in the high group and missed by everyone in the low group. Thus the fraction of the high group answering correctly would equal 1.00 and the fraction of the low group would equal 0.00; the discrimination index would thus be maximized at 1.00 and the proportion passing would be .50. Although none of the above items performed in this way, the closest approximation was New Mexico, which produced an impressive discrimination index of .8.

We will next illustrate item analysis with a Track C, 50-item, multiple-choice test administered to several classes totaling 77 people. Twenty-seven percent of 77 is 20.8. This might best be "rounded" down to 20 in order to simplify computation. Data for three items of this test are shown in Figures 9–5, 9–6, and 9–7. Letters of keyed responses are marked with asterisks.

First, consider the item data reported in Figure 9–5. The asterisk identifies Option B as the keyed response. Of the 20 examinees in the high group, 2 marked "A," 17 chose "B," and 1 chose "D." Of the low 20, 3 marked "A," 7 selected "B," 5 selected "C," and 5 chose "D." Each of these numbers was divided by 20 to obtain the decimal fractions displayed in Figure 9–5. The item discrimination index was computed by subtracting the fraction of the low group answering the item correctly from the fraction of the high group answering it correctly. The fraction of the entire class answering correctly was estimated by computing the mean of the fractions of the high and low groups. The data for this item look very satisfactory.

	Option A	Option B*	Option C	Option D
High	.10	.85	.00	.05
Low	.15	.35	.25	.25
Disc. Index		.50		
Proportion passing		.60		

Figure 9–5. Item-Analysis Data for a Satisfactory-Appearing, Four-Optioned, Multiple-Choice Item. Asterisk indicates letter of keyed response.

Next consider the five-option item data displayed in Figure 9–6. This item introduces the additional idea of computing a discrimination index for each foil as well as for the total item. Overall, the item functioned very well; its discrimination index was .60. Yet Option B contributed nothing to the question's discriminatory power; as many high as low students chose "B." This fact should direct the teacher's attention to Option B. Studying it may reveal a flaw that can be corrected. If not, the item might well be left unedited.

	Option A	Option B	Option C	Option D*	Option E
High	.00	.15	.05	.75	.05
Low	.25	.15	.20	.15	.25
Disc. Index	−.25	.00	−.15	.60	−.20
Proportion passing				.45	

Figure 9–6. Item-Analysis Data for a Good-Discriminating, Five-Optioned, Multiple-Choice Item Having One Suspect Option. Asterisk indicates keyed response.

Finally, consider the data shown in Figure 9–7. This figure introduces a mechanism for dealing with omissions; they are tallied like options. The item discrimination index is a very modest .10. In looking for a reason, attention is riveted on Option D, which was chosen by *more* high scoring students than low scoring ones. This foil should be studied to discover what makes it more attractive to good students than to poor ones. Or, since Option C also failed to help the question discriminate between high and low achievers, the item might well be examined with an eye to discarding it altogether.

	Option A*	Option B	Option C	Option D	Omit
High	.70	.05	.00	.25	.00
Low	.60	.10	.00	.15	.15
Disc. Index	.10	−.05	.00	.10	−.15
Proportion passing	.65				

Figure 9–7. Item-Analysis Data for a Poor-Discriminating, Four-Optioned, Multiple-Choice Item Having Omissions. Asterisk indicates keyed response.

In these kinds of ways, item-analysis data can *direct attention* to questions or options that may be flawed, but *content decisions should be made mainly from the perspective of validity.* Items should never be deleted, edited, or certified as valid on the basis of item analysis data alone.

A caution should be sounded concerning the limited stability of item-analysis data obtained from single classes. Discrimination indices will vary somewhat from class to class owing to the instability of data from small samples. Also, slight class-to-class variations in instruction can influence student performance on items. It is important, therefore, to avoid overinterpreting data gathered from single classes. The best practice is often to record the data with the item in the file and await the accumulation of data from two or more classes before taking them very seriously.

What Difficulty Level Enables Good Discrimination?

As noted above, an item that is correctly answered by everyone cannot discriminate among students whose achievement differs. Nor can one that is missed by everyone. Nor can any other item answered correctly by the same fraction (whatever it might be) of high and low scoring examinees. The "ideal" item—from the rather narrow perspective of discrimination power—is one that would be answered correctly by all the high scorers and missed by all the low scorers. However, this is wildly improbable because students who do not know the answer often guess, and some of those who guess get it right. Thus the "ideal" fraction passing is more than 50% (except on those completion items on which guessing is not a factor).

Experts do not fully agree on what the "ideal" fraction passing should be in order to maximize possible discrimination power of tests. Many adhere to the rule of thumb that the fraction passing should ideally be midway between the chance level score and a perfect score. Others accept Lord's (1952) more sophisticated technical rationale, which leads to somewhat higher recommended fractions answering correct. Figure 9–8 shows the fraction passing that is recommended by each system.

Item Type	(Traditional Target) Fraction Passing	(Lord's Target) Fraction Passing
Completion or Short-Answer Items	.50	.50
Alternate-Choice Items	.75	.85
Three-Option Items	.67	.77
Four-Option Items	.63	.74
Five-Option Items	.60	.69

Figure 9–8.   Recommended Ideal Fraction Passing (Lord's Target) Objective Items

Of the two sets of recommended *target* fractions passing, I prefer Lord's values. For one thing, his values seem to yield tests having very slightly greater reliability (if other things are equal). The other bases for my preference are two closely related, nonmeasurement reasons. First, student morale is higher if the mean raw scores are higher, and less time is lost to defensive bickering when the test is discussed. Second, in schools where students are accustomed to percentage grading schemes,[2] they tend to panic when the mean score is lower than their expectation of what the average performance should be. True, one can and should explain that it is the norm-referenced meaning rather than the raw or percentage score that is important, but this takes time and the concept often proves to be quite difficult for students to grasp in environments where most other teachers use percentage grading (pseudo) standards.

Using Item-Analysis Data to Improve Teacher-Made Tests

Miss Tamblyn teachers a fifth-grade unit on vertebrates and uses a test that contains (among other things) a matching exercise in which pupils are shown pictures of *un*studied vertebrates to be classified. (Laudably, she is testing for transfer of learning.) Since she did not happen to revise this unit and the test had no obvious flaws, Miss Tamblyn used this test for three consecutive years and then pooled the three sets of answer sheets for an item analysis before revising and refining it. Figure 9–9 presents the results for selected items.

The first of these pictures was a frontal view of an armadillo. The data in Figure 9–9 show that the item did not discriminate well between high and low scoring pupils. *The value of the item analysis in this case would be the attention it attracts to the item.* What is wrong with the item?

Reflection brings to mind the validity issue that it *is* appropriate to expect pupils to recognize nursing as a clue, but what would be the corresponding clue from a front view of an armadillo? None are obvious enough to render the item *valid* for fifth-graders. The item is unreasonably hard. Pupils could eliminate fish, bird, and

---

[2]Actually, I contend that percentage grading systems lack a rational foundation for courses consisting of Track C content. The rationale for this bold assertion was provided in Chapter 3, and the topic will be explored more fully in Chapter 12. The point here, however, is that percentage grading systems (although usually irrational) are a fact of life in most schools, and student expectations concerning test difficulty are formed on the basis of the percentage grading systems with which they are familiar.

Front View of Armadillo

	Option A* (Mammal)	Option B (Bird)	Option C (Reptile)	Option D (Amphibian)	Option E (Fish)
High	.45	.00	.55	.00	.00
Low	.40	.00	.55	.05	.00
Disc. Index	.05	.00	.00	−.05	.00
Proportion passing	.425				

Unfamiliar Mammal Nursing Her Young

	Option A* (Mammal)	Option B (Bird)	Option C (Reptile)	Option D (Amphibian)	Option E (Fish)
High	1.00	.00	.00	.00	.00
Low	.90	.00	.05	.05	.00
Disc. Index	.10	.00	−.05	−.05	.00
Proportion passing	.95				

Unfamiliar Mammal With Udder Visible

	Option A* (Mammal)	Option B (Bird)	Option C (Reptile)	Option D (Amphibian)	Option E (Fish)
High	1.00	.00	.00	.00	.00
Low	.65	.05	.20	.10	.00
Disc. Index	.35	−.05	−.20	−.10	.00
Proportion passing	.83				

Figure 9–9. Item-Analysis Data for Several Five-Optioned Matching Items. Asterisk indicated keyed response.

amphibian from consideration, but the distinction between reptile and mammal was simply too hard. What to do? The item might well be discarded. Or a picture of a mother armadillo nursing her little ones could be substituted. Or at least a picture of a mother caring for her young.

This item illustrates how item-analysis data can direct attention to malfunctioning items. Once such items are subjected to scrutiny, the reason for the disappointing performance often becomes apparent, but sometimes it does not. In such cases a colleague can sometimes be helpful in identifying a flaw. Or high scoring students who missed the item can be asked why they chose their responses. The point is that an item should never be revised solely on the basis of its item-analysis data; rather its inadequate performance should be brought to light and thoughtfully considered. This is usually sufficient to identify flaws.

The second item whose data are displayed in Figure 9–9 is a picture of an unfamiliar mammal nursing her litter. The discrimination index for this item (.10) is also disappointing. The problem is that the item is too easy; the nursing litter seems to be too obvious a clue. Too obvious, that is, from the narrow perspective of discrimination. But is it a *valid* item? Provided that some students did not know this distinction before the unit and provided it was an instructional objective, then it certainly seems to be a valid idea to test. This validity consideration supersedes the issue of discrimination; Miss Tamblyn might quite properly decide to leave the item intact.

On the other hand, she might reason that this huge Track C domain has more potential items than she could ever use and, therefore, that she might seek a replacement item that is *both* valid *and* more discriminative. The third item whose data are shown in Figure 9–9 meets these two criteria. The nursing clue is very much present, yet it is not so blatant. As a result, the item is just as valid as the preceding one and it is also much more discriminatory.

Mr. Fong taught his 28 elementary pupils to make rough visual estimates of linear measures. He tested this skill with multiple-choice items. Twenty-seven percent of 28 rounds to 8, so he tallied the responses of the top and bottom 8 answer sheets. With such small numbers, he was very careful not to overinterpret the results.

Figure 9–10 shows one of his items and its data. The item had a very modest discrimination index because it was very hard for the high and low groups alike. Mr. Fong realized that he could render the item easier or harder by changing the value of the distractors. Because he decided that a somewhat easier version of the item would be just as valid as the original version and would also probably be more discriminating, he pursued *both validity and discriminatory power* by modifying the distractors. He used the revised item the following year with a class of 30. As shown in Figure 9–10, it functioned much more adequately.

Original Item: The approximate height of the teacher's desk is:

  A. 2 feet.
  B. 2½ feet.
  C. 3 feet.
  D. 3½ feet.

	Option A	Option B*	Option C	Option D
High	.25	.375	.25	.125
Low	.25	.25	.25	.25
Disc. Index	.00	.125	.00	−.125
Proportion passing		.31		

Revised Item: The approximate height of the teacher's desk is:

  A. 1½ feet.
  B. 2½ feet.
  C. 3½ feet.
  D. 4½ feet.

	Option A	Option B*	Option C	Option D
High	.00	.875	.125	.00
Low	.125	.375	.375	.125
Disc. Index	−.125	.500	−.250	−.125
Proportion passing		.63		

Figure 9–10. Item-Analysis Data for Item before and after Revision. Asterisk indicates keyed response.

Are Hand-Analyzed Item Analyses Worth the Trouble?

Many a thoughtful reader has been wondering how a busy teacher could find time to analyze every item of every test given and to thoughtfully use the results. Certainly, one's tests would be improved from year to year by conducting item analyses, but would it take more time than it was worth? Would it divert too much effort away from other aspects of instruction? It probably would.

I, therefore, do not encourage teachers to item analyze every test they give, but I do urge them to conduct an occasional analysis on at least some questions and to consider thoughtfully the findings. The number should be greater for teachers having computer capability to do the job.

Thoughtful consideration of item-analysis data serves two purposes. First, item analysis improves the quality of particular tests upon which it is performed. It helps teachers to decide better which items to retain intact in their item files, which to attempt to improve by editing, and which to discard outright.

Second, item analysis serves the less obvious function of helping teachers gain insights concerning such things as the student's option-selection process, characteristics of effective questions, and item-writing errors they commit. Studying the results of an item analysis on one's test provides instruction in test making. Thus, contemplating the findings of an occasional item analysis is a good professional development activity over and above its contribution to the particular test.

QUIZ 9–2

Suppose the following three questions were administered to 88 students in several sections of a high school English class. Twenty-seven percent of 88 is 23.76; to facilitate computation, the teacher would best round this up to 25. Examine the item-analysis data for each item. Where the data are worrisome, examine the content of the item to determine what should be done. (The asterisk indicates the keyed response.)

1. Return your application either to Rev. Stith or to
   A. I.
   B. me.
   C. myself.
   D. we.

	Option A	Option B*	Option C	Option D
High	.00	.92	.08	.00
Low	.04	.60	.32	.04
Disc. Index	−.04	.32	−.24	−.04
Proportion passing		.76		

QUIZ 9–2 (cont.)

2. The monkey scampered up the rope, leaped to the swing, grasped the other beast by the collar, and ripped *it* off. The *it* stands for:
    A. monkey.
    B. rope.
    C. swing.
    D. other beast.
    E. collar.

	Option A	Option B	Option C	Option D	Option E*
High	.00	.00	.00	.00	1.00
Low	.04	.00	.00	.00	.96
Disc. Index	−.04	.00	.00	.00	.04
Proportion passing					.98

3. The correct spelling of the possessive of Gladys is:
    A. Gladyss
    B. Gladyses
    C. Glady's
    D. Gladys's
    E. Gladyss'

	Option A	Option B	Option C*	Option D	Option E
High	.00	.00	.12	.88	.00
Low	.08	.04	.44	.40	.04
Disc. Index	−.08	−.04	−.32	.48	−.04
Proportion passing			.28		

KEY TO QUIZ 9–2

1. The item discrimination index of .32 signifies adequacy. Although Options A and D contributed little to the item's power, no substitute distractors come to mind. The item would likely be retained without revision. Or if the test contains an alternate-answer section, the item could well be converted into, "Return your application either to Rev. Stith or to (myself, me)."

2. The data reveal that the question discriminated poorly because it was so easy that it could not reveal individual differences among students in these classes. Examination of the item suggests two hypotheses. First, students at this level may have a good command of identifying most antecedents of pronouns.

KEY TO QUIZ 9–2 (cont.)

Second, close inspection of the item reveals a flaw. The noun that immediately precedes the pronoun is the keyed response; therefore, students who have the misconception that the antecedent to a pronoun is always the noun that immediately preceded it will get the item right for the wrong reason. This would suggest the use of a revised stem such as "The monkey scampered up the rope, leaped to the swing, grasped the other beast by the collar, and bit *it* on the head."

3. This item appears to be terrible; it discriminates in the wrong direction! One occasionally encounters a negatively discriminating item. When this happens, the first thing to do is to check the key. In this case, the only thing wrong with the item is that the teacher miskeyed it.

   When the key is changed to Option D, the discrimination is seen to be a very respectable .48. The fraction passing is now .64.

   When this is not the explanation for negative discrimination in a good-sized sample, scrutiny usually reveals some other serious item flaw(s).

Chapter Summary

An effective teacher-made test does not just happen. It is thoughtfully designed to be a contributing component of an integrated instructional effort to enhance student learning. The examination is then skillfully crafted item by item. Appropriate directions to accompany the test questions are created. It is then carefully assembled, edited, and formatted. Finally, the test is reproduced in a way that renders it legible and attractive.

Effective classroom testing also requires teacher attention to test administration. The work environment must be conducive to maximum performance. Above all, testing conditions must be uniform from student to student; thus every effort should be made to ensure that all have a fair chance to do their best and that none have unfair advantage over others. This concern for fairness obviously requires the prevention of cheating. It also directs attention to the need to eliminate disabling test anxiety; a calm, serious, and relaxed atmosphere should be established. Concern for fairness also dictates that all examinees operate on the same footing with regard to guessing; none should have a systematic advantage because of individual differences in guess-making tendency when in doubt.

After a test has been administered, its accurate scoring requires close attention. Likewise, the recording of scores in grade books must be done with care to ensure accuracy.

Finally, a teacher can gain considerable insight into test making by studying item-analysis results. In addition, investing some time in analyzing students' test performance can enable one to flag poor items, spot ways in which other questions can be edited and improved, and identify adequate and outstanding items that should be saved for reuse.

Suggestions for Further Reading

Ebel, R. L., & Frisbie, D. A. (1991). *Essentials of educational measurement* (5th ed.). Englewood Cliffs, NJ: Prentice-Hall. Chapter 13, "Evaluating Test and Item Characteristics," places the topic in a broader perspective and provides good examples of constructive use of item-analysis results.

Gronlund, N. E. (1988). *How to construct achievement tests* (4th ed.). Englewood Cliffs, NJ: Prentice-Hall. Chapter 7, "Assembling, Administering, and Evaluating the Test," provides sound coverage of most of the same topics as this chapter. In addition, item analyses for domain-referenced tests are considered—an area of validity that will be introduced in Chapter 14 of this book.

Hopkins, K. D., Stanley, J. C., & Hopkins, B. R. (1990). *Educational and psychological measurement and evaluation* (7th ed.). Englewood Cliffs, NJ: Prentice-Hall. Chapter 10, "Item Analysis for Classroom Tests," provides a good, focused treatment of item analysis. In addition to topics considered in this book, the validity issue of item analyses with external criteria is addressed.

Millman, J., & Greene, J. (1989). The specification and development of tests of achievement and ability. In Linn, R. L. (Ed.), *Educational measurement* (3rd ed.). New York: Macmillan. This authoritative chapter provides a brief, yet sophisticated treatment of most of the topics considered in Part II of this book.

Interpreting, Reporting, and Using Student Achievement Information

Some of the most widely cited findings of teacher effects research concern the favorable impact of frequent monitoring of student progress. This monitoring can take the form of informal observation and oral questioning or the more formal forms of structured testing by means of objective tests, product assessments, or performance evaluation. Regardless of which means of tracking student achievement are appropriate in a given situation, the need to assess achievement is always present.

Some purposes of educational measurement are best served by formative testing, which is designed to be relatively continuous and to provide immediate assistance to instruction and learning. Other purposes of student assessment are best achieved by summative testing, which is designed to be relatively episodic and to assist in keeping and reporting records of student status. Both formative and summative assessment share the fundamental purpose of enhancing student learning, albeit by rather different means.

Proper interpretation of test scores requires familiarity with certain concepts of elementary statistics. Similarly, proper use of assessment data for student grading purposes requires familiarity with basic concepts of data management. Part III, therefore, presents a few concepts of elementary statistics needed for use and interpretation of scores from both teacher-made measures and from published instruments.

Two of teachers' most important responsibilities, and ones for which they are held most accountable, are marking and reporting. Part III will culminate with consideration of grading practices that enhance learning, development, and communication.

10

Using Summative and Formative Measurement in Teaching

This chapter focuses on the use of teacher-made achievement measures to enhance student learning. Appropriately used classroom tests are potent instructional tools. However, in order for student assessment practices to realize their potential in enhancing learning, they need to be carefully *planned at the same time that instruction is planned*, not as an afterthought. While a teacher develops a unit's content and methods, some of the design activities should focus on complementary testing methods. This includes considering the types of tests, their content vis-à-vis the content of the learning materials, and their timing and frequency (Nitko, 1989).

Summative instruments are used to assess learning after it has taken place—to sum it up. **Formative measures** are designed to assist learning while it is still in progress—still being formed. Although these summative and formative varieties of evaluation differ in the means they use, they each can contribute to effective teaching through effective measurement. Therefore, the planning of each should be conducted with an eye to its instructional impact.

In practice, the distinctions between formative and summative evaluation are not as clear-cut as definitions may imply. David (1986) illustrated this point with a can opener. As a consumer, you evaluate a new can opener to see how well it works. The can opener has already been manufactured; if it does not work, you will return it. Yours is therefore a summative evaluation. Now imagine that you could adjust various parts of the device, for example, how it hooks to the can or how easily the handle turns. You use the same test—opening a can—but this time conclude that the handle needs to be adjusted. Now, although you are doing the same thing to test how well the can opener works—opening cans—you are using the information to change the product. Therefore, you have done a formative evaluation. Although the distinction between summative and formative evaluation can be stated clearly, in practice whether a test is summative or formative depends more on *how the information is used* than on what the information is.

Another illustration of the blurring between formative and summative testing is found in the quizzes in this book. On the summative side, the content is Track C, there is no need for precise diagnosis and prescription, and no "passing" standards are established. On the formative side, many of the items were designed to reveal common misconceptions and to provide "remedial" comments/instruction. Too, they are not used for grading. So are the quizzes predominantly formative or summative? Perhaps the question is best addressed by thinking of them as instructional quizzes because instruction was their primary purpose. This gives them a formative tilt.

Using Summative Measurement in Teaching

Before examining the role of summative assessment in the classroom, it should be mentioned that many important non-classroom uses exist for summative data. For example, summative tests are used to certify competence to enter occupations such as teaching, law, or real estate sales. Summative measures, of course, are used to provide records of level and breadth of school achievement. And they inform institutional decisions such as which students shall receive scholarships or which job applicants will be hired.

Our present interest, however, is mainly those classroom uses of summative evaluation that are designed to help teachers decide "where to go from here." This help in deciding "what to do next" is based on measuring "where are we now." A *sum*mative measure *sums* up a person's status to date.

Summative decisions in the classroom can take such forms as "Into which reading group should Melliana be placed?" "Would Juston benefit from the alternative lesson more than from the standard one?" "What grade should be awarded Fran for the term's work?" "Is Clark ready to take the lead in the school play?" "Have the pupils gained a satisfactory command of reading digital clock faces?" or "Has the class learned to factor common monomials out of polynomials well enough to be able to start factoring trinomial squares?"

Classroom Decision Making

Summative achievement measurement, then, provides help in reaching varied kinds of educational decisions. Consider the examples below in more detail.

Grading

Perhaps the most obvious kind of decisions aided by summative assessment concerns student grading. Should Madge receive an A or a B in chemistry? Is Eric's second-grade reading satisfactory? Teacher-made tests provide the foundation upon which sound grading practices are built.

Promotion

Closely related to grading judgments are promotion decisions. Should Heather be promoted from kindergarten to first grade? That is, would she benefit next year more from (a) a regular first-grade class, (b) a transition class, or (c) a repeat of kindergarten?

Many educators believe in providing a "gift of time" to enable slow developers to become ready before being thrust into first grade. However, the alleged benefits of delaying kindergarten entry, repeating kindergarten, and attending transition classrooms are more apparent than real (e.g., Mantzicopoulos & Morrison, 1992). Most low achieving students experience better cognitive and affective learning from regular promotion than from retention (Shepard & Smith, 1990).

Exceptions do exist, however. Although the best decision-making rule is "When in doubt, promote," there is an occasional youngster for whom retention offers the better chance of fostering desired development. Summative tests of student achievement provide one of the several important data sources that should be considered by teachers, principals, parents, and school psychologists in reaching wise promotion decisions.

Classification

Students are classified whenever decisions are made concerning their assignment to one category rather than another. Several terms, focusing on various aspects of decision making, refer to kinds of classification (Cronbach, 1990). Summative tests facilitate *selection* decisions when some students are accepted (e.g., for a school team or participation in an academic contest) and others are not.

Summative tests are used to make *screening* decisions to decide which individuals should be studied more closely (e.g., which may qualify for placement in a gifted program or which may have a hearing problem). Summative measures are used for *certifying* when results are used to allow students to participate in some activity, such as driving or intermural athletics.

Summative testing is used in *diagnosis* to identify what a student has and has not learned. Summative diagnosis differs in emphasis from the ongoing diagnosis of specific learning difficulties within a unit. In summative diagnostic testing, the focus may be broader than a particular lesson or unit. It may deal with an entire area such as reading, spelling, or arithmetic.

Summative assessment is used to help make *placement* decisions concerning levels of instructions, such as which students would benefit most from the lower reading group or from ninth-grade general math rather than algebra. Another kind of placement decision that teachers make with summative tests concerns assignment of students to cooperative learning groups. If each group is to contain one high student, about two average ones, and one low student, then the teacher judges the status of each student on the basis of prior summative data in the subject content.

Other Instructional Decisions

Teachers use results of summative tests for a myriad of other instruction decisions. Suppose a high school or community college civics instructor is appalled by a class's low performance on interpretive exercises in summative tests concerning First Amendment protection provided by the Constitution. The teacher might make a decision that the group's achievement was not high enough.[1] If the instructor values this topic more than others to come, then more exercise in understanding and practice in applying the First Amendment might be provided.

Notice that this use of the results to modify instruction is formative. The test, having been designed mainly to measure student achievement after it was all over, was said to be summative, and its use to grade students was summative. However, for the teacher, who will teach the unit again, it is not "all over." The instructor's use of the results to formulate better teaching is, of course, formative.

Consider how a middle school English teacher might use prior summative assessment of a class's performance in reading comprehension as a basis for deciding which of several novels to use for the particular class. Which novel would best match student capabilities? Should some students be assigned a more challenging work? Will others not be able to handle the standard assignment and benefit more from an easier one?

A fifth-grade teacher planning a unit on comma usage might use results of prior summative testing to decide whether to use a challenging section of the unit or to use some supplementary basic material instead. Thus the prior knowledge of pupils' capability in language arts would be used to decide which option would better serve the needs of the greater number of students.

---

[1] We might digress to consider an apparent contradiction. Application exercises concerning the First Amendment are surely Track C content—and thus not very amenable to domain-referenced interpretation. The teacher, however, has made a domain-referenced interpretation and an instructional decision based on it. The instructional/evaluation model presented in this book denies the appropriateness of such interpretations *for purposes of assessing individual students,* but the model is too restrictive in this regard for evaluating curricular programs or instruction.

How else could one judge the appropriateness of students' relative success on subtopics? Just as the physical-education instructor might wisely judge that soccer should be introduced into the program (presumably because it merits some time vis-á-vis other content) the civics instructor might soundly judge that the First Amendment should be introduced or given expanded coverage because it merits more time in comparison to other content.

The last two examples involve proper aiming of the level of instruction. The situations illustrate how important prior summative assessment is in helping teachers wisely target their teaching. Instructional level is appropriate when a lesson is neither too difficult nor too easy for students. A teacher's decisions concerning the instructional level at which a class or an individual will most benefit are of the utmost importance. If the teacher aims either too high or too low, teaching effectiveness will be gravely impaired (Slavin, 1987a). Thus a major contribution of summative evaluation to effective teaching is the assistance it offers teachers in appropriately setting their instructional levels.

Enhancing Self-Understanding

Summative measurement plays a prominent role in self-concept formation. Teacher-made and published tests provide information that helps students gain realistic insight concerning their strengths and weaknesses. Summative assessment yields information such as "I am tall for my age," "I'm poor in baseball," "I'm good in math," "My verbal aptitude is about average," and "I would probably not enjoy a job that required a lot of persuasive activity."

Although the last two of these examples concern aptitude and interest measurement—the subjects of Chapters 18 and 19—all of the judgments about self-status are summative in nature. Each describes status after it has been attained without any particular emphasis on altering that status.

The attainment of self-understanding is a very important goal of school. So is self-acceptance, especially in those attributes that are not amenable to alteration. Every teacher contributes to some aspects of students' developing self-concept. School counselors have special responsibility in this sphere.

Using Test Power

Summative measurement of student achievement provides valuable bases for several kinds of informed decision making *by teachers*. In addition, it serves several functions related to student decision making, including those decisions that are caused by student knowledge of the evaluation process. As emphasized repeatedly in this book, to a substantial extent summative *evaluation drives student effort*. The following discussion focuses on three closely related motivational impacts of classroom assessment practices.

Defining Important Learning Outcomes

Most students usually study what they believe will be assessed. They are adaptive. They do not study what teachers say they should learn merely because teachers say it is important. Nor do they necessarily study what they themselves think is important, nor what their parents say is important. Rather, they tend to study what pays off—what contributes to good grades. In this sense teachers' evaluation activities "speak" much more loudly than their words. Tests have this kind of power (Sadler, 1983).

Of course, test power is not absolute. It is not the only thing that guides and drives the efforts of most students. Indeed, for a few people, it is not even a major source of guidance. Yet by and large, evaluation has great power.

Effective teachers recognize this motivating and guiding power of tests. And they harness it. Good teachers exploit test power by ensuring that it causes students to conform to what the teachers want them to do. They do this by creating tests that measure the blend of content and mental processes they wish students to pursue. Astute teachers ask themselves two key questions about each measure of student achievement: "What does this assessment tell students about the achievement outcomes we value?" and "What is likely to be the effect of this assessment on students?" (Stiggins, 1991, p. 535).

Less expert teachers often use tests that emphasize mere recall or recognition of isolated bits of information. This approach encourages surface memorization of isolated details.

What is wrong with that? Unfortunately, isolated surface learning is destined to be rapidly forgotten. In contrast, *information that is learned within a broader framework of meaningful interrelationships is better retained*. Moreover, the factual knowledge that students acquire in school may be less important than the skills that can help them continue to grow and adapt. For these reasons, *we need to make deep learning a central goal of education, and to foster its development through the student evaluation*. This objective requires us to emphasize understanding, transfer of learning to untaught problems or situations, and other thinking skills. Moreover, it requires us to evaluate the development of these skills through tasks that demand more than recognition or recall of facts (Crooks, 1988, pp. 467–468).

This effect on learning was a major reason why so much space in Chapter 4 was devoted to the topic of planning classroom tests. Although most teachers rather adequately sample the content they have taught, many are less successful in sampling the mental processes, tasks, or instructional objectives they espouse (Nitko, 1989, p. 447). Test content is important, of course, in order for tests to validly measure student achievement. The complementary point here, however, is that *test content is important because it directs students* to pursue some kinds of objectives and it diverts them from the study of other possible goals (Lundeberg & Fox, 1991, p. 102). Therefore, teachers who make constructive use of measurement in their teaching make sure that their tests "send the desired messages" to students concerning what is important.

QUIZ 10–1

1. Jim Robinson teaches a one-semester, sixth-grade health class for 45 minutes a day. He has decided to use 20-minute tests. He wonders what the optimum testing frequency should be *in order to maximize student learning*. With which frequency would students probably learn the most?

   A. Twice a week.

   B. Once a week.

   C. Every two weeks.

   D. Every three weeks.

   E. Every four or five weeks.

QUIZ 10–1 (cont.)

2. Marge Johnson teaches eleventh-grade United States History. She is considering whether or not to give a cumulative final examination at the end of the year. Would a comprehensive final exam enhance the long-term memory of her students more than other worthwhile uses she could make of the time?

   A. Definitely.

   B. Probably.

   C. Probably not.

   D. Definitely not.

3. A typical, traditional, elementary school weekly spelling lesson consists of a list of words and one or two spelling rules. Students are to master the spelling of the words and to learn to *apply* the rules, yet the tests generally ignore the rules and do not require their use with any new, unstudied words. Rather the tests are based solely on the studied words. Is this wise?

4. Are the above three items designed to serve formative or summative purposes?

KEY TO QUIZ 10–1

1. A or B. Read on; this issue will be addressed in the next section.

2. B. Read on; this issue will be discussed in the section after next.

3. No. It not only fails to harness test power, but it actually creates a situation in which test power pulls students away from desired learning of rules. This issue is taken up later in this chapter.

4. Formative. They are intended to prompt thinking about topics about to be taken up in order to enhance learning while study is in progress. (In summative testing, it would not be fair to ask questions on material before it is studied.)

Pacing Student Effort

It is widely recognized that most students study more when the day of reckoning looms near than when the testing day exists only in the distant future. Even you and I, who should know better than to mass our practice rather than to distribute it more evenly, tend to study more just a day or two before a test than a week or two before. Alas, that is an understatement. Many of us do not study at all until the test approaches. It is shameful, but true. And, of course, this regrettable tendency is at least as true of our immature students as it is of us.

However, let us waste no class time scolding students about this shortcoming. Empty words have little impact. Rather, we must *engage summative test power to prompt students to pace their study.* How? Simply by testing rather often.

Perhaps the most vivid examples of the benefit of more frequent testing can be found at the college level, at which it is common for courses to have only two or three exams. In such classes it is not unusual to find students who do not "crack the textbook" until shortly before the midterm. Rather than lament this deplorable reality, an instructor can *do* something to change it—test more frequently. For example, replacing 3 50-minute tests with 15 10-minute weekly quizzes can do wonders to keep students up to pace. Although the total amount of testing time can remain the same, the impact can be great in causing students to distribute their study time more evenly. At the college level, more frequent testing can also improve attendance.

Although most of the research on the impact of testing frequency on learning has been conducted at the college level (Bangert-Downes, Kulik, & Kulik, 1986), enough has been done in grades 9 through 12 to enable generalization there too. "Overall, the evidence suggests that a moderate frequency of testing is desirable, and more frequent testing may produce further modest benefits" (Crooks, 1988, p. 449). Moreover, students themselves tend to favor more frequent testing.

What advice should be derived from this line of research? The many secondary school teachers who test only every three to four weeks are not testing often enough. A quiz or test every week or two might be considered a minimum for most academic classes. Slight additional benefit would likely result from even more frequent testing, such as once to twice a week.

Suggestions at the elementary level are more speculative, owing to lack of research evidence. It seems reasonable to believe, however, that younger children will not be any more self-directed than older ones. Therefore, more, rather than less, frequent testing seems prudent.

Other factors, of course, also should be considered. On the one hand, the impact of testing frequency seems likely to be great for teachers who use few other means of monitoring student progress, of pacing their study, or of influencing what they study. On the other hand, the impact of testing practices would probably be less for teachers who employ several methods (e.g., homework correction, oral classroom questioning, and group discussions) of tracking student progress, providing feedback, and motivating students to study appropriate material in a timely fashion.

Prompting Review

Just as tests prompt students to study, they can prompt students to review. Review provides an opportunity to *practice* before material has been forgotten. Review also causes students to *relearn* important material that has already faded from memory. Very important also, review provides an opportunity for students to *integrate* material across lessons and units. Not only does review provide an opportunity for integration to occur, but it can also prompt students to integrate if they know they will have to do so on the upcoming test. Along the same lines, review can motivate students to *build connections* among topics, events, facts, and principles. Again, however, students are generally motivated to seek meaningful content bridging only to the extent that they expect to be evaluated on their ability to make meaningful connections.

Cumulative tests, such as comprehensive final examinations or review tests, are therefore useful teaching devices insofar as they prompt students to review. And, like other summative tests, cumulative examinations are effective in directing student attention to what they believe is going to be tested. It therefore behooves teachers to ensure that such measures do assess higher order learning and that students know this in time to let it guide their study.

Here, too, other factors merit consideration in deciding how beneficial review tests are likely to be in given situations. It seems reasonable to expect the most benefit of review tests such as cumulative final examinations in subjects that are not highly sequential, yet have richly meaningful connections. Social studies, literature, and science might be examples. Review might be expected to be less beneficial with content in which the use of requisite material is inherent in the study of advanced topics. Algebra and instrumental music might be examples. Yet even here, review is likely to prove very useful.

Avoid Exclusive Reliance on Test Power

A major theme of this book is that summative test power should be harnessed and used to inspire, motivate, prod, or coerce students to try to learn what we want them to learn. Our tests should be a preplanned integral part of our instructional activities. A little of this is good. More is better. A lot is better still.

However, teachers should not rely exclusively on this (or any other one) technique to motivate students. Effective educators command a rich variety of techniques to stimulate students to want to learn—testing is only one. Used in isolation, it is not sufficient.

Likewise, teachers should not rely wholly on test power to communicate to students what subject matter and mental processes are important. Good teachers employ several means of doing this. Testing is but one of these means.

Likewise, teachers should not depend solely on their tests to prompt students to seek applications, connections, and other kinds of higher-order learning. Effective teachers have skill in using several methods of helping students to learn how to transfer their learning, to find meaning in it, to note and value connections, and so on. Testing is only one of these methods.

It is unreasonable to hold students accountable for command of higher-order learning if they have not been helped to attain it. If higher mental processes have not been taught, it is unfair to test them. There should be consistency among (a) the objectives of a unit, (b) the content and methods with which the unit is taught, and (c) the means by which student achievement is assessed. Therefore, if the objectives and content of a unit have stressed deep learning, then deep learning should be tested. If the objectives and content have failed to penetrate beneath the surface, then only surface learning should be tested. *(In this case the teacher might want to rethink the objectives and content before teaching the unit again.)*

Using Formative Measurement in Teaching

Consider a traditional, weekly, elementary school spelling unit. A list of words is assigned. On Monday and Tuesday, the words and rules governing their spelling are studied. On Wednesday, a practice (i.e., formative) test is administered to identify words that each pupil has not yet mastered. Thursday each child is expected to study and remediate the words missed on the practice test. The summative test is given Friday. It is exactly the same test as the one given Wednesday, but its purpose is for grading. (Strictly speaking, of course, it was test use—not the test—that was formative or summative.)

As the name implies, *form*ative evaluation is designed to provide feedback at points in time when it can still be used to improve the learning. Its purpose is not to judge final adequacy of student learning; its aim it to improve that learning. Thus the tone of formative assessment is *diagnostic* and *corrective*. The coach who says to the baseball batter, "keep your elbow up," "turn a little to the left," or "you're too near the plate," is making observation-based judgments concerning the batter's performance and providing feedback aimed at making an immediate improvement in that performance. This is evaluation aimed at improving achievement while it is still in an alterable, formative stage—formative evaluation.

It is important to realize that much useful formative evaluation data are gathered by informal means. We have seen that ongoing observation of students is one. Another important data source is direct personal communication with students which can take the form of oral questioning, interviews, and conversation (Stiggins, 1991, pp. 536–537). Because formative data do not ordinarily count for grades, student-supplied information is relatively trustworthy.

To be useful in diagnosing and correcting specific learning difficulties, a diagnostic assessment needs to be given early enough for its feedback to still be used. It also has to be closely targeted to the specific learning. Consequently, formative tests are mainly teacher-made. The feedback or corrective purpose of formative measurement militates against the use of such tests for grading. Grading is best based on *terminal* student status. Formative assessment occurs *during* instruction, not at the end. For example, a driver education teacher will provide much verbal feedback to a student learning parallel parking. The student's final grade in parking obviously should not be based on the average of the practice parkings. It should be based on how well the student is able to park at the end of the unit. Likewise, students' final grade in spelling should be based on the sum of their performance on the Friday summative tests, not on the Wednesday formative tests.

Will students work hard to prepare for formative tests if the results are not counted in grading? When the answer to this question is "No," teachers sometimes find it necessary to count the formative test for grades in spite of the logic against doing so. However, the best approach, where possible, is to manage the situation so that the answer to the above question is "Yes." How, for example, is this done for the traditional spelling unit? First, those receiving perfect scores on Wednesday's practice test are sometimes exempted from the Friday test. But this method only motivates the better spellers who stand a chance to receive this reward. Too, one may worry about the short-term "learning" this practice may foster. Second, the amount of work to be done on Thursday is an inverse function of the pupil's performance on the practice test, which can motivate all to study before Wednesday.

Traditional classroom emphasis on evaluation has been summative in nature. Indeed, words such as "testing" and "evaluation" are so closely associated with summative evaluation that many people have difficulty applying them to useful feedback or unthreatening assistance aimed at improving performance rather than at judging it. Student learning is, however, enhanced by timely use of formative assistance.

Throughout instruction, teachers have two tasks: (a) provide the instruction they have planned and (b) constantly assess their success so that they can modify their teaching if needed (Airasian, 1991, p. 123). Thus, formative evaluation can have a beneficial influence on learning in all three tracks.

Formative Measurement in Each Track

Although formative evaluation is needed in various kinds of teaching, its role is more important in some than in others. This section will examine the role of formative assistance in each track.

Track A

The general climate in Track A is extremely hospitable to formative evaluation. Minimum essential goals are identified and meaningful standards are established. Individual differences are forced into the time-it-takes-to-reach-the-standard dimension. Thus at the end of instruction, all or most students achieve about the same—they have mastered the small, essential, well-defined domain of content or skill. In this context, tests serve to pinpoint weaknesses to be remedied—to assist teacher and pupil in identifying deficiencies in order to overcome them.

An example is mastery of the 10 Hindu-Arabic numerals, their meaning, and their English names. Throughout this unit, the young child might be "tested" repeatedly with such questions as "Hold up four fingers," "Point to the numeral that stands for the number of fingers I am holding up," "What is the name of this numeral (showing a numeral)," and "Make this many marks on the board (showing a numeral)." Several items of each type could enable difficulties to be pinpointed. For example, a pupil might have mastered the numerals and their meanings, but not their spoken English names. Such knowledge would lead to remedial instruction. No sharp distinction would exist between a formative "test" and instructional practice.

Another example is a Spanish unit on conjugating regular *-ar* verbs. During the unit the teacher might administer one or more formative tests involving the conjugation of half a dozen regular *-ar* verbs, perhaps half of which have been specifically studied and half of which are unfamiliar, but are given to be regular. Each student's errors would be diagnostically helpful. If Jon missed the second person plural of one word and the third person plural of all six, then his study would be directed to second and especially third person plurals. If Max missed nothing, then he might be exempted from further study in the unit. If Fran performed perfectly on the three familiar words, but had several scattered errors on the three unfamiliar ones, then her study should be directed to seeking the generalizability of the rules to all regular *-ar* verbs, not just to memorize the ones presented in class or text.

In Track A, a given test can serve both formative and summative purposes. If the examinee exhibits mastery on the test, then the summative decision-making function is to certify mastery; the unit is completed. However, if he or she fails to demonstrate mastery, then the decision-making function may be twofold. First is the summative decision that more study is needed. Second is the formative, diagnostic decision concerning what needs to be remediated.

Because we are determined that each child master the unit, no "score" need be kept for purposes of grading. Eventually nearly everyone will receive a "pass" or "master" score. Formative assessment concerns "coaching," not "score keeping."

Track B

The climate in Track B is also quite receptive to formative evaluation. Behavioral developmental objectives are used to channel individual differences into level of achievement. Thus at the end of instruction, students differ in their competence, and these differences are assessed with discriminative summative tests. Formative tests also are discriminative. In addition, they may have a diagnostic element and serve to identify some of the more important weaknesses that should be remediated in order for performance to improve.

An example would be a physical education teacher's observation of each middle school student's basketball free throws. These observations would provide data to enable such formative suggestions as "Arch the ball more," or "More wrist action." Such formative evaluations would probably not be used for grading. Rather, students' terminal level of skill (say, number of free throws out of 10) would be more appropriate.

Another example is the situation described on pages 115–116 of a nonmastery unit on state capitals that was to have a 12-item quiz on five different occasions during a unit. Table 4–3 presented the specification for each of these five parallel quizzes. Any form of this quiz could be used formatively to identify for each pupil certain states whose capitals are not known. The items specified in the top part of the table would most appropriately be remediated because they are deemed most important. Similarly, any of the forms of this quiz could be used summatively to assess terminal achievement. This might be a situation in which the teacher would decide (in spite of misgivings) to use all five forms for grading in order to prompt study. In addition, however, each would also be used formatively to pinpoint deficiencies.

In Track B, a given test can serve both formative and summative purposes. Since total mastery is either impossible or unnecessary, no summative "pass/fail" decision is made. However, summative assessment is made of each student's level of achievement and the formative decisions concerning what might best be improved. In Track B formative evaluation, the results are usually not used for grading. Formative evaluation is aimed at fostering improvement, not at keeping records of achievement.

Track C

Formative evaluation does not play the central role in Track C that it does in Tracks A and B. Nonbehavioral developmental objectives are used for large, ill-defined, unmasterable content domains. Subject matter is not highly sequential; therefore, it is not critically important that students attain specified levels in earlier units before undertaking later ones. Individual differences are exhibited as level and breadth of achievement and are assessed by discriminatory survey tests.

The lack of dominating inherent sequence in the subject matter is the key reason why formative evaluation is less important in Track C than it is in Track A. It is not vital to diagnose or remediate weaknesses. If Joanne's competence on the subject of the Civil War is lower than on any other historical period, the deficit does not demand remedy. This situation is probably the reason that formative evaluation has typically been neglected in Track C teaching. Is this neglect desirable?

To an extent, it is. The "Teach, test, reteach" model is not suited to Track C material because it lacks strong inherent sequence. The behavioristic teach-test-reteach model assumes that all the elements—including important insights and understandings—can be broken down and taught one at a time. The application of such a theory to Track C content "is severely flawed and has a deadening effect on instruction, especially because it postpones attention to thinking and problem solving" (Shepard, in Kirst, 1991, pp. 23 & 27).

Yet some sequence assuredly exists among Track C topics. Great holes of knowledge do tend to handicap students. Some attempt to "fill in the gaps" is desirable when sequential connections exist among topics. Recall the advice given on page 34 for those who failed to grasp an important concept: Re-study the material to allocate *some* of the individual differences into the time dimension so that they would not be quite so great in achievement. Thus formative assessment has a significant contribution to make in Track C, and it probably should be used more than it is.

For an example of how formative testing could be used to good advantage in Track C, return to the spelling lesson mentioned earlier in this chapter. The typical lesson consists of words to be mastered and a couple of rules governing their spelling. I contend that the usual formative test given on Wednesday communicates a very *un*desirable message to pupils: "You are *not* accountable for being able to use the spelling rule(s) with new words; you are going to be tested only on the specific words contained in the lesson." In other words, the formative test indicates that transfer of learning is *not* important.

Such a message is deplorable! Transfer of spelling rules is vitally important to pupil ability to spell regular words. That is why the rules were included in the spelling lessons in the first place.

A more enlightened use of formative evaluation would provide formative tests designed to perform two functions. The first is the Track A function of testing mastery of the specific words provided in the lesson. Second is *the Track C function of testing pupil ability to transfer knowledge of the rules to new words*. Thus the formative test should have some words in it that were *not* studied but which can be spelled by use of the rules. Similarly, the summative test should contain some additional rule-governed words that were neither studied nor contained in the formative test.

Such testing would harness test power by sending pupils the clear messages that *ability to use the rules is an important outcome of the lesson* and *students are accountable for this outcome*. It would cause pupils to do what we want them to do rather than divert them from desirable practice in applying the rule.

(A public relations issue might be mentioned. If a teacher were going to adopt this unorthodox suggestion, the rationale should be clearly explained *before* to students, parents, and principal. Moreover, since the practice is unusual, it might be wise to "start slowly," perhaps only including a couple of new words in each test until the idea becomes familiar. To the complaint that "We didn't study that word," the answer is a patient re-explanation of the idea that "We *did* study the rule by which it is spelled. If the rule is to be useful, you must be able to use it to spell *new* words.")

QUIZ 10–2

1. Which of the following colorful descriptors (from Chapter 3) best describes effective teaching of elementary school spelling?
   A. Amphibious teaching
   B. Hybridized teaching
   C. Double-exposure teaching
   D. Multilevel teaching

2. The statement was made that formative evaluation is aimed at "coaching," not at "score keeping." Here is a troublesome application of that principle:

   The seventh-grade math faculty of a large middle school are discussing homework policy. John Stunkle argues eloquently that the purpose of homework is to provide practice and feedback—homework is formative. Therefore, it should *not* be counted for grading. Rather, grades should be pure measures of terminal student achievement as measured by summative tests.

   If you were one of the teachers on this math faculty, how might you best reply to John's contentions?

KEY TO QUIZ 10–2

1. D. Mastery of specific words in Track A; transfer of rules in Track C.

2. John's argument has obvious merit. It is just as inappropriate to count the practice (i.e., homework) in math as it would be for the driving instructor to count the early practice attempts in parallel parking. What teachers are really interested in is the terminal level of student achievement. This, of course, must be measured at the end of instruction.

   However, there is a major practical problem. To a nontrivial extent, if teachers do not count homework, students will not do it. Yes, we can and should explain that homework provides the means by which they learn the material needed on the tests. While students will understand this, many will still not do the homework if it does not count.

   What to do? Most thoughtful teachers who have been caught in the confrontation between the logic of not counting the homework and the practical reason to count it, have compromised logic and expediency. They have counted homework for grading, but only enough to prompt students to do it. Those of us who have experimented with classes to find how little we could count it in the total grades without experiencing a sharp drop-off have generally arrived at answers of one-fifth, one-fourth, or one-third.

Effects on Student Learning

Classroom evaluation practices, both summative and formative, impact student learning. When teachers carefully design student assessment practices to reinforce other aspects of effective teaching, evaluation powerfully enhances learning. But when educators are careless, the potential benefits of measurement are lost. Worse still, poor assessment practices actually interfere with desired student learning. Recall the example of the Wednesday formative spelling tests that do not assess applications of rules; such tests direct students away from efforts to learn to use the rules.

Common Desirable Effects

Formative student evaluation practices facilitate student learning and retention in several ways. Some overlap those discussed earlier in this chapter for summative student evaluation practices. Others are largely distinctive to formative evaluation.

First, consider those impacts of effective measurement that are redundant with summative evaluation. Like summative testing, formative testing may prompt review. In general, however, formative measures are less likely to do so than are summative tests that count toward grades.

Like summative tests, formative tests help to pace student study. However, formative tests that do not contribute directly toward grades may also have limited impact on some students in this regard in comparison to summative tests that do "count."

An impact of formative testing that is less relevant to summative testing is the testing phenomenon described in Chapter 1. The mere act of taking a test, even if one has not reviewed for it, can enhance long-term retention (Glover, 1989). This effect occurs when the act of retrieving material from memory is performed under conditions where the retrieval is difficult, yet possible. That is, taking a quiz just when its content is about to slip from memory is more beneficial than the same amount of time spent in drilling on the content when it is well within reach or in taking a quiz after the content can no longer be retrieved. A formative test that does not count toward a grade can prompt this kind of practice in active retrieval of material from long-term memory whether or not students have studied for it.

A major distinctive contribution of formative classroom testing is the direct feedback it provides to students. Where formative evaluation is appropriately used, this corrective feedback, especially in Tracks A and B, is extremely helpful to students as they work to identify and overcome their deficiencies. This feedback is the central aim of formative evaluation. However to seek only this one benefit would be to overlook many other useful potential contributions of effective classroom formative evaluation.

Yet another sense in which student assessment practices can aid learning concerns the feedback that teachers obtain from formative testing. Not only does this information help identify which problems need to be remediated for individual pupils, but it also reveals which difficulties are common to several students and therefore merit whole-class time.

From a different angle, teachers receive formative feedback from summative tests (summative, that is, from the students' perspective). Typical teachers will teach their units again and again. Hence the results of a summative test, even though they will not prompt review this term, may help a teacher to judge the adequacy of methods and materials used in the unit.

A final important sense in which formative testing practices influence student learning concerns the role tests have in communicating to students "what is important." That is, students tend to study what they think will be assessed with summative tests. Formative tests are very effective ways to communicate to students the blend of content that will be assessed in subsequent summative tests that "count." They also communicate the relative importance of the mental processes that will be called forth. Thus, formative tests provide a "preview" of the summative test—they can vividly communicate what the summative test will be like. They serve to focus student study on that which will appear in the formative test. Properly used, this focusing function of formative tests is highly desirable, but it should be recognized as a tool requiring skillful professional use.

Focus: A Two-Edged Sword

Formative feedback focuses student attention and effort. A comment by a speech teacher to "establish eye contact with your audience," focuses the learner's efforts on eye contact. A note from an algebra teacher on a practice test or homework assignment to "remember to divide the denominator into *each term* of the numerator," alerts the student to a common error. The verbal feedback of the driving instructor that "the parallel parking attempt did not work because your car was too far back before you started to turn the wheel," focuses the learner's attention on where the car is to be when the wheel is first turned. The formative test of regular *-ar* Spanish verbs directed Jon's attention to third person plurals, and it focused Fran's efforts on transferring use of the rule rather than memorizing particular verbs.

The direction provided by feedback is usually desirable. Thoughtful feedback is designed to focus effort and attention. That is its purpose.

However two cautions should be noted. First, ill-considered feedback obviously has the potential to focus the student on the wrong thing. If the speaker's faults include several that are more serious than eye contact, then focusing effort on eye contact is ill-advised. A widely recognized rule of good teaching is to focus feedback on only the one or two most serious faults and to get them under control before moving on to lesser deficiencies. For example, an English teacher's comments on a student's theme might focus on only the one or two aspects of the composition that most need attention.

The other caution concerns the frequent mismatch of Track A mastery teaching methods with Track C content. In Track A, the formative test and the subsequent summative test can be highly similar because the content domain is small and little if any sampling is ordinarily involved in item selection.[2] In this context, the teach-test-reteach model works well.

But in Track C, a formative test and the corresponding summative test should *not* be any more similar than would occur if different competent teachers developed the two forms independently by reference to the table of specifications on which the tests are based. Some teachers who (mis)use mastery strategies with Track C content merely create an illusion of mastery. This illusion is strongest when the identical test is used formatively during instruction and summatively after instruction. The

---

[2] The unfamiliar *-ar* verbs in the Spanish test were an exception to this generalization. In that case it was a simple rule that was to be mastered, not the large domain or words to which it applies. (Alternatively, the conjugation of regular *-ar* verbs could be thought of as a multilevel, Track A and Track C unit.) Hence in Track A, there is little danger associated with the focus provided by formative evaluation.

formative test provides a very sharp focus of student learning. When the summative test measures only that material on which study was focused, it yields scores that *misrepresent* student status on the broader content domain. This is nothing more or less than teaching to the test—an unprofessional behavior in the context of Track C instruction.

A more subtle variety of teaching to the test with Track C content occurs when a formative test and its summative counterpart are not identical, but are excessively and inappropriately similar. In this case too, the formative test functions to artificially focus student study on the material that happens to be sampled in the summative test. This emphasis is a somewhat diluted version of teaching to the summative Track C test.

If a teacher takes care not to make the formative and summative forms of a test any more similar than random chance would do within the constraints established by the test's specifications, then the danger of inappropriate focus is averted. Yet some who advocate indiscriminate use for mastery methods with all kinds of content (e.g., Guskey, 1985) do not take this precaution. On the contrary, they go out of their way to make the formative and summative forms of the test artificially similar, thus assuring that the summative form will not serve as a representative, honest sample of student competence in the entire content domain. This kind of misuse of formative testing tends to give it an undeserved bad name.

QUIZ 10–3

1. In which track is the diagnostic feedback focus provided by formative tests the most helpful?

   A. Track A.
   B. Track B.
   C. Track C.

2. In which track is the danger of inappropriate focus greatest?

   A. Track A.
   B. Track B.
   C. Track C.

3. Regarding your answer to Item 2, should formative evaluation still be used in that track in spite of this danger of misuse?

   A. Yes.
   B. No.

4. In which track does formative evaluation offer the **least** assistance to learning?

   A. Track A.
   B. Track B.
   C. Track C.

QUIZ 10–3 (cont.)

5. Regarding your answer to Item 4, is formative evaluation nevertheless useful in that track?

    A. Yes.
    B. No.

6. One of the cautions about focus concerned teaching to the test. It was illustrated in Track C. Does the same danger exist in Track B? If so, for which kind of Track B content is the danger greater?

    A. Yes, mainly for unmasterable motor skills.
    B. Yes, mainly for masterable cognitive content that is not important enough to warrant mastery.
    C. No.

7. In Chapter 9, a test-organization rule indicated that alternate-choice items should precede multiple-choice questions. This rule was violated in this quiz. Was the violation justified? If so, why?

    A. No, Items 3 and 5 should have come first.
    B. Yes, because item-type variety keeps examinees "on their toes."
    C. Yes, because the rule lacks rationale.
    D. Yes, because Item 3 logically had to follow Item 2, and Item 5 had to follow Item 4.

8. Which item-writing rule from Chapter 6 is violated by **both** items 6 and 7?

    A. Avoid clueing with length of keyed response.
    B. Avoid clueing with familiarity of keyed option.
    C. Express ideas clearly, unambiguously, and briefly at as low a readability level as possible.
    D. Formulate the issue in the stem.
    E. Measure significant student learning.

KEY TO QUIZ 10–3

Answers		Comments
1.	A	Where everything is vital, identifying and remediating weaknesses is most important.
2.	C	See pages 295–296.
3.	A	See pages 291–292.
4.	C	See pages 291-292.
5.	A	See pages 291–292.

KEY TO QUIZ 10–3 (cont.)

6. B   This is a place where survey testing samples a domain. If the test is to be representative of the domain, then one must not teach to the test.

7. D   One should feel free to violate the item-writing rules when there is compelling reason to do so.

8. A   If a test systematically violates this rule, a worrisome advantage exists for test-wise examinees. The remedy to occasional items such as 6 and 7 is to make sure that one's tests on balance do not violate the rule. For example, students using the same "clue" for Item 8 would be led to miss it; this tends to cancel out their advantage on Items 6 and 7.

Chapter Summary

Tests and other means by which students are evaluated are valuable and powerful teaching tools. The fundamental purpose of classroom use of formative and summative achievement tests is to enhance student learning.

Summative assessment helps teachers in two general ways. First, *summative tests help teachers make instructional and grading decisions.* Decisions such as level at which instruction should be aimed can "make or break" a teacher's effectiveness. Second, *summative tests exert influence over what students study and how they pace their study.* In most settings, summative tests are one of the teacher's most effective means of influencing such vitally important student effort variables.

Formative assessment provides feedback to the learner and/or the teacher at a time when learning is still in a formative stage. Its purpose is to facilitate the learning.

Formative assistance helps identify learning problems that have diagnostic significance. Once a deficit is identified, it can be remediated. For Track A content, in which each bit of information is deemed to be vital, a sensible strategy is to teach, then to give a formative test, then (if necessary) to reteach. In Track B, especially in motor skill acquisition, recognition and correction of poor habits in their formative stage is also extremely useful. In this case, the formative measure is likely to be a performance test. For Track C content and for masterable Track B content that is not important enough to master, formative evaluation has a smaller role in teaching. Yet it is still useful in identifying sources of relative weaknesses, especially if content is to any extent interconnected or sequential.

In all kinds of subject matter, formative assessment is useful in communicating to students the kinds of learning for which they will be accountable in subsequent summative tests. It also provides a helpful means of invoking the testing phenomenon.

Suggestions for Further Reading

Airasian, P. W. (1991). *Classroom assessment.* New York: McGraw-Hill. Chapter 3, "Assessment for Instructional Planning" and Chapter 4, "Assessment during Instruction," provide a somewhat different and useful perspective on a variety of kinds of evaluation other than summative.

Crooks, T. J. (1988). The impact of classroom evaluation practices on students. *Review of Educational Research, 58,* 438–481. This detailed and far-ranging article reviews and integrates a remarkably diverse and massive literature. It summarizes much of the research basis for the "use test power" theme of this book.

Nitko, A. J. (1989). Designing tests that are integrated with instruction. In Linn, R. L. (Ed.), *Educational measurement* (3rd ed.). New York: Macmillan. This excellent chapter addresses a variety of relevant topics from a relatively advanced perspective.

Stiggins, R. J. (1991). Assessment literacy. *Phi Delta Kappan, 72,* 534–539. Because assessment practices have a major impact on student learning, Stiggins argues that we should allocate more resources to the training of teachers in sound methods of assessing student learning.

Data Management

This book concerns using measurement effectively in teaching. This central goal requires quantitative capabilities in: (a) managing data suitably for purposes of reporting student achievement, (b) comprehending descriptions of reference groups, (c) understanding various kinds of derived scores, (d) knowing how an instrument's reliability and validity are investigated and reported, and (e) understanding and evaluating what test manuals and research articles report about tests' reference groups, reliability, and validity. To assist teachers in achieving these aims, a few statistical concepts are presented. Statistics are tools to pursue measurement goals; the study of statistics per se is not the aim. This focus of purpose allows the selection of only those topics that provide keys to educational measurement.

Some confusion exists regarding the relationship between measurement and statistics. **Measurement**, as discussed in Chapter 1, typically concerns *assessing* the size, degree, or amount of things by use of numbers. **Statistics**, on the other hand, concern the *analysis* of data by use of mathematics. An example or two will highlight the distinction. The height of each person in a class can be measured by use of a meter stick. Determining the class's average height is a problem of statistics. Statistics thus provide the mathematical tools by which the results of measurement are studied or analyzed. Or suppose we were interested in the amount of relationship between pupils' silent reading comprehension of (a) purely factual material and (b) inferred meaning. We would first construct or find tests of factual and inferential reading comprehension by which to measure. Then we would use statistics to reveal the amount of relationship, or correlation, between the two sets of measures. (In Chapter 14 the surprising results of such investigations are reported.)

Before plunging into selected statistics topics, some reassurance may be helpful. Mathematics and statistics strike terror in the hearts of many education students. Old, deep-seated fears and feelings of inadequacy are not uncommon. Be reassured. First, the treatment of statistics as such will be brief; computation is a minor topic in this book. Second, it is not assumed that readers are skilled in mathematics; about all that is assumed is that readers have had a semester or so of high school algebra *and forgotten most of it*. Third, the arithmetic will be kept very simple. To keep examples easy, very small numbers of cases will be used, usually between 4 and 10; this provides less opportunity for simple arithmetic mistakes to obscure what is being studied. To keep the calculations simple, the examples have also been "rigged" so that all means will come out to be whole numbers and all numbers for which square roots are needed will be perfect squares.[1] Readers will not be expected to extract a root of 5, 12, 200, etc. It will be unnecessary, therefore, to use a calculator or to "master" yet again[2] the little-used algorithm for extracting square roots. Knowing that an answer will be a whole number, readers can obtain it with a minimum of trial and error.

---

[1] I am indebted to Dr. John T. Roscoe for many of the frequency distributions used in this chapter.

[2] In most groups, very few people can extract a square root by use of the oft-memorized algorithm. Yet most people have "mastered" the topic several times. This provides a meaningful review of two important principles. First, "mastery" is not always forever. When something is only retained temporarily, there is reason to question whether it was really vital in the first place. If it was, then sufficient review should have been provided to ensure its permanent retention. If not, then it should not be treated as Track A content.

Second, a useful filter by which to evaluate potential curriculum is how well the subject matter is retained. (Of course, other criteria also merit consideration.) Some content, like state capitals and extraction of square roots, is not well retained by most people. In general, meaningful material is better retained than subject matter learned by rote. Other things being equal, it is far better to teach what will better be retained than what will soon be lost.

This curriculum filter is the rationale for this chapter's emphasis on meaning rather than calculation.

A few somewhat technical words of explanation at this point are in order, mainly for those readers who have taken a statistics course. First, descriptive statistics are the main concern of this chapter; therefore, N, rather than $N - 1$, will be used in several formulas. This emphasis also renders unsuitable for present purposes the standard deviation and r formulas programmed for many calculators and computers. Second, ungrouped data will be used because they better enable a clear view of what formulas do. Third, discussion will avoid various technical issues (e.g., interpolating medians among tied scores) not central to measurement purposes of this book. The focus will be the meaning of statistics as applied to educational measurement; this emphasis is likely to provide some new or better insights even for readers who have a good background in statistics.

Frequency Distributions and Percentile Ranks

When a group of people has taken a test, the resulting set of scores must be organized in some way. Suppose that a group of 50 students took the State Capitals Test presented in Chapter 1. A single list of the scores, such as 4, 8, 6, 9, 5, etc., is unbearably awkward. The first step taken to render the "basket full" of scores more manageable is to arrange them vertically in numeric order. It does not matter whether they are organized into ascending or descending order. Thus, scores could be tallied in a **frequency distribution** as shown in Table 11–1.

Although the derived scores and their interpretation will be treated fully in Chapter 16, it will be helpful at this time to introduce percentile ranks and standard scores. Recall that derived scores are used in making norm-referenced interpretations. **Percentile ranks (PRs)** are a kind of derived score that is particularly well suited for providing norm-referenced interpretations of student performance on published instruments.

PRs can be defined as the percent of a reference group that an examinee excelled or equaled.[3] Thus if Simone obtains a PR of 38, she performed as well as or better than 38 out of every 100 students in a particular reference group.

Table 11–2 shows the next step in developing PRs. The first two columns of the table are headed with the conventional symbols. Upper-case *"X"* (or some other letter near the end of the alphabet) stands for "raw score" and lower-case *"f"* represents "frequency." The tally marks have been converted into numerals and entered in the *"f"* column of Table 11–2. The last column of Table 11–2 indicates the percentage of the total group that obtained each raw score. Each entry is found by dividing its frequency by the number of people in the group and multiplying the resulting fraction by 100. Thus 1 divided by 50 yields the first entry of 2%, 3 divided by 50 = 6%, etc.

Table 11–3 provides the next step. For the new column, we add the percentage of persons who received each raw score to the percentage who received all lower scores. This step simply involves adding the percentage entry in each row to the entries in all rows below it and entering this sum in the right-hand column.

---

[3]These are technically known as top-of-interval PRs. The definition of bottom-of-interval PRs does not include the phrase "or equaled." Mid-interval PRs are defined as the percent of the reference group excelled plus one-half the percent tied. Mid-interval PRs and top-of-interval PRs are the more common kinds. In longer instruments, the distinction among the varieties of PRs is not very important.

Table 11–1

Frequency Distribution

Raw Score	Frequency Tally
10	/
9	///
8	//
7	//
6	HHT HHT
5	HHT HHT //
4	HHT HHT
3	HHT
2	////
1	
0	/

Table 11–2

Percentage Frequency Distribution

X	f	Percentage
10	1	2
9	3	6
8	2	4
7	2	4
6	10	20
5	12	24
4	10	20
3	5	10
2	4	8
1	0	0
0	1	2
	50	

TABLE 11-3

Cumulative Percentage Distribution

X	Percentage	Cumulative Percentage
10	2	100
9	6	98
8	4	92
7	4	88
6	20	84
5	24	64
4	20	40
3	10	20
2	8	10
1	0	2
0	2	2

One thing remains to be done. There is a convention of avoiding PRs of 0 and 100. All other numbers are rounded to the nearest whole percent, but PRs are never rounded to 0 or 100. Rather, the bottom of the range is defined as 1 (or 1−, .1, .01, etc.) and the top is set at 99 (or 99+, 99.9, etc.). The middle column of Table 11–4 contains this feature.

Table 11-4

Unsmoothed and Smoothed Percentile Ranks

X	Percentile Ranks	Smoothed PRs
10	99+	99+
9	98	98
8	92	94
7	88	88
6	84	80
5	64	64
4	40	40
3	20	20
2	10	10
1	2	4
0	2	1

This example will be carried one minor step further in order to provide understanding of a procedure that is commonly applied to data for published instruments. In Table 11–1, scores of 9 would not be expected to be more common than scores of 7 or 8. Nor would scores of 1 be expected to be less frequent than scores of 0. These features of the data are most probably anomalies caused by the small sample size. Test publishers often smooth out a distribution in an attempt to make it better represent the population of people from which the particular sample was selected.

The right-hand column of Table 11–4 contains **smoothed PRs**. Smoothing of normative data by any of a variety of techniques is common in published tests. It should be understood that no one correct smoothed distribution of PRs exists for a given data set. A reader would *not* be expected to start with the data shown in Table 11–1 and end with the exact smoothed data shown in Table 11–4. Indeed, I came up with slightly different results on two occasions. The reassuring point is that any reasonable smoothing of the raw data is likely to enhance the extent to which they represent the population of people from which the sample of examinees was drawn. It is also comforting to note that real reference groups ordinarily contain at least several hundred cases. With large reference groups, much less smoothing is generally needed.

Although other features of PRs will be addressed in Chapter 16, this introduction will suffice to provide a good general sense of what they are. This type of derived score will be called on further to illustrate various issues.

QUIZ 11–1

1. Ten students have taken the State Capitals Test and obtained the following scores. Make a table showing the *un*smoothed percentile rank associated with each possible raw score.

Student	Raw Score
Alma	6
Bert	5
Chuck	10
Dennis	3
Frank	1
Gladys	5
Henry	8
Irma	2
Jennifer	4
Kelly	7

2. Describe in words what Gladys's PR means.

KEY TO QUIZ 11–1

1. The major steps for producing unsmoothed PRs are shown below.

X	f	Percentage	Cumulative Percentage Frequency Distribution	PRs
10	1	10	100	99+
9	0	0	90	90

KEY TO QUIZ 11–1 (cont.)

8	1	10	90	90
7	1	10	80	80
6	1	10	70	70
5	2	20	60	60
4	1	10	40	40
3	1	10	30	30
2	1	10	20	20
1	1	10	10	10
0	0	0	0	1–

2. Gladys performed on this particular sample of questions as well as or better than 6 out of every 10 (or 60 out of every 100) students who took the test.

Measures of Central Tendency

Suppose four classes have taken the same test and comparison is sought of the resulting sets of scores. If the groups were large, it would be difficult to hold the several frequency distributions in mind. Rather than compare full distributions, **summary statistics** are usually compared. This section and the next describe measures by which distributions are condensed or summarized.

Measures of central tendency, or **averages**, provide one set of helpful methods of condensing entire frequency distributions into single numbers. If a random person on the street were asked what an "average" was, the response would probably be something like, "You get the average of several numbers when you add them up and then divide by the number of them there are." Actually, this is a description of only one kind of average—the mean. The word "average" is a nonspecific general term that stands for all three of the common measures of central tendency (as well as some uncommon ones). In this book, "average" will be used only in this generic sense; to sharpen our concepts and thinking, specific terms—mean, median, or mode—will be used to refer to particular kinds of averages.

Assume that the 10-item State Capitals Test has been given to each of four classes. To make the calculations easy, the illustrative classes are very small. The distributions of scores are listed below. Because the class sizes are so small, it will be more convenient to re-list ties (such as the two 6s in Class A) than to provide separate "X" and "f" columns.

Class A	Class B	Class C	Class D
10	7	9	10
9	7	4	10
7	5	4	9
6	5	4	5
6		4	5
4			4
			3
			2

The Mean

As mentioned above, the most widely known measure of central tendency is the **mean**. This kind of average is computed by use of the formula

$$M = \frac{\Sigma X}{N},$$ where M stands for the mean,

Σ is an operation symbol meaning "the sum of,"
X denotes raw score, and
N is the number of cases (or examinees).

For Class A, the mean is computed by adding the six scores and dividing this sum (of 42) by the number of examinees (which is 6). Thus in Class A, $M = 7$; in Class B, $M = 6$; in Class C, $M = 5$; and in Class D, $M = 6$.

Means, like other measures of central tendency, enable us to compare the average performance of groups. The four class means reveal that Class A evidenced the most knowledge of state capitals and that Class C showed the least.

The Median

The **median**, symbolized *Md,* is the point in a distribution that divides it into two equal parts. In frequency distribution having an odd number of cases, the middle score divides it into two parts having equal number of cases. For example, if seven people wish to find their median height, they could arrange themselves into order by stature. The height of the middle person would be the median height. To find the median of a distribution of scores, simply arrange the scores into ascending or descending order, and then take the middle score(s). In distributions having an odd number of scores, the middle score is the median. In those having an even number of cases, the median is the midpoint between the two middlemost scores.[4]

For Class A, the median is halfway between the two middlemost scores, 6 and 7; therefore, $Md = 6.5$. For Class B, the median is halfway between 5 and 7; thus, it is 6. Class C contains an odd number of students; therefore, its median is the middle score—one of the 4s. For Class D, the median is midway between the two scores nearest the middle of the distribution—5.

The Mode

The third common measure of central tendency is the **mode**. The mode, symbolized *Mo,* is the most frequently occurring score. In Class A, the mode is 6 because more people obtained that score than any other. In Class B, there is a tie between 5 and 7; thus, the modes are 5 and 7; the distribution is bimodal. Notice that intermediate value is *not* taken between the two modes. In Class C, the mode is 4, while Class D is bimodal with modes of 5 and 10.

If the information is now entered concerning central tendencies of the four illustrative classes, the results are:

---

[4]This is a simplified method of determining a median; it does not ordinarily yield exactly the same value as the more complex standard method.

Class A	Class B	Class C	Class D
10	7	9	10
9	7	4	10
7	5	4	9
6	5	4	5
6		4	5
4			4
			3
			2
$M = 7$	$M = 6$	$M = 5$	$M = 6$
$Md = 6.5$	$Md = 6$	$Md = 4$	$Md = 5$
$Mo = 6$	$Mo = 5 \& 7$	$Mo = 4$	$Mo = 5 \& 10$

Notice that in some distributions, two or more of the average may be identical, while in other distributions all three values may differ.

Evaluation of Measures of Central Tendency

Reflection on the distribution for Class A will permit readers to intuit the relative power or adequacy of the three kinds of average. The mode is inherently unstable from sample to sample because it is based on few cases. In Class A, the mode of the entire distribution was determined by only two persons. The mode ignores most of the cases, but is supersensitive to a minority of cases. For instance, if the person receiving a 4 had instead attained 8 points, the distribution's mode would not have changed at all. Yet if one of the people who received a 6 had instead scored 7, the mode of the entire class would have been altered.

The median is somewhat more consistent from sample to sample because it is based on all the data (albeit not with maximum efficiency). Again consider Class A. If the person receiving 4 points had instead obtained 7 or 10 points, the distribution's median would have been altered. But if the person's score had changed from 4 to 0 or 5, the median would have been unaffected. This is inconsistent because the median is sensitive only to which half of the distribution contains each score; it is indifferent to where, within that half of the distribution, each lies.

Finally, the mean is the most dependable of the three summary statistics because it efficiently uses all cases in a distribution. If *any* person's score were to change, the mean would change in the same direction. Moreover, the impact of a change in any score on the mean would be exactly proportional to the amount by which the score had changed.

When to Use Each Kind of Average

It is apparent that the mean enjoys superior statistical properties over the other measures of central tendency. Why, then, are the other statistics used? There are two general reasons.

First, there are occasions when the median or even the mode better serves one's purpose. Consider a distribution of ages at which youths drop out of secondary school. Which kind of average is best? It depends on one's purpose. For an administrator computing the cost of educating students for the years they remain in school, the mean would be indicated. For a sociologist concerned with the typical dropout's unreadiness to cope with the adult world, the median might be more meaningful. For an educator seeking to target a timely intervention just before the age at which the greatest number terminate, the mode would be best. The point is that we should use the kind of average that best suits our purpose. When it is legitimate, the mean serves most, but not all, purposes best.

Mortality data provide another example of a situation in which an average other than the mean is preferable. When a newspaper reports that the average American female now lives to be, say, 79 years old, which kind of average is being used? It is the median. This is appropriate because the focus of interest usually concerns the age at the time of death of the most typical female in the distribution. For example, out of the next 99 baby girls born, what will be the actual death age of the 50th to die? This example also illustrates the virtue of avoiding the generic term "average" when reference is made to a specific kind of average; it would have been clearer if the newspaper had reported the median to be 79 rather than the "average" to be 79.

The second reason why the median and the mode are sometimes needed arises in situations in which the mean cannot be computed. Because the mean is sensitive to the exact size of each score, its proper use requires measures that have equal units or intervals of measurement. Fortunately, most common measures have equal units of measurement. For example, money comes in equal units; thus, the difference between \$1 and \$2 is exactly the same as the difference between \$1566 and \$1567. Because money is measured with a scale that has equal intervals, we can compute means of amounts of money, such as the mean daily balance in a checking account. Similarly, temperature is measured with equal units of measurement. The difference between $-100°$ C and $-99°$ C equals the difference between $+1000°$ C and $+1001°$ C. Thus, the mean of several temperatures can be found. Likewise, time, distance, volume, pressure, weight, etc., are measured with equal interval scales. Finally, raw test scores are generally considered to have equal units of measurement.[5]

When measures lack equal units, however, the mean may not legitimately be used. What, then, should one do? Where the cases can be arranged into order, the median can be employed. Thus, if an odd number of students in a class arrange themselves from shortest to tallest without use of a measuring instrument, they could determine whose stature was at the median. Without a suitable measuring instrument, they could not, however, find the mean height. Medians are often used in situations where scores can be rank ordered, but lack equal units of measurement. In such cases, the median is attractive because it is the more powerful of the suitable kinds of average.

Several kinds of derived scores do not have equal units of measurement. One example is the common grade equivalent. This is dramatically illustrated by visiting four classes in a school district while oral reading is taking place. The difference between the typical first-grader's reading and that of the median second-grader is great enough to be readily apparent even to the novice. Much less difference exists, however, between the median ninth-grader and the typical tenth-grader. A basic developmental trend is that growth slows down during the growing years and stops,

---

[5]Technically, raw scores do not provide perfectly equal units of measure. Intervals tend to be larger near the extremes of a distribution than near its center. However, this departure is minor and is wisely ignored by practitioners (Nunnally, 1978).

of course, when maturity is reached. The absence of equal amounts of grade-to-grade growth renders the mean inappropriate for summarizing a distribution of grade-equivalent scores.

Ranks are another kind of derived score that lack equal units of measurement. That PRs lack equal units is evident from examining a frequency distribution such as that shown in Table 11–4. In the final, smoothed distribution, one raw score point equates to very few PR units in the extremes of the distribution but to many PR units in the center of the distribution. To illustrate, suppose your score on the State Capitals Test were 0; this equates to a smoothed PR of 1. Had you earned one more point, your raw score of 1 would convert to a PR of 4. Thus, 1 point of raw score amounted to only 3 PR units. Now suppose your original raw score had been 5; this yields a PR of 64. Had you received one more point, your raw score of 6 would equate to a PR of 80. This 1 point of raw score amounted to 16 PR units. Since PRs lack equal units of measurement, neither the mean nor any statistic based on it may be used to summarize distributions of PRs.

In addition to being used by default when the mean is inappropriate, however, medians are sometimes used for two other reasons even where means could be computed. First, the median is the best kind of average to show the status of the most typical individual in a group. Second, the median is sometimes used as a convenient, rough measure of central tendency.

Alas, situations exist in which the "scores" cannot even be arranged into order. In such cases, only one thing is left to do—use the mode as the only suitable measure of central tendency. For example, what is the average state of birth of the members of a class? We cannot add states and divide to get a meaningful mean. The only meaningful way to address the issue of the average state of birth in a group is to use the mode.

When the data being summarized cannot be put into order, neither the mean nor the median can be computed. In situations in which the cases are not orderable, only the mode can be used legitimately.

QUIZ 11–2

For Items 1–9, which measure of central tendency would best serve for each purpose?

1. A principal reporting a school's average daily attendance

2. A teacher reporting the number of addition facts known by typical members of the class

3. A teacher wanting a quick, rough average of a group's performance on a spelling test

4. A teacher reporting the average percentile rank of the class on a published test

QUIZ 11–2 (cont.)

5. An assistant superintendent of schools estimating the average tax revenue to be realized in a new housing development in the district

6. A psychologist reporting the average mental age of a group of children

7. A teacher discussing the average ethnicity of the children in a class

8. A researcher's report of average age of teenage pregnancy

9. A report of your class's average raw score on this quiz

10. Find the mean, median, and mode of the distribution to the right.

10
10
9
8
4
4
4

KEY TO QUIZ 11–2

1. Mean. Because children come in equal intervals, the mean is legitimate. For most purposes, the mean would best capture the intent of averaging, but for a few, the median might be preferred.

2. Median. Although the scores are considered to have equal units of measure and the mean could properly be computed, the teacher's interest was on the skill possessed by the typical child in the class.

3. Median. Although the mean is appropriate and preferable, the median provides the quick, rough estimate desired.

4. Median. The teacher wishing to focus on the most typical student would prefer the median. One thinking of the class as a whole might prefer the mean. The mean is not mathematically legitimate, however, because PRs do not have equal units of measure.

5. Mean. The mean or the total revenue would be the focal interest. Yet to a member of the city council or board of education interested in the tax burden per typical homeowner, the median would also be of interest.

6. Median. Mental ages and other age and grade equivalent scores lack equal units of measure; therefore, the mean is not appropriate. The median is the best by default. (The psychologist thinking of the group as a whole might prefer the mean if it were legitimate. One could compute the mean of the *raw* scores, then convert this mean of raw scores

> ### KEY TO QUIZ 11–2 (cont.)
>
> into an age equivalent. In this case it would be the age equivalent corresponding to the mean raw score, not the mean age equivalent.)
> 7. Mode. Ethnic groups are not orderable, hence only the mode can be used.
> 8. Median. Although the mean could legitimately be computed, educational interest is in age of pregnancy of the most typical individual in the group.
> 9. Mean. Raw test scores are generally considered to have approximately equal measurement intervals. Hence, one would opt for the most sensitive summary statistic available for the class.
> 10. $M = 7$, $Md = 8$, and $Mo = 4$.

Measures of Variability

Useful as measures of central tendency are, they do not condense or summarize all important aspects of information contained in frequency distributions. Consider again the data for two classes.

Class B	Class D
7	10
7	10
5	9
5	5
	5
	4
	3
	2
$M = 6$	$M = 6$

Examination of the classes' distributions reveals some important similarities and differences. Each class has a mean of 6. However, measures of central tendency reveal nothing of the conspicuous difference between the classes in another dimension. Class B is obviously less variable than Class D. The much greater heterogeneity of Class D would require a lot more effort by its teacher to provide for individual differences.

It is a serious oversight to attend only to central tendency and to ignore differences in diversity within distributions. This point is illustrated by the story of the statistician who drowned while trying to ford a river with a mean depth of only 6 inches!

Measures of variability, or scatter, provide methods of condensing into single numbers this second aspect of distributions. Two such measures that summarize the extent of distributions' dispersion will be considered.

Range

The **range** describes the number of unit intervals over which the scores of a distribution vary. This is obtained by subtraction. To find the range of a group of scores, subtract the smallest score from the largest score.[6] Thus the range of scores for Class B is $7 - 5 = 2$. Class D's range is 8. This confirms what can be noticed concerning relative variability in these very small distributions simply by inspection; in larger, more typical distributions, the differences are less likely to be evident from inspection.

The range, as a statistic that summarizes distributions' dispersion or variability, has the advantages of being widely known, easily understood, and easily computed. Unfortunately, it is a very crude measure because it is based on only two cases—the highest and the lowest. It thus ignores most of the data. Because the range is based on so few cases, it is a poor summary statistic. For an illustration, compare Classes E and F.

Class E	Class F
10	10
10	9
10	5
10	5
0	4
0	4
0	3
0	0
$M = 5$	$M = 5$

Class F contains only a few examinees whose scores differed markedly from its mean. On the other hand, Class E consists entirely of persons who deviate greatly from its mean. Yet the classes have identical ranges of 10. This demonstrates how the range is insensitive to most of the available data.

In spite of its limitations, the range can be used for some "rough and ready" purposes in which great precision is not needed. Such use is most defensible when the user takes note of anomalies such as the excessive contribution to the range made by the bottom score in Class F.

Another disadvantage of the range is that it leads to a statistical dead-end; it does not provide a stepping stone to other statistics. We clearly need a more powerful measure of variability. This need gives rise to the widely used standard deviation.

Standard Deviation

As a statistic that describes a distribution's variability or scatter, the **standard deviation** is free from the problems that plague the range. Unfortunately, its computation is somewhat more involved. Class B will be used to illustrate the computation of the standard deviation. First, compute the mean of the raw scores; this is shown in the Computation Box 11–1 below. (Do not worry about the formula at the bottom of the box; it will be explained below.)

---

[6]Alternatively, the range is often defined as one more than the difference between the largest and smallest scores.

Computation Box 11–1

Standard Deviation of Class B

X	x	x^2
7	$+1$	1
7	$+1$	1
5	-1	1
5	-1	1
—		—
		$\Sigma x^2 = 4$

$$M = \frac{\Sigma X}{N} = \frac{24}{4} = 6$$

$$SD = \sqrt{\frac{\Sigma x^2}{N}} = \sqrt{\frac{4}{4}} = \sqrt{1} = 1$$

Next, find the amount by which each raw score (symbolized X) deviates from the mean score. This second column is headed x to stand for deviation score of variable X. Enter the amount and direction of each raw score's deviation from the mean of 6. The first score, 7, is 1 more than the mean, so enter a plus 1. Likewise for the second raw score. The two scores of 5 are each one point below the mean of 6, so enter a *minus* 1 for each.

Except for one problem, the mean of these deviation scores could be computed, and a good measure obtained of the distribution's variability expressed in raw-score units. The problem is that the mean of deviation scores is the same for all distributions. Hence, the simple mean of the algebraic values of the x-scores would not discriminate among distributions of differing variability. What to do?

One solution is to compute the mean of the absolute values of the x-scores. This statistic, known as the average deviation or mean deviation is a fine method of quantifying variability; but, because it forsakes the algebraic values of the x-scores, it does not provide a good foundation for more complex statistics such as measures of relationship.

Another solution to the problem of x-score distributions always having a mean algebraic value of 0 is to find another way to get rid of the negative signs in this distribution of deviation scores. This can be accomplished by squaring each x-score. In Computation Box 11–1, the third column contains the squared deviation scores and is appropriately headed x^2. The mean of these squared deviations is another fine descriptor of variation. Moreover, it paves the road to more advanced statistics. This mean of x^2 scores is known as the **variance (V)**. Its formula is:

$$V = \frac{\Sigma x^2}{N}$$

Useful as it is, this statistic will not be used in this book because its values are not interpretable in terms of raw score units. Instead, its positive square root will be used.

The square root of the mean squared deviations is known as the **standard deviation**. This widely used statistic reports a distribution's variability in terms of raw score units. Aside from being a bother to compute if one has to do it by hand, the standard deviation (*SD*) has no significant disadvantages. After one grows accustomed to it, the *SD* is easily understood and easily interpreted. The basic formula for the standard deviation is:

$$SD = \sqrt{\frac{\Sigma x^2}{N}}$$

In Computation Box 11–1, the third column of data consists of the squared *x*-scores. Each of the first two entries is the square of +1; this is +1. Each of the last two entries is the square of −1; this too is +1. The sum of these squared deviation scores is 4. The *SD* is therefore found to be the positive square root of the sum of the squared deviation scores (4) divided by the number of cases (4).

Computation Box 11–2 demonstrates the calculation of the standard deviation for another distribution. In this distribution of Class D, the mean is 6. Therefore, each entry in the *x*-score column is the amount by which the corresponding raw score differs from this mean, and the algebraic sign of each *x*-score indicates the direction by which its raw score differs from the mean. For example, 10 is 4 more than the mean of 6; therefore a +4 is entered in the *x*-score column. When all of the *x* entries have been made, one can check the work. The sum of the *x*-score column should always equal 0 (within the tolerance of rounding error). If it does not, one or more errors have been made.

Computation Box 11–2

Standard Deviation of Class D

X	x	x^2
10	+4	16
10	+4	16
9	+3	9
5	−1	1
5	−1	1
4	−2	4
3	−3	9
2	−4	16
$M = 6$		72

$$SD = \sqrt{\frac{\Sigma x^2}{N}} = \sqrt{\frac{72}{8}} = \sqrt{9} = 3$$

The next column consists of the squares of these *x*-scores. Since the squares of all positive real numbers are positive and the squares of all negative real numbers are also positive, no entries in x^2 columns will ever be negative. When this column is completed its sum is found.

The *SD* is computed by dividing this sum of the x^2 column (72) by the number of cases (8) and extracting the positive square root of the quotient. This yields a *SD* of 3.

For the benefit of readers who still feel insecure about their ability to compute *SD*s, the computation of the *SD*s for Classes E and F is provided. If you have achieved a command of this process, skip the next two boxes. Otherwise, it is suggested that you first try to compute the *SD* for Class E by yourself and then check your work in Computation Box 11–3. If necessary, this process can be repeated for Class F with Computation Box 11–4.

<table>
<tr><td colspan="3">

Computation Box 11–3

Standard Deviation of Class E

</td><td colspan="3">

Computation Box 11–4

Standard Deviation of Class F

</td></tr>
<tr><td>X</td><td>x</td><td>x^2</td><td>X</td><td>x</td><td>x^2</td></tr>
<tr><td>10</td><td>+5</td><td>25</td><td>10</td><td>+5</td><td>25</td></tr>
<tr><td>10</td><td>+5</td><td>25</td><td>9</td><td>+4</td><td>16</td></tr>
<tr><td>10</td><td>+5</td><td>25</td><td>5</td><td>0</td><td>0</td></tr>
<tr><td>10</td><td>+5</td><td>25</td><td>5</td><td>0</td><td>0</td></tr>
<tr><td>0</td><td>−5</td><td>25</td><td>4</td><td>−1</td><td>1</td></tr>
<tr><td>0</td><td>−5</td><td>25</td><td>4</td><td>−1</td><td>1</td></tr>
<tr><td>0</td><td>−5</td><td>25</td><td>3</td><td>−2</td><td>4</td></tr>
<tr><td>0</td><td>−5</td><td>25</td><td>0</td><td>−5</td><td>25</td></tr>
<tr><td>$M = 5$</td><td></td><td>200</td><td>$M = 5$</td><td></td><td>72</td></tr>
<tr><td colspan="3">

$$SD = \sqrt{\frac{\Sigma x^2}{N}} = \sqrt{\frac{200}{8}} = \sqrt{25} = 5$$

</td><td colspan="3">

$$SD = \sqrt{\frac{\Sigma x^2}{N}} = \sqrt{\frac{72}{8}} = \sqrt{9} = 5$$

</td></tr>
</table>

Some readers may be wondering, "Why bother with computation in this age of calculators and computers? We don't compute *SD*s by hand anymore, do we?" No, we do not. The computations *with simplified data* offered in this book are designed to reveal and illustrate the *meaning behind* the calculations so they will not be shrouded in mystery.

QUIZ 11–3

1. Compute the mean and standard deviation for Class A.

   Class A
   10
   9
   7
   6
   6
   4

2. Find the range and *SD* for Class C.

   Class C
   9
   4
   4
   4
   4

KEY TO QUIZ 11–3

1. $M = 7$; $SD = 2$.
2. Range $= 5$; $SD = 2$.

So What?

"OK," some disgruntled reader is thinking, "I understand how the standard deviation is computed and what it means, but so what? Who wants a standard deviation anyway? What is it for?" The answer from the first paragraph of this chapter may merit repetition. The *SD*, like other statistics introduced in this chapter, is used to describe reference groups used in making norm-referenced interpretations, to describe samples used in estimating test reliability and validity, to derive some kinds of scores, and sometimes to compute student grades. Such statistics thus provide tools by which to pursue the goal of using measurement to improve teaching. The next section concerns a kind of derived score.

Standard Scores

A few varieties of derived scores have already been encountered. Percentile ranks and grade equivalents exemplify two of the three general kinds of converted scores that were outlined in Chapter 3. Standard scores are the third general group of derived scores.

As their name suggests, **standard scores** are closely associated with, and arise from, the standard deviation. This is, therefore, a convenient and logical place in which to introduce the concept of standard scores and their computation. They will then be referred to as the need arises in subsequent chapters. However, the full development and explanation of their uses will be left for Chapter 16.

Standard scores are a group of derived scores that are particularly useful when computations need to be performed. The prototype of the standard score group is the **z-score**; *z-scores are derived scores expressed in terms of distance from the mean in* SD *units.* The formula for the *z*-score is:

$$z = \frac{x}{SD}$$

Computation Box 11–5 shows the calculation of a set of *z*-scores for one of the classes used before. First, the mean must be computed (or found on a calculator). Next, the *SD* is computed by use of the now familiar formula (or calculator). Finally, the new step is performed; the *z*-score corresponding to each raw score is calculated by dividing its *x*-score by the *SD* of the distribution. (Caution: It is the *x*, not the x^2 that is divided by the *SD*.) The top raw score of 10 is 3 raw score units greater than the mean of 7; thus, its deviation score is +3. This +3 is divided by the *SD* of 2 to obtain the *z*-score of +1.5. The next case is 2 raw score units above the mean. When this +2 is divided by the *SD* of 2, the *z*-score is found to be +1. The third score is equal to the mean. Thus 0 divided by 2 equals 0. The next two cases have raw scores that are 1 point *below* the mean; when −1 is divided by the *SD* of 2, the quotient is found to be −.5. Finally, the last score is 3 raw score units below the mean. When −3 is divided by the *SD* of 2, −1.5 results. A final check on one's work can be made by algebraically adding the *z*-score column; its sum should be 0 (within the limits of rounding error).

Computation Box 11–5

z-scores of Class A

X	x	x^2	z
10	+3	9	+1.5
9	+2	4	+1.0
7	0	0	0.0
6	−1	1	−0.5
6	−1	1	−0.5
4	−3	9	−1.5
$M = 7$		24	

$$SD = \sqrt{\frac{\Sigma x^2}{N}} = \sqrt{\frac{24}{6}} = \sqrt{4} = 2$$

$$z = \frac{x}{SD}$$

It was seen in the previous section that deviation scores (i.e., *x*-scores), expressed normative status in terms of distance from the mean measured in *raw score units.* By contrast, z-scores express normative status in terms of distance from the mean measured in *standard deviation units.* This conversion of raw score units of the x-score into standard deviation units of the z-scores is achieved by dividing the x-score by the SD in the formula:

$$z = \frac{x}{SD}$$

"So what?" some readers may wonder. The advantage of expressing deviation scores in terms of standard deviation units is one of *comparability.* Suppose, for example, that a 7-year-old girl is found to be 5 pounds lighter than the national mean for her age and gender; i.e., her x-score for weight is -5 *pounds.* Suppose also that she is 2 inches shorter than the mean of this reference group. Thus, her x-score for stature is -2 *inches.* These metrics of pounds vis-à-vis inches are useless for comparing her *relative status* on weight and height. We are tied to the artifacts of the metrics with which she was measured. Now, suppose we knew for this reference group that the SDs of weight in pounds to be 4 and its SD of height in inches to be 3, then we could convert each of the x-scores into a z-score as follows:

Weight

$$z = \frac{x}{SD} = \frac{-5\text{lb}}{4\text{lb}} = -1.25$$

Stature

$$z = \frac{x}{SD} = \frac{-2\text{in}}{3\text{in}} = -.67$$

This shows her relative status in weight and height with respect to the reference group. Notice in the calculation above how the *units of measure cancel out.* By dividing the deviation score (which is expressed in whatever unit of measure that happened to be used) by the SD (which is expressed in the same unit of measure), the unit of measure cancels out. We are thereby liberated from the artifact of the original metric.

One final point remains regarding this example. Two domain-referenced scores that are referenced to different domains cannot be *compared.* The only meaningful way by which to achieve comparability is by use of a common reference group (or at least highly similar groups) of people that bridge the incommensurate domains. Even though each separate measure was admirably suited to domain referencing, pounds could not be compared with inches. Comparability was achieved by norm referencing both measures to the same reference group of people. This is an important use of norm referencing that was not mentioned in Chapter 3, but which will resurface in Part V when test batteries are discussed.

Some readers may feel a need to think their way through Computation Box 11–6, which is another example of the calculation of z-scores.

A Preview of Correlation

One major statistics topic remains to be treated. It is the measurement of relationship between two variables—**correlation**. An understanding of a way by which relationship is quantified is necessary for later work with validity and reliability.

The study of co-relation follows nicely from the topic of standard scores, and it could well be taken up at this time. The correlation between two variables will, when we get to it, turn out to be nothing more complicated than the mean of the products of corresponding z-scores.

However, the topic will not be used until Chapter 14, and some readers will be eager to return to measurement issues at this time. Therefore, consideration of correlation will be delayed until it is needed.

Computation Box 11–6

z-scores

X	x	x²	z
16	+8	64	+1.33
16	+8	64	+1.33
14	+6	36	+1.00
6	−2	4	−0.33
6	−2	4	−0.33
4	−4	16	−0.67
2	−6	36	−1.00
0	−8	64	−1.33
$M = 8$		288	

$$SD = \sqrt{\frac{\Sigma x^2}{N}} = \sqrt{\frac{288}{8}} = \sqrt{36} = 6$$

$$z = \frac{x}{SD}$$

Chapter Summary

Raw data are often condensed by use of summary statistics. Two dimensions of a distribution—central tendency and variability—are usually summarized. Three widely used measures of central tendency are the mean (*M*), median (*Md*), and mode (*Mo*). The mean is permissible whenever a scale has equal units of measure. The median is possible whenever ordering of scores is possible. The mode is most often used when neither of these conditions is present. Most applied uses are best served with the more powerful mean where it is permissible, but occasionally the median or even the mode is the more meaningful.

Group variability or individual differences are often summarized by use of the rough-and-ready range or the much more adequate standard deviation (*SD*). Most of the more advanced statistics that teachers encounter are based on the mean and the standard deviation.

Of the several kinds of derived scores used for norm-referenced interpretation, two were introduced in this chapter. Percentile ranks (PRs) provide easily understood statements concerning the percent of a reference group that examinees excelled or equaled. For most *interpretive* purposes, PRs are the derived score of preference.

The prototypic kind of standard scores—z-scores—provide a measure of examinee deviation from a group mean; this deviation is measured in standard deviation units. For most *computational* or *research* purposes, standard scores are the derived score of preference.

Suggestions for Further Reading

Ferguson, G. A., & Takane, Y. (1989). *Statistical analysis in psychology and education* (6th ed.). New York: McGraw-Hill. A basic text in statistics that treats topics in much greater depth and breadth than does this book.

Hopkins, K. D., Glass, G. V., & Hopkins B. R. (1987). *Basic statistics for the behavioral sciences* (2nd ed.). Englewood Cliffs, NJ: Prentice-Hall. Another sound, basic text in statistics that focuses on use of statistics in education and related fields.

Lyman, H. B. (1991). *Test scores & what they mean* (5th ed.). Englewood Cliffs, NJ: Prentice-Hall. Chapter 5, "A Few Statistics," provides readable, elementary coverage of most of the same topics as does this book (in Chapters 11, 14, and 16). It uses examples that are more realistic, but harder to compute.

Sax, B. (1989). *Principles of educational and psychological measurement and evaluation* (3rd ed.). Belmont, CA: Wadsworth. Chapter 7, "Summarizing and Interpreting Measurements," provides an introduction to a slightly broader set of topics than does this book. It contains a helpful short section on selecting an electronic calculator.

Thorndike, R. M., Cunningham, G. K., Thorndike, R. L., & Hagen, E. P. (1991). *Measurement and evaluation in psychology and education* (5th ed.). New York: Macmillan. Chapter 2, "Measurement in Numbers," also provides a survey of a slightly broader selection of topics than does this book. It addresses those statistical concepts treated in this chapter as well as those taken up in our Chapter 14.

Marking and Reporting

Teachers are expected to provide periodic summative reports of student achievement. Educators spend much time computing, recording, explaining, and defending the grades they award. The primary function of these activities is to communicate effectively to various audiences the level and breadth of student achievement (Hills, 1981, p. 283). Hence teachers need to be skilled in developing valid grading procedures that are solidly based in student assessment (Sanders, et al., 1990). The measurement upon which marks are based should be an integral part of teaching, being directly linked to instructional goals that reflect both subject matter content and the cognitive complexity of the learning outcomes (Terwilliger, 1989).

The communication function of grades is best served when grading practices are harmonious with the kind of subject matter, type of instructional objective, appropriate manifestation of individual differences, type of measuring instruments, and their kind of interpretations. Too often, however, marking practices and policies are inconsistent with other elements of teaching and thereby become distracting, counterproductive, and/or confusing. The purpose of this chapter is to pursue the former conditions.

It is an understatement to say that professional consensus has not emerged concerning the purposes of grades, how they should be determined, and how they are best used. Achievement of a given amount and kind can yield a C from one teacher and an A from another. The difference may reside in various sources of confusion about grades (Hills, 1981, pp. 332–343), in teachers' differing standards, and/or in conflicting definitions of what constitutes grades.

In addition to professional disagreement concerning marking practices, a number of out-and-out mistakes occur as teachers compute student grades (Stiggins, Frisbie, & Griswold, 1989). Marking is an aspect of professional practice in which many teachers' competence is not adequate (Hills, 1991).

This important and controversial topic will be opened by considering the functions that grades serve. Knowing what we are trying to achieve will help us to develop practices that contribute to our goals. Next, the topic of marking will be related to the instructional/evaluation model developed in Chapters 2 and 3 in order to formulate criteria of effective grading systems. These criteria will lead to grading practices that are rational and constructive. Some sources of ambiguity in grades will then be examined. Awareness of things that cloud the meaning of marks will help us avoid pitfalls. Finally, the issue of how to combine scores into total grades will be explored to find ways that achieve the desired relative weight of each component part.

Once a teacher has determined the purpose of his or her grades, developed a rational basis for marking that avoids the common sources of confusion, and acquired skills in combining the component parts into total grades, an important task remains—communication. An evaluation plan should be developed in order to inform students and parents of the basis of grading. Terwilliger (1989) helpfully enumerated the following essential elements about which a classroom evaluation plan should be explicit:

1. The timing of data collection (e.g., dates for tests, due dates for assignments and projects.)

2. Conditions under which data will be collected (e.g., kinds of tests, availability of reference materials and computational aids during tests, whether late homework and projects will be accepted and the penalties for lateness.)

3. Methods by which the data will be used to arrive at summative grades (i.e., the relative weights of the items of data).

Purposes and Functions of Grades

The primary reason that grades are virtually universal in elementary, secondary, and higher education is their role in communication. Many significant needs are met in whole or part by school marks; therefore, there is a demand for grades and a convention of providing them. The varied purposes of communicating student achievement can be grouped into three types: (a) directly benefiting individual students and their parents, (b) facilitating the work of the school, and (c) meeting needs of the broader society. Diverse as these purposes are, they are all based on the supposition that grades reflect the extent to which students have achieved the instructional goals that guide curriculum development, teaching methods, and assessment practices.

Benefit to Students and Parents

Marks provide feedback concerning student achievement to students and their parents (or guardians). This important reporting function helps parents monitor student effort, give encouragement, and remain informed.

The feedback also enables young people to gain self-knowledge. Grades provide achievement information by which students learn more about their capabilities and limitations in comparison with others as well as their own relative strengths and weaknesses. This information facilitates important decisions concerning course selection, future education, and career choice. Developing a realistic self-concept is an important part of growing up.

Some educators resist giving informative feedback via grades and other means for fear it will damage self-concept. A sharp distinction between self-concept and self-esteem is helpful in this connection. Positiveness of self-esteem is desirable—the more the better. When it comes to self-concept, however, we seek realism. If Joe is an inept speller or driver, he should know this. He is best served by honest feedback about his skills so that he can make realistic provisions for living with them and/or for overcoming them. Grades should enhance realism of self-concept concerning achievement.

Yet even when grades are low, high self-esteem is possible and desirable. Molly could be inept at spelling, sports, or math and still believe herself to be a very worthwhile person. Positive self-esteem is something that educators should value and work for, but it does not happen to be a purpose of grading.

Benefit to the School

Grades are a major way by which schools track student progress. This institutional function has several constructive purposes. For one thing, it enables teachers to individualize instruction. Effective teaching needs to be aimed at a level appropriate to the learner. Recent grades provide a means of estimating what level of instruction will best meet the needs of each student.

Another way schools use marks concerns entry requirements for certain courses. This, of course, is most common at the secondary and college levels where many courses have prerequisites. For example, a high school might not allow students to enroll in an academic physics course unless they have at least a "C" in first-year algebra.

Schools also use marks to determine eligibility for various activities such as athletics and student government. In college, grades also often serve as the primary determinant of scholarships, probationary status, and suspension from school.

Some elementary teachers group their pupils within classes into less heterogeneous subgroups for reading and mathematics instruction. This so-called homogeneous grouping enables teachers to instruct subgroups in which student capabilities are more similar so that the level of instruction can better be targeted to the capabilities of the respective subgroups.

Grades at both elementary and secondary level are sometimes used for grouping students in the same course or grade. For example, a middle school might offer three levels of seventh-grade English and mathematics designed to meet the needs of students having differing levels of past achievement in the respective subjects.

Although it is beyond the scope of this book to evaluate research on such controversial practices, mention will be made of two key points. If so-called homogeneous grouping is used, then it is essential to provide appropriately targeted instruction to the respective groups; obvious as this is, it is often violated. For example, suppose a school offers four levels of an American history class—a decision that would probably be unwise (Slavin, 1990). In this case, these classes should *not* all use the same textbook. Even if the general developmental objectives are identical across levels, the most suitable means of pursuing these objectives will differ with student characteristics.

The other key point is that group assignment should be done separately for each subject involved. That is, there should be no day-long groups. Suppose a high school were to group students into three levels for social studies, English, math, science, and physical education. A given youngster could well be in the low stratum in social studies and English, the middle one in math and science, and the high one in physical education. Even when students are grouped relatively homogeneously with respect to one school subject (e.g., reading), the members of each group will still be highly variable with respect to other subjects (e.g., math).

Benefit to the Larger Community

Although grades are confidential and can generally be released only with permission of students (in the case of adults) or parents (in the case of minors), they are used by institutions outside the school for important functions. For example, when a person applies for admission to college, a transcript of secondary school records is usually required. In some instances grades serve as a basis for reaching selection decisions regarding whether to admit the student. In other cases, the marks help colleges make placement decisions, such as which math course would be most appropriate. And, of course, grades are one basis by which scholarship recipients are chosen.

Business, industry, and government also have frequent occasion to request transcripts of those who apply for jobs. The grades students receive in high school and college provide prospective employers with much valuable information.

Another use of marks involves licensing or certification of competence. Before people are legally allowed to practice a variety of occupations, such as electrician, teacher, or physician, governmental regulatory agencies assess qualifications. Grades from occupational preparation programs (e.g., trade schools, teacher education programs, or medical schools) help to certify competence, thereby protecting the public from deficient practitioners.

Toward a Rational System of Grading

It has been observed that grading practices, like most deeply ingrained features of a culture, are often accepted with little thoughtful analysis of their nature, rationale, and functions. In examining marking practices, the perspective might best be similar to that of cultural anthropologists who examine a set of behaviors and try to understand their functions and the way in which they fit into the total culture of which they are a part. Grading practices should be looked at through the objective eyes of a social scientist (Thorndike, Cunningham, Thorndike, & Hagen, 1991, p. 176).

It is well known that it is easier to earn a given grade from some teachers than from others; a common and major defect of grades is the lack of clear understanding of what they mean (Stiggins, Frisbie, & Griswold, 1989). It is clearly undesirable for a student's grade to be an artifact of who taught a course and/or which other people were enrolled in it. Measurement authorities generally agree that *grades should be pure measures of achievement* uncontaminated by such extraneous issues as teacher-to-teacher variations of standards and achievement of classmates. (Ebel & Frisbie, 1991; Gronlund & Linn, 1990; Thorndike, Cunningham, Thorndike, & Hagen, 1991).

Many issues relate to grading. The most fundamental decision a teacher must make may be the choice between an absolute or a relative grading method. If an absolute method is chosen, the methods of evaluation should be designed to yield meaningful domain-referenced interpretation. If a relative method is selected, then the system should be fashioned to provide meaningful norm-referenced interpretation. As discussed in Chapters 2 and 3, however, a teacher cannot rationally choose between these major approaches without considering the kind of subject matter. To a large extent, the nature of the subject matter dictates the kind of referencing that is appropriate.

Where grades report achievement in small, well-defined, masterable, vital domains (i.e., Track A content), domain-referenced grading should be used *for each minimum essential objective separately.* Report cards can state each minimum essential objective and provide places to check mastery or nonmastery (and perhaps borderline) status. At the lower elementary level, portions of report cards sometimes consist of such domain-referenced checklists for reporting attainment of specific minimum essential objectives. Figure 12–1 shows a section of a report card designed to report separately the mastery status on each of several minimum essential objectives.

When grades report achievement in well-defined, nonessential or unmasterable domains (i.e., Track B), it is not necessary to report achievement for each objective separately. This kind of subject matter can be interpreted either by means of domain referencing and/or norm referencing. If domain referencing is chosen, report cards should be designed to be referenced clearly to each domain separately with a report of achievement for each. Figure 12–2 illustrates such a section.

MATHEMATICS

Grade Two, Third Quarter

Skill	Not Mastered	Partial Mastery	Mastered
Uses communitive property of addition (e.g., if 6 + 3 = 9, then 3 + 6 must = 9)	____	____	____
Explains place value (e.g., 52 = 5 tens + 2 ones)	____	____	____
Supplies missing addends under 10 (e.g., 3 + ? = 8)	____	____	____
Adds three 1-digit numbers	____	____	____
Adds two 2-digit numbers without regrouping	____	____	____
Adds two 2-digit numbers with regrouping	____	____	____
Supplies missing subtrahends under 10 (e.g., 6 − ? = 2)	____	____	____
Supplies missing minuends under 10 (e.g., ? − 3 = 8)	____	____	____
Subtracts 1-digit numbers from 2-digit numbers without regrouping	____	____	____
Subtracts 2-digit numbers from 2-digit numbers without regrouping	____	____	____
Reads conventional clocks at quarter hours	____	____	____
Determines value of combinations of coins up to a dollar	____	____	____
Constructs simple pie graph	____	____	____
Reads simple pie graph	____	____	____

Figure 12–1.   Portion of Report Card Suitable for Track A Content. Adapted from Millman J. (1970). Reporting student progress: A case for a criterion-referenced marking system. *Phi Delta Kappan, 52,* pp. 226–230.

Although the approach illustrated in Figure 12–2 is appropriate, it is not the choice of most teachers or schools. Since Track B goals are not essential, little reason exists to go to the trouble of domain-referencing reports of student achievement for each separate objective. Rather, it is common to combine achievement across several objectives and to report each student's composite status by means of norm referencing.

Where grades are used to report student achievement of developmental objectives for large, open-ended, unmasterable, nonessential content domains (i.e., Track C), meaningful reporting demands norm referencing. Referencing to ill-defined content domains is not viable. Much confusion would be avoided if this fact were more widely recognized.

PHYSICAL EDUCATION
Eighth-Grade Boys' Track

Event	Status on Best of Three Attempts
100-meter dash	_____ Seconds
200-meter dash	_____ Seconds
400-meter dash	_____ Seconds
800-meter dash	_____ Seconds
1600-meter dash	_____ Seconds
High jump	_____ Meters
Long jump	_____ Meters
Shot put	_____ Meters
Discus	_____ Meters
100-meter low hurdles	_____ Seconds
100-meter high hurdles	_____ Seconds

Figure 12–2.   Portion of Report Card Suitable for Domain-Referencing, Track B Content. This is not the method of choice of most teachers.

Since Track C objectives are not essential, no need exists to report student achievement separately for each objective. Here too, it is common practice to combine achievement across several objectives.

But what if, as is often the case, the content taught during a reporting period is drawn from two or three of the tracks? In this case, it may make the best sense to separate the report of Track A content from the rest. The Track A material can be organized into a checklist indicating the mastery or nonmastery of each minimum essential objective. Alternatively, in those cases in which almost all students have mastered all of the Track A objectives, it is often easier to gloss over minimum essential objectives with a mere comment that all *except those listed* have been met.

Another option would be to fail any student who does not master each and every minimum essential objective. This decision could be seen as a logical consequence of the contention that such objectives are truly vital. A major difficulty with this approach is that many schools overuse Track A objectives. Many of the so-called minimal essential objectives really are not essential. Thus, a person who fails to master a mislabeled "essential" objective does not necessarily merit failure in a whole course or subject. Another trouble with such a hard-line approach concerns the arbitrary periodicity of school reporting cycles. Mastery learning is designed to bring nearly everyone to mastery *eventually.* In this context in which individual differences are directed into the time dimension, it is not consistent to demand mastery at some arbitrary point such as the end of a reporting cycle.

Once the Track A content of a course or subject has been handled, it is customary and sensible to *combine achievement in all Track B and Track C objectives into one composite grade.* The rest of this section is devoted to the issue of how this composite grade—which usually reflects achievement in several developmental objectives—is best determined.

Consider the two most common methods of assigning such grades to students, and scrutinize the advantages and disadvantages of each. From an analysis of the virtues and vices of each method, a set of goals for rational and effective marking systems will be derived. The concept of anchor measures will then be developed. Finally, illustrative grading systems will be presented and evaluated by use of the above criteria.

Two Prototypic Grading Systems[1]

Two widely used groups of methods are used to determine grades.[2] **Percentage grading** is the most common variety of a group of methods based on attempts to orient grades to absolute standards. **Grading on a class curve** is the most common of those methods based on relative, norm-referenced orientations. These two common systems will be the focus of this section. Although each system has numerous variants, most teachers fall quite neatly into the percentage grading camp or the class curve camp.

Percentage Grading Systems

Percentage grading systems are the most widely used basis for assigning grades, yet "textbooks on teaching in general, as well as textbooks on measurement in particular, are highly critical of this approach" (Thorndike, Cunningham, Thorndike, & Hagen, 1991, p. 179). In such systems, teachers use alleged "absolute standards" in the form of the percentage of possible points required for each grade. Advocates believe this provides advance notice to students of what they have to do in order to earn various grades.

This information would indeed be desirable, but does an announcement that "you will need to average at least 90% to earn an A," really communicate what students have to learn or how hard they will have to work? Does it tightly specify the content? Does it communicate the difficulty of the tests on which this "standard" must be maintained? No, it does not.

It does not answer—or even address—the crucial question: "Ninety percent *of what?*" It does not because most courses or subjects cover broad, variable ranges of Track C content. The difficulty of the content and its exact composition appropriately varies from teacher to teacher and from year to year. The objectives of most elementary and secondary school subjects are nonbehavioral and developmental. They can be pursued by any of several content routes; thus, the exact content is not tightly specified.

Such large, open, vaguely described, Track C content domains do not give rise to meaningful interpretation of student achievement in terms of either raw or percentage scores. Recall that to be useful, domain-referenced statements must relate to a content domain that is *very clearly specified.* "The domain definition should be sufficiently detailed and delimiting to show clearly what facets of behavior are included

---

[1]Most of the remainder of this section on developing a rational grading system is based on Hanna, G. S., & Cashin, W. E. (1988). Improving college grading. IDEA Paper No. 19. Manhattan, KS: Kansas State University, Center for Faculty Evaluation and Development. Used with permission.

[2]In addition, there are other methods used by relatively few teachers; McKeachie (1986) and Terwilliger (1971) discussed several of these less-common grading methods (e.g., grading on progress and contract grading) and their problems.

and what facets are excluded in the domain" (American Psychological Association, 1985, p. 26).

An important consequence of the size and lack of incisive description that characterizes Track C content is *uncontrolled item difficulty*. A teacher can (intentionally or inadvertently) develop a test on which no student is likely to obtain even 70% of the possible points. Likewise, an instructor can create a test on which most students easily attain over 90%. Raw scores and percentage scores are "as dependent on test characteristics as on student characteristics" (Mehrens & Lehmann, 1991, p. 484); i.e., raw scores are *artifacts of test difficulty*. For this reason, announcements concerning "absolute standards" such as, "you must average at least 84% to earn a B," creates only an *illusion* of informative clarity; it really tells nothing because it does not answer the question, "Eighty-four percent of what?"

Such statements tell nothing, that is, unless an implicit understanding exists concerning test difficulty. Difficulty, of course, is inherently norm referenced. Thus, for a percentage marking system to convey information, it must *violate its intrinsic domain-referenced nature and be rendered covertly norm referenced.*

As testimony to the truth of this claim, consider what happens when a test turns out to be too hard. Suppose a teacher uses percentage grading in a class that has always exhibited normal competence. Now, on a certain 40-item test, the top score is only 80%. Does the teacher assign unusually low grades? Often not. Most teachers who find themselves in this predicament do one or another form of *violence to the meaning of percentage grading*. That is, after they paint themselves into a corner, they walk on the wet paint. How?

A few void the test. More go ahead and count it, but "rig" the next one to be very easy in order to compensate. Some let students correct their errors for partial credit on (only) this hard test. Others are more generous than they would otherwise be in awarding partial credit. Many teachers engage in such "eccentric" arithmetic practices as counting each of the test's 40 items at 3% rather than the proper 2.5% or giving everybody a 10% to 25% bonus.

Perhaps the most common "adjustment" is to scale the "percentage" grades to the top person in the class (80% in this example). Thus, a score of 60% would be elevated to 75% (60/80). *This*, of course, *is norm referencing*. While norm referencing makes excellent sense, one could not do worse than to select a single individual for the reference "group"!

None of these and similar "adjustments" are compatible with the basic rationale of absolute standard, domain-referenced, percentage grading. They do not represent true percentage grading; they represent pseudopercentage grading systems. They are ways people find out of the messes that they get into by use of a fundamentally flawed system. It would be preferable to employ a grading system that avoids both the predicaments and the deceptions.

In most subjects, the content is variable in difficulty; for example, one could test knowledge or application of given facts or principles with easy questions or with difficult ones. Large, open, ill-defined content domains do not tie down test item difficulty. Thus interpreting student performance in terms of either raw or percent scores (i.e., domain referencing) cannot be meaningfully achieved. There is simply no statistical, educational, or psychological basis for linking arbitrary percentages to grades (Mehrens & Lehmann, 1991, p. 484). Since true domain referencing is neither feasible nor meaningful for the kinds of content most teachers teach most of the time, the pursuit of a rational system of grading leads to an examination of norm referencing.

QUIZ 12–1

Several common methods of "adjusting" (pseudo)percentage grading have been sketched. Most have unintended consequences. Identify any undesirable effect on students of each of the following ways teachers "walk on the wet paint."

1. Voiding the test that turns out to be too difficult
2. Rigging the next text to be much easier
3. Awarding partial credit unusually generously
4. Performing "eccentric" arithmetic
5. Scaling to the top student

KEY TO QUIZ 12–1

1. If the test is voided, students who have not prepared for it are rewarded, while those who have conscientiously studied are punished. This may impact undesirably on their future study behavior. Voiding also reduces the validity of the grades as balanced measures of achievement.
2. The resulting feedback is very misleading. A given level of performance would result in unrealistically adverse feedback on the first occasion and unrealistically favorable feedback on the second. Such erratic feedback tends to hinder students' development of self-monitoring and realistic self-appraisal.
3. Being generous with partial credit may be a reasonable thing to do. Although it usually would not suffice to solve the problem, it would help.
4. Awarding 3% for each of 40 items "teaches" that 100% of something may not be all of it. What kind of arithmetic modeling is this?
5. Scaling everyone's grade to the performance of the top student sets this individual up for group censure. Such a student may learn that it is unwise to perform at one's best because it earns peer disfavor.

Class-Curve Grading Systems

Teachers who use class-curve grading often understand that domain referencing is not ordinarily meaningful for grading and that norm referencing is the only viable alternative. (They may also recognize some or all of the problems of class-curve grading discussed in this section, but they may seem to be the lesser evil.)

As do those who use percentage grading, teachers who grade on class curves usually value advance notice to students regarding what is required to receive various grades. They seek this by such statements as, "To earn an A, you must be among the top 20% of the people in this class in total end-of-term points." Does such information really communicate how hard students must work in order to receive a given grade? No. Not unless students have prior knowledge of the academic capabilities, motivation, and resources of others who happen to be enrolled in the particular section of a class.

At the elementary level, the children assigned to a given teacher may be more or less capable than those assigned last year. At higher levels, some sections of a course often contain better students than others. Persons in classes having many poor students can more easily rise to the top than can those in better classes. For example, a student in the A stratum in the poor section might well receive only a B or even a C in a high section. This section-to-section fluctuation commonly *makes a one-grade difference for several students per section.*

We have an apparent paradox. On the one hand, norm referencing is the only logical foundation upon which to base grades for Track C content. On the other hand, the only method of achieving norm referencing of which most teachers are aware—grading on a class curve—is ordinarily unsatisfactory because it introduces instability arising from small class sizes. Do not despair; there *is* a way out. First, however, the other major problems associated with class-curve grading must be identified.

Grading on a class curve forces students to compete for grades. Yet *learning* is not inherently competitive.[3] One person's success in learning does not predispose others to less success. In class-curve grading, however, a predetermination of a section's grade distribution exists—*regardless of student learning.* Such "reality" causes students to feel a sense of helplessness and to lack a sense of efficacy.

Perhaps the greatest evil of class-curve grading is its impact on interpersonal relations. Suppose there can be only four A grades in a certain class, and Sue ranks fifth. The only way she can earn an A is by "bumping" someone else. The "bumped" person need learn no less, but in class-curve grading someone must receive a lower grade in order for Sue to receive a higher one. Thus in such a system, a grade not only reflects a student's achievement, it is also a function of the achievement of others in the class.

Having to "bump" others and being "bumped" foster ill will. Marking on a class curve does not encourage group study or cooperative learning; instead, it encourages isolation and exclusion. Class-curve grading does not motivate students to help one another to learn; on the contrary, self-interest is "best" served by interfering with the learning of one's fellows.

Many teachers who use (pseudo)percentage grading systems recognize the grave evils of class-curve marking and seek to avoid them. (They may also recognize some or all of the problems of so-called percentage marking discussed above, but these problems seem to them to be the lesser evil.)

---

[3]I have no universal objection to competition. Where there can be only one first-chair clarinetist in the band, competition is inherent. If only one person can be elected class president, again competition makes sense. Learning, however, is not inherently competitive; one person's success in learning need not doom another to learn less.

QUIZ 12–2

1. If there were no way out of the paradox and you had to choose a (pseudo)percentage grading system or a class-curve system, which would be the lesser evil?

2. Ms. Jenkins uses domain referencing for setting a passing (pseudo)standard (e.g., 60%) and class-curve grading for differentiating among the other grades. How do the problems of this system compare in seriousness with those of percentage grading or class-curve grading?

3. Mr. Khalaf uses (pseudo)domain referencing to establish the standard necessary for an "A" (e.g., 90%) and a class-curve system for distinguishing among the other grades. How do the problems of this system compare in seriousness with those of percentage grading or class-curve grading?

4. Miss Hebart computes grades by use of both class-curve grading and by percentage grading. She then computes the mean of the two to determine each student's grade. How do the problems of this system compare in seriousness with those of percentage grading or class-curve grading?

KEY TO QUIZ 12–2

1. There probably is no best answer. This is my personal response: So-called percentage grading has serious problems. Class-curve grading not only has problems, it has *evils*. I abhor its impact on the interpersonal relations of children. I would therefore reluctantly choose one or another of the adulterations of percentage grading.

   One common "adjustment" I would assuredly *not* use is to scale the percentages to the performance of the top student. This covert norm referencing to a sample of one person represents the worst of both systems. It sets the top student up to be disliked (if not persecuted) by peers.

2 and 3. Such grading schemes as these have the advantage and limitations of one system in one part of the distribution of grades and the benefits and problems of the other system in other parts of the distribution. These mixes of two inadequate systems do not produce hybrid vigor; rather, they produce a more confusing set of problems than either system used by itself.

4. Such schemes as this succeed in diluting the problems of each approach. The cost of this dilution of disadvantages, however, is a simultaneous dilution of the advantages of each. Moreover, her system takes more effort.

Characteristics of Sound Grading Systems

In seeking better systems of grading, we should strive not to dilute, but to *avoid* the pitfalls identified for percentage and class-curve grading practices. At the same time, we should seek to tap the full, undiluted values of each approach. Our pursuit of this dual aim will be assisted by the recognition of attributes of effective grading systems.

Obtain Relevant Norm Referencing

The content domains of most courses are large and flexible.[4] Instruction is typically aimed at transfer of learning rather than mere recall. It is not possible to describe the domains with sufficient precision either to render domain referencing meaningful or to make the establishment of content mastery standards appropriate. Hence the only viable means of interpreting performance is by means of norm referencing.[5]

A sound system of grading must be referenced to a *relevant* group of other people. The pursuit of relevance usually dictates that the reference group consist of other (past and/or present) students in the grade or course.

Avoid Instability of Small Samples

Sound grading systems must also be referenced to *stable* groups. This requires groups large enough to avoid marked group-to-group fluctuation. The need for stability dictates that reference groups *not* consist of individual classes. The grades awarded to students in a given section should be free to reflect the group's achievement if it turns out to be unusually high or low. Similarly, grades should reflect section-to-section peculiarities in variability.

Avoid Psychological and Social Evils of Fixed-Sum Systems

There is no predetermined total amount that students in a class can achieve. Grading systems should reflect this reality. Cooperation should not be thwarted by systems of reporting achievement. Counterproductive competition among peers should be avoided. These considerations dictate that the reference group be (at least largely) external to the section being graded (unless the section is enormous, as in some college courses).

Provide Sense of Efficacy

Students should have a sense of control over their learning and over the grades that report this achievement. They should know that if the achievement is unusually high or low in their class, then the grade distribution will faithfully reflect this reality.

Be Defined and Interpretable

A standard of any marking and reporting system is that it be highly interpretable (Thorndike & Hagen, 1977, p. 590). A system's meaning should be communicable. It

---

[4]Recall that earlier in this chapter separate approaches were described (and illustrated in Figure 12–1) for handling grading of Track A material.

[5]Note that "norm referencing" *per se* does *not* require that the individual class serve as the reference group. Nor does it dictate the shape of the distribution of grades or suggest that the symmetric bell-shaped "normal" curve requires some specific fraction of students to fail (Mehrens & Lehmann, 1991, p. 484).

is also desirable that the definition of grades be consistent from section to section and from teacher to teacher. This consistency is achieved by norm-referenced definition of grades' meaning by comparison to a stable, relevant reference group.

Anchorage to a More Inclusive Reference Group

Analysis of the two common grading systems leads to a dilemma. Norm referencing is found to be the best foundation on which to base grades in courses having Track C content. Yet the best known means of achieving norm referencing—class-curve grading—is wholly unsatisfactory. Anchor measures provide an escape from the apparent dilemma by permitting referencing to a larger, external reference group. Instead of section-by-section referencing, a more inclusive reference group is sought upon which to base norm referencing. "This group might include (a) all of the students in various sections of the same general course for whom common performance data are available or (b) all students who have taken a particular course under the same instructor over a specified period of time" (Terwilliger, 1989, p. 18).

An **anchor measure** is a device with which one can judge or "take bearings" of a class's status. As an example, suppose all the sections of the same high school biology course (i.e., sections taught from the same syllabus, same text, etc.) took the same final exam. This test could be used to reveal if and how the groups differed in achievement. The grade distributions in the several sections could be adjusted accordingly. An exam used in this way would be said to be an anchor test. Or suppose prior mean grade-point-averages (GPAs) were available for the students in each section. If some sections were found to have higher mean GPAs than others, then the section-to-section distributions of biology grades could thereby be adjusted.

To provide anchorage, a variable need have only one attribute: It must correlate with performance in the course being graded. The greater the relationship, the better. Thus, common tests across sections would provide stronger anchorage than would prior grades.

Notice that some anchor measures (e.g., common tests or projects) can and should contribute to the evaluation of each student, while others (e.g., aptitude test scores, grades in prerequisite courses, or GPAs) clearly should *not* be used to evaluate student course work.

Anchor measures can help to meet each characteristic of sound grading systems. When a course achievement variable is used to anchor achievement of students in one section of a course to a large number of other students who have taken (or are taking) essentially the same course, the anchor provides the needed link to satisfy all of the above listed criteria. The group of relevant other people who have had the same course provides meaningful, interpretable, and appropriate norm referencing; this satisfies the first and fifth criteria. The large size of the reference group provides stability; this meets the second criterion. The ability of each section's grades to rise or fall with student achievement liberates students from a need to compete with peers; this meets the third criterion. This capacity of a class's grades to reflect its achievement also provides its members with a realistic sense of control over their destiny; this satisfies the fourth criterion.

The statistical processes by which anchor measures are used can be relatively simple and intuitive. This is the approach used in the following examples that illustrate their use.

Example 1: Teacher's Use of Own Unit Test as Anchor Measure

Mrs. Frank teaches in a small middle school. Each year she teaches her well-polished "Life in the Kalahari" unit to her two sections of seventh-grade social studies. The test for this unit provides a measure with which the classes across the years are linked. She could use the test to anchor her two small sections to each other, but she prefers a larger, more stable reference group. Since this test is revised only every several years, Mrs. Frank uses it to anchor each section to all of her past sections over the past several years.

Mrs. Frank announces at the beginning of the school year that the distribution of grades in *typical* (or average) classes contains about 20% A, 30% B, 30% C, 19% D, and 1% F. She explains that comparison is *not* within each small class, but with several previous years' classes. If a class's achievement is unusually high or low, its grades will reflect this—grading is *not* on a *class* curve.

This year there were only 12 pupils in a particular section. Table 12–1 shows the cumulative distribution of test scores for a few previous years' classes and the distribution for this section. The percentage of previous pupils receiving each grade on the test approximates the announced distribution of grades for typical classes.

Table 12–2 provides the distribution of *total* points accrued in the seventh-grade social studies course. (Discussion does not need to digress to how these points were assigned or summed.) These totals include pupil performance not only on the summative test for the anchoring unit, but also on tests for other social studies units, written assignments, and oral reports. The question is, where should Mrs. Frank draw the lines separating the A, B, C, D, and F grades for the report card grade?

The general aim is to draw the lines in places where the resulting distribution of grades will most closely coincide with the shape of the class's distribution on the anchor test. In addition, it is conventional wisdom that one should draw the lines that separate adjacent grades in parts of the distribution where there are relatively large gaps.[6]

Mrs. Frank's class this year is clearly superior. Note that 5 out of 12 received grades of A on the anchor test. Therefore she would want to award more than the typical 20% (i.e., 2 or 3) A grades. Given the reasonable break in the distribution of total points shown in Table 12–2 between the fifth and sixth pupils, she would probably award five A grades; this, fortunately, nicely coincides with the number of pupils who received A marks on the anchor test.

In deciding how many Bs to assign, Mrs. Frank would note that 4 pupils earned this grade on the anchor test, and in the distribution of total points a reasonable break occurs with 4 Bs. Since there was little difference between the Bs and Cs in the anchor scores, she would have felt very free to deviate from the exact number of 4 had the break been a bit higher or lower.

---

[6]It is widely believed that the separation of adjacent grades should be made where large gaps occur. This seems like common sense to teachers and students alike. There is also an important public relations point. Larger breaks between grades reduce the tendency of persons who fall at the top of a grade interval to argue, trying to salvage the point or two that would put them into the next higher grade interval. It is good to avoid unproductive bickering over grades.

From a statistical point of view, however, the large gaps in a distribution of a single class usually reflect nothing more than the instability of small samples. From this perspective, it can be soundly argued that gap size should be ignored (except for ties, of course).

I find the statistical argument persuasive, yet the public relations issue is very important. In my ambivalence, I take the expedient course and yield to the "conventional wisdom."

Table 12-1

Example of a Teacher's Use of a Test As an Anchor Measure

Distribution of Scores for 6 Previous Classes			Scores of Present Class
X	f	Grade	Frequency
40	1		
39	0		1
38	3		1
37	3	A (20%)	
36	4		1
35	3		2
34	4		
33	4		
32	5		1
31	3	B (30%)	
30	7		1
29	7		2
28	5		
27	6		1
26	5		1
25	4	C (30%)	
24	3		
23	5		1
22	3		
21	2		
20	4		
19	2		
18	1		
17	2	D (19%)	
16	1		
15	1		
14	0		
13	0		
12	1		
11	0		
10	0	F (1%)	
9	1		

For C grades, this occurred. Although the bottom 3 pupils received Cs on the anchor test, they were medium to low Cs. The relatively large break in the distribution of totals between the bottom two people prompted Mrs. Frank to draw the line between them, giving only 2 Cs and 1 D. This illustrates the common situation in

Table 12–2

Points Earned by this Year's Class

Distribution of Total Points	Grade
349	
337	
330	A
317	
311	
299	
287	
276	B
268	
255	
230	C
202	D

which the distribution of grades on the anchor measure does not perfectly coincide with the distribution of final grades.

It should be understood that the five pupils who received A grades for the course are not necessarily the exact ones who received A grades on the unit test. Anchor measures are used to "get a fix on" *classes*. They are not, of course, the sole means of assigning course grades to individuals.

All five criteria of sound grading systems were satisfied. The grades were rendered interpretable by being norm referenced to the larger, more stable, highly relevant group of previous youngsters who had studied the unit and taken the test. At the same time, the psychological and social evils of putting children in a fixed sum pit to "fight it out" were avoided. Finally, pupils were provided with a realistic sense of efficacy.

Example 2: Sections of Second-Year Algebra Taught by Several Teachers

Suppose a large secondary school has nine sections of second-year algebra taught by four different teachers. With so many teachers who may have differing orientations toward grading, a need exists to define a common norm-referenced meaning of grades. As counselors and administrators can attest, many students attempt "migration" from "stingy" teachers to "generous" ones. This can be avoided by common norm-referenced grading standards. Moreover, consistent definitions of grades' meaning will make the grades more able to serve their primary purpose—communication.

Consider the (unlikely) worst-case scenario in which the nine sections do not all use the same text, symbols, or terminology. Even here, anchorage can be achieved. One attractive approach would be for each teacher to anchor this year's classes to his or her own prior students, as Miss Frank did.

Another approach would be to find some limited common test content (e.g., story problems or factoring) that could be used for the nine concurrent sections. If an occasional common quiz is used or if some portions of selected tests are common across the several sections, a basis for linkage enables estimations of the sections' relative achievement status, helping each teacher know how to scale letter grades for assignments and tests given throughout the term.

Even in this worst-case scenario, two means have been shown by which anchor measures could be used to satisfy each of the five criteria of good grading systems. In the more likely cases in which the teachers use the same text and terminology, occasional common quizzes or tests would more easily satisfy all the criteria.

Anchorage in the Context of Ability Grouping

Some schools engage in systematic homogeneous ability grouping of students. For example 22 sections of sophomore English could consist of 5 enriched sections, 12 regular sections, and 5 basic ones. In this situation, it is imperative *not* to grade all sections on the same curve. We obviously do not expect or desire similar distributions of grades in sections that have systematically been created to be dissimilar. Any reasonable anchor measure would suffice. The techniques of anchoring are fully applicable and especially important in the context of ability grouping.

QUIZ 12–3

1. Suppose you are a first-year teacher in a small elementary school and you teach the only section of third grade. You have informed yourself of the local customs concerning grade distributions, but you do not know how typical your 19 third-graders are. What are some of the ways by which you could "get a fix on" your class?

2. The four sixth-grade teachers in a school have decided to anchor their English grades to the sum of the four classes. For an anchor measure, they are considering use of (a) an objective mechanics of expression test that they all use and find to be valid, (b) an out-of-class assignment they all use which involves an oral report on a book, or (c) an essay test they all use with each teacher scoring his or her own class's papers.

    Assume that all three measures correlate about the same with overall achievement in sixth-grade English and that all three could count equally in contributing to English grades as defined by each teacher. Which measure would be the best anchor?

3. In using anchor measures, should one seek to have distributions of grades reflect differences among classes in standard deviations as well as differences in means?

KEY TO QUIZ 12–3

1. Prior data (e.g., the opinion of the experienced second-grade teacher who taught most of the children last year or last year's published achievement test scores) could be used to estimate the level of your class's achievement. However, this would only satisfy some of the criteria of effective grading systems; it would not provide a realistic sense of efficacy or avoid the evils of fixed-sum systems. Use of published achievement test scores during the current school year would, therefore, be preferable. Although scores of published instruments are seldom appropriate for use in assigning grades to individual pupils, they can be quite useful in assessing a class's status.

2. The key factor to consider here is the likely differences in generosity of the four teachers in assessing the oral reports or the essays. It is probable that some will be systematically more generous than others in awarding points. This would create an artifact in the scores that would gravely limit their utility as anchor measures. For this reason, projects, oral reports, essays, etc., are not nearly as satisfactory for anchoring as are objective measures.

3. Yes. Although group-to-group fluctuation is not as great in variability as it is in central tendency, it is certainly the secondary purpose of anchoring to account for this issue. This will be illustrated later in this chapter.

An Alternative Approach

The above method of anchoring a class's grades is, in my opinion, the preferred approach, yet many competent and conscientious practicing teachers reject it. Some believe it is too complex and takes too much time from other things they should be doing. (And it must be conceded that the method is relatively complicated.) Others contend that the method prevents immediate and clear feedback to students about progress. (And it is true that it does *not enable* such feedback at all times, but neither does the alternative of percentage grading, which often enables only an *illusion* of meaningful feedback, as pointed out by Thorndike, Cunningham, & Hagen, 1991, p. 179.) Still others fret that the use of anchor measures prevents them from being able to summarize a student's overall standing at any point in time. (And before the anchor data are available, this is a real problem.)

So what advice might best be given to those who reject the recommended use of anchor measures to achieve meaningful norm-referenced grading? Or to teachers who work in schools where percentage grading is required? Or to those who think it wise not to deviate too much from their colleagues in grading practice? Item 1 of Quiz 12–2 on page 333 provides some help. So does Quiz 12–1 on page 331.

The problems of (pseudo)percentage systems seem far preferable to the problems and evils of class-curve systems. If users of (pseudo)percentages understand their logical shortcomings and grasp the need for covert norm referencing, the system can be improved. Recognizing the "standards" to be illusory, we are liberated from rigid, superstitious, literal adherence to arbitrary standards; we are free to manipulate the data to serve socially constructive ends.

Experienced teachers with a lot of trouble could carefully select from their files items that had known percentages of examinees passing. Similarly, teachers having access to large, computerized item banks could also know something about item difficulty before a test is administered. If most of a test's items are thus chosen to yield a desired shape of distribution, the result will usually turn out to be reasonably close to the desired shape. Such indirect norm referencing can be quite sound and still provide the illusion of being criterion referenced in settings where such a fiction is required. For example, such "rigging" is needed for civil service exams for which there is a pre-set "passing" score such as 70%. However, this method is not practical in most teaching settings.

A less formal and easier approach is widely used to make so-called percentage systems less problematic. First, the teacher tries to create tests just hard enough to make the distribution of percentage scores conform with his or her norm-referenced judgment of what the students in the class merit. When the aim is good, no adjustments are needed.

However, if the test turns out to be too hard (or too easy), the teacher adds (or subtracts) some constant number of percentage points to each score. (Needless to say, students will be more understanding of the propriety of awarding extra percentage points to their scores on a hard test than to subtracting them from their scores on an easy one. Therefore, teachers who use this approach may tend to aim their tests a little too hard because the resulting adjustments can be made more harmoniously.)

This method is similar to the method of "eccentric" arithmetic (e.g., awarding 6% for each of 20 items). But "eccentric" arithmetic models bad math. A simple additive adjustment can be an open and honest recognition of the need to adjust scores because the teacher's aim (with respect to test difficulty) was off-target.

The adjustment is usually based informally on the teacher's best guess. *This guess should be a norm-referenced estimate of the status of the particular class in comparison to a larger, external reference group.* This estimate may be based on systematically collected anchor data; more often it is based on the teacher's informal perception of the class's status.

By using informal, rough-and-ready estimates for any adjustments that are needed, experienced teachers can achieve some of the benefit of anchoring by means of their past knowledge of students and their crude estimates of the status of a particular class. At the same time, they can preserve the illusion of percentage grading with absolute standards. In ways such as these, those who feel compelled to use a bad system can make it less unacceptable.

Sources of Ambiguity in Grades

The teachers in a school may differ sharply in their operational definitions of the meaning of grades (Stiggins, Frisbie, & Griswold, 1989). It has been shown that many teachers attempt to define them as representing absolute status, while others use them to represent relative status. This section will provide a discussion of some of the issues involved in relative, anchored, norm-referenced meanings of grades such as those advocated in this book.

Effort vs. Achievement

Fourth-grader Fran works very hard in math, but has great difficulty with the subject. She tries harder and spends more time on math than any other pupil in the class. She gets much good help at home in the subject; therefore her homework is exemplary. However, on quizzes and tests, her performance hovers in the next-to-bottom tenth of her rather typical class. What letter grade should she receive in math? (For purposes of discussing this and later examples, the common A, B, C, D, and F grades will be used.)

Some teachers would assign Fran about a D on the grounds that her achievement was higher than only 10 to 20% of typical fourth-graders. A few might award her an A because her effort was superb. Many would assign her a B or a C in the belief that both her achievement and her effort are relevant. Thus one year Fran may receive a C or D and the next year an A or B even though she performs consistently. How well do these grades serve their primary purpose of communicating? Alas, not nearly as well as they would if teachers could agree on the basis for grading.

Next consider tenth-grader Hank who has verbal aptitude scores in the top 1% of students his age. He works very little in social studies, yet he has no difficulty with the subject. In class he often "acts up" and causes mild disturbances and distractions. He rarely turns in assignments or homework. However, on tests, his performance is at the very top of his rather typical class. What letter should he receive?

Some teachers would award Hank an A on the basis of his very high achievement test scores. Many others would argue that his homework should count as part of his achievement measure and that it, averaged in some way with his high tests, would lower his grade to a B or even a C. A few would suggest that he should receive a very low grade—D or F—because he is not using his ability. A few others would favor awarding a D or an F to reflect (or even to punish) his unsatisfactory behavior. Many teachers would take more than one of these criteria into consideration, compromising among them.

If the Frans and the Hanks can both bring home the same C grade, one has to question what a C means. A need exists for clarification of what marks are supposed to communicate. Clearly a single letter grade cannot adequately represent both achievement and effort without suffering from grave ambiguity. On the one hand, achievement is too important to have its report obscured by mixing it with anything else. On the other hand, such attributes as effort, classroom behavior, and deportment are also important and should be reported; information about them should not be clouded by being mixed with anything else. Thus single letter grades do not suffice. A **multiple marking system** is needed to do justice to the multiple dimensions of importance; each major dimension merits a separate, unambiguous grade (Gronlund & Linn, 1990).

This clarity of reporting is best achieved by defining the main letter grade to be a *pure measure of achievement* (Gronlund & Linn, 1990; Terwilliger, 1989). Such a definition prevents its meaning from being confounded with information about student aptitude, motivation, behavior, and so forth.

If this definition is applied to Fran and if homework did not count, she would most likely receive about a D to reflect her low achievement in math. Hank would receive an A to report his high attainment in social studies. Yet situations are complicated by legitimate differences among teachers concerning whether they count the formative homework as part of the summative grade. Recall that Chapter 10 presented the pros and cons of doing so. If the homework did not count some modest amount, then Fran would probably get about a C and Hank would probably receive a B.[7]

Adequate reporting systems must not stop with the D or C for Fran and the A or B for Hank. They must also provide for reporting the important information about student effort and behavior. Hence, more than one mark is needed. This can be accomplished in a number of ways. Some schools enable notes to be written on report cards. Many have a second category, such as effort, deportment, or citizenship, with which to report on a second important dimension of student activity. If the same letter grades are used for this second dimension, Fran would merit an A and Hank an F. To avoid confusion between systems, many schools use a different set of symbols for the citizenship or effort mark, e.g., O (outstanding), G (good), S (satisfactory), and U (unsatisfactory).

By providing for the *separate* reporting of at least two dimensions of student activity, reporting systems can provide much clearer information. For example, Hank's academic grade of B coupled with an effort grade of U tells us much more about his performance than a single symbol could. It helps explain why his achievement was not higher.

QUIZ 12–4

A suggestion often made for reporting achievement of students like Fran is to note the level at which they have been working and the success they have achieved at that level. Thus Fran's report card might indicate that even though she is in the fourth grade, she has been working on second-grade arithmetic and has achieved about average compared with second-graders who are working on second-grade math. Evaluate this suggestion.

KEY TO QUIZ 12–4

This method is used in some report cards. It probably has more merit for highly sequential content like math than it does for less linear subject matter like social studies. This approach certainly has the attraction of offering the slow student the opportunity to make good grades (on easier work).

---

[7]Hank's situation would be further complicated if the homework he was assigned were the same that other students are assigned. He could very logically argue that the purpose of (formative) homework is to enable him to learn; his learning is assessed on the (summative) tests. Since he performed extremely well on the tests, the homework was obviously unnecessary. I would not want to have to dispute this point.

On the other hand, if his homework was individualized to the extent of being something from which he would likely benefit, his argument would not refute the legitimacy of counting homework as an achievement measure and lowering his grade if he did not do it.

> ### KEY TO QUIZ 12–4 (cont.)
>
> The major problem with this approach is that it uses a reference group to which the student does *not* belong. For many purposes people would not much care how Fran compares with second-graders; they would have much more use for norm-referenced statements concerning her status among fourth-graders.

Terminal Level of Achievement vs. Progress

Sixth-grader Stella has always found spelling difficult. At the end of fifth grade, her spelling was about average for beginning third-graders. Late this year, it has improved to the point of being about average for beginning fifth-graders. What letter grade should she receive in spelling?

Many teachers would award Stella a D or C because her achievement is still somewhat low for her grade. Others would suggest an A to reflect the excellent gain she made in a single year. Still others would find merit in both of these ideas and settle for a middle-ground B or C.

The issue here is whether Stella's achievement mark should represent her terminal level of achievement or her progress. Several reasons explain why *grades are better based on terminal level of achievement*. First, such marks better convey information about student status and the level of learning experiences from which they will now most benefit. The purposes of grades to communicate to students and parents, to help the school, and to assist external agencies are all better served if the grades clearly report student terminal status. Thus Stella should receive a D or a C. An A for her spelling progress would report nothing about her present status.

Second, progress is fakable. For example, if a physical education teacher announces that grades will be based on improvement during the term, some students may deliberately perform poorly on the pretests in order to be able to "improve" during the term. Recall the discussion in Chapter 3 concerning instructional objectives. They are best phrased in terms of *terminal* student behaviors. Grading and reporting, of course, should reflect the extent to which students have achieved objectives (Terwilliger, 1989); hence grades should also be conceived in terms of terminal student status.

Third, determination of progress, improvement, gain, etc., requires comparison of pre- and posttest scores. Difference scores (e.g., posttest score minus pretest score) are always less reliable than either the pretest scores or the posttest scores. Thus any system of marking based on difference scores (e.g., progress or comparison of aptitude measures with achievement measures) will be less accurate than either of the measures on which they are based.

Finally, few teachers who use the verbiage of gains really mean it. For example, suppose a keyboarding teacher has an objective that each student will *learn* the home position of the eight fingers, but Sarah enters the class already *knowing* them. Since she does not *learn* them in the class, should she be penalized? Of course not. This demonstrates that the real objective was not that she would learn the home positions so much as that she would exit the class knowing them.

Distribution Shape

Mr. Moore and Mr. Duncan both teach senior English. They are equally competent teachers, and their students, on average, are equally capable. In typical sections, however, their respective grade distributions might be:

	Mr. Moore	Mr. Duncan
A	5%	40%
B	15%	45%
C	40%	15%
D	30%	0%
F	10%	0%

Joe is a rather poor student in English, typically achieving better than only about one-fifth of his peers. What grade should he receive?

The answer, of course, is a matter of normative definition. The way Mr. Moore defines grades, Joe merits a D. The way Mr. Duncan defines them, he should receive a B. What are Joe's parents, not knowing the peculiarities of particular teachers, to make of his grade of D or B?

The remedy to this problem lies in the attainment of greater similarity of definitions. Unfortunately, this is easier said than done. Teachers often exhibit a lot of (not particularly rational) ego involvement in their grading practices. For example, Mr. Moore may pride himself on his high expectations and high standards. He might be extremely resistant to "cheapening" the value of grades. Mr. Duncan, on the other hand, may take pride in his high grades, thinking they somehow evidence successful teaching and successful student learning. In reality, of course, their grade distributions probably reflect little more than the artifact of their respective definitions or conceptions of the "proper" meaning of grades.

Both teachers will agree that there is a problem. Any progress they can make toward converging their definitions would help grades to better communicate to the several important audiences. Although it may not prove feasible to get Mr. Moore and Mr. Duncan to agree to the same shape of grade distribution, it would probably be possible to get each to compromise a little in the direction of the other. In-service educational programs can help teachers understand that no "cosmic" right distribution of marks exists; rather, distributions are matters of social convention.

The fact that grade meaning is simply a cultural convention leads to a suggestion for teachers who are new to a school. Since grade distributions in a given school depend more on cultural milieu than on any other factor, the new teacher is well advised to explore the local meaning of grades and to stay within tolerated limits (Thorndike, Cunningham, Thorndike, & Hagen, 1991, p. 186). Avoiding unacceptable deviations from the convention helps achieve better communication (not to mention fewer waves).

Thus if I were a new teacher in a school where most of the faculty grade much like Mr. Moore (who gives much lower grades than I would prefer), I would tend to maintain the local meaning of the grades by largely conforming. On the other hand, if I were to teach in a school where most teachers award grades like Mr. Duncan (who awards higher grades than I would prefer), I would seek to maintain the meaning of the grades by largely conforming.

QUIZ 12–5

Three teachers instruct a total of five sections of eighth-grade history. There are 20 youngsters in each section. Teacher X uses a point system of one sort, Teacher Z has a point system of another variety, and Teacher Y uses a (pseudo)percent system. They seek anchorage among their five classes, but they do not wish to have to conform in their record-keeping practices.

After extensive discussion and compromise the teachers reach consensus that *in typical sections* the distributions of grades should approximate:

A = 20%
B = 25%
C = 30%
D = 20%
F = 5%

They choose for anchorage a particular unit in which their content and methods are highly similar. They cooperate in devising an objective test for the unit, and they agree that it is equally valid for their respective classes. The distribution of grades on this anchor measure of the five sections is:

In Typical Sections	Teacher X Section 1	Teacher X Section 2	Teacher Y Section 1	Teacher Y Section 2	Teacher Z Section 1
A = 20%	A = 20%	A = 15%	A = 25%	A = 15%	A = 25%
B = 25%	B = 25%	B = 20%	B = 30%	B = 20%	B = 30%
C = 30%	C = 30%	C = 30%	C = 30%	C = 50%	C = 10%
D = 20%	D = 20%	D = 25%	D = 15%	D = 15%	D = 25%
F = 5%	F = 5%	F = 10%	F = 0%	F = 0%	F = 10%

Combining Data for Grades

People in many walks of life are called on to combine several component elements of data into summary composites. An application of major relevance to teachers involves figuring term grades by combining scores for paper-pencil tests, daily work, homework, book reports, products, performances, and other criteria. The mechanics of such a task are not as simple as most people tacitly assume.

Two major steps are involved in combining parts into totals or averages. First, a decision or judgment is made as to how much weight each part merits. Second, the decision must be competently carried out. Teachers often lack understanding of principles of weighting grades; many use procedures that do not accomplish their intent (Stiggins, Frisbie, & Griswold, 1989). Before focusing on these two steps, some situations will be considered in which the several components should not be combined at all.

QUIZ 12–5 (cont.)

Below for each class is the distribution of total points for the grading period. Use the anchorage information above to draw the cut-off line in the most suitable places in each column to indicate final report-card grades below.

Class X–1	Class X–2	Class Y–1	Class Y–2	Class Z–1
345	349	99	98	1107
339	340	98	96	1099
337	338	96	95	1090
336	330	96	95	1081
336	327	92	91	1077
325	321	92	90	1076
320	315	91	86	986
315	299	91	85	980
309	290	91	85	960
283	283	89	85	925
280	276	88	85	871
265	271	87	82	865
265	266	84	82	851
264	259	82	80	843
262	252	79	79	801
249	252	79	78	737
241	239	76	74	732
240	233	71	70	649
238	199	68	68	510
105	170	65	64	305

When Combining Data Does Not Make Sense

The issue of combining elements into total scores is relevant only to those situations in which measures of Track B or Track C content domains are combined for norm-referenced interpretations. When assessing achievement in Track A, one should not combine measures of the respective objectives. This follows from the kind of objectives used in Track A. Each objective is deemed to be minimally essential. Therefore, in Track A teaching and testing, one should not add or average students' achievement across several objectives; to do so would allow superiority in some domains to compensate for deficiencies in others. Permitting compensation is sensible in most situations, but not in those where mastery of each objective is judged to be essential.

KEY TO QUIZ 12–5

This task is not entirely objective. The classes are roughly ordered from easy-to-grade to hard-to-grade. Thus teachers would probably be in close agreement concerning the places the lines should be drawn in the first two classes, while differences of opinion would be greater for the other three. Following is one reasonable way to do the job. If your lines for the last classes are slightly different than those below, it is not necessarily cause for concern. The key considerations follow the table.

Class X–1	Class X–2	Class Y–1	Class Y–2	Class Z–1
345	349	99	98	1107
339	340 A (15%)	98 A (20%)	96 A (20%)	1099
337 A (25%)	<u>338</u>	96	95	1090 A (30%)
336	330	<u>96</u>	<u>95</u>	1081
<u>336</u>	327 B (20%)	92	91	1077
325	321	92	90 B (15%)	<u>1076</u>
320 B (20%)	<u>315</u>	91	<u>86</u>	986
315	299	91 B (40%)	85	980 B (20%)
<u>309</u>	290	91	85	960
283	283 C (30%)	89	85	<u>925</u>
280	276	88	85	871
265 C (30%)	271	<u>87</u>	82 C (50%)	865 C (20%)
265	<u>266</u>	84	82	851
264	259	82	80	<u>843</u>
<u>262</u>	252	79 C (25%)	79	801
249	252 D (25%)	79	78	737 D (20%)
241 D (20%)	239	<u>76</u>	<u>74</u>	732
240	<u>233</u>	71	70	<u>649</u>
<u>238</u>	199 F (10%)	68 D (15%)	68 D (15%)	510 F (10%)
105 F (5%)	170	65	64	305

X–1. This class's distribution should, according to the information provided by the anchor test, be as close as feasible to that of typical classes. The only deviation arose from a tie.

An effort should be made to avoid cumulative deviation from the distribution in the anchor test; thus, if one has to award an extra A, then one would aim to award one B less than the target.

X–2. The notable thing about this class is its slightly below-average status. The breaks in the distribution enable the distribution of final grades to exactly parallel the distribution of grades in the anchor measure.

Y–1. The key thing about this class is its slightly above-average status. The breaks in its distribution of total scores did not enable a very close parallel with the distribution of grades for the anchor measure. Teachers might differ somewhat in where they separated consecutive grades.

KEY TO QUIZ 12–5 (cont.)

Y–2. The salient feature of this distribution is not its central tendency, but its variability. It is center-heavy; i.e., its distribution of anchor test scores has a much smaller standard deviation than that of typical classes. The natural breaks in the distribution of final scores would enable this to be paralleled quite closely.

But one final thing should be noted. Assuming that the points in both of Teacher Y's classes have identical meaning, then a number of points needed to achieve any given grade in one section must yield the same grade in the other section. This consideration limits the extent to which one can use the natural gaps in each class's distribution. When both of Teacher Y's classes are combined, it is seen that no natural break separates B and C grades. That is why I would give 3 B grades rather than only 2 in Class Y–2.

Z–1. This class is unusually heterogeneous; its anchor scores were much more variable than those of typical sections. The distribution of grades in the final distribution should reflect this feature of the class. It turned out, however, that the natural breaks did not accommodate a very exact match between the shapes of the distributions of grades for the anchor test and course grades.

Establishing Intent

A teacher responsible for collapsing several data sources into one summary score must first address the issue of how much each component should contribute to the composite. In some schools, this is entirely the teacher's choice. In others, policy dictates some of the weights; for example, a school might have a rule that homework will count one-third of the grade in seventh-grade math.

The composite measure may be either a mean or a total; the relative weights of the contributing parts are the same. Because it is easier to compute totals than means, the following discussion and illustrations use totals.

The issue of relative weight has no quantitative solution; it involves judgment. It is to be expected that reasonable people may differ somewhat. How much should the final examination in a first-semester, high school Spanish course contribute to the semester grade? Although there is no one right answer to such validity questions, people who know the context are likely to have similar opinions. Thus Spanish teachers familiar with the course and a particular high school's 50-minute final exam period would probably find a 10% weight to be skimpy. Likewise, they would probably consider a 40% weight to be too much. However, whether it should be 15%, 25%, or any other figure is not something on which perfect consensus is likely (or very important).

Ms. Lenelli needs to assign term science grades to her fourth-graders. For the last nine weeks, the class has conducted experiments of the effect of light and water on plant growth, completed five work sheets, and taken a summative test on the term's work. How much should each of these elements count?

Ms. Lenelli considers the relative amounts of time spent on the various worksheets and judges it reasonable to count each the same amount. She similarly decides to assign equal weights to the two experiment reports. After brief but thoughtful consideration, she decides that the relative allocation of credit among the parts will be:

Each of the 2 experiment reports	15%
Each of the 5 worksheets	6%
Test	40%

Several things merit consideration in allocating weight. First is the time devoted to each facet. This, of course, includes homework time as well as class time. If other things are equal, it makes sense to count components in proportion to the time allotted them. In Ms. Lenelli's case, other things were judged to be equal.

Second is the relative importance of the objectives assessed by each component. Other things being equal, components that tap major objectives should receive more weight than those assessing less important goals. For example, in a driver education course, the portion of the behind-the-wheel performance test that concerns response to various emergencies might be weighted far more than instructional time or testing time might imply.

Another consideration is component uniqueness. When important objectives are assessed by only one element—such as a single oral test in a foreign-language course—the element may merit more weight than it otherwise would. (Alternatively, of course, the teacher may wisely consider assessing the important goal by additional methods.) On the other hand, when several measures tap the same objective, then each should be assigned less weight than it would receive if it were unique.

The final issues to be considered in assigning weights are reliability and validity of the elements. Other things being equal, it makes sense to give more weight to measures judged to be more valid and reliable than to those thought to be less valid and/or less reliable.

For a second example of establishing relative weights among components, we will consider a high school English class. Mr. Wendt wants the nine-week grades for each term to be based on (a) an oral report, (b) a written book report, (b) 20 daily class or homework assignments, (d) three quizzes, and (e) a major examination. How much should each count?

On the basis of the main consideration of time spent, Mr. Wendt tentatively assigns weights as follows:

Oral report	5%
Written book report	11%
Each of 20 daily assignments	2%
Each of 3 quizzes	8%
Major exam	20%

However, when he contemplates the criteria of importance and uniqueness of the components, he decides to allocate a great deal more credit to the oral component and somewhat less to the daily work.

When he considers component validity, he recalls his frequent suspicion that some of the book reports were plagiarized and that substantial amounts of homework reflect more than optimum help from others. Accordingly, he decides to weight them a little less. Finally, the criterion of reliability of marking prompts him to acknowledge that the grading of the oral report is probably less reliable than that of other components. This consideration moderates his earlier decision to greatly increase its weight; he finally decides to increase it only moderately. After taking all of these issues into account, he arrives at the following weights.

Oral report	10%
Written book report	10%
Each of 20 daily assignments	1.5%
Each of 3 quizzes	10%
Major exam	20%

As mentioned above, students should be given advance notice regarding how important each element is (Terwilliger, 1989). This information reduces the number of complaints and increases the ease of defending those grades that may be disputed. More important, *advance knowledge of relative weight of assignments guides student effort*. Grading practices influence most students. This impact should be thoughtfully used by teachers to enhance student learning. Just as test power can be harnessed by informing students what will be tested, *grade power should also be harnessed*.

These two examples illustrate how teachers should thoughtfully decide how much emphasis they want to give each of several components. Attention can now be turned to means of achieving the intended weights.

The Mechanical Problem

Before addressing how to achieve the desired weights for the above two examples, it will be fruitful to focus for a time on the problem and the common misconceptions. A certain teacher has given four tests. Term grades are based on the total number of points earned in the four tests. The possible points, means, and standard deviations for the four tests are reported below. Answer this question before proceeding: *Which test(s) counted the most?*

Information	Test 1	Test 2	Test 3	Test 4
Points	100	90	60	50
M	50	70	58	30
SDs	10	6	1	12

Now use the paragraph heads below to select the section that corresponds to your answer. *Go directly to that section now.*

Test 1. If you think Test 1 is the most influential in determining the total or mean grade, you probably are responding to the fact that it has the greatest number of points possible. This is the modal response among educators; most think the weights that components carry are proportional to their possible points. Although your answer is modal, it is wrong!

It is wrong, that is, in the context of grading on the basis of *relative* standing. In the context of Track C, meaningful marks must be norm referenced. Thus grading on the basis of total raw or percentage scores is *not* appropriate. If it were sensible to grade on the basis of percentage or total raw scores, then your answer would be correct. When grades are based on percentage of possible points that students have earned, the weight each score contributes is a function of its maximum points possible (Oosterhof, 1987).

To see why your answer is wrong for norm-referenced grading, consider two students' performance on Tests 1 and 4. Each performed quite erratically, 1 *SD* above the mean on one test and 1 *SD* below the mean on the other.

Student	Test 1	Test 4	Total
Tweedledee	60	18	78
Tweedledum	40	42	82

If Test 1 carried more weight than any other test (as you thought it did), then it would follow that Tweedledee, who did well on Test 1, should have a larger total than Tweedledum, who did well on Test 4. But that is not the case, Tweedledum has the larger total. Therefore, the test on which Tweedledum did well (Test 4) counted a bit more than the one on which he performed poorly (Test 1).

Since you missed the question, go back and select another answer, this time from a norm-referenced perspective. Then find the section that corresponds to your new answer and read it.

Test 2.   If you think Test 2 counts the most in determining the total grade, you probably are responding to the fact that it has the largest mean score. This is a common misconception; many teachers think the weights that elements contribute to a total are proportional to their means. This concept and your answer are wrong!

To see why this is wrong, consider two students' performance on Tests 1 and 2. Each performed rather erratically, 1 *SD* above the mean on one test and 1 *SD* below the mean on the other.

Student	Test 1	Test 2	Total
Tweedledee	60	64	124
Tweedledum	40	76	116

If Test 2 carried more weight than any other (as you thought it did), then it would follow that Tweedledum, who did well on Test 2, would have a larger total than Tweedledee, who did well on Test 1. But that is not the case, Tweedledee had the larger total. Therefore, the test on which Tweedledee did well (Test 1) counted more than the one on which he performed poorly (Test 2).

Since you missed the question, go back and select another answer. Then locate the section that corresponds to your reconsidered answer and read it.

Test 3.   If you think Test 3 is the most important influence on the total grade, you likely are attending to the fact that its mean score yielded the largest percentage correct. This is irrelevant; your answer is wrong!

To see why it is wrong, consider two students' performance on Tests 2 and 3. Each performed rather erratically, 1 *SD* above the mean on one of the two tests and 1 *SD* below the mean on the other.

Student	Test 2	Test 3	Total
Tweedledee	64	59	123
Tweedledum	76	57	133

If Test 3 carried more weight than any other test (as you thought it did), it would follow that Tweedledee, who performed well on Test 3 should have a larger total than Tweedledum, who "hit" on Test 2. However, look at the totals; Tweedledee got the short end of the stick. Very little individual differences were manifest on Test 3; Tweedledee's high score is, therefore, very little superior to the lower scores of other examinees. The main thing that influences the relative total scores of these two students is their relative performance on the test that revealed more individual differences. In other words, when the scores of a test have little or no variation, they contribute little or nothing to the variability of the total scores.

Since your answer was incorrect, go back and choose another answer. Then find the section that corresponds to your new answer and read it.

Test 4. If you think Test 4 is the most influential, you are right! This fact can be demonstrated by arranging it successively with each other test. It can be shown that a student who performs any specified number of *SD* units above the mean on Test 4 and an equal amount below the mean on the other test will have a larger total than a student whose performance is the opposite.

Why does Test 4 weigh the most? The answer relates to the variability of its scores vis-à-vis the variability of scores of the other components. In general, the element with the most variable scores will contribute the most.

Solutions to the Mechanical Problem

The above example demonstrated that the method of weighting components that seems intuitively appropriate to most people cannot be depended on to achieve the intent. How, then, can teachers achieve desired relative weight? How can Ms. Lenelli and Mr. Wendt make their composite grades reflect their intent? Here is the rule of thumb: When several scores are combined, *the relative weight of the components is proportional to their standard deviations*[8] (Hopkins, Stanley, & Hopkins, 1990, p. 332).

Since the elements of a composite score contribute in proportion to their *SD*s, the way to control the contribution of each part is to control the size of its *SD*. Fortunately, *SD* size is easily manipulated. If each score in a distribution is multiplied (or divided) by any number, the *SD* is multiplied (or divided) by that number. An example may be persuasive.

The left column in the distribution list below has a *SD* of 1. The distribution on the right was obtained by multiplying each score in the left-hand distribution by 5. As a result of multiplying each score by 5, the *M* and the *SD* were each multiplied by 5. The energetic reader can verify these statistics by using the formulas given in Chapter 11. The principle can be demonstrated with any frequency distribution. If each score is multiplied by any constant, then the *M* and the *SD* will be multiplied by the same constant.

---

[8]Actually, weights are influenced by both the variability of the respective components and the intercorrelations among them. Since a serviceable approximation is provided by the *SD*s alone, it is customary to ignore the intercorrelations.

X	Y
6	30
6	30
8	40
8	40
$M = 7$	$M = 35$
$SD = 1$	$SD = 5$

Now the question can be answered: How can a teacher make each of several sets of scores contribute the same amount to a total (or average) score? Suppose the teacher whose test data were reported on page 351 wanted to have Tests 2 and 4 count the same amount. How can this be accomplished? The number of points possible in each test is irrelevant to the issue. So is the mean score of each test. What is germane to the question is the relative variability of scores in the two distributions.

The SD for Test 2 is 6; the SD for Test 4 is 12. The easiest way to cause the SDs to become equal is to multiply each student's Test 2 score by 2. Where did the 2 come from? We saw that the SDs were 6 and 12, respectively. Wanting them to be equal (because the teacher wished the tests to count the same), we ask, "By what number must the 6 be multiplied to change it to 12?" To change 6 to 12, multiply by 2. Therefore, the easiest way to achieve equality between the tests is to multiply each student's Test 2 score by 2.

For a second example, suppose a teacher wanted to count Test 2 (whose $SD = 6$) twice as much as Test 1 (whose $SD = 10$). By what number must the SD of 6 be multiplied to yield 20 (i.e., two times Test 1's SD of 10)? The answer is 3 and one-third. One would probably choose to round this to an even 3, and to multiply each student's Test 2 score by 3.

The practical-minded reader may be doubting that it is realistic to expect a busy classroom teacher to know the SD of each distribution in the grade book. For teachers whose records are kept on computers, as discussed in Appendix C, it *is* indeed realistic. But for the shrinking majority of teachers who still figure grades with hand calculators, a simpler statistic may be more attractive than using an inexpensive statistical calculator to compute each standard deviation. The range is usually quite serviceable, especially if one verifies that a very extreme score does not radically change a class's range.

To illustrate, suppose the range for one test is 48–81 and the range for another is 45–55. The range for the first (i.e., 33) is about three times that of the second (whose range is 10). If one wanted the tests to count the same toward the total score, approximate equality would most easily be achieved by multiplying each student's score on the second test by 3.

Ms. Lenelli's Science Grades

Recall Ms. Lenelli's thoughtful intent of weighing the components as follows:

Each of 2 experiment reports	15%
Each of 5 worksheets	6%
Test	40%

It has been shown that distributions of scores can be adjusted after the data are in. This is sometimes necessary, but advance planning can obviate the need for most of these after-the-fact data manipulations. Much time and effort can be saved with foresight.

A simple rule of thumb can provide the light necessary to foresee and prevent the need for most such after-the-fact data manipulations. The rule is that variables of the same kind are likely to have *SD*s that roughly correspond to intended weight (assuming that one uses longer tests for more important components, etc.). However, components of different kinds may *chance* to have *SD*s that differ wildly. The opportunity to avoid labor concerns the word "chance" in the previous sentence; with foresight, components of different kinds can be manipulated into having *SD*s that are roughly what is desired. If this is achieved, then alteration after the fact are not necessary.

Ms. Lenelli wants the two experiment reports to count the same. She presumably will have pupils do them with similar formats and will assess them with comparable standards. To make them count approximately the same, all she probably will have to do is give them equal possible points. Suppose she allocates 10 points on each experiment report and expects a range from about 3 to 10 for each. If nothing unusual happens, she can reasonably assume (even without bothering to verify) that their *SD*s and ranges are about equal and that they therefore count approximately the same amount.

Similarly if the worksheets are similar in content and format, then allowing the same number of possible points for each will probably cause them to have roughly equal *SD*s and ranges. How many points for each should be possible? To achieve equality *among* the worksheets, it does not matter. With foresight, however, Ms. Lenelli can probably approximate the desired balance *between* worksheets and experiment reports at the same time. Suppose she considers a 5-point scale for each worksheet and expects the ranges to hover around 3 (e.g., the scores to range from 2 to 5). This range is a little less than one-half that of the 7 anticipated for each experiment report; she therefore might expect each worksheet to count a bit less than one-half as much as each report. So it appears that the contemplated 5-point scale for the worksheets would serve nicely to approximate the intended 15%:6% ratio.

Finally, she can determine the range that is desired for the test. The test is to count nearly three times as much as either experiment report (i.e., 40% is $2\frac{2}{3} \times$ 15%). The anticipated range for each report is 7, thus the desired range for the test would be estimated from this source to be about 19. For the worksheets-test comparison, the test is intended to count nearly 7 times as much as any one worksheet (i.e., 40% is $6\frac{2}{3} \times$ 6%). The range for each worksheet is 3; thus the desired range for the test would be estimated from this source to be about 20. Taking the two rough estimates, 19 and 20, Ms. Lenelli has a range within which to aim the final distribution of test points.

Suppose she used a very similar test last year. It had 25 objective items, and the scores ranged from 14 to 24. This is a range of 10. The simple and adequate thing to do would be to give 2 points per item; this would have yielded a range of 28 to 48, which equals 20.

With this kind of *forethought*, Ms. Lenelli can achieve a very adequate approximation to her intended weights with very little actual work. On the other hand, if she waits until the end of the term to address the issue, she will probably have to alter the variability of one or more of the components in order to achieve the desired balance among them.

Two issues that surface in this example remain to be addressed. First, were you worried by the fact that Ms. Lenelli will have only a possible 50 points for her test rather than the more usual 100? If so, you are suffering from a percentage grading hangover! Recall that the grading of this unit takes place in the context of Track C, where norm referencing is necessary.

In Track C, component scores need not be changed into percentages. Track C domains are ill-defined and content difficulty is not fixed; therefore, meaningful domain-referenced interpretation via raw scores or percent scores is not possible. There is no good reason why Track C elements should be reported in percent scores; doing so adds no meaning and creates unnecessary work and opportunity for computational errors. Nor does converting each element into a percent assure equality among them. The component-to-component *SD*s of percent scores is just as variable as (and perfectly correlated with) the component-to-component *SD*s of raw scores.

The final issue arising from Ms. Lenelli's example concerns the wisdom of basing this year's scaling of components on data from previous years. Might not one class be more or less variable than past groups? Yes, it well might, but the *relative* size of the *SD*s or ranges of the respective elements does not ordinarily vary much from group to group. Admittedly, it would be preferable to assure exact proportionality among the *SD*s, but unless calculations are being done by computer, it is probably not worth the effort.

If however, Ms. Lenelli's grades at Utopia Elementary School were kept on computer and she had software with which easily to specify the *SD* of any set of scores entered, then it would be sensible and adaptive for her to be more perfectionistic. For example, she could specify that whatever scale entered for the worksheets be converted into derived scores with a *SD* of 6, that whatever scale entered for the experiment reports be transformed into derived scores having a *SD* of 15, and that whatever set of scores entered for the test be converted into scores with a *SD* of 40. Then, thanks to the magic of technology and her knowledge of this topic, she would nicely approximate her intent without doing much work at all.

Mr. Wendt's English Grades

After a few minutes' deliberation, Mr. Wendt has decided on the desired weights for the parts of his high school English term grades. If he can anticipate the original ranges or *SD*s of the elements and transform them into ones that have the desired relative values, he can save himself the trouble of manipulating scores during the end-of-term rush. Listed below are his desired weights for each part and the range of scores he has commonly obtained for each in the past (before he resolved to save labor via foresight).

Component	Desired Weight	Typical Old Range
Oral report	10%	2–10
Written book report	10%	5–20

Component	Desired Weight	Typical Old Range
Each of 20 daily assignments	1.5%	0–3
Each of 3 quizzes	10%	6–15
Major exam	20%	29–70

Mr. Wendt can start with any one of the ranges and alter the others into the desired proportionality with it. It is usually easiest to start with one of the least important components or with one having raw scores that would be awkward to alter. He decides to start with the daily work and to retain the 0–3 scale he has always used; this yields a range of 3 for each assignment.

He considers the other components in turn. For the oral report, he wants the range to be 6 or 7 times as great as the one for daily work (because 10% is 6.67 × 1.5%). He asks himself, "What do I have to do to the present range of 8 to make it 6 or 7 times 3, or about 20?" "Multiply it by about 2.5," he calculates. He therefore alters his former 10-point rating scale into a 25-point scale. Assuming he uses about the same fraction of the scale as he did before, the resulting range should be about 5–25. This is the intended range of about 20 points.

For the book report, he again needs a range that is 6 to 7 times that of each homework assignment. His old 20-point scale produced a range of 5–20. He decides to go to a new 25-point scale. Its range will likely be about 6–25. This 19-point range is the desired size.

Let us digress here to consider a public relations issue along with the measurement one. Suppose that in the past, Mr. Wendt has experienced some ill will when he awarded only 5 or 10 points out of a possible 20 for the book report. Could he sweeten the taste without changing the normative meaning? Sure. Instead of using a 25-point scale with a typical range of 6–25, he could employ a 50-point scale for which a typical class's range would be 31–50 or a 100-point scale for which most classes would have a range from about 81 to about 100. Or if he were a negative sort who wanted to sour the taste without changing the normative meaning, he could go to a 20-point scale with a typical range of 1–20. In all of these cases, the range is 19.

In norm-referenced assessment, the differences are purely cosmetic. Which would be best? In view of the fact that many students suffer from a (pseudo)percentage grading system orientation (hangover), a range that reasonably approximates the expectations it creates might be desirable. Perhaps 31–50.

Now before reading on, put yourself in Mr. Wendt's place and decide what he might most easily do for the quizzes and the exam. Then proceed.

For each quiz, he needs the range to be about 6 or 7 times 3 (again because the desired 10% weight for each quiz is 6.67 × the desired 1.5% weight for each homework assignment). The old range of 9 was only about three times that of each homework assignment. If he doubles it (either by doubling each quiz score as he enters it into the grade book or by counting twice as many points for each question), its range will become 12–30. This 18-point range is the desired 6 or 7 times the 3-point one for homework.

Finally, he wants the range for the exam to be somewhere around 40 (because the 20% weight for the exam is 13.33 × the 1.5% weight for each homework assignment which has a range of 3; thus, 3 × 13.33 = 40). Its old range is 41. That is close enough; he decides to leave it alone.

Many educators assume the weight of each graded element is determined by its possible points. This is untrue in norm-referenced assessment. Parts contribute to a composite score approximately in proportion to their *SD*s or roughly in proportion to their ranges. If a computer is doing the work, one can afford to be precise in controlling the weight of the parts. When teachers do the calculations by hand, rough approximations are sensible.

Actually, the misconception that the parts contribute in proportion to the number of points possible works quite well *if* all the parts consist of the same kind of material. Thus, a 15-item, multiple-choice test is likely to have a *SD* that is very roughly half that of a 30-point, multiple-choice test if the items of the respective tests are similar in discrimination power. Similarly, a woodshop teacher might use a 0–4 rating scale for a small project and a 0–16 scale for a major one intended to count four or so times as much; this is reasonable if the instructor uses about the same proportion of the respective scales.

The misconception gets teachers into trouble when the elements being combined are expressed in very different kinds of scales. Thus it is *not* safe to assume that the *SD* of a 50-item, true-false test will approximate that of a 50-item, multiple-choice test. Nor is it appropriate for a physical education teacher to assume that performance ratings of game skill will combine with scores from an objective test in proportion to the points possible on the two measures. Finally, it is *not* prudent to assume that a 30-item, objective test will contribute the same as a 30-point essay test.

A Special Problem

Teachers who use percentage grading systems are vulnerable to an additional hazard of intended weights not coming out as desired. In the case of daily work or homework, many teachers would want all assignments to contribute equally to the final grade. When each is recorded as a percentage, the teacher understanding the above recap might conclude that the intended equality of weights would likely come close to target. Alas, this is not necessarily so, if, as is common, the range of percentages is much greater for F grades than for other grades.

To illustrate, suppose a teacher has the following range.

$$A = 90-100$$
$$B = 80-89$$
$$C = 70-79$$
$$D = 60-69$$
$$F = 0-59$$

In a given week, Brian's three homework grades are 92%, 79%, and 0% (because he did not turn it in). His mean for the week is 57%. Does it seem fair that his grades of A, C, and F should average F? No, to most of us it would seem more proper for him to receive a C.

The problem arises because the range of F grades is about six times as great as the range of any other grade. Hence, the adverse impact of a missing grade is far greater than the beneficial impact of a perfect grade. In seeking to avoid this problem, it is helpful to make a sharp distinction between an F (which Brian may deserve for the missing assignment) and a 0 (which may carry too severe a penalty).

Three methods of avoiding the excessive impact of very low grades (often reflecting missing assignments) will be sketched. First, some authors have recommended that percentage grades be redefined into uniform 20-point intervals. Although this would solve the immediate problem, it might create others (e.g., give the appearance of lowering "standards").

Another solution might be to transform the percentage grades into another scale such as A+ = 15, A = 14, A− = 13, B+ = 12, . . . F = 2, and F− = 1. Then at the end of the term, one could transform the mean back into a percentage and letter grade. The disadvantages of this is the work it would cause and the slight increase of grouping error that would result in using only 15 intervals rather than 101. (The topic of grouping error will be taken up in Chapter 16.)

Perhaps the best solution would be for the teacher to record the actual percentage if it is 60 or greater. If it is between 0 and 59, however, one would transform the percentage to a proportional amount between 50 and 59. Thus all the grade book entries would be between 50 and 100, and all the grade ranges would be equal. Following is the table to provide this transformation.

Original %	Transformed "%"
0– 6	50
7–12	51
13–18	52
19–24	53
25–30	54
31–36	55
37– 42	56
43– 48	57
49–54	58
55–59	59

Under this system Brian's 92%, 79%, and 0% would be recorded as 92%, 79%, and 50%. The mean of these is about 74%. This figure would yield the C that most of us thought was fair.

Chapter Summary

Providing meaningful reports of student achievement is a time-consuming part of teachers' work. Yet this time is well spent because of the several important functions that grades serve.

To achieve their important purposes, grades need to be rooted in a rationale consistent with the course's subject matter, kind of instructional objectives, and kind of scores and interpretations. At the same time, grading needs to be structured to avoid adverse impact on interpersonal relationships and mental health. And marks need to be meaningful and interpretable. These multiple aims are best achieved when grades reflect student achievement reported by means of norm referencing to large, stable, well-described, relevant groups of other students, an objective often best achieved by use of anchor measures.

Like testing practices, *a teacher's grading system should be planned carefully at the time instruction is designed*. This thoughtfully established student evaluation system should be communicated to students very early in the term, and it should be exploited as a means of enhancing learning.

The meaning of marks is greatest when a faculty shares similar normative perspectives concerning appropriate distributions in typical classes. The meaning of grades is also maximized if each mark represents some discrete and important student attribute. *Thus it is desirable for a grade to represent a pure measure of terminal student achievement*. In addition, one or more other marks are needed to report on other important aspects of student behavior, such as apparent effort or citizenship.

Appropriately combining the elements in a term grade is not as simple as it may appear. First, a teacher should thoughtfully decide how much each component should contribute to the total grade. Then this intent must be achieved. For components to make the intended relative contributions, their standard deviations need to be proportional to their desired weight. Practical means of approximating this without undue labor were illustrated.

Suggestions for Further Reading

Ebel, R. L., & Frisbie, D. A. (1991). *Essentials of educational measurement* (5th ed.). Englewood Cliffs, NJ: Prentice-Hall. Chapter 15, "Grading and Reporting Achievements," provides a sound, succinct, middle-of-the-road treatment of the topic, including a brief discussion of grading software.

Hills, J. R. (1981). *Measurement and evaluation in the classroom* (2nd ed.). Columbus: Merrill. This basic text offers an exceptionally thorough treatment of grading, with six short chapters (14–19) addressing functions of grading, processes of grading, grade reporting systems, useful technical practices in grading, faulty grading practices, and legal aspects of grading.

Mehrens, W. A., & Lehmann, I. (1991). *Measurement and evaluation in education and psychology* (3rd ed.). New York: Holt, Rinehart and Winston. Chapter 20, "Marking and Reporting the Results of Measurement," provides sound and even coverage of the many issues involved in grading. Although organized differently from this book's chapter or Hills' chapters, the same general middle-of-the-road positions of measurement authorities are reached.

Oosterhof, A. C. (1987). Obtaining intended weights when combining students' scores. *Educational Measurement: Issues and Practice, 6,* 29–37. This self-contained instructional module provides explanation and practice in combining components elements into totals.

Terwilliger, J. S. (1971). *Assigning grades to students*. Glenview, IL: Scott, Foresman. A very insightful and helpful short classic that introduces a number of grading systems and analyzes the problems associated with each.

Terwilliger, J. S. (1989). Classroom standard setting and grading practices. *Educational Measurement: Issues and Practices, 8*, 15–19. A thoughtful article that provides a brief rationale for referencing grades to groups larger than the individual class. It also suggests how a file of test items can be used for this kind of anchorage.

Thorndike, R. L., & Hagen, E. P. (1977). *Measurement and evaluation in psychology and education* (4th ed.). New York: Wiley. Chapter 15 provides an unusually helpful discussion of grading practices and rationale. In addition, it is a major

Characteristics of Good Measuring Instruments

The first three parts of this book have focused on classroom testing. The final one, Part V, concerns various kinds of published instruments. The present Part IV provides a transition; each of its four topics is germane both to the construction and use of teacher-made tests as well as to the selection, use, and interpretation of published instruments.

There are several widely recognized features of all effective measures—be they simple measures such as rulers, attendance records, or completion tests or more sophisticated ones such as individually administered tests of academic aptitude, tryouts for school musicals, or electrocardiographs. Although authors tend to organize these desirable attributes of measuring instruments into somewhat differing lists, their lists contain much the same content. In this section, the "pie" is cut into four pieces: practicality, interpretability, validity, and reliability.

Various *practical considerations* such as ease of use, cost, and time requirements are examined in Chapter 13. *Interpretability* is also treated in Chapter 13. The point that educational measures must be interpretable via either domain referencing and/or norm referencing is reviewed and elaborated. Chapter 14 concerns *validity* and ways in which it is demonstrated. In addition, another statistics topic necessary to an understanding of some of the materials which follow on validity and reliability is developed.

Chapter 15 addresses *reliability*. Although the topic is inherently quantitative, formulas and their use are minimized; the underlying concepts of test reliability, its enhancement, and its assessment are amplified.

These four characteristics of effective measures are relevant to measures in any field, not just education. As you study this section, keep in mind that each feature applies not only to educational measures, but to measures of distance, speed, pitch, weight, time, pressure, vision, body temperature, earthquake intensity, or stock market performance.

Thus you should "think big" when studying these characteristics of effective measuring instruments. In addition to applying the topics broadly to fields outside of education, you should seek to apply them to the full spectrum of educational measures. To teacher-made tests and to published tests. To measures of maximum performance and to measures of typical performance. To objective paper-pencil tests and to product and performance measures. To instruments that tap cognitive attributes and to those that assess affect and motor skills. To power tests and to speed tests. To summative measures and to formative ones. To mastery tests and to discriminatory tests. The characteristics of good measuring instruments have very broad application.

13

Practicality and Interpretability

This chapter addresses two of the four characteristics of effective measuring instruments. Since the ordering of these four features is arbitrary, the easiest topic—practical considerations—will be considered first.

Practicality

The least important feature of measuring instruments is **practicality**—that collection of practical considerations variously referred to as practical features, administrative issues, and logistic considerations. This potpourri of test features affects the extent to which the use of a test is practical.

Cost

Published tests vary in their costs, and schools are rightly influenced by this factor. Yet the money outlay for a published test, its answer sheet, and its machine scoring are rarely more than a minor part of the total costs associated with its use. The value of student time devoted to taking a test and the value of professional time spent in administering and interpreting it are usually far greater than the value of the money spent in purchasing the test and its answer sheet. It is therefore appropriate for potential test purchasers to give relatively little weight to the money cost of instruments unless other things are equal (which they rarely are).

One aspect of money cost is the reusability of testing materials. Some instruments can be used only once, while others are designed to be reused over and over again. The purchase of durable, reusable test booklets can involve significant "up front" investment and thereby make a test appear to be very expensive, but the per-student cost is often much less when the investment is figured over the expected life of the booklets.

A type of money outlay that often deserves more attention than it gets is that of answer sheets. Although per-pupil cost of answer media appears small in comparison with the original cost of durable test booklets, the answer media, of course, are consumed and must continuously be replenished.

When issues of cost and economy are applied to teacher-made tests, the merit of separate answer sheets discussed in Chapter 9 takes on a new dimension. Not only are separate answer sheets often easier and faster to mark, but they may enable larger, more costly test booklets to be reused.

A final aspect of cost is that of scoring. Many published tests are scored locally and/or by the publisher by machine and/or computer. Publishers typically offer a variety of scoring services from which users may select those desired. This expense, like the purchase of answer sheets, is a recurring one. As the years go by, the cost of buying and scoring answer sheets often becomes more significant than the price of the original test booklets.

Time

When teachers develop classroom tests, they naturally make their length convenient. When schools purchase published tests, however, the length is set. At the elementary level, schedules are relatively flexible. Whether a given test requires a little more or less working is not ordinarily critical. However, at the secondary level, classes adhere to a rigid schedule. If a test requires more continuous time than a single class period, the whole school timetable must be disrupted. In such a case one would want to think twice before purchasing the instrument.

In addition to the actual working time, allowance must be made for handing out materials, reading directions, answering questions, and collecting materials after the test. These activities usually require from 5 to 15 minutes, depending on test complexity and examiner efficiency. In middle schools where class periods are often 40 minutes or less, this may leave only 20 to 30 minutes for working time. High school periods are usually longer, so 30 to 45 minutes of working time can usually be accommodated.

If the continuous time required to administer a test exceeds the length of a class period, use of the test is extremely disruptive to the entire school. For this reason, publishers of longer tests often organize subtests into lengths that can fit conveniently into class periods.

Although test brevity is a virtue, the inherent trade-off between length and reliability must be understood. Short tests tend to be unreliable; longer ones tend to be more reliable. The most effective way to make any given test more reliable is usually to lengthen it. Therefore, persons selecting published tests must not pursue brevity with a singleness of purpose. Nor should they expect to find a test that is both short and reliable. (To so expect is as naive as to expect to find a automobile that, on the one hand, is large, safe, and comfortable and, on the other hand, has a low initial cost and good fuel economy.) This topic will resurface in Chapter 15.

Ease of Administration

Published instruments differ considerably in the ease with which they can be administered. Some require substantial preparation time and tedious attention to detail in order not to depart from the standard procedures. For example, I once used a group-administered geometry aptitude test that had 17 separately timed subunits in 40 minutes of working time. With this many opportunities to err in timing, errors are not unlikely. (Alas, I forgot to start the stopwatch for one of the sections.)

Some tests, such as individually administered aptitude tests like the Wechsler Intelligence Scales, demand great skill and experience of examiners/scorers. For this reason, such devices should be used only by those who have had additional course work devoted to their use. Even among the kinds of instruments that regular classroom teachers are qualified to administer, score, and interpret, there is considerable variation in demands. Therefore, the ease with which a test can be administered is a practical consideration that merits attention when selecting tests.

Ease, Speed, and Accuracy of Scoring

Chapter 9 discussed formatting teacher-made tests and answer sheets to accommodate easy and speedy scoring. Teachers should avoid making needless work. So should commercial test publishers. If potential users of published tests wish to hand score answer sheets for speedy results, then availability of appropriate answer media and scoring devices, such as overlay stencils, are important. Yet some published tests can be scored only by machine.

Once a raw score is obtained, it must, if interpretations are to be norm referenced, be converted into some sort of derived score. Some test manuals make this task quite easy and error-free, while others require users to enter a sequence of two or even three tables to make successive conversions. Moreover, the ease of using tables varies substantially as a function of print size, spacing, and use of guide lines, shading, and color. If errors creep into the scoring process, then the problem is more than one of mere convenience and time; *scoring errors reduce reliability and validity.*

If a potential test user wishes to have answer media machine scored and converted into derived scores, then the availability of necessary answer media and scoring services is an important thing to consider in selecting a test. Yet some published tests can be scored only by hand.

If suitable scoring services are available, then cost, accuracy, and turn-around time become important considerations. Some scoring services provide admirable speed and accuracy of service, while others require worrisome amounts of waiting time before test results become available.

Availability of Desired Derived Scores

Not all publishers provide the kinds of derived scores that informed users desire. As will be seen in Chapter 16, test manuals and scoring services commonly provide several kinds of derived scores. Percentile ranks and percentile bands are the derived scores of choice for most interpretive purposes (Lyman, 1991), while standard scores are needed for most research or computational uses. Before purchasing a test, users should verify that the kind(s) of scores needed are available.

Availability of Interpretive Aids

After tests are administered and scored, the results often need to be interpreted to interested parties such as students and parents. Some published tests are accompanied by extremely helpful devices to aid interpretation of scores to lay people. Such interpretive aids are usually designed to simultaneously highlight both (a) what is revealed by the test scores and (b) the limits of what is known from the scores.

Several tests have interpretive aids that provide vivid graphic displays of confidence bands of percentile ranks. As will be seen in Chapter 16, such percentile bands help students and parents understand the fundamental truth that one must allow for a margin of error in the scores.

Some publishers provide computer-generated prose printout interpretations as an option that can be purchased along with scoring. In general, these interpretive aids explain to parents and students what the scores mean. It is important to realize that the quality of such prose interpretive aids can be no better than the sophistication of the program that generates them. There is great variation in the adequacy of such interpretations. Prospective users would be wise to consider carefully whether a given service is of sufficient merit to be beneficial.

Interpretability

The second feature of good measuring instruments to be discussed is **interpretability**. To be useful, measures must yield results that are meaningful; they must produce interpretable scores. Two major bases for score interpretation were introduced in Chapter 3—domain referencing and norm referencing.

The topic of interpretability is important because some tests lack *both* bases of meaningful interpretation. This deplorable condition occurs in both teacher-made instruments and in published ones. Some tests that are alleged to be criterion or domain referenced simply do not define a domain clearly enough to provide a basis for an informed referencing of the interpretation to a domain (Forsyth, 1991; Nitko, 1980). Likewise, some tests said to be norm referenced simply do not describe the reference groups in enough detail to enable users to judge relevance to their interpretive purpose.

There are thus two roads to interpretability, the domain-referenced and the norm-referenced. Any useful educational measure—be it teacher-made or published—must be accompanied by at least one of these means of meaningful interpretation. Performance on some kinds of test content can be meaningfully referenced to content domains; performance on other content cannot be. Similarly, achievement on some kinds of test content can be meaningfully referenced to the performance of other people, while achievement on other test content cannot be.

Domain Referencing in Tracks A and B

Recall that domain-referenced interpretations relate to content or skill domains. Such a domain must be described in enough detail to indicate very clearly what it includes and what it excludes (American Psychological Association, 1985, p. 26). When a test's content or skill domain is tightly specified, interpretation can be meaningfully referenced to its content (i.e., content or domain referenced). When test content is not clearly delimited, interpretation cannot meaningfully be domain referenced.

Content of Tracks A and B is clearly specifiable. Performance can therefore be referenced to the domain. Would it also make sense to reference performance to that of other people?

In Track A there would be no point in referencing performance to the performance of other people[1] because by the end of successful instruction nearly all students have achieved mastery of the essential content. Where everybody is virtually perfect, everybody is average, and there is nothing to be gained from so describing them.

In Track B there can be sound purpose in referencing performance to that of other people because significant amounts of individual differences in achievement exist after effective instruction. Since people differ, reporting relative status conveys information.

Norm Referencing in Tracks B and C

Recall that norm-referenced interpretations relate examinee performance to the performance of other people. A reference group of other people must be described in enough detail to enable test users clearly to know its nature. When a norm group is adequately described and relevant to the interpretive purpose, interpretation can be meaningfully people referenced (i.e., norm referenced). On the other hand, interpretation cannot meaningfully be norm referenced when there is no reference group, where one is not adequately described, or where it is not relevant to the purpose of interpretation.

---

[1]It should be recognized, however, that the process of selecting goals and setting standards does not occur in a vacuum; when well done, it is undertaken with full cognizance of how well learners at a particular level of maturity can handle the content.

Individual differences in achievement clearly exist in Tracks B and C. Performance therefore can meaningfully be norm referenced. Would it also make sense to reference performance to content or skill domains?

In Track C, it is not possible to reference interpretation to the ill-defined content domains.[2] An illusion of domain referencing can be created by such statements as "Mary has achieved a 75% mastery of current events." But such utterances are meaningless because the content domain is not sufficiently laid out to identify what she has achieved 75% of. Nor do we know the difficulty of the items with which her achievement was assessed.

In Track B there can be good reason to reference performance to content. Since the content of Track B is well described, it is possible and meaningful to reference performance to it.

Norm Referencing to the Class

As discussed in Chapter 12, when interpretations of teacher-made tests are to be norm referenced, they are often referenced to the teacher's own class. For grading purposes, this is extremely undesirable. For some other purposes, such as dividing a fourth-grade class into three instructional groups for mathematics, the class at hand is not only the most obvious and easiest reference group to use, it is the most appropriate one as well.

When interpretations of published tests are to be norm referenced, they too could be referenced to single classes. This, however, is uncommon because larger, more stable groups are ordinarily more desirable for referencing. Published tests are, therefore, usually accompanied by data from larger reference groups.

Norm Referencing to Larger External Groups

As explained in Chapter 12, interpretations of teacher-made tests can, by use of anchor measures, be indirectly norm referenced to larger external reference groups. It was seen that this is often highly desirable.

For published tests, it is seldom necessary for teachers to go to this trouble themselves because national reference-group data are ordinarily supplied by the publisher. Moreover, the scoring services that are available for many published tests provide, in additional to national norms, optional reference-group data for such groups as the user's own class, the user's own school, and the user's own school district.

National Norms

By far the most common comparative data accompanying published instruments are national norms that enable an examinee's performance to be compared with that of a *representative sample* of other examinees of a *given description*. This section is devoted to the issue of the representativeness of the sample. The next section will be

---

[2] That is, in Track C domain referencing does not suffice. Yet is obviously necessary to have some sense of test content. The statement that "Anna scores higher than 35% of a national sample of seventh-graders" needs to be accompanied by a description of test content—e.g., spelling vs. running vs. math. That was the point in Chapter 4 of careful planning and description of the content of Track C tests. Their domains should be described as clearly as is practical; the point is that this is not clear enough to enable domain referencing to suffice.

devoted to the topic of the relevance of the reference group to one's interpretive purpose.

Although teachers do not conduct national norming studies, they should be able to judge the adequacy of published normative data. Schools usually rely on the accuracy of national norms, yet too few users critically evaluate the norming study described in test manuals. Following is a description of things to look for in evaluating the adequacy of a test's reference group as a representative sample.

Samples can be categorized into two groups, random samples and nonrandom samples. In **random samples** each person in a population (such as all fifth-graders in the United States) has a known (and usually equal) probability of being selected; who gets selected is a matter of blind chance. In **nonrandom samples**, people are selected on some basis other than chance; who gets selected is usually a matter of convenience or economy. Nonrandom samples may or may not be similar to the populations of interest, and there is no way to know just how much they may misrepresent the populations. Publishers who sample nonrandomly are often less than candid in describing their samples; the user must be astute enough to detect it from the procedures described in the test manual or to deduce it from the inadequate description.

Reputable test publishers usually attempt to gather national normative data from random samples. For example, the publisher of a fifth-grade math test should provide national normative data that are based on a random sample of fifth-grade students. If, as is usually the case, the test is to be marketed nationally, the random sampling is ordinarily national in scope.

Conceptually, this is simple. To illustrate, suppose a sample of 5000 fifth-graders is being sought. Suppose a list exists of all the fifth-graders in the country, all their names are put in the proverbial hat, 5000 names are drawn out, and the test is given to each of these children. Although conceptually simple, this simple random research design is wholly impractical for several reasons.

First, there is no such master list of all fifth-graders, and obtaining one would be prohibitively costly. Second, it would be outrageously expensive and inconvenient to test 5000 pupils scattered in nearly that many schools all over the country. Third, some schools would decline to participate in the study.

To circumvent the first two of these problems, the publisher would likely use **cluster sampling** by obtaining a list of all the school districts in the country and choosing only a sample of, say, 100 districts. Within each selected school district, participation might be sought for only one randomly selected school. (We will delay for a time the matter of replacing those who decline.) Within each selected school each fifth-graders might be asked to participate.

A major concern with such a practical research design is the error that can result from the small number of sampling units (100 in this case). To protect against this source of error, **stratification** is often used. A stratified random sample is selected randomly, but in a way that assures proportional representation of each subgroup into which the population is divided.

To illustrate, consider a historical fact in test norming. Cognitive performance of students in some parts of the country averages lower than performance of students in other regions (Hopkins, Stanley, & Hopkins, 1990, p. 62). To protect against a chance over-representation or under-representation of any region, publishers have long divided the country up into several geographical regions, determined the fraction of the population in each, and then sampled that fraction of people from each region (Peterson, Kolen, & Hoover, 1989, p. 240). This stratification of the random sampling procedures enhances the adequacy of the sample.

Another common stratification variable is population density (Peterson, Kolen, & Hoover, 1989, p. 240). On average, suburban students perform better on cognitive measures than rural students, and inner-city students perform worst of all. Therefore, most publishers stratify all the school districts of the country into several sizes and select the desired proportion from each size category. This action ensures the appropriate representation of students from each size of district. Another common basis for stratification is public vs. nonpublic schools. Ethnicity is another that receives considerable attention.

The stratification variable of greatest importance is socioeconomic status (SES). It is well known that cognitive performance is correlated with SES (Cronbach, 1984). This correlation is moderate when individuals serve as the unit of analysis. In test standardizations, however, whole schools or school districts are the unit of sampling, and the correlation of school averages of SES and test performance is relatively high.

If SES influence is held constant, the other stratification variables become much less important. For example, if school districts in the deep South are compared with those from other parts of the country having the *same SES*, there is likely to be little or no systematic differences in cognitive performance. Similarly, if minority children are compared with nonminority children of the *same SES*, large differences in performance are unlikely. Therefore test *users should attend most closely to a research design's treatment of SES.*

To stratify for SES, publishers estimate average SES of school districts. Since SES is a complex and subtle attribute, publishers have to settle for a crude estimate of the mean or median SES of persons in each school district. This is commonly achieved by use of two indicants that are available from U.S. census data. One indicant is income, either per capita or family. The other is education (e.g., median number of years of school completed by adults over 25 years of age). Such indicants enable publishers to quantify all school districts in the country on the basis of estimated average SES, to separate this list into several SES strata, to determine the fraction of the population enrolled in schools within each stratum, and to seek participation of a corresponding fraction of the sample from each stratum.

Most major publishers stratify samples on the bases of three or more variables, such as SES, geographic region, public versus nonpublic schools, and ethnic group. Professionals who are considering the purchase of a test should examine the manual of cognitive tests to verify that SES was a stratification variable. Mere assurance that such variables were considered in selecting the sample does not suffice. In addition, authors should report in the manual the success of the stratification efforts. This is best achieved by use of a table for each stratification variable that shows the percentage of the population and the percentage of the sample in each stratum. Wise prospective users are deeply suspicious of the adequacy of a test's reference group data unless they are described by such tables.

Indeed there are manuals in which few if any aspects of the norming study are described in sufficient detail to enable their adequacy to be judged. In general, one can assume that authors and publishers who have gone to the trouble and expense of conducting careful norming will be willing to follow the dictates of *Standards of Educational and Psychological Testing* (American Psychological Association, 1985) and report their efforts. Those who resort to vague, glossed-over description of their norming research usually have reason to avoid scrutiny of the details of their work. Other things being equal, such tests should be avoided.

The issue remains of what publishers can best do about districts or schools that choose not to participate in norming studies. This is a serious problem because of the very real danger that those who decline to participate may differ in some systematic ways from those who are willing to take part. This lack of participation risks systematic error or **bias** in the reference group data. First, the problem should be minimized by making participation attractive. The test booklets and scoring service should, of course, be offered to participating schools free of charge. Additional incentives are possible, such as discounts on other purchases. Second, publishers can minimize the potential bias resulting from nonparticipation by replacing schools that choose not to cooperate with others *from the same strata* (Peterson, Kolen, & Hoover, 1989, p. 241).

QUIZ 13–1

Following are three true stories about standardization of well-known tests. First, identify the fault in the norming procedure. Then speculate on the likely *direction*, if any, of the bias that may have been introduced. That is, indicate whether a typical class's status would be reported to be too high or too low as a result of the norming defects.

1. A major achievement battery was normed on a sample drawn by use of a random sampling design that was well stratified for SES and other appropriate variables. Selected schools were invited to participate for less charge than normal use of the test would entail.

2. A test was normed on children in and around Nashville, Tennessee, and was still being used thirty years later throughout the country.

3. A major publisher normed a test on a carefully selected, stratified, cluster, random sample. Schools invited to participate were supplied all testing materials free of charge, but a condition of participation was that they would not receive student scores.

KEY TO QUIZ 13–1

1. Although the sample selection procedures were adequate, bias would be introduced by requiring schools to pay in order to participate in the norming. It is not only necessary to avoid bias in sample selection, but also to do what can be done to avoid its introduction by schools declining to participate. One might speculate that poorer schools would be less able to afford the bargain than more affluent ones. This would yield

KEY TO QUIZ 13–1 (cont.)

normative data that were too high. Therefore a typical class's scores would appear to be lower (in comparison with this too-high reference group) than they should.

2. Such geographically restricted normative data usually reflect sampling by convenience. The extent to which the resulting data are representative of the country is unknown.

   Use of very old normative data is another source of concern. Even when test content has not changed (and in most aptitude and achievement areas, it has), current curricular emphases may have. It is not much of an exaggeration to say that using normative data several decades old is engaging in cross-cultural testing.

3. The issue here is the similarity of motivational efforts by teachers and others for (a) the norming sample and (b) subsequent users of the test. Many teachers resent administrators' agreeing to devote class time for test-norming research. If they are not going to receive potentially helpful scores for their students in return for this time, then some teachers might well exhibit less enthusiasm for the endeavor than would teachers in classes that subsequently use the test. Thus one might speculate that the norming sample would perform less well than normal and that groups compared with it would appear to be higher than they really are.

Normative Samples Should Be Relevant to the Purpose of Interpretation

The previous section focused on representative national reference-group data. These are desirable when educators wish to compare a student's performance with a national cross-section of students in the same grade or subject. The broader issue is that normative comparisons should be made with respect to a relevant group of other examinees. No matter how adequately sampling has been conducted, the resulting reference-group data will be helpful only if the population sampled is one with which the user wishes to compare examinees (Peterson, Kolen, & Hoover, 1989, p. 236). Test users must, therefore, always be acutely aware of what reference group was used to obtain derived scores.

To illustrate, suppose you have just taken a reading test and are told that you performed at the 90th percentile. Should you be elated? Not until you know what the reference group is. If it is one of reading-disabled seventh-graders, you probably would not be thrilled to learn that you out-performed 9 out of every 10 of them. On the other hand, if it were a reference group of Ph.D. candidates, you might have cause for elation.

Or suppose I have just taken a personality inventory and am told that my profile is very strange, being two or three *SD*s above average on several subscores and the same amount below average on several others. Should friends and colleagues be alarmed about my mental health? Not until they inquire about the reference group. If it were a carefully selected sample of middle-aged, white American male professors (all of which I am), then they would have cause for concern. But if it turns out to be a sample of outback Australian aborigines or a sample of European Nobel laureates, then I should be unconcerned that my profile differed markedly from that of an irrelevant reference group.

But now suppose I were a professor of anthropology planning to spend three years on field research among outback Australoids; now the Australoid reference group would be useful. In judging how I would fit into that culture, the Australoid norms would be relevant. That I have no known Australoid ancestry is immaterial. The principle can be put this way: If we want to know how a fish will get along in a particular pond, then compare it with the fish in that pond. If we want to know how it will fare in another pond, then compare it with the fish in the other pond.

This principle prompts some test users to compare students' performance with that of samples that are *not* representative of all age- or grade-mates in the country. For example, a principal of a Bureau of Indian Affairs reservation school might wish to compare local pupils with a sample of other Native American, reservation youth. That is, the administrator would wish the publisher to disaggregate this kind of youth from the national normative data.

This comparison is not often feasible because there are not likely to be enough Native American reservation pupils in the national normative sample either (a) to provide stable data or (b) to be representative of reservation-dwelling Native American students. There are, however, certain groups for whom disaggregated normative data are sometimes available.

Inner-City School Norms.   Like the reservation principal, educators who work with disadvantaged inner-city students sometimes contend that it is unfair to compare them with a national cross-section of other students, most of whom have far greater educational advantages. From one point of view, of course, they are right. No question about it, our society does not distribute opportunity equally to all its young. Life is not fair to many inner-city students. But that is not the issue.

The issue of which reference group is preferable depends largely on the intent of the norm-referenced interpretations. On the one hand, if the purpose is to judge how each person stands in comparison with other grade-mates across the country, then aggregated national norms make the most sense. On the other hand, if the goal is to judge how each student has progressed *in the disadvantaged context of the inner city and its schools*, then inner-city or local norms would indeed make good sense (Ricks, 1971). However, one would not want to rely *exclusively* on inner-city norms. The typical inner-city school would be average in comparison with other such schools, and this could obscure the very real educational, economic, and social disadvantages of inner-city life. It would not be helpful to use the special norms to obscure the problem. On the contrary, solving the problem demands awareness of it.

Fortunately, inner-city educators need not decide between inner-city norms and national norms. They can both be used simultaneously, and this often makes the best sense.

Ethnic Norms.   Along the same lines, spokespersons for various minorities sometimes suggest that it would be more fair to compare a child from a given group with others from the same group than to compare him or her with a national cross-section. The issues here are similar to those concerning inner-city norms.

For example, suppose one were interpreting an aptitude test score for an achievement test for a group of rural Hispanic students. For the purpose of judging how well they can function in their present situation, local norms or Hispanic norms would be suitable. But for predicting how well they might at first function if they should attempt to enter the mainstream, national norms would be preferable (Ricks, 1971).

Occupational Norms.   In some uses of published tests, there is merit in comparing an individual with persons who work in a particular occupation. Suppose a person were to take a spatial aptitude test for the purpose of vocational counseling to consider entry into training in drafting. In this situation it would be useful to compare the person's score with those of people who work in this field. One might also want to use national norms, but the occupational norms would be especially useful.

Gender-Specific Norms.   In this culture at this time gender differences exist in some kinds of achievement and aptitude tests, some favoring males and some favoring females (Cronbach, 1990). Even greater gender differences exist in some kinds of interest inventories. It is, therefore, common for interest and aptitude measures to provide separate norms for males and females. While interpretation is usually based on same-gender reference group data, it is occasionally productive to employ cross-gender, norm group data as well.

As an example, suppose eleventh-grader Estell has taken a mechanical aptitude test and is seeking advice from her counselor concerning her aptitude for (a) car mechanics and (b) engineering. Since males tend to receive higher mean scores than females on mechanical aptitude tests, test publishers often provide separate male and female norms. Estell's counselor would, of course, want to report her status in comparison with other eleventh-grade girls; suppose her percentile rank (PR) in this reference group is 99.

In an ideal situation, the counselor would also have data with which to compare her score to those received by successful car mechanics *when they were in the eleventh grade.* (Of course most of them would be male, but the occupational group might best be taken as a whole.) Suppose her PR in this reference group were 95. Suppose also that her PR in comparison with those received by successful engineers when they were high school juniors was 70. Her performance in comparison with these latter two groups would certainly be more helpful for her in judging how her mechanical aptitude compares with persons in those occupations than would her performance in comparison with high school girls.

Alas, the counselor probably would not have the desired occupational reference-group data. However, she or he would have data for high school males. Suppose Estell's PR in comparison with eleventh-grade boys were 93. The counselor might reason that because she is considering entry into what have traditionally been male-dominated fields, her prognosis would better be assessed by reference to male norms than by female reference group data. In the absence of the more desirable occupational reference group data, the cross-gender data—along with the female data—would be useful.

Course-Based, Grade-Based, and Age-Based Reference Group Data

National reference group data are commonly based on people who are enrolled in a given course, people who are in a given grade, or people who are in a given age. Which makes the best sense?

At the secondary and college level, many courses are not taken by all students. For example, only some high school students elect chemistry. If a chemistry teacher administers a published chemistry test, the reference group providing the most meaningful interpretations would be one consisting of other students in high school chemistry, not 16-year-olds or high school juniors (many of whom have not studied chemistry). Similarly, in other elective courses, references groups best consist of representative samples of students who have taken the respective subjects.

For courses studied by all students (e.g., secondary subjects such as history and English and virtually all elementary subjects), normative data can be based either on others of the same age or grade. Most achievement tests in this country are accompanied by reference group data based on others of the same grade. Virtually all aptitude tests in this country have reference group data based on others of the same chronological age. In addition, many aptitude tests also provide grade-based normative data.

These conflicting traditions of aptitude tests being referenced to same-age peers and achievement tests being referenced to same-grade peers is unfortunate because simultaneous use of different bases can render comparison of aptitude and achievement hazardous. For example, suppose Jake is a 12-year-old fourth-grader. If his national PR on a reading test is 50 and his national PR on a verbal aptitude test is also 50, one is prone to conclude that his reading and his verbal aptitude are very similar. Not necessarily true! If, as is usual, the achievement test provides national PRs based on others of the same grade, then his reading PR of 50 indicates that he performed about *average for fourth-graders*, most of whom are only about 10 years old. And if, as is usual, the aptitude test provides national PRs based on others of the same grade, then his aptitude PR of 50 indicates that he performed about *average for 12-year-olds*. Thus his reading score is not as high as his aptitude score.

This difficulty is avoided if both the achievement and the aptitude test are referenced the same way. It does not matter whether this be by age or grade. Whenever one wishes to compare aptitude with achievement (as in judging whether a child is underachieving or in establishing eligibility for a learning disabilities program), it is important to ensure that the normative data are either both age based or are both grade based. This rule is especially important if the student is significantly underaged or overaged for his or her grade.

Comparability of Norm Groups

Another issue involved in comparing scores of different tests concerns the comparability of their normative data. Suppose that Anwar obtained a PR of 75 on a reading test and a PR of 50 on a math test. In judging whether he is stronger in reading than math, two issues must be considered. One concerns whether the difference is large enough to merit confidence that it was not just a chance happening. (This topic will be addressed in Chapter 15.) The other issue is whether the normative samples for the two tests were equally capable. If one test had been normed with a brighter sample than the other, then the comparison between scores would be distorted.

Ideally, we would like for the reading and math tests to have been normed on the *same sample*. Then comparability between the two PRs would be certain. As will be seen in Chapter 17, a major advantage to the use of achievement batteries (consisting of several different subtests measuring various subjects) is that the whole battery is normed on the same sample. With batteries, comparability of normative data is assured.

If the two tests have been normed on different samples, then comparability merits intense consideration. Descriptions of the norming studies should receive even greater scrutiny than normal in order to judge whether interpretation of both tests is referenced to samples that are comparable in representing the same population.

Closely related is the issue of comparing aptitude and achievement scores, as in Jake's case. Such aptitude-achievement comparisons are used to identify underachievers and to quantify aptitude-achievement discrepancies for identification of students eligible for learning disability programs. Three problems have been identified that can distort such comparisons. First, the respective tests' scores must be referenced to the *same population*, such as people in a given grade. Second, allowance must be made for measurement error of the difference between the scores. Finally, the standardization designs of the two tests should be highly similar in order to produce *comparable samples* of the normative population. Persons contemplating such test uses should also be familiar with a number of additional technical pitfalls that make comparisons of aptitude and achievement measures hazardous (Thorndike, 1963).

Chapter Summary

Of the four characteristics of good measuring instruments to be treated, a test's practical features were the first to be considered. Although less important than the topics that follow, features such as time and cost, ease and convenience of use, speed and accuracy of scoring, and compatibility of time limits with school schedules all impact significantly on test feasibility.

Interpretability is another characteristic of all effective measures. Unless there is a basis by which to interpret the scores, a measure is useless. Two roads to interpretability are domain referencing and norm referencing. There is no "best" kind of referencing. The nature of the subject matter and the purpose of the interpretation must be considered before deciding on a kind of interpretation a test's scores should be given.

Norm-referenced interpretations can be based on national norms, local norms, gender-specific norms, ethnic group norms, etc. Reference groups should be relevant to the purpose of the testing. They should provide assistance in answering the question(s) that use of the test was intended to address.

Publishers providing derived scores for tests are obliged to describe the reference groups on which these scores are based. This description should be detailed enough to allow prospective test users to (a) judge the relevance of the reference group(s) to their needs and (b) evaluate the adequacy with which the normative data were gathered.

Suggestions for Further Reading

Gronlund, N. E., & Linn, R. L. (1990). *Measurement and evaluation in teaching* (6th ed.). New York: Macmillan. Pages 101–103 give good coverage of the major practical issues that should be considered in selecting a published test. Chapter 14, "Interpreting Test Scores and Norms," provides a sound introduction to derived scores and their use as well as perspective vis-á-vis raw scores and domain-referenced interpretation.

Mehrens, W. A., & Lehmann, I. (1991). *Measurement and evaluation in education and psychology* (4th ed.). New York: Holt, Rinehart and Winston. Chapter 2, "Norm- and Criterion-Referenced Measurement," provides an informative and balanced discussion of the rightful place and limitations of each kind of interpretation.

Peterson, N. S., Kolen, M. J., & Hoover, H. D. (1989). Scaling, norming, and equating. In Linn, R. L. (Ed.), *Educational measurement* (3rd ed.). New York: Macmillan. Pages 236–241 provide relatively succinct and technical coverage of sampling.

Ricks, J. H. (1971). Local norms—when and why. *Test Service Bulletin No. 58*. San Antonio: The Psychological Corporation. A readable discussion and rationale for the limited use of local norms.

Thorndike, R. L. (1963). *The concepts of over- and under-achievement*. New York: Columbia University. A classic treatment of the myriad problems facing those who wish to compare student achievement with aptitude.

Validity

Validity is an essential feature of satisfactory measuring instruments. It has often been described as the extent to which a device measures what it is being used to measure. Along these lines, validity has been characterized as how well a test "fulfills the function for which it is being used" (Hopkins, Stanley, & Hopkins, 1990, p. 76). Thus it is not a test itself that is valid to some extent; rather, it is the various uses to which it may be put that are valid to various extents. An instrument could be highly valid for some purposes, fair for other uses, and worthless for still others.

An example may clarify this important point. Suppose a person buys a bathroom scale, but does not know quite what it measures. If it were used to rank-order a group of third-graders by height, it would function rather poorly. If it were used to put them in order by weight, the device would be much more valid for this task. If it were used to predict their grades in spelling next semester, the device would be worthless for this job. Thus it is not the scale itself that is valid to some extent; it is the uses to which it might be put that are valid to various extents.

The concept of validity is broader in scope than focus on mere scores. It also concerns *inferences* from the scores and *usefulness* of the inferences. Thus validity "refers to the appropriateness, meaningfulness, and usefulness of the specific inferences made from test scores. Test validation is the process of accumulating evidence to support such inferences" (American Psychological Association, 1985, p. 9).

Validity is multifaceted. Recall from Chapter 1 the wide variety of uses of educational tests. Recall also the important idea that tests and other measures are useful only to the extent that they improve decision making. The concept of validity is relevant to each of these uses and to each resulting decision. "The extent to which a test improves the accuracy of decisions is the extent to which it provides useful information and, hence, has practical validity" (Hopkins, Stanley, & Hopkins, 1990, p. 76).

Validity thus concerns the extent to which test scores lead to adequate and appropriate inferences, decisions, and actions. It concerns evidence for *test use* and judgment about *potential consequences* of score interpretation and use. Tests, as such, are not validated. What is validated is the inferences about the meaning of test scores or interpretation about the implications for action that arise from the interpretations (Messick, 1989, p. 13).

To illustrate, return to the example of the bathroom scale. Since the scale was not at all valid for predicting next semester's spelling grades, one would rightly denounce its use for assigning suitable spelling tasks to individual pupils. The measure would not do this job adequately, and the consequences of using it for this job would be highly undesirable; thus this *use* of the scale is invalid.

On the other hand, the scale was very satisfactory for assessing weight. Suppose it were used to measure weight and its "scores," along with height measures, were used for screening children for obesity with the purpose of dietary and exercise intervention for those diagnosed as obese. The device would contribute very helpfully to this job, and the consequences of its use would be highly desirable. Thus this *use* of the scale would be quite valid.

Validity data are grouped into categories called **content-related**, **criterion-related**, and **construct-related** validity evidence. An important relationship exists between the kind(s) of interpretation to be made from a test's scores and the kind(s) of validity evidence most relevant to the test's use(s) (Goldman, 1971). For example, if a test is employed to predict next year's college grades of high school seniors, then the validity evidence of primary interest concerns how well the test forecasts next year's college grades. On the other hand, if a test is used to measure pupil knowledge of this week's spelling lesson, then the kind of validity evidence of most interest focuses on how well the test matches the objectives and content of the spelling lesson. Although validation should often include several kinds of evidence (American Psychological Association, 1985, p. 9), the one(s) of primary concern relate to the anticipated interpretation(s) or decision(s) to be made from the scores.

Recent scholarly thinking has stressed that *validity is a unitary concept.* Although the rubrics of content-related, criterion-related, and construct-related *validity evidence* are convenient, their use does not imply that distinct types of validity exist or that a particular method of validation is sufficient for each specific test use. Moreover, rigorous distinctions among the categories are not possible (American Psychological Association, 1985, p. 9). In this chapter, discussion will be loosely organized around these three types of validity evidence, but no effort will be made to force each source of evidence into only one category or to worry unduly over the classification of borderline sources of useful information.

First, the three kinds of validity evidence will be discussed. Then examination will center on the important issues of the relationship between validity and educational decision making. Finally, the validity of a test use will be considered in view of the likely consequences of that use.

Content-Related Validity Evidence

Attention in this section is focused on achievement tests. Whether achievement measures are commercially developed or are created by classroom teachers, they are best evaluated by considering (among other things) how well they measure the kind of achievement they are used to assess. This applies equally to objective tests, to essay and other product assessments, and to performance tests; to mastery tests and to discriminatory tests; to pretests and posttests; and to formative and summative tests.

When a test is used to measure achievement, most interest should focus on content-related validity evidence. *Content-related evidence concerns the degree to which the sample of test questions or tasks is representative of the content domain of interest.* Validation of achievement tests often relies on expert judgments to assess the relationship between the test and the content domain (American Psychological Association, 1985, p. 10).

Building Validity into Teacher-Made Achievement Tests

Validity is built into achievement tests. The most persuasive evidence that an achievement measure is valid is usually a consideration of how thoughtfully its specifications were drawn up, how faithfully the test was constructed to conform to these plans, and how skillfully its questions or tasks were crafted to tap the targeted content domain(s) *and nothing else.*

So how does a teacher build content-valid tests? By attending carefully to the test-development procedures. Chapter 4 focused on planning classroom tests so they will reflect the content and mental processes that teachers intend. Chapters 5 to 8 attended to methods of preparing items and tasks that tap the content domain on which instruction has focused and nothing else (such as test-wiseness). Chapter 9 addressed a variety of issues, such as directions concerning guessing, that influence what tests actually measure.

A major purpose of this book is to enable teachers to build validity into teacher-made achievement tests. The topic is given little space here because Part II has already treated it at length. It is, of course, important for the reader to realize that Part II relates directly to validity. It concerns building classroom tests that validly assess achievement.

Assessing Validity of Published Achievement Tests

When a teacher, school, or district selects an achievement test or battery of tests from among several competing instruments, validity should be a central consideration. The kind of validity evidence of greatest relevance to this task concerns how well the test content matches the curricular objectives. The professional task is to *judge* how well the author(s) built validity into the test.

Achievement tests are typically used to measure how well examinees can handle specific content or skill domains. Content-related validation involves the systematic examination of a test and its manual in order to judge how well it samples the domain of interest. At one level, this task of evaluating the content-related validity evidence of a published instrument is achieved by studying the test. Each item should be scrutinized. This examination gives a sense of how expertly the items were crafted and reviewed, of content balance, and of relative weight allotted to various mental processes.

At another level, the manual's description of the test's development procedures facilitates the task of judging the content-related validity evidence of commercially prepared instruments. Knowing how the domain to be assessed was identified and delimited, precisely what the test plans specified, how items were developed, edited, field-tested, revised, etc., helps one judge *some* dimensions of the answer to the question, "Was validity built into this test?"

This would help in judging how adequately the content domain was described in advance. Such advanced specification provides protection against a test being overloaded with content that lends itself most readily to being assessed with objective items. "A well-constructed achievement test should cover the objectives of instruction, not just its subject matter." Content should, therefore, have been "broadly defined to include major objectives, such as the application of principles and the interpretation of data, as well as factual knowledge" (Anastasi, 1988, p. 140). Potential test users should attend closely to such matters.

Another dimension to the question, "Has validity been built into this test?" concerns the achievement indicants that are actually measured (in contrast to the instructional objectives). For example, commercially distributed achievement tests tend to rely mainly on objective items. If the main instructional objective concerns students' ability to *express* themselves orally, to *produce* correctly spelled words from dictation, or to *develop* logical mathematical proofs, then selection-type items are not likely to assess the entire achievement domain. In such cases no amount of authorial care in developing excellent test items that adhere to test specifications can rectify a mismatch between the specifications and the achievement domain. One should be careful not to overgeneralize from the indicants sampled.

As stated above, knowing how the content domain was specified, precisely what was included in the specifications, how items were developed, edited, field tested, revised, etc., aids in judging *some* aspects of an achievement test's validity in a given situation. These important facets of the validity picture involve judgment about the interface of test content with instructional objectives. Thus *content-related validity evidence is judgmental,* not quantitative.

Validity Is Situationally Specific

Another angle of content-related validation concerns the situationally specific nature of validity. A test that is highly valid for assessing student achievement in some settings may be seriously inadequate for measuring achievement in other situations. Two examples may help to illustrate this important point.

Suppose a published test in first-year, high school French focuses exclusively on the written language. Miss Foix's French course heavily emphasizes the written language. She may (if other things are satisfactory) find the test to be highly valid for measuring how well her students have achieved her instructional objectives. Mr. Hwang's French course gives heavy emphasis to the written language, but he also seeks to develop knowledge and appreciation of French culture. He may (if other things are satisfactory) find the test to be valid for assessing how well his students have achieved *some* of his instructional objectives and ill-suited for assessing their achievement of other objectives. Finally, Mrs. Dubois's course gives equal attention to the oral language, to the written language, and to French culture. She therefore will find the test to be relatively *in*valid for assessing her students' achievement of major goals of the course even if it is exemplary in other respects; it matches her curriculum poorly.

The point is that the test was not valid or invalid. That cannot be judged in the abstract. What is properly judged is the *match* of the test with some particular use to which the test is to be put. Thus validity is not an attribute of a test; it is an attribute of the *interaction* of a test with a situation in which the test is used to make decisions.

For another example of achievement tests' situationally specific validity, consider two elementary schools that have different emphases in their math curriculum. School A focuses heavily on computational skills (and achieves good results thereon) and gives less attention to math applications (on which its pupils perform less well). School B emphasizes application of math to real life situations (and achieves good results thereon) and gives less emphasis to computation (on which its pupils perform less well). Now suppose each school is looking for a math test that matches its curriculum. Test X emphasizes computational skills, giving less attention to application. Test Y emphasizes application and provides less coverage to computation. Test Z provides a balanced assessment of computation and applications. If other things are equal, Test X will be best suited to School A and Test Y will best meet the needs of School B.

Tests X, Y, and Z are not valid or invalid in any absolute sense. That you or I might prefer Test Z is irrelevant. What must be judged is the *interaction of test content with the proposed test use.* Test Z is not the most valid measure of achievement in either school because its content is not well matched to either school's instructional objectives.

Face Validity Is Not Validity

Face validity refers to what a test *appears superficially* to measure and should not be confused with validity. In other words, "face validity" is a misnomer. Nonetheless, it is an important test attribute. If a test "looks valid" to examinees, better rapport and public relations result. "If test content appears irrelevant, inappropriate, silly, or childish, the result will be poor cooperation, regardless of the actual validity of the test" use (Anastasi, 1988, p. 144). For example, a test of basic arithmetic for use in adult basic education programs should not have some application questions that would be appropriate only for children. (e.g., Mother gave Mary $20.00 to buy a skirt costing $13.95 with tax. How much change should Mary receive?)

It is appropriate to consider the extent to which a test will superficially appear to examinees to measure something worthwhile. However, this consideration should not be confused with content validation.

Necessary But Not Sufficient

Content considerations are indispensable to understanding what content and mental processes achievement tests measure and which they may neglect. However, they do not highlight, and may not even reveal, some of the subtle excess things that may inappropriately influence achievement test scores.

For example, the impact on test scores of examinee test-wiseness, the effect of test reading level, the influence of prior familiarity with stimulus material in interpretative exercises, and the consequences of cultural bias may not come to light from the judgmental processes described above. Some authorities address such contaminating factors under the topic of content-related validation; others consider them to be issues more relevant to construct-related validation. It is not important how they are classified, but it is very important that they be considered. We shall delay treatment of such topics until construct-related validity evidence is taken up.

QUIZ 14–1

1. In which track—A, B, or C—is it most difficult to build validity into an achievement test? Why?

2. For each of the following classroom achievement measures, assess the importance of content-related validation.

   A. A primary teacher's Track A unit test on knowledge of fire exit route

   B. A high school physical education teacher's Track B test of shooting accuracy (in a given range) in archery

   C. A primary teacher's observations of pupil's typical behavior in interpersonal relations

   D. Your final examination in this course

   E. High school debaters' performance in a tournament

KEY TO QUIZ 14–1

1. As discussed in Chapter 4, Track A and B domains are quite clearly specified; it is therefore relatively easy to develop test content that matches the clearly delimited instructional domain. Moreover, sampling is often unnecessary because an entire Track A domain or Track B skill can be included in the test.

   But in Track C, the content and boundaries of domains are not as tightly described. It is therefore more difficult to develop test content that closely parallels the less clearly defined instructional domain. Moreover, sampling is necessary because the Track C domains are too large to be tested in their entirety.

   For these reasons, two-way tables of specification are drawn up for Track C tests. They provide control over the sampling of content topics and over the sampling of mental processes.

2. The first measure is performed in the context of Track A instruction. The second is a Track B skill. The final three measures are based on Track C domains. In all five of these situations, content validation concerns the extent to which a measure assesses student performance on the instructional objectives and nothing else. (In Track C the issue of balance of topics and mental processes comes into the picture, but the basic issue is the same: How well does the test assess student performance on the objectives and nothing else?) Thus the issue of content-related validity evidence is vital to all five examples, regardless of track.

A Little More Statistics: The Pearson r

Several different kinds of data are used to assess test validity. It has been shown that judgment about the appropriateness and balance of test content provides a very important kind of validity consideration, especially for achievement tests. Other approaches to test validation (including those to be taken up next) employ the **correlation coefficient**. A grasp of correlation is therefore requisite to understanding some kinds of validity evidence. An understanding of correlation is also vital to the topic of reliability, which will be treated in Chapter 15. Discussion, therefore, digresses to complete the background in statistics, started in Chapter 11, that provides the necessary tools for an understanding of validity and reliability.

Correlation[1] (or co-relation), represented by the letter r, is a measure of relationship. It is an index of the degree of "in commonness" or "going togetherness" between two measures. When a quantitative statement of the degree of "going togetherness" or "correlation" between two variables is needed, a correlation coefficient is calculated. In this section, the meaning of correlation will first be treated. Then attention will be turned briefly to calculation. Finally, some interpretive

---

[1] Although there are other kinds of correlation coefficients, this book will treat only the Pearson correlation. The versatility, power, and widespread use of the Pearson product-moment coefficient of correlation nicely serve our purposes.

considerations involved in using concepts of correlation in educational measurement will be discussed.

The Meaning of Correlation

A good way to give meaning to the topic of correlation is to use graphic aids called scattergrams, bivariate distributions, correlation plots, or scatterplots. Of these synonyms, bivariate (i.e., two variable) distribution may best capture the meaning. The simultaneous graphing of two variables will now be reviewed.

Suppose a class of six students has taken two forms of the same 10-item test. The students' scores on the two alternate forms are displayed below.

Student	Form X	Form Y
Amy	9	7
Brett	5	5
Cindy	3	7
Dwight	5	5
Ellen	5	5
Fran	3	1

From "eyeballing" the patterning of co-relationships, we get a general sense that persons with high scores on one measure (e.g., Amy) tend to get high scores on the other measure, while persons who perform poorly on one variable (e.g., Fran) also tend to function poorly on the other. We might also notice from casual inspection of the distributions that Cindy is an exception to this trend of relationship between scores. If the number of persons were larger, it would be harder to secure information from a simple inspection of the data. Fortunately, two more effective ways show the amount of co-relationship or correlation, one graphic and one numeric. First, consider the graphic method.

Recall from elementary algebra that pairs of points can be graphed on coordinates. Two perpendicular axes are arbitrarily labeled as shown in Figure 14–1. From the point of intersection, equal units or intervals are laid out and numbered on each axis. Positive values are conventionally assigned to the right-hand region of the horizontal axis and negative values to the left-hand region. Similarly, custom dictates that the upper portion of the vertical axis represent positive numbers and the lower region represent negative numbers. A final convention is to let the first of the two variables, Form X scores in this case, be graphed on the horizontal axis, while the other variable is graphed with respect to the vertical axis; this was the basis of labeling the axes.

The points can now be plotted, with each point representing the two scores earned by a student. First is Amy, whose respective scores on Forms X and Y are 9 and 7. Brett, Dwight, and Ellen are all represented by the same point, 5 for each test form. Cindy's respective scores were 3 and 7, while Fran's were 3 and 1.

Figure 14–1 can be simplified in appearance by eliminating the negative portion of each axis (which is possible because all entries were positive), by omitting the detail in numbering points on each axis, and by "closing up" the resulting box. Figure 14–2 shows this simpler representation of the data for these six students. Another simple way by which the same data can be put into a bivariate distribution or scatterplot is shown in Figure 14–3. Whether dots or tally marks are used, the resulting

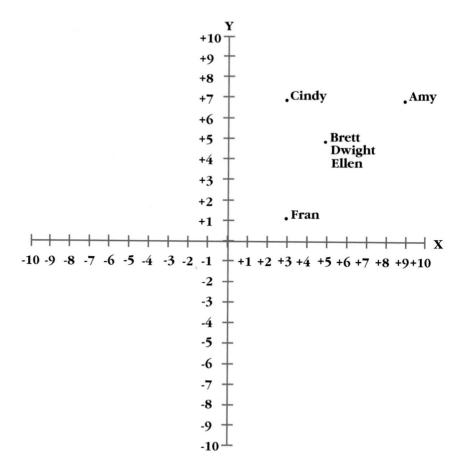

Figure 14–1. Graph on Cartesian Coordinates

visual displays of the data are much the same. In these ways, the amount of co-relationship or correlation between two variables is represented visually.

Now some experience is needed in associating scattergram or bivariate distribution pictures of amount of relationship with correlation coefficients that numerically represent amount of relationship. The following correlation plots are designed to help clarify the nature and meaning of the correlation coefficient. In Figure 14–4, no relationship exists between the variables of academic aptitude and shoe size for a sample of fourth-graders. Knowledge of a pupil's foot size provides no hint regarding his or her present aptitude for school work. Likewise, aptitude is a useless predictor of foot size. The two measures do not co-vary; they are uncorrelated. This fact is represented by a correlation coefficient of .0.

The values of the measures plotted in the scattergram are laid out so the larger values are upward and to the right. When the correlation coefficient, *r*, is positive, high scores on one variable tend to occur most often with high scores on the other measure, and low scores likewise tend to go together. Most of the dots or tally marks therefore fall near the diagonal that extends from the lower left part of the scatter diagram to its upper right region. When most of the entries lie on or near this positive diagonal, the correlation or relationship is a positive one.

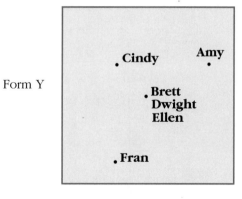

Form Y

Form X

Figure 14–2. Scattergram without Detail

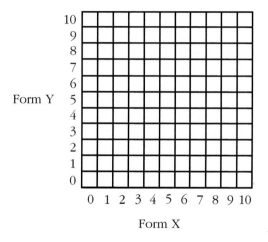

Form Y

Form X

Figure 14–3. Scatterplot with Tally Marks

Figure 14–5 shows the relationship between two measures when $r = 1.0$, that is, when all the entries lie on the positive diagonal. The graphed dots show the co-relationship between people's ages with their ages five years ago. Notice that each person's status on either variable can be predicted perfectly from knowledge of her or his status on the other variable. The relationship is therefore perfect. Since high values on one measure go with high values on the other measure, the correlation is a positive one. Such a perfect positive correlation is represented as $r = 1.0$.

Figure 14–6 displays the covariation between two measures when $r = -1.0$, that is, when all the entries lie on the negative diagonal, which extends from the upper-left to the lower-right portions of the graph. The cases graphed show the relationship between children's ages in years and the number of years remaining until reaching their eighteenth birthdays. We see that each individual's value on one measure can perfectly predict his or her value on the other measure. For example, a child of 10 has 8 years left as a minor, a youth of 16 has 2 years remaining, and a baby of 1 has 17 years to go before attaining majority. The relationship between the two

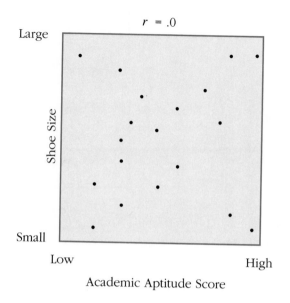

Figure 14–4.   Bivariate Distribution for Academic Aptitude Scores and Shoe Sizes

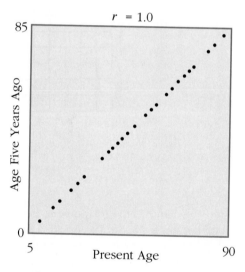

Figure 14–5.   Scattergram between Present Age and Age Five years Ago

measures is again a perfect one; prediction is perfect. But in this instance, high values on one variable are associated with low values on the other; the relationship is therefore negative. Such a perfect negative correlation is represented as $r = -1.0$.

Figures 14–5 and 14–6 show the limits within which correlation coefficients can vary. The smallest possible value is $r = -1.0$, signifying a perfect negative relationship. The largest possible value is $r = +1.0$, representing a perfect positive correlation. Either of these extreme values enables perfect prediction of one variable from the other. Midway between these extreme values is $r = 0.0$, which represents the absence of any relationship and the complete inability to predict a person's status on

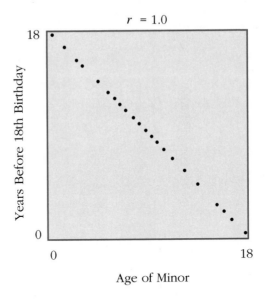

Figure 14–6. Bivariate Distribution for Age of Minor and Number of Years Remaining in Minority

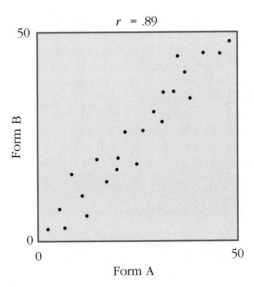

Figure 14–7. Scatter Diagram for Forms A and B

one variable from his or her status on the other. Selected other values of *r* are pictured in Figures 14–7, 14–8, and 14–9.

Figure 14–7 shows a typical correlation between two equivalent forms of a 50-item, published achievement test administered to the same students on two different occasions. The correlation pictured is about .89. The relationship is a positive one (i.e., high scores on one form tend to go with high scores on the other form, and low scores on one form tend to be found with low scores on the other form). However,

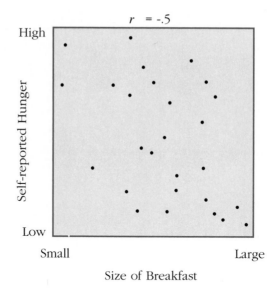

Figure 14–8.   Scatterplot between Size of Breakfast and Midday Hunger

knowledge of a person's score on one test form does not enable perfect prediction of status on the other form; the correlation is imperfect. These last two sentences characterize correlation coefficients that lie between 0.0 and +1.0.

Figure 14–8 displays a hypothetical relationship between the rated size of the breakfast eaten by students and their self-reported hunger at 11:00 A.M. The correlation shown is about −.5. The relationship is negative; high ratings on one variable are most often associated with low ratings on the other variable. Yet knowledge of a particular student's rating on one measure does not enable perfect prediction of her or his rating on the other measure; predictability is imperfect. These last two sentences describe correlation coefficients that fall between 0.0 and −1.0.

For a final example, Figure 14–9 shows a correlation that is about .5.

Computing Pearson r

Our interest is primarily concerned with the meaning of correlation. Therefore, computation will be illustrated by use of a formula that highlights meaning. Recall from Chapter 11 that z-scores express individuals' deviancy from a group mean in standard deviation units. Thus $z = \frac{x}{SD}$. This statistic is very helpful in seeing the meaning of correlation.

The Pearson r is the mean of the products of corresponding z-scores. The form of the formula for *r* that emphasizes this is:

$$r = \frac{\sum z_x z_y}{N}.$$

Suppose we were interested in the relationship between the height and weight of the members of a class. To calculate *r*, we would find each person's height *z*-score, find each person's weight *z*-score, then multiply each person's two *z*-scores together, and finally compute the mean of these products.

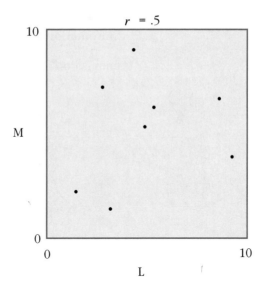

Figure 14–9. Scatterplot between Forms L and M

To work out a simple example, suppose a class of six students has taken quizzes of current events on two consecutive weeks. Their scores are shown below. To compute the r, we convert each person's raw scores into z-scores, multiply these two sets of corresponding z-scores together, and take the mean of their products. This computation is shown in computation Box 14–1.

	Quiz X	Quiz Y
Lousie	8	7
Maxine	10	9
Nicole	7	7
Olive	8	9
Phil	8	7
Quinton	7	3

For readers who may wish to examine another example, Computation Box 14–2 provides one for the correlation between Variables 1 and 2.

Interpreting Pearson r

There are two issues that surface with high frequency when one interprets correlation coefficients. One involves the question of causation. The other concerns the impact of sample variability on correlation size.

Correlation Does Not Imply Causation

When two variables—call them A and B—are correlated, three possible causal explanations exist. A positive or negative relationship between A and B may be caused by any one of more of these three causative patterns:

1. Variable A may cause Variable B.
2. Variable B may cause Variable A.

Computation Box 14–1

Computation of Pearson r

	Quiz X				Quiz Y			
X	x	x^2	z_x	Y	y	y^2	z_y	$z_x z_y$
8	0	0	0	7	0	0	0	0
10	+2	4	+2	9	+2	4	+1	+2
7	−1	1	−1	7	0	0	0	0
8	0	0	0	9	+2	4	+1	0
8	0	0	0	7	0	0	0	0
7	−1	1	−1	3	−4	16	−2	+2
$M_X = 8$		6		$M_Y = 7$		24		+4

$$SD_x = \sqrt{\frac{\Sigma x^2}{N}} = \sqrt{\frac{6}{6}} = \sqrt{1} = 1 \qquad SD_y = \sqrt{\frac{\Sigma y^2}{N}} = \sqrt{\frac{24}{6}} = \sqrt{4} = 2$$

$$r_{xy} = \frac{\Sigma z_x z_y}{N} = \frac{4}{6} = .67$$

Computation Box 14–2

Computation of Pearson r

	Variable 1				Variable 2			
X	x	x^2	z_1	X	x	x^2	z_2	$z_1 z_2$
25	− 4	16	−0.33	30	0	0	0.00	0.00
45	+16	256	+1.33	42	+12	144	+1.33	+1.77
45	+16	256	+1.33	45	+15	225	+1.67	+2.22
17	−12	144	−1.00	27	− 3	9	−0.33	+0.33
21	− 8	64	−0.67	27	− 3	9	−0.33	+0.22
41	+12	144	+1.00	30	0	0	0.00	0.00
25	− 4	16	−0.33	24	− 6	36	−0.67	+0.22
13	−16	256	−1.33	15	−15	225	−1.67	+2.22
232		1152		240		648		+6.98

$M_1 = 29$ $\qquad\qquad$ $M_2 = 30$

$$SD_1 = \sqrt{\frac{1152}{8}} = \sqrt{144} = 12 \qquad SD_2 = \sqrt{\frac{648}{8}} = \sqrt{81} = 9$$

$$r_{12} = \frac{6.98}{8} = .87$$

3. Some other variable(s), C or Cs, may cause A and B to covary (i.e., to be correlated).

As an example, suppose a high school counselor has conducted a study of the relationship between high school grade point average (GPA) and car ownership. Among junior males, the r is found to be $-.4$. It may be tempting to leap to a causal conclusion, particularly if it coincides with one's prior opinion, but the finding does not justify it. It may indeed be true that A causes B along such lines as car ownership diminishes study and grades (perhaps because of "cruising" time as well as time spent working to support the vehicle). Alternatively, it may be that B causes A because persons with poor academic records seek satisfaction elsewhere and are therefore more likely to get cars. Finally, one or more C factors may cause GPA and car ownership to correlate negatively; certain kinds of family values might be plausible candidates for C. In this example, while one might suspect one or another of these causal explanations or suspect that the relationship has more than one cause, the correlational data do not demonstrate which causal explanation is true. Correlation shows relationship; it does not explain the underlying mechanism of the relationship.

For another example, suppose a study was done in an elementary school of the correlation between scores on an academic aptitude test and GPA among fifth-grade students. The r is found to be $.5$. Again it is tempting to leap to a causal explanation such as "high intelligence enables one to earn higher grades." This "A causes B" explanation seems plausible, but the correlation does not prove it.

The opposite explanation—that high academic achievement enables good performance on academic aptitude tests—may not be as appealing, but it *is* plausible to those who realize that the content of tests of cognitive aptitude include many items learned in school. (E.g., "About how long did the Civil War last?" "At what temperature does water freeze?" "Who created Mickey Mouse?" "Why is Martin Luther King, Jr., famous?")

The third alternative, that some other factor(s) cause(s) scores on aptitude tests and GPA to go together, is also plausible. Factors such as intellectual stimulation in the home, achievement motivation, academic interests, encouragement, and books in the home appear to help account for the correlation. Again, however, the mere presence of the correlation does not demonstrate any one or any combination of the causal explanations.

Sample Variability Affects Correlation Size

Another issue that influences interpretation of r concerns variability. The variability of a sample influences the size of the correlation coefficient that will be found in the sample. The more individual differences present among the members of a sample, the greater will be the absolute value of the correlation coefficient if any relationship exists. This feature of rs has widespread application; it influences the interpretation properly given to validity coefficients, reliability coefficients, and innumerable other estimates of relationships between variables.

Suppose, for example, that you attempted to guess the correct age of 10 people. How well would the guess correlate with their actual ages? That is, how valid are the estimates? *It depends on the variability of the group.* If the people were all between 35 and 40, little individual differences in age would be present; as a result you would not be very effective at differentiating among the people who do not differ much. On the other hand, if the people varied in age from 10 to 90, you would have much less trouble recognizing the differences, and the estimates would correlate quite highly with their actual ages.

As another example, suppose Mrs. Kanomaka teaches two sections of physical education. Her second-period class is extraordinarily homogeneous; the class consists almost entirely of average students. Her third-period class is unusually heterogeneous; the class has many excellent students and many inept ones. Suppose Mrs. Kanomaka used her knowledge of students' status during the year to make predictions of how students in each class separately would place in a final-day race. She will likely do much better in her third-period class than in her second-period class. Where great individual differences are present, they are easier to measure and easier to forecast.

QUIZ 14–2

1. The correlation shown in the scatterplot to the right is about
   A. −1.0
   B. −.5
   C. 0.0
   D. +.5
   E. +1.0

2. The correlation in this plot is about
   A. −1.0
   B. −.9
   C. −.5
   D. .0
   E. +.5

3. The correlation in this plot is about
   A. +.9
   B. +.7
   C. +.4
   D. .0
   E. −.3

4. In the plot displayed in the previous item, a particular examinee is above the median on the horizontal variable. On vertical Variable 2, she or he is
   A. certain to be below the median.
   B. likely to be below the median.
   C. equally likely to be above or below the median.
   D. likely to be above the median.
   E. certain to be above the median.

QUIZ 14–2 (cont.)

In the following questions, guess. You are not expected to know the answers. Do not spend time researching the answers. Just guess. The feedback will help you develop a "feel" for the meaning of correlational data.

5. Among adults, arm length and leg length correlate about _____.

6. Independent measures of reading rate and reading comprehension in adults correlate about _____.

7. Scores on a modern language aptitude test and grades received in a foreign language a year later correlate about _____.

8. The strength of grip at age eight of identical twins correlates about

    _____.

9. Adult stature of same-gender siblings correlates about _____.

10. Among all the children in a K–6 elementary school, scores on a wide-range vocabulary test and weight correlate about _____.

KEY TO QUIZ 14–2

1. C. No relationship is evident.

2. B. There is a strong, albeit imperfect, negative relationship.

3. C. The relationship is definitely positive, but it is weak.

4. D. This is best shown by drawing a vertical line at about the median for Variable 1. Now, of those persons above the median on Variable 1 (i.e., those to the right of the line), how many are above and below the median on Variable 2? This is best revealed by drawing a horizontal line at about the median for Variable 2. This leaves 6 dots in the upper-right cell versus 4 in the lower-right cell. Thus a person who is to the right of the vertical line is most apt to be above the horizontal line.

5. About .7. People with long arms tend to have longer-than-average legs, and inversely. Any guess from about .4 to about .9 is reasonable.

6. About .5. In general, good readers are both good at comprehending and fast; poor readers tend to be both slow and limited in comprehension. Any guess from about .3 to about .7 is good.

7. About .5. The predictability of most secondary school subjects is represented by a correlation between the prediction—e.g., an aptitude test score—and the subsequent criterion measure—e.g., grades. Guesses between .3 and .7 are reasonable.

8. About .9. Knowledge of the strength of grip of one identical twin enables quite accurate prediction of the strength of grip of the other. Guesses between about .8 and .99 are reasonable.

KEY TO QUIZ 14–2 (cont.)

9. About .5. Knowledge of the height of one sibling is helpful in guessing the height of others, but considerable differences will exist. Guesses between about .3 and .7 are good.

10. About .9. Does it surprise you that weight and vocabulary—two seemingly unrelated attributes—would correlate?

    Among persons of the same age, they would not be expected to correlate; if you guessed .0, this was probably your perspective. But the question specified all the children from kindergarten through Grade 6. In general the sixth-graders will know many more words and weigh much more than the kindergartners. Because of the extraordinary variability in each variable among *all* the children in the school, the correlation is great. (Of course, the variability only influences non-zero correlations. If two variables were totally unrelated, then no amount of variability would create a correlation.)

    This question provides an opportunity to review two important points. First, the variability of a group influences the correlation. As just noted, among children of the *same* age or grade, the correlation between weight and vocabulary would be negligible. Similarly, among children whose vocabulary scores and/or weights are all quite similar (i.e., among those who do not vary much on vocabulary and/or on weight), there will be little correlation between vocabulary and weight; *when there is little or no variation, there can be little or no co-variation.* This is not a mere play on words, it is at the heart of the relationship between sample variability and *r.*

    Second, correlation does not demonstrate causation. If it did, then a physician concerned about a child being underweight might reasonably prescribe vocabulary drill! Likewise, a teacher who believed that correlation proved causation might attempt to remediate a vocabulary deficiency by prescribing a high caloric diet!

Criterion-Related Validity Evidence

Many tests (usually published ones) are used to make predictions. Some predictive uses help examinees make better decisions, as in educational or vocational counseling. Other predictive uses enhance institutional select/reject decisions, as in educational admissions decisions and in business, industry, and government hiring decisions. Still other predictive uses of tests help institutions make better decisions about how to serve their clients. For example, a diagnostic test ought to be capable of prediction; as noted in Chapter 1, there would be no constructive point in labeling a problem if the label did not suggest a helpful intervention. "Validity of predictions is checked by follow-up" (Cronbach, 1984, pp. 126–127).

This follow-up, known as **predictive validation**, compares the original test scores with scores of one or more criterion measures. "In this context the criterion is the variable of primary interest. . . . The choice of the criterion and the measurement procedures used to obtain criterion scores are of central importance" (American Psychological Association, 1985, p. 11). The criterion measure should be dependable, free from bias, and credible (Cronbach, 1990, p. 153).

Other tests (usually published ones) are sometimes used as substitutes for measures that would be preferred if they were equally inexpensive, safe, and convenient. For example, a paper-pencil test about cooking might be used as an economical substitute for a more "authentic" performance test. A skin patch test may be used in tuberculosis screening as a cost-effective and safer substitute for a chest X-ray. A short paper-pencil personal adjustment survey could be used as a substitute for a lengthy interview by a skilled clinician. When substitute measures are used, their validity should be checked.

Such checking, known as **concurrent validation**, compares the results obtained with the substitute measure with those secured from the variable of primary interest. Here too, the criterion measure should be dependable, free from bias, and credible.

The above examples may give the impression that criterion-related validation is less relevant to teacher-made tests than is content-related validation. That is correct. Why then do classroom teachers need to know about criterion-related validation? The main reason is that teachers use, and at times must evaluate the adequacy of, published instruments. They should be able to judge the adequacy of published tests by use of *all three* kinds of evidence. Professionals who use a test must be able to evaluate its validity and judge the extent to which the scores support various kinds of decisions (American Psychological Association, 1985, p. 41).

Two kinds of criterion-related validity evidence have now been identified. These can be outlined, and put in perspective, as follows:

Kinds of Validity Evidence:

I. Content-Related
II. Criterion-Related:
    A. Predictive
    B. Concurrent
III. Construct-Related

Before examining predictive and concurrent validation in more detail, a caution may be helpful. Do *not* anticipate a one-to-one correspondence between the three kinds of validity evidence and the three tracks of the model of relationships. There isn't one. This point was inherent in Item 2 of Quiz 14–1.

Predictive Validation

Many educational decisions are based on forecasts. Following are examples of the kinds of questions that call for predictions. In each case, the prediction would assist the decision-making process. Educators want the forecasts to be as accurate as possible. Moreover, they want to know just how accurate their imperfect predictions are.

- What grade in first-year, high school French would Agnes most likely receive if she takes the course?

- Would Amanda benefit more from regular instruction in math than from acceleration?

- How much earnings per year would Beth average if she enters job X?

- About what freshman GPA would Del earn at College A? At College B?

Many predictive situations call for personnel-type decisions that are made by institutions concerning selection or hiring. Others are made by institutions regarding how best to meet the needs of their clientele (e.g., "Should John be classified as learning disabled?"). Still other predictive situations require decisions by clients themselves (e.g., "Should I go to College X?" or "Should I take algebra next year?").

Investigating Predictive Validity

How might a researcher go about investigating the validity of a test for certain predictive purposes? Clint Weber is an eighth-grade counselor. He helps students decide whether to elect French in ninth grade. Prominent among the considerations is the question of how well each student would perform in French if the course were elected. (Of course, this is not the only consideration. For example, one might also well ask if the student has any need to know French.)

Mr. Weber might consider several reasonable predictors. He could use grades in eighth-grade English to predict grades in French. He could use scores on an English achievement test. He could employ scores of a commercially marketed modern language prognosis test. He might use results of a general academic aptitude test. He decides to consider two: first-semester grades in eighth-grade English and scores on a modern language aptitude test.

The research design is a follow-up study conducted in a way that does not let the study itself influence the findings. The predictive validation of eighth-grade English grades could be conducted with "canned data." Mr. Weber need only go to past records to secure information about previous students' (a) grades in eighth-grade English and (b) subsequent grades in French. This provides two variables for each student. When these two variables are correlated (after converting grades into numbers; e.g., A = 4, B = 3, C = 2, D = 1, and F = 0), the resulting r is a **predictive validity coefficient**. Suppose Mr. Weber's computations based on the 150 students who took French during the past two years reveal that $r = .49$. This figure provides an answer to the question, "How valid is his use of eighth-grade English grades to forecast grades in first-year French?"

The predictive validation of the scores of the modern language aptitude test would require Mr. Weber to administer the predictive test to a sample of eighth-grade students. He might administer it to the eighth-grade class in March or April and put the results aside *without reporting them to anyone.* (If the participating students' aptitude scores were known to themselves or to their French teacher, this information might influence how hard the students would work or how the teacher might treat them or perceive their work. The researcher must safeguard against possible contamination of the criterion measure.)

Once the criterion measure has matured (i.e., after the midyear French grades become available), Mr. Weber can convert these grades to numbers and compute the correlation between the French grades and the aptitude test scores. This *r* is a predictive validity coefficient.

First-semester French grades served as the criterion of success in the course. They are, of course, not the only criterion that might be considered. Suppose Mr. Weber also had a published French achievement test that was suitable for midyear administration. The scores of this test could be correlated with each predictor. He would now have a total of four predictive validity coefficients. Typical results might be:

Predictor	Criteria	
	French Grades	French Achievement Test Scores
English Grades	.49	.52
Aptitude Scores	.52	.54

These results conform to the general findings that test scores are, other things being equal, better predictors than are grades in individual courses. Also, they illustrate the generalization that, other things being equal, test scores are predicted more accurately than are grades. In view of the discussion in Chapter 12 of some of the common faults with grades, it should not be surprising that they often prove to be less adequate than test scores as either predictors or criteria.

Validity Generalization/Situational Specificity of Criterion-Related Validity Findings

If you worked in another school, would you be safe in assuming that Mr. Weber's findings of a .49 *r* between eighth-grade English grades and French grades would generalize to your school? To some extent, yes, but a number of factors can cause substantial school-to-school variations in findings.

One is random simple sampling error. Mr. Weber's study was based on 150 students. While this should give reasonably stable or generalizable findings, one would not expect them to replicate perfectly if he were to repeat the study. Some inconsistency of findings would be expected because of chance factors associated with the sample. (Consider, for example, the presence in one group of a highly gifted student for whom an A is forecast but who experiences a severe emotional disturbance and receives an F. This one extreme person can markedly impact the size of the *r* in a sample of Mr. Weber's size.) Of course, other things being equal, greater confidence can be placed in the generalizability of findings from larger samples than from findings from smaller samples.

Another factor that can cause validity findings to differ from school to school concerns the reliability and validity of French teachers' grading practices. The results reported for Mr. Weber's school were rather typical. If the French teacher in School X had grading practices that do not focus on terminal level of student achievement, then, other things being equal, the validity findings in School X would be depressed. Or if the French teacher in School Y practiced unusually sound grading procedures, then the extent to which the predictor could forecast French grades in School Y would be enhanced.

Another thing that causes teacher-to-teacher variation is the composition of the criterion measure. Recall the differences among Miss Foix, Mr. Hwang, and Mrs.

Dubois in their emphasis of the written language, the oral language, and French culture. In a school where the predictive English grades were based mainly on written work, they would do a much better job, other things being equal, in predicting French grades in a course with a heavy orientation toward the written language than in one directed more toward other outcomes.

Another reason for significant situation-to-situation fluctuation in validity findings is the reliability of the predictor measure—the eighth-grade English grades in Mr. Weber's case. Even where predictor measures have a given composition, their reliabilities may differ. Other things being equal, more reliable predictive measures forecast more accurately than less reliable ones.

Yet another factor that can cause great situation-to-situation variation in predictive validity findings concerns the variability of the samples. Other things being equal, samples that are more heterogeneous with respect to the predictive and criterion measures will yield greater predictive validity findings than will samples that are more homogeneous.

Concurrent Validation

Many educational decisions are based on measures that substitute for the "real things." Following are examples of the kinds of questions that call for substitute measures. In each case, the substitute measure would assist in decision making. For each example it will also be seen that some considerations relevant to construct-related validation and/or content-related validation would also be helpful in judging the validity of a given test use.

> Example 1: How well do the scores on a short paper-pencil aptitude test correlate with the Full Scale IQs of the *Wechsler Intelligence Scale for Children–III (WISC–III)*?

This is a relatively straightforward situation in which concurrent criterion-related validation would assess the adequacy of a test in a given situation. The indicated research design calls for a sample of examinees to take both the paper-pencil test and the more highly regarded WISC–III. The two sets of scores are then correlated to find a concurrent validity coefficient. This provides information with which to judge the adequacy of the substitution of the paper-pencil measure for the more costly one. Of course, validity is being traded for economy; the findings of the study would inform the decision concerning the acceptability of the trade-off.

One could well argue that the WISC–III really is not the ultimate measure and that the original question would better have been, "How well do the scores on this short paper-pencil test represent the domain of content assessed by the WISC–III?" Phrased in this way, the WISC–III is no longer seen as *the* criterion, but is conceptualized as a fallible *criterion estimate*. In this case, the methods of construct validation would also be applicable.

> Example 2: How well does a 10-minute test measure knowledge of algebra as assessed with a two-hour final examination?

In this example too, the criterion measure—the two-hour final—is clearly imperfect. One can have a group of students take both tests and correlate the two sets of scores. While this will provide an indicator of how good the short test is *as a substitute*, it will not address the question of how adequate the shorter measure is as a survey of the entire domain (including aspects not sampled by the criterion measure). The latter concerns content-related validation.

Example 3: How good an indicator is a short paper-pencil woodworking test of actual woodworking skill?

Here too, a criterion-related validation study would involve giving two tests to a group of persons similar to those for whom the short paper-pencil test was intended. The Pearson *r* would be a concurrent validity coefficient.

Is this, however, as much of the "whole picture" as was the case in the above two examples? No, because no criterion measure is specified in the research question. The findings of the validation study will depend in large measure on the characteristics of the criterion measure(s) selected or created. What blend of woodworking skills should the criterion test contain? For a given sample in a given situation, there are as many possible concurrent validity coefficients as possible criterion tests. Considerations of what should be used for the criterion test(s) involve both content and construct validation issues.

QUIZ 14-3

1. Suppose you have just purchased a bathroom scale and are having second thoughts concerning how good a buy it was. How might its validity best be investigated? What kind of validity evidence would be most relevant to answering this question?

2. Would the variability of the sample used to validate your scale influence your findings?

KEY TO QUIZ 14-3

1. This calls for concurrent validation. Have a group of people weighed on both your scale and on a recognized one (such as the one in your physician's office). Correlate the two sets of scores. This *r* is a criterion-related (and, of course concurrent) validity coefficient.

2. Yes. To illustrate why, consider two small samples, one homogeneous and one heterogeneous.

Homogeneous Sample	Heterogeneous Sample
99 lbs.	50 lbs.
100 lbs.	100 lbs.
101 lbs.	150 lbs.
102 lbs.	200 lbs.
103 lbs.	250 lbs.

KEY TO QUIZ 14–3 (cont.)

Suppose your scale typically errs by a pound or two in either direction. In the homogeneous sample, this much error will likely cause several people in your sample to be wrongly rank-ordered. In the heterogeneous sample, however, this much error will not cause anyone to be wrongly ranked.

Here is another way of looking at it. In the homogeneous sample the amount of error of measurement—a pound or two—is great in *comparison* to the minor individual differences present. In the heterogeneous sample, however, this same amount of measurement error is minor in *comparison* to the great individual differences present.

Construct-Related Validity Evidence

Some devices are designed to measure abstract psychological characteristics such as abstract reasoning, numerical ability, introversion, reading comprehension, physical endurance, and leadership. Attributes such as these are called constructs because they are theoretical constructions about the underlying nature of observable behavior (American Psychological Association, 1985, p. 9). Construct validation concerns the extent to which such devices assess the targeted constructs—and nothing else.

Construct validation *consists of building a strong logical case based on circumstantial evidence that a test measures the construct it is intended to measure.* It involves explaining test scores and revealing the network of their relationships with other variables. Like other scientific exploration, it involves interactions among curiosity, speculation, data collection, and critical review of possible interpretations of the evidence (Cronbach, 1990).

Construct-related validity evidence is widely applicable; it spans the psychomotor, affective, and cognitive domains. It is central to the study of measures intended to assess abstract constructs, such as academic aptitude, anxiety, or dogmatism. In addition, construct-related validation is used to supplement the content-related validation of achievement tests and the criterion-related validation of tests used for prediction or as substitutes for preferable tests.

Content-related validity evidence has been shown to be judgmental, while criterion-related evidence is always quantitative, usually correlational. Construct-related validity evidence is quantitative, sometimes correlational and sometimes not. It also has a foundation in logic.

Examples of Construct-Related Validation Studies

Many kinds of logical evidence are useful in construct-related validation, and an introductory treatment can only scratch the surface. Following are five disparate examples selected to (a) illustrate some educationally important kinds of construct-related validity evidence, (b) show the breadth of kinds of evidence used, and (c) provide the flavor of the process of simultaneously building a circumstantial case that a construct and the device used to assess people's status on it are both valid.

Construct-Related Validity Evidence for an Intelligence Test

Suppose a new individually administered test of general academic aptitude (i.e., present aptitude for school-type learning) has been devised for use with 6- to 12-year-old children. The author is planning to conduct construct-related validation studies in order to build a circumstantial case that anticipated uses of the test will be valid. An early step might be to contemplate the nature of the construct and to speculate on its relationship to other constructs. This kind of thinking might lead to several expectations:

1. We conceive of aptitude between ages 6 and 12 to be in a *state of growth.* Therefore, the raw scores of the test should increase with age between ages 6 and 12.

2. We think of academic aptitude at these ages as being an *increasingly stable* attribute. Therefore, we predict that the consecutive-year correlations between scores will increase with age. For example the *r* between scores of children tested at age 7 and retested at age 8 will be a little lower than the *r* between scores secured at ages 10 and 11.

3. When children at each age are considered separately, scores will *not* correlate significantly with those variables thought to measure attributes that are *un*related to academic aptitude. Examples of such variables are weight, height, and strength of grip.

4. When children at each age are considered separately, scores will correlate in the low positive range (say from +0.1 to +0.4) with those of variables thought to measure constructs only modestly correlated with academic aptitude. Examples of such constructs are interpersonal relations, some kinds of creativity, leadership, and family socioeconomic status.

5. When children at each age are considered separately, scores will correlate in the moderate range (say from +.3 to +.7) with those of constructs believed to be moderately correlated with academic aptitude. Examples are recent school grades, near future school grades, and scores of achievement batteries that assess present achievement status.

6. When children at each age are considered separately, scores will be moderately highly correlated (say +.6 to +.8) with those of variables that measure similar constructs. Examples would be other tests of academic aptitude. (Note these are not necessarily concurrent validation studies because the other tests are not necessarily considered to be superior criteria by which the new test can be assessed. Nor would they likely attempt to assess the same blend of aptitude components. Therefore the author would not want extremely high *r*s. Indeed if the new, individually administered test's scores correlated very highly with those of more convenient and less expensive group-administered ones, it would be cause *not* to use the new test.)

Readers will have arrived at the impression that this construct-related validation example could continue indefinitely. Construct validation is open-ended. Networks of meaningful relationships can be explicated indefinitely.

Partial Construct Validation of an Anxiety Scale

Suppose a new instrument is designed to measure, via self-report, questionnaire items, college students' typical anxiety. Suppose its manual reports results of the following three construct-validation studies with suitable samples of college students.

First, a sample was given a simple, global self-report item involving typical level of anxiety. This self-rating correlated .4 with the total score on the new anxiety scale. This finding suggests that the scale measures something that people could self-rate, but does not agree very well with it. The scale author would have anticipated such a finding because the new scale was designed to be superior to simple self-reports. Hence this is not a concurrent-validity coefficient because the other variable was not a highly credible criterion.

Next the manual reports a correlational study in which each person was rated on several anxiety-related items by at least three roommates or others living in the same dormitories. The mean peer rating for each person was correlated with the scale's scores; the $r = .7$. This measure comes closer to being a criterion, and this study could be said to provide criterion-related validity evidence. Yet there are surely, aspects of anxiety of which peers may ordinarily be unaware; this fact would show that the mean of peer ratings is not a fully adequate criterion measure and that the study is, therefore, one yielding construct-related validity evidence.

Finally, suppose each person in a sample took the anxiety scale and provided her or his GPA. Figure 14–10 shows (and exaggerates) the resulting relationship; people with middle-level anxiety scores tend to have higher grades than do those with either higher or lower anxiety scores. Summarizing this relationship with a *linear* correlation such as the Pearson *r* would be a mistake because it would obscure the very real relationship that is present. Fortunately, the scatterplot reveals the curvilinear relationship (and nonlinear statistics exist to report it).

Does this relationship evidence validity or invalidity of the anxiety scale? It depends on the nature of the construct the scale is supposed to tap. If the scale had been designed to assess only negative attributes that are universally distracting, dis-

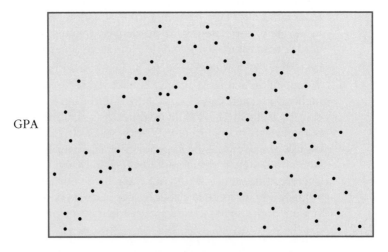

GPA

Anxiety Score

Figure 14–10.   Scatterplot between Anxiety and GPA

abling, and harmful, the finding would erode the claim of validity for the scale and/or the construct. On the other hand, if "anxiety" had been conceptualized to include qualities that are beneficial in small amounts (e.g., challenge, engagement, attentiveness, motivation) as well as negative if present in excessive amounts, then the above findings would support the validity of the scale and the construct.

Construct Exploration of a Geometry Aptitude Test

Suppose we are considering use of a geometry aptitude test to help high school students decide whether to take geometry. The kind of evidence in which we are most interested (and most expect to find in the test manual) is predictive. Assume the manual reports predictive validity coefficients for end-of-year geometry grades. In the total sample, consisting of 12 schools, $r = .51$. The findings for the grades criterion range from .34 to .65 in the 12 schools. These predictive validity findings are consistent with expectations.

Suppose in one large school, the validity of the aptitude test for predicting geometry grades was .53. In addition, its correlation with several other end-of-tenth-grade grades are:

Geometry	.53
Biology	.45
Social Studies	.45
English	.38
Physical Education	.22
Keyboarding	.21

Although the first entry above reports a predictive, criterion-related validity finding, the constellation of correlations serves a different purpose. The test did the best job in doing the thing it was designed to do, and it did successively poorer jobs in doing things less related to the thing it was designed to do. Collectively, these findings not only support use of the test as a predictor of geometry grades, but further suggest that it is discriminating in predicting geometry grades. This is what one would expect of a test purporting to measure geometry aptitude.

Now suppose I become concerned about possible speededness of the test. My concept of geometry aptitude involves a construct much more of power than speed. Yet I suspect that the test is somewhat speeded. If the manual indicates that 89% of the reference group attempted at least one of the last three items of the 50-item test, I might put my concern to rest.

To pursue the matter, a random half of a sample of typical examinees could be tested with standard time limits, while the other half would take it with much more time. (Of course, the scores of this latter group would not be used for counseling. The standard directions were violated, so the use of reference-group data would be meaningless.) Suppose the mean raw scores for the two groups are 36.2 and 37.0. The generous amount of extra time only enabled students to get an average of .8 more items correct, further suggesting that the scores are not very influenced by speed.

Construct Clarification of a Test of Silent-Reading Comprehension

Suppose a reading comprehension test consists of 40, 4-option, multiple-choice items. Of course, the kind of validity evidence of primary interest for an achievement test is content-related. Assume that scrutiny of the test reveals that it is a good measure of our notion of what silent-reading comprehension is. However, before adopting the test, we check some research studies of this test reported in journals in order to supplement the content-related evidence with construct-related evidence.

Suppose a well-designed study of passage dependence is found. A sample of 400 pupils was randomly assigned to two groups. One group took the test under standard conditions. The other took it with the passages removed in order to see how well the items could be answered without access to the materials on which they are based. The chance-level score for this 40-item, four-option, multiple-choice test is 10. It would, therefore, be expected that the mean score of the group that took the test without the passages would be near 10. Suppose, however, that their mean score turns out to be 20, while that of the group taking the test under standard conditions is 30.

The mean of 30 is more than 20, so the researchers conclude that the test measures reading comprehension. Recall, however, that it is supposed to measure reading comprehension *and nothing else*. The mean of 20 is so much more than the chance-level score of 10 that the investigators conclude that the test measures something other than reading comprehension—and a lot of it! Such findings would, if replicated, be quite damaging to validity claims.

Recall from Chapter 6 the recommendation to ensure context dependence of teacher-made interpretive exercises by using novel stimuli and being sure items are based on these stimuli. Teachers who do this for their classroom tests are attending to this important aspect of validity.

Now suppose that the test (like many reading tests) provides separate scores in six "subskills" (e.g., reading for literal meaning, reading for inferred meaning, identifying passage themes, and recognizing cause-effect relationships), and that a profile of the scores is provided for each examinee so that teachers "can remediate specific weaknesses." Such scores, being based on only six or seven items each, would rightly be suspect. How reliable are such short measures likely to be? Not very. Moreover, over half a century of attempts have failed to produce tests that are very effective in differentially assessing reading-comprehension subskills.

For a construct-related validity study of the profile of subscores, suppose a researcher administered one form of the test to a sample of students and then (without teachers having results of the test) administered the other form two days later. What fraction of examinees should have the same lowest "subskill" on the two profiles? Certainly much more than the chance-level one-sixth. When the results are tallied, only one-sixth of the examinees has the same lowest subtest on the two forms. In other words, the lowest subscore could be predicted just as well by rolling a die as by consulting the results of the test! The profile appears to be totally worthless and should not be used. (*Aside:* Many published reading tests and informal reading inventories provide such profiles, and they would fare little better than this imaginary test if the above study were conducted. Teachers should beware (e.g., see Cummings, 1982; Schreiner, Hieronymus, & Forsyth, 1969).

Construct Explication of a Social Studies Test

A published test of middle school social studies will serve as the final example of construct validation. As with the previous examples, only a few of the many kinds of possible data will be illustrated. Those that follow have been selected to illustrate additional aspects of construct validation.

1. To help prospective users judge how well the test measures the local curriculum, the authors provide in the test manual a detailed description of how content specifications were drawn up and how they allocated relative emphasis among several levels of mental processes. (This information relates to content-related validity evidence.)

2. The manual also describes how the test items were reviewed for accuracy and item flaws by experts in the social sciences and by measurement specialists. (This in itself is only mildly reassuring.) An empirical study is also reported in which examinees were given the social studies test and were independently assessed for test wiseness. These two measures correlated only a trivial .09. (This adds much credence to the claim that the test's scores are not impacted by individual differences in test-wiseness, which, of course, is something the test is not supposed to measure.)

3. The manual further describes how representatives of various minority groups reviewed the test content for "bias." (Although appropriate, this, in itself, does not guarantee the absence of some of the kinds of detrimental bias that will be discussed later in this chapter.)

4. For each student participating in the norming, the most recent social studies grade was secured. These grades correlated .48 with the test scores. (If social studies grades were deemed to be better measures of those aspects of achievement assessed by the test, this would best be called a criterion-related validity finding. However, since grades in hundreds of different classes do not represent a uniform attribute, they are not in any sense an "ultimate" criterion against which to evaluate the new test. Therefore, this might be regarded as a construct-related validation study.)

5. The manual reports that the social studies test scores correlated .47 with scores of a critical thinking test and .51 with scores of a reading comprehension test. (The constructs of critical thinking and reading comprehension would reasonably be thought to be positively correlated with, yet distinct from, social studies achievement. This would lead us to expect correlations that represent significant relationship, yet are much lower than the reliabilities of the respective tests. Since the findings were consistent with expectations, they add credence to the belief that the test is valid.)

6. The manual reports that 80% of the norming sample attempted one or more of the last five items. For at least 20% of examinees, its scores appear likely to be influenced by speed. For those whose definition of social studies achievement focuses on power and explicitly excludes consideration of speed, this degree of speededness would evidence invalidity. On the other hand, for teachers whose construct of achievement includes student ability to work at a reasonable pace, this degree of speededness might enhance validity.

A Different Perspective

The last three examples illustrated how construct-related validation is appropriate for special-purpose aptitude tests (which are mainly validated with predictive studies) and for achievement tests (which are primarily validated on the basis of content considerations). These examples illustrate the important point that it is not sufficient to rely on only one category of evidence of the validity of a particular test use (Messick, 1989).

While this point was being driven home, some readers may have wondered where content- or criterion-related evidence leaves off and where construct-related notions begin. The boundaries are blurred. Traditional ways of categorizing validity evidence have led to the three major categories. "However, because content- and criterion-related evidence contribute to score meaning, they have come to be recognized as aspects of construct validity. In a sense, then, this leaves only one category, namely, construct-related evidence" (Messick, 1989, p. 20). This leads to an alternative outline to the one shown on page 397.

Traditional View	Alternative View
Kinds of Validity Evidence:	Kinds of Construct-Related Validity Evidence:
I. Content-Related	I. Content-Related
II. Criterion-Related	II. Criterion-Related
A. Predictive	A. Predictive
B. Concurrent	B. Concurrent
III. Construct-Related	III. Other

How can common usage, outlined on the left, be reconciled with the newer thinking outlined on the right? Most scholars continue to use the notions of content- and criterion-related validity evidence, but do not consider either to be wholly discrete. It is acceptable for different persons to classify a given kind of information (e.g., context dependence) in alternative ways (e.g., content- or construct-related).

Instructional Sensitivity

Chapter 9 presented item analysis rationale and procedures as they relate to internal consistency of tests. This, of course, concerns reliability.

At this time, a very different rationale and set of procedures are presented that pertain to instructional sensitivity—a variety of construct-related validity evidence.[2] The rationale for collecting instructional-sensitivity data is based on the construct of academic achievement. Achievement is viewed as something that is enhanced by instruction.[3] Therefore, a valid measure of achievement should yield larger scores for examinees who have been exposed to relevant instruction than for those who have not.

Suppose a test is administered to some students who are about to start a unit. It is also given to an equally capable group that has just completed the unit. The fraction passing each item in each group can be calculated. Here are data for a hypothetical six-item, completion, mastery test.

[2]Many authors refer to these procedures as "item analysis for criterion-referenced tests" (e.g., Gronlund & Linn, 1990; Haladyna & Roid, 1981). I prefer to emphasize that they do not concern reliability by providing them with an entirely different name—instructional sensitivity. I also stress that these procedures are applicable to discriminatory tests having norm-referenced interpretation as well as to mastery tests having domain-referenced interpretations (Hanna & Bennet, 1984).
[3]Achievement is a special case of a large group of construct validation procedures that investigate the impact of various kinds of intervention. Instruction can be viewed as an "intervention."

	Pretest *p*-values (Fraction Passing)	Posttest *p*-values (Fraction Passing)	Instructional Sensitivity (Posttest *p* Minus Pretest *p*)
1.	.00	1.00	1.00
2.	.20	.98	.78
3.	.14	.85	.71
4.	.88	.91	.03
5.	.88	.99	.11
6.	.40	.44	.04

What information can be teased out of such a table? In considering Item 1, notice that the item was perfectly learned *during the unit*—nobody knew it before instruction and everybody knew it after instruction. Thus the item was instructionally sensitive *and* the data suggest that the instruction was effective.

A few students knew Items 2 and 3 before instruction and most did after. The findings suggest that all is well.

The data for Item 4 suggest two problems. First, most knew it before the unit; hence its study might waste their time. Second, 12% did not initially know the item, and 9% still did not on the posttest. Hence the unit seems to have been ineffective in this regard.

Item 5's data are less worrisome. Although most students knew it before the unit, virtually all did after the unit. If its mastery is important, its inclusion in the unit would be appropriate. Some provision for skipping the content would be helpful for the 88% who already knew it.

The data for Item 6 are troublesome in that few examinees seem to have learned its content during the unit. Such findings direct attention (a) to the item (scrutiny of which may reveal a flaw) and (b) to the instruction (contemplation of which may suggest why it seems not to have been effective).

Should maximum instructional sensitivity be sought? In Track A units that deal with novel material, instructional sensitivity should be very high. An example would be knowledge of English equivalents of a dozen Japanese verbs. Initial knowledge may be near zero and terminal knowledge may be nearly perfect. In such a context, it is reasonable to look on instructional sensitivity as an attribute to be maximized.

In Track C units that involve more familiar material that cannot be mastered, instructional sensitivity cannot be as high. Moreover, it is not desirable to maximize it. An example would be applications of the First Amendment to the U.S. Constitution. Instructional sensitivity cannot be maximized because some students will have already gained some grasp of the content. Thus the pretest *p*-values will tend to be well above zero.

Moreover, a posttest should not be so easy that everyone receives nearly perfect scores on it. That event would render the test completely *un*reliable; it would not reveal the individual differences in achievement that are present. As was shown in Chapter 9, pursuit of discriminatory items leads test makers to seek items of moderate levels of difficulty.

Therefore, in the context of discriminatory testing in Tracks B and C, instructional sensitivity is desirable only in moderation. While items are expected to be somewhat easier after instruction than before, all students are not expected either to be ignorant of every item before a unit or to have achieved perfect command of all items after the unit (Bennett, 1984).

QUIZ 14–4

For each of the following test uses, select the one most appropriate kind of validity evidence, using the following key.

A. Content-related validation

B. Predictive criterion-related validation

C. Concurrent criterion-related validation

D. Construct-related validation

1. A test used to assess students' creativity

2. This quiz used to assess comprehension of this section

3. An inexpensive device used for home self-measurement of blood pressure

4. A mastery test used to measure student achievement in a fifth-grade social studies unit

5. A discriminatory test used to measure achievement in a fifth-grade social studies unit

6. An aptitude test used to predict success in the study of bookkeeping

KEY TO QUIZ 14–4

1. D   Creativity is a psychological construct.

2. A   Content considerations dominate (although they do not monopolize) the validation of achievement tests.

3. C   Focus would probably be on how well the "scores" agree with those of the physician's better device used by a qualified nurse. However, a case could be made for direct assessment of the instrument's adequacy similar to the way it might be done for the physician's own sphygmomanometer.

4. A   Content-related validation is the most relevant to classroom achievement tests, regardless of track. Of course, various kinds of construct-related evidence, such as instructional sensitivity, would also be helpful.

5. A   Content-related evidence is the most relevant to typical achievement test uses, regardless of whether the tests measure Track A, Track B, or Track C content.

6. B   Since the test is designed for prediction, concern will focus on predictive validity in the kinds of situations in which the test will be used. Of course, various kinds of construct-related evidence would be useful to supplement the predictive evidence.

Validity and Decision Making

Repeated emphasis has been directed to the important principle that tests should be used to facilitate better decision making. Ordinarily, one should not use a test unless it is likely to help someone make a better decision. A physician should not order a blood test for anemia unless she or he intends to receive the results and use them to take appropriate action. Nor should a teacher administer a classroom or published test if the results are not intended to be useful in making a decision.

Before proceeding, a delimitation is in order. The above does not argue that tests serve *only* this decision-making function. Repeated emphasis has also been given to the role that tests play in prompting, guiding, and pacing student study. Such roles are vital to informed professional use of tests.

Nonetheless, the present focus is on the use of tests as *instruments that inform decisions*. Four examples will highlight the conceptualization of validity in terms of the extent (if any) to which *use* of a data source enlightens decision making.

Example: Mastery Test for Track A Content

In teaching content that is essential in its own right or is essential for subsequent work in the subject because the subject matter is highly sequential, mastery testing makes good sense. Use of a mastery test is *valid* to the extent it helps the teacher make wise instructional *decisions* regarding whether to advance individual pupils to the next topic.

One should consider carefully which kind of error is the more serious, recycling a pupil who could succeed if advanced or advancing one who will later falter. *This is the underlying consideration in establishing passing standards for mastery tests.* In some circumstances (e.g., a unit on capitalization of proper nouns), the consequences of premature advancement are minor; the pupil would be quickly recognized and given additional instruction. In other situations (e.g., knowing how to use the brake of a car before driving it), the consequences of premature advancement are disastrous.

Example: Mastery Test for Track B and Track C Content

In teaching content that is not vital, mastery testing does *not* ordinarily make good sense. When the decision to advance is appropriate for all the students, preventing some from advancing is counterproductive. One does not have to master *Catcher in the Rye* (whatever "mastery" would mean) before studying *Robinson Crusoe*. Nor does one have to "master" basketball dribbling before practicing free throws. Therefore, use of mastery tests with Track B and C content is *not* ordinarily valid.

Example: Modern Language Aptitude Test

Next, reconsider Clint Weber's use of an aptitude test to predict students' success in French. His predictive validation studies yielded coefficients of about .5. Here too, one should consider which kind of error is more serious—a student who would do poorly in French decides to take it or a student who would do well in the subject decides not to take it. This is probably not a question we should ordinarily answer for others. Such questions are usually best decided by individual students and their parents. Their differing answers will reflect their various levels of interest in and/or need for French, as well as the degrees to which they are willing to take risks. Thus in this counseling application, good decisions may best be conceptualized in terms of what is good *in the client's value system.*

Another issue meriting attention concerns **incremental validity**. Mr. Weber found the test to have predictive validity coefficients of about .5 in his school. But what would have been the predictive validity of the method(s) of prediction he would have used if the test were not available? Suppose that merely asking students, "If you were to take French next year, what grade do you think you would most likely receive?" yielded results that correlated about .5 with next year's French grades. So how much does Mr. Weber's simple use of the aptitude *improve* decision making? Not at all.

Before deciding not to use the test, however, he might well ask, "If I base predictions on the joint use of the test and student self-predictions, what will be the resulting predictive coefficient?" Suppose he decided to weight the two predictors equally[4] by the methods described in Chapter 12. Further suppose this composite prediction is found to correlate .65 with French grades. He wonders if the predictions he could provide his counselees would be *sufficiently better* than the ones from the self-predictions alone to merit the use of the predictive test. That is, he wonders if the incremental validity of the test improves decision making enough to justify its use.[5] If he decides it is, then he should adopt the test.

Example: Teacher Referral of Pupils for Assessment

In this final example of the validity of decision making, the concept of validity is applied to procedures and processes rather than to test usage. Consider the role that classroom teachers play in referring students who *may* need various kinds of special services, ranging from reduced price school lunches to programs for the mentally retarded to speech therapy. The ideas associated with validity are applicable to such decisions of whether to refer for fuller assessment.

Classroom teachers cannot be familiar with the exact criteria for reduced lunch prices, hardness of hearing, giftedness, behavior disorders, mental retardation, and so forth *ad infinitum.* Various specialists are needed to help make such decisions. *The classroom teacher's job is to refer the pupil to a specialist.* This referral, of course, requires awareness of the possible problems that students may have and a commitment to notice enough to alert the specialists when they are needed.

Screening procedures should result in the referral of more people than actually turn out to be diagnosed as having the problem. To see why, consider the two kinds of errors that the screening process can make in, say, identifying primary pupils who may have undiagnosed vision defects. First, it (mis)identifies some children who have adequate vision as having a problem. Second, it fails to identify some children who have a defect. Which kind of error is more serious? They both erode a correlation coefficient the same amount, but they are not equally serious in human

---

[4]The method of determining the relative weight that ideally should be assigned to the separate predictors is beyond the scope of this book. This topic is addressed in most elementary statistics texts under the topic of multiple-regression analysis.

[5]*Caution:* Do not merely subtract .50 from .65 to answer this question. Pearson *r*s do not have equal units of measure and cannot be subjected to arithmetic of this nature. A better way to address the question would be to compare the experience tables (or the corresponding scatterplots) of the .5 and .65 predictive validity coefficients. This comparison will provide a sense of the incremental benefit of the use of the second predictor. It is substantial.

consequences. Flagging a child who ultimately turns out not to have a problem causes no serious harm because the comprehensive assessment that follows will reveal and correct the error. But failing to identify a child who really suffers from a deficit can be very damaging because no subsequent attention is given the case. Thus good *ultimate* decision making is facilitated by screening and referral processes that overidentify more than they overlook.

Consequential Bases of Judging Validity of Test Use

It is hard to disentangle issues of the value implications of test score interpretations from issues of the validity of those interpretations. Even the words "valid" and "value" are derived from the same Latin root. Since validity and values go hand in hand, validation processes should address the value implications of score interpretations (Messick, 1989, pp. 58–59).

For example, it was suggested above that it is better to go to the expense of providing complete vision examination for a youngster who does not turn out to have a defect than to overlook a child who has a vision problem. That contention, of course, reflects my values. Because this value is widely shared, its subjective nature may not attract much attention. Yet it is good to recognize that *values drive interpretations of validity.* For example, a faculty might accept as valid a screening process that picks up all the youngsters who have hearing defects as well as twice that number of others. However, it might reject as invalid a process that identifies three quarters of the children who have problems and no others. This reflects its values, not merely the size of validity coefficients.

Many consequences of test use have not traditionally been considered to be issues of validity. It is perhaps less important to argue that all consequences should be considered under the topic of validity than to insist that *all consequences of test use should be considered,* including unanticipated side effects. Following are examples of appropriate consideration of consequences of test use. The first three examples provide reviews of ideas from earlier parts of this book that are directly relevant to classroom use of teacher-made tests.

Example: Frequent Testing

One reason why teachers engage in classroom testing is to improve decision making. The extent to which the resulting decisions are improved provides one way to assess the validity of the tests. Recall that classroom tests are also "the ring in the nose of the bull." They have power over students. Hence, another way to evaluate validity concerns the desirability of the impact(s) of test use.

Testing frequency influences student learning. In a typical high school class, giving a test every week or two is superior to giving only one a month (Bangert-Drowns, Kulik, & Kulik, 1986), probably owing to its tendency to prompt and pace study and review. The impact of test frequency on learning should be a major factor in deciding how often to test. This consequence of test use is no mere "side effect." It is central to the teacher's purpose.

Example: Offering a Choice of Essay Questions

Many teachers offer students a choice of essay questions on which to write. This practice enables foresightful students to exempt themselves from studying some of a unit's content. In some contexts this will be desirable; in others, it will be undesirable. Either way, *wise teachers anticipate consequences, judge their desirability, and then design testing practices that foster desirable student outcomes and inhibit undesirable ones.*

Example: Assessing Higher Mental Processes

The third example of validity "side effects" emphasizes that teaching is enhanced by harnessing test power so that it "pulls" students in desired directions. If a teacher's tests consistently tap higher levels of mental processing, then the students will be more likely to pursue higher mental processes. Less expert teachers, however, are prone to overemphasize surface learning in their tests. This emphasis tends to direct student effort toward the acquisition of less important material that is likely to be quickly forgotten. Such unfortunate direction of effort is obviously an *un*intended side effect.

As discussed in Chapter 4, effective teachers anticipate the consequences of alternative student assessment practices so that their actions can be fashioned to produce desired effects. They seek this impact. Far from being a mere side effect, this consequential basis for evaluating the validity of test use is central to the integration of student assessment practices into other aspects of effective teaching. Our professional challenge is to foresee the consequences of alternative student assessment practices so that our actions can be fashioned to produce desired effects.

Example: Testing Student Achievement to Evaluate Teachers and Principals

It seems reasonable for society to want to hold schools accountable for the vast resources they receive. In pursuit of accountability, it is sometimes suggested that, since schools are supposed to cause student learning, student learning should be measured in order to judge the success of the schools. This is not a stupid idea, but its advocates are often dangerously naive because such accountability suggestions often neglect to anticipate foreseeable, unintended, undesirable consequences. Reflection brings to light several related reasons for the inadequacy of this suggestion. First, only *some* of a school's outcomes can be tested by means of inexpensive objective paper-pencil questions. Other outcomes (e.g., psychomotor goals, affective outcomes, typical performance objectives, long-term goals) can be assessed with sufficient resources, but not with multiple-choice items. Objective testing would, therefore, provide a valid way to assess *some* of the very important outcomes of schooling, but such tests would have to be supplemented by other assessment techniques (which tend to be more costly).

Next is the issue of input versus output. School populations differ with respect to prior student achievement and aptitude. Advantaged students tend to exit school with superior achievement even if the quality of instruction is only fair. Any competent use of test scores for assessing teaching must make allowances for the unequal entry status of students from teacher to teacher and school to school.

Similarly, differences exist in the resources society invests in education from district to district. Sophisticated evaluation techniques that allow for such differences are needed. Unfortunately, those who propose simplistic use of student achievement measures to hold schools accountable often fail to recognize that the task is not as simple as it may seem.

Third is the reasonable and adaptive tendency for people to be sensitive to the means by which they are evaluated. (Indeed, that is the whole point of the test power theme.) This tendency is not limited to students; it extends to teachers, principals, and superintendents, too.

Now this tendency interfaces with an unfortunate fact that those who seek to hold schools accountable are seldom willing to spend enough on the endeavor to do the job well; they often are looking for "cheap fixes," therefore, assessment is often limited to objective paper-pencil testing.

Given the sensitivity to the test and the desire for a "cheap fix," these two forces can converge to cause evaluation power to push schools to overemphasize easily tested outcomes and to neglect those that are not. Thus use of tests to evaluate schools can cause a serious distortion of the curriculum. Evaluation processes can subvert the thing being evaluated (Smith, 1991).

Fourth, if one's salary or job is dependent on "producing" better test scores, one's goal may well become the production of better test scores. That is *not* the proper aim of education! Schools should be concerned with producing better student learning, of which test scores are a mere indicant (indeed a fairly good indicant *if* they are not distorted).

An analogy may clarify this key point. A physician treating a patient for a temperature might have the proper aim of reducing the temperature. The objective is not merely to reduce the reading of the thermometer. If it were, it could be achieved by having the patient take a sip of cold water before placing the thermometer in the mouth (analogous to teaching to the test). The proper goal is temperature reduction, of which thermometer reading is a mere indicant (indeed a very good one *if* it is not distorted).

The problem then is that using tests to evaluate schools creates a strong temptation to teach to the test. This contaminates the test as an estimate of goal attainment (Haladyna, Nolen, & Haas, 1991), and it distorts the very learning the test is designed to assess. Thus another case arises of validity being situation-specific. A test that is quite valid as one of several low-stakes measures of pupil achievement can become quite invalid if it is used as a high-stakes measure of teacher, school, or district adequacy (Linn, Baker, & Dunbar, 1991). These factors lead most educators to conclude that student achievement test scores should not be used (especially in isolation) to evaluate teachers, schools, or school districts (Madaus, 1991).

Example: Test Bias

Test bias is an aspect of validity that has generated substantial discussion, heat, and research in the past generation. The term "test bias" has so many alternative meanings (Flaugher, 1978) that its unqualified use often results in confused quarreling rather than informed discussion.

One way the term is used by some is closely related to the notion of discrimination. Track B and C tests are designed to reveal relevant individual differences. In this sense, a spelling test is supposed to discriminate against poor spellers, and it should not be criticized for doing so. Yet in one meaning of the word, the test is biased against poor spellers. This is not the way the term is usually used in measurement discussions. The word "fairness" may better capture our meaning.

Bias in Content.   Another way the term "test bias" is used concerns superficial aspects of test content. In this sense a science test that contains traditional gender-role stereotyping in all its application problems might be said to be biased. If this impacts on the relative scores of males and females, then the stereotyping creates a validity issue.

Even if it does not affect scores, the stereotyping is an aspect of face validity that, although not validity, is nevertheless important.

Differences in Groups' Status.   Another meaning of "test bias" concerns mean difference among groups. If whites obtain higher mean scores than blacks on a given test, some would say it is biased. Whether this has anything to do with test validity depends on *why* a mean group difference exists. Suppose the "test" were longevity data. On average, in the United States whites live longer than blacks. That is a fact, and it does not seem sensible to condemn demographers who collect or publish the data. On the contrary, knowledge of such facts promotes awareness of a minority health problem.

Now suppose the test showing the black-white difference is an academic aptitude test. On average, whites receive higher scores than blacks. That is a fact, and it does not seem sensible to condemn the test or its author for the fact. On the contrary, knowledge of the fact promotes the realization that a problem exists. (At least those whose values lead them to consider the inequity undesirable regard it as a problem.) Yet it seems reasonable for minority spokespersons to fear that some people will interpret the fact to mean that there is an inherent superiority of whites over blacks involving aptitude. That *use* of the test data, without consideration of economic, cultural, language, educational, and social differences would, of course, be invalid.

Bias in Screening.   Yet another aspect of bias concerns differential sensitivity of screening mechanisms. Whether screening is done by teachers or by tests, it is possible that a screening process may be more apt to identify a needy person in one group than in another.

For example, teachers may be more apt to notice signs of learning disability in boys than in girls. Thus more boys get referred and identified. Of course, this greater referral of males would not be a source of gender bias if the gender ratio were equal between referral and incidents. However, if a male learning disabled student has a greater chance of being identified than a female one (as Shaywitz, Shaywitz, Escobar, & Fletcher, 1990, found to be the case for reading disability), then selection bias exists. Assuming the interventions for learning disabilities are beneficial, the bias would work to the disadvantage of females with unidentified learning disabilities.

Bias in Scoring.   Whenever test scoring procedures are not completely objective, possible bias in scoring should be considered (Cole & Moss, 1989, p. 207) and, where possible, prevented. It was recommended in Chapter 7 that teachers scoring essay tests should not know whose paper is being read. This also provides protection against ethnic bias, gender bias, and so forth.

Predictive Bias.   A variety of potential test bias that has received much attention concerns systematic underprediction or overprediction for groups. An analogy may provide focus on the predictive aspects of this issue.

Suppose a meteorologist makes daily forecasts of the next day's maximum temperature for Phoenix, Arizona, and for Fairbanks, Alaska. On most days, the predicted temperature for Phoenix is greater than that of Fairbanks. Does this prove the meteorologist is biased? Of course not. The job is to predict. The validity of the enterprise resides in the degree to which the prophecies come true. If the temperatures of the two cities are really going to be different, the job of the forecaster is to predict them correctly.

If, however, the forecaster consistently predicts that one city is going to be cooler than it turns out to be, then there is consistent underprediction for that city. This is the essence of **predictive bias**. This was a rather simple illustration because the validity of the criterion measure was virtually unassailable. Alas, this is rarely the case in education.

Here is a more realistic example (adapted from Cole & Moss, 1989). Suppose the black students in a school score, on average, lower on an academic aptitude test than the white students. Suppose also that the groups differ in the same direction and amount on GPA the following year. The conclusions people draw from these findings will depend on their prior assumptions. To some, the grade difference demonstrates a lack of test bias. (And among those who reject the notion of test bias, some may explain the differences in grades by differences in student opportunity and experience. Others may see them as race-related capacities.) To others, the test score and grade differentials clearly indicate bias in *both* the test and the high school grades.

The topic of bias arising from over- or underprediction is very complex and takes one far beyond consideration of the test under investigation. It also calls attention to issues of fairness in the criterion measures.

Much of the research on this topic has focused on college admission tests. It can be summarized as follows *if* one is willing to accept the validity of the criterion measures (typically college GPA). Empirical investigations of actual test use have typically found either no significant bias of this kind or a slight tendency for the future status of members of minority groups to be *over*predicted (Anastasi, 1988, p. 198).

Differential Validity.   Space permits mention of only one more variety of bias, differential predictive validity among groups. When the predictive validity of tests has been compared between males and females, consistent differences have been reported. In general, the future grades of females have proven more predictable than those of males (Anastasi, 1988, p. 182). Mr. Weber would likely find that the grades his eighth-grade girls will earn in French are forecast more accurately than are those that will be earned by his eighth-grade boys. However, since this difference does not create a systematic advantage for either sex, it is not cause for concern.

That is, the difference is not cause for much concern in Mr. Weber's situation in which (a) the test content is directly relevant to the thing being predicted and (b) the predictive validity coefficients between the sexes do not differ greatly. However, when a predictive test is not intrinsically relevant to criterion performance, there is greater likelihood of finding differences in the validity among ethnic, racial, or gender groups (Anastasi, 1988, p. 194), and this irrelevance of the predictor is a cause for concern about fair test usage. At such times, a predictive test can correlate with some future criterion measure, yet not measure appropriate material.

For an example, consider the selection process for a middle school's boys' basketball team. If a study were done between eighth-grade boys' amount of facial hair at the beginning of the basketball season and their value to the team at mid-season, it would probably be positive. Thus the "test" has predictive validity. Of course, this is not the way to pick the team. It merely capitalizes on a coincidental correlation (for a few years) of facial hair and height (both of which, of course, are caused by puberty). Even though the "test" use would predict, it is not appropriate to use it because it does not measure the right thing—basketball skill. Its irrelevance to the criterion (a) makes it likely to correlate less highly with the criterion than more suitable selection techniques would and (b) creates an unnecessary hazard of unanticipated outcomes.

The unanticipated consequences might be that the facial hair "test" systematically underpredicts the mid-season basketball skill of boys of Asian, African, and Native American descent (who tend to have less facial hair than whites). Therefore, this use of the "test" must be judged to be *in*valid because of its consequences.

In general, well-designed research has not found widely used predictive tests, such as college admissions tests, to be more or less predictive for minority group members than for others (Anastasi, 1988, p. 197).

Chapter Summary

The unitary concept of validity concerns the extent to which tests and other assessment devices measure what they are used to measure and nothing else. Validity can be thought of as the extent to which tests facilitate desirable decision making. Contemporary conceptualization of validity also encompasses the consequences, sought as well as unanticipated, of test use and of test score interpretation. In addressing consequences of test use, values are inevitably blended into the process of making validity judgments.

Three traditional kinds of validity evidence exist. Content-related validity evidence concerns judgments regarding the match between test content and instructional objectives. Content-related validity evidence is the kind of evidence of greatest (but not exclusive) relevance for achievement tests. Appropriate content is built into tests. Part II of this book was devoted to building classroom tests that were valid from a content perspective.

Criterion-related validity evidence is appropriate when one or more credible criterion measures exists against which the utility of a test can be evaluated. For tests used to predict future events, predictive validity coefficients are obtained by correlating the forecasts with the subsequent criterion measures. For tests used as substitute measures, concurrent validity coefficients are computed by correlating the tests' scores with those of the recognized criterion measures. Such coefficients utilize the Pearson r, which is the mean of the product of corresponding z-scores.

Construct-related validity evidence concerns the extent to which a test assesses a psychological construct. A rich diversity of sources of evidence can be used to build a circumstantial case that a test measures what it is being used to measure and nothing else. Such cases are founded in logic and are built with quantitative data. The process tends simultaneously to validate both the test and the construct being assessed.

Suggestions for Further Reading

American Psychological Association. (1985). *Standards for educational and psychological testing.* Washington, DC: Author. Pages 9–18 give a succinct, current, readable statement of professional thinking on the topic of validity and enumerate standards by which the validity evidence of published instruments can be evaluated.

Anastasi, A. (1988). *Psychological testing* (6th ed.). New York: Macmillan. Chapters 6 and 7 take the reader through basic and advanced concepts in an extremely comprehensive, well-organized, comprehensible manner.

Cole, N., & Moss, P. A. (1989). Bias in test use. In Linn, R. L. (Ed.), *Educational measurement* (3rd ed.). New York: Macmillan. This sophisticated analysis of bias provides insights into the multifaceted topic and helps readers realize that there are no simple answers.

Cronbach, L. J. (1990). *Essentials of psychological testing* (5th ed.). New York: Harper & Row. Chapter 5 provides an extraordinarily thoughtful, integrated, and sophisticated treatment of the topic in a remarkably readable style.

Hopkins, K. D., Stanley, J. C., & Hopkins, B. R. (1990). *Educational and psychological measurement and evaluation* (7th ed.). Englewood Cliffs, NJ: Prentice-Hall. Chapter 4 offers a very sound introductory treatment of validity.

Reliability

This chapter completes the treatment of characteristics of effective measuring instruments. Chapter 13 addressed the varied kinds of practical considerations that contribute to or detract from a scale's attractiveness to practitioners. In addition, Chapter 13 addressed the vital factor of interpretability—the need for a test's scores to be referenced either to a tightly defined content domain (to enable meaningful domain referenced interpretation) and/or to a well-described and relevant reference group of other people (to enable meaningful norm-referenced interpretation). Chapter 14 concerned validity, sometimes described as the extent to which a device measures what it is being used to measure and nothing else. Discussion is now turned to reliability.

Basic Concept

Whenever anything is measured, the result contains a certain amount of chance error (Stanley, 1971, p. 356). This chance error makes all measures in all fields of study less than perfectly reliable. *A device's reliability is the extent to which its scores are consistent. Un*reliability, on the other hand, concerns the extent to which measurements are *in*consistent.

Reliability is described as the *consistency* with which a device measures *whatever* it measures. Notice that validity concerns the extent to which an instrument measures what it is supposed to measure, while reliability concerns only the consistency with which it measures. Thus a test that consistently measured the wrong thing (and is therefore invalid) might be highly reliable.

It is unfortunate that the word "reliability" was adopted for the attribute under discussion. To the lay person, the word *reliability* refers to a concept much closer to the measurement concept of *validity*. Feldt and Brennan (1989, p. 106) provide an example from weather prediction. To illustrate the difference in usage between standard English and measurement jargon, the same statement will be made in each dialect:

> *Standard American English:* A meteorological prediction based on accurate and replicable measures of temperature, air pressure, etc., can lead to very unreliable predictions.

> *Measurement jargon:* A meteorological prediction based on reliable measures of temperature, air pressure, etc., can lead to very invalid predictions.

Readers should take pains to use the technical terms in the ways they are defined in the discipline of educational and psychological measurement.

In developing the concepts of reliability and validity, it is critical to grasp the distinction between them. For an extreme but vivid example, suppose a vocabulary test were somehow believed to measure running speed. It would likely be reasonably reliable as a measure of what it measures, yet it would be wholly invalid as a measure of running speed.

For a more realistic example, suppose a poorly constructed vocabulary test contains many item clues. Test-wise students would be at an advantage (as, of course, would students having good vocabularies). The test might be highly reliable, in part because it consistently measures vocabulary (a source of validity) and in part because it consistently measures test-wiseness (a source of invalidity).

Figure 15–1 shows the results of four students' archery tests. Student A consistently hits the bull's eye; this performance is consistently on target—both valid and reliable. Student B is just as consistent as Student A, but is consistently off-target. This performance is reliable but *in*valid. The performance of Student C is much less consistent than that of A and B, yet it centers approximately on target. This performance might be said to be somewhat reliable and somewhat valid. Student D's consistency equals that of Student C, but is off-center as well. This performance is somewhat reliable and quite invalid.

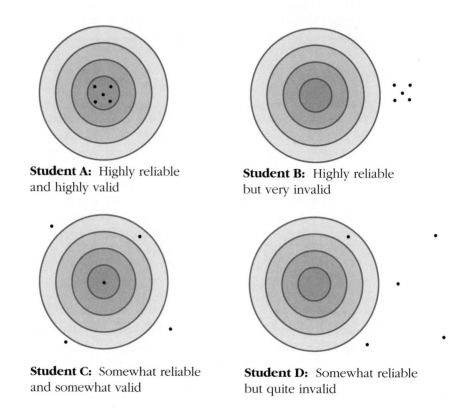

Student A: Highly reliable
and highly valid

Student B: Highly reliable
but very invalid

Student C: Somewhat reliable
and somewhat valid

Student D: Somewhat reliable
but quite invalid

Figure 15–1.   Reliability and Validity of Four Archery Students' Performance

Notice that there can be no student whose performance is always on target yet inconsistent. *Validity cannot exist in the absence of reliability.* Reliability is, therefore, sometimes said to constitute a necessary but not sufficient condition for validity. Although helpful, this fails to emphasize that both reliability and validity exist on continua, not as dichotomies. Thus it might be better to say that the limits of a test's reliability create limits on its potential validity. It is important to realize that consistency does not guarantee validity; consistency merely enables validity.

Nonetheless, reliability is an essential attribute of any measuring instrument in any field. Without some consistency of measure, instruments have no value. A completely unreliable test would be one whose scores are entirely random; use of such a test would be a total waste of time. A table of random numbers or a roulette wheel would provide information just as useful.

Part II of this book has examined ways to make classroom tests as reliable as they can reasonably be. Similarly, published tests should be made as reliable as feasible. The manuals that accompany published instruments should include information about the reliability in enough detail to enable test users to judge whether scores are consistent enough to justify the intended use of the test. The phrase "test scores" in the previous sentence includes the total score, each subscore, and each reported cluster of item scores (American Psychological Association, 1985, p. 20).

Typical users of published tests, such as teachers, do not conduct reliability studies. However, they do have a responsibility to determine that the available information regarding reliability is relevant to their intended test uses and interpretations (American Psychological Association, 1985). If a manual does not supply information concerning reliability, the test should not be used until and unless its reliability is investigated and found to be adequate. "Lack of knowledge *about* measurement error does not remove it from any set of scores" (Feldt & Brennan, 1989, p. 105). Test users need to know how much confidence they can place in the consistency of the scores.

The topic of reliability has very practical implications for teachers' development of effective classroom tests. It also has practical implications for teachers' ability to soundly judge published measures. Knowledge about a test's reliability enables teachers to exercise appropriate caution in interpreting its scores—a topic to be taken up in the next chapter. The topic also has great transfer potential to other fields because imperfections of reliability are common to the instruments in all fields. A universal need exists to enhance reliability of measures and judgments to the extent that (a) practical constraints enable and (b) the importance of the decisions to be made from the test scores merit.

Major Sources of Measurement Error

We will identify four common sources of random measurement error that erode the reliability of educational measures. These are content sampling error, occasion sampling error, examiner error, and scorer error. Although other sources of error exist (e.g., see Stanley, 1971), these four are the most significant for both teacher-made and published measures. They will be presented in a nontechnical manner.

Content Sampling Error

In the context of Track C, *a test is a sample of behavior.* The plans used for developing tests are designed to assure that they appropriately sample their content domains. However, even the best of samples can happen to hit on a disproportionate fraction of an examinee's strong or weak topics. A student can be lucky or unlucky in the "luck of the draw" of items that appear in a test—and pupils understand this at a young age. Witness common comments such as "If Mrs. Stone asks so and so, I'm dead" or "I hope the test has a big essay on such and such."

Because of **content sampling error**, some scores overrepresent student status, while other scores underrepresent examinee competence. Such error is inevitable in Track C tests where the domains are too large to be tested in their entirety. The tests must sample, and wherever there is sampling, sampling error will occur. Content sampling error is, therefore, a fact of life that cannot be avoided.

Nonetheless, it is a contaminant. To the extent that scores are a function of which form of a test happens to be administered rather than pure measures of examinee competence, the scores cannot be relied on to perfectly represent examinee status on the domain. Thus content sampling error limits the extent to which appropriate generalizations can be made from the content sampled to the domain of interest.

Minimizing Content Sampling Error.   An obvious way by which to reduce content sampling error is to test more content. A longer test obviously can, other things being equal, more adequately sample a domain's content than a shorter test can.

It is equally obvious, however, that enhancement of reliability—that is, reduction of measurement error—should not be pursued with a singleness of purpose. For example, it would not be productive to spend all available time in testing, leaving none for instruction. Thus a tradeoff must be reached between the undesirable presence of content sampling error and the undesirable expenditure of time for testing.

A Common Mistake.   People who lose sight of this unavoidable tradeoff are at risk of making serious errors. A common mistake along these lines is to seek a published test that will provide several reliable subscores in very little testing time. It is a fact of life that a reliable score can be secured only by investing adequate testing time. If one is only prepared to ask three or four questions per score, one must be prepared to live with scores that have an enormous element of chance in them. In Track C, it would be more realistic to plan for 10, 20, or more items per useful score. The highly *un*reliable scores from 3-to-5-item subsets can do much more harm than good if the users do not realize their grave limitations and make allowance for a huge margin of error in their interpretation.

Professional educators should be very skeptical of those who make claims that commercial instruments are conveniently brief *and* highly reliable. A given test can quite readily be *either* short *or* reliable, but not both. Beware of pies in the sky.

Measuring Content Sampling Error.   The research design by which the amount of content sampling error is investigated is relatively simple. To use it, however, one first needs two parallel forms of the test under investigation—namely, forms that have been constructed to conform to the same table of specifications. An appropriate group of examinees is administered both of these forms, one right after the other. This yields two scores for each examinee. These two sets of scores are then correlated. This Pearson *r* is also a **reliability coefficient**, more specifically, an alternate-form reliability coefficient.

If there were no error of measurement in either form, then each person would achieve identical status on the two forms and the correlation would be 1.0. The extent by which the resulting equivalent-form reliability coefficient is less than 1.0 reflects content sampling error.

Research estimates of this and other kinds of measurement error are important for published tests. However, such investigations are not ordinarily conducted on classroom tests. Teachers typically lack the time, resources, and need to do such studies. Their time is better spent in enhancing reliability than in estimating it.

Typical Values and Classroom Implications.   Values for total scores on full-period published tests usually fall between about .85 and about .95. Period-long, teacher-made objective tests more often have parallel-form-with-no-time-interval reliability coefficients in the .5 to .9 range. Classroom tests tend to suffer from more content sampling error largely because (a) they often are not built to conform to tables of specification, (b) their items are typically not as expertly crafted, and (c) their items usually have not been subjected to expert editorial review, tryout, and revision. Of course, teachers who conscientiously implement the test-making procedures described in Part II of this book will, other things being equal, produce much more reliable (and valid) instruments than those who are careless.

Essay tests suffer from more content sampling error than objective tests because they can provide fewer content "chunks." In general, many small chunks of information provide a better basis for generalizing than do fewer larger chunks. This is one of the reasons why teachers should ordinarily use objective items whenever they are adequate to assess instructional objectives.

Occasion Sampling Error

Just as there is "luck of the draw" from one sample of content to another, there is a corresponding element of luck with respect to when one happens to be assessed. Everyone has good days and bad days. Behavior is influenced by such things as illness, fatigue, motivation, domestic stress, weather, and social factors. If other things are equal, tests administered on a person's good days are likely to overrepresent status, while those hitting the bad days are prone to underestimate it.

Among well-motivated students, the impact of **occasion sampling error** is rarely great. However, among poorly motivated individuals, it can be significant.

One could argue that it is not the fault of the test or its author that student performance differs from one occasion to another. True, but irrelevant. The point is that test scores are ordinarily obtained in order to *generalize about examinee status over a period of time.* To the extent that scores are a function of when people happen to be assessed rather than a pure function of their status on the content domain, the scores cannot be trusted to represent status on the domain. Thus occasion sampling error limits the extent to which safe generalizations can be made from the particular occasion when the test happened to be given to the period of time in question.

Minimizing Occasion Sampling Error.   An obvious way to reduce occasion sampling error is to test on more occasions. Suppose, for example, that a middle school social studies teacher has been giving four, 50-item objective tests per semester. The teacher could reduce occasion sampling error if testing were conducted on more occasions. If it were desired to maintain the same amount of testing time (and content sampling error), the same 200 items could be redistributed among, say, eight, 25-item tests or quizzes during the semester.

It is doubtful that the enhancement of reliability resulting from the reduction of occasion sampling error would compensate for the added work of testing more frequency. Recall, however, that more frequent testing also tends to enhance learning (Bangert-Drowns, Kulik, & Kulik, 1986). The benefits derived from pacing student study, motivation, etc., may well justify more frequent testing, and the reduction on occasion sampling error might better be considered to be a desirable side effect.

Measuring Occasion Sampling Error.   The research design for investigating occasion sampling error is also simple. A sample of examinees is given the same form of the test on two occasions. This provides two sets of scores that are correlated. The r is a test-retest reliability coefficient. If each person performed consistently in comparison with the others, then relative status would be identical between the two administrations and r would equal 1.0. The extent by which r is less than 1.0 reflects inconsistency of examinees from one occasion to the other.

How far apart should the two occasions be? Ideally test-retest reliability would be researched for several different time intervals. The interval of greatest interest to a given user may depend largely on (a) the length of time over which the scores are to be used and (b) the extent to which interventions (such as instruction) are changing the attribute measured.

Test scores should be used only during their period of currency. Some tests serve only short-term purposes. One would not, for example, take very seriously the scores from a long-past early unit vocabulary test in Spanish concerning relatives (*tia* = aunt, etc.). Such scores age rapidly. A test-retest interval of overnight or a few days would seem reasonable for such a test. Other tests are intended to serve longer-term purposes. For example, a state may require retesting only every three years for students classified mentally retarded or gifted. In this case, we would be interested in how consistent the scores were over a three-year period (in spite of the fact that it is not the fault of the test that students' real relative status changes during a period this long).

The time interval between testing and retesting in most published cognitive tests is a week or two—time enough to get over a common cold or to catch one. Common values for scores based on full-period testing times would range from about .85 to about .95.

Examiner Error

Test scores ought to generalize across examiners; that is, scores ought to be a function of student status, not of who happened to test them. Therefore, any differences in scores that arise from differences in examiners is a source of measurement error. One meaning of **examiner error** that springs to mind involves examiner mistakes (e.g., allowing more or less time for a standardized test than the directions specify). Examiner error also includes other impacts on scores deriving from who administered the test. These differences include examiner elicitation of maximal effort through prompting, reduction of test anxiety through advance "stage setting," and establishment of good rapport.

Examiner error is not a very worrisome source of unreliability in typical, group-administered, published or teacher-made instruments. It is not, that is, when examiners prepare carefully and follow standardized instructions conscientiously. Examiner error is, however, a major source of concern in individually administered aptitude and achievement tests such as those commonly administered by special education teachers and by school psychologists. It is also a source of great potential measurement error in such events as athletic tryouts and musical auditions.

Minimizing Examiner Error.   The fundamental way by which to minimize examiner error in published instruments is to follow the administration instructions to the letter and to adhere to sound practices on issues not addressed by the directions. Persons whose work requires use of individually administered tests that are very vulnerable to examiner error often take special courses devoted to their use. For example, school psychologists who administer individual aptitude tests such as the Wechsler and Stanford-Binet Scales ordinarily have taken whole courses devoted exclusively to these instruments.

Measuring Examiner Error.   An examiner's performance can be witnessed or recorded while a test is being administered. This performance can then be critiqued. Such practice is common in learning to administer instruments such as projective techniques and individual aptitude tests. However, there is no direct research design for isolating the amount by which examiner error reduces reliability.

Scorer Error

Just as test results ought to generalize across (a) the particular form of the test that happens to be used, (b) the occasion on which it happens to be administered, and (c) the particular examiner who chances to administer it, they should also generalize across scorers. Students' scores should be a function of their achievement, not a function of who happened to mark their work.

For objective tests, **scorer error** is of minor concern. That is why such instruments are said to be objective—the scores are not sensitive to the scorer. However, scorer error is a major contributor to unreliability of essay and other product measures and of performance assessments. At times, scores can depend more on the quirks of the marker than on examinee performance.

Minimizing Scorer Error.   A widely recognized way to reduce scorer error is to use multiple markers and average the results. Unfortunately, this is very costly—so much so that the tradeoff between enhancing reliability and spending professional time typically renders it impractical to have even two scorers for typical classroom tests. Yet for assessments that yield highly important results, such as a state bar examination, it is important to use multiple markers.

A more practical means of reducing errors of scoring classroom tests is to follow the relevant recommendations from Part II of this book. An example would be having students circle **T** or **F** for true-false items rather than having them write **T** or **F**; this avoids errors in deciphering their marks (and saves time). Another example that teachers can readily use with their own tests involves the recommended methods of scoring essays; these procedures were developed for the express purpose of minimizing scoring errors.

Measuring Scorer Error.   The impact of scorer error can be studied by having a single set of products (e.g., essays) or performances (e.g., auditions) independently assessed by two raters. This yields two sets of scores that are correlated. The r is an interrater reliability coefficient. The extent by which it is less than 1.0 indicates the extent to which inconsistencies in marking detract from the reliability of the scores.

Correlation and Quasi-Correlation Methods of Assessing Reliability

The consistency or reliability of a set of measures can be approached from two somewhat different viewpoints. One perspective focuses on the size of measurement error; it will be taken up in the next section of this chapter. The other approach concerns the consistency with which individuals maintain their positions in a group on repetition of a measurement procedure (Stanley, 1971). In this section this interindividual approach will be explored by examining the common methods of assessing reliability. Discussion will involve the methods sketched above as well as others that will be introduced.

An important point should be kept in mind as the various methods of investigating reliability are discussed. Reliability coefficients are **correlation** or **quasi-correlation coefficients**, and their size is dependent on the variability of the research group. A test author or publisher may be tempted to investigate a test's reliability with an unusually heterogeneous group so that it will seem to be more reliable than it will actually be with typical users. In order to enable informed test users to monitor the characteristics of research groups and to judge their relevance, test manuals should adequately explain the studies reported. The sample used to make each reliability estimate must be described, including a report of the number of persons, the mean, and the standard deviation (American Psychological Association, 1985, p. 20).

A vital concept concerning reliability is that a given test does not have *a* reliability coefficient. Since reliability can be estimated in many ways—and these ways report different sources of error—it is not appropriate to say a test's reliability *is* so and so (American Psychological Association, 1985, p. 21). Nor would it even if its use were restricted to a given sample. As seen in the last section, reliability can be investigated in different ways, and these are reflected in different kinds of reliability coefficients. A systematic discussion follows on means by which an instrument's reliability can be assessed.

Test-Retest

As noted above, the **test-retest approach** requires only one form of a test. It is administered on two occasions with a time interval in between. The two resulting sets of scores are correlated. This test-retest reliability coefficient reflects the extent to which individuals maintain their same relative positions across the two occasions. Thus test-retest coefficients measure occasion sampling consistency. Since content sampling error does not reduce them, they tend to be relatively high.

Alternate-Form-Immediate

As mentioned earlier, the **alternate-form-immediate approach** requires two equivalent forms of the test. They are administered back-to-back to a group of persons, and the two resulting sets of scores are correlated. This alternate-form-immediate reliability coefficient reflects the extent to which individuals maintain their same relative positions across the two forms. Parallel-forms reliability coefficients, therefore, measure content sampling consistency. Since occasion sampling error does not erode them, equivalent-form immediate reliability coefficients tend to be relatively high.

Alternate-Form-with-Interval

The **alternate-form-with-interval approach** also requires two parallel test forms. They are given to a group of people with a time interval between. The two resulting sets of scores are correlated. This alternate-form-with-interval reliability coefficients reflect the extent to which individuals maintain their same relative positions across the two forms and across two occasions. Equivalent-forms-with-interval reliability coefficients thus simultaneously measure content sampling consistency and occasion sampling consistency. Since they are eroded both by content sampling error and occasion sampling error, coefficients tend to be relatively low.

This fact makes alternate-form-with-interval coefficients *more realistic* as estimates of reliability because *both content sampling error and occasion sampling error really do occur when people are tested.* We should be aware of the kinds and amounts of error present in the measures we use. Consequently, we prefer to have reliability assessed by methods that reflect all of the major sources of error that are present in test scores.

Content and occasion sampling error are the two major sources of error in most group-administered objective tests. Therefore, as practitioners who want to have an appropriately healthy respect for such tests' lack of perfect reliability, we prefer the manual to report alternate-form-with-interval reliability coefficients (see American Psychological Association, 1985). Typical values of parallel-form-with-interval reliability for published tests with scores based on full-period length range from about .80 to about .92.

What about essay tests? Their reliability also suffers from scorer error. Realism therefore argues for a research design that also allows imperfect reliability of scoring to erode the reliability coefficient in the same way it erodes the test's reliability in the real world. An appropriate research design would involve two forms of the test administered on different occasions and scored independently by different persons. The correlation between the resulting two sets of scores is low enough to reflect the error from content sampling, occasion, and scorer sampling.

Finally, consider an individually administered performance test, such as an audition or an individually administered aptitude test. Its reliability also suffers from examiner error. Therefore, we seek a research design that also permits inconsistency across examiners to be revealed. A research study capable of yielding a realistic estimate of the consistency across content samples, time, examiners, and scorers requires having people assessed on two different occasions with different forms of the test or task by different examiners/scorers.

Internal Consistency

The above approaches are conceptually simple. Unfortunately they present logistic difficulties in execution because they require each examinee either to take a test twice or to take two forms of a test. It is hard for publishers to secure schools' cooperation in allowing this much research testing. There is therefore great practical attraction to a set of methods that require only one form of a test to be administered once. Collectively known as **internal consistency estimates**, these methods are based on the internal relationships among the parts of tests.

Internal consistency estimates are commonly reported for published instruments. They can also be used to study the reliability of teacher-made tests.

An important caution applies to internal consistency reliability estimates. *They are inflated by speed.* If a test's scores are markedly impacted by speed, none of the internal consistency estimates can appropriately be used (American Psychological Association, 1985, p. 21) because they will seriously exaggerate the test's reliability. The reliability of such tests should be estimated by one or more of the above methods.

For this reason it is to be expected that any test manual that reports an internal consistency coefficient for a timed test will supply evidence regarding the degree to which scores are influenced by speed. Many timed tests provide generous time, and their scores are not markedly influenced by speed. For example, if a manual reported that 96% of a norming sample attempted at least one of the test's final three items, it would be reasonable to report a measure of internal consistency (although it would be very slightly inflated). On the other hand, if a test is highly speeded (say, less than 70% or 80% finish), then its internal consistency estimates will seriously overrepresent the consistency of scores and should not be reported.

Split-Half.   One approach to studying internal consistency is the **split-half method** in which a test's scores are split, for research purposes only, into two half-scores. One could be obtained from the first half of a test and the other from the last half. However, this partitioning would probably cause the halves to have dissimilar content, and speed would impact on the second half, but rarely on the first; the halves would therefore lack parallelism in what they measure. A better method is to secure the subscores respectively from the test's odd- and even-numbered items. This common method equalizes the potential impact of speed and tends to distribute content more equally between the halves. Or the test could be divided into halves that are as equivalent as possible in content.

The two sets of subscores are then correlated. Except for one problem, the results are conceptually similar to those obtained from parallel-form-immediate reliability studies. The resulting split-half coefficient is the reliability of only a half test, not the full test. Fortunately, there is a formula (known as a special case of the Spearman-Brown Formula) that (given some realistic technical assumptions) enables the half-test reliability to be adjusted to estimate the corresponding reliability of the full test. To make this adjustment, the half-test r is substituted in the expression, $\frac{2r}{1+r}$. For example, if the correlation between scores of the odd-numbered items and the even-numbered items on a test is .6, then the adjusted (usually called a corrected) estimate of the full test's internal consistency reliability is

$$\frac{2 \times .6}{1 + .6} = \frac{1.2}{1.6} = .75$$

Kuder-Richardson 20.   A formula called **Kuder-Richardson 20** (1937) avoids the need to split the test for scoring; it yields results that (with minor technical qualifications) are the average of all the split-half coefficients that would result from different splits of a test (Anastasi, 1988, p. 124). This coefficient is not a Pearson r, but it has relevant features of correlation coefficients and, for this book's purposes, can be treated as though it were one.

Many computerized scoring programs routinely provide Kuder-Richardson 20 (K-R 20) reliability coefficients. Provided an instrument is not speeded and the assumptions specified below are met, it can be interpreted somewhat like a parallel-form-immediate coefficient or a corrected odd-even coefficient would be. The only difference is that K-R 20, by virtue of being an average of all ways of splitting a test, is depressed if the content is not homogeneous. Thus if a test consists of dissimilar kinds of content, such as a few spelling words, a few arithmetic skill problems, and a few items measuring social studies knowledge, then K-R 20 would yield lower results than would the alternate-form or odd-even methods.

K-R 20 requires that all items count the same amount, that all items be scored dichotomously (i.e., no partial credit), and that all items be independent (e.g., no blocks of items such as those found in interpretive exercises). These conditions are usually met in objective tests lacking interpretive exercises, but not in tests containing interpretive exercises, in essay tests (where items may not count the same and where partial credit is common), in mathematical proofs, or in various kinds of rating forms.

Coefficient Alpha.   Cronbach (1951) provided a generalization of the K-R 20 that is free of the limitations specified in the last paragraph. This internal consistency measure, known as **coefficient alpha**, also requires only one administration of one form. This quasi-correlation is routinely provided by many computer programs for scoring and analyzing test data. It can be interpreted much like an odd-even or alternate-form reliability coefficient, except that it, like the K-R 20, (a) is depressed by content heterogeneity and (b) is inflated by speededness.

TO RECAP

Several factors contribute to error of measurement. Alternative methods of assessing reliability take different combinations of these factors into account. Table 15–1 summarizes these methods and the kinds of measurement errors that impact them.

Practitioners need realistic estimates of the amount of measurement error present in tests. This leads to a preference for estimates that are conservative in their claims of reliability. That is, methods that realistically reflect the inconsistencies that operate in the applied use of tests provide a sound basis for knowing how much confidence to place in scores. On the other hand, methods that take only some of the relevant sources of error into account tend to make tests appear to be more reliable than they really are in use. Such a false impression can cause practitioners to neglect to allow for proper margins of error in the interpretations.

In the case of published tests, the authors and publishers are expected to invest the time and money necessary to provide a variety of informative reliability information about their products.

In the case of teacher-made tests, it is often impractical to compute even internal consistency estimates. However, with increasing numbers of teachers accessing computerized scoring of their classroom tests, the simultaneous computer report often provides a measure of internal consistency. Where this is available, teachers can have a better sense of the degree to which the scores from their tests reflect content sampling error. This is good. At the same time they should be aware that internal consistency estimates do not reflect occasion sampling error, examiner error, or scorer error.

**TO RECAP
(cont.)**

Table 15–1

**Selected Reliability Coefficients and the
Sources of Measurement Error that Impact Them***

Kind of Reliability Coefficient	Kinds of Measurement Error Taken into Account
Test-retest	Occasion sampling
Test-retest with different scorers	Occasion sampling Scorer
Parallel-form-immediate	Content sampling
Parallel-form-immediate with different scorers	Content sampling Scorer
Parallel-form-with-interval	Occasion sampling Content sampling
Parallel-form-with-interval and different scorers	Occasion sampling Content sampling Scorer
Parallel-form-with-interval and different examiners/scorers	Occasion sampling Content sampling Examiner Scorer
Split-half	Content (Heterogeneity of content unless halves are parallel)
Kuder-Richardson 20	Content Heterogeneity of content
Coefficient Alpha	Content Heterogeneity of content

*Adapted from A. Anastasi, *Psychological Testing* (6th ed.). New York: Macmillan, 1988, p. 126.

QUIZ 15–1

Following is information for five hypothetical published tests. It is difficult to compare their reliability findings because they report different kinds of studies. Assume each test used suitable random subsamples of students from their norming samples. Also assume these samples to have equal variability.

QUIZ 15–1 (cont.)

Test V reports a K-R 20 reliability coefficient of .90.

Test W reports a corrected odd-even reliability coefficient of .88.

Test X reports a test-retest coefficient of .92.

Test Y reports an alternate-form-immediate coefficient of .88.

Test Z reports an alternate-form-with-interval coefficient of .88.

1. Which test had its reliability assessed by a method that always causes heterogeneity of content to erode the coefficient?

2. Which test had its reliability assessed by the most rigorous method?

3. Among Tests V, Y, and Z, which test appears to have the *least* adequate reliability?

4. For which test is no information concerning content sampling error presented?

5. Among Tests W, Y and Z, which probably has the *least* content sampling error?

KEY TO QUIZ 15–1

1. Test V. K-R 20 and alpha always are reduced when content is heterogeneous.

2. Text Z. Alternate-form-with-interval assessment takes account of both content sampling error and occasion sampling error.

3. Text Y. Content sampling error alone reduces its reliability to .88. Occasion sampling will surely influence its scores further.

4. Text X. Only occasion sampling is reflected in its test–retest study.

5. Text Z. Its coefficient is similar to the other two, but it also reflects occasion sampling error. Therefore its content sampling error is probably smaller.

The Standard Error of Measurement: The Other Side of the Coin

As mentioned before, the reliability of a set of scores can be approached from alternative perspectives. In the one examined in the last section, which is based on *inter*individual variability, attention is directed to the consistency with which people maintain their relative positions in a group on repetition of a measurement procedure. The focus is on *consistency*, and results are expressed in correlation or quasi-correlation coefficients.

The alternative perspective[1] will now be examined; it is based on *intra*individual variability, or the consistency among repeated measures of the same person. In this approach, attention is directed to the size of measurement error expressed in the same units as scores (Stanley, 1971).

Error of measurement is the flip side of reliability. Reliability coefficients quantify the extent to which test scores are consistent. In contrast, standard errors of measurement report the extent to which the scores are contaminated by error.

If it were feasible to make an infinite number of measures of a thing, some variation among the fallible or obtained measures would surely result. That is, there is always some error of measurement regardless of what is being measured. To illustrate, suppose Steve weighs himself 10 times on a scale, one time right after another. The resulting distribution is displayed below:

Distribution of
Repeated Measures

186
187
187
189
187
185
187
187
188
187

$M = 187$
$SD = 1$

This standard deviation is computed by the formula given in Chapter 11. Yet this *SD* is a very unusual one because it does *not* represent interindividual differences. Only one person has been measured, hence there are no individual differences. The only thing that prevented the 10 measures from agreeing perfectly with each other is measurement error. This standard deviation of measurement error is called a standard error of measurement.

For another illustration, suppose each of 500 machinists were asked to use his or her own micrometer to measure the diameter of a particular steel ball. If the distribution of these 500 "scores" were obtained, its mean and standard deviation could be computed. The mean would be a good approximation of the true diameter.

The only thing that would cause or enable the 500 obtained scores to differ from this mean is measurement error. (The main sources of measurement error may be the machinists and their micrometers.) If there were no error of measurement, then all the raw scores would be identical, and the *SD* of their frequency distribution would be zero. To the extent that the *SD* of the 500 fallible scores is greater than zero,

---

[1]Parts of this section are adapted from (Hanna) *Journal of Counseling and Development*, Volume 6, 1988, pages 477-483. ©AACD. Reprinted with permission. No further reproduction authorized without written permission of American Association for Counseling and Development.

error is present. Again, the standard deviation of this distribution of repeated measures is called a **standard error of measurement (*SEM*)**.

In any set of normally[2] distributed scores, 68% (or roughly 2 out of 3) of the scores fall within 1 *SD* of the mean. Similarly in the distribution of independent multiple measures of the same thing, such as the steel ball, the shape of the distribution of obtained scores will usually be such that about the same figure holds for the *SD* of the measurement errors—the *SEM*.

A "true" or infallible score is an abstraction. All that any examiner can have is a fallible or obtained score that is a mere estimate of the "true" score. To secure an interval within which the true score probably lies, a confidence band is constructed around the obtained score.[3] Confidence bands of various widths are then a direct function of how many *SEM*s are included on either side of the obtained score. The most common intervals are:

1. The obtained score plus and minus 1 *SEM*. This provides an interval within which the probability is .68 that the "true" score falls; these 68 chances out of 100 are often rounded to 2 out of 3.

2. The obtained score plus and minus 2 *SEM*s. This yields a range within which the probability is .95 that the "true" scores lies; this is often reduced to 19 chances out of 20.

3. The obtained score plus and minus 2.6 *SEM*s. This gives a confidence band that has .99 probability of containing the true score.

It is sometimes assumed that the size of a test's *SEM* will be the same at all score levels, but this is not always the case. A device can be considerably more precise in measuring persons at some levels of functioning than at others. In general, tests tend to have smaller *SEM*s for raw scores near the center of the distribution of scores than in the extremes of the distributions (Feldt & Brennan, 1989). While it is highly desirable for test manuals to report *SEM*s at several score levels, when only a general *SEM* is reported, it can be used as an approximation.

"OK," some readers are thinking, "*SEM* is the flip side of the reliability coin, but why bother to look at both sides? Wouldn't one side be enough?"

Actually, the two approaches to the topic richly complement each other. Reliability coefficients provide a good way of comparing the consistency of different tests. However, they have little utility in interpreting scores to parents and students because they are based on technical concepts and jargon.

*SEM*s, by contrast, have two significant advantages. First, they can be used to meaningfully interpret scores to lay people without resorting to esoteric ideas and language. This is possible because *SEM*s report error of measurement in the same unit of measure that is used for the test scores themselves. Chapter 16 will show how *SEM*s can be used to provide confidence bands, or margins for error, within which examinees' true statuses probably lie.

---

[2]A normal distribution is the familiar, bell-shaped curve that is approximated in many varied circumstances when a large number of independent events collectively determine an outcome.

[3]This procedure reverses the theoretical but wholly impractical process that is conceptualized in which the confidence band is constructed around the "true" score.

Second, unlike reliability coefficients, *SEM*s are not influenced by the variability of the group with which they were computed (Anastasi, 1988, p. 134). As will be noted in the next section, this has important implications for mastery tests.

The two examples given above, weight and micrometer measures, were both remote from educational applications. Similar examples for attributes that are not influenced by being measured could be based on oven temperature, height, and readings of light meters. However, in typical educational testing, students experience a practice effect, and their scores improve if they are retested. That is, the attribute being measured is influenced by the measurement process. It is therefore not practical to estimate the *SEM* of teacher-made or published instruments by the method of repeated measurement.

The examples were very useful to reveal the meaning of the concept of *SEM*, but they did not show how to go about finding *SEM*s of educational and psychological measures. These are found by first conducting a reliability study and computing a reliability coefficient. This reliability coefficient is then entered in the formula $SEM = \sqrt{1 - r}$ to determine the *SEM*.

Just as there are reliability coefficients and reliability coefficients (i.e., some reflect different and more sources of measurement error than others), there are also *SEM*s and *SEM*s. When a reliability coefficient has been determined by a method that allows all of the major sources of error to depress it, it may not superficially look as impressive as one that takes account of only some error sources. However, it is more realistic. Similarly, the corresponding *SEM* that reflects all of the major sources of measurement error will be larger than one that takes account of only some of the error present, but it provides a more realistic basis to estimate the amount of error that contaminates our measures.

QUIZ 15–2

1. The manual of a published test reports a *SD* of 4 and a parallel-form-immediate-reliability coefficient of .91. What is the corresponding *SEM?*
2. What main source of error does the *SEM* in Item 1 account for?
3. A teacher investigating a test obtains a *SD* of 5 and a alternate-form-with-interval reliability coefficient of .64. What is the corresponding *SEM?*
4. Which sources of error does the *SEM* in Item 3 account for?

KEY TO QUIZ 15–2

1. $SEM = SD\sqrt{1 - r}$. Therefore, $SEM = 4\sqrt{1 - .91} = 4\sqrt{.09} = 4\,(.3) = 1.2$.
2. Since parallel-forms-immediate reliability reflects content sampling error, the *SEM* computed from it reflects the same source of error.

> ### KEY TO QUIZ 15–2 (cont.)
>
> 3. $SEM = 5\sqrt{1 - .64} = 5\sqrt{.36} = 5\,(.6) = 3.0.$
> 4.   The *SEM* is based on equivalent-form-with-interval reliability findings. The *r* will be eroded by content sampling error and occasion sampling error. The corresponding *SEM* will therefore be enlarged (to a realistic degree) by these same two sources of error.

Reliability of Mastery Tests

Mastery tests have a distinctive feature that renders some statistics inappropriate. In the context of Track A instruction, individual differences have been channeled into the time dimension; therefore little individual differences are found in achievement. When a mastery test is given after effective instruction has taken place, most of the scores cluster near the ceiling—that is, most are perfect or near perfect.

The *inter*individual differences approach to reliability is based on people's maintenance of the same relative position in a group. When almost everyone has nearly the same score, few individual differences exist. Hence, reliability coefficients hover near zero. This outcome can make mastery tests undeservedly look bad. Thus reliability coefficients are not ordinarily appropriate for mastery tests because they report amount of interindividual discrimination in a situation where discrimination was not sought.

Yet score consistency is just as important for mastery tests as it is for discriminatory tests. Users have just as urgent a need to know how much confidence to place in scores—all of the scores, including subscores based on instructional objectives. The need is particularly acute because many objectives-based diagnostic tests are plagued with measurement error, mainly because they have too few items per score (Nitko, 1989, p. 458).

Manuals of some poorly prepared mastery tests dismiss the topic of reliability on grounds that correlational approaches are not appropriate. It is true that correlational methods are typically inappropriate for mastery tests, but this in no way exempts authors of master tests from reporting information about score consistency. Lack of knowledge about measurement error does not remove it from scores (Feldt & Brennan, 1989, p. 105). *Test manuals should provide* SEMs *for the total score and each subscore that is reported* (American Psychological Association, 1985, p. 20).

Since ignoring the topic is not a responsible option, what are the authors of mastery tests to do? Several legitimate approaches can be taken. First, a number of specialized coefficients are deemed appropriate for mastery tests. (For a brief presentation, see Feldt and Brennan, 1989.) Authors of mastery tests can use one of these methods. Although this approach is appropriate, it has the disadvantage of using statistics unfamiliar to most users of mastery tests.

Second, the agreement in pass-fail decisions between two administrations or (preferable) between two forms can be computed. Such a percentage of agreement in classification serves as a measure of consistency of decisions made from a mastery test. Unsophisticated use of this method, however, tends to make scores of mastery tests look much more consistent than they deserve. Here is an example of how.

Suppose each form of a mastery test passes 90% of examinees and fails 10%. The authors report that the two forms, administered on consecutive days, classifies 85% of examinees the same on both forms. This may superficially look respectable, but actually it represents very little reliability. If both forms were completely *un*reliable in their selection of which 90% to pass and which 10% to fail, agreement would be expected 82% of the time [(.9 × .9) + (.1 × .1)]. Since a totally unreliable test that passes 90% would agree with itself 82% of the time, the reported value of 85% represents only a very modest increment over a total lack of consistency.

What is needed is one of the specialized coefficients mentioned above that will index the contribution to consistency that the test makes *over what a random process would yield*. One such statistic is **Kappa** (Cohen, 1960), which is the ratio of the actual gain in consistency to the maximum possible gain over chance. For the above example, the actual gain was .03 (i.e., .85 − .82), and the maximum possible gain was .18 (i.e., 1.00 − .82). Therefore, Kappa $= \frac{.03}{.18} = .17$.

Another approach to investigating the reliability of mastery tests involves conventional correlation methods that can be rendered appropriate by expanding the examinee pool to include some *un*instructed individuals. The logic of this orientation is that all tests—including mastery tests—are designed to reveal individual differences *when and if* individual differences are present. By using a sample consisting of instructed and uninstructed examinees, individual differences in achievement are assured. Persons using this method often secure half of their research sample from special pretesting with the test and the other half from regular posttesting with the test. When these groups are pooled, individual differences in achievement are present and correlational methods are appropriate.

Finally, the simplest approach to reporting the consistency of mastery test scores is based on *SEM*s. Recall that *SEM*s are not sensitive to group variability (Payne, 1992, p. 183). They therefore can be used as readily with mastery tests as with any other. When a pass-fail standard is recommended for a mastery test, the *SEM at that point* is particularly helpful in expressing the amount by which use of the test's cut score is contaminated by error (American Psychological Association, 1985, p. 20).

Reliability of Difference Scores

In many practical situations, test users wish to compare two or more scores. Following are examples of comparative statements.

Horace is taller than Jim.

Horace is taller than he was last year.

Horace's *z*-score for height compared with age mates is greater than his *z*-score for weight.

Helen's reading has improved this year.

Helen reads better than she spells.

Helen reads better than Joe reads.

Helen reads better than her aptitude test scores would lead us to expect.

Some examples involve a person's *gain* over time. Others concern a *comparison* between two people. Still others compare a person's *relative status* on two attributes. Regardless of which variety of comparison is used, all involve a *difference* between two scores.

The fact that two scores are being compared creates double jeopardy from measurement error. Either of the two scores can, and usually does, err. If they happen to err in opposite directions the difference between them is seriously distorted. To illustrate, consider a simple example.

Ruth is trying to improve her keyboarding speed. Last week she entered 24 words per minute on a five-minute timed test. This week she managed 27 words per minute on a parallel test. How much, if any, has she really improved? The most likely source of measurement error in this example is occasion sampling error. It can cause either score to overestimate or to underestimate her status.

Of course, it is not known how much, if any, she has truly improved. On either occasion, her performance may have been unusually good or unusually poor. If she had a good day last week and a bad one this week, her actual rate may have improved much more during the week than the difference score of 3 (i.e., $27 - 24$) indicates. If her score overestimated her status on both occasions, then she probably improved a bit. If her speed was underestimated both times, she has likely improved a little. Finally, if her rate was underestimated last week and overestimated this week, then she may actually have gotten slower. The *double jeopardy of measurement error* from both measures renders our conclusions more error prone than they would be if they were focused on either of the scores separately.

If measurement errors of the two measures are unrelated, then the *SEM* of the difference between measures 1 and 2 is:

$$SEM_{\text{diff}} = \sqrt{SEM_1^2 + SEM_2^2}.$$

Notice that this relationship is the same as the relationship, expressed by the Pythagorean Theorem, among the three sides of a right triangle. The hypotenuse is always the longest side of a right triangle, just as the *SEM* of a difference between two scores is always greater than either of the score's *SEM*s. However the hypotenuse of a right triangle is never as long as the sum of the two legs, just as the *SEM* of a difference between two scores is never as great as the sum of the scores' *SEM*s.

The relatively low reliability of difference scores has many important practical implications. One of the reasons that instructional objectives should be stated in terms of *terminal* student behavior (in contrast to gain) concerns the greater reliability of terminal status measures. Similarly, one of the reasons that grades should be based on terminal status rather than on improvement concerns the greater reliability of terminal status assessments.

Another hazard involved in use of difference scores is found in such statements as "John is not achieving up to expectancy." Such statements regarding underachievement (in which achievement scores are lower than aptitude scores) or overachievement (in which achievement scores are higher than aptitude scores) are based on a comparison of two scores and therefore have larger *SEM*s than either of the scores on which they are based.

Recall the point that tests can be properly used to generate hypotheses or to test hypotheses, but not for both at the same time. Underachievement is a case in point.

If a counselor were to thumb through cumulative records of many students to identify underachievers, there would be great (indeed reckless) risk of misidentification owing to large measurement error of the achievement-aptitude discrepancies. This problem arises from the exclusive use of a difference score for identification.

A sounder practice would be for the counselor to use this method to identify *possible* underachievers for further study. If the students picked up with this crude screening method were referred for more intensive assessment with other (likely individually administered) tests, then the original test data would be utilized only for hypothesis formation. The subsequent test data would be used for hypothesis testing. The very real hazards of interpreting difference scores still are present, but they are greatly reduced when this problem is not confounded by the simultaneous use of test for hypothesis formation and hypothesis testing.

Similarly, suppose a teacher notices that Hubert does not seem to work up to his apparent ability and refers him for testing. Here too, the counselor or psychologist has a hypothesis to investigate. If tests given to investigate this hypothesis reveal the aptitude score to be significantly higher than the achievement score, then a *much* better basis exists to consider Hubert to be underachieving.

Another practical implication of the relative unreliability of difference scores concerns profile analysis. When a test battery provides several scores (or a test provides several subscores), interpretation can focus on the one-by-one interpretation of these scores or on comparisons among them. The former creates no unusual hazards, but comparative statements among several scores place the interpretation in multiple jeopardy of measurement error.

For example, if a profile contains scores A, B, C, D, E, and F, even the seemingly innocuous statement that Sue's strongest area is Subtest C is tantamount to saying "C is greater than A," "C is greater than B," "C is greater than D," "C is greater than E," and "C is greater than F." Thus five comparisons were implicit, *each having double jeopardy from measurement error.* Unless her obtained score on Subtest C was much greater than *each* of the others, the statement that her strongest area is C is likely to err. In interpreting profiles, it is extremely helpful to use graphic interpretive aids to show appropriate margins of error. This important topic will be taken up in the next chapter.

Although C has the greatest probability of being the strongest area, there are five opportunities for it not to be. Even though it is the place to "put your money" (if you have to bet), it usually is not wise to give even odds. An everyday analogy may be helpful. A pregnancy's due date is the most likely delivery date, but the baby may be born on any of many other dates. Even though the due date is the most likely *single* date, only about one baby in ten is born on it.

The inherently low reliability of interpreting profiles is a major reason why many test users would better interpret the scores in a test or battery one at a time without comparative statements or implications. Indeed, wherever practitioners can avoid the use of difference scores, they often would be well advised to do so (Cronbach, 1984).

Chapter Summary

Reliability, like validity and interpretability, is an essential attribute for any measuring instrument. While limitations of a test's reliability place limits on its possible validity, high reliability findings do not demonstrate that a device measures what it is supposed to measure; thus reliability does not ensure validity.

Reliability involves several kinds of consistency. The most important are consistency from one content sample to another, from one occasion to another, from one examiner to another, and from one scorer to another. In considering the reliability of a given test, we should judge which of these sources of error are likely to be significant. The most useful reliability studies for published tests are those that take each of the significant relevant sources of measurement error into account.

A standard error of measurement is a statistic that is useful in establishing confidence bands within which an examinee's true status is likely to fall. About two-thirds of examinees' true scores fall within one *SEM* of their obtained scores. This provides interpreters a means of simultaneously communicating to students and parents both (a) the amount of confidence that can be placed in a score and (b) the caution that should be exercised in accepting the score. The interpretive use of *SEM*s will be developed more fully in the next chapter.

Suggestions for Further Reading

American Psychological Association. (1985). *Standards for educational and psychological testing.* Washington, DC: Author. Pages 19–23 give a brief, current, and readable statement of current thinking concerning reliability. In addition, standards are provided by which readers can judge the adequacy of published tests' provision of reliability information.

Feldt, L. S., & Brennan, R. L. (1989). Reliability. In Linn, R. L. (Ed.), *Educational measurement* (3rd ed.). New York: Macmillan. This reference contains a succinct, relatively advanced, and current treatment of the topic.

Frisbie, D. A. (1988). Reliability of scores from teacher-made tests. *Educational Measurement: Issues and Practice, 7,* 25–35. An elementary treatment of reliability focusing on classroom tests; provides formulas for estimating reliability of teacher-made tests.

Payne, D. A. (1992). *Measuring and evaluating educational outcomes.* New York: Merrill. Chapter 12, "Defining and Assessing Reliability," provides a relatively quantitative elementary approach with formulas and numeric examples. It also contains a good description of the use of Cohen's Kappa to investigate the reliability of mastery tests.

Thorndike, R. M., Cunningham, G. K., Thorndike, R. L., & Hagen, E. P. (1991). *Measurement and evaluation in psychology and education* (5th ed.). New York: Macmillan. Chapter 4, "Qualities Desired in Any Measurement Procedure: Reliability," offers a good introduction to the topic, with unusual clarity of the topics of reliability of difference scores and the percentage-agreement method of assessing reliability of mastery tests.

Choosing and Using Published Instruments

The first three sections of this book focused on teacher-made tests and their use in facilitating student learning. Part IV, concerning characteristics of effective measures, was relevant to the informed use of both classroom and published instruments.

Part V now deals with choosing and using published instruments. Chapter 16 will complete the transition to published measures by explaining the meaning and use of various kinds of widely used derived scores by which norm-referenced interpretations are made. In addition, Chapter 16 will address some important principles of score interpretation that are widely applicable both to teacher-made measures and published devices. This topic of interpreting test results will link closely with the last two chapters' treatment of validity and reliability.

Chapter 17 will focus on commercially distributed achievement tests. Attention in Chapter 18 will be directed to a variety of published aptitude tests. Finally, Chapter 19 will feature selected other published instruments, mainly those that tap various affective attributes. As particular measures are used to illustrate classes of instruments, meritorious features and common pitfalls also will be pointed out. Discussion of various published measures will also provide a meaningful context in which to further consider the merits of various kinds of reference groups and principles of sound interpretation. And, as has been the case throughout this book, attention will continue to be drawn to the use of measurement to enhance student learning.

16

Derived Scores and Their Interpretation

When the boundaries and difficulty of content domains are not tightly specified, raw and percent scores lack domain-referenced meaning because interpretation cannot be referenced to ill-defined domains. Interpretation of discriminatory survey tests of open-ended, unmasterable content is therefore referenced to the performance of other people. Thus meaningful interpretation of Track C achievement tests must be norm referenced, as must interpretations of measures of aptitude, attitude, interest, adaptive behavior, and temperament, which also sample large, imperfectly described constructs.

Derived scores are essential to norm referencing. In order to achieve comparative, people-referenced interpretation, raw scores are transformed into derived scores, which are then converted or derived by use of a reference group of other people whose test performance is known. As seen in Chapter 13, the reference group(s) used to interpret a test's scores should be relevant to the purpose(s) of the interpretation. This important topic will be further discussed in later chapters.

There exists a perplexing variety of derived scores, and many educators are confused about their relative merits. Two goals of this chapter are to complete the elementary presentation of the major kinds of derived scores, started in Chapter 11, and to suggest when each kind should be used.

Many educators are also unacquainted with principles of sound interpretation. However, every teacher should be competent in interpreting student performance on published tests (Sanders et al., 1990). Another major purpose of this chapter is to make recommendations concerning the appropriate use of derived scores. This topic of interpretation is closely related to the content of the last two chapters on reliability and validity.

Kinds of Derived Scores and Their Features

Test scores can be classified as follows:

I.   Raw and Percent Scores (used in making domain-referenced interpretations)

II. Derived Scores (used in making norm-referenced interpretations)

   A. Simple ranks and percentile ranks

   B. Developmental grade and age equivalents

   C. Standard scores

The vast majority of derived scores fit quite neatly into one of these three subdivisions. We shall examine them in turn.

Ranks

A simple **rank** indicates an individual's standing in a group, *counting from the top.* Thus Hazel's rank of 3 in a race signifies that she was the third person to finish the race. Likewise, Mark's rank of 46 in his high school graduating class indicates that he was 46th from the top of his class. The ease with which ranks are understood explains their popularity.

Although they are conceptually simple, ranks have the awkward feature of requiring a second number. How good was it for Hazel to place third? It depends, of course, on the number of people in the race. (As an aside, it also depends on the nature of the group; that is why reference groups must be not only relevant to the purpose of the interpretation but also described in sufficient detail so that prospective test users can evaluate their relevance.)

Likewise, Mark's class rank of 46th will mean one thing if obtained in a class of 1000 and a vastly different thing if attained in a class of only 46. It is therefore necessary to indicate the size of the group along with the rank (e.g., 3rd in 25 and 46th in 50). For this reason, simple ranks are uncommon in test score reporting.

This inconvenience can be avoided if each group's size, and people's rank within it, is altered to make all groups equivalent to 100. Thus Hazel's 3rd in 25 can be viewed as equivalent to 12th in 100. Likewise, Mark's 46th in 50 is the same as 92nd in 100. With the understanding that the rank is always in a group of 100, the need to indicate the group size is obviated.

As the name implies, a **percentile rank (PR)** indicates rank per 100, but reports the individual's rank *counting from the bottom* of the distribution. Thus Hazel's rank of 12 in a group of 100 is equivalent to a *percentile* rank of 88. That is, she beat 88 out of every 100 people in the race. Likewise, Mark's simple rank of 46 in a group of 50 equates to a PR of 8; he outperformed only 8% (4 out of 50) of the people.

The above examples are based on a variety of PRs defined as the percent of the reference group excelled. As noted in Chapter 11, PRs can also be defined as the percent of the reference group excelled or equaled. Another widely used kind is defined as the percent excelled plus half the percent equalled. Fortunately, differences among them are usually minor in measures having many items.

It is important to keep in mind the fact that *PRs count from the bottom of distributions*—opposite from the familiar convention of counting from the top in indicating simple ranks.

Major Strengths of PRs

PRs, sometimes called **centiles**, have an important feature that enhances their utility: They are easily understood. Neither esoteric jargon, intimidating technical explanations, confusing figures of normal curves, nor anxiety-provoking mathematical symbols are necessary for the meaningful interpretation of students' PR scores.

Another desirable feature of PRs is their widespread applicability. They do not suffer from traditions that restrict their use to certain kinds of instruments (e.g., as IQs are limited to aptitude tests and grade equivalents are limited to achievement tests). Rather, PRs are widely employed to interpret scores of achievement tests, aptitude tests, interest inventories, and personality surveys.

Limitations of PRs

PRs, nonetheless, are not without their limitations. For one thing, they lack equal units of measure. Like simple ranks, PR units tend to be small near the center of distributions and large near the extremes.

To make this intuitively obvious, imagine a group of 25 or so adults who are to be rank-ordered for stature. As they are arranged in a line from tallest to shortest, it is likely to be easy to get the tallest few into the correct order. Likewise, each of the several shortest people is likely to differ from the next by enough to make ordering relatively easy. The difficulty is most apt to occur near the middle of the line, where adjacent people tend to differ very little.

Or imagine about one hundred children running a race. It is relatively easy to identify and rank-order the first several and the last several. But think how hard it would probably be to identify the middle child who finishes among the great thundering stampede in the central part of the distribution.

For a final example of unequal PR units, review the frequency distribution for the State Capitals Test in Table 11–1 on page 303. Notice how more people cluster near the center than at the extremes. That is why, in Table 11–4 on page 304, the corresponding PRs are more widely separated by single raw points near the center of the range than near its ends.

The normal curve will be introduced at this time because it further reveals the *in*equality of PR units. The normal distribution is the familiar bell-shaped, unimodal, symmetric distribution that occurs whenever a large number of independent events (e.g., test items) collectively determine an outcome (e.g., a test score). Its formula and detailed explanation (e.g., see Hopkins, Glass, & Hopkins, 1987) are not central to our purposes.

Figure 16–1 reveals how PRs relate to selected *z*-scores *in normal distributions.* The area enclosed by the curve and the base line represents 100% of the scores in a distribution. The vertical lines partition the total area into *SD* intervals. The percent of the total area enclosed by each section is displayed. This reports the percentage of a normally distributed group that will have scores between successive whole *z*-score intervals.

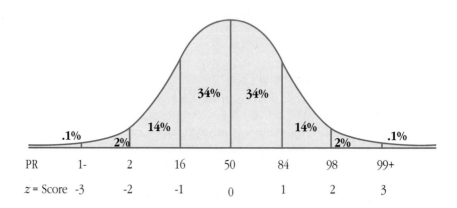

Figure 16–1.   Corresponding Percentile Ranks and *z*-Scores in a Normal Distribution

Notice how two people who differ by, say, 1 *SD* would be separated by a variable number of PR units, depending on their place in the distribution. For example, between *z*-scores of −3.0 and −2.0, there are only about 2 PR units, but the difference between *z*-scores of 0.0 and 1.0 is about 34 PR units.

Another limitation of PRs is their appearance of great precision. With 99 PR intervals, a parent or student can reasonably, but incorrectly, infer that the test is accurate enough to classify examinees this precisely.

Recommended Uses of PRs

Because of their unequal units, *PRs are not suitable for calculation.*

　　Because of the ease with which students and parents can understand them, PRs are recommended for making interpretations. Their only interpretive disadvantage is the implied precision by their fine units. A solution to this problem will be offered in the final major section of this chapter.

Grade and Age Equivalents

A contrast will be useful. PRs and standard scores are typically used to show a person's status in a group to which he or she belongs. In contrast, a *developmental* score indicates the group within which an examinee's performance would be at the median.[1] For example, if fifth-grader John takes a fifth-grade math test and earns the same raw score on it as the median eighth-grader would obtain on it, then his grade equivalent is 8.

　　The school year is customarily divided into 10 intervals to enable decimalized reporting of **grade equivalent scores (GEs)**. Thus a GE of 1.0 is the level of performance exhibited by the typical beginning first-grader. A GE of 9.7 signifies median achievement among students who are in the seventh month of ninth grade. (A few tests omit the decimal and report GEs as two-digit numbers. Thus 1.0 becomes 10 and 9.7 becomes 97.)

　　An **age equivalent** indicates the chronological age at which a given youngster's status would be at the median. For example, if four-year-old Lucy takes a listening vocabulary test and obtains the same raw score as typical five-year-olds receive, then her age equivalent is five.

　　The calendar year is divided into 12 months. Thus an age equivalent of 4–2 is the level of performance typical of children who are four years and two months old. An age equivalent of 8–11 signifies median status among children who are eight years and eleven months old. Notice that a dash, not a decimal point, is used in age-equivalent scores.

　　Certain derivatives of age equivalents were once widely used. The best known of these was the (original kind of) IQ, which meant "intelligence quotient." It was called a quotient because it was obtained by dividing a child's mental age (i.e., the age equivalent obtained from an intelligence test) by her or his chronological age and multiplying the result by 100. This original kind of IQ is now called a "ratio IQ," but it has not been used in reputable tests published during the last 30 years.

Strengths of GEs and Age Equivalents

Responsible advocates of GEs defend them primarily as measures of growth during elementary school. The advocates believe that GEs are useful indicators of pupil growth, but they also point out that GEs should not be used to assess pupils' standing in their grades or their relative performance on different tests. PRs should be used for the latter purposes (Hieronymus, Hoover, & Lindquist, 1986, p. 26).

---

[1] A few tests have developmental scores defined in terms of means rather than medians.

Limitations of GEs and Age Equivalents

Age and grade equivalents enjoy great popularity "because they seem so blessedly simple to understand" (Popham, 1990, 164). But this appearance is deceptive. "They have many limitations which are not immediately apparent" (Lyman, 1991, p. 110). These lead to widespread misunderstanding, misinterpretation, and misuse. Several limitations most relevant to classroom teachers are examined below.

A feature that contributes to age and grade equivalents' apparent simplicity is an illusion of being domain-referenced standards that everyone should meet. While a spelling GE of 5.9 sounds to many people like a statement of what the examinee can or should do, it is not. The GE indicates the norm-referenced information that the examinee performed as well on the test as the typical end-of-fifth-grade pupil performs on it. Nobody would suggest that everyone should be above the 50th percentile. "Yet, people talk continually as if all sixth-graders should be reading at or above the sixth-grade equivalent" (Mehrens & Lehmann, 1991, p. 237). GEs, like all derived scores, provide normative information, not standards.

Like PRs, GEs and age equivalents lack equal units of measure. Figure 16–2 provides a generalized growth curve for school-aged people. A widely observed developmental trend is that growth slows as maturity is approached. By the time maturity is attained, growth stops altogether. For example, considerable difference exists between the spelling skill of first- and second-graders. There is much less difference between eleventh- and twelfth-graders' average spelling. Grade- and age-equivalent scores therefore have unequal units. This precludes their use for computational purposes.

Another ramification of the unequal units of measure concerns the impossibility of expressing the status of superior adults in age or grade equivalent units. I am 6'2" tall. How could you represent my stature as an age equivalent? At what age is the

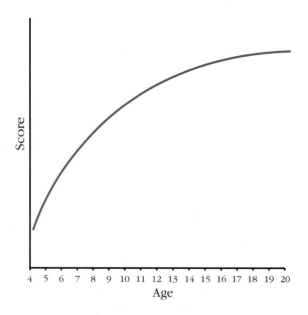

Figure 16–2. Generalized Growth Curve

median American male 6'2" tall? Likewise, how could the mental age of the average reader of this book be expressed as an age equivalent? It cannot.

Another problem with GEs is school attrition. Sad to say, many youths drop out of high school. Therefore, the difference between the median scores obtained by eleventh- and twelfth-graders on a test may be more a function of attrition than of growth between the grades. Of course, attrition is an even bigger factor in the college years.

A logical issue concerns the most relevant reference group for interpretive purposes. Suppose a boy aged 4–0 is measured for height and is tall for his age. How would his norm-referenced status best be reported? His age equivalent could be reported to be 5–0. This would report the group within which he would be at the median. It would provide a comparison with a group to which he does *not* belong. It would seem preferable for most purposes to report his status within the group to which he does belong (e.g., "compared with other age 4–0 males, he is taller than 90 out of every 100").

Yet another difficulty with GEs is the frequency with which they are misunderstood by parents and students. Let us return to our opening example. Fifth-grader John took a fifth-grade math test and obtained the same raw score that the median beginning eighth-grader receives; his grade equivalent is therefore 8.0. When his parents hear this they are likely to think they have been told that their prodigy is capable of doing eighth-grade math (and perhaps to wonder why he has not been double promoted).

Consider more carefully what the interpretation actually stated: John performed as well on the *fifth-grade* math test as the average eighth-grader would *on a fifth-grade math test.* He did not take an eighth-grade test that would include content that fifth-graders have not yet studied. Therefore, the test results report nothing about how well he handles eighth-grade work. However, the likely misinterpretation is not stupid. The problem is that GEs veritably beg to be misinterpreted.

Another major limitation of age- and grade-equivalent scores is their unequal variability across different attributes. In general, the variability of GEs is less for some subjects, such as math, than it is for others, such as reading. Here is an example. Brice, who is in the middle of the eighth grade took the *Iowa Tests of Basic Skills.* His GEs for the major divisions were all 10.0. The typical teacher, parent, principal, or student would interpret this to mean that Brice performed uniformly across the subject-matter areas. Not so! The PR equivalents of these GEs range from 77 in Language Skills to 87 in Mathematics Skills (Hieronymus & Hoover, 1990, p. 107). It is seen that developmental scores are ill-suited for profile interpretation.

Recommended Uses

Age and grade equivalents are inadequate for calculation because of their unequal units. For a variety of reasons they are also ill-suited for the majority of the interpretive purposes to which they are put; they are widely misunderstood and misinterpreted. Cronbach (1984, p. 102) summed it up well by saying that "professional opinion is critical of grade conversions."

Their *only* legitimate use is in the assessment of growth in elementary (and possibly middle) school children—and even this use is controversial. Many authorities (e.g., Cronbach, 1990) do not favor even this use, while others (e.g., Hoover, 1984) defend it.

Standard Scores

A **standard score** indicates an individual's deviancy from a group mean expressed in standard deviation units. The kind of standard score introduced in Chapter 11 was the z-score, which is the prototype of all standard scores. Recall the formula:

$$z = \frac{x}{SD}$$

where x is the individual's deviation score expressed in the metric of the raw score and SD is the standard deviation, also expressed in terms of the raw score units. When the two units of measurement cancel out, the z-score is left free of any unit-of-measure artifact.

Because z-scores are accompanied with algebraic signs and are expressed in such large units that they usually are reported to at least one unit beyond the decimal point, they are inconvenient to use in hand calculations. Various transformations are used to create more convenient kinds of standard scores. Some of the more common ones will now be introduced. Others will be presented in Chapters 17 and 18 when a test using them is presented.

Decimalized scores can be eliminated if z-scores are multiplied by a specified number. Common multiplicative constants are 10, 15, 16, and 100.

Negative z-scores can be eliminated if a specified number is added to each z-score. Common additive constants are 50, 100, and 500.

Table 16–1 provides the constants that are used to develop several of the common varieties of standard scores.[2]

Table 16–1

Defining Constants for Selected Standard Scores

Kind of Standard Score	M	SD
z-score	0	1
T-score	50	10
DIQ_{15}	100	15
DIQ_{16}	100	16
Stanine	5	2
CEEB	500	100

---

[2]Some standard scores are normalized; others are not. Non-normalized standard scores are derived by the formulas using the constants presented in Table 16–1. It is they that are described in this section.

However, the standard scores provided with most published instruments are normalized. They are obtained first by computing the *PR* corresponding to each raw score. Then each *PR* is converted into the z-score equivalent in a *normal distribution*. This z-score is then transformed into any of several other kinds of standard scores as explained in this section.

The relative advantages of normalized and non-normalized standard scores involve technical issues to which practitioners need not attend. They rarely differ significantly, and test users generally do not need to be aware of which kind of standard score is provided for a given test.

T-Scores.   A kind of standard score known as the **T-score** is used in many psychological tests and a few education ones (e.g., the PSAT, to be discussed in Chapter 18). T-scores are obtained by multiplying the z-score by 10 and then adding 50. The formula is expressed as $T = 10z + 50$. The second row of Table 16–1 provides information about T-scores; their standard deviation is 10 (achieved by multiplying by 10) and their mean is 50 (achieved by adding 50).

It is useful to have some sense of how T-scores correspond to PRs. Figure 16–3 provides the corresponding values at selected points in a normal distribution. Figure 16–3 also clarifies the fact that T-scores and other varieties of standard scores are really just relabeled z-scores.

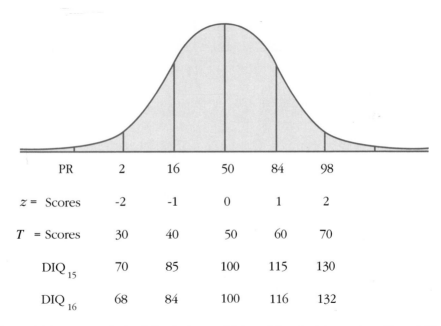

PR	2	16	50	84	98
z = Scores	-2	-1	0	1	2
T = Scores	30	40	50	60	70
DIQ_{15}	70	85	100	115	130
DIQ_{16}	68	84	100	116	132

Figure 16–3.   Percentile Rank Equivalents of Selected Standard Scores in a Normal Distribution

Deviation IQs.   A half-century ago, authors of some then-advanced intelligence tests began to seek better derived scores for their tests than the old IQs (now called ratio IQs). In order to attain public acceptance of the newer scores, a system of standard scores was developed to mimic ratio IQs. These standard scores were assigned a mean of 100 and a standard deviation of 15 or 16. The third and fourth rows of Table 16–1 provide the data for these scores.

Although they were true standard scores, they were called **deviation IQs (DIQs)**. Their computational properties are far superior to those of old ratio IQs, which have fallen into disuse since about 1960. Figure 16–3 shows the relationship of DIQs to PRs, z-scores, and T-scores.

As will be mentioned in Chapter 18, newer aptitude tests and recent editions of most older ones have retained the kind of standard score known as DIQs but have replaced their *name* with terms that more aptly describe the scores' meaning in terms of what the tests really measure.

Stanines.   Another type of standard score has a *M* of 5 and *SD* of 2, as shown in the fifth row of Table 16–1. Limited to 9 intervals, these "standard nines" are called **stanines**. Figure 16–4 shows their relationship to PRs.

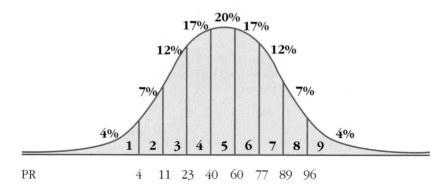

Figure 16–4.   Relationship of Stanines to the Normal Curve and Percentile Ranks

CEEB Scores.   The College Entrance Examination Board devised a novel kind of standard score for its college admissions Scholastic Aptitude Test (SAT). The same system is used for the Graduate Record Examination, which is widely used for admission to graduate programs. These standard scores have a *M* of 500 and a *SD* of 100.

In addition to their main use in predicting academic success of examinees, these tests are used to study trends in applicant test performance. They provide a fixed reference against which year-to-year averages can be compared. In the case of the SAT, this is achieved by using the original 1941 examinees as the reference group for the standard scores (Anastasi, 1988).

Useful as this is for research purposes, it is of much less importance for a contemporary high school senior to know how he or she compared with a (much more selective pre-World War II) sample from the past than it is to know how he or she compares with contemporary peers. For this purpose the SAT soundly provides PRs based on current samples of college preparatory examinees.

Strengths

Standard scores have equal units of measure and are therefore suitable for calculation purposes. With the exception of stanines, which have larger units and accompanying grouping error, one kind of standard score is about as good as another.

Limitations

An understanding of standard scores requires technical knowledge. Hence, they are generally unsuitable for interpretive purposes to lay people.

Two kinds of standard scores merit special caveats. First, IQs and scores that simulate them "are especially open to misinterpretation" (Cronbach, 1990, p. 117). Although DIQs have great *technical* merit over ratio IQs, they are, nonetheless, questionable for interpretive purposes. PRs serve much better.

Second, stanines are sometimes used for interpretations because they do not overrepresent test precision. However, stanines suffer from grouping error (with an accompanying loss of reliability). Moreover, they are rather esoteric. To give them meaning, most people who interpret stanine scores to students or parents use a figure like Figure 16–4. Aside from the intimidating and needlessly distracting impact that a normal curve can have, it should be noted that stanines are thus given *meaning via definitions in terms of PRs*. It seems more parsimonious simply to use the PRs. In my judgment, the important goal of avoiding the impression that a test is more accurate than it really is is better met by use of confidence bands, a topic addressed below.

Recommended Uses

Because of their equal units, standard scores are recommended for computational purposes.

Because of their technical nature, standard scores are ill-suited for interpretive purposes. It is especially wise to avoid interpretive use of kinds of standard scores that are misunderstood to signify that a test measures attributes that it does not, in fact, measure. Thus DIQs are particularly ill-advised for interpretive purposes.

QUIZ 16–1

For each of Items 1–4, select the kind of derived score that would best be used for the indicated test use.

A. Percentile ranks
B. Grade or age equivalents
C. Standard scores

1. A teacher wants to calculate the mean class score on a published reading test from individual student scores.
2. A teacher wants to explain to a pupil how she scored on the published reading test.
3. A teacher wants to show a couple their child's relative status on scores of an achievement battery's subtests on several school subjects.
4. A school psychologist wants to compare Fred's verbal aptitude test score with his silent reading comprehension test score to determine if there is enough difference between the scores for him to qualify for a learning disabilities program.

For each of the following items, select the best option. Use Figure 16–3 as needed.

5. A DIQ of 100 is equivalent to a *z*-score of
    A. -2.
    B. -1.
    C. 0.
    D. 1.
    E. 2.

QUIZ 16–1 (cont.)

6. A DIQ of 70 is equivalent to a PR of about

   A.   1.
   B.   2.
   C.   50.
   D.   70.
   E.   98.

7. A PR of 98 is equivalent to a DIQ of approximately
   A.   2.
   B.   70.
   C.   98.
   D.   100.
   E.   130.

8. Which has the largest units?
   A.   Stanines.
   B.   *T*-scores.
   C.   CEEB scores.
   D.   DIQs.

9. Scores of three children on a math test are given below. The same reference group was used to derive each kind of score. Which child performed the best?
   A.   Adam had a PR of 30.
   B.   Beth had a *T*-score of 30.
   C.   Chad had a stanine of 8.

KEY TO QUIZ 16–1

1. C   Because standard scores have equal units of measure, only they are suitable. (A teacher not wanting to use them might consider use of the class median rather than the mean. It could be obtained for PRs.)

2. A   Comparison with a pupil's grade-mates is best achieved by PRs.

3. A   Such profile interpretation is best done with PRs drawn on a scale that compensates for their unequal units of measure. This will be illustrated in Figures 16–5 and 16–6 below. (A case could possibly also be made for standard scores, but, being much more technical, they are less suited for lay people.)

4. C.   This numerical comparison is best conducted with a scale having equal units of measure. The school psychologist would be acquainted with the technical features of the various kinds of standard scores.

> ## KEY TO QUIZ 16–1 (cont.)
>
> 5. **C.** From Figure 16–3 it is seen that a DIQ of 100 is at the mean. The corresponding z-score is 0.
>
> 6. **B.** Figure 16–3 shows that a DIQ_{15} of 70 and a DIQ_{16} of 68 equates to a PR of 2.
>
> 7. **E.** Figure 16–3 shows that a PR of 98 represents the same degree of superiority as a z-score of 2, a T-score of 70, or DIQs of 130 or 132.
>
> 8. **A.** Since stanines have only 9 possible values, these nine intervals must cover the entire distribution. Thus each unit is large. (If you chose C, you might think through this analogous question: Which has the larger units, weeks or months?)
>
> 9. **C.** A PR of 30 is a little below average. A T-score of 30 is two full standard deviations below average. A stanine of 8 is well above average (actually between 1.25 and 1.75 *SDs* above average).

Appropriate Computational Uses of Derived Scores

Recall from Chapter 11 that the computation of the mean and statistics based on it (e.g., *SD* and *r*) require equal units of measure. We have seen that simple ranks and PRs lack equal units of measure. Rank units tend to be smaller near the center of distributions than at the extremes. Ranks and PRs, therefore, have extremely limited utility for data management and data summary. For example, the median is the most powerful measure of central tendency that can legitimately be used with PRs.

We have also seen that age- and grade-equivalent scores lack equal units of measure. Units tend to be smaller in size as maturity is approached (and to have zero size after maturity is reached). Developmental scores therefore have only meager computational utility. For example, the median is the most powerful appropriate measure of central tendency for age- and grade-equivalent scores. Similarily, Pearson *r* is not suitable for scales lacking equal units of measure.

Finally, the various kinds of standard scores are blessed with equal units of measure.[3] This renders them suitable for the kinds of data manipulations educators often perform. Therefore, *standard scores are the preferred score to use when calculations are performed.*[4]

Of the various kinds of standard scores, two are notably less suitable for computation than others. As mentioned above, one is stanines. The other is a variety of

---

[3]As noted in Chapter 11, raw scores often do not have perfectly equal units. Similarly, non-normalized standard scores (being derived via linear transformations of raw scores) lack perfectly equal units of measure. However, unit inequality is minor and is wisely ignored by practitioners (Nunnally, 1978).

[4]Some authorities, therefore, urge the use of standard scores for combining components for grading purposes. Because most teachers prefer not to routinely convert their raw scores into standard scores, the approach presented in Chapter 12 avoided use of standard scores for computation of grades. This was achieved by attending very closely to variability—something inherent in the use of standard scores.

standard score used to report subtests of certain aptitude tests. These standard scores have a *M* of 10 and a *SD* of 3. It is the small *SD* (making each unit large) that renders them relatively inaccurate.

The alleged advantage of stanines is their broad units that do not imply undue precision. The concomitant problem is that broad intervals create grouping errors. That is, they hide differences within each interval, and they exaggerate trivial differences between borderline cases of adjacent intervals.

Appropriate Interpretive Uses of Derived Scores[5]

One who interprets test scores has several simultaneous concerns. Brief mention will first be made of two that do not happen to be central to this chapter. First, it is necessary for the recipient of the interpretation to understand clearly the content domain measured by the test. Even in norm-referenced interpretation, substantial information about the content domain is necessary for the derived scores to have meaning. "Your national PR of the math test was 73" is meager. Does the test focus on computation, concepts, problem solving, or some blend of these? Even large and ill-defined domains can be clarified (e.g., "As you know, the test assessed your ability to apply the Bill of Rights to a wide variety of current-event-type situations.")

Second, the reference group needs to be identified. Derived scores can be based on local, regional, or national groups. They can be gender specific or combined. They can be based on age-based peers or on grade-based peers. Certain combinations of these are suitable for some interpretive needs. The point is that any reference group used should be relevant to the purpose of the interpretation, and this reference group should be identified (e.g., "Compared with other fourth-graders in our school district . . . ," "In comparison with a national cross-section of eighth-grade girls . . . ," or "Compared with a national sample of second-year, high school German students . . . "). Use of large-city norms, gender-specific norms, etc., will be illustrated in the next two chapters as specific published tests are discussed.

Following are interpretive suggestions that are central to this chapter on derived scores and their interpretation.

Replace Misleading Names with Descriptive Ones

The names given tests, the names given constructs, and the kinds of derived scores used for interpretations can lead to misunderstandings. Following are some cautions concerning how certain terms often lead to serious misunderstanding regarding what a test measures or what its scores mean.

Names of Constructs.   The distinction between aptitude and achievement is unclear to some people. (The achievement-aptitude continuum will be discussed in Chapter 18.) Persons receiving interpretations should be helped to understand the nature of

---

[5]Parts of this section are adapted from (Hanna) *Journal of Counseling and Development*, Volume 6, 1988, pages 477-483. ©AACD. Reprinted with permission. No further reproduction authorized without written permission of American Association for Counseling and Development.

the test under discussion. The word "ability" is especially likely to blur distinctions because, depending upon context, it can mean either aptitude or achievement. The word is often better avoided.

Similarly, as will be emphasized in Chapter 19, students who have taken an interest inventory are apt to forget the nature of its items and think it is a measure of achievement or aptitude. The distinctions often has to be pointed out more than once during an interpretation.

Perhaps the most commonly misunderstood construct name is "intelligence." To many people, this word stands for far more than present aptitude for school-type learning. Yet that is what most so-called intelligence tests are designed to assess. The *Cognitive Abilities Test* and the *Otis-Lennon School Ability Test* are laudable examples of contemporary tests that now avoid altogether the oft-misunderstood word "intelligence."

Names of Derived Scores.   Certain derived scores have names that are often misunderstood. "IQ" tops the list. "The intelligence quotient (IQ) is one of the most misunderstood concepts in measurement" (Mehrens & Lehmann, 1991, p. 234). Vast numbers of lay people, forgetting that aptitude tests only *sample current behavior,* think of "IQ" as a genetically fixed attribute that is unaffected by environment. Moreover, contemporary tests' "IQs" (i.e., DIQs) are not "quotients" at all; rather they are standard scores. Many of the better tests now available use more descriptive terms such as "Standard Age Score" or "School Ability Index" instead of the widely misunderstood "IQ." I urge educators to avoid the term "IQ" for interpreting scores to parents or students. More descriptive terms that are more easily grasped should replace this obsolete and widely misunderstood term.

Another term that is often misunderstood is "percentile rank." Although PRs are the kind of derived score of preference for most *interpretive* purposes, they have some minor problems. For one thing, the term "percentile rank" seems to demand a grasp of the concept of percent of the reference group. For young children and older persons for whom math is only a bad memory, this term can be an affective and conceptual obstacle to a clear understanding. Fortunately, this problem is easily circumvented by avoiding the terms "percentile," "centile," and "percent." *PRs can be used without use of their name.* For instance, one might say, "Pedro ran the lap faster than 79 out of every 100 eight-year-old boys in the country," or "Muriel scored better on the reading test than 25 out of every 100 tenth-graders in our school." By avoiding use of words such as "percent," the confusion can be avoided.

Another problem is that the term "percentile" often causes lay people (including well-educated ones) to confuse the idea of percent of a reference group of other people with the notion of percent of test items. The unfamiliar word "percentile" is decoded as "percent," and people's prior associations in test interpretations with "percent" scores are retrieved with the consequence that thinking shifts to a percent score. Such a percent-of-raw-score interpretation would be suitable for a domain-referenced interpretation of Track A content rather than for a people-referenced interpretation necessary of Track C content.

Fortunately, this confusion is also easily forestalled by avoiding the word "percentile" with people who may not understand it. *Use the concept of PR without necessarily employing its troublesome name.* For example, the statement "Harry received a percentile score of 65 on a nationally normed seventh-grade math computation test," may elicit an anguished parental response of, "Heavens! That's barely passing." The parent has apparently interpreted the statement to mean that Harry answered 65% of the items correctly. The misunderstanding could be corrected by explaining that percentile scores do not refer to percent of items answered correctly, but rather to percent of other examinees that his performance equaled or surpassed. It would have been preferable, however, to have prevented the confusion in the first place by avoiding the word "percentile"; e.g., "Harry's math computation score was equal to or better than 65 out of every 100 seventh-graders in the country." If greater simplicity were sought, the "65 out of 100" could be reduced to "13 out of 20," or rounded to "about 2 out of 3."

Avoid Jargon

Those who interpret test scores need to communicate what scores mean as simply as possible without introducing esoteric symbols or jargon. We need to go to pains not to overwhelm or confuse students or parents. On the contrary, the purpose is to aid understanding.

It is helpful for those of us who interpret test scores to put ourselves in the shoes of the lay person who is receiving an interpretation. This can be achieved by moving outside one's own professional field. When, for example, you or I receive an X-ray interpretation from our dentist, we do not want to be "snowed" by technicalities; rather we need the *meaning* of the findings as *simply and completely* as possible.

Here is a useful self-test for professionals: *If an expert cannot provide an interpretation in nontechnical language that typical lay people can understand, then there is reason to doubt how well the professional understands the material.* Thus if your dentist cannot explain the meaning of your X-rays in terms you understand—costs, inconvenience, discomfort, cosmetics, and durability of alternative treatments (or non-treatment)—then you may need a new dentist. If your attorney cannot explain the meaning of a rental agreement or a will in ways you can understand, then you have cause to wonder just how well the attorney understands the document beyond the surface level of being able to parrot jargon. And if a teacher, counselor, or administrator cannot explain the meaning of a test score in terms that typical parents or students can readily grasp, then the educator likely does not have an adequate command of the underlying concepts.

A central goal of test interpreters is thus to reveal the meaning of the test scores in *ways that are meaningful to the recipient.* Recipients vary in their background knowledge. Interpretations should, therefore, be varied to be appropriate to the particular audience.

Provide for a Margin of Error

Another goal of interpretation involves avoidance of overinterpretation. Many students and parents are prone to attribute greater validity and reliability to test scores than is justified. Thus we need to take care to communicate the presence of measurement error.

Although measurement error is ubiquitous, many lay people tend to take test scores far too seriously—to forget that tests provide only imperfect, fallible measures. Test interpreters have the joint responsibility of (a) reporting as much as the test scores reveal and (b) disclosing the limits of confidence that should be placed on this information. In other words, a need exists to point out the implications of the score and to allow a margin of error in these interpretations.

This "balancing act" is best achieved by somewhat different means in interpretations designed to describe an examinee's current status than in ones that forecast the future. The foundations for status interpretations were laid in Chapter 15, while those of prediction are rooted in Chapter 14. Thus the topics of this section could have been treated in the last two chapters. They have been juxtaposed and located here to emphasize their central relevance to score interpretation and to highlight their common purposes: (a) to convey what a score reveals and (b) to communicate a healthy respect for the limits thereof.

Making Descriptive Interpretations

As seen in Chapter 15, standard errors of measurement provide a good way to express amount of measurement error in terms of a test's raw scores. Recall that out of every 100 people who obtain a given score, 68 will have true status that lies within the plus and minus 1 *SEM* range. Similarly, about 95% of people's true status on what a particular test assesses will lie within the range created by adding and subtracting 2 *SEM*s from their obtained scores.

Such ranges provide intervals within which the correct values probably lie. A **confidence band** or **confidence interval** is a range of values that probably contains the true status. An everyday example is provided by someone asking, "How old would you estimate Professor Brown to be?" A common answer might be, "Oh, I'd say about 43, give or take five years." Or you are asked, "About what is your status in spelling?" You might answer, "Probably between the 65th and 80th PRs of the adult population of college graduates."

In each case, a confidence band has been offered (although the likelihood of it containing the true status is unknown). Confidence intervals can use either raw scores (as in the first example) or derived scores (as in the second example). Confidence bands based upon *SEM*s, which enable one to know the likelihood of the band containing the true status, are used in a wide variety of situations to report simultaneously (a) what is known from a measurement and (b) the extent of uncertainty that accompanies this knowledge.

Reporting test results without an accompanying emphasis on measurement error often leads to naive misuse of test results. Providing only a specific PR misrepresents the tests as being reliable enough to pinpoint a person's status. The problem, then, is that in trying to communicate what has been learned from a test with a single number that represents the examinee's most likely status, an interpreter can easily imply much more precision of measurement than is actually present.

The remedy is to report scores in such a way that a lay person will be sure to understand the key point that *we do not know the examinee's exact status;* we only know how he or she scored on a particular occasion on a certain form of the test administered by a given examiner and scored by a particular scorer. The goal and challenge is to openly report all that is known from a test score about the person's true status without fostering overconfidence in an exact score. This is best achieved by reporting a range that probably contains the score the examinee would have received on a perfectly reliable form of the test. In essence, this indicates that no score is free of error, so it is best to think of a score not as a discrete number but as a range of numbers, any one of which could represent the examinee's true status on an error-free test (Airasian, 1991, p. 383).

Some published tests provide percentile bands for this purposes. PR intervals can be presented as numeric ranges, such as 55–79 and/or represented graphically in a variety of ways. When they are depicted with visual aids, it is usually beneficial to use a scale that adjusts for the unequal units of measure. Figure 16–5 shows a vertical bar graph used for showing a percentile band of 66–96 based on the obtained score plus and minus 1 *SEM*; the "odds" are thus about 68 in 100 that the examinee's true status lies within this range.

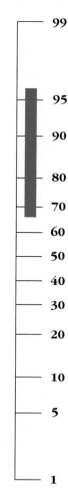

Figure 16–5. Vertical Bar Graph of Percentile Band

Figure 16–6 displays a two-level confidence band. The heavy, dark segment (19–66) is based on an obtained score plus and minus 1 *SEM*. The chances are thus about 2 in 3 (i.e., 68 in 100) that his or her true level of functioning lies within this range. The light segment (8–84) is based on the obtained score plus and minus 2 *SEM*s. The odds are therefore about 19 in 20 (i.e., 95 in 100) that the person's true status lies within this interval.

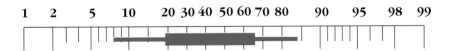

Figure 16–6. Two-Level Confidence Band

Notice the trade-off. If a very precise statement is made (e.g., "Your PR is 43."), it has little chance of being true. If a somewhat less precise statement is ventured (e.g., "Out of every one hundred people obtaining the same score as you, about two-thirds would get PRs between 19 and 66 on an error-free form of the test"), then better odds of being correct are obtained. In order to secure decent odds of being correct, the price was a somewhat vague statement. If still better odds are desired, further trade-off with vagueness must be made (e.g., "Out of every 100 students scoring like you, about 95 would receive PRs between 8 and 84 on a perfectly reliable form of the test").

Mention should be made of a public relations and rapport problem that sometimes attends use of confidence bands. Some test interpreters fear that reporting broad ranges of scores within which a person's real status probably lies is not specific enough to provide the examinee with needed information about her or his performance. To say that Maria's PR is somewhere between 50 and 78 is so vague that it appears to some people to constitute an admission of inadequacy of the test and/or the person interpreting its scores. On the contrary, it is a *disclosure* of the extent to which the particular test, like all measures, is not totally reliable. Qualified professionals honestly reveal the limitations of their knowledge. To obscure these limitations is to deceive and to misrepresent. *Competent test interpreters meaningfully disclose the fact that scores lack precision.*

If Maria's parent is dismayed that the test is so inaccurate, then it should be explained that this and similar tests *are* that imprecise and that it is therefore very important to *recognize* and allow for this reality. The greater the distress over the size of a confidence band, the greater was the naivete about the reliability of the scores. The greater the outrage because of crudeness of measuring devices, the greater the need for the person to realize the extent of tests' crudeness of measurement. It is usually feasible to refer to some kinds of measures with which the person is more familiar to illustrate the need to allow for a *margin of error.*

Suppose Jane Quigley took a mechanics-of-expression test and earned a PR of 58 with respect to a representative national reference group of tenth-grade students. Suppose the *SEM* at this score level yields a band of 38–76. (Notice that 38–76 is not exactly symmetrical around the score of 58. This is because the PR units near the center of the distribution are smaller.)

Following is an example of how the interpretation of Jane's percentile band might be made with each of the aims discussed in this section in mind. Note (a) the domain description, (b) the description of the reference group, (c) the explanation of PRs, and (d) the introduction of the notion of measurement error (in content sampling and occasion sampling) in terms that a lay person can readily understand.

As you know, Mrs. Quigley, Jane took the *Mechanics of Expression Test* to give us an estimate of how well she manages such things as capitalization, punctuation, noun-verb agreement, and word choice (such as who vs. whom and me vs. myself). We interpret performance on this kind of subject matter by seeing how students compare with a national sample of other tenth-graders.

The way we show how a person's performance compares with that of others is to report a percentile rank, which is the percentage of students that was outperformed or equaled. For example, if we said Joe's percentile rank was 15, it would mean that his status on this particular sample of behavior was as good as or better than only 15 out of every 100. If we said that Al's percentile rank was 50, it would mean that his performance was average. In this way, we are able to show how a student's score on the test compares with the scores of a large group of grade-mates across the country.

It is important to realize that Jane's performance on the particular form of the test that happened to be administered on this particular day does not provide the last word on her true command of mechanics of expression. It is always possible that the test may have caught her on an unusually bad (or good) day. Or the questions in a certain form of the test could happen to hit on a disproportionate fraction of the things she knows best (or least). Achievement tests, like measures in every field, are not completely accurate. Wise use of any kind of measure makes allowance for error of measurement.

Whenever we measure anything, we should think of a margin of error to allow for imperfect accuracy. For example, an oven thermometer will give slightly different readings depending on its location in an oven. In the same way, the odometers of several cars making the same trip will show slightly different mileage readings. Or several carpenters measuring a board are not likely to agree exactly on its length. Thus error of measurement is present in all fields, and education is no exception.

Now if we placed 100 different thermometers in various parts of an oven and read each, we could establish a range of scores within which most of the readings would lie. Similarly, if the odometer readings for a given trip were secured from many different cars, we could make a range of values—such as 345–348 miles—within which most of the distances would agree. If we asked many carpenters to measure the board, we could express its length as a range of scores within which some fraction—say, two-thirds—of the carpenters agreed.

That is what we will do with Jane's test score. Judging from her performance on the form of the test she was given on one particular day, we can say the chances are about 2 out of 3 that her true score lies within a certain range. That is, we can be moderately confident that the score she would have received on an error-free form of the test would have been within this band of scores.

Jane's percentile band is 38–76. Thus the percentage of tenth-graders she excels or equals is probably between 38 and 76. We are, therefore, quite confident that her status is *not* in the bottom third or so of the representative national sample of tenth-grade students. We are also reasonably assured that her true achievement is *not* in the top fourth. Her mechanics of expression appears to be somewhere in the average range. If her status differs from the average, it is a little more likely to be slightly above average than below, but in any case it is probably fairly close to average.

TO RECAP

To summarize, percentile bands combine the utility of PRs with an emphasis that a score should not be considered precise. They also have the advantage over coarse-unit scores such as stanines of having consecutive bands differ only slightly. This is possible because percentile bands are centered on actual obtained score, not on pre-established gross intervals (Lyman, 1991, p. 104). Percentile bands therefore provide a fine way of communicating to students and parents both what scores reveal and the limits of what they reveal. They are recommended for use in interpreting examinee status.

Making Predictive Interpretations

Recall Clint Weber from Chapter 14, the counselor who used eighth-grade English grades to predict students' grades in first-year French. He looked up the two grades for each of 150 recent students and computed the Pearson r between them, finding r to equal .49. Unfortunately, this predictive validity coefficient does not help Mr. Weber foster student understanding of the degree to which the predictor correctly forecasts future achievement and the degree to which a margin for predictive error should be allowed. To aid students and parents in understanding the meaning of the predictive measure, Mr. Weber might wisely format his findings concerning the past experience of his sample of former students into an **experience (or expectancy) table** (American Psychological Association, 1985, p. 53; Cronbach, 1990).

The first step in developing an experience table is to cross-tabulate each person in the sample with respect to the two variables. This is shown in section (a) of Figure 16–7. Next, the tally marks in each cell of the resulting scattergram are converted into a numeral as shown in (b) of Figure 16–7. In addition, the total number of persons represented in each row is entered. Then the number of persons in each cell is divided by the number of persons in its row. The resulting decimal fraction for each cell is shown in (c). Finally, these decimal fractions are converted into percentages as shown in (d). It is also useful for the final expectancy table to report the number of cases on which the data in each row are based so that users can know how much confidence to place on each row's entries.

Such a table enables the student or parent simultaneously to understand two critical things about the prediction. First, experience tables show just how valid the test was in predicting the criterion. Second, expectancy tables reveal with equal clarity the extent to which the predictions were imperfect. These two concerns, the amount of confidence to have in a score and the amount of margin to allow for error, are both indispensable to informed use of data.

Suppose Samantha had a B in eighth-grade English and Mr. Weber is explaining to her what this means in terms of her likely grades in French. He can use Figure 16–7(d) to show her that out of every 100 students who received a B in eighth-grade English 3 failed first-semester French, 16 were awarded grades of D, 26 obtained grades of C, 34 received B grades, and 21 earned grades of A. Such a walk through a row of an experience table will do much to help Samantha understand both the amount of forecasting power the predictor has and the limits of this power.

(a) A scattergram with tally marks

Grade in English		Grades in French — F	D	C	B	A
	A	/	///	卌	卌 ///	卌 卌
	B	/	卌 /	卌 卌	卌 卌 ///	卌 ///
	C	/	卌 卌 ////	卌 卌 卌 /	卌 卌	卌 /
	D	卌 ////	卌 卌	卌 ////	///	//
	F	///	/	/		

(b) A numeric representation of the same data

Grade in English		Grades in French — F	D	C	B	A	Totals
	A	1	3	5	8	10	27
	B	1	6	10	13	8	38
	C	1	14	16	10	6	47
	D	9	10	9	3	2	33
	F	3	1	1	0	0	5

(c) Decimal fraction representation of same data

Grade in English		Fraction Receiving Each English Grade Who Later Received Each French Grade — F	D	C	B	A
	A	.04	.11	.19	.30	.37
	B	.03	.16	.26	.34	.21
	C	.02	.30	.34	.21	.13
	D	.27	.30	.27	.09	.06
	F	.60	.20	.20	.00	.00

(d) Experience table from scattergram

Grade in English		No.	Percent Receiving Each English Grade Who Later Received Each French Grade — F	D	C	B	A
	A	27	4%	11%	19%	30%	37%
	B	38	3%	16%	26%	34%	21%
	C	47	2%	30%	34%	21%	13%
	D	33	27%	30%	27%	9%	6%
	F	5	60%	20%	20%	0%	0%

Total No. 150

To Use Table for Predictions: Locate student's eighth-grade English grade at left. Then read across that row to find the percentage of students who received that English grade who later received each grade in French.

Figure 16–7. Development of Experience Table from Scattergram: (a) a scattergram with tally marks; (b) a numeric representation of the same data; (c) decimal fraction representation of same data; (d) experience table from scattergram.

QUIZ 16–2

Following is an experience table that can be used to predict grades in the first semester of first-year algebra. Use the table to answer the questions that follow it.

QUIZ 16–2 (cont.)

Experience Table Showing Percentages of Students in the Combined Eighth-and Seventh-Grade Validity Sample Earning Each Final Course Grade in Algebra at Successive Intervals of the *Algebra Prognosis Test* Scores*

Prognosis Test Score		*Final Algebra Grade*				
Total Raw Score (0–100)	*Number of Students*	*Percentage Earning Each Grade*				
		F	*D*	*C*	*B*	*A*
96–100	74	0	0	4	23	73
91–95	100	0	2	15	35	48
86–90	159	1	3	29	43	25
81–85	162	2	12	33	39	14
76–80	145	1	12	41	32	14
71–75	124	8	21	42	23	6
66–70	102	11	25	40	19	5
61–65	72	11	26	39	21	3
56–60	51	14	27	49	10	0
51–55	45	22	38	22	16	2
41–50	56	32	29	29	9	2
21–40	22	41	36	14	5	5

Total N = 1112

$M = 76.0$ $M = 2.3$
$SD = 15.0$ $SD = 1.2$

*Adapted from the *Orleans-Hanna Algebra Prognosis Test Manual.* Copyright © 1968, revised 1982 by The Psychological Corporation. Reproduced by permission. All rights reserved.

1. Chi received a prognosis test raw score of 68. What grade is he most likely to receive in algebra?

2. Out of every 100 students receiving a score of 45, how many fail algebra?

3. If Mary receives a score of 98 on the prognosis test, can we be *certain* that she will pass algebra with at least a grade of C?

4. From "eyeballing" the experience table, guess the size of the Pearson *r*.

KEY TO QUIZ 16–2

1. Chi is more likely to receive a C than any other grade.
2. 32.
3. No. Of the 74 youngsters in the validation sample who scored at about this level, none received grade of less than C, but it is possible. With a much larger sample, some probably would have. It would be best simply to indicate that fewer than 1% (or fewer than one-half of 1%) who scored as well as she did would be likely to learn a grade lower than C.
4. Any guess between about .5 and .7 is good. The actual *r* is .61.

Chapter Summary

Derived scores are obtained from raw scores by use of normative information. *Derived scores are necessary for norm-referenced interpretation because they are the means by which examinee status relative to other people is reported.* Hence, derived scores are always based on the performance of people in a reference group, and interpreters should ensure the relevance of the reference group for the interpretive purpose.

One way of categorizing derived scores is provided by the distinction between status scores and developmental scores. Percentile ranks are a kind of status score that indicates the percentage of a reference group (usually grade, age, or course peers) that an examinee equaled or excelled. *PRs and/or percentile bands are widely regarded as well suited for interpreting scores to students and their parents.* PRs are poorly suited for data computation because they lack equal units of measure.

Standard scores are status scores that indicate examinee deviancy from a (usually grade, age, or course peer) group mean in standard deviation units. *Standard scores are generally considered to be the best suited kinds of derived scores for computation because they have equal units of measure.* Standard scores are ill-suited for interpretive purposes because they are based on technical concepts that pose unnecessary obstacles to meaningful communication.

Developmental derived scores, unlike status scores, indicate the group within which the examinee would be average. They are popular with many teachers, administrators, and school psychologists, but they have grave limitations. *Grade-equivalent and age-equivalent scores should not be used to interpret a person's status, to analyze relative strengths and weaknesses, or to perform statistical calculation.* If they have any legitimate function, it is in the assessment of growth at the elementary school level.

Persons responsible for interpreting test scores to students and parents have a responsibility not only to report what the scores indicate but also to disclose the extent to which the scores are unreliable or invalid. In making descriptive interpretations of current examinee status, percentile bands provide the best way to simultaneously accomplish these two important functions. In making predictive interpretations, expectancy tables offer the best means of revealing the extent to which the test forecasts validly.

Suggestions for Further Reading

Lyman, H. B. (1991). *Test scores and what they mean* (5th ed.). Englewood Cliffs, NJ: Prentice-Hall. A very readable paperback book focused on scores and their meaning. Chapter 5, "Derived Scores," is particularly relevant to this book's Chapter 16.

Mehrens, W. A., & Lehmann, I. J. (1991). *Measurement and evaluation in education and psychology* (4th ed.). New York: Holt, Rinehart and Winston. Chapter 11, "Norms, Scores, and Profiles," provides a sound introduction to derived scores and their interpretive uses.

Seashore, H. G. (1955). *Methods of expressing test scores.* Test Service Bulletin No. 48. San Antonio: The Psychological Corporation. This classic description of several kinds of derived scores contains sound cautions about possible misinterpretation. It also provides a widely reprinted conversion chart.

Thorndike, R. M., Cunningham, G. K., Thorndike, R. L., & Hagen E. P. (1991). *Measurement and evaluation in psychology and education* (5th ed.). New York: Macmillan. Chapter 3, "Giving Meaning to Scores," gives a good introduction to derived scores and their interpretive uses.

17

Achievement Tests

As mentioned in Chapter 4, published achievement tests are, by and large, summative instruments designed to assess broader segments of content than teacher-made unit tests (e.g., whole courses rather than short units). The decisions they are designed to inform are, therefore, of the broad-stroke type rather than detail type (e.g., what level of reading would most benefit Tyron rather than does Tyron know how to pronounce a particular diphthong).

Since published tests tend to cover whole courses (e.g., biology) or broad content areas (e.g., social studies or reading), they typically span large, ill-defined content domains and are therefore given norm-referenced interpretations. Herein is the major advantage of published tests—they ordinarily supply reference-group data for groups larger than individual classes. In addition, commercially developed tests are usually developed by specialists in instrument construction and subject matter. They therefore tend to exhibit higher technical quality than teacher-made tests in such matters as freedom from major item flaws, item discrimination, formatting, printing, and reliability.

These generalizations have exceptions. Some published tests are designed to yield domain-referenced interpretations and are not accompanied by normative data. Some focus on separate objectives and/or small instructional segments rather than broad content areas. And some are ineptly prepared. Nonetheless, the generalizations offered above are ordinarily true.

This chapter will present general information about published achievement tests and offer selected examples of widely used ones. The examples are designed to illustrate a variety of instrument features and to provide some familiarity with certain well-known tests. In keeping with this book's primary focus on better teaching through better testing (in contrast to the study of tests *per se*), no effort will be made to systematically survey all widely used instruments or to address all of the major characteristics of those that are discussed. Topics will be included for their ability to illustrate points, not for comprehensiveness of coverage.

Separate Tests

On occasion, educators use specialized tests of particular subjects, such as biology, American history, reading, or algebra. Such tests have their greatest use at the secondary level in subjects not taken by all students, such as chemistry, French, or trigonometry. Because the market of potential buyers of some such tests is limited, there are fewer such instruments than teachers might wish, and they often become quite aged between revisions.

Four examples of separate tests will be examined, including two survey tests and two diagnostic. Categorizing these tests another way, three are group administered and one is individually administered.

Sequential Tests of Educational Progress End-of-Course Tests: Biology

Achievement in elective high school subjects cannot, of course, be surveyed by batteries designed for all students. Special end-of-course tests are needed for use with students enrolled in the respective elective subjects. Interpretation of such tests' scores is best referenced to the performance of other students who have taken the respective courses. The biology test accompanying the *Sequential Tests of Educational Progress* (Educational Testing Service, 1979), a major achievement battery, is an example of an end-of-course test for an elective academic subject.

Most such tests are published and normed separately. The end-of-high-school course tests accompanying the *Sequential Tests of Educational Progress* are an exception. Of course, the biology test could not be normed on the same students as the chemistry or physics test, because different students enroll in the courses. However, they could be on students in the same schools; this provides greater comparability than would otherwise be the case.

Recency of any test merits attention for two reasons. First, course content changes over time and can become obsolete. This will obviously be true in such subjects as chemistry, recent history, or biology. It is even true in more stable content areas such as French or geometry because curricular emphases tend to change over time; a test developed 10 or 20 year ago cannot be assumed necessarily to adequately reflect contemporary content emphases. One would worry that curricular and content developments since the 1979 date of publication may limit its utility.

Second, student achievement may change over time. Norming studies conducted for achievement test batteries provide evidence concerning national trends in achievement. Several test publishers have reported increases in achievement based on the results of their norming studies in the 1980s (Linn, Graue, Sanders, 1990, p. 11). Therefore, recency of a test's normative data is also important because student achievement may be in a state of change. If reference group data are seriously aged, there is cause to wonder if contemporary students would perform the same as those used for the norm-referenced interpretation.

Watson-Glaser Critical Thinking Appraisal

The *Watson-Glaser Critical Thinking Appraisal* is an interesting instrument for high school and college students and is probably the best known and most widely used measure of its kind. The 40-minute device has two alternate forms that assess five subdomains (inference, recognition of assumptions, deduction, interpretation, and evaluation of arguments). The authors discourage efforts to use subscores to evaluate individual status on subskills because the subscores are based on too few items to be very reliable. "The authors should be complimented for including this important caveat" (Berger, 1985). One can, however, use these subscores to analyze the performance of a class to judge the types of critical thinking instruction that are most needed by the group.

Reliability is not as high as one might wish, probably owing both to the difficulty (and potential ambiguity) with which the construct of critical thinking is measured and to the fact that most of its items have only two options. For example, alternate-form reliability for a typical group of high school seniors (apparently administered without a time interval) was only .75 (Watson & Glaser, 1980).

Validity may appropriately be considered from a content-related perspective. Prospective users should judge for themselves the extent to which the test content matches what they seek to teach and to measure.

Construct-related validation is also highly relevant. Substantial research has been conducted with the test and with its earlier editions. Here are samples. First, as one would expect from the nature of the construct, college students' *Critical Thinking Appraisal* scores correlated more highly with a verbal aptitude test than with grades in English composition. Second, again as one's understanding of the construct of critical thinking would lead one to predict, high school students' *Critical Thinking Appraisal* scores correlated with scores of an aptitude test more highly than they did with achievement measures. Yet the correlation with the aptitude scores was not as high as the reliabilities of the two tests would have allowed if the two measures had been assessing the same construct (Watson & Glaser, 1980, p. 12).

The most recent edition of the *Watson-Glaser Critical Thinking Appraisal* was published in 1980. Therefore, persons considering its use should carefully consider whether the content of critical thinking instruction has undergone changes. My guess is that most such persons would conclude that the test content is not seriously aged. It is, however, entirely possible that more instructional emphasis has been given to critical thinking in the 1980s and 1990s than before. If so, the aged reference-group data would cause contemporary students to appear to be more capable than they really are.

KeyMath–Revised

KeyMath–R (Connolly, 1988a), for Kindergarten through Grade 9, illustrates separate subject tests that are diagnostic in orientation and that are administered individually. It is designed to provide, in less than an hour of testing time, a comprehensive assessment of a pupil's understanding and application of major math concepts and skills. Unlike group-administered tests, it must be administered one-on-one.

The test yields (a) a total score, (b) scores for the three broad areas of basic concepts, operations, and applications, (c) a score for each of 13 subtests, and (d) a subscore for each of three or four domains within each subtest, each being represented by a set of 6 test items.

A strength of the manual is its provision of both internal consistency coefficients and alternate-form-with-interval reliability coefficients for the first three of these levels of scores. Of course, the internal consistency coefficients, which reflect only content sampling error, tend to be higher than do the alternate-form reliability coefficients with two to four weeks between the sittings. Since the latter provide more realistic data, they are summarized here. The alternate-form-with-interval reliability coefficient reported for the grade-based derived scores is .90 for the total test. The median for the three broad areas is .82 and the median for the 13 subtests is .69. *Reliability data for the domain subscores are not reported.*

The author does a fine job of fostering awareness of measurement error for the first three levels of scores. Users are urged to use confidence bands, and interpretive aids simplify responsible use of these scores.

Enigmatically, this commendable allowance for measurement error is abandoned in the place it is most needed—in interpreting the three or four domain subscores of each subtest. These subscores, based on only six items each will, of course, be less reliable; thus more caution concerning imperfect reliability is needed. Yet these distributions of relatively unreliable raw scores are rendered even less useful by trichotomizing each into only three broad categories: "weak," "average," and "strong." It seems doubtful that such crude scores based on so few items would lead to sound instructional decisions.

Still worse, users are provided a behavioral objective for *each item* that can be used to analyze strengths and weaknesses. When one is tempted to use subscores based on as few as one or six items, one especially needs confidence intervals to emphasize the enormous amount of measurement error that is present. When this problem is brought to light, most people will be dissuaded from using such unreliable subscores.

The norming of *KeyMath–R* was stratified with regard to several variables including socioeconomic status. A meritorious feature of the *KeyMath–R Manual* is the provision of tables that report for each stratification variable the degree of congruence between the norming sample and the national population. For example, four strata of parental educational level were used; the comparison between the sample and the population is condensed in Table 17–1.

Table 17–1

Representation of the Norming Sample by Parental Education Level*

Parental Education Level	*% of Sample*	*% of U. S. Population*
Less than high school	18.2	16.8
High school graduation	40.9	40.6
One to three years of college or technical school	19.3	19.2
Four or more years of college	21.6	23.4

*From *KeyMath–Revised* by Austin J. Connolly, © 1988b American Guidance Service, Inc., Circle Pines MN 55014-1796. All rights reserved.

Two separate points are to be made. First, the manual laudably supplies information enabling users to judge the adequacy of the reference group. The *provision of data* such as that displayed in Table 17–1 is a virtue regardless of what the data reveal. Second, the data in this particular example show substantial parallelism between the sample and the population and therefore enhance one's confidence in the representativeness of the reference group.

Burns/Roe Informal Reading Inventory

Informal reading inventories are reading tests designed to supply teachers with information on such things as: (a) the level at which students read fluently with excellent comprehension, (b) the level at which they can make maximum progress in reading with teacher assistance, (c) the level at which they are unable to pronounce many of the words and/or are unable to comprehend adequately, (d) their strengths and weaknesses in phonic analysis, use of context clues, and structural analysis to pronounce words, (e) their strengths and weaknesses in answering various types of comprehension questions, and (f) the highest level of material that they can comprehend when it is read to them (Johns, 1988, p. 3).

Unlike most published tests, informal reading inventories are domain referenced. "The individual is evaluated against pre-established standards which must be met" in order to become a successful, accomplished reader in the classroom (Burns & Roe, 1989, p. 1). Informal reading inventories attempt to identify students' specific word-recognition and comprehension skills (Silvaroli, 1986, p. 1).

Many critical comments could be made about a variety of informal reading inventories. To give a flavor of the measurement qualities of many tests in this category of instruments, discussion will focus largely on one feature—reliability—of a particular, widely used instrument—the *Burns/Roe Informal Reading Inventory* (Burns & Roe, 1989).

The diagnostic uses of scores obviously require that they be sufficiently reliable. Therefore authors should provide evidence concerning reliability. Prevailing professional standards dictate that all scores and subscores be accompanied by reliability estimates so that test users can judge whether scores are sufficiently accurate for their intended uses (American Psychological Association, 1985, p. 20). Reliability data are just as necessary for domain-referenced interpretations as for norm-referenced ones.

The *Burns/Roe Informal Reading Inventory* is typical of many informal reading inventories in blatantly disregarding this need. As reviewers of an earlier edition said, "There is no technical manual. There are no data on reliability, standard errors of measurement, comparability of the four forms, or relationship to other measures. No basis for the criteria used to determine levels is given. . . . As a consequence, use of the *Burns/Roe Informal Reading Inventory* must be an act of faith." It "falls far short of accepted standards for test development and revision" (Murphy & Bruning, 1989, p. 116).

This instrument is not an unusually poor informal reading inventory. Typical instruments of this type suffer from equal poverty of reliability data, information or rationale concerning standards, and data demonstrating equivalence of the raw scores used to make domain interpretations of the "parallel" forms. (E.g., see review by Norris, 1989, of Silvaroli's *Classroom Reading Inventory*, 4th ed., and reviews by Marr, 1985, and Fuchs, 1985, of the *Ekwall Reading Inventory*.)

Nor, sad to say, are informal reading inventories the only instruments having authors who exhibit a wholesale disregard (or ignorance) of prevailing professional standards of test development. Test users should develop a healthy skepticism. We should not take a published instrument's adequacy on faith, even if its author is respected and it is published by a reputable firm. Professional standards of test development are applicable to all those who write tests, and we who use tests should demand that authors meet these standards. When an author fails to report reliability or other technical data, it is not prudent to assume that all is well; it usually is not!

QUIZ 17–1

1. Focus on interpretability. Review the first two paragraphs in this section on the Burns/Roe. Is there an appropriate match between the kind of content and the kind of interpretation for informal reading inventories?

KEY TO QUIZ 17–1

1. As Forsyth (1991, p. 9) said in another context, "No one challenges the idea that it would be desirable to have educational measurements which accurately describe what examinees can and can not do." The point is that when the content domains are open-ended, as many skills of reading comprehension are, we do not have the means of achieving meaningful domain referencing. (Similarly, it would be desirable to have a prosperous society with a twenty-hour work week, but we do not know how to achieve it.)

   I simply do not know how to domain-reference interpretation of a test that assesses a domain such as student strengths and weaknesses in answering various types of reading comprehension questions. "Comprehension questions" constitute a *very* ill-defined domain. It therefore is not amenable to domain referencing. Yet that is the only avenue to interpretation offered by typical informal reading inventories. Thus the absence of adequate normative data to enable meaningful interpretation is a problem as serious as the reliability issue discussed above.

Commercially Prepared Customized Tests

Several publishers market customized test-making services. These are organized to allow school districts to custom order their content-area tests. Typically, school personnel examine a list or catalog of instructional objectives and select those deemed relevant to the local curriculum. The publisher then prints a test consisting of about three items per objective, and the district sets a passing standard for each (e.g., 3 out of 3 or 2 out of 3). Student answer sheets are then scored in terms of mastery of the separate objectives.

This kind of publishing service is especially attractive to districts faced with a mandate to engage in some of the less sound varieties of outcomes-based assessment. In some such schemes, districts are required to document each student's mastery of each objective. If enough items per objectives were provided to yield reliable subscores, this approach would, of course, be reasonable *if the objectives pertain to delimitable, masterable, essential, subject matter.* But unfortunately, the method is often used indiscriminately rather than being reserved for Track A content.

Following are tightly paraphrased versions of three reading objectives found in catalogs of objectives issued by three major test publishers.

1. Given a short passage, the student will identify the answer to a question that requires an inference or conclusion to be drawn.

2. The student determines the meaning of an unfamiliar phrase from the context of the passage.

3. Given a reading passage, the student will identify a cause-effect relationship.

QUIZ 17–2

1. How adequate is the match of these objectives with the kind of subject matter they concern? That is, is this the most useful kind of objective for silent reading comprehension?
2. How reliable are the scores for each objective likely to be?
3. In some content, it is worthwhile to diagnostically pinpoint subskills (e.g., subtraction of one-digit numbers from two-digit numbers with and without the need to "borrow"). Is this degree of subskill identification helpful in silent reading comprehension?

KEY TO QUIZ 17–2

1. Silent reading comprehension represents a large, open-ended, unmasterable content domain. Nonbehavioral developmental objectives are appropriate. Yet these objectives are minimum essential, mastery goals. Hence they are not suitable for the subject matter.
2. How broadly can three or four items survey with such large and varied domains? How consistently is a three- or four-item subtest likely to be? Not very!

   It would be irresponsible to base serious decisions on such unreliable data. Yet if decisions were not needed for the separate subscores, the total score would suffice.
3. No. Recall the discussion in Chapter 14 of the construct validity of such subscores. Although it seems intuitively sensible to try to identify subskills of silent reading comprehension and to "remediate" the weak "subskills," half a century of research has generally been unsuccessful in empirically identifying components of reading comprehension (e.g., see Schreiner, Hieronymus, & Forsyth, 1969, or Cummings, 1982, for numerous citations). Therefore, a survey approach rather than a diagnostic one is called for.

It seems to me that such commercially prepared customized tests have little to offer. Here is the double-bind problem. On the one hand, consider Track A content that really is vital and for which minimum essential mastery objectives are needed. What is vital in School District X in Maine is, for the most part, also vital in District Y in California and District Z in Mississippi. So where is the need to customize? Published tests would suffice without the trouble and expense of customizing.

On the other hand, consider Track C content for which minimum essential objectives are ill-suited. In this context, there is little merit in having unneeded subscores or meaningless "standards" of "mastery."

There is, however, merit in commercially marketed *collections of test items* from which a district can select those that help to fulfill the testing needs established by its two-dimensional table of specifications. Such item banks can have items classified by content areas and mental processes without engaging in the meaningless ritual of matching each item to a behavioral objective. Good items are hard to write, and commercial item banking is a way to share them. Some such banks are discussed in Appendix C.

Achievement Batteries

Most schools elect to test achievement with coordinated sets of tests, called batteries. **Achievement batteries** are widely used prior to high school for the assessment of the regular academic subjects. Their use at the high school level is limited to those subjects that constitute the common core of the curriculum. Separate tests are needed to assess achievement in elective courses such as physics, Spanish, and algebra.

Achievement batteries offer significant advantages over separate, cafeteria-style, collections of uncoordinated tests for the several content areas. For one thing, content can be "dovetailed" so that it neither overlaps redundantly between tests nor "gets lost" between areas. For instance, the topics of charts, tables, and graphs can fit in math, social studies, science, or study skills. In a coordinated battery, the topic can be adequately covered without redundancy; in a collection of separate, uncoordinated tests, it is likely either to be overemphasized or neglected.

Another advantage of achievement batteries over separate tests concerns intraindividual comparisons such as, "Is my child better in reading than in math?" If the reading and math tests had been normed on different reference groups—as would likely be the case for separate tests—then the difficulty of the comparison is compounded by possible differences in the capabilities of the respective reference groups. A major advantage of using a battery of subtests is that *the subtests have all been normed on the same reference group*. This greatly simplifies the task of interpreting difference scores—an enterprise that is hazardous enough under the best of conditions.

Another reasonable question that parents, teachers, and students themselves ask concerns year-to-year growth. A pupil might well ask, "Has my reading improved adequately during the past year?" If each grade's reading test is well targeted in difficulty for that grade, then the pupil may not have taken the same test in successive years. Rather, she or he may have taken successive *levels* of the same test—tests articulated to be parallel except insofar as grade-to-grade changes of instructional content and optimal difficulty dictate. For example, a math subtest at one grade might not include "borrowing" across zero; the next higher level of the subtest for the next grade or two might.

Since various levels assess slightly different content domains, scores of different levels are not directly equivalent. Comparison is achieved by statistical linkage of derived scores among levels. Most batteries accomplish this technical feat of grade-to-grade linkage of scores by means of one or another variety of standard score. Because the industry has no one common system, these kinds of standard scores were not discussed in Chapter 16.

The plotting of growth is, of course, also complicated by the reduced reliability with which it is measured. (Recall from Chapter 15 the difficulties inherent in the assessment of difference scores.) This reduced reliability creates a set of hazards aside from those of content comparability and score linkage. All things considered, the assessment of year-to-year growth is a very technical, problematic, and important enterprise.

This is as good a place as any to note that the raw scores of alternate forms of the same test also may not be assumed to be equivalent or interchangeable. Even if parallel forms have been carefully based on the same specifications, the forms may happen to differ slightly in difficulty and/or in variability. Publishers have statistical methods to render the derived scores equivalent. However, only the derived scores of alternate forms—not the raw scores—may safely be considered to be interchangeable. (Recall that one of the criticisms of the *Burns/Roe Informal Reading Inventory* was the unsubstantiated assumption that raw scores of the forms were interchangeable.)

Four widely used group achievement batteries will now be examined. To avoid redundancy, different things are illustrated in the various group batteries, and no attempt is made to address all the important features of each. For the most part, what is said about one, such as time needs, purposes, reliability, or item types, will be true for most similar tests as well.

Comprehensive Tests of Basic Skills

The *Comprehensive Tests of Basic Skills* (CTBS) (California Test Bureau, 1989a) are a widely used achievement battery that measures basic skills in reading, language, spelling, mathematics, study skills, science, and social studies from kindergarten to Grade 12. The battery is designed to provide information useful in (a) determining educational progress of students, classes, schools, and districts, (b) planning program improvement, (c) identifying common and individual needs, (d) evaluating special programs, and (e) reporting to parents, the community, and government agencies.

The battery is unusual in having a short and a long version. The short one requires about two and one-half hours of testing at most grades, while the longer versions take about five hours. The shorter time seems scanty for a reliable survey of each pupil's achievement, although it would be more than sufficient for evaluating the achievement of a class, school, or district. For example, 10 subscores are reported for seventh-graders, each based on 20 items. The Kuder-Richardson reliabilities of these subscores have a median value of only .70 (California Test Bureau, 1989b, pp. 109 & 116).

QUIZ 17–3

1. Recall the special case of the Spearman-Brown Formula given on page 430, which enables one to estimate how reliable a test would be if its length were doubled. Use it to estimate the median reliability of the subscores of the longer versions of the *Comprehensive Tests of Basic Skills.*

QUIZ 17–3 (cont.)

2. What sources of measurement error do these Kuder-Richardson reliability coefficients reflect? Which important sources of error do they neglect?

KEY TO QUIZ 17–3

1. $\dfrac{2r}{1 + r} = \dfrac{2(.7)}{1.7} = \dfrac{1.4}{1.7} = .82+$

The *estimate* is therefore .82. Actually the median of the actual rs was slightly higher, .85 (California Test Bureau, 1989b, pp. 123, 130, & 137).

2. Recall from Table 15–1 on page 432 that Kuder-Richardson reliability coefficients take account of (i.e., are reduced by) content sampling error and content heterogeneity. The most important source of error not registered is probably occasion sampling error (although examiner and scoring error might also be mentioned). It would be far better for the publisher to report alternate-form-with-time-interval reliability findings.

The *Comprehensive Tests of Basic Skills* are typical of achievement batteries in providing a variety of interpretive information spanning norm referencing and domain referencing (or curriculum referencing, as it is called in these tests). It might be noted—and lamented—that several batteries supply domain- or criterion-referenced interpretation quite indiscriminately, without regard to the meaningfulness of such referencing for the kind of subject matter tested. To illustrate, CTBS curriculum objectives include:

"The student will identify the meaning of affixes,"

"The student will demonstrate understanding of measurement concepts and their application in problem solving," and

"The student will demonstrate understanding of the structures and functions of various political systems, and will be able to identify responsible decisions based on situations or criteria" (California Test Bureau, 1990).

The scoring services that users may purchase include mastery information for individual students concerning these and similar open-ended, unmasterable objectives. Such information, of course, has very limited meaning since a student's raw or percentage score will depend upon the difficulty of the items that *happen* to be used in the test. Yet the availability of this questionable scoring service need not be a disadvantage to knowledgeable users. Users who understand that Track C content should be given only norm-referenced interpretations will know better than to purchase such scoring services for this or other tests.

On the other hand, a student's norm-referenced status on such objectives could be useful *if* it were sufficiently reliable, which is highly unlikely given limitations of test length. Norm-referenced assessment of classes, schools, or districts on such objectives could also be useful, and it would probably be highly reliable. Suppose, for example, that Ms. Jackson notices that her class performed considerably below the national average in use of affixes. This could prompt useful consideration of the appropriate curricular emphasis on this topic. If she did not intend to slight it, she might decide to give it more emphasis next year. On the other hand, if the local curriculum calls for a major unit on prefixes and affixes in the next higher grade, then she might well decide not to alter her instructional emphasis.

Stanford Achievement Test Series

The *Stanford Achievement Test Series* (The Psychological Corporation, 1988–1990) is another battery that measures the goals of general education from kindergarten through Grade 12. The middle portion of this test, covering elementary and junior high school years, dates back to 1923 and is now in its eighth edition. A downward extension, the *Stanford Early School Achievement Test*, measures cognitive development of children in kindergarten and Grade 1. An upward extension, the *Stanford Tests of Academic Skills*, measure achievement in basic or core subjects at the high school level. This battery's structure of subtests and levels is fairly typical, so it will be used for illustration. Table 17–2 presents the subtests, the recommended grades for each level, and the length of each subtest in time and in test items.

A feature of this battery that is somewhat unusual is the inclusion of listening in Grades 1 through 9. Many batteries do not provide a separate measure of listening comprehension, perhaps because it is usually not taught as a separate subject. However students' ability to gain information from the spoken word is a critically important skill that may merit more attention than it gets. Even at the college level, students may learn as much from listening as from reading. A deficit in reading comprehension may be especially disabling for the person whose listening comprehension is also weak.

In order to illustrate selected features in more detail, discussion will focus on Intermediate 1 level of the *Stanford Achievement Test*, designed for Grades 4.5 to 5.5. Table 17–2 shows that 12 different subscores are provided in addition to various subtotals and totals. Our knowledge of reliability should prevent a naive expectation that several reliable scores can be secured without the investment of considerable testing time. How much time would one realistically expect to have to invest in the Intermediate 1 level?

In total, nearly six hours of working time are needed. Another hour or so is needed for distributing booklets, reading directions, answering preliminary questions, and so on. This administration time is distributed among 6 to 12 different testing sessions.

The sample items used in administering the test provide an idea of what each part actually assesses. It should be recognized, however, that sample items are generally easier than most of those that appear in the tests that follow them. And, of course, a few sample items cannot fully reveal the breadth of content coverage; they

Table 17–2

Scope and Sequence Chart (Stanford Achievement Test Series, Eighth Edition)*

Subtest/Total	SESAT 1		SESAT 2		PRIMARY 1		PRIMARY 2		PRIMARY 3		INTERMEDIATE 1		INTERMEDIATE 2		INTERMEDIATE 3		ADVANCED 1		ADVANCED 2		TASK 1		TASK 2		TASK 3	
Grade (Content)¹	1st half K		2nd half K / 1st half 1		1		2		3		4		5		6		7		8		9		10		11–12	
Recommended Administration Points	K.0–.5		K.5–1.5		1.5–2.5		2.5–3.5		3.5–4.5		4.5–5.5		5.5–6.5		6.5–7.5		7.5–8.5		8.5–9.9		9.0–9.9		10.0–10.9		11.0–12.9	
	Items	Time*	Items	Time*	Items	Time*	Items	Time*	Items	Time*	Items	Time*	Items	Time*	Items	Time*	Items	Time*	Items	Time*	Items	Time*	Items	Time*	Items	Time*
Sounds & Letters/Word Study Skills	48	30	40	25	36	20	48	25	48	25																
Word Reading/Reading Vocabulary³	30	15	40	25	30	20	40	30	40	25	40	25	40	25	40	25	40	25	40	25	40	25	40	25	40	25
Sentence Reading/Reading Comprehension			30	30	40	35	40	35	54	45	54	50	54	50	54	50	54	50	54	50	54	40	54	40	54	40
Total Reading	78	45	110	80	106	75	128	90	142	95	94	75	94	75	94	75	94	75	94	75	94	65	94	65	94	65
Language Mechanics									30	20	30	20	30	20	30	20	30	20	30	20						
Language Expression									30	25	30	25	30	25	30	25	30	25	30	25						
Language/English/Total Language²					44	40	44	40	60	45	60	45	60	45	60	45	60	45	60	45	54	30	54	30	54	30
Study Skills³									30	25	30	25	30	25	32	25	32	25	32	25	34	25	34	25	34	25
Spelling					30	20	30	20	36	15	40	15	50	15	50	15	50	15	50	15	40	15	40	15	40	15
Listening³	45	30	45	30	45	30	45	30	45	30	45	30	45	30	45	30	45	30	45	30						
Concepts of Number					34	25	34		34		34	20	34	20	34	20	34	20	34	20						
Mathematics Computation					26	30	36	30	44	35	44	40	44	40	44	40	44	40	44	40						
Mathematics Applications⁴	21**		22**		30	30	35	25	38	35	40	35	40	35	40	35	40	35	40	35	18**		18**		18**	
Mathematics/Total Mathematics	42	30	44	30	90	85	105	85	116	90	118	95	118	95	118	95	118	95	118	95	48	40	48	40	48	40
Environment	40	30	40	30	40	30	40	30																		
Science									50	30	50	30	50	30	50	30	50	30	50	30	50	25	50	25	50	25
Social Science									50	30	50	30	50	30	50	30	50	30	50	30	50	25	50	25	50	25
Partial Battery⁷,⁸																										
Basic Battery⁴	165	105	199	140	315	250	352	255	429	300	387	285	397	285	399	285	399	285	399	285	270	175	270	175	270	175
Complete Battery⁵	205	135	239	170	355	280	392	285	529	360	487	345	497	345	499	345	499	345	499	345	370	225	370	225	370	225
Using Information⁶											×	×	×	×	×	×	×	×	×	×	×	×	×	×	×	×
Thinking Skills⁹											×	×	×	×	×	×	×	×	×	×	×	×	×	×	×	×

1 For Fall testing, we recommend use of the previous grade level. For example, use Primary 3 for testing in the fall of grade 3, since most students will not have been exposed to the content on Primary 3 (3rd Grade).
2 A total Language score is also available that includes Spelling, which can be substituted for the regular Total Language score.
3 Auditory Vocabulary is included in the Listening subtest.
4 The Mathematics Applications subtest is available with or without calculator norms.
5 Complete Battery includes all subtests. Basic Battery excludes Environment, Science, and Social Science.
6 Basic Battery excludes Environment, Science, and Social Science.

7 Partial Battery excludes Study Skills, Listening, Environment, Science, and Social Science.
8 Separate Partial Battery booklets are not available at Primary 1, Primary 2, or TASK levels.
9 Using Information and Thinking Skills are "embedded subtests" that do not require additional administration time.
10 They are available from the Basic or Complete Battery (Stanford Abbreviated).
* All items in the SATB Abbreviated TASK Mathematics subtest meet Chapter 1 Advanced Skills requirements.
* Time for each subtest is in minutes.
** A separate Mathematics Applications score is available for these items embedded in the SESAT and TASK Mathematics subtests.

serve better to illustrate item types. Figure 17–1 provides all of the sample items of the Intermediate 1 level.

Why is the "not here" response option offered only in the math subtest? Recall from Chapter 6 that the "none of the above" option and its variants are suitable only in right-answer items. Math subtests are often the only ones that contain no best-answer items. Therefore, this option and its directions tend to be more suitable in math content than in most other content areas.

Iowa Tests of Basic Skills

The *Iowa Tests of Basic Skills* (ITBS) (Hieronymus, Hoover, & Lindquist, 1986) is a widely used and highly regarded achievement battery for kindergarten through Grade 9. Evolving out of an early statewide testing program, it provided a pioneering example of a test that assessed a broader spectrum of educational outcomes than knowledge of factual material. For example, its study skills subtests provided interpretive exercises to assess student ability to cope with maps, tables of contents, charts, graphs, and indexes.

An interesting feature of the ITBS is its provision of multiple levels of the battery in one multilevel booklet. Levels typically suitable for Grades 3 to 9 are published in one booklet. This facilitates the three ways under which the battery can be administered:

First is graded testing in which a single level of the test is given (indiscriminately) to all the pupils in a grade; the level is determined by their grade. This method is the most common one, not only for the ITBS, but for other batteries as well.

Second is functional level testing in which all the pupils of a class take the same level of the test, but the level is determined by the level of achievement typical of the class (rather than by its grade). Like graded testing, this is convenient. Functional level testing provides the opportunity for the level used to be better targeted in difficulty to the average pupils in a class; this tends to enhance reliability slightly.

Third is individualized testing in which the optimum level *for each pupil* is sought, either on the basis of the teacher's assessment of the pupil's achievement or by use of previous test results. Each child is given the answer sheet appropriate to her or his level; this indicates for each subtest the item numbers on which to start and stop. Since the directions, sample items, and time limits are identical for the levels, students taking different levels can be tested simultaneously. Although more trouble to plan, this option provides the most reliable information because of its superior targeting of test difficulty for individual students.

A feature the ITBS shares with other batteries is computerized reporting to pupils and parents. Figure 17–2 provides an example of the reporting options that schools may purchase. Such reports provide a prose interpretation to parents with a minimum of professional time. Interview time can then be used for follow-up problems or for dealing with matters of interpretation that go beyond the routine. Nonetheless, teachers and administrators should realize that the *computerized reports are no better than the sophistication of the program from which they are generated.*

As an example, the report shown in Figure 17–2, although reasonable, could be faulted on several bases. First, the use of the GE (mercifully only once) is questionable in view of the high frequency with which they are misunderstood. Second, the bar graphs for PRs are not confidence bands and, therefore, give no indication of the

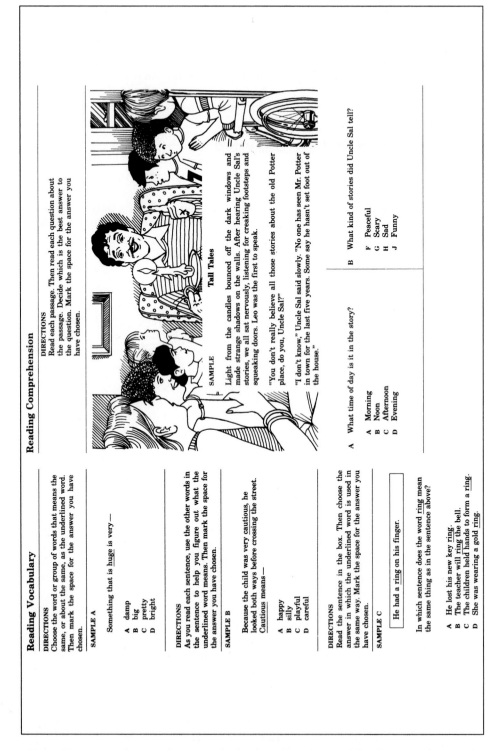

Figure 17–1. Sample Items from *Stanford Achievement Test*, Eighth Ed. Copyright © 1988 by Harcourt Brace Jovanovich, Inc. Reproduced by permission. All rights reserved.

Concepts of Number

DIRECTIONS
Read each question and choose the best answer. Then mark the space for the answer you have chosen.

SAMPLE

Which is the numeral for twenty-three?

A 23
B 203
C 230
D 2003

Mathematics Computation

DIRECTIONS
Read each question and choose the best answer. Then mark the space for the answer you have chosen. If a correct answer is *not here*, mark the space for NH.

SAMPLE A

$$\begin{array}{r} 15 \\ + 3 \\ \hline \end{array}$$

A 12
B 18
C 22
D 28
E NH

SAMPLE B

$$\begin{array}{r} 29 \\ - 5 \\ \hline \end{array}$$

F 14
G 23
H 25
J 34
K NH

Mathematics Applications

DIRECTIONS
Read each question and choose the best answer. Then mark the space for the answer you have chosen. If a correct answer is *not here*, mark the space for NH.

SAMPLE

Jan had 7 posters. Then she gave 3 to Dan. How many posters does Jan have left?

A 10
B 9
C 5
D 4
E NH

Spelling

DIRECTIONS
Read each group of phrases. Look at the underlined word in each phrase. One of the underlined words is not spelled correctly for the way it is used in the phrase. Find the word that is *not* spelled correctly. Then mark the space for the answer you have chosen.

SAMPLE A

A a ship at <u>sea</u>
B over his <u>eye</u>
C <u>buy</u> a ticket
D <u>one</u> the game

DIRECTIONS
Look at the four words in each question. Decide which word is *not* spelled correctly. Then mark the space for the answer you have chosen.

SAMPLE B

A move
B hand
C gurl
D north

Language Mechanics

DIRECTIONS
Read each sentence. Decide which word or group of words belongs in the blank. Then mark the space for the answer you have chosen.

SAMPLE A

He is a student in _____.

A Elementary school
B Elementary School
C elementary School
D elementary school

SAMPLE B

The bank will open at nine _____.

F oclock'
G o'clock
H oc'lock
J oclock

SAMPLE C

The wind _____ through the trees.

A rustles
B are rustling
C do rustle
D rustle

Figure 17–1. *cont.*

Language Expression

DIRECTIONS
For each question, read all four groups of words. One group of words forms a correct sentence. Each of the other choices is wrong because it does not form a complete sentence, or because it forms more than one sentence. Decide which group of words forms a correct sentence. Then mark the space for the answer you have chosen.

SAMPLE A

  A Since early this morning.
  B Brian opened the package.
  C Coming down the street.
  D Somewhere in the house.

SAMPLE B

  F Scott needs a pencil he wants to draw.
  G The boy smiled the girl laughed.
  H Laura came to the party with us.
  J Jim saw a horse it was black.

DIRECTIONS
For each of the following questions, first read the sentences that are in the box. Then choose the answer that *best* joins the sentences in the box into one clear sentence without changing their meaning. Mark the space for the answer you have chosen.

SAMPLE C

> He is my friend.
> He won the race.

  A My friend, he won the race.
  B My friend won the race.
  C He won the race, my friend.
  D By my friend, the race was won.

Study Skills

DIRECTIONS
Read each question. Choose the best answer. Then mark the space for the answer you have chosen.

SAMPLE
Look at these guide words from a dictionary page.

> hobby – honest

Which word could be found on the page?

  A hoarse
  B hog
  C hotel
  D howl

Science

DIRECTIONS
Read each question and choose the best answer. Then mark the space for the answer you have chosen.

SAMPLE

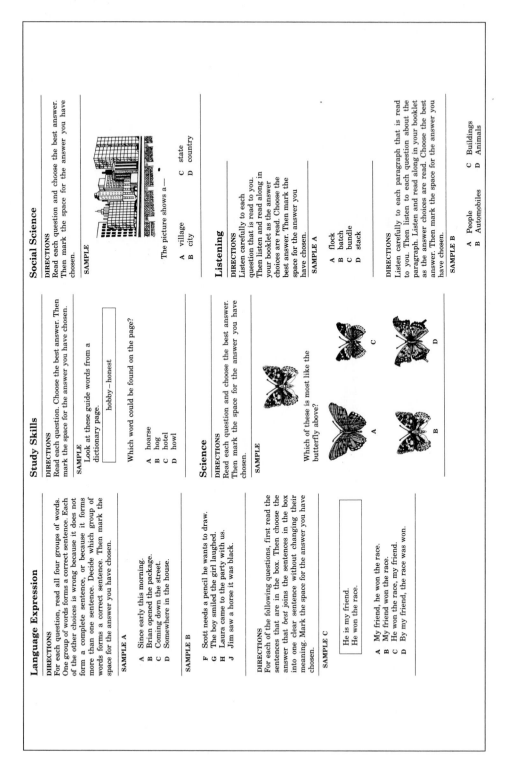

Which of these is most like the butterfly above?

Social Science

DIRECTIONS
Read each question and choose the best answer. Then mark the space for the answer you have chosen.

SAMPLE

The picture shows a —

  A village   C state
  B city   D country

Listening

DIRECTIONS
Listen carefully to each question that is read to you. Then listen and read along in your booklet as the answer choices are read. Choose the best answer. Then mark the space for the answer you have chosen.

SAMPLE A

  A flock
  B batch
  C bundle
  D stack

DIRECTIONS
Listen carefully to each paragraph that is read to you. Then listen to each question about the paragraph. Listen and read along in your booklet as the answer choices are read. Choose the best answer. Then mark the space for the answer you have chosen.

SAMPLE B

  A People   C Buildings
  B Automobiles D Animals

Figure 17–1. *cont.*

COPY FOR THE PARENTS OF SHARON JOHNSON

DEAR PARENTS:

YOUR DAUGHTER SHARON WAS GIVEN THE IOWA TESTS OF BASIC SKILLS (FORM G, LEVEL 12) IN OCT. 1984, BY MR GARZA. SHARON IS IN THE SIXTH GRADE AT WASHINGTON ELEM SCHOOL IN MAIN TOWNSHIP ISD. THIS REPORT WILL EXPLAIN THE DETAILS OF THE TEST RESULTS.

SHARON'S COMPOSITE SCORE IS THE BEST INDICATOR OF HER OVERALL ACHIEVEMENT ON THE TESTS. SHARON EARNED A COMPOSITE GRADE EQUIVALENT OF 66, WHICH MEANS THAT HER TEST PERFORMANCE WAS APPROXIMATELY THE SAME AS THAT MADE BY A TYPICAL PUPIL IN THE SIXTH GRADE AT THE END OF THE SIXTH MONTH. SHARON'S PERFORMANCE WAS MEASURED WITH THE LEVEL 12 TEST. SHARON'S STANDING IN OVERALL ACHIEVEMENT AMONG SIXTH GRADE PUPILS NATIONALLY IS SHOWN BY HER COMPOSITE PERCENTILE RANK OF 59. THIS MEANS THAT SHARON SCORED BETTER THAN 59 PERCENT OF SIXTH GRADE PUPILS NATIONALLY AND THAT 41 PERCENT SCORED AS WELL OR BETTER. SHARON'S OVERALL ACHIEVEMENT APPEARS TO BE ABOUT AVERAGE FOR HER GRADE.

THE SCORES OF ONE PUPIL ARE OFTEN COMPARED WITH OTHER PUPIL'S SCORES. GENERALLY, SHARON'S SCORES ARE ABOUT AVERAGE WHEN DESCRIBED IN THIS WAY. HOWEVER, SKILLS CAN ALSO BE COMPARED WITH EACH OTHER TO DETERMINE AN INDIVIDUAL'S STRENGTHS AND WEAKNESSES. IN SHARON'S CASE, THE HIGHEST SCORE IS IN READING. THIS IS A STRONG POINT WHICH CAN BE USED TO IMPROVE OTHER SKILLS. SHARON'S LOWEST SCORES ARE IN SPELLING, CAPITALIZATION, MATH COMPUTATION AND SOCIAL STUDIES. THESE ARE AREAS IN WHICH SHARON APPEARS TO NEED THE MOST WORK.

A PUPIL'S COMMAND OF READING SKILLS IS RELATED TO SUCCESS IN MANY AREAS OF SCHOOL WORK, SINCE MOST SUBJECTS REQUIRE SOME READING. SHARON'S READING SCORE IS SOMEWHAT ABOVE AVERAGE WHEN COMPARED WITH THOSE OF OTHER SIXTH GRADE PUPILS NATIONALLY AND ABOVE AVERAGE WHEN COMPARED WITH HER OWN TEST PERFORMANCE IN OTHER AREAS.

IF YOU WOULD LIKE MORE INFORMATION ABOUT SHARON'S PERFORMANCE IN SCHOOL, PLEASE CONTACT MR GARZA.

SINCERELY,
WASHINGTON ELEM SCHOOL

PROFILE NARRATIVE REPORT

Iowa Tests of Basic Skills
Published by THE RIVERSIDE PUBLISHING COMPANY

Pupil SHARON JOHNSON
I.D. No
Grade 6
Sex F
Birth Date 09/73
Age 11 yrs 1 mos
Test Date 10/84

Teacher MR GARZA
School WASHINGTON ELEM
System MAIN TOWNSHIP ISD
Order No 001-0001-000
Level/Form 12/G
Norm FALL

Subtests	GE	NP	National Percentile Rank (1 25 50 75 99)
VOCABULARY		59	
READING		73	
SPELLING		35	
CAPITALIZATION		39	
PUNCTUATION		59	
USAGE/EXPRESSION		40	
LANGUAGE, TOTAL		43	
VISUAL		68	
REFERENCES		53	
WORK-STUDY, TOTAL		63	
MATH CONCEPTS		61	
MATH PROBLEMS		67	
MATH COMPUTATION		44	
MATHEMATICS, TOTAL		59	
COMPLETE COMPOSITE	66	59	
SOCIAL STUDIES		43	
SCIENCE		50	

GE=Grade Equivalent, NS=National Stanine, NP=National Percentile Rank

Figure 17–2. Sample Student Report of the *Iowa Tests of Basic Skills.* Copyright© 1986 by the Riverside Publishing Company. Reproduced by permission of the Riverside Publishing Company.

need to provide for a margin of error. In the same amount of space, confidence bands could have been provided.

Finally, after reporting Sharon's overall status, the report focuses attention on Sharon's highest and lowest scores. This is a good interpretive technique that avoids a tedious recitation of the examinee's status on each and every variable. For example, "In general, Travis performed in the high-average range on the 15 measures except for X and Y, on which his status was very superior, and Z, on which his performance is slightly below average."

It is useful to emphasize the outlier scores *if they significantly deviate from the person's own mean.* Many students do indeed have uneven profiles worth noting; Sharon is not conspicuous among them. Her spread of PRs (from 35 to 73) is relatively narrow, and it does not seem prudent to lead parents to think that her strongest and weakest scores clearly represent higher and lower status from all other subscores. For example, attention is directed to her low scores in spelling (PR 35), capitalization (39), math computation (44), and social studies (43). However, her usage/expression (PR 40) and references (PR 53) scores do not differ from her other relatively low PRs by enough to leave one confident that those mentioned are really her weakest areas. Or that they are *enough lower* to be educationally significant even if they really are her lowest.

The report thus fails to provide cautions against overinterpretation of minor differences. Provision is needed for the modest reliability of difference scores. Again, the use of horizontal bar confidence bands in the report would have been a significant improvement.

Another feature common to most published batteries is the provision of a variety of optional scoring services that users may purchase. One of the most common and least expensive is district normative data based on the current group whose answer sheets are sent to the publisher for centralized scoring. This enables the provision of local as well as national PRs. Another scoring service that is widely available for various achievement batteries are class summaries. These often summarize all the subscores of all the children in a class on a single sheet.

Another scoring option made practical by modern computer technology is a detailed "diagnostic" analysis of each pupil's performance. As mentioned above, such detail could be very useful *if it were reliable.* But a survey test can only survey broad content domains; it does not have enough time to assess each small content subdomain with enough items to provide reliable subdomain scores. As a result, many of the optional computer-generated reports provide information based on too few items to be useful.

Not only is such information prone to be unreliable, but several publishers fail to provide information concerning the reliability of *each score reported* as they should (American Psychological Association, 1985, p. 20). All in all, users should be wary of reports that provide too much information from too little testing time. With only a few hours of testing time, one cannot expect more than a few reliable scores. (Remember the old adage, "If it seems too good to be true, it probably is.")

Several publishers, however, sell gullible users detailed reports of dubious utility. Figure 17–3 provides a fairly typical example. Several problems render the use of such reports very questionable. First is the attempt to domain-reference open-ended, ill-defined content. Raw scores and percent scores are not meaningful ways by which to interpret Track C content. (Interestingly, there is an implicit recognition of this

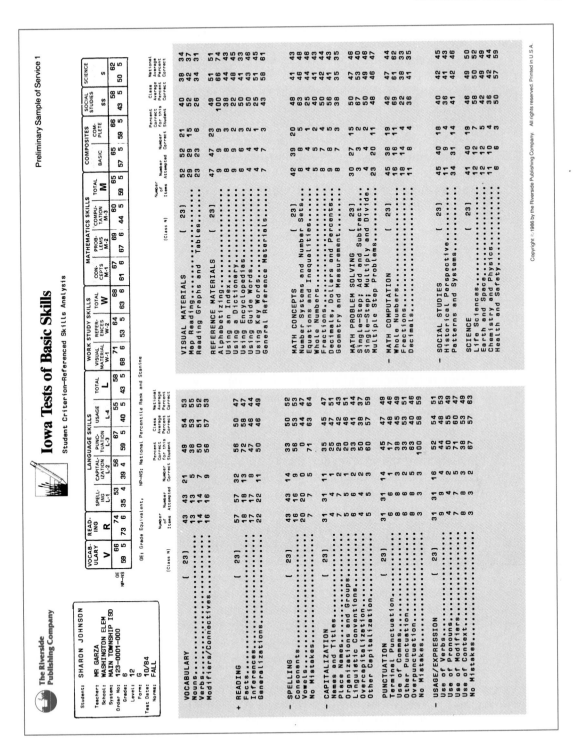

Figure 17–3. Sample Skills Analysis Report for the *Iowa Tests of Basic Skills.* Copyright© 1990 by the Riverside Publishing Company. Reproduced with permission of the Riverside Publishing Company.

point in the provision of reference-group data for the class and for the nation. However these averages provide no information on the norm-referenced extent of an individual's deviancy. For example, we have little idea of where Sharon's 38% correct on nouns—contrasted with 55% correct for the national sample—places her within the bottom half. Such normative data are very meager.)

Second is the point made above that the identified "subskills" of reading comprehension have not been demonstrated empirically to exist. Third is the issue of reliability. These subscores are based on as few as three or four items. How adequately, for example, can a mere four items survey a student's achievement in the use of pronouns? (There is nothing wrong with having so few items on a survey test of punctuation. The complaint concerns the inappropriateness of supplying a separate subscore.) Or how reliably can a mere six items assess a pupil's command of health and safety? It is naive to think that subscores based on so few items would be reliable enough to be very helpful in making educational decisions for individual students.

It will be worthwhile to reiterate that this kind of *score reporting service* is common among achievement batteries; it was illustrated with one particular test. It should also be repeated that the mere availability of such scoring services does not in any way handicap informed test users who know better than to purchase them. Thus the norm-referenced use of this and similar batteries' major subscores is not compromised by the supplementary availability of dubious scoring services.

The ITBS can also serve to illustrate the availability of more than one kind of "national" reference group data (often called norms). In addition to the carefully selected stratified random cluster sampling of school children, special reference groups are also available for supplementary comparisons. ITBS users can elect to use large-city reference group data, norms based on Catholic school, high socioeconomic norms, or low socioeconomic norms.

The ITBS was used in pioneering efforts to base derived scores of an achievement battery and an aptitude battery on the same reference group. The ITBS has long been co-normed with the *Cognitive Abilities Test.* Use of the identical reference group renders aptitude-achievement comparisons less hazardous. This feature is now common with major achievement batteries.

Tests of Achievement and Proficiency

The *Tests of Achievement and Proficiency* (TAP) (Scannel et al., 1986a) are a high school achievement battery that is a companion test to both the *Cognitive Abilities Test* and the ITBS. To attain maximum similarity of its reference group with that of the ITBS (in order to facilitate measurement of growth), the TAP is normed in the same national sample of school districts. Moreover, the students who participate in the norming of the *Tests of Achievement and Proficiency* also take the *Cognitive Abilities Test.*

Like the ITBS, the TAP is available in a multilevel booklet with a separate level for each grade that overlaps adjacent levels. Thus the four levels provided for Grades 9 to 12 offer unusually good targeting of test difficulty to each grade.

The TAP consists of six regular subtests, each requiring 40 minutes of working time. Table 17–3 summarizes descriptions of these subtests and information concerning their reliability. (In addition to the standard battery, the TAP also has optional subtests in listening and writing.)

Table 17-3

K-R 20 Reliability of the *Tests of Achievement and Proficiency* *

Test Name and Description	K-R 20 at Grade 11
Reading Comprehension: Understanding of everyday materials such as labels, advertisements, and newspapers as well as textbook materials from literature, social studies, and science	.93
Mathematics: Use of basic mathematics in managing the quantitative aspects of everyday living as well as understanding of mathematical principles	.90
Written Expression: Ability to express ideas in writing including the organization of ideas, letters, and themes, and the mechanics of word usage, word order, and punctuation	.89
Using Sources of Information: Skill in obtaining and interpreting information from maps, charts, tables, graphs, and common references such as dictionaries, tables of contents, and indexes	.93
Social Studies: Knowledge and skills in history, economics, political science, geography, and sociology	.93
Science: Knowledge of concepts and techniques of biology, earth and space science, physics, and chemistry	.87

*Condensed from *Tests of Achievement and Proficiency, Form G* (1986a, p. i), *Tests of Achievement and Proficiency: Directions for Administering Separate Level Booklets* (1986b, p.7) by D. P. Scannel, O. M. Haugh, A. H. Schild, & G. Ulmer, and The Riverside Publishing Company (1990, p. 26). Reproduced with permission of The Riverside Publishing Company.

In reporting results, one could easily give a false impression that a Written Expression Test directly measures student's writing. Not so. The TAP Written Expression Test is a multiple-choice test that might be more accurately described as a test in *editing* written expression. The following example gives the flavor of an important attribute the test assesses; although important, it is not the student's own written expression.

Example of Editing Item

1. Our country's bicentennial
2. celebration of the
3. Bill of Rights occurred
4. in December 1992.

Which is the correct way to write Line 4?

A. in December 1992.

B. in December, 1992.

C. In December of 1992.

D. in december of 1992.

Of course, the reliability coefficients reported in Table 17–3 would be lower if more realistic ones were reported—such as alternate-forms-with-interval. Even so, the level of the K-R 20s is meritorious. This reflects the fact that 40 minutes of testing time are invested in each score.

Finding and Evaluating Published Tests

Finding published instruments from which to make an informed selection requires certain knowledge. This section describes the major sources of information about published measures and how they can be used to locate tests.

The subsequent task of evaluating available instruments in order to select the one that best meets one's needs requires much more knowledge. That material has already been covered in Part IV of this book. Recall the characteristics of good measuring instruments: practical considerations, a basis for meaningful and relevant interpretation, validity, and reliability. Attention now focuses on finding the tests and locating information about these evaluative criteria. This discussion is not only applicable to achievement tests, but also to other kinds of instruments.

Analysis of Need for Testing

Before embarking on a search for "the right" test, one needs to determine if a published test is needed at all. Recall from Chapter 1 that a test should not be used unless it is reasonable to expect it to help in decision making. As an example, the following list contains some of the reasons a school or district might have for considering use of an achievement battery.[1]

To provide parents with information concerning their child's achievement status

To monitor student progress in basic skills

To provide teachers with information that will help in establishing instructional groups for certain subjects (e.g., reading and math)

To provide teachers with information useful in individualizing instruction

To identify each student's relative strengths and weaknesses in broad areas of achievement

To assess the extent to which each student is working up to her or his measured aptitude for schoolwork

To assess strong and weak features of a school's curriculum in comparison with a national cross-section of schools

To assist in identifying students needing referral for special services

To provide information to governing bodies and the general public concerning student achievement

---

[1]Adapted from parts of Stanford Achievement Test Series Test Coordinators Handbook (The Psychological Corporation, 1990a).

These and other reasons lead most schools to administer an achievement battery at least on alternate years between at least Grades 3 and 8. Many schools test annually and many do so from Grades K to 12.

The first and most important step in test selection is to consider why a test is needed, what type of information it is likely to yield, and how that information will be used (Mehrens & Lehmann, 1991, p. 292). These considerations will go far to prevent the use of tests whose results serve few if any useful purposes.

Locating Available Tests

Having decided to select a test, a school or district next needs to locate those instruments from which the choice can be made. Two primary sources of information about available published instruments are publishers' catalogs and *Tests in Print*. These may be consulted in either order, depending on convenience.

Test Publishers' Catalogs.   Test publishers and distributors, like other merchants, advertise their products in a variety of media. The medium most helpful to people in search of prospective tests is the test catalogs. Publishers are generally willing to supply free catalogs on request.

Many school districts maintain a collection of current catalogs from several large publishers of educational tests. Although well over one hundred test publishers do business in the United States (Kramer & Conoley, 1992), four are the giants in the educational testing industry. These are California Test Bureau, Educational Testing Service, The Psychological Corporation, and The Riverside Publishing Company. Appendix A provides a list of names, addresses, and phone numbers of these and a few other major test publishers.

Test catalogs are, of course, good resources for learning about available tests. They are the best means of learning the current prices. They are also an excellent way to learn the types of derived scores supplied with a test and the amount of time it takes to administer it.

Beyond that, one is well advised to remember that catalogs are designed to sell tests; they are promotional. Hence they are *not* good sources of information on such attributes as the validity for various uses, the excellence of the normative data, and the degree to which the test is reliable. Such information is not neatly summarized in a catalog. For such information, the test manual(s) must be consulted.

Tests in Print.   A particularly useful reference is a series which lists tests that are commercially available. Revised at irregular intervals, *Tests in Print IV* is likely to be published in 1993. At times when its latest edition is very recent, this is a singularly effective resource for learning of the existence of tests one might wish to consider. Between editions, it needs to be supplemented with current catalogs.

The first two steps in a test-selection process have now been addressed. Figure 17–4 pictures these and the remaining steps. After analyzing the needs for a test and deciding one is needed, one learns of the available instruments from which to choose. The next two steps—reading reviews about the tests under consideration and studying them and their manuals—can be undertaken in either order.

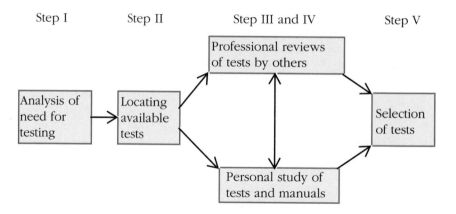

Figure 17–4. Flow Chart for Test Selection

Test Reviews

It is a good idea to get some expert opinions before making a final test-selection decision. Such opinions are most readily available in the form of test reviews. Unless a test is very new, it is likely that reviews of it (or, at least, of its earlier edition) have been published.

Test reviews ordinarily result from a journal or book editor inviting an expert to review a particular test. The reviewer ordinarily attempts to evaluate the major features of the instrument by use of the professionally recognized criteria that are summarized in *Standards for Educational and Psychological Testing* (American Psychological Association, 1985).

Several professional journals publish test reviews. A reading journal may contain reviews of reading tests, a journal in the field of learning disabilities might provide occasional reviews of tests that are used by workers in this field, and a counseling journal may offer reviews of instruments of interest to counselors. *Education Index* provides the best way to locate journal-published reviews of a particular test.

The other major place to locate reviews or critiques of particular tests is in published volumes of test reviews. By far the best known of these is a series, published at irregular intervals since 1938, known as the *Mental Measurements Yearbooks*. Founded and long edited by O. K. Buros, the "yearbooks" are now targeted for publication in odd-numbered years with the *Twelfth Mental Measurements Yearbook* scheduled for publication in 1993. Each contains critical evaluations of a few hundred tests, typically by two independent reviewers each. Between editions, *Mental Measurements Yearbook* reviews can be accessed by means of an on-line computer service through Bibliographic Retrieval Service available in most research libraries.

Another source of published reviews is a set of volumes known as *Test Critiques* (Keyser & Sweetland, 1985–1987). The reviews in *Test Critiques* tend to be descriptive. The *Mental Measurements Yearbooks*, in contrast, provide descriptive information for each test, but the reviews focus on critical evaluation of the merits of the tests. Such volumes are housed in most research libraries in the reference sections (with encyclopedias, dictionaries, etc.) where they cannot be checked out. Because they are relatively specialized reference resources, many small libraries do not have even the *Mental Measurements Yearbooks*.

A word might be imparted concerning the sophistication of persons who are invited to review tests. Their insightfulness varies greatly. Most are highly competent professionals whose reviews share considerable consensus. However, a few are written by persons who are relatively unsophisticated in educational and psychological measurement. It is therefore wise to take the contents of a review as points to be given serious consideration, but not to blindly accept a reviewer's assessments.

A word about style may also be helpful. Reviewers usually try to be generous and mannerly. Most are reluctant to say anything as strong as, "In the total absence of reliability data, this test should not be employed for any applied use" or "In view of the confused and confusing discussion of validity, this test is not recommended for any foreseeable purpose." About the strongest condemnation that most reviewers are willing to make is something along the lines, "The release of this instrument was seriously premature," or "This test can be recommended for research purposes only." Readers should understand that such statements are strong indicators that caution or avoidance is being advised.

At this point it would be worth your while to read the most recent *Mental Measurements Yearbook* reviews of a few tests that are of interest to you. Compare and contrast the comments of different reviewers of the same test.

Figure 17–4 shows Steps III and IV to be parallel in that their order is variable. Persons considering tests may choose to obtain copies of the instruments and their supporting publications or to read reviews first. The choice may well be based on convenience. Regardless of order, however, both steps are important. On occasion, a relatively new instrument may not have published reviews. In that case, the next step becomes even more critical.

Appendix B summarizes parts of the above discussion regarding sources of information about published instruments. It lists major sources of information for (a) learning of the existence of measures, (b) finding critical reviews of particular measures, and (c) locating research about particular instruments.

Specimen Sets

Just as a prospective house buyer will make a very careful inspection of the house, prospective test buyers should make a very detailed examination of any test being considered. This is enabled by securing from the publisher or distributor an examination kit or specimen set of the test. This should include (a) a copy of at least one form of the test (at the level(s) of interest if the instrument has multiple levels), (b) a copy of the answer media available, (c) a manual containing administration and scoring information, and, if such data are not provided in the general manual, (d) additional manual(s) or technical supplement(s) that provide information concerning reference group sampling, reliability, and validity.

To be useful, a test must be interpretable. Interpretability via domain referencing is best evaluated by examining the domain description in the manual, considering the domain specifiability, and judging the match between the test content and the domain that should be incisively defined. Interpretability via norm referencing is best judged by examining the manual's description of the kind(s) of reference group(s) provided, evaluating the adequacy with which sampling was conducted, and judging the relevance of the reference group(s) for the intended test use(s).

Validity is also an essential characteristic of effective measures. In the case of achievement tests, validity interest focuses largely on content-related validity evidence. This is investigated by studying the rationale and methods of content selection explicated in the manual, examining the table of specifications in the manual, and, especially, *scrutinizing the content of the test, item by item.* In the case of predictive tests, interest focuses mainly on criterion-related, predictive validity evidence. Data concerning this are most often available in the test manual or technical supplements. In the case of tests designed to assess other constructs, construct-related validity evidence will probably be the most important. It is most commonly found in the technical manual and/or in cited research literature.

Finally, reliability is an essential feature of all effective measures, and it is a fundamental obligation of authors and publishers to supply such information. Test manuals and technical supplements are the primary source of information concerning reliability and standard errors of measurement. Regardless of whether the test is designed for norm- or domain-referenced interpretation, information about the consistency of all of its scores is essential. Prudent prospective buyers will study such data carefully—or deplore its absence—before deciding for or against purchase.

Selection

The final step in the test-selection process comes after reviewing the test and its manual(s) and after studying the reasoned evaluations of others (if available). In most cases, those making the selection decision experience some ambivalence. One competitor may be the most reliable, another the easiest to interpret, and yet another the least expensive. Final decisions are often prefaced with phrases like, "All things considered" and "On balance." Such phrases catch the spirit of what informed test selection involves—a balanced consideration of all the pertinent characteristics of effective measures.

QUIZ 17–4

1. It is time to apply Part IV of this book to the topic of test selection. Fill in the following table to indicate the major source(s) of information concerning each of the characteristics of good measuring instruments.

Characteristic	*Sources of Information*
Practical concerns	
Interpretability	
Reliability	

QUIZ 17–4 (cont.)

2. Validity was not included above because its answer depends upon the kind of test. In the table below indicate the kind of validity evidence of greatest interest for each kind of test and the source of information concerning that kind of validity evidence. (There often would be secondary sources of information of interest, but focus on the primary source for each case.)

Kind of Test	*Validity Evidence of Greatest Importance*	*Primary Source of Information*
Domain referenced achievement test		
Norm referenced achievement test		
Computer programming aptitude test		
General academic aptitude test		
Self-concept scale		
A "quick and dirty" screening test		

KEY TO QUIZ 17–4

1.

Characteristic	*Sources of Information*
Practical concerns	Test catalog, manual, answer sheets, interpretive aids
Interpretability	Manual
Reliability	Manual

KEY TO QUIZ 17–4 (cont.)

2.

Kind of Test	Validity Evidence of Greatest Importance	Primary Source of Information
Domain referenced achievement test	Content-related	Test
Norm referenced achievement test	Content-related	Test
Computer programming aptitude test	Criterion-related (predictive)	Manual
General academic aptitude test	Construct-related or Criterion-related (predictive)	Manual
Self-concept scale	Construct-related	Manual
A "quick and dirty" screening test	Criterion-related (concurrent)	Manual

Chapter Summary

Published tests are often technically superior to teacher-made tests and are typically accompanied by reference-group data external to the particular class. The trade-off is that they are not customized to the needs of the individual class. Published achievement batteries offer the major additional advantage of enabling norm-referenced comparison of achievement among several content areas, between achievement in successive years, and/or between achievement and aptitude measures. These interpretations involve difference scores, and each has its hazards. Nevertheless, the importance of such comparisons prompts most users of achievement batteries to use them.

Commercially produced instruments vary greatly in quality. Professionals who use published tests should adopt a cautious attitude toward evaluating them. The merits of each test should be thoughtfully considered in light of evidence that the authors and others provide. Test users can obtain much help in evaluating tests by studying the criteria by which instruments are evaluated. The best compilation of professional opinion concerning bases for evaluating published tests is *Standards for Educational and Psychological Testing* (American Psychological Association, 1985). Having decided to adopt a given test, one should maintain an evaluative mode in considering various interpretive aids, reports forms, and scoring services that can be purchased for the test. Appendix B provides a summary of sources of information about published instruments.

Suggestions for Further Reading

Gronlund, N. E., & Linn, R. L. (1990). *Measurement and evaluation in teaching* (6th ed.). New York: Macmillan. Chapter 11, "Achievement Tests," provides an introduction to the major published achievement tests. Chapter 13, "Test Selection, Administration, and Use," offers a sound elementary treatment of the processes involved in test selection as well as the uses and misuses of published achievement tests.

Haladyna, T. M., Nolen, S. B., & Haas, N. S. (1991). Raising standardized achievement test scores and the origins of test score pollution. *Educational Researcher, 20,* 2–7. A thoughtful consideration of the problems created by high-stakes external testing programs in which the elevation of test scores is an end in itself rather than a mere *indicant* of *some* important kinds of achievement. A variety of test preparation activities are analyzed from the perspective of their impact on the extent to which they cause test scores to misrepresent the domains they are designed to sample.

Hopkins, K. D., Stanley, J. C., & Hopkins, B. R. (1990). *Educational and psychological measurement and evaluation* (7th ed.). Englewood Cliffs, NJ: Prentice-Hall. Chapter 14, "Standardized Achievement Tests," offers an integrated treatment of achievement tests, kinds of derived scores, and kinds of reference groups.

Mehrens, W. A., & Lehmann, I. J. (1991). *Measurement and evaluation in education and psychology* (4th ed.). Fort Worth: Holt, Rinehart and Winston. Chapter 16, "Standardized Achievement Tests," provides thorough coverage of the topic with a particularly sound discussion of the problems encountered in diagnostic testing.

Salvia, J., & Ysseldyke, J. E. (1988). *Assessment in special and remedial education* (4th ed.). Boston: Houghton Mifflin. Chapter 16, "Assessment of Academic Achievement: Screening Devices," provides brief descriptions of a large number of specific tests, particularly those useful in special education. Chapters 17 and 18, concerning diagnostic assessment in reading and math, provide more comprehensive treatment than general introductory chapters typically can. It would be particularly useful to juxtapose reading these chapters with Chapter 16 in Mehrens and Lehmann (1991), which offers astute treatment of cautions to be observed in diagnostic testing.

Smith, M. L. (1991). Put to the test: The effects of external testing on teaching. *Educational Researcher, 20,* 8–11. This article presents a very worrisome description and discussion of the educationally adverse consequences that can result from externally mandated, high-stakes achievement testing programs at their worst. Persons reading this article will benefit from first reading Mehrens and Kamanski (1989) and/or Haladyna, Nolen, and Haas (1991).

18

Aptitude Tests

The last chapter showed that published achievement tests and those that teachers produce are more alike than different. This chapter and the next will focus on instruments that teachers do not ordinarily produce, devices that are available mainly from test publishers. There is also substantial similarity between classroom achievement tests and a wide variety of commercially marketed measures of other attributes. For example, the universal characteristics of good measures (i.e., reliability, validity, practical features, and a basis for interpretation) all apply to aptitude tests, interest inventories, etc., as much as to published or teacher-made achievement tests. Moreover, the similarity between achievement and aptitude tests turns out to be much greater than their names may imply.

Like achievement tests, aptitude tests should be used only when they are likely to improve decision making. Some of the decisions facilitated by aptitude tests are instructional in nature and are made by teachers, some are administrative decisions, and some are made by individual students and their parents. Most involve prediction of one sort or another. Aptitude test interpretations are norm-referenced because the instruments assess large, ill-described domains. Like other measures, aptitude tests lack perfect reliability and validity; therefore, in using them for decision making, allowance must be made for measurement error.

This chapter provides general information about aptitude tests. In addition, selected examples will highlight features of aptitude measures and provide familiarity with certain tests that are widely used in schools.

The Achievement-Aptitude Continuum

If asked, "What is the difference between achievement and aptitude?" the proverbial person on the street might answer along the lines, "Achievement is what you have learned; aptitude is your ability or capacity to learn." While this understanding is not entirely wrong, it is very deficient; psychologists have long understood that intelligence (i.e., aptitude) tests do not provide simple and direct measurement of potential in any valid sense (Stanovich, 1991). This section will pursue clarification of what aptitude tests actually measure by two means. First, aptitude will be compared and contrasted with achievement. Second, attention will focus on what aptitude is not.

What Is Achievement?

Perhaps the clearest way to define **achievement** is in terms of the processes, methods, and operations by which it is measured. The way to be clearest concerning "What is achievement in fifth-grade language arts?" is to agree on the way it is to be measured. Once the parties to the discussion can agree on the measure, they have an operational definition—achievement in fifth-grade language arts is that which is measured by the test. Such operational definitions may seem circular to people who do not understand their purpose, but their aim is clarity and that aim is nicely achieved.

Although clear, an operational definition may be poor. Thus if the test does not measure what educators agree constitutes fifth-grade language arts, the test is not valid and the operational definition is poor. Yet it is clear, and this clarity provides a means to improve the test/definition and the impact it has on student effort. *A test that is a valid measure of a construct is a good operational definition of that construct.*

Much of this book has been devoted to making classroom achievement tests valid—that is, good operational definitions of the kinds of achievement that educators value. Thus we want achievement tests to focus on important material, to tap higher mental processes, to be free of item flaws that enable content-ignorant persons to deduce the keyed responses, to reflect the objectives of instruction, to be instructionally sensitive, and so forth.

Recall from Chapter 14 that instructional sensitivity is the extent to which persons who have been instructed perform better than those who have not. We saw that discriminatory tests for Track C content should be instructionally sensitive, but not to an extreme. The assessment of higher mental processes requires transfer of learning. The tests must go somewhat beyond what was specifically taught. Therefore, specific rote learning does not, in itself, guarantee ability to apply all instances of the learning.

Thus begins the continuum shown in Figure 18–1. At one end are achievement measures that are extremely sensitive to instruction—mastery tests on which well-prepared students get perfect or near-perfect scores. Near this end of the continuum are achievement tests that require a little processing of material beyond what was specifically taught. Still further from the instructionally sensitive endpoint are achievement measures that require more transfer of learning to make less direct applications.

There comes a point, of course, at which teachers would consider problems to demand too much transfer and not enough of what was taught. Such items would not be considered to measure course achievement (enough) and would be considered to be more measures of aptitude or problem solving.

It might also be mentioned that achievement tests are reasonably focused. A math test is limited to math, a biology test is limited to biology, and so on.

What Is Aptitude?

One way to characterize aptitude or "intelligence" tests is as tests that move too far from the instructional sensitive end of the continuum to be considered legitimate measures of achievement in a particular subject.

Another way of defining "intelligence" involves descriptions of intelligent behavior. Although no one such definition has achieved universal acceptance, the flavor of the construct was captured by Binet's pioneering description. To him, intelligent behavior involved the tendency to take and maintain direction; the ability to

Content highly instructionally sensitive		Content only somewhat sensitive to specific instruction, but very sensitive in general culture		Content only somewhat sensitive to general culture	
Mastery achievement test	Achievement test requiring some processing or transfer	Achievement test requiring deep processing and transfer	Aptitude test tapping much heterogeneous achievement	Aptitude test requiring novel problem solving	Non-verbal aptitude test
Used to assess past learning				Used to predict future learning	

Figure 18–1.   Achievement-Aptitude Continuum

adapt; and the capacity to judge well, to reason well, and to comprehend well (Binet & Simon, 1916; Terman, 1916).

Still another way to think of aptitude tests concerns their function. The main legitimate uses to which "intelligence" tests are put involve prediction of future success in more or less academic settings. Much misunderstanding concerning "intelligence" and "IQ" would be avoided if discussion were to shift away from an abstract psychological construct and come to focus on the *purposes of aptitude testing.* Such tests are used to predict; they produce forecasts. *"Intelligence" testing is primarily a forecasting endeavor.* This point is also made in Figure 18–1.

Yet another way to characterize aptitude tests is as tests that are not ordinarily focused on particular content fields but that often span many fields and include out-of-school learning as well as school-type learning. Aptitude tests are thus *not* very sensitive to instruction in *any one* subject. Yet it is important to realize that most aptitude or so-called intelligence tests do measure broad-scope achievement that is very influenced by the general intellectual, educational, and cultural environment.

Here are several examples of some of the kinds of questions that appear in major "intelligence" tests. They could be fashioned either as oral completion items for individual administration or as written multiple-choice questions for use in paper-pencil tests.

At what temperature does water freeze?

What country is also an entire continent?

Who was Moses?

Monarch is to country as mayor is to _____ .

Jim and Bob Brown are brothers. What is the relationship between Jim's daughter and Bob's daughter?

Who wrote *Tom Sawyer?*

What is the name of your state's governor?

What is photosynthesis?

What is the main source of income of most newspapers?

What is an ideograph?

What number comes next in this series: 1, 3, 7, 15, 31?

What purposes are served by a U. S. Federal census?

This is the kind of material measured in most "intelligence" tests. Such questions clearly measure learning, much of which is school learning. Operationally, intelligence is what is measured by valid tests of the construct. If a test samples *acquired behaviors* that psychologists agree to label intellectual, then the test provides a good operational definition of intelligence (Mehrens & Lehmann, 1991, p. 307). The sample items listed above thus help to convey what "intelligence" is—*and what it is not.*

What "Intelligence" Is Not

Clearly, intelligence is not "something you are born with." Nor is it "capacity." Nor is it unchangeable. Nor is it neural tissue. Intelligence is evidenced by ability to handle the kind of material assessed by leading "intelligence" tests. Since the word "intelligence" (and the term "IQ") are so widely misunderstood to mean some of the things that intelligence is not, it may be better to avoid the word altogether and to use others that better convey what is measured. As mentioned in Chapter 16, such terms as "academic aptitude," "cognitive abilities," and "scholastic aptitude" serve quite well.

Scholars agree that it is not possible to assess genetic endowment or so-called innate potential. Rather, intellectual development is understood to involve "a dynamic interaction of heredity and environment beginning with the prenatal environment. Trying to separate the relative influence of each for a given person is a futile task, particularly in view of the mutual interdependence of these variables in contributing to any individual's score on any intelligence or achievement scale" (Kaufman & Kaufman, 1983, p. 20).

Even if we could separate the impact of heredity and environment, this dichotomy would *not* equate to a distinction between things that are alterable and those that are fixed at conception. "Many inherited characteristics are changeable, and conversely, many environmentally acquired characteristics are extremely resistant to change" (Angoff, 1988, p. 713).

Why Aptitude Tests Measure What They Measure

Many people have wondered why "intelligence" tests are not constructed so as to avoid past achievement. They could be based on completely novel material. (A test that pursues this approach, the *Progressive Matrices*, will be described later.) As shown in Figure 18–1, such tests lie at the end of the continuum opposite achievement.

A test with completely novel material was a good idea that had to be tried to determine that it was no panacea to environmental inequities. Such tests can be constructed, but they are not as effective as conventional aptitude tests in fulfilling their primary function—academic prediction. Recall from Chapter 14 that predictive measures tend to work best when they are intrinsically related to the thing being predicted (Anastasi, 1988, p. 194). Hence if we want to predict school learning in the future, tests that assess past learning tend to do the job better than tests that assess something else.

Then why have aptitude tests at all? Why not base all predictions on measures of relevant past achievement? In point of fact, it is often possible to make better predictions based on past achievement than on aptitude measures. For example, college freshman grades are generally predicted a little more validly from high school grades than from college admissions tests. Aptitude tests are used for two reasons.

First, at times there is no past achievement in the subject being predicted. Suppose we need to predict how well students will do in first-year German, computer programming, geometry, or bookkeeping. We cannot administer an achievement test because they have not yet studied the subject. Aptitude tests are valuable in providing predictions in settings where there is no past achievement to measure.

Second, even where there is past achievement to measure, better predictions can be made with a suitable weighted combination of predictors than with one alone. Thus college freshman grades are predicted more validly by simultaneous use of high school grades and college admissions test scores than by either alone. Similarly, second-year German grades can be forecasted more accurately by joint use of first-year grades and verbal aptitude measures than by grades alone.

It has been said that aptitude tests that tie into past school learning are generally superior for mainstream students over those that are not academic in flavor. Yet there is an important place for tests that are less loaded with school learning than the illustrative items provided above. Culturally loaded tests are clearly inappropriate for examinees who do not have the common background of experience in the culture for which the test was developed. Nonverbal or "culture-fair" tests may be the only available measures suitable for students who are not conversant with Standard American English or with the mainstream United States culture. Tests that are less saturated with a particular culture than the sample items provided above would be valuable for such examinees.

However, beware of so-called culture-free tests; "tests are culture-free in name only—there are no tests that measure potential or aptitude directly" (Hopkins, Stanley, & Hopkins, 1990, p. 373). Tests are cultural artifacts; how then could one be culture-free?

A test such as the *Progressive Matrices*, described below, would be suitable for a pupil who speaks little English. But what about pupils who speak a variant dialect, or ones for whom English is not the first language, or ones whose homes are culturally unusual? Is a culturally saturated test fair to them?

From one angle, of course not. Their cultural differences place them at a disadvantage over which they have little or no control.

From another angle, definitely. Of course their circumstances will have placed such people at a cultural disadvantage. Recall, however, that *the purpose of aptitude tests is to predict.* Such people's circumstances will usually also place them at a disadvantage in schools. The main job of aptitude tests is to forecast school success. Therefore, for a test to be able to do its predictive job, such persons should be at an equal disadvantage on the aptitude test. Recall that one would not condemn the weather forecaster who systematically (yet correctly) predicts lower temperatures for Minneapolis than for Miami. Nor would one condemn a physical exam whose results lead to consistent predictions that lame students will not, on average, learn to run as fast as those having no physical impairment.

For typical examinees who share reasonable amounts of the culture for which the test is developed, a culturally relevant test will predict academic success better than one that is less culturally loaded. Schools, after all, are culture-saturated.

Tests of General Academic Aptitude

In this section four widely used scholastic aptitude tests are briefly described. With no attempt at comprehensiveness, selected features of each test are addressed in order to illustrate various points.

Otis-Lennon School Ability Test

The name of the *Otis-Lennon School Ability Test* (OLSAT) reflects an evolution from its origins in 1918 when the word "intelligence" was used in its title. Then it changed to "mental abilities," and finally to "school abilities." The change to "school ability" reflects the purposes for which the test is most appropriate. The use of "school ability" rather than "mental ability" is also intended to discourage overinterpretation of the nature and breadth of the attributes being assessed (Otis & Lennon, 1990, p. 9). Such tests assess only a rather narrow (albeit very important) spectrum of abilities; they do not tap all important aptitudes as the word "intelligence" implies to many people.

The Otis tests were originally based on a construct of "intelligence" as a unitary trait that is best reported globally. However, the OLSAT now has two part scores—verbal and nonverbal—in addition to the total score.

Traditionally, academic aptitude tests have been interpreted mainly with respect to reference groups of other students of the same age. The OLSAT thus provides age-based standard scores having $M = 100$ and $SD = 16$. These scores, previously called "deviation IQs," are now more descriptively called "School Ability Indexes." Like most aptitude tests, the OLSAT manuals also supply age-based percentile ranks and stanines.

In addition to age-based derived scores, the OLSAT also provides grade-based derived scores. Of course, pupils whose ages are about average for their grade will receive very similar grade-based and age-based derived scores. For those who are underaged or overaged, status in comparison with age peers will not be identical to status vis-à-vis grade peers. This point is particularly important when teachers or counselors compare achievement scores (which are usually referenced to grade peers) to aptitude scores (which are usually referenced to age mates). In this case the grade-based aptitude scores are very useful.

The OLSAT is accompanied by high quality normative data. Its excellent norming design was conducted concurrently with the *Stanford Achievement Test*. Therefore, users who wish to compare school aptitude scores with achievement scores can be confident that the normative samples are comparable.

Raven's Progressive Matrices

Various editions since 1938 of the *Raven's Progressive Matrices* have provided for examinees aged six and over. Items consist of arrangements of designs in rows and columns. Each item has one of its parts missing, and the examinee is required to

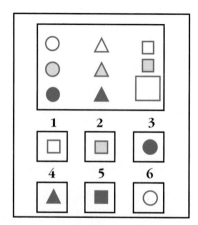
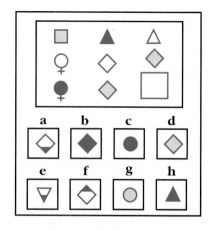

Figure 18–2.   Items Illustrating item type typical of *Progressive Matrices*

select the correct option with which to complete the matrix. This intriguing item type enables the assessment of abstract, logical reasoning abilities without use of language. Figure 18–2 provides two examples of the general item type.

Such items are less culture-saturated than are most verbal and quantitative questions. Other things being equal, they would therefore be expected to correlate less adequately with criteria of school-type learning than would more verbal, educationally relevant tests. However, such devices are valuable for assessing people whose cultural or linguistic background is too atypical to enable valid use of more culturally specific measures. They are also useful with examinees who have a language disability.

Most of the reference group data for this series of nonverbal tests have been based on United Kingdom populations. This and the lower predictive validity to be expected from such tests explains why the *Progressive Matrices* have not achieved widespread group usage in United States schools. They have, however, often been used by school psychologists to assess individual children (e.g., see Kaufman, 1979).

Wechsler Scales

Unlike the group-administerable tests described above, assessment of individual children for special education classification and other purposes is ordinarily conducted with instruments designed to be administered one-on-one. Such tests not only yield quantitative scores, but also provide rich clinical data from the highly structured interview—that is, the examination.

Individual intelligence tests require much more knowledge, skill, and practice to correctly administer and score than do group tests. For example, typical classroom teachers who have taken a course in educational measurement are qualified to use most group tests. However, qualifications to administer, score, and interpret individual intelligence tests typically require two or more additional courses of specialized work.

Perhaps the most widely used individual intelligence tests are those developed by David Wechsler. The current Wechsler scales are the *Wechsler Preschool and Primary Scale of Intelligence–Revised* for youngsters 3 to 7 years of age, the *Wechsler Intelligence Scale for Children–Third Edition* (WISC–III) for ages 6 to 16, and the *Wechsler Adult Intelligence Scale–Revised* (WAIS–R) for age 16 into old age. Use of Wechsler scales typically involves administering 10 to 12 subtests, which are grouped into two main categories—Verbal and Performance. Aged-based deviation *IQs* are provided for each of these major sections as well as for the total score.

Terms such as "verbal," "performance," and "nonverbal" as used in various tests do not have uniform meaning. In some tests, "nonverbal" includes quantitative measures, in others it does not. In the Wechsler scales, the verbal section includes mental arithmetic. It is, therefore, important for users to become very familiar with a test's contents before attempting to use its subscore titles meaningfully.

In most respects the Wechsler scales are exemplary in their development, standardization of administration and scoring procedures, and norming. On the negative side, it might be noted that they still use the older, oft-misunderstood word "intelligence" in their titles, and the obsolescent term "deviation IQ" is still used to described these derived scores (which are standard scores having $M = 100$ and $SD = 15$).

Fortunately, the new WISC–III also provides PRs and percentile bands to facilitate interpretation.

K–ABC

The *Kaufman Assessment Battery for Children* (Kaufman & Kaufman, 1983) avoids these problems. Designed for individual administration to children aged 4 to 12, the K–ABC is intended to perform many of the same functions as the Wechsler scales. Its aged-based total score, like Wechsler DIQs, have $M = 100$ and $SD = 15$. But the K–ABC scores are more accurately identified as "standard scores." In addition, age-based percentile ranks are provided. Note too that the word "intelligence" is laudably avoided in the name of this instrument.

The K–ABC is a relatively modern instrument that has the advantage of sound anchorage in well-defined psychological theory (Coffman, 1985, p. 771). In addition, it addresses contemporary emphases in making relatively sound provisions for "certain emerging testing needs, such as use with handicapped groups, application to problems of learning disabilities, and appropriateness for cultural and linguistic minorities" (Anastasi, 1985, p. 769). Exemplary provision is made for profile interpretation with full cognizance of measurement error.

A novel feature of the K–ABC is the inclusion of achievement measures. More than most aptitude tests, it seeks to separate achievement from problem solving. This may be a reason for the notably lower correlation of socioeconomic status with K–ABC mental processing scores than with scores of most general aptitude tests.

The reference group data were, in general, gathered in conformity to the best of current practice (Page, 1985, p. 775). An interesting feature of the norming was the development of supplementary reference groups to provide subgroup normative data for a black-white dichotomy and for two parental educational levels. Thus, for example, if one were testing a black child whose parents did not graduate from high school, it would be possible to compare him or her with other black children whose parents did not graduate from high school. In addition, of course, one would ordinarily want to compare such an individual with the total national sample of age peers.

QUIZ 18–1

1. In identifying students for programs for the learning disabled, behavioral disordered, or gifted, it is customary to use individually administered aptitude tests. For which of these would the use of a test administered one-on-one be *least* important? Why?

2. Individual intelligence tests are generally regarded as much superior to group-administered ones. With regard to reliability, which would likely be superior—a well-designed, objective, group test or a well-designed individually administered oral one? In considering your answer, consider the four major sources of measurement error discussed on pages 423–427.

KEY TO QUIZ 18–1

1. Individual testing with concurrent skilled clinical observation is vital to the assessment of some kinds of learning disabilities. To take an obvious example, suppose a child is suspected of having reading disabilities. Use of conventional group paper-pencil tests would put him or her at a potential disadvantage because reading problems could interfere with performance on the aptitude test. The confounded results of the aptitude test would therefore not be very interpretable.

    Insightful clinical observation is also vital to the assessment of behavioral disorders. For example, suppose an aptitude measure is needed for a child suspected of having a behavioral disorder. Short attention span could seriously interfere with performance on a group-administered, paper-pencil test. The one-on-one administration by a highly skilled examiner provides more opportunity for rest breaks, motivational encouragement, re-focus of attention, etc., with which to get the child's best effort. Then, too, if attention could not be focused long enough for a valid assessment, the clinical observations would probably bring this to light; on a group test the cause of the low score would be much less likely to be recognized.

    Individual testing for classification of gifted students is also common but much less important. *Unless* such a child is suspected of having a disability that would interfere with performance on a group-administered, paper-pencil aptitude test, there does not seem to me to be any compelling reason to demand an individual test.

2. Myth has it that individual tests are more reliable; they are not. Their superiority rests on other attributes such as (a) the examiner's greater opportunity to obtain the examinee's best effort and (b) the wealth of clinical observations and inferences that a skilled examiner can obtain from the testing session.

    Let us compare individual and group aptitude tests on the four major sources of measurement error. They would suffer from comparable amounts of content sampling error and occasion sampling error. Examiner error is very likely to be greater in individual tests in which the examiner has to manipulate materials, clock response times for individual items, give many detailed verbal instructions, ask appropriate follow-up questions, and record responses. Similarly, scoring error is much greater for the open-ended responses that are typical of individually administered aptitude tests than for the objective, paper-pencil, group tests that are scored with very little measurement error.

    So individual tests are often superior in spite of their reliability, not because of it.

Tests of Specific Aptitudes

A number of so-called **special aptitude tests** are available for school and college use. Some are designed to help institutions such as medical and law schools make wise selection decisions. Others are designed to help students make wise educational and occupational decisions (e.g., tests of mechanical aptitude, musical aptitude, algebra aptitude, artistic aptitude, and modern language aptitude).

Many special aptitude tests, such as those used to predict success in algebra or law school, are better described as tests with specialized purposes than as tests that measure unique aptitudes. For example, a modern language aptitude test is dedicated to the function of predicting success in the study of modern foreign languages. The attributes it assesses are not likely to be peculiarly relevant to this field. The general verbal aptitude on which it would probably focus are also important to the study of history, English, or even geometry. It would not probably be much more valid than a general verbal aptitude test in predicting French grades.

Advantages exist, however, to the use of such a specialized test over a general verbal aptitude test. One advantage of a language aptitude test is its customization to provide an optimal content blend for predicting success in languages as distinct from other courses. Another advantage is its face validity or credibility to students and parents as a predictor of success in languages. Also very important is the likely inclusion in its manual of validity data that focus on the test's predictive validity for its specialized purpose. Finally, such a test would probably be accompanied by an expectancy (or experience) table to aid in its meaningful interpretation to students and parents.

For these reasons, some schools use specialized aptitude tests for such subjects as modern languages and algebra. Others may predict grades in these subjects nearly as well by use of general aptitude tests and/or past grades. Remember Mr. Weber who used eighth-grade English grades to predict French grades.

Aptitude Batteries

Tests of general academic aptitude, such as the OLSAT, were historically based on the view that "intelligence" is a general attribute. Such tests always provide a total or composite aptitude score. Most older measures of general intelligence were consistent with the notion that intelligence is a unitary attribute and provided only this total score. In contrast, most contemporary instruments depart from this purely unitary view of "intelligence" and offer some subscores (e.g., the OLSAT's verbal and nonverbal subscores and the Wechsler scales' verbal and performance scores).

Multiple **aptitude batteries**, on the other hand, are based on the belief that "intelligence" is multifaceted and that it is useful to assess various aptitudes separately. Such testing always leads to an aptitude **profile**—an integrated presentation of several scores. Some such tests, being consistent with the belief in multiple aptitudes, provide no total score.

The main purpose of an aptitude profile is differential prediction. To illustrate, suppose a student is going to do better (or worse) next year in Spanish than in geometry. A single-score test could not predict this difference. Multiple aptitude batteries have a chance. The extent to which they can correctly forecast such a difference is a manifestation of their differential validity. Unfortunately, a common feature of multiple-score aptitude batteries is their disappointing performance in this regard (Anastasi, 1988, p. 395).

Another major purpose of aptitude profiles involves educational and occupational counseling. In educational and vocational planning, it is useful to know a person's relative strengths and weaknesses.

In this section four popular aptitude batteries are described. Selected features of each test are addressed in order to illustrate various points, but no attempt is made to provide a comprehensive description of the batteries.

Cognitive Abilities Test

The *Cognitive Abilities Test* (Thorndike & Hagen, 1986) is the K–12 aptitude companion of the ITBS and the TAP. All three group tests are normed on the same sample of schools. In addition to providing for identical reference groups for achievement and aptitude scores, the exemplary norming design of the *Cognitive Abilities Test* pioneered in using stratified random sampling to ensure proportional representation of students with respect to size of school, region of the country, and, most importantly, socioeconomic status.

Like its achievement counterparts, the *Cognitive Abilities Test* is published in a multilevel booklet that accommodates out-of-level and individualized testing.

Like other aptitude batteries, the *Cognitive Abilities Test* is founded on the belief that "intelligence" or aptitude is multifaceted rather than global and that it is useful to measure various kinds of cognitive abilities separately. It consists of three separate parts—verbal, quantitative, and nonverbal—each requiring 30 minutes of testing time. Each of these major parts includes three separate subtests at most grade levels, each designed to tap a distinct kind of verbal, quantitative, or nonverbal aptitude. Thus each subconstruct is assessed in multiple ways. The authors are to be commended for not reporting the scores based upon these nine short (hence unreliable) subtests.

This test was first published in 1954 as the *Lorge-Thorndike Intelligence Test*, and is now in its fourth edition. Its authors pioneered in avoiding two major problems of so-called intelligence tests, misunderstood titles and misleading names of derived scores. Because "intelligence" was so widely misunderstood, the more descriptive term *cognitive abilities* was adopted. By providing a name that more clearly describes what the test measured, the authors helped to prevent some of the grave misinterpretations given to scores of tests with the title "intelligence."

Along the same lines, the name of the *Cognitive Abilities Test*'s standard scores (which have $M = 100$ and $SD = 16$) was changed from the widely misunderstood term "DIQ" to the more descriptive term "standard age scores." This clearly denotes what the scores are—standard scores based on reference groups of age mates. Although the statistical characteristics of the scores did not change, the new name represented a great improvement that has been emulated by several other tests (e.g., the OLSAT's School Ability Index).

The Differential Aptitude Tests

The *Differential Aptitude Tests* (DAT), since the first edition in 1947, have probably been the most widely used of all multiple aptitude batteries designed mainly for school use. They include eight tests, and require nearly four hours of time for administration. The current edition (Bennett, Seashore, & Wesman, 1990) has two levels, one for Grades 7 to 9 and one for Grades 10 to 12. Separate norms tables are provided for males and females because gender differences occur on several of the tests.

Unlike most aptitude batteries, its scores are grade based. They are therefore more suitable for comparison with scores of achievement measures.

The DAT can be used at various points in testing programs. Often it is used in Grades 8 or 9 as one source of information to aid students and parents in planning high school programs of studies. It is also often used near the end of high school to supplement grades and achievement test scores in informing the planning of post-secondary occupation and education.

Either of these uses of the DAT is enhanced if it is used in conjunction with an interest inventory. The *Career Interest Inventory* was designed for use with the DAT and can be administered as part of the battery. Its interpretation is integrated with that of the DAT.

Like several other tests, the DAT has been revised often enough so that each revision is not radical. Thus the validity data for the immediate past edition or two remain reasonably relevant to the current edition. "The amount of validity data available on the DAT is overwhelming, including several thousand validity coefficients" (Anastasi, 1988, p. 394).

The DAT manual has long been considered a model to be emulated in providing interpretative aids, sound suggestions, unexaggerated descriptions of the test and its attributes, and cautions regarding common misuses and interpretive errors. For example, the DAT was among early tests to introduce percentile bands for interpretive uses. In general, the interpretive hazards are much greater in interpreting profiles of scores than in interpreting individual scores. The various editions of the DAT manuals have done much to minimize the risks of misuse and to prompt proper use.

Armed Services Vocational Aptitude Battery

The *Armed Services Vocational Aptitude Battery* (ASVAB) is a battery consisting of 10 aptitude and achievement subtests designed to serve recruitment and classification needs of the armed services. Four of the subtests provide a qualifying composite score used in all the services. Each branch of the military then uses various combinations of subscores from this battery to form aptitude composites that meet its needs for classifying enlisted personnel (Anastasi, 1988, p. 400).

This battery has credible technical data, although its criterion-related validation consists mainly of studies of predicting success in military training programs. It is made available for high school use at no cost or obligation. In some schools it is routinely administered to all students in Grade 11 or 12; in others it is made available for those considering military enlistment. "The results of the ASVAB are used by the military to assist in recruiting and to stimulate interest in the services" (Mehrens & Lehmann, 1991, p. 335).

The ASVAB's widespread use by high schools has been rather controversial for reasons that lie outside its technical attributes. The ASVAB thus serves to illustrate how the *consequential basis of validity* discussed in Chapter 14 enter into consideration to use or not to use a test.

One source of dispute concerns the ethical issue of whether schools should feature a test that is designed to serve the recruiting and classification needs of particular employers (i.e., the armed services) rather than to meet the educational and counseling needs of youth. Many schools have accommodated this concern by administering the battery selectively to only those students who are considering enlisting.

Another source of controversy that focuses on a nonmeasurement, ethical issue involves questions concerning the propriety of assisting the recruiting efforts of employers that have explicit policy commitments to discriminate against gay men and lesbians. This source of sharp differences of opinion illustrates how people on both sides of an issue attend to the consequential basis of validity. It also brings home the point that validity and values are closely linked.

Woodcock-Johnson Psychoeducational Battery–Revised

The *Woodcock-Johnson Psychoeducational Battery–R* (Woodcock, 1989) is a relatively comprehensive, individually administered battery designed for use between ages 3 and 80. It consists of 12 cognitive ability subtests, 9 achievement subtests, and 5 interest subtests.

Used extensively in special education, the Woodcock-Johnson provides an individual assessment that enables comparison of aptitude, achievement, and interest scores that were derived from the same reference group. It is similar in this regard to the K–ABC in being an individually administered battery that accommodates comparison of comparable derived scores for aptitude and achievement.

College Admissions Tests

As students near the completion of high school, many consider applying to post-secondary educational institutions. At this point, college admissions testing becomes a central part of most high school testing programs. That is, information about the tests is disseminated and enrollment to take the tests is often coordinated. Unlike all other instruments (aside from the ASVAB) discussed in this and the past chapter, however, college admissions tests are not bought by the school, nor does the school control them. They are controlled and managed very tightly by their publishers in order to ensure test security.

A new edition is typically prepared for each of the several dates a test will be administered nationally. The tests are given only at designated, supervised testing centers. Test booklets are kept sealed until administration time, which takes place simultaneously in all testing centers. Following the administration, answer sheets are sent for centralized scoring.

This section will briefly described the two nationally used college admissions tests.

Scholastic Aptitude Test

Prior to the 1920s, each college and university that wanted to use an admissions test had to develop, administer, and score its own. A student applying to several colleges would have to take several such tests. Then several colleges cooperatively formed the College Entrance Examination Board, which published a common exam for use by all member institutions. This instrument, the *Scholastic Aptitude Test* (SAT), has been improved over the decades and has undergone extensive research.

The SAT is a three-hour test having two major sections, Verbal and Mathematical, designed to assess cognitive attributes that develop slowly over time through students' in-school and out-of-school experiences. Unlike achievement tests, the SAT is not linked to the content of specific courses or fields of study—only to common curricular goals (Anastasi, 1988, p. 330).

Scores of each section are reported by means of a system of standard scores having $M = 500$ and $SD = 100$ *based on a 1941 reference group of high school seniors who took the test.* This fixed reference group has enabled the charting of the much-publicized, significant decline of SAT scores that took place from the mid 1960s to the late 1970s, followed by the slowing decline, then leveling, and finally slight ascent that has since occurred.

Because the SAT is used as a basis for admissions decisions in some of the nation's most prestigious universities, the stakes are high for examinees. Many efforts have been made to provide assistance to future examinees in order to improve their scores. This assistance can take the form of sound, balanced *instruction designed to raise the examinee status on the attributes* sampled by the test. Of course, this laudable approach is not prone to yield dramatic short-term results.

On the other hand, assistance can take the form of *coaching designed to impact the scores without having comparable influence on the attribute being assessed.* In other words, coaching is designed to cause test scores to *mis*represent the domains from which they sample and therefore to overpredict examinee success in college. Like teaching to the test, coaching aims to *in*validate test use. Specific, test-focused instruction—coaching—tends to have greatest impact on scores of tests containing certain unusual item types and with examinees who are unfamiliar with objective testing practices. The former is minimized in tests such as the SAT by avoidance of item types that are particularly vulnerable to coaching. The latter is minimized by providing all examinees with preliminary descriptive and practice materials.

Many studies have been conducted on the impact of coaching. A summary conclusion is that intensive drill on items similar to those of the SAT is not likely to produce much greater gains than those associated with a year of regular high school instruction (Anastasi, 1988, p. 44).

The technical quality of the SAT is very high. The new forms developed each year are linked statistically to past forms in order to accommodate the indirect referencing to the 1941 norm group. Since the SAT is used to forecast success in college, predictive validation is of prime importance, and studies in many colleges are conducted each year. Freshman grade point average is the criterion typically used. Table 18–1 provides average validity findings from over two thousand studies for SAT composite alone, high school records alone, and the joint use of SAT scores and high school records.

The College Entrance Examination Board also publishes the Advanced Placement Program tests for students who take high school courses for college credit and/or advanced college placement. Since the courses taken for advanced placement differ in content and quality, the advanced placement tests provide a means of "authenticating" the courses.

The Preliminary Scholastic Aptitude Test (PSAT) is a shortened version of the SAT designed for use a year or more before the SAT. It provides a basis to predict how

Table 18–1

Average Correlations of Freshman GPA with SAT Scores Alone, With High School Records Alone, and With SAT and High School Records Combined*

Predictors	Average Correlation in All Colleges
SAT scores alone	.42
High school records alone	.48
SAT scores and high school records	.55

*From *The College Board Technical Handbook for the Scholastic Aptitude Test and Achievement Tests* by T. F. Donlon (Ed.), 1984, New York: College Entrance Examination Board. Copyright 1984 by the College Entrance Examination Board.

well students will do on the SAT and thus enhances educational planning. In addition, of course, it provides experience with the test format, procedures, and item types.

The PSAT also is used as the National Merit Scholarship Qualifying Test for identifying national merit semifinalists. As such, it is taken by students seeking a wide variety of college scholarships. Like the SAT, PSAT normative data are based on the relatively select college-bound students who typically take the test.

QUIZ 18–2

Use Table 18–1 to answer the following questions.

1. Why does the joint use of SAT scores and high-school records yield higher validity coefficients than the use of either alone?
2. Compared with the data reported in Table 18–1, would each predictor's validity in colleges that are highly selective tend to be higher, about the same, or lower?
3. Suppose you are a counselor in a typical high school. Some of your seniors have taken the SAT and you wonder how good its predictive validity will be for them in predicting their freshman GPAs in typical colleges. Will the validity most likely be lower than, equal to, or higher than that reported in Table 18–1?

> ### KEY TO QUIZ 18–2
>
> 1. A general rule of prediction is that several predictors, properly weighted, are collectively more valid than any one alone. They tend to tap different attributes and consequently can collectively provide more information than any one alone.
>
> 2. Lower. Selective colleges tend to reject applicants whose scores are relatively low. This selectivity results in reduced variability among those admitted. That is, there is less variability among students in selective institutions than among those in less selective ones. When less variability is present, neither predictive tests nor criterion grades can detect differences among people as reliably. Thus validity is reduced in restrictive samples.
>
> 3. Higher. Students in typical high schools have not yet been "homogenized" on the bases of selective college admissions practices or self-selection for college. They are thus more heterogeneous than the sample of college students for whom validity data are available. Consequently, predictive validity would be larger.

American College Testing Assessment Program

The *Enhanced American College Testing (ACT) Assessment* consists of tests in English, mathematics, reading, and science reasoning, a student profile section, and an interest inventory. This recently restructured version replaced the original ACT design used since 1959.

The ACT's purposes are similar to those of the SAT. Both tests assess cognitive attributes that are a bit right-of-center of the achievement-aptitude continuum pictured in Figure 18–1. Both are designed to assess present readiness for college work. Both are best used along with high school grades in predicting college achievement.

They occupy somewhat different niches; traditionally, colleges and universities using the ACT have been less selective, on average, in their admission practices than have those using the SAT. There is also a geographic correlate to their adoption; although both are used nationally, the SAT is most used by colleges in the Northeast, especially Ivy League ones, while the ACT is more popular in the Midwest.

In technical aspects, the ACT probably is a little inferior to the SAT (Anastasi, 1988, p. 331). To illustrate, the ACT is scored for number right, yet it has not been unusual for 25% or more of examinees to fail to complete the various subtests (Kifer, 1985). Thus test-wiseness in reserving a few seconds at the end of each subtest to wildly guess on remaining items would enhance examinee scores. (The problem of *wild* guessing is largely avoided in the SAT by use of a correction-for-guessing formula.)

ACT results are reported with standard scores based on self-identified, college-bound, high school seniors. The scores have a range of 1 to 36, with the means for the various scores being at or near 18. Statistical linkage from year to year enables the plotting of performance trends. ACT scores, like SAT scores, declined during the 1970s. The statistical linkage of the various new forms developed each year also allow for a score adjustment among the several annual administrations so that students tested earlier in the school year will not be at a disadvantage compared with those tested later (Aiken, 1985).

Much like the SAT is accompanied by the PSAT, the Enhanced ACT is accompanied by the P-ACT. This new test is designed to help tenth-graders in planning their post-secondary education.

Chapter Summary

Aptitude tests differ from achievement tests more in degree than in kind. In contrast to achievement tests, *aptitude tests are designed mainly for predictive uses*, have scores that are less sensitive to short-term instruction, and are usually broader in scope.

Aptitude tests differ in the kinds of scores they yield. Some provide only a global score, others are designed to profile several different kinds of aptitude, and still others serve both purposes. Aptitude tests also differ in their aims. Some serve only narrow purposes (e.g., dental school admissions). Others are used to make many different kinds of academic predictions. And some, in addition to being used to help make a variety of kinds of scholastic predictions, are intended for use in the measurement of psychological aptitude or intelligence constructs. Scores of most aptitude tests are interpreted with respect to age-based reference groups.

Intelligence tests and the IQ scores that have traditionally accompanied them have been misunderstood by large segments of the lay public to represent (a) a much wider spectrum of valued attributes than tests really measure, (b) inborn capacity, and (c) something that is relatively unchangeable. Users of such tests need to take pains to ensure that people who receive the scores understand the falsity of each of these ideas. This communication is best achieved by avoiding the term "intelligence," replacing it with more accurate descriptive terms such as "scholastic aptitude," "academic aptitude," and "cognitive abilities." Similarly "IQs" are derived scores that are best avoided; percentile ranks serve much better for interpretation without misconceptions.

Suggestions for Further Reading

Anastasi, A. (1958). Heredity, environment, and the question of "how?" *Psychological Review, 65,* 197–208. This classic article brilliantly reveals how heredity and environment interact to produce development. It shows that the productive question is not "How much do heredity and environment each contribute to development?" but "How do heredity and environment interact to cause development?"

Cronbach, L. J. (1990). *Essentials of psychological testing* (5th ed.). New York: Harper Collins Publishers. Chapters 7–10 give a richly integrated treatment of the construct of general ability, the methods by which it is appraised, kinds of intellectual abilities, and the interpretation and fostering of individual development.

Mehrens, W. A., & Lehmann, I. J. (1991). *Measurement and evaluation in education and psychology* (4th ed.). Fort Worth: Holt, Rinehart and Winston. Chapter 15, "Standardized Aptitude Measures," provides a balanced and thorough coverage of the constructs of intelligence and of the devices used to measure them.

Salvia, J., & Ysseldyke, J. E. (1988). *Assessment in special and remedial education* (4th ed.). Boston: Houghton Mifflin. Chapters 9, 10, and 11 concern assessment of "intelligence" and provide descriptions of major group and individual aptitude tests.

19

Interest, Self-Concept, and Adaptive Behavior Scales

The achievement and aptitude tests discussed in the last two chapters are similar in being cognitive tests of maximum performance that tap a wide range of thinking activities. Other parts of this book have discussed psychomotor tests of maximum performance that assess how well pupils can perform various acts such as holding a pencil, playing a musical instrument, keyboarding, or dancing. In contrast to these measures of maximum performance, most of the instruments considered in this chapter are affective measures of typical performance. In addition, published adaptive behavior scales will be examined briefly. Such scales achieve indirect measurement of certain important self-help motor activities, such as zipper use and teeth brushing, and mixed cognitive, psychomotor, and affective activities such as street crossing.

The affective domain encompasses values, feelings, attitudes, interests, preferences, motivation, self-control, temperament, and other noncognitive personality attributes. In general, the development and use of affective scales are afflicted with difficulties over and above those common to educational and psychological testing (Anastasi, 1988, p. 560); these problems render affective measures relatively less refined. Part of this assessment difficulty results from the use of direct observation of various affect-prompted behaviors; as seen in Chapter 8, observation tends to be both expensive in time demands and relatively low in reliability. Some of the assessment troubles also stem from lack of clarity concerning the meaning of some abstract affective constructs. And much of the difficulty associated with measuring affect arises from the fact that *many affective measures are fakable.* They are fakable because affective measures tap *typical behaviors*, not maximum behaviors.

A test of maximum cognitive or motor activity is administered with examinees' knowledge that they are being tested under rules and expectations that make it proper and adaptive for them to do their best. For example, students running a race or taking a reading test are supposed to perform at their maximum capability. A measure of typical affective behavior, in contrast, is designed in one way or another to avoid examinees' "best" efforts and get their *typical* state of mind, reactions, or feeling (Lyman, 1991).

As seen in Chapter 8, this can be achieved by observing people when they do not know they are being evaluated. This approach is often used to assess students for reporting or grading purposes. For example, a primary teacher may make systematic surreptitious observations of pupils' interpersonal relations, posture, etc., in order to identify problems for correction and/or to record and report status. Along these lines, standardized, published rating forms can elicit ratings of past, nonsystematically observed behaviors. For example, parents or teachers can rate a child's typical performance in activities such as dressing, getting to the seat on time, or voluntarily taking turns. This approach is used by one of the instruments described below.

Alternatively, measurement of typical performance can be secured by eliciting honest, undistorted self-reports. This approach can be helpful in circumstances where examinees lack motive to fake, as in counseling or other situations in which grades are not at stake. This technique is widely used to assess occupational interests, attitudes, temperament, self-concept, etc. It is used in most of the published instruments discussed in this chapter.

This chapter will introduce a few of the myriad of published affective instruments. First, occupational interest inventories will be addressed. Then measures of self-concept will be considered. Finally, the assessment of adaptive behaviors will be briefly taken up.

Interest Inventories

The selection and preparation for a career is a major developmental task facing adolescents. Educational and psychological measurement can contribute several things to the related tasks of choosing an occupation and planning the educational preparation for it. Of course, achievement testing provides useful objective data concerning a person's command of occupationally significant subject matter and skills. And aptitude testing facilitates prediction of how well a person would be able to perform in educational preparation for a given occupation. These are vital components of informed occupational planning.

However, they are not enough. One may have the aptitude to learn a job and acquire the necessary knowledge and skills to do it, yet be miserable in the work. For example, a person may not like the content of the work; e.g., someone capable of becoming proficient in math may not like it. Or an individual may dislike the mix of people, data, and things with which jobs are concerned; for example, a person with good math aptitude and achievement may also like math, yet not want to become a math teacher because of not enjoying constant work with people. Or one may dislike the kind of co-workers found in a field. Other dimensions on which people differ is the relative value they place on variety versus consistency in work, on supervision versus independence, on job security, and on income. Interest surveys get at some of these dimensions of affect that are so important in choosing a congenial career.

One of the difficulties in measuring occupational interests is the fact that examinees often have no prior experience with the occupation being considered; hence they have little way to know whether they would like it. For example, how would eleventh-grade Sue know how well she might enjoy the field of plant pathology when she has had only one introductory biology course? Or how would she know her preference for the kinds of work typically performed by attorneys when her only exposure to the field is the glamorized image depicted in the media? Hence it does not suffice to ask direct questions such as "Do you enjoy studying plant diseases?" or "Do you like legal work?" and to interpret the answers at face value. Vocational interest inventories have to pursue less direct means of assessing preferences.

Interest inventories help people organize what they already know about themselves. They typically provide norm-referenced interpretation for responses to objective standardized items. Many of these items concern common activities that secondary students understand from their personal experience. Such self-report surveys can provide information useful to stimulate thinking about careers and about educational planning. The variety of scoring scales draw attention to many vocations the youth might not otherwise consider (Cronbach, 1990, p. 463).

In receiving and understanding the results of interest inventories, students need to understand what was measured—their self-reports of interests, preferences, and so forth. It is common for them to "jump track" and think of the inventory as an assessment of maximum performance like those of an achievement test. For example, the student who asks "How did I do?" has likely forgotten that the interest inventory is designed to assess interest, not achievement or aptitude. It is important to clarify that there are no good or bad areas of vocational interest, no right or wrong answers.

Students and their parents often think that interest scores tell what they can do best. Not true. Interest scores tell nothing about achievement or aptitude; the correlations between interest scores and corresponding abilities are close to zero. Nor are they good predictors of success in academic work or in vocational training. Rather than telling what a person *can* do, interest scores indicate what people would *enjoy* doing if they survive the training (Cronbach, 1990, pp. 478–480). Sight must never be lost of the fact that *interest inventories measure typical performance.*

In pursuit of this understanding that typical performance is being assessed, it is usually a good idea to avoid the word "test." To many people, "test" implies measure of maximum performance. Words like "inventory," "scale," or "survey" help to set the stage for student thinking along lines other than test of maximum performance.

The goal of a study of careers is enhanced self-knowledge, not a firm career decision. It often takes years to mold a career with many successive decisions being made along the way. Youths should be encouraged to engage in broad-spectrum exploration that identifies promising options. "Concentration comes gradually, first as choice of a broad area, then of a vocational line, and ultimately of a specialized or personalized role" (Cronbach, 1984, p. 412).

Before specific instruments are examined, a discussion is in order of a measurement technique often used in affective assessment. In this **forced-choice** item type, examinees are required to choose from two or more options the one they most prefer, the one most descriptive of them, or the one they like best.

Some forced-choice measures require choices between opposites. The assumption that certain pairs of traits are polar opposites has come under increasing criticism. For example, we no longer define masculinity and femininity as polar opposites; they are now regarded as independent variables (Anastasi, 1988, p. 592). Other attributes that many scholars no longer consider to be polar opposites include liberalism and conservatism, introversion and extroversion, and heterosexuality and homosexuality.

Many older personality measures are based on conceptions of each of such pairs as representing opposite ends of the *same continuum* and use forced-choice items to assess people's status on each resulting bipolar scale. Before using such an instrument, users should carefully consider whether each pair of "opposite" labels are indeed opposite. That is, would *independent measures* of the pair of opposites really yield scores that were correlated as near -1.00 as their reliabilities would allow (as, for example, would be the case for tall-short or young-old).

Yet forced-choice items have a place. Consider the meal planner for a school cafeteria. He or she might survey the students on which they liked most and least of yellow or red fruits and vegetables, including carrots, corn, squash, and tomatoes. Such a forced-choice survey would not reveal which students love them all and which hate them all. This, however, is not a problem if the dietitian has decided to use some yellow or red vegetables or fruits because of their nutritional properties regardless of students' absolute preference. If a student has to eat one of them, then a forced-choice determination of which is liked best (or disliked least) makes good sense.

Similarly, in interest assessment, most of us have to earn a living. The person who may loathe all kinds of gainful employment still has a need to find a job, preferably one that is less loathsome than other options. Likewise, the fortunate individual who finds many fields interesting still has a need to select one occupation from among those that are most fascinating.

This section provides very brief descriptions of three interest inventories, one of which is based on the forced-choice technique. They are intended to provide a sense of some of the methods used to measure vocational interests, but not a detailed knowledge of these scales or a consideration of their reliability or validity.

Kuder General Interest Survey

A group of inventories developed by G. Fredrick Kuder has been widely used in secondary schools for several decades. The *Kuder General Interest Survey* (1987), intended for Grades 6 to 12, will be considered here.

Rather than focusing on the myriad of specific occupations a person could consider, scores are provided for 10 broad categories of jobs: outdoor, mechanical, computational, scientific, persuasive, artistic, literary, musical, social service, and clerical. Students are then encouraged to focus on the occupations in the one to three groups in which their scores suggest the highest interest, giving particular consideration to jobs that relate to more than one of their high areas. Percentile ranks for the 10 scales are referenced to four reference groups—boys in Grades 6 to 8, girls in Grades 6 to 8, boys in Grades 9 to 12, and girls in Grades 9 to 12.

The Kuder is typical of interest inventories in providing gender-specific reference group data because the sexes differ considerably in their affect toward some fields. There are times, however, when one might be more interested in comparing a student's scores with people of the gender that dominates a given occupation rather than with her or his own. For example, a female considering auto mechanics might want to compare her mechanical interest scores not only with females, but with males as well. The Kuder, like most interest surveys, makes provision for both same-gender and cross-gender profiling of scores.

The *Kuder General Interest Survey* employs a forced-choice technique by means of groups of three activities from which the examinee is to indicate the most preferred and the least preferred. Figure 19–1 provides two sample triads of Kuder items.

Like most affective surveys, the *General Interest Survey* is administered without a time limit. Most people complete it in less than an hour.

Many affective measures have special keys to identify people who answer carelessly, do not comprehend the questions, answer items in inconsistent ways, or try to represent themselves in an unrealistically favorable light. Along these lines, the *General Interest Survey* provides a scale to indicate whether the responses were marked carefully and sincerely.

As mentioned above, interest measures—and affective measures of typical performance in general—tend to be somewhat fakable. This is generally not a problem

---

The instructions direct students to indicate which of the three things in each set they like *most* and which they like *least.*

Visit an art gallery	Collect signatures of famous people
Browse in a library	Collect coins
Visit a museum	Collect butterflies

Figure 19–1. Sample Items from *Kuder General Interest Survey.* Copyright © G. F. Kuder, 1987. Reprinted by permission of CTB Macmillan/McGraw-Hill, 2500 Garden Road, Monterey, CA 93940-5380.

in situations where examinees are seeking career guidance because in that context they correctly perceive their self-interest to be served by truthfulness. However, if the same instruments are used for employment purposes, the fakability becomes a problem. Suppose, for example, that Annica is applying for a job as a sales representative for a life insurance company and she is taking an inventory as part of the application process. She is asked which activity she would most prefer, planning a pancake feed, selling tickets for a pancake feed, or cooking pancakes for a pancake feed. It does not require a great deal of psychological sophistication to deduce that the second option is the one to choose if she wants a job selling life insurance.

Recall from Chapter 14 that validity is situationally specific. This principle applies with special force for self-report affective measures. In general, the validity of self-report affective measures depends on the context. The above triad might be quite invalid where self-interest is served by faking. Yet "it is generally safe to assume that normal people are truthful unless they perceive it in their best interest to be otherwise" (Hopkins, Stanley, & Hopkins, 1990, p. 439). Hence the same triad would likely be valid in an interest inventory if the scores were to be used for vocational counseling.

Career Interest Inventory

One of the newest interest scales on the market is the *Career Interest Inventory* (The Psychological Corporation, 1990b). Level 1 is for Grades 7 to 9 and Level 2 is for Grades 10 to 12. Students are asked to indicate preference, or lack of preference, for items consisting of job activity statements, school activity statements, and school subject statements. Figure 19–2 shows several sample activity items from the scale.

The *Career Interest Inventory* was designed for use in conjunction with the *Differential Aptitude Tests.* The two instruments have derived scores referenced to the *same norm group.* This provides the major advantage of comparability of the reference groups when aptitudes and interests are juxtaposed—as they usually are in career counseling.

The scores of the *Career Interest Inventory* are used to help students select courses, identify careers to investigate, and make educational plans. Figure 19–3 shows a computerized prose and graphic report of a student's interest scores interpreted against the backdrop of his DAT scores and self-reported educational plans.

The instructions ask students to select from five levels of responses ranging from *like very much* to *dislike a great deal.*

Join a computer club
Write reports on how people behave
Take a course in creative writing
Organize books in a library
Operate an X-ray machine
Help families choose homes to buy

Figure 19–2. Sample Items from *Career Interest Inventory,* Levels 1 and 2. Copyright © 1990 by The Psychological Corporation. Reproduced by permission. All rights reserved.

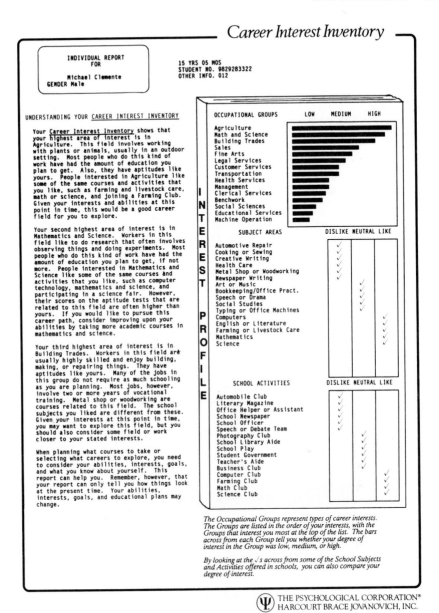

Figure 19–3. Individual Report for the *Career Interest Inventory.* Copyright © 1990 by The Psychological Corporation. Reproduced by permission. All rights reserved.

The Self-Directed Search

The Self-Directed Search (Holland, 1985) is a vocational counseling instrument for high school and college students. It is simple to use; students simply rate themselves on their (a) preference for various activities (b) knowledge of how to do or desire to learn how to do various things, (c) interest in various jobs, and (d) abilities.

Simple scoring procedures enable the student to add the results of these four parts to obtain total scores for six scales—realistic, investigative, artistic, social, enterprising, and conventional. These scales are the cornerstones of Holland's model of occupational themes. This hexagonal model not only provides the foundation for the *Self-Directed Search*, but for several other inventories as well.

Each of the six occupational themes corresponds to a cluster of personal attributes. The themes also correspond to features of occupations in terms of which different occupational environments can be categorized. The purpose of *The Self-Directed Search* is to help young people identify jobs to consider that are relatively congruent with their personalities on the assumption that this congruence enhances work satisfaction, job stability, and achievement (Anastasi, 1988, p. 578).

The examinee is instructed to consider her or his highest scores and to enter the *Occupations Finder* to find the titles of many occupations that involve these kinds of preferences. Use of the *Occupations Finder* is intended to encourage consideration of whole categories of occupations rather than premature focus on only one or two occupations (Dolliver, 1985, p. 1347).

The Self-Directed Search is unusual in its being self-administered, self-scored, and self-interpreted—or at least it is for many students. However, others require supervision and assistance in its scoring and interpreting. And many of those who use it successfully will have follow-up needs to take up with a counselor. However, the latter is by no means a fault of the instrument; the search for a congenial occupation may be assisted by several successive guides, and the instrument is only one.

Considerable research attests to the effectiveness of the approach, and the *Self-Directed Search* "has become the prototype of a self-administered, self-reported, self-scoring, and self-interpretive vocational measure" (Dolliver, 1985, p. 1347).

QUIZ 19–1

1. Which instrument, the *Kuder General Interest Survey* or the *Career Interest Inventory,* could show a student's interests to be uniformly low?

   A. *Kuder General Interest Survey.*

   B. *Career Interest Inventory.*

2. Which of the following scales could show a student's interests to be uniformly high?

   A. *Kuder General Interest Survey.*

   B. *Career Interest Inventory.*

3. Which of the two scales below is more likely to be mistaken for an achievement test at the time of interpretation by students or parents?

   A. *Kuder General Interest Survey.*

   B. *Career Interest Inventory.*

KEY TO QUIZ 19–1

1 and 2. The Kuder is based on forced-choice items; thus from each triad one must indicate which activity is least preferred and which is most preferred. Therefore all students' answer sheets will have the same number of most- and least-preferred items. It is not possible on forced-choice scales to indicate low interest in all activities. Nor is it possible to report high interest in all activities.

The *Career Interest Inventory*, in contrast, consists of *independent* items. A person could indicate preference for most or all of the activities or dislike for most or all. Hence on this instrument, one could have a uniformly low or high set of scores.

3. Students and their parents are prone to slip into the familiar rut of thinking of paper-pencil scales as tests of maximum performance. Continuous care is needed to prevent this and to maintain the posture that there are no good or bad scores on an interest inventory. There does not appear to be any reason to expect one instrument to be more vulnerable to this problem than the other.

Measures of Self-Concept

Prior to the 1960s, many schools routinely screened for personal adjustment or self-concept in an effort to identify students in need of special attention. Then an interesting convergence of attitudes from conservative and liberal groups raised a number of concerns about invasion of student and family privacy and intrusiveness in general (Cronbach, 1990, p. 522). The political climate now leads most schools to either avoid measures of personal adjustment and self-concept or to use them sparingly, usually after securing written consent from parents or guardians.

Measures of self-concept tend to be more intrusive and more threatening than interest inventories. They are more socially and politically sensitive. They tend also to be more vulnerable to distortion. Some possible responses to items are clearly more socially desirable than others, and there is, in this culture, a natural tendency for persons to tilt their responses in socially desirable directions. This not only includes intentional falsification, but also the general adaptive tendencies to present the self in a favorable light. Thus, as mentioned before, personality measures in general are afflicted with more serious technical measurement problems than are achievement tests, aptitude tests, or even interest inventories.

Piers-Harris Children's Self-Concept Scale

The *Piers-Harris Children's Self-Concept Scale (The Way I Feel About Myself)* (Piers & Harris, 1969–1984) is a self-report measure designed to help assess the self-concept of students in Grades 4-12. Based on 80 yes-no self-referent statements, the scale is intended to reveal students' conscious self-perceptions concerning both descriptions and evaluation of their behaviors and attributes. High scores suggest positive self-evaluations, while low scores indicate negative self-concepts. Compared with other affective measures (aside from interest inventories), the Piers-Harris is widely used and is regarded by many (e.g., Jeske, 1985) to be the best children's self-concept measure available.

The Piers-Harris is recommended for three purposes. It can be used for routine screening in high-risk settings. It can serve as one component of a thorough individual assessment in a clinical or counseling setting. And it can be used in research; it is a common criterion measure used to assess the impact of experimental interventions on self-concept.

A praiseworthy feature of the manual is its stress that *"the Piers-Harris should never be used as the sole method for assessing self-concept where this is being used to influence important decisions about a child.* The scale is designed to supplement skilled clinical judgments, not replace them" (Piers, 1984, p. 2). Of course, no single instrument should ever be used as the sole basis for a major decision. This principle applies with special force in the affective domain where measurement is relatively primitive.

The reference group used for providing norm-referenced interpretations leaves a great deal to be desired. It consisted of children from one Pennsylvania town assessed in the 1960s. Fortunately, this grave limitation does not detract from the scale's use for research studies in which the mean raw scores of experimental and control groups are compared or in which before-after comparisons are made.

Reliability is relatively high, as affective instruments go. Internal consistency coefficients of total scores hover around .9, but test-retest correlations average in the low .70s. It is clear that the caveat concerning the use of the Piers-Harris is well advised for an instrument having scores with such limited stability.

In addition to the total score, six subscores are available. However, their very modest reliability renders their use questionable for purposes other than research.

The computerized scoring service for the Piers-Harris, like that of many affective instruments, provides cautionary scales to alert interpreters of possible problems. In the Piers-Harris, attention is directed to the possibility of "faking good" (i.e., distorting one's answers in a socially desirable direction), "faking bad," acquiescence (i.e., the tendency to say "yes" to almost any item), negative response bias (i.e., the tendency to say "no" to most stimuli), and random responding.

Scales designed to reveal random responding or failure to understand an instrument's items are often based on comparisons of examinee responses to similar items. For example, it is inconsistent to respond "no" both to Piers-Harris Item 5 ("I am smart.") and to Item 53 ("I am dumb about most things."). Answer sheets containing several such inconsistencies should be questioned.

The Adjective Checklist

An adjective checklist is simply a list of adjectives for which respondents are asked to check those that apply. They can be applied to almost anything (e.g., brands of soap, one's students, political parties, religious groups, one's ideal self, or one's real self). In completing a checklist, the respondent simply marks the adjectives that apply to the person or thing being rated. Personality checklists, of course, apply to people, and can be administered as self-report or as observer-report instruments. Such devices are relatively easy to construct, consume little administration time, and are sometimes just as valid as other kinds of personality inventories (Aiken, 1991, pp. 352–353).

The best-known instrument of this type is *The Adjective Checklist* (Gough & Heilbrun, 1980), which is suitable for high school and college ages. Respondents are directed to mark those of the 300 adjectives that they consider to be self-descriptive. The device yields derived scores for 37 scales covering a wide range of attributes (e.g., Dominance, Aggression, and Self-Confidence). Some of these scales are designed to check for various sources of invalidity such as random responding.

One of these scales—Achievement—will serve to illustrate more closely the nature of the instrument. Achievement is defined as striving to be outstanding in pursuit of socially recognized significance. This scale is made up of some adjectives for which checking increases one's score on this scale (e.g., assertive, self-confident, and energetic) and some for which checking reduces one's Achievement score (e.g., awkward, considerate, and modest) (Gough & Heilbrun, 1980, p. 8).

The Adjective Checklist reference group consisted of several thousand respondents who were selected by rather arbitrary, nonrandom means. The group appears to poorly represent the national population of high school and college-aged people. This unfortunate condition is not unusual with affective instruments designed for adults.

Internal consistency averages about .75 for the scales. Test-retest correlations over a six-month interval averaged .65. On the one hand, these figures seem very modest. They should prompt great caution in interpreting scores for *individual students*. Both content sampling error and occasion sampling error are considerably higher than one would desire.

On the other hand, the cost effectiveness of the ACL is astonishing in that it yields 37 scores in under half an hour of administration time. This is a very attractive feature of the instrument for *research purposes* (where time is often short) and helps to explain its popularity in studies that focus on group changes or group differences. It has been used in several hundred studies. The reliability of group means is, of course, much higher than the reliability of individual scores.

The primary strength of *The Adjective Checklist* has always been as a research instrument concerning psychological theory. As such, researchers and theoreticians are likely to find the device more interesting than are practicing school psychologists or counselors (Zarske, 1985, p. 52). This would be true of many affective instruments. *The Adjective Checklist* is as far afield from school measurement as will be explored in this book.

QUIZ 19–2

1. It was stated that the reliability of group means is much higher than the reliability of individual scores. Why is this true?
2. How did this principle apply to the use of anchor tests in Chapter 12?
3. How did it apply to the use of stratification variables in Chapter 13?

KEY TO QUIZ 19–2

1. Simply because more data are summarized in group means than in scores for individual students. To illustrate, suppose an eight-item survey quiz has been given to a 25-pupil class. Each pupil's scores should be treated with great caution; it will be relatively unreliable because it is based on only eight bits of information. The class mean, however, is based on 25 times 8 bits of information—200 in all. It will be approximately as reliable as a 200-item test would be for an individual pupil.

2. One practical application involves the (formal or informal) statistical linking used with anchor tests to achieve norm-referenced grading without permitting the evils of class-curve grading. A mean score or standard deviation for the class—even if it is based on a short, not-too-reliable quiz or assignment—provides a reasonable way to compare the class performance with that of a larger and/or external reference group of other students.

3. Another practical application of the greater reliability of group data than of individual data concerns the use of stratification variables in selecting a norming sample for cognitive tests. Recall that socioeconomic status is a very important variable for ensuring representativeness of the sample in comparison to the population. Yet the correlation of SES and cognitive test scores would not be great for individuals, perhaps .4 or less. Yet for school or district means, the correlation would be very great. To illustrate, suppose a town has five elementary schools. Within each of these schools the correlation between SES estimate and achievement estimate for individual pupils would be only modest. Yet the *mean* SES for the schools would probably correlate almost perfectly with their *mean* achievement. For example, tell me which school has the highest (or lowest) average SES, and I can probably tell you which one has the highest (or lowest) achievement.

Measures of Adaptive Behavior

Another important realm of behavior concerns children's self-help skills, how well they look after their own practical needs, and how dependable they are in taking responsibility for themselves in their daily routines. These domains encompass both maximum behavior skills (e.g., knowing how to lock the house door, take turns on the swing, or feed the pet) and typical behaviors (e.g., remembering to lock the house, being willing to take turns, or remembering to feed the pet).

Measures of adaptive behavior contribute to the comprehensive picture of a child's functioning. Many such socialization behaviors are part of the school curriculum and are important to successful living. The systematic assessment of adaptive behaviors would help to balance schools' natural but undesirable overemphasis on cognitive achievement. Inadequacies in some everyday living behaviors (e.g., remembering one's keys and interpersonal relations) cause most people far more trouble in life than inadequacies in academic skills (e.g., spelling or computation). Schools would better serve their clients if they spent more energies in assessing and enhancing important adaptive behaviors and less in assessing the easier-to-measure, low-level cognitive outcomes of schooling.

Yet the major uses of published adaptive behavior scales focus on persons who are thought to have various handicaps. The assessment of children with intellectual, emotional, or physical handicaps has become both more common and more comprehensive as a result of the 1977 enactment of the Education for All Handicapped Children Act (Public Law 94-142), which fostered more comprehensive assessment. Decisions regarding admission to special treatment and training programs for the mentally retarded must, of course, take into account the individual's intellectual function. In addition, sound classifications must be based on a consideration of the person's adaptive behavior, emotional adjustment, and physical conditions (Anastasi, 1988, pp. 284–286). Adaptive behavior assessment is an essential part of a comprehensive evaluation of a person suspected of mental retardation because measures of social competence help to determine the extent to which a handicap affects everyday coping.

Vineland Adaptive Behavior Scales

The *Vineland Adaptive Behaviors Scales* (Sparrow, Balla, & Cicchetti, 1984) is a revision and major improvement of the *Vineland Social Maturity Scale*, first published in 1935. It assesses the social competence of handicapped and nonhandicapped persons from birth to age 19 as well as that of low-functioning adults.

Two of the three instruments in the current Vineland series, the Survey Form and the Expanded Form, use the measurement technique developed for the original Vineland. Ratings are secured by means of semi-structured interviews in which a professional interviewer questions a child's parent or other caregiver concerning the child's regular performance of various activities. Figure 19–4 provides several illustrative items. Scoring of individual items generally follows the rule of awarding 2 points if the activity is habitually performed, 1 point if it is performed sometimes or with partial success, and 0 if it is never performed.

The economy of this interview-of-caregiver approach to measurement is impressive, and it is common to several competing instruments. The scales tap typical performance by means of interviewing persons who have had ample opportunity to observe the behaviors in question when the child did not know she or he was being assessed and had no motive to behave atypically. An interview of only 20 to 60 minutes for the Survey Form or 60 to 90 minutes for the Expanded Form produces a breadth of information that would require much more time in direct observation. Moreover, this "third party" method of administration allows assessment of persons who cannot or will not perform on command during direct administration, such as infants, severely retarded persons, or emotionally disturbed individuals (Sparrow, Balla, & Cicchetti, 1984, p. 7).

A Spanish-language version of the Survey Form is also available. This provides a means of utilizing Spanish-speaking parents as sources of information concerning their children's adaptive behaviors. When a child whose native language is not Standard American English is being evaluated for possible mental retardation, it is, of

Communication Domain Items
> Listens to a story for at least five minutes
> States telephone number when asked
> Addresses envelopes completely

Daily Living Skills Domain Items
> Feeds self with fork
> Makes own bed when asked
> Looks both ways and crosses street or road alone

Socialization Domain
> Laughs or smiles appropriately in response to positive statements
> Shows a preference for some friends over others
> Apologizes for unintentional mistakes

Motor Skills Domain
> Walks as primary means of getting around
> Screws and unscrews lid of jar
> Uses eraser without tearing paper

Figure 19–4.   Sample Items from the *Vineland Adaptive Behavior Scales* by Sara Sparrow, David Balla, Domenic Cicchetti, © 1984, 1985 American Guidance Service, Inc., Circle Pines, MN 55014-1796. All rights reserved.

course, especially important to consider adaptive behavior. This helps to make a distinction between clinical retardation and mere deficit in the language of the school.

The third Vineland instrument is the Classroom Edition, which consists of a paper-pencil questionnaire that the teacher can complete. Appropriate for ages 3 through 12, this instrument requires about 20 minutes to complete. It provides a means of securing information about adaptive behavior in the classroom without going to the considerable expense of sending someone to the classroom to observe the child.

Each of the three instruments assesses four domains of adaptive behavior: Communication, Daily Living Skills, Socialization, and Motor Skills. The sample items displayed in Figure 19–4 are grouped by domain. The interview forms also provide a maladaptive behavior score to assess undesirable behaviors that can interfere with a person's adaptive functioning. An adaptive behavior composite is provided with each of the instruments. In addition to domain scores, various subdomain scores are provided with the longer versions of the Vineland.

Chapter Summary

Interest inventories comprise the majority of published affective instruments used in schools. These self-report instruments provide a useful way to prompt secondary students to confront their future. Fortunately, the measurement of vocational interests is less intrusive than the assessment of other aspects of personality.

Interest scores from self-report instruments provide a very useful source of information to be considered along with other information about interest (e.g., professed interest, hobbies, reactions to work experience, and interest reported by others). Student interests also need to be considered along with information concerning their achievement and aptitudes in order to facilitate wise educational planning and career decision making.

Self-concept measures are less commonly used in schools, but are widely used in research. A variety of techniques have been developed for assessing self-concept. Two were briefly sketched, one involving yes-no responses to self-referent statements and one involving indicating which adjectives on a list are self-descriptive. Instruments can be administered individually or in groups and may yield from one to many scores. In general, their reliability does not compare favorably with that of cognitive instruments, and the sampling procedures used for selecting the reference groups used for their interpretation are often deplorable.

While interests and self-concept measures focus on typical behaviors, adaptive behavior scales tap both maximal behaviors (e.g., can cross streets safely) and typical behaviors (e.g., ordinarily does cross safely). Standardized, norm-referenced assessment of everyday adaptive behavior in the home, classroom, and playground is often achieved by interviewing a parent or other caregiver. Informal evaluation of adaptive behaviors may merit more evaluation time than it typically receives in schools.

Suggestions for Further Reading

Aiken, L. R. (1991). *Psychological testing and assessment* (7th ed.). Boston: Allyn and Bacon. Chapters 9–11 of this introductory test in psychological measurement provide a broader elementary treatment of methods and instruments used in affective assessment than space in this chapter permitted.

Anastasi, A. (1988). *Psychological testing* (6th ed.). New York: Collier Macmillan. Chapters 17–20 of this more sophisticated text provide a rich description and analysis of the efficacy of a wide variety of techniques used to assessing interests, values, attitudes, opinions, situational behaviors, and other personality attributes.

Cronbach, L. J. (1990). *Essentials of psychological testing* (5th ed.). New York: Harper Collins Publisher. Chapters 12–16 offer a broad-scope consideration of a variety of means of measuring several kinds of typical performance. Chapter 12, "Interest Inventories," is highly recommended for persons who will be using interest inventories in career study units or in counseling.

Hopkins, K. D., Stanley, J. C., & Hopkins B. R. (1990). *Educational and psychological measurement and evaluation* (7th ed.). Englewood Cliffs, NJ: Prentice-Hall. Chapter 15, "Standard Interest, Personality, and Social Measures," provides a solid, broad survey of instruments and topics.

Mehrens, W. A., & Lehmann, I. J. (1991). *Measurement and evaluation in education and psychology* (4th ed.). Fort Worth: Holt, Rinehart and Winston. Chapter 17, "Interest, Personality, and Attitude Inventories," contains a particularly good analysis of problems and descriptions of instruments used to assess interests.

Major Test Publishers and Selected Instruments

Following is a list of the largest publishers of educational and psychological tests in the United States. Following each publisher's name is listed a selection of its better known titles.

Most major test publishers provide free catalogs of their instruments upon request. Several major publishers also distribute instruments published by others and list them in their catalogs.

American College Testing Program. Box 168, Iowa City, IA 52243.
 (319) 337-1000
 Enhanced ACT Assessment

American Guidance Service. Publishers' Building, Circle Pines, MN 55014.
 (800) 328-2560
 Bruininks-Oseretsky Test of Motor Proficiency
 Kaufman Assessment Battery for Children (K–ABC)
 Kaufman Test of Educational Achievement (K–TEA)
 KeyMath–Revised
 Peabody Individual Achievement Test–Revised (PIAT–R)
 Peabody Picture Vocabulary Test–Revised (PPVT–R)
 Vineland Adaptive Behavior Scales

Consulting Psychologists Press, Inc. 577 College Ave., Palo Alto, CA 94306.
 (800) 624-1765
 Adjective Checklist
 Embedded Figures Test

CTB/McGraw-Hill. Del Monte Research Park, Monterey, CA 93940.
 (800) 538-9547
 California Achievement Tests
 Career Maturity Inventory
 Comprehensive Tests of Basic Skills
 Kuder General Interest Survey
 Kuder Occupational Interest Survey
 SRA Achievement Series
 Survey of Basic Skills

Educational Testing Service. Princeton, NJ 08541.
 (609) 921-9000
 College Board Scholastic Aptitude Test (SAT)
 Graduate Record Examinations (GRE)
 School and College Ability Tests–Series III (SCAT–III)
 Sequential Tests of Educational Progress, Series III (STEP–III)

The Psychological Corporation. 555 Academic Court, San Antonio, TX 78204.

(800) 228-0752
Career Interest Inventory (CII)
Differential Aptitude Tests (DAT)
Metropolitan Achievement Tests (MAT)
Ohio Vocational Interest Survey, Second Edition (OVIS–II)
Orleans-Hanna Algebra Prognosis Test
Otis-Lennon School Ability Test (OLSAT)
Self-Directed Search
Stanford Achievement Test
Stanford Diagnostic Mathematics Test
Stanford Diagnostic Reading Test
System of Multicultural Pluralistic Assessment (SOMPA)
Watson-Glaser Critical Thinking Appraisal
Wechsler Adult Intelligence Scale–Revised (WAIS–R)
Wechsler Intelligence Scale for Children–III (WISC–III)
Wechsler Preschool and Primary Scale of Intelligence–Revised (WPPSI–R)

The Riverside Publishing Co. 8420 Bryn Mawr Ave., Chicago, IL 60631.

(800) 323-9540
Cognitive Abilities Test
Gates-MacGinitie Reading Test
Iowa Tests of Basic Skills (ITBS)
Iowa Tests of Educational Development (ITED)
Nelson-Denny Reading Test
Tests of Achievement and Proficiency (TAP)
Stanford-Binet Intelligence Scale: Fourth Edition
Study of Values

Western Psychological Services, 12031 Wilshire Blvd., Los Angeles, CA 90025

(800) 648-8857
Auditory Discrimination Tests
Piers-Harris Children's Self-Concept Scale
Tennessee Self-Concept Scale

Locating Information About Published Instruments

The table below lists selected major sources of information about published educational measures.* Sources are largely limited to those relevant to professional practitioners. For each source listed, a rating is given if it is deemed to be fair or better in providing (a) information about the availability of instruments, (b) critical reviews of measures, or (c) research about particular instruments.

	Availability of Tests	Critical Reviews	Research about Particular Tests
Compilations of Reviews			
Bibliographic Retrieval Services		Good	
Mental Measurements Yearbooks	Fair	Very Good	Good
Test Critiques	Fair	Good	
Miscellaneous			
Test Manuals			Very Good
Publishers Test Catalogs	Very Good		
Journals			
Educational and Psychological Measurement			Very Good
Journal of Counseling and Development		Good	Fair
Journal of Reading		Good	
Measurement and Evaluation in Counseling and Development		Good	Good
The Reading Teacher		Good	

---

*This appendix is patterned after a course handout once used by K. D. Hopkins

Reference Sources

Current Index to Journals in Education		Fair	Good
Education Index		Fair	Good
ERIC			Very Good
Psychological Abstracts		Fair	Very Good
Tests in Print	Very Good		

Computer Applications for Record Keeping, Item Banking, and Item Analysis

by Charles R. DuVall

This appendix is designed to acquaint the reader with the rudiments of use of personal computers in keeping records, preparing tests, and analyzing test data. The material is organized under three basic topics:

1. **Grade Book**. Probably the most basic measurement application of the computer is that of maintaining grade books (student records).
2. **Test Item Bank**. The second computer application is the maintenance of banks of test items as well as the classification of these items.
3. **Data Analysis**. The third, and most complex topic is that of item and/or group data analysis through the use of appropriate statistical procedures.

Before analyzing selected software programs for these topics, suggestions for implementing any or all of these procedures will be presented.

IMPLEMENTATION SUGGESTIONS

The first thing that must be determined is the type of computer(s) available. These can be broken into two major classifications, the Apple series and IBM and IBM compatible (OS-2/MS-DOS operating systems) machines. A third, but less frequently found computer is the Tandy family of machines. The available computer will usually determine the software (programs) you will use in your work. Ideally, if you are starting with neither a computer nor software, you should pick the major software programs and then obtain the computer that best operates with that software. However, most teachers find the computer is already chosen; they must then look for software that is compatible with the machine and its operating system.

When you begin to shop for software, start by determining the software available to you.

Perusing reviews of the latest software in journals at local university or public libraries is a good place to begin. One good source, available at most libraries, is *Software Reviews on File.* Another good source is the reviews in *Technology & Learning,* a journal devoted to the needs of educators. Most professional association journals contain one or more columns specifically dealing with software. These journals may be either discipline specific (e.g., *Social Studies and the Young Learner*) or general in nature (e.g., *Instructor*). A helpful source of indexes of these reviews is the *Cumulative Index to Journals in Education* (CIJE) and *Education Index,* both of which are available in hard copy as well as on *ERIC on CD-ROM* and *Wilsondisc* disks for easy searching. In addition, when looking for software it is a good idea to read not only the columns but also the advertisements in journals.

Daily newspapers also run computer columns. One example is *"Computers"* by Terkel and Peterson. The authors of computer columns will often answer queries from readers who have specific questions. Finally, you may wish to obtain copies of catalogs of software (e.g., *Macintosh Administrative & Teacher Productivity Software Guide* and *IBM Software for Education Guide*). After consulting such sources you will have a general idea of the software programs available in your chosen area. Because of the large number of companies developing software for IBM compatible computers (MS-DOS), one catalog listing all available educational software does not exist. For this reason either a database literature search for software reviews or a bulletin board query is recommended.

When looking for software it is advisable to be aware of your operating system—MS-DOS (MicroSoft-Disk Operating System), Apple (several versions), Macintosh, or Tandy. Most systems do not operate interchangeably with ease, if at all, and some software will not operate on earlier versions of selected operating systems (e.g., MS-DOS is now at Version 5.0+). When purchasing software it is a good idea to ask the vendor about the compatibility of the software with your machine and operating system. Obtain a copy of a "demo" disk if it is available. Many software vendors provide these if asked. These demos provide the opportunity to test before buying.

Software usually is not sold, but rather licensed to the original purchaser. This means that when you "open" the package you have agreed to the licensing agreement terms contained in the package. Be sure to read these terms carefully as they usually preclude returning software when the package has been opened (broached).

Other sources of information about computers, their use, and the programs to use with specific tasks are colleagues, local user groups (usually "networked" through friends or colleagues), want ads in the newspaper, and local computer/software dealers. Additional information may be obtained through the use of subscription on-line services such as *Compuserve, Newsnet,* and *Prodigy.*

In summary, it is a very good idea to understand clearly exactly what you want the software program to do for you before you purchase it. Computers and software are regularly updated or "modernized" at fairly frequent intervals. Since individual purchasers and school systems cannot afford to update their software constantly, it behooves the purchaser to examine thoroughly all options available, carefully plan all purchases, and be sure the software purchased will fully meet the needs of the educational program, teacher, and students for several years. This goal can best be accomplished by examining all available sources of information and making purchase decisions based upon both present needs and future plans.

The following three sections contain brief reviews of grade book software programs, data bank programs, and analytical (data analysis) programs. These reviews are not intended to be comprehensive, but are presented to give an idea of the wide range of features available to teachers. Such uses of computers and appropriate software provide teachers the dual opportunity to (a) spend less time recording data, preparing tests, and analyzing data and (b) perform these tasks more thoroughly and appropriately. In all cases, where programs are mentioned, a complete bibliographic entry is presented in the list of sources at the end of this appendix. It is suggested that interested individuals contact the source for more complete information as well as demo disks where available. Comprehensive reviews of most of the software mentioned in this appendix are available in one or more of the review sources mentioned above.

GRADE BOOKS

The program *Grade Machine* is available for Apple IIe/IIc/IIgs, Macintosh, as well as IBM compatible machines. Capacity for reporting scores and data vary among the programs for the different operating systems, but all appear to be more than adequate for single teacher use. School licenses are also available. This program permits the preparation of individual progress reports, group reports, statistical analyses, and graphic presentation of data for class comparisons and communication with parents.

MECC (Minnesota Educational Computing Consortium) offers a program titled *Grade Manager*. This program is available for the Apple, IBM, and Tandy computers. It offers attributes similar to *Grade Machine* mentioned above. In addition, the Apple version permits transferring data from MECC's program *Labels, Letters, and Lists* to labels, badges, lists, and form letters. MECC's catalog lists over 140 software packages available to schools, as well as several attractive "membership" packages.

IBM offers the program *grade2* to handle this repetitive and time-consuming task for teachers. It is advertised as providing four functions: student data base, grade data management, test scoring and analysis, and report generating capabilities.

Still another grade book program is *MacRegistrar*, which also has features similar to those described above. Internally it can handle the creation of free-form notes on individual students or class groups as well as the creation of histograms and descriptive statistics. This program also permits the importing and exporting of data.

Other programs include *Mac School Marks 3.0*, *Grade Book 1.2*, and *VAR Grade 4.6*. These programs have many similar features as well as some differences. They vary widely in price. In some cases demo disks are provided for review. The bibliographic citation lists all pertinent data regarding each program publisher, which should permit the interested reader to obtain sufficient data to make an informed choice.

TEST ITEM BANK

When considering use of test item banks there are two possible approaches to take. One is to use already prepared questions, which are usually contained in the teacher's manual or an accompanying item booklet that supports the adopted text. Many publishers now supply these item banks on disk designed for many popular word processing or database programs.

Another choice that schools may wish to make is to purchase collections of test items. An example of these types of tests is provided by Tom Snyder Productions. These item banks are called the *Exam in a Can* series. These are available in several different discipline areas. One example is the following series of topics available for use with mathematics classes: "Basic Math Skills," "Applications in Basic Math," "Pre-Algebra," "Algebra I Skills," "Algebra II Skills," "Geometry," "Pre-Calculus," and "Calculus." Some of the above titles are available in both English and Spanish versions for Apple, IBM compatible, and Tandy computers. Because of the price of individual "cans," purchase by individual teachers may be prohibitive. Purchase of these item banks is most feasible for schools and/or school systems. One advantage of using prepared item banks is that the keyboarding of all questions is already accomplished. In the case of math the particular signs and symbols are provided, rather than the teacher being forced to obtain a software program containing these symbols. A second advantage is that most questions have already been provided with logical distracters.

Another alternative available to teachers is to use a software program specifically designed (dedicated) to generate many types of tests, handle graphics, and use mathematical and scientific notation/symbolism. Most programs of this type will permit the use of an answer scanning device or will also permit student answers to be entered manually. One such program is the *LXR TEST 4.1* for the Macintosh. Similar programs for IBM compatible machines are also available. When choosing to generate their own item bank and prepare their own tests, teachers should be sure that the software program contains the ability to generate within itself, or the capability to be used in conjunction with a painting or drawing program and a special character generator for math and science symbols. These types of programs permit teachers to keyboard test items provided in hard copy.

Another alternative available for consideration is the creation of separate item banks and individual tests for pupils to take using the computer rather than printed copy. One program that provides this service is *Multiple Choice.* This program requires the use of another program for the Macintosh called *HyperCard.* Students go to the computer, take the test (on screen), and the results are recorded for individual students. Group results and comprehensive analysis are also recorded. This program cannot be used to print hard copies of tests, but results and analyses can be printed. The program also can be programed to provide students instant feedback with explanations (drill and practice). Results may also be saved to a text file for grade book recording.

Another possible way to establish a test item bank is to use a word processing program to create the item bank. This process is far from ideal, and the use of programs specifically developed for this purpose is far more satisfactory. However, if you have limited funds and an available program the following is a suggested process.

1. Set up the test bank in different files, titling them by broad categories. As you type the items identify each item by one or more concept terms.
2. When you begin to assemble the test from one or more categories, establish a file for the particular test. Do a "find" search, using the concepts you wish to test. Transfer the items from the item bank to the test file by "marking the text" and then transferring the marked sections (test questions) to the test file. You can arrange test items in any order you wish by again using the "mark and block transfer" commands within the test file.

This procedure is very rudimentary and is not ideal. Any of the above mentioned programs, as well as others on the market, will do this job with much greater ease. The advantage that this process has over non-computer test making is that it makes keyboarding/rekeying and proofreading individual course examinations unnecessary. One common word processing software program that has gained wide-spread popularity in schools is *Bank Street Writer;* however, any word processing program that has block transfer and file insert commands can be used for this purpose.

At a slightly more sophisticated level, but still below the dedicated program level, is the use of a "general" database program to store the bank of items and generate, through "form or report design" capabilities, individual tests for duplication. With some databases the materials can be exported to a word processing program after the data have been entered and classified. The key to using a "general" database is to design the fields so that they represent the data (questions) you wish to enter, the concepts you wish to use for classification purposes, and the way in which you wish to have results analyzed. If you use a relational database powerful enough, you can use it to maintain your grade book as well as store your item banks. In most cases general database programs do not have mathematical and scientific notations available within their word processing programs.

If the use of general database programs is chosen over a dedicated program, three programs of differing levels of complexity merit consideration. The first is *Data Manager PC*, which is a relational database with adequate capabilities. The second is *FoxPro*, which is also a relational database but with more capabilities and expanded programing requirements. Finally the "freeform" database program *askSam* is available. In using this program it is not necessary to structure fields, although it is possible, but the data entered are still available for use. This program, however, requires higher-level programing skills and uses its own command structure. These three software programs are by no means the only available ones, but they illustrate the differing levels of complexity. They have a wider range of adaptability than do dedicated programs, but they also require more programing skills and, depending upon user requirements, may impose some limitations upon the output.

DATA ANALYSIS

Item analysis may be accomplished in several ways using several different analytical approaches and tools. The first is using a tool like *LXR TEST 4.1*. This program offers the additional feature of machine-scoring capabilities, which eliminates the necessity for manually posting individual test scores and item analysis results into the database.

JMP IN is a statistical analysis tool that can display data visually. It can import data from text files or they can be entered manually. Use of this program allows for the examination of data for relationship among variables (test scores).

The Disaggregation Calculator contains spreadsheet templates designed to help analyze student data, such as normal curve equivalents, and compare student data on tests from year to year. It is available to work with *MicroSoft Works* (Mac), *MicroSoft Excel* (Mac) and *Lotus 1-2-3* (MS-DOS).

Of course any spreadsheet program can be programed to analyze test scores, as well as individual question analysis if the person wishes to design programs for this type of analysis. One such program is *SwiftCalc PC*, which, while designed for use with financial data, could be adapted to test data analysis with little difficulty. Again, there are choices available in programs or spreadsheet templates available for purchase that relieve the individual of this task. Most of these programs are more appropriate for purchase by school districts than by individual teachers.

Other programs are highly relational in nature and are most definitely for school and/or district use. These involve programs for item bank development, machine scoring of tests, automatic recording to grade books, and complete statistical analysis of individual, classroom group, school and district performance analysis. These can be located in schools and be a part of a school-wide or district network.

One program not directly related to record keeping, item banking, or item analysis merits mentioning because of its great potential for use by teachers. It is called *Ideafisher*. Through a series of questions it works as a one-person "think tank." The program is designed to help in task definition and examining alternatives while working toward problem solution. It has great potential for course development and planning.

SUMMARY

This presentation was prepared to acquaint you with some basic ideas for using your personal computer and software in making you a more effective teacher. An attempt was made to lead you from the first tentative steps in computer use through a logical developmental sequence of ideas and software programs. No attempt was made to represent the programs presented as complete, merely representative at differing levels of expertise. No prices for programs were presented because pricing is a highly flexible and ever changing matter, as is the state of development in software, computers, and operating systems.

SOURCES

askSam 5.0, askSam Systems, 119 South Washington Street, Perry, FL 32347, (800) 800-1997.

Bank Street Writer III, Scholastic, P.O. Box 7502, 2913 East McCarty Street, Jefferson City, MO 65102, (800) 541-5413.

"Computers," Judi K. Terkel and Franklynn Peterson, nationally syndicated newspaper column (back issues of columns available from *Newsnet* or by writing the authors at 3006 Gregory Street, Madison, WI 53711-1847, enclose SASE).

Compuserve, Inc., 500 Arlington Centre Blvd., P.O. Box 20212, Columbus, OH 43220, (800) 848-8199 (on-line service).

Cumulative Index to Journals in Education (CIJE), ORYX, 4041 North Central Indian School Road, Phoenix, AZ 85012-3397 (also available on ERIC on CD-ROM).

Data Manager PC, Timeworks, Inc., 625 Academy Drive, Northbrook, IL 60062.

Disaggregation Calculator, Center for Total Development, 22W280 Birchwood Drive, Glen Elyn, IL 60137.

Education Index, H. W. Wilson Company, 950 University Ave., Bronx, NY 10452 (also available on WILSONDISC {CD-ROM search software}). (800) 367-6770.

ERIC on CD-ROM, SilverPlatter International, 100 River Ridge Road, Norwood, MA 02062-5026, (617) 769-2599.

Exam in a Can, Tom Snyder Productions, Inc., 90 Sherman Street, Cambridge, MA 02140, (800) 342-0236. Request catalog for complete list of titles.

FoxPro and *FoxBASE+,* Fox Software, Inc., 134 West South Boundary, Perrysburg, OH 43551, (419) 874-8678. Demos available.

Grade Book 1.2, Bobbing Software, 67 Country Oaks Drive, Buda, TX 78610, (512) 295-5045 (demo disk provided).

Grade Machine, The, Misty City Software, 10921 129th Place NE, Kirkland, WA 98033, (206) 828-3107.

Grade Manager (Apple/IBM/Tandy), MECC, 3490 Lexington Avenue, St. Paul, MN 55112, (800) 685-MECC (6322).

grade 2, see *IBM Software for Education Guide* for details.

HyperCard 2.0, Claris, 5201 Patrick Henry Drive, Santa Clara, CA 95052, (800) 544-8554 (program included w/Macintosh computer purchase).

IBM Software for Education Guide, IBM Direct, PC Software Department, One Culver Road, Dayton, NJ 08810, (800) 426-2468 (catalog and information).

Instructor, Scholastic, Inc., 730 Broadway, New York, NY 10003 (column: "Software Workshop").

JMP IN, SAS Institute, SAS Campus Drive, Cary, NC 27513

Labels, Letters, and Lists, see *Grade Manager* for MECC information.

Lotus 1-2-3, Lotus Development Corporation, 55 Cambridge Parkway, Cambridge, MA 02142-1295, (800) 872-3387, ext. 6384 or (800) 345-1043.

LXR TEST 4.1, Logic Extension Resources, 9651 Business Center Drive, Suite C, Rancho Cucamonga, CA 91730, (714) 980-0046.

Macintosh Administrative & Teacher Productivity Software Guide, Apple Computer, Inc., 20330 Stevens Creek Blvd., M/S 36-AN, Cupertino, CA 95014 (catalog).

MacRegistrar, Cooke Publications, P.O. Box 4448, Ithaca, NY 14852, (800) 482-4438, ext. 15.

Mac School Marks 3.1.1, Chancery Software, 1168 Hamilton Street, Suite 500, Vancouver, BC, Canada, V6B 2S2, (800) 663-8831 (demo disk provided).

Microsoft Works & Microsoft Excel, Microsoft Corporation, One Microsoft Way, Redmond, WA 98052, (800) 426-9400.

Multiple Choice, Symposia, 4259 Andover Terrace, Pittsburgh, PA 15213.

Newsnet, 945 Haverford Road, Bryn Mawr, PA 19010, (800) 345-1301 (on-line-service).

Prodigy, Prodigy Services Co., 445 Hamilton Avenue, White Plains, NY 10601, (800) 776-3693 (on-line service).

Social Education, National Council for the Social Studies, 3501 Newark Street NW, Washington, DC 20016 (column: "Instructional Technology").

Social Studies and the Young Learner, National Council for the Social Studies, 3501 Newark Street NW, Washington, DC 20016 (column: "Media Corner").

Software Reviews on File, Facts on File, 460 Park Avenue South, New York, NY 10016 (monthly, cumulative index).

SwiftCalc PC, see *DataManager PC* for information.

Technology & Learning, 2451 East River Road, Dayton, OH 45439.

VAR Grade 4.6, Reasonable Solutions, 2101 West Main Street, Medfore, OR 97501, (800) 876-3475.

Wilsondisc, see *Education Index* for information.

References

Aiken, L. R. (1985). Review of ACT Assessment Program. In Mitchell, J. V., Jr. (Ed.), *The ninth mental measurements yearbook*, Volume I, 29-31. Lincoln, NE: The University of Nebraska Press.

Aiken, L. R. (1991). *Psychological testing and assessment* (7th ed.). Boston: Allyn and Bacon.

Airasian, P. W. (1991). *Classroom assessment*. New York: McGraw-Hill.

American Psychological Association. (1974) *Standards for educational & psychological tests*. Washington, DC: Author.

American Psychological Association. (1985). *Standards for educational and psychological testing*. Washington, DC: Author.

Anastasi, A. (1958). Heredity, environment, and the question of "how?" *Psychological Review, 65,* 197–208.

Anastasi, A. (1985). Review of Kaufman Assessment Battery for Children. In Mitchell, J. V., Jr. (Ed.), *The ninth mental measurements yearbook*, Volume I, 769–771. Lincoln, NE: The University of Nebraska Press.

Anastasi, A. (1988). *Psychological testing* (6th ed.). New York: Macmillan.

Angoff, W. H. (1988). The nature-nurture debate, aptitudes, and group differences. *American Psychologist, 43,* 713–720.

Arlin, M. (1984). Time, equality, and mastery learning. *Review of Educational Research, 54,* 65–86.

Baker, F. B. (1990). Some issues in the application of microcomputerized testing packages. *Educational Measurement: Issues and Practice, 9,* 18–19.

Bandura, A. (1977). *Social learning theory*. Englewood Cliffs, NJ: Prentice-Hall.

Bangert-Downs, R. L., Kulik, J. A., & Kulik, C. C. (1986). *Effects of frequent classroom testing*. (ERIC Document Reproduction Service No. 274 672.)

Bayer, L. M., & Bayley, N. (1976). *Growth diagnosis* (2nd ed.). Chicago: University of Chicago Press.

Bennett, G. K., Seashore, H. G., & Wesman, A. G. (1990). *Differential Aptitude Tests* (5th ed.), Form C. San Antonio: The Psychological Corporation.

Bennett, J. A. (1984). Assessment of instructional sensivity in three standardized algebra achievement tests. Unpublished doctoral dissertation, Kansas State University.

Berger, A. (1985). Review of the Watson-Glaser critical thinking appraisal. In Mitchell, J. V., Jr. (Ed.), *The ninth mental measurements yearbook*, Volume II, 1692–1693. Lincoln, NE: The University of Nebraska Press.

Berger, S., Dertouzos, M. L., Lester, R. K., Solow, R. M., & Thurow, L. C. (1989). Toward a new industrial America. *Scientific American, 260,* No. 6, 39–47.

Berk, R. A. (1986). *Performance assessment: Methods and applications*. Baltimore: Johns Hopkins University Press.

Bigge, M. L. & Shermis, S. S. (1992). *Learning theories for teachers* (5th ed.). New York: Harper-Collins.

Binet, A., & Simon, T. (1916). *The development of intelligence in children*. Baltimore: Williams & Wilkins.

Bloom, B. (1971). Mastery learning and its implications for curriculum development. In E. W. Eisner (Ed.), *Confronting curriculum reform*. Boston: Little, Brown.

Bloom, B. S. (1976). *Human characteristics and school learning*. New York: McGraw-Hill.

Bloom, B. S., Engelhart, M. D., Furst, E. J., Hill, W. H., Krathwohl, D. R. (1956). *Taxonomy of educational objectives, handbook 1; Cognitive domain*. New York: McKay.

Boyer, E. L. (1987). *College: The undergraduate experience in America*. New York: Harper & Row.

Burns, P. C., & Roe, B. D. (1989). *Burns/Roe Informal Reading Inventory: Preprimer to twelfth grade* (3rd ed.). Boston: Houghton Mifflin.

California Test Bureau. (1989a). *Comprehensive Tests of Basic Skills*. Monterey, CA: McGraw-Hill.

California Test Bureau. (1989b). *CTBS Technical Bulletin 1*. Monterey, CA: McGraw-Hill.

California Test Bureau. (1990). *CTBS Class Management Guide*. Monterey, CA: McGraw-Hill.

Chase, C. I. (1968). The impact of some obvious variables on essay-test scores. *Journal of Educational Measurement, 5*, 315–318.

Choate, J. S., Enright, B. B., Miller, L. J., Poteet, J. A., & Rakes, T. A. (1992). *Curriculum-based assessment and programming* (2nd ed.). Boston: Allyn and Bacon.

Coffman, W. E. (1985). Review of Kaufman Assessment Battery for Children. In Mitchell, J. V., Jr. (Ed.), *The ninth mental measurements yearbook*, Volume I, 771–773. Lincoln, NE: The University of Nebraska Press.

Coffman, W. E. (1971). Essay examinations. In Thorndike, R. M. (Ed.). *Educational measurement* (2nd ed.). Washington DC: American Council on Education.

Cohen, J. (1960). A coefficient of agreement for norminal scales. *Educational and Psychological Measurement, 20*, 37–46.

Cole, N. S., & Moss, P. A. (1989). Bias in test use. In Linn, R. L. (Ed.), *Educational measurement* (3rd ed.). New York: Macmillan.

Connolly, A. J. (1988a). *KeyMath–Revised*. Circle Pines, MN: American Guidance Service.

Connolly, A. J. (1988b). *KeyMath–Revised manual*. Circle Pines, MN: American Guidance Service.

Conoley, J. C., & Kramer, J. J. (in press). *Tests in Print IV*. Lincoln, NE: The Buros Institute of Mental Measurements.

Conoley, J. C., & Kramer, J. J. (1989). *The tenth mental measurement yearbook*. Lincoln, NE: The Buros Institute of Mental Measurements.

Cook, W. W., & Clymer, T. (1962). Accelerating and retardation. In Henry, N. B. (Ed.). *Individualizing instruction: The sixty-first yearbook of the National Society for the Study of Education, Part 1*. Chicago: The National Society for the Study of Education.

Cox, W. F., Jr., & Dunn, T. G. (1979). Mastery learning: A psychological trap? *Educational Psychologist, 14*, 24–29.

Cronbach, L. J. (1942). Studies of acquiescence as a factor in true-false tests. *Journal of Educational Psychology, 33*, 401–415.

Cronbach, L. J. (1951). Coefficient alpha and the internal structure of tests. *Psychometrika, 16*, 297–334.

Cronbach, L. J. (1971). Comments on mastery learning and its implications for curriculum development. In E. W. Eisner (Ed.), *Confronting curriculum reform*. Boston: Little, Brown.

Cronbach, L. J. (1977). *Educational psychology* (3rd ed.). New York: Harcourt Brace Jovanovich.

Cronbach, L. J. (1984). *Essentials of psychological testing* (4th ed.). New York: Harper & Row.

Cronbach, L. J. (1990). *Essentials of psychological testing* (5th ed.). New York: HarperCollins.

Cronbach, L. J., & Furby, L. (1971). How we should measure "change"—or should we? *Psychological Bulletin, 74*, 68–80.

Crooks, T. J. (1988). The impact of classroom evaluation practices on students. *Review of Educational Research, 58*, 438–481.

Cummings, O. W. (1982). Differential measurement of reading comprehension skills for students with discrepant subskill profiles. *Journal of Educational Measurement, 19*, 59–66.

David, J. L. (1986). Making teacher evaluation useful: A national perspective. *Keynote Address, Kansas–NEA Conference*, Salina, KS, October 18, 1986 (available from KNEA, Topeka, KS).

Dolliver, R. H. (1985). Review of the Self-Directed Search. In Mitchell, J. V., Jr. (Ed.), *The ninth mental measurements yearbook*, Volume II, 1346–1347. Lincoln, NE: The University of Nebraska Press.

Donlon, T. F. (Ed.). (1984). *The College Board technical handbook for the Scholastic Aptitude Test and achievement tests*. New York: College Entrance Examination Board.

Dorr-Bremme, D. W., & Herman, J. (1986). *Assessing school achievement: A profile of classroom practices*. Los Angeles: Center for the Study of Evaluation, UCLA Graduate School of Education.

Ebel, R. L. (1975). Can teachers write good true-false test items? *Journal of Educational Measurement, 12*, 31–36.

Ebel, R. L., & Frisbie, D. A. (1991). *Essentials of educational measurement* (5th ed.). Englewood Cliffs, NJ: Prentice-Hall.

Educational Testing Service. (1973). *Multiple-choice questions: A close look*. Princeton, NJ: Educational Testing Service.

Educational Testing Service. (1979). *Sequential Tests*

of Educational Progress End-of-Course Tests: Biology. Princeton, NJ: Educational Testing Service.

Ericksen, S. C. (1983). Private measures of good teaching. *Teaching of Psychology, 10,* 133–136.

Feldt, L. S., & Brennan, R. L. (1989). Reliability. In Linn, R. L. (Ed.), *Educational measurement* (3rd ed.). New York: Macmillan.

Ferguson, B. A., & Takane, Y. (1989). *Statistical analysis in psychology and education* (6th ed.). New York: McGraw-Hill.

Fitzpatrick, R., & Morrison, E. J. (1971). Performance and product evaluation. In Thorndike, R. L. (Ed.), *Educational measurement* (2nd ed.). Washington, DC: American Council on Education.

Flaugher, R. L. (1978). The many definitions of test bias. *American Psychologist, 33,* 671–679.

Fleming, M., & Chambers, B. (1983). Teacher-made tests: Windows on the classroom. In W. E. Hathaway (Ed.), *Testing in the schools.* San Francisco: Jossey-Bass.

Forsyth, R. A. (1991). Do NAEP scales yield valid criterion-referenced interpretations? *Educational Measurement: Issues and Practices, 10,* 3–9, 16.

Frary, R. B. (1988). Formula scoring of multiple-choice tests (correction for guessing). *Educational Measurement: Issues and Practice, 7,* 33–38.

Frisbie, D. A. (1988). Reliability of scores from teacher-made tests. *Educational Measurement: Issues and Practice, 7,* 25–35.

Fuchs, L. S. (1985). Review of Ekwall Reading Inventory. In Mitchell, J. V., Jr. (Ed.), *The ninth mental measurements yearbook,* Volumn I, 541–542. Lincoln, NE: The University of Nebraska Press.

Gettinger, M. (1984). Individual differences in time needed for learning: A review of literature. *Educational Psychologist, 19,* 15–29.

Glaser, R. (1963). Instructional technology and the measurement of learning outcomes: Some questions. *American Psychologist, 18,* 519–521.

Glass, G. V., & Smith, M. L. (1978). The technology and politics of standards. *Educational Technology, 18,* 12–18.

Glover, J. A. (1989). The testing phenomenon: Not gone but nearly forgotten. *Journal of Educational Psychology, 81,* 392–399.

Goldman, L. (1971). *Using tests in counseling* (2nd ed.). Pacific Palisades, CA: Goodyear.

Gough, H. G., & Heilbrun, A. B., Jr. (1980). *The Adjective Checklist.* Palo Alto, CA: Consulting Psychologists Press.

Gronlund, N. E. (1970). *Stating behavioral objectives for classroom instruction.* New York: Macmillan.

Gronlund, N. E. (1985). *Stating objectives for class-room instruction* (3rd ed.). New York: Macmillan.

Gronlund, N. E. (1988). *How to construct achievement tests* (4th ed.). Englewood Cliffs, NJ: Prentice-Hall.

Gronlund, N. E., & Linn, R. L. (1990). *Measurement and evaluation in teaching* (6th ed.). New York: Macmillan.

Gullickson, A. R. (1984). Teacher perspectives of their instructional use of tests. *Journal of Educational Research, 77,* 244–248.

Gullickson, A. R. (1985). Student evaluation techniques and their relationship to grade and curriculum. *Journal of Educational Research, 79,* 96–100.

Guskey, T. R. (1985). *Implementing mastery learning.* Belmont, CA: Wadsworth.

Haertel, E. (1986). *Choosing and using classroom tests: Teachers' perspectives on assessment.* Paper presented at the annual meeting of the American Educational Research Association, San Francisco.

Haladyna, T. M., Nolen, S. B., & Haas, N. W. (1991). Raising standardized achievement test scores and the origins of test score pollution. *Educational Researcher, 20,* 2–7.

Haladyna, T. M., & Roid, G. (1981). The role of instructional sensitivity in the empirical review of criterion-referenced test items. *Journal of Educational Measurement, 18,* 39–52

Hales, L. W., & Tokar, E. (1975). The effect of the quality of preceding responses on the grades assigned to subsequent responses to an essay question. *Journal of Educational Measurement, 12,* 115–118.

Hanna, G. S. (1988). Using percentile bands for meaningful descriptive test score interpretations. *Journal of Counseling and Development, 66,* 477–483.

Hanna, G. S., & Bennett, J. A. (1984). Instructional sensitivity expanded. *Educational and Psychological Measurement, 44,* 583–396.

Hanna, G. S., & Cashin, W. E. (1988). *Improving college grading.* IDEA Paper No. 19. Manhattan, KS: Kansas State University, Center for Faculty Evaluation and Development.

Hanna, G. S., & Orleans, J. B. (1982). *Orleans-Hanna algebra prognosis test manual.* San Antonio: The Psychological Corporation.

Hargenhahn, B. R., (1988). *An introduction to theories of learning* (3rd ed.). Englewood Cliffs, NJ: Prentice-Hall.

Harrow, A. J. (1972). *A taxonomy of the psychomotor domain: A guide for developing behavioral objectives.* New York: McKay.

Hieronymus, A. N., & Hoover, H. D. (1990). *Iowa Tests of Basic Skills teacher's guide with 1988 norms.* Chicago: Riverside.

Hieronymus, A. J., Hoover, H. D., & Lindquist, E. F. (1986). *ITBS preliminary teacher's manual.* Chicago: Riverside.

Hills, J. R. (1981). *Measurement and evaluation in the classroom* (2nd ed.). Columbus: Merrill.

Hills, J. R. (1991). Apathy concerning grading and testing. *Phi Delta Kappan, 72,* 540–545.

Hively, W. (1974). Domain-referenced testing: Part one. *Educational Technology, 14,* 5–10.

Holland, J. L. (1985). *The Self-Directed Search–Form E.* Odessa, FL: Psychological Assessment Resources.

Hoover, H. D. (1984). The most appropriate scores for measuring educational development in the elementary schools: GE's. *Educational Measurement: Issues and Practice, 3,* 8–14.

Hopkins, K. D., Glass, G. V., & Hopkins, B. R. (1987). *Basic statistics for the behavioral sciences* (2nd ed.). Englewood Cliffs, NJ: Prentice-Hall.

Hopkins, K. D., Stanley, J. C., & Hopkins, B. R. (1990). *Educational and psychological measurement and evaluation* (7th ed.). Englewood Cliffs, NJ: Prentice-Hall.

Hsu, T., & Yu, L. (1990). Using computers to analyze item response data. *Educational Measurement: Issues and Practice, 8,* 21–28.

Jeager, R. M. (1987). Two decades of revolution in educational measurement. *Educational Measurement: Issues and Practice, 6,* 6–14.

Jeske, P. J. (1985). Review of the Piers-Harris Self-Concept Scale (The Way I Feel About Myself). In Mitchell, J. V., Jr. (Ed.), *The ninth mental measurements yearbook*, Volume II, 1169–1170. Lincoln, NE: The University of Nebraska Press.

Johns, J. J. (1988). *Basic reading inventory* (4th ed.). Dubuque, IW: Kendall/Hunt.

Johnson, F. R. (1976). The reliability and concurrent validity of multiple-choice tests derived by four distractor selection procedures. Unpublished doctoral dissertation, Kansas State University.

Kaufman, A. S. (1979). *Intelligent testing with the WISC–R.* New York: Wiley.

Kaufman, A. S., & Kaufman, N. L. (1983). *Kaufman Assessment Battery for Children interpretive manual.* Circle Pines, MN: American Guidance Service.

Keyser, D. J., & Sweetland, R. C. (Eds.). (1985–1987). *Test critiques.* Kansas City, MO: Test Corporation of America.

Kifer, E. (1985). Review of the ACT Assessment Program. In Mitchell, J. V., Jr. (Ed.), *The ninth mental measurements yearbook*, Volume I, 31-36. Lincoln, NE: The University of Nebraska Press.

Kirst, M. W. (1991). Interview on assessment issues with Loria Shepard. *Educational Research, 20,* 21–23, 27.

Kramer, J. J. & Conoley, J. C. (1992). *The eleventh mental measurements yearbook.* Lincoln, NE: The Buros Institute of Mental Measurements.

Krathwohl, D. R., Bloom, B. S., & Masia, B. B. (1964). *Taxonomy of educational objectives, handbook II: Affective domain.* New York: McKay.

Krathwohl, D. R., & Payne, D. A. (1971). Defining and assessing educational objectives. In Thorndike, R. L. (Ed.), *Educational measurement* (2nd ed.). Washington, DC: American Council on Education.

Kuder, G. F. (1987). *Kuder General Interest Survey.* Monterey, CA: Macmillan/McGraw-Hill.

Kuder, G. F., & Richardson, M. W. (1937). The theory of estimation of test reliability. *Psychometrika, 2,* 151–160.

Linn, R. L., Baker, E. L., & Dunbar, S. B. (1991). Complex, performance-based assessment: Expectations and validity criteria. *Educational Researcher, 20,* 15–21.

Linn, R. L., Graue, M. E., & Sanders, N. M. (1990). Comparing state and district test results to national norms: The validity of claims that "everyone is above average." *Educational Measurement: Issues and Practice, 9,* 5–14.

Lord, F. M. (1952). The relation of the reliability of multiple-choice tests to the distribution of item difficulties. *Psychometrika, 17,* 181–194.

Loree, M. R. (1948). A study of a technique for improving tests. Unpublished doctoral dissertation, The University of Chicago.

Lundeberg, M. A., & Fox, P. W. (1991). Do laboratory findings on test expectancy generalize to classroom outcomes? *Review of Educational Research, 61,* 94–106.

Lyman, H. B. (1991). *Test scores and what they mean* (5th ed.). Englewood Cliffs, NJ: Prentice-Hall.

Madaus, G. F. (1991). The effects of important tests on students: Implications for a national examination system. *Phi Delta Kappan, 73,* 226–232.

Mager, R. F. (1975). *Preparing instructional objectives* (2nd ed.). Belmont, CA: Fearon.

McCammon, R. W. (1970). *Human growth and development.* Springfield: Thomas.

McKeachie, W. J. (1986). *Teaching tips* (8th ed.). Lexington, MA: Heath.

Mackenzie, D. E. (1983). Research for school improvement: An appraisal of some recent trends. *Educational Researcher, 12,* 5–17.

Mantzicopoulous, P., & Morrison, D. (1992). Kindergarten retention: Academic and behavioral outcomes through the end of second grade. *American Educational Research Journal, 29,* 182-198.

Marr, M. B. (1985). Review of Ekwall Reading Inventory. In Mitchell, J. V., Jr. (Ed.), *The ninth mental measurements yearbook*, Volume I, 542–543.

Marshall, J. C. (1967). Composition errors and essay

examination grades re-examined. *American Educational Research Journal, 4,* 375–385.

Marshall, J. C., & Powers, J. M. (1969). Writing neatness, composition errors and essay grades. *Journal of Educational Measurement, 6,* 97–101.

Mehrens, W. A., & Kaminiski, J. (1989). Methods for improving standardized test scores: Fruitful, fruitless, or fraudulent? *Educational Measurement: Issues and Practice, 8,* 14–22.

Mehrens, W. A., & Lehmann, I. (1991). *Measurement and evaluation in education and psychology* (4th ed.). Fort Worth: Holt, Rinehart and Winston.

Messick, S. (1989). Validity. In Linn, R. L. (Ed.), *Educational measurement* (3rd ed.). New York: Macmillan.

Millman, J. (1970). Reporting student progress: A case for a criterion-referenced marking system. *Phi Delta Kappa, 52,* 226–230.

Millman, J., & Greene, J. (1989). The specification and development of tests of achievement and ability. In Linn, R. L. (Ed.), *Educational measurement* (3rd ed.). New York: Macmillan.

Murphy, C. L., & Bruning, R. H. (1989). Review of the Burns/Roe Informal Reading Inventory: Preprimer to Twelfth Grade (2nd ed.). In Conoley, J. C., & Kramer, J. J. (Eds.), *The tenth mental measurements yearbook,* 116.

Nitko, A. J. (1980). Distinguishing the many varieties of criterion-referenced tests. *Review of Educational Research, 50,* 461–485.

Nitko, A. J. (1989). Designing tests that are integrated with instruction. In Linn, R. L. (Ed.), *Educational measurement* (3rd ed.). New York: Macmillan.

Norris, J. A. (1989). Review of the Classroom Reading Inventory (4th ed.). In Conoley, J. C., & Kramer, J. J. (Eds.), *The tenth mental measurements yearbook,* 178–180.

Nunnally, J. C. (1976). Vanishing individual differences—just stick your head in the sand and they will go away. *Journal of Instructional Psychology, 3,* 28–40.

Nunnally, J. C. (1978). *Psychometric Theory* (2nd ed.). New York: McGraw-Hill.

Oosterhof. A. C. (1987). Obtaining intended weights when combining students' scores. *Educational Measurement: Issues and Practice, 6,* 29–37.

Otis, A. S., & Lennon, R. T. (1990). *OLSAT technical manual.* San Antonio: The Psychological Corporation.

Page, E. B. (1985). Review of Kaufman Assessment Battery for Children. In Mitchell, J. V., Jr. (Ed.), *The ninth mental measurements yearbook,* Volume I, 773–777. Lincoln, NE: The University of Nebraska Press.

Payne, D. A. (1992). *Measuring and evaluating educational outcomes.* New York: Macmillan.

Petersen, N. S., Kolen, M. J., & Hoover, H. D. (1989). Scaling, norming, and equating. In Linn, R. L. (Ed.), *Educational measurement* (3rd ed.). New York: Macmillan.

Piers, E. V. (1984). *Piers-Harris Children's Self-Concept Scale.* Los Angeles: Western Psychological Services.

Piers, E. V., & Harris, D. B. (1969–1984). *The Piers-Harris Children's Self-Concept Scale.* Los Angeles: Western Psychological Services.

Pomerance, H. H., & Krall, J. M. (1979). *Growth standards in children.* New York: Harper & Row.

Popham, W. J. (1978). *Criterion-referenced measurement.* Englewood Cliffs, NJ: Prentice-Hall.

Popham, W. J. (1990). *Modern educational measurement: A practitioner's perspective* (2nd ed.). Englewood Cliffs, NJ: Prentice-Hall.

Popham, W. J., & Baker, E. L. (1970). *Establishing instructional goals.* Englewood Cliffs, NJ: Prentice-Hall.

Priestley, M. (1982). *Performance assessment in education and training: Alternative techniques.* Englewood Cliffs, NJ: Educational Technology Publications.

The Psychological Corporation. (1988–1990). *Stanford Achievement Test Series.* San Antonio: The Psychological Corporation.

The Psychological Corporation. (1990a). *Stanford Achievement Test Series test coordinators handbook.* San Antonio: The Psychological Corporation.

The Psychological Corporation. (1990b). *Career Interest Inventory.* San Antonio: The Psychological Corporation.

The Psychological Corporation. (1991). *Education tests, products, and services 1991 catalog.* San Antonio: The Psychological Corporation.

Pyrczak, F. (1972). Objective evaluation of the quality of multiple-choice test items designed to measure comprehension of reading passages. *Reading Research Quarterly, 8,* 62–71.

Raven, J. C. (1983). *Standard Progressive Matrices.* London: Lewis & Co.

Ricks, J. H. (1971). Local norms—when and why. *Test Service Bulletin No. 58.* San Antonio, The Psychological Corporation.

The Riverside Publishing Company. (1986). *Preliminary technical summary: The new Riverside basic skills assessment program 12.* Chicago: Riverside.

The Riverside Publishing Company. (1990). *Test catalog.* Chicago: Riverside.

Sadler, D. R. (1983). Evaluation and the improvement of academic learning. *Journal of Higher Education, 54,* 60–79.

Salomon, G., & Perkins, D. M. (1989). Rocky roads to transfer: Rethinking mechanisms of a neglected phenomenon. *Educational Psychologist, 24,* 113–142.

Salvia, J., & Ysseldyke, J. E. (1988). *Assessment in special and remedial education* (4th ed.). Boston: Houghton Mifflin.

Sanders, J. R., Hills, J. R., Nitko, A. J., Merwin, J. C., Trice, C., Dianda, M., & Schneider, J. (1990). Standards for teacher competence in educational assessment of students. *Educational Measurement: Issues and Practices, 9,* 30–32.

Sax, G. (1989). *Principles of educational and psychological measurement and evaluation* (3rd ed.). Belmont, CA: Wadsworth.

Scannel, D. P., Haugh, O. M. Schild, A. H., & Ulmer, G. (1986a). *Tests of Achievement and Proficiency,* Form G. Chicago: Riverside.

Scannel, D. P., Haugh, O. M., Schild, A. H., & Ulmer, G. (1986b). *Tests of Achievement and Proficiency: Directions for administering separate level booklets.* Chicago: Riverside.

Schreiner, R. L., Hieronymus, A. N., & Forsyth, R. (1969). Differential measurement of reading abilities at the elementary school level. *Reading Research Quarterly, 4,* 84–99.

Seashore, H. G. (1955). Methods of expressing test scores. *Test Service Bulletin No. 48.* San Antonio: The Psychological Corporation.

Shaywitz, S. E., Shaywitz, B. A., Escobar, M. D., & Fletcher, J. M. (1990). Prevalence of reading disability in boys and girls. *Journal of the American Medical Association, 264,* 998–1002.

Shepard, L. A. (1990). Inflated test score gains: Is the problem old norms or teaching the test? *Educational Measurement: Issues and Practice, 9,* 15–22.

Shepard, L. A. (1991). Psychometricians' beliefs about learning. *Educational Researcher, 20,* 2–16.

Shepard, L. A., & Smith, M. L. (1990). Synthesis of research on grade retention. *Educational Leadership, 47,* 84–88.

Silvaroli, N. J. (1986). *Classroom Reading Inventory* (5th ed.). Dubuque, IA: Brown.

Slavin, R. E. (1987a). A theory of school and classroom organization. *Educational Psychologist, 22,* 89–108.

Slavin, R. E. (1987b). Mastery learning reconsidered. *Review of Educational Research, 57,* 157–213.

Slavin, R. E. (1990). Achievement effects of ability grouping in secondary schools: A best-evidence synthesis. *Review of Educational Research, 60,* 417–499.

Smith, M. L. (1991). Put to the test: The effect of external testing on teachers. *Educational Researcher, 20,* 8–11.

Smith, M. L., & Shepard, L. A. (1987). What doesn't work: Explaining policies of retention in the early grades. *Phi Delta Kappan, 69,* 129–134.

Sparrow, S. S., Balla, D. A., & Cicchetti, D. V. (1984). *Vineland Adaptive Behavior Scales.* Circle Pines, MN: American Guidance Service.

Stanley, J. C. (1971). Reliability. In Thorndike, R. L. (Ed.), *Educational measurement* (2nd ed.). Washington, DC: American Council on Education.

Stanovich, K. E. (1991). Discrepancy definitions of reading disability: Has intelligence led us astray? *Reading Research Quarterly, 26,* 7–29.

Starch, D., & Elliott, E. (1912). Reliability of grading high-school work in English. *School Review, 20,* 442–457.

Starch, D., & Elliott, E. (1913a). Reliability of grading work in history. *School Review, 21,* 676–681.

Starch, D., & Elliott, E. (1913b). Reliability of grading work in mathematics. *School Review, 21,* 254–259.

Stiggins, R. J. (1987). Design and development of performance assessments. *Educational Measurement: Issues and Practice, 6,* 33–42.

Stiggins, R. J. (1991). Assessment literacy. *Phi Delta Kappan, 72,* 534–539.

Stiggins, R. J., & Bridgeford, N. J. (1985). The ecology of classroom assessment. *Journal of Educational Measurement, 22,* 271–286.

Stiggins, R. J., & Bridgeford, N. J. (1986). Student evaluation. In Berk, R. A. (Ed.), *Performance assessment.* Baltimore: The Johns Hopkins University Press.

Stiggins, R. J., Conklin, N. F., & Bridgeford, N. J. (1986). Classroom assessment: A key to effective education. *Educational Measurement: Issues and Practice, 3,* 5–17.

Stiggins, R. J., Frisbie, D. A., & Griswold, P. A. (1989). Inside high school grading practices: Building a research agenda. *Educational Measurement: Issues and Practice, 8,* 5–14.

Stiggins, R. J., Rubel, E., & Quellmalz, E. (1986). *Measuring thinking skills in the classroom.* Washington, DC: National Education Association.

Terman, L. M. (1916). *The measurement of intelligence.* Boston: Houghton Mifflin.

Terwilliger, J. S. (1971). *Assigning grades to students.* Glenview, IL: Scott, Foresman.

Terwilliger, J. S. (1989). Classroom standard setting and grading practices. *Educational Measurement: Issues and Practices, 8,* 15–19.

Thorndike, R. L. (1963). *The concepts of over- and under-achievement.* New York: Columbia University.

Thorndike, R. L. (1969). Helping teachers use tests. *NCME Measurement in Education, 1,* 1–4.

Thorndike, R. L. (1971). Editor's note. In Thorndike, R. L. (Ed.), *Educational measurement* (2nd ed.). Washington, DC: American Council on Education.

Thorndike, R. L. (1982). *Applied psychometrics.*

Boston: Houghton Mifflin.

Thorndike, R. L., & Hagen, E. P. (1977). *Measurement and evaluation in psychology and education* (4th ed.). New York: Wiley.

Thorndike, R. L., & Hagen, E. P. (1986). *Cognitive Abilities Test.* Chicago: Riverside.

Thorndike, R. M., Cunningham, G. K., Thorndike, R. L., & Hagen, E. P. (1991). *Measurement and evaluation in psychology and education* (5th ed.). New York: Macmillan.

Tinkelman, S. N. (1971). Planning the objective test. In Thorndike, R. L. (Ed.), *Educational measurement* (2nd ed.). Washington, DC: American Council on Education.

Tuinman, J. J. (1974). Determining the passage dependency of comprehension questions in 5 major tests. *Reading Research Quarterly, 9,* 206–223.

Tyler, R. W. (1931). A generalized technique for constructing achievement tests. *Educational Research Bulletin, 10,* 199–208.

Watson, G., & Glaser, E. M. (1980). *Watson-Glaser Critical Thinking Appraisal manual.* San Antonio: The Psychological Corporation.

Wesman, A. G. (1971). Writing the test item. In Thorndike, R. L. (Ed.), *Educational measurement* (2nd ed.). Washington, DC: American Council on Education.

Woodcock, R. (1989). *Woodcock-Johnson Psychoeducational Battery–Revised.* Hingham, MA: Teaching Resources Corporation.

Zarske, J. A. (1985). Review of The Adjective Checklist. In Mitchell, J. V., Jr. (Ed.), *The ninth mental measurements yearbook,* Volume I, 52–53. Lincoln, NE: The University of Nebraska Press.

Index of Subjects

Index of Names